THIRD EDITION

Characteristics of and Strategies for Teaching Students with Mild Disabilities

Martin Henley

Westfield State College

Roberta S. Ramsey

Muscogee County School District, Columbus, Georgia

Robert F. Algozzine

University of North Carolina

Allyn and Bacon

Boston ▪ London ▪ Toronto ▪ Sydney ▪ Tokyo ▪ Singapore

Series Editor: *Ray Short*
Editorial Assistant: *Karin Huang*
Marketing Manager: *Ellen Mann Dolberg/Brad Parkins*
Editorial-Production Administrator: *Mary Beth Finch*
Editorial-Production Service: *Modern Graphics, Inc.*
Composition and Prepress Buyer: *Linda Cox*
Manufacturing Buyer: *Megan Cochran*
Cover Administrator: *Linda Knowles*

Library of Congress Cataloging-in-Publication Data

Henley, Martin. 1943-
     Characteristics of and strategies for teaching students with mild
disabilities / Martin Henley, Roberta S. Ramsey, Robert F. Algozzine.—3rd ed.
         p.   cm.
     Includes bibliographical references (p.) and index.
     ISBN 0–205-29066-3 (pbk.)
     1. Learning disabled—United States. 2. Mainstreaming in
education—United States. 3. Behavior modification—United States.
I. Ramsey, Roberta S. II. Algozzine, Robert. III. Title.
LC4705.H46 1998
371.9—dc21   98-25248
                                                                           CIP

Printed in the United States of America

10 9 8 7 6 5 4 3 2 1   03 02 01 00 99 98

To
Margaret, Bobby, Kathryn,
Michael, Randy, and Carl

CONTENTS

PREFACE

This book is written for general and special education majors, both undergraduate and graduate, who want to learn how to effectively teach students with mild disabilities. Aside from speech and language problems, mild disabilities are the most common disabling conditions found in schools. The mild disabilities are: mild mental retardation, behavior disorders, and learning disabilities. Due to the nature of their learning problems students with mild disabilities spend the major portion of their school day in their general education classrooms. This means that the responsibility for educating these students is shared by general and special educators. The recent emphasis on inclusion makes it imperative that general and special educators share a common knowledge base about the nature and needs of these hard-to-teach students.

Our purpose is to provide in a single volume a comprehensive overview of educational practices that influence the identification, placement, and teaching of students with mild disabilities. No other text details both characteristics of and strategies for teaching students with mild disabilities. Our emphasis on characteristics separates this text from others in the same genre. Too often key issues that influence the placement and teaching of students with mild disabilities are muddled by misinformation. One such issue is eligibility criteria. One of the most troublesome aspects of special education today is the misidentification of students as mildly disabled. In some cases students with legitimate disabilities are overlooked. In other instances problem learners are called mildly disabled without sufficient supportive evidence. It is crucial that both general and special educators develop a clear understanding of the types of learning problems that characterize students with mild disabilities. Many special education programs sag under the weight of misplaced students and unfulfilled expectations.

This book is divided into two parts. The first part addresses the characteristics of students with mild disabilities. Chapter 1 explains the basic principles of special education, including its history, legal mandates, and descriptions of various types of disabling conditions. Chapters 2 through 4 present detailed information on each of the three mild disabilities, including practical teaching strategies for each. Although some states subscribe to a nonlabeling approach when serving students with mild disabilities, the reality is that learning problems are constantly addressed by educators and parents in terms of one of the specific mild disabilities of mild mental retardation, learning disability, or behavior disordered. There are many reasons for this shifting back and forth between avoiding and using categorical terms to discuss students with mild disabilities. Chapter 5 details those reasons and highlights similarities and differences found within the three mildly disabling conditions.

The second part of this book details effective teaching practices for students with mild disabilities. The research basis for instruction of students with mild disabilities indicates that good teaching works for all youngsters regardless of the reason for their learning problems. Although categories of disabilities help determine eligibility for special education and provide direction for the prevention of mild disabilities, teaching concerns are best addressed noncategorically. Such classroom practices as cooperative learning, peer tutoring, career education, and computer-assisted instruction are equally effective for all learners with mild disabilities.

Chapter 6 explains how to set up mainstreaming and inclusion programs. Chapter 7 looks at teaching from the point of view of the learner, and Chapter 8 highlights instructional modifications. Classroom management practices are detailed in Chapter 9. The emphasis is on actions by the teacher that prevent discipline problems, and information on such classroom management practices as behavior modification and life space intervention is presented. Chapter 10 extends the classroom management discussion to an analysis of social skills instruction. The final chapter, 11, describes the value of family–school cooperation. It describes programs for helping families and gives an overview of issues that surface when a family discovers that a child has a mild disability.

This book is organized with the needs of the reader in mind. Visual organizers highlight how concepts tie together. Figures and tables summarize information. Anecdotes help the reader get a feel for events that affect the lives of youngsters with mild disabilities. Case studies provide models for problem solving. We have attempted to achieve a writing style that is readable without sacrificing content. Many issues relating to the education of students with mild disabilities require thoughtful analysis. As in most educational concerns the "right" answer is elusive. Our goal is to present an honest and straightforward picture of the issues that confront teachers and families as they strive to provide mildly disabled students with the education they need to live successful lives.

We want to acknowledge and thank those who reviewed an earlier draft of the manuscript: Ann Boyer; Florida Atlantic University and Catherine Medina: Northern Arizona University.

We owe sincere thanks to our families, who supported us during the writing of this third edition. As always we are in debt to our college students who, in their quest for knowledge and practical solutions, have pushed us to expand our awareness. We owe special thanks to our editor Ray Short. He foresaw the need for this book when no one else did. His encouragement and support were instrumental in seeing this project reach a successful conclusion. Karin Huang, editorial assistant, provided us with the structure, the help, and limits we needed to move from cut and paste to third edition. Finally we want to thank our college and university colleagues who provide us with both inspiration and challenge. We are keenly aware that in the final analysis the value of our work rests on their judgment. We hope we have met their expectations.

PART ONE

Characteristics of Students with Mild Disabilities

1 Foundations of Special Education for Students with Mild Disabilities

Advance Questions

Answer the following questions as you read this chapter:

1. What factors led to the development of special education?
2. What are the key principles that drive special education today?
3. Why do some students receive special education?
4. Who is eligible for special education?

Chapter Web

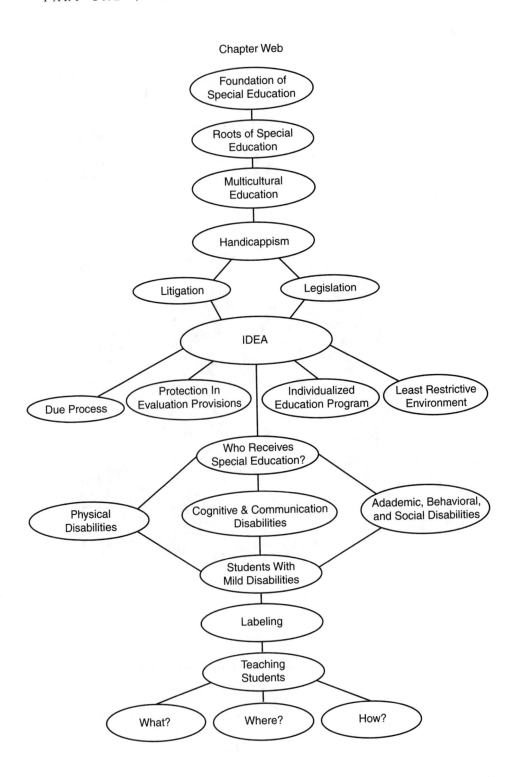

5. What are mild disabilities?
6. What are the advantages and disadvantages of classifying students for special education?
7. How do school personnel decide what special education services are appropriate for students with mild disabilities?
8. What are some key differences between general and special education?

Vignette: Jake, Mary, Felipe

Jake always seems to be one step behind the other students in his seventh-grade class. Despite the slowness that is a part of Jake's performance and social development, his teacher enjoys having him in class. Because Jake is talkative with a good sense of humor, many of his schoolmates enjoy helping him. Jake's teacher likes teaching him because he responds favorably to efforts to help him develop new skills. Jake's classroom performance is similar to many students with mild mental retardation.

Jake's class contains a mixture of students who are easy to teach and students who are hard to teach. Mary is one of the difficult kids. When she was younger she was diagnosed as "hyperactive," and she was put on medication to control her behavior. She comes from a home where both parents work hard to maintain a comfortable lifestyle. There is a lot of pressure put on Mary to succeed. Both of her parents are upwardly mobile professionals who have little time for parenting. Mary does not trust adults and often takes her anger out on her classmates. When she is not physically disrupting the classroom, Mary is socially withdrawn, isolated, and unhappy. Mary's teacher believes that Mary has emotional problems.

Felipe is also difficult to teach—not because of what he does, but because of what he does not do. Felipe does not read or write as well as his seventh-grade classmates. He has never done well in reading, but his scores on ability tests and tests of achievement in other areas (e.g., mathematics) have always been average when compared to his peers. Now that Felipe is in junior high school, his difficulties are particularly troublesome, because he is expected to read and complete homework assignments in English, history, science, psychology, and economics. Felipe appears to have a learning disability.

Each of these students, Jake, Mary, and Felipe, is difficult to teach. They are constantly at-risk of failing, and they are potential school dropouts. Jake, Mary, and Felipe have mild disabilities that are interfering with their progress in school.

Now that you have read the vignette about Jake, Mary and Felipe, see how many problem-solving questions you can answer. For those questions you cannot readily answer, try to find some additional information to use in answering them as you read the chapter. The experiences of Jake, Mary, and Felipe are typical of students with mild disabilities.

1. What should be done to help students like Jake, Mary, and Felipe?
2. Who should teach them?
3. Do all schools provide special education services for students with mild disabilities?

4. What expectations would you have for students like Jake, Mary and Felipe if you were teaching in their junior high school?
5. Should students with mild disabilities be included in classes with students without disabilities?

Every classroom contains students like Jake, Mary, and Felipe. Helping students with learning problems is part of the motivation that stimulates many to become teachers. As one experienced teacher put it, "some teachers like the underdog." The purpose of special education is to help students achieve success in school. Special educators and their general classroom peers want to see all students stay in school, graduate, and succeed in life; but because of differences between the two systems of education, they sometimes work at cross-purposes. When special and general educators communicate and share responsibility for educating students with special needs, everybody benefits.

The Roots of Special Education

Origins of the United States's national education system date from the colonial days. Early schools educated a select, limited segment of the population—white, male children of upper class families (Smith, Price, & Marsh, 1986). Before 1815, schools serving this small proportion of school-aged youth were primarily church sponsored.

Public support of schools by local taxation began during the first half of the nineteenth century. Children previously excluded from schooling—middle class, poor, female, or culturally different—were included. During the mid-nineteenth century, states began enacting compulsory education laws (e.g., Rhode Island in 1840, Massachusetts in 1852). A change in the values and economic thinking of our society was reflected by this Common School Movement.

These early common schools educated students of all ages in the same classroom. In the one-room schoolhouse, students of different ages, different abilities, and different backgrounds learned side by side. Horace Mann, the architect of American public education, believed universal education was the great equalizer. Cremin (1961) characterized this early vision.

> Mann's school would be common, not as a school for the common people—for example, the nineteenth-century Prussian Volksschule—but rather as a school common to all people. It would be open to all, provided by the state and the local community as part of the birthright of every child. It would be for rich and poor alike, not only free but as good as any private institution. It would be nonsectarian, receiving children of all creeds, classes, and backgrounds. (p. 10)

Mann's humanitarian ideal began to take hold, and by 1860 a majority of the states had established public school systems. Throughout this period of rapid growth, Mann advised that instruction be adapted to meet the needs of children who differed in temperament, ability, and interests.

As the United States grew, the one-room schoolhouse was replaced by graded elementary, middle, and high schools. Explicit academic requirements were established for each grade level of the common public school. Students were taught a specific curriculum, and that curriculum was organized into graded units. Educators believed that grouping students by age would make the task of teaching easier (Sarason & Doris, 1979; Ysseldyke & Algozzine, 1982). Achievement was determined by how well children learned the predetermined, graded curriculum. This curriculum-centered characteristic of the new schools made it difficult for many children to keep pace (Smith, Price, & Marsh, 1986; Ysseldyke & Algozzine, 1984).

Immigration and compulsory school attendance broadened the school-aged population to a larger, more variant membership. With the influx of immigrants during the early twentieth century, cultural and ethnic differences in students created a mismatch between teacher expectations and student performance. Some children adapted to school and learned; others dropped out. Many children worked in factories; others took to the streets. Few of the absent students were missed. Little concern was shown for children with disabilities and what we now refer to as at-risk youth.

The influence of social reformers, such as Jane Addams, encouraged some cities to establish alternative instructional programs for "special cases." The superintendent of the Baltimore schools wrote, "Before the attendance laws were effectively enforced there were as many of these special cases in the community as there is now; few of them, however, remained long enough in school to attract serious attention or to hinder the instruction of the more tractable and capable" (Van Sickle, 1908–1909, 102). Early public educational programs offered two choices. Students either received and profited from instruction in lock-step, curriculum-centered classes, or they were placed in a special class. Many administrators believed that these first special education programs were proper preparation for institutionalization. In a speech to the National Education Association, E. R. Johnstone stated that the special education class

> must become a clearing-house. To it will be sent the slightly blind and partially deaf, but also incorrigibles, the mental deficients, and the cripples. . . . The only thing to do is to give them the best of care and training possible. Keep them in the special classes until they become too old for further care in school, and then they must be sent to the institutions for safety. (Johnstone, 1908, 114–118)

A few early special programs were set up for children with specific disabilities, such as deafness or blindness. However, many early public school special classes were repositories for diverse youngsters who did not fit into the regular classroom. In 1899, Elizabeth Farrell described students in her first special education class in New York City:

The first class was made up of the odds and ends of a large school. There were the over-age children, the so-called naughty children, and the dull, and stupid children. They were taken from any and every school grade. The ages ranged from eight to sixteen years. They were the children who could not get along in school. They were typical of a large number of children who even today are forced directly or indirectly out of school; they were the children who were interested in street life; many of them earned a good deal of money in one way or another. While some of them had been in trouble with the police, as a class they could not be characterized as criminal. They had varied interests but the school, as they found it, had little or nothing for them. (Farrell, 1909, 91–96)

From the first decades of the twentieth century until the mid-1970s, students who were different— the odds and ends of society—were ignored, placed in isolated special classes, or transferred to state institutions. In Pennsylvania, for instance, legislation provided for the exclusion of specific children from school. Children evaluated as uneducable because of below-average IQ scores were assigned to the Department of Public Welfare for training in state-run institutions. Most notable about the process of classifying and rejecting students who didn't fit the standard public school curriculum was the lack of due process in educational decisions.

Diversity in the Schools

In 1970, the Task Force of Children Out of School studied the Boston Public School System. The Task Force report— *The Way We Go to School: The Exclusion of Children in Boston*— found over ten thousand students excluded from public school classrooms because they didn't match school standards for the normal student. Patricia Reilly, age sixteen, was told to leave school because she was pregnant. Kathy Fitzgerald, age nine, was excluded from public school because she had a seizure disorder (i.e., epilepsy). Richard, eleven years old, was placed in a special class for the retarded because he was emotionally disturbed; and no other program was available. These children were denied the right to an appropriate education because they were different. In 1974, Congress estimated that over a million school-aged youngsters were denied a proper education in America's schools.

How could a nation based on equal opportunity for all its citizens support such discriminatory practices toward children? The answer is found in attitudes toward people who are different. Prejudice, like creeping shadows, can take many forms. The public school system mirrors our society. Schools reflect the attitudes and prejudices of teachers, administrators, and parents. Students who are different often have special needs, and those special needs have been used as a rationale to exclude them from mainstream life in American schools.

Education once intended for a small, elite sector of the population is now mandated for all children. During the past century, the curriculum-centered format of public schools has remained static while the needs of students have changed significantly. School dropouts, discipline problems, low achievement, and increased referrals to special education are a concern to educators and the public at large. Diversity of students, simply defined as the condition of being different, is at odds with a system of education that requires conformity and assimilation of an unyielding curriculum.

Smith-Davis (1989a) identified some important events and acts of legislation that increased diversity in United States' education. The *Brown v. Topeka Board of Education* decision in 1954 radically altered the national school population. This landmark case, acted upon by the U.S. Supreme Court, decreed that "segregated but equal" school facilities for black and white schoolchildren were discriminatory and unconstitutional. *Brown v. Topeka Board of Education* reversed a prior decision rendered in *Plessy v. Ferguson* in 1894 that legalized separate schools based on racial lines.

The Civil Rights Act of 1964 gave support to advocates who pushed for the inclusion of students with disabilities in public schools (Smith-Davis, 1989a,b; Smith, Price, & Marsh, 1986; Ysseldyke & Algozzine, 1990). Mainstreaming, a term used to promote the integration of school-aged youth with disabilities into classrooms with nondisabled peers, followed on the heels of successful efforts to deinstitutionalize programs for adults and children with disabilities. Placement of youth and adults with moderate and severe disabilities within community settings dramatized their capability to live normal lives. These changes diversified the student population in the nation's schools and emphasized the need for schools to accommodate children with special learning needs (Ysseldyke, Algozzine, & Thurlow, 1983). Yet changes in public school practices toward students with disabilities have been slow to come. For instance, the steady increase each year in youngsters identified with mild disabilities and placed in special programs is testimony to the intractability of a system of education that looks first to blame the student for failure.

Multicultural Education

In 1987, 47 percent of the workforce was comprised of white Americans; in the twenty-first century 85 percent of new workers will be people of color. By the year 2020 almost half of the school-aged population will be young people of color (Pallas, Natriello, & McDill, 1989). This "browning of America" is a reality that signals profound change in our American culture. Multicultural education, with its attendant emphasis on gender, race, and bilingualism is aimed at preparing today's youth for a future characterized by diversity. Ford (1992) defines multicultural education as school "practices and policies that transform the school so that male and female students, social class, racial, and ethnic groups will experience an equal opportunity to learn" (p. 108).

Advocates for multicultural education believe that all students should learn to adapt to the reweaving of our country's social and economic fabric. The purpose of multicultural education is to restructure schools so that students will acquire the knowledge, attitudes, and skills needed to function in an ethically and racially diverse nation and world (Banks, 1993, 27). How this is to be accomplished is a matter of some dispute. Some educators argue that textbooks and curriculums should emphasize the contributions and lifestyles of such diverse groups as gays, women, and people of color. Others oppose curriculums that give equal time to such controversial topics as homosexuality or replace traditional Western European thinking with "Afrocentric" texts and learning materials.

A multicultural issue that affects all populations is lack of equal rights for women. Even though men and women have equal ability, men continue to make higher salaries and have easier access to promotion. Stereotypes about women begin in infancy, with pink birth ribbons signifying daintiness and beauty. These initial views are strengthened throughout childhood through toys, sports, and leisure activities. Consider a nine-year-old boy who chooses ballet over baseball, or a ten-year-old girl who wants to play football. Each of these youngsters will face opposition and ridicule as they attempt to oppose gender barriers. Look around your education classes. If you are an elementary or early childhood major you probably have five times more females than males in your class. Why do more women than men select education as a major? An analysis of explanations is certain to highlight some of the gender barriers girls and women must overcome in order to achieve an equal position in our society.

As the debates continue about how multicultural issues should be dealt with, the major hurdle to the educational progress of many people of color continues to be poverty. Hu-DeHart (1993) succinctly illustrates the chasm that separates rich and poor in America, "Today 1% of the population of the U.S. has 'gained control' of more of the nation's wealth than the bottom 90%. This situation parallels the stark and painful inequality in much of the Third World" (p. 51). Multicultural proponents point to inequities of school funding as evidence that today's poor schoolchildren (many of whom are minorities) are at a distinct disadvantage in their preparation for tomorrow's workplace. Property taxes fund schools. Children who live in destitute communities are unable to break the cycle of poverty because their education is as bleak as their neighborhoods.

Placement of students in special education programs represents one of many multicultural problems that confront our schools. African American children, particularly boys, are overrepresented in special education programs for students with mild mental retardation and behavior disorders. Paradoxically, females and children with limited English proficiency (e.g., Hispanic) are underrepresented in special education programs. This trend of over- and underrepresentation means that many African American children may be inappropriately placed (see Lloyd Dunn's remarks in the chapter on mild mental retardation), while females and Hispanic students who require special education are overlooked. The uneven distribution of students in special education has created a confusing picture about the educational needs of females of all races, African Americans, Hispanics, and Native Americans (see Figure 1.1).

	Native American	Asian	Hispanic	African American
M.R.	1	1	11	34
B.D.	1	1	6	22
L.D.	1	1	11	17

FIGURE 1.1   Ethnic Percentages Receiving Special Education Services (Within Each Mild Disability Category, 1990)

Source: Adapted from Supplement to *Teaching Exceptional Children, 26*(3) (January 1994).
Note: Females of all races are underrepresented in special education placements.

In an optimistic scenario, twenty years from now America will be built on a strong foundation of respect for individual differences. The positive outcomes of multicultural education could help alleviate sexism and racism. In such a society all individuals regardless of gender, ethnic origin, or sexual preference would have an equal opportunity to succeed. As educators, the choices we make now will determine our ability to adapt to fundamental changes in American society. Diversity in color, culture, and language is an ever-growing educational reality that requires careful consideration as we plan for the future.

Handicappism

Advocates for individuals with disabilities use the word "handicappism" to refer to the perception that a person is incompetent because of a physical or psychological impairment. When asked about their most difficult adjustments, adults with disabilities invariably comment about dealing with the prejudices of the population. For example, friends and neighbors may refer to Elise Jones, who has a visual impairment, as "poor, blind Elise!" Condescending remarks about individuals with disabilities may be masked as sympathy, but the message is a clear illustration of handicappism. In fact, Elise's visual impairment is only a part of her individuality, not the sum total of what Elise is as a person.

Sooner or later, most of us will experience a disability. Old age, injuries, or illness are inescapable aspects of the human condition. Although the idea that at some point in your life you will experience a disability might seem remote, the simple truth is that we are not talking about infrequent or isolated cases. The number of U.S. citizens with disabilities is equal to the combined population of New York City, Los Angeles, Chicago, and Miami.

Despite the hurdles of handicappism, examples of magnificent accomplishments by individuals with disabilities abound. Although Stephen W. Hawking is incapacitated by motor neuron disease, he was invested as a fellow in the Royal Society, one of the oldest and most prestigious scholarly societies. Hawking is considered one of the most brilliant physicists of the 20th century.

Individuals with disabilities are people first and people with a disability second. The label assigned to their disability should not be used to replace all their other characteristics. Franklin D. Roosevelt guided the United States through the Second World War from the vantage point of a wheelchair. Einstein was considered too slow to attend school with his peers. Nelson Rockefeller and Thomas Edison had learning disabilities. These extraordinary people were not limited by their disabilities. Throughout this book, we highlight the individual first and the disability second by our phrasing "student with a disability." We do this because language shapes expectations and expectations shape actions. Our persistent theme is that students with mild disabilities are more like their peers than different from them. This is the most important lesson you can learn from reading this book. Your language, your expectations, and your actions when you teach students with mild disabilities will determine their success or failure. Remember, a disability is a problem that can be overcome; don't handicap your students by limiting your expectations for their personal growth or your interactions with them.

Litigation and Legislation

Prior to the early 1970s, handicappism, the notion that individuals with disabilities were severely limited in their ability to learn, was the predominant educational perspective. Most notable about this view was that the lack of due process afforded students as educators either excluded them from school or placed them in dead-end special classes. Due process is a constitutional right guaranteed by the Fourteenth Amendment. During the 1970s, concern about the legal rights of students with special needs spurred several significant class action suits that challenged due process procedures in school evaluation and placement practices. A class action suit is litigation on behalf of a class or group of individuals. For example, when a small group of students who were classified as mentally retarded won a class action suit, all other students with mental retardation within the court's jurisdiction benefitted.

Highlight 1.1 Francis

Francis enjoyed going out to eat with his friends. However, he often encountered difficulties because few restaurants were accessible to his wheelchair. Curbs, narrow doors, stairs, and small public restrooms were all obstacles for Francis. One evening Francis and his friends were ordering dinner. When the waitress came to Francis, she asked one of his friends, "What would he like to eat?" The waitress assumed that because Francis was in a wheelchair he was incapable of ordering his own dinner! Just as physical obstacles impaired Francis's ability to live a normal life, so did stereotypes by well-meaning but thoughtless people. A disability may be born, but society handicaps.

In *Diana v. California State Board of Education* (1970), the issue of Mexican American student overrepresentation in special classes for students with mild retardation was addressed. The plaintiffs were nine children who came from homes where Spanish was the primary language. The class action suit alleged that Mexican American students had been improperly categorized as mildly retarded on the basis of invalid IQ testing. In a consent agreement, the opposing parties agreed that schoolchildren should be tested in their native language. This case laid the groundwork for future lawsuits based on cultural bias in educational evaluations.

The following year, 1971, fourteen families sued the State of Pennsylvania on the basis that their children with mental retardation were denied equal access to a public education. This case, *Pennsylvania Association for Retarded Children (PARC) v. Commonwealth of Pennsylvania* was prompted by the state policy of denying a public education to youngsters with mental retardation. During the legal proceedings, parents described their futile attempts to fight a system that arbitrarily and callously excluded their children from school.

Nancy Beth Bowman was expelled from kindergarten because she wasn't toilet trained. The fifteen-year-old daughter of Leonard Kalish was never allowed to enroll in school. It cost him $40,000 to have her educated in private schools. The parents of David Tupi said their son was expelled from school without notice. One morning the school bus just stopped coming to pick him up. The three-judge panel, in a consent decree, ruled that the state could not predetermine educability. In their decision the judges stated that Pennsylvania must:

1. Admit all children with mental retardation into public school.
2. Place students with mental retardation in regular classrooms when possible.
3. Make all school records accessible to parents.
4. Provide preschool programs for children with mental retardation when such programs were available to nondisabled children.
5. Precede all placement decisions with a hearing to allow parental participation and consent.

The PARC decision emphasized the due process rights of parents to review and challenge placement decisions regarding their children.

In *Mills v. the Board of Education of the District of Columbia* (1972), litigants challenged the exclusion of children identified as mentally retarded, emotionally disturbed, learning disabled, visually impaired, hearing impaired, and physically disabled from Washington, D.C., schools. As in the PARC case, Mills demonstrated the unconstitutionality of school exclusion procedures. Both the PARC and Mills "right to education" cases highlighted the right of students with disabilities to due process in educational decisions.

By 1973 thirty-one similar court cases constituted a groundswell of political activism on behalf of students with disabilities (Taylor & Searle, 1987). It was clear to Congress that schools could no longer be allowed to violate the Fourteenth Amendment rights of students with disabilities. The Fourteenth Amendment states that "no state shall make or enforce any law which shall abridge the privileges or immunities of citizens of the United States; nor shall any state deprive any person of life, liberty, or property without due process of law."

The Individuals with Disabilities Education Act (IDEA)

The culmination of many years of struggle on behalf of children with disabilities occurred on November 29, 1975, when President Ford signed into law Public Law 94–142, The Individuals with Disabilities Education Act (IDEA). This landmark federal legislation mandates a free and appropriate education for all students with disabilities aged three to twenty-one. The Individuals with Disabilities Education Act (IDEA) has been called the "first compulsory special education law," and much of what happens in special education classes today is a direct response to the provisions embodied in it (Ysseldyke & Algozzine, 1984). All Handicapped Children Act, provides students with their families with special rights.

By law, school personnel must prepare an **individualized education program** for every student enrolled in a formal special education program. This means that teachers must have clearly documented plans for how instructional time in special education will be used. A written document, the individual education plan (IEP), specifies long-range goals and short-term objectives for the student, the kinds of services to be provided, the personnel who will deliver the services, an indication of how much time will be spent in general education classed, and a plan for evaluating student's progress.

By law, students with disabilities and their families are entitled to **protection in evaluation** activities that are part of the educational experience. This means that students cannot be placed in special programs in an arbitrary and capricious manner. Students with disabilities and their families are entitled to a multidisciplinary evaluation. Each evaluation must be a team effort comprising the expertise of any school professional who can help decipher the needs of a student with a disability. Occupational therapists, school psychologists, special education teachers, general classroom teachers, and speech clinicians are examples of professionals that contribute to a multidisciplinary evaluation. The evaluation methods used to make educational decisions must be appropriate for use with students with disabilities, and they must be made in an unbiased fashion (e.g., without regard to ethnic, cultural, or racial characteristics).

By law, students with disabilities and their families are guaranteed rights of **due process**. This means that these students and their families have the same Fourteenth Amendment rights enjoyed by all citizens. School personnel cannot change the educational placement of students with disabilities without the informed consent (i.e., written permission) of the students' parents or guardians. Parents are also entitled to independent assessments and impartial hearings when decisions about their children are being made. If needed, states must provide mediation services to resolve disputes with families regarding special education services.

By law, students with disabilities must be educated in the **least restrictive environment**. This means that students with disabilities should be educated to the maximum extent feasible with nondisabled students. Students with disabilities receive special education in a variety of settings. Some are enrolled full time in general education classes and receive only indirect services from special education personnel. Many students with mild disabilities are pulled out of their general education classes daily to go to resource rooms for special education services. Still others are enrolled in self-contained special education classes but, to the maximum extent possible, attend general education classes for part of the school day for certain kinds of instruction. For example, a student might be enrolled in a special class but attend a general education class for instruction in math, music, art, or physical education. Table 1.1 lists key provisions of IDEA. In addition to IDEA, other significant federal legislation promotes the rights and services for individuals with disabilities. The mandate for a free, appropriate public education for adults with disabilities is also paralleled in the Vocational Rehabilitation Act of 1973 (P.L. 93–112). Section 504 of this act made it illegal for institutions or organizations that receive federal funds to discriminate against citizens with disabilities.

In 1990 Congress passed the Americans with Disabilities Act. This law gives civil rights protection to individuals of all ages with disabilities in public services,

---

TABLE 1.1   Major Provisions of IDEA

Due Process Provisions
Right to examine all pupil records
Right to independent assessment of pupil
Right to written notice of any program change
Right to impartial hearing on any school decisions

Protection in Evaluation Provisions (PEP)
Right to individual assessment before placement
Right to assessment with appropriate instruments
Right to unbiased assessment and team decisions

Individualized Education Program (IEP) Provisions
Right to written statement of present functioning
Right to written statement of goals and objectives
Right to written statement of services expected
Right to written statement of expected time frame
Right to written statement of annual monitoring

Least Restrictive Environment (LRE) Provisions
Right to education as much like normal as possible

transportation, private sector employment, public accommodations, and communications. The Americans with Disabilities Act (ADA) is modeled after Section 504 of the Rehabilitation Act of 1973. The Americans with Disabilities Act is sweeping in its authority and might rightly be called the civil rights act for persons with disabilities. Every sort of public accommodation and commercial facility from automatic teller machines to football bleachers must be accessible to individuals with disabilities.

In 1990 Congress amended IDEA in several significant ways. The Individuals with Disabilities Education Act (IDEA) (Public Law 101–476) replaced the original title of the law which was the Education for all Handicapped Childrens Act. The name change reflects the need to emphasize the person first and the disability second. Amendments in IDEA included an expansion of related services such as therapeutic recreation, social work services, and rehabilitation counseling. Transition services were mandated to be written into individual education plans (IEPs). Transition services begin at age sixteen (fourteen when appropriate). These services coordinate rehabilitative services—for example, supported employment and independent living—beyond the school years. The purchase or leasing of customized equipment to support educational services (e.g., computers, wheelchairs, adaptive equipment) is also authorized by this federal law. The Individuals with Disabilities Education Act adds students with autism and traumatic brain injury to the list of populations provided special education.

In June of 1997, President Clinton signed the Individuals with Disabilities Education Act Amendments (P.L. 105–17) into law and reauthorized the IDEA. The amendments added a number of provisions designed to change the education of students with disabilities (see Table 1.2). Key improvements included a strengthening of the role of parents, ensuring the access to general education, focusing the efforts on teaching and learning rather than paperwork and compliance requirements, giving greater attention to racial, ethnic, and linguistic diversity and encouraging the parents and educators to work out their differences using nonadversarial means (Yell & Shriner, 1997).

By now it should be clear that legal mandates to educate and provide services to individuals with disabilities have been the driving force to provide equal opportunities for all school-aged children. The Individuals with Disabilities Education Act is continually being reviewed in state and federal courts. For example, overrepresentation of African American students in special classes and the use of IQ tests to identify minorities as mildly retarded have been scrutinized by federal courts. Such key provisions of as "appropriate education" and "nondiscriminatory assessment" have also spurred important judicial decisions. There is no end to this refinement of the Individuals with Disabilities Education Act. Table 1.3 lists some court cases that have influenced the delivery of special education services to students with mild disabilities.

Special education is a complex alternative for providing instruction to students who fail to profit in general education classes. Students with special

TABLE 1.2   Key Additions In Public Law 105 -17

Area	Provisions
Due Process	■Parental consent is required when a school system evaluates a child and when it places a child for the first time ■Consent for evaluation is not consent for placement ■Parents continue to have right to impartial hearing to challenge school district decisions ■States must also provide mediation services to resolve disputes with parents regarding provision of special education services
Protection in Evaluation	■Parental consent is required evaluation and reevaluation unless school can demonstrate that parents failed to respond to reasonable notice ■If parents refuse, schools must provide mediation services or follow other due process procedures to secure permission to evaluate or reevaluate ■Student can not be declared eligible because of a lack of instruction in reading or math or because of limited English proficiency ■Reevaluations must be conducted at least every three years, more frequently if conditions warrant or if parents or teachers request ■A variety of assessment information must be gathered relative to current levels of functioning and development, including data on general education involvement
Individualized Education Program	■Central focus is participation in general education ■Required participants include parents, general education teachers, special education teachers, local education agency representative knowledgeable in general curriculum, person who can interpret instructional implications of evaluation results ■When behavior is an issue, supports must be included ■Must include measurable annual goals, benchmarks, and objectives related to meeting child's needs in general curriculum

TABLE 1.2   Continued

	▪Must include explanation of the extent to which child will not participate in general education ▪Must include explanations of modifications required in testing and assessments ▪ Must include measure of progress toward annual goals and how parents will be kept informed of progress. ▪Transition services must be included when student reaches age of 14
Least Restrictive Environment	▪Parental participation in decision-making must be ensured ▪General education curriculum is presumed to be appropriate beginning point for educational plans ▪Removal to alternative curriculum should be considered only when participation in general curriculum with supplementary support and services demonstrated not to be beneficial ▪Participation of students with disabilities in state and district assessments is required similar to their general education peers ▪State Education Agencies expected to report to public assessment performance of students with disabilities as often and in same detail as it reports performance of students without disabilities

Source: Adapted from material in M. L. Yell & J G. Shriner (1997), The IDEA Amendments of 1997: Implications for special and general education teachers, administrators, and teacher trainers. *Focus on Exceptional Children, 30*(1), 1–19.

needs are served in a variety of special education settings, and they receive differing of the Individuals with Disabilities Education Act. Table 1.3 lists some court cases that have influenced the delivery of special education services to students with mild disabilities.

Special education is a complex alternative for providing instruction to students who fail to profit in general education classes. Students with special needs are served in a variety of special education settings, and they receive differing amounts of special education assistance. Two kinds of services are available.

TABLE 1.3   Selected Judicial Decisions Since Passage of Public Law 94–142 Focus on Students with Mild Disabilities

1975	*Issac Lora et al. v. The Board of Education of New York et al.* Nondiscriminatory assessment procedures must be used when placing minority students with emotional problems in special education programs.
1976	*Frederich L. v. Thomas* (Philadelphia). Class action suit that reaffirmed the right of students with learning disabilities to have appropriate education programs.
1979	*Larry P. v. Riles* (California). Intelligence tests banned in California when assessing African American students as mildly retarded. Disproportionate numbers of African American students were placed in special classes for the mildly retarded.
1981	*Luke S. and Hans S. v. Nixe et al.* (Louisiana). Prereferral interventions, curriculum-based assessment, and direct classroom interventions were mandated for students with mild disabilities.
1982	*Board of Education of the Henrick Hudson School System v. Rowley.* This Supreme Court decision clarified "appropriate" education by determining that the intent of P.L. 94–142 is to open the doors of public schools to students with disabilities, not to provide opportunities for students to reach maximum potential. Due process procedures to determine an appropriate education were reaffirmed by the Court.
1984	*Smith v. Robinson.* Supreme Court decision that restricted the ability of students and their families to recover legal fees incurred in due process hearings. This decision was negated in 1986 when Congress passed the Handicapped Children's Protection Act, which restored the courts' authority to award legal fees to parents who succeed in lawsuits or administrative hearings.
1984	*Marshall et al. v. Georgia.* Judge Edenfiel ruled that the overrepresentation of African Americans in special classes was not discriminatory. In his view, lower socioeconomic conditions rather than discriminatory assessment and placement practices was the reason African American students were placed in programs for the mild mentally retarded. This was the first court case that highlighted the need to include a measure of adaptive behavior within the classroom as part of the criteria for determining mild mental retardation.
1985	*Burlington v. Department of Education, Massachusetts.* The Supreme Court found that parents had the right to public school reimbursement of private school tuition if the public school program rejected by parents was inappropriate.
1988	*Honig v. Doe. Supreme Court* decreed that school systems may not unilaterally exclude children with disabilities from the classroom for dangerous or disruptive behavior. Any programmatic changes because of behavior disturbances must follow due process procedures outlined in P.L. 94–142. In drastic situations the school can suspend a student for up to ten days.

TABLE 1.3   Continued

1989   *Daniel R. R. v. State Board of Education.* District and appeals court upheld hearing officer decision that general education curriculum was beyond abilities of a student with retardation and that he would receive little benefit from mainstreaming. The courts found that for some children placement in general education environment would not provide a free appropriate education.

1990   *Moore v. District of Columbia. Reversing an earlier decision, federal appeals court ruled that prevailing parents were entitled to recover attorney fees when a final resolution of their special education dispute came at the administrative hearing level.*

1993   *Zobrest v. Catalina Foothills School District* The court held that provision of a sign language interpreter in a parochial school was not an entitlement under IDEA; the decision was reversed in a finding that services of an interpreter were part of a general government program that distributed benefits to any child qualifying for services regardless of the school the student attended.

1997   *K. R. v. Anderson Community School Corp.* The Seventh Circuit court decided that a student with disabilities was not entitled to a publicly-funded personal assistant while attending a parochial school. The ruling set forth that under the IDEA, students with disabilities who choose to attend religious schools need not receive the full range of services they would receive if they attended public school, but they must receive some services.

Direct services are provided by working with students to correct or compensate for the problems that have caused them to fall behind in school. Indirect services are provided by special education personnel to others who are working with students in their general or special education classes—for example, consultation services. Appendix A gives a chronology of educational services provided youngsters with disabilities since the eighteenth century.

Who Receives Special Education?

During the past twenty years, the politics of disabilities have undergone considerable study (Lipsky & Gartner, 1989). Activists and academicians have insisted that the disabilities (biological conditions) be conceptually untangled from the social ramifications (handicappism) experienced with the condition. A person with a disability usually has a problem, either temporary or permanent, that requires special devices (e.g., wheelchairs, prostheses) or specialized instruction.

In the United States, school-aged children with disabilities are entitled to a free, appropriate public education. It is illegal to discriminate against individuals with disabilities. This means that an individual cannot be denied an education or a job because of a disability. When thinking about who receives these services, remember that special education is a subsystem of general education. Special education is mandated to provide services to students who have been identified as unable to progress effectively in the general classroom as a result of that disability. It is important to note that the presence of a disability alone is not sufficient reason to initiate special education services. Special education is warranted only after all attempts to help a youngster within the confines of the general classroom have proved ineffective.

In the first textbook dealing with the "education of exceptional children," Horn (1924) observed that mental, temperamental, and physical differences were the bases for some students needing special education. Today, many states organize their special education departments along similar categorical lines. A category is a descriptor or label assigned to a group of students. Although the names of the categories vary slightly from state to state, special education is generally provided for children within each of the following categories:

1. Students with visual impairments or blindness.
2. Students with hearing impairments or deafness.
3. Students with deafness and blindness.
4. Students with physical or other health impairments.
5. Students with multiple disabilities.
6. Students with language or communication impairments.
7. Students with learning disabilities.
8. Students with behavior disorders or serious emotional disturbances.
9. Students with mental retardation.

Physical Reasons for Needing Special Education

Special learning needs in areas of physical abilities (e.g., seeing, hearing, moving) are the basis for several categories of students with special needs. Most of us take normal vision and hearing for granted. The expression "20/20 vision" is used to describe normal visual functioning. Vision is measured by having people read letters or discriminate objects at a distance of twenty feet. The task is not difficult for most people. There are people, however, who must stand closer to see what others see easily from twenty feet away. These differences in visual functioning are the basis of deciding whether a student is blind or visually impaired. There are also people who even at a louder volume cannot hear what can easily be heard by the majority. Between normal hearing and deafness are various degrees of hearing loss, and it is these differences in degrees of hearing that are the basis for another category of exceptional students (i.e., deaf or hearing impaired).

How different do vision or hearing have to be before a person is considered blind or deaf? A person who, even with correction (e.g., glasses), must be twenty feet from a target that a person with normal vision can see at two hundred feet or more is considered blind. People with corrected vision better than 20/200 but not better than 20/70 are considered *visually impaired*. Ability to hear is measured along two scales: intensity and frequency. Intensity or loudness is measured in decibels (dB), and frequency or pitch is measured in hertz (cycles per second). Moores defines deaf and hard of hearing in terms of the effects on hearing loss:

> A deaf person is one whose hearing is disabled to an extent (usually 70 dB or greater) that precludes the understanding of speech through the ear alone, without or with the use of a hearing aid. A hard of hearing person is one whose hearing is disabled to an extent (usually 35–69 dB) that makes difficult, but does not preclude, the understanding of speech through the ear alone, without or with a hearing aid. (Moores, 1982)

For practical purposes, deafness means the absence of hearing in both ears; people with deafness have great difficulty hearing conversational speech without the assistance of a hearing aid. People with hearing impairments experience significant difficulty in hearing.

There are other disabling conditions that are of a physical nature. For example, *arthritis* is a measurable inflammation of a joint that limits movement. *Cerebral palsy* is impaired motor function due to brain damage; it produces difficulties in motor control that are observable in movement of large and small muscle groups. *Seizure disorder* (i.e., epilepsy) is also a brain disorder that results in convulsive episodes and periods of unconsciousness. Other health impairments include severe orthopedic problems that adversely affect educational performance and limit strength, vitality, or alertness. Special education may be provided to people with physical differences caused by congenital anomalies (e.g., spina bifida) as well as other general health and physical problems, (e.g., heart disease, asthma, diabetes, traumatic brain injury, autism).

Cognitive Reasons for Needing Special Education

Differences in intellectual performance or mental abilities are the bases for identifying a special need. To be considered mentally retarded, an individual must demonstrate subaverage intellectual functioning and delayed social development. Intelligence tests are frequently used to determine if an individual's intellectual performance is below that of peers. Students with scores from 75–50 on an intelligence test fall within the mild range of mental retardation. Students with more complex forms of mental retardation are often categorized as moderately, severely, or profoundly disabled. Besides the differences in severity linked to IQ scores, students with moderate to profound mental retardation usually have communication and health problems. We refer to these students as having clinical mental retardation because they have serious physical and medical complications that are identified by a physician at birth or soon afterwards (e.g., fetal alcohol syndrome, Down syndrome).

Highlight 1.2 Evan

Evan is a fourteen-year-old resident of a Catholic residential facility for youngsters who require child care in Syracuse, New York. Tall and athletic, Evan is a leader among the other boys. Mark Costello, a first year child care worker, describes his response to Evan's invitation to come see the puzzle he has just completed.

As Evan led me over to a card table sitting in the middle of the living room, it was obvious how proud he was of his accomplishment. Eager to lavish him with praise, I looked down at the table to see the three-hundred jigsaw pieces carefully connected after many evenings of effort. Pride quickly turned to confusion, however, when it became apparent that the picture was face down on the card table.

"What picture, Mr. Cos?" Evan asked.

"Do you see the picture on the top of the box the pieces came in, my friend?" I asked.

"Sure, what about it?"

"Well, that picture is now upside down on this card table and you old buddy, have just completed one heck of a tough task."

While the other boys were trying to read Evan's reaction to this perplexing bit of news, I began to internalize my first real lesson about the significance of mental retardation. Naive but determined, he had stuck to a task few if any youths of normal intelligence could tolerate. Was this just a glimpse of his true potential? How hard it was that night to convince Evan of how proud we were of his somewhat tarnished accomplishment.

From *Confessions of a Special Eddie: Reflections in Appreciation of Human Difference*, p. 19, by T. Mark Costello, copyright 1994, New York: Wizard Press. Reprinted with permission.

These students demonstrate deficits in adaptive behavior (i.e., social development). There is no formal definition of adaptive behavior, but the term generally refers to the way in which an individual functions in his or her community. As with intelligence tests, adaptive behavior evaluations are based on age-group comparisons. Formalized inventories of functional abilities (such as dressing oneself, using the telephone, or independently moving about the neighborhood) help educational evaluators determine adaptive behavior. Any determination of mental retardation must include a measure of intelligence and a measure of adaptive behavior skills (Robinson & Robinson, 1976). No student should be identified as mentally retarded solely on the basis of an intelligence test. Just as there are students with low intelligence test scores, there also are students whose intellectual performance is above that of their classmates. Historically, giftedness was determined by high IQ test scores. This approach is no longer favored by many educators because intelligence tests sample too narrow a range of abilities. Creativity, musical talent, leadership skills, and problem-solving abilities are a sample of talents not measurable through intelligence testing. More recently, experts in the field of giftedness recommend a multidimensional approach to establishing criteria for identification of students with special gifts or talents.

According to Renzulli, Reis, and Smith (1981), in order to be identified as gifted, students should demonstrate:

1. High ability including measured intelligence evaluation.
2. Creativity in the development and implementation of innovative ideas.
3. High task commitment—perseverance or diligence.

Students with special talents are not disabled; consequently, they do not receive federally mandated special education, although your state or local school system might subsidize a special education program for gifted students and talented students. Four groups of students are underrepresented in gifted education programs: culturally different, female, disabled, and underachieving (Patton, Kauffman, Blackbourn, & Brown, 1991).

How different do measures of intelligence have to be before an individual is considered mentally retarded or gifted? Differences in scores on intelligence tests and measures of adaptive behavior are evaluated in the same way as differences in scores on hearing, vision, or physical performance tests. Standards for normal intelligence and adaptive behavior are set by testing large groups of individuals. Professionals then set criteria for retardation or giftedness that are based on differences from mean intelligence or adaptive behavior ratings. For example, the common standard for normal performance is a score of 90–110 on an intelligence test; scores below 75 or above 130 are considered reflective of mental retardation or giftedness. It is important to remember that special education services for students identified as gifted are not mandated by federal legislation. Figure 1.2 traces the normal curve distribution of IQ scores used to determine degrees of mental retardation and giftedness.

Academic Reasons for Needing Special Education

With the categories of mental retardation and gifted, it is assumed that the individual's performance on achievement tests will be consistent with the performance on intelligence tests. This means that if a student obtains a high score on an intelligence test, high performance on an achievement test is also expected. If students perform poorly on intelligence tests, it is expected that their achievement test scores will also be low. There are students whose performance on achievement tests is not consistent with their performance on intelligence tests. When the difference between ability (e.g., intelligence test performance) and achievement (e.g., reading, math) is significant, the student may be identified as learning disabled.

How different do scores on ability tests and scores on achievement tests have to be before a student is classified as learning disabled? Although officials of the federal government have provided guidelines for use in identifying students with learning disabilities, no specific criteria have been provided for judging

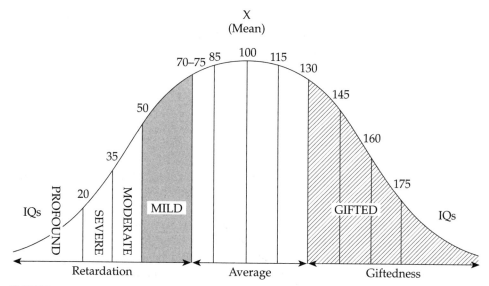

FIGURE 1.2   Normal Curve Distribution of IQ Scores

when discrepancies between ability and achievement are severe enough to call a student learning disabled. Criteria differ from state to state for determining the identification of a learning disability.

Students are considered eligible for special education if they meet guidelines spelled out in state regulations. Due to a lack of consistent criteria between and within states, it is likely that many students in special education programs for students with learning disabilities are misplaced. Students with learning disabilities comprise the largest subgroup of students with mild disabilities.

Communication Reasons for Needing Special Education

Just as there are differences in the reading, writing, and mathematical skills of students, there are also differences in the ways students speak and express themselves. Some people speak clearly, enunciating each part of their speech. Others speak quickly, making it difficult for listeners to understand them. Some children use speech as a means of making their desires, feelings, and opinions known. Others are less adept at verbalizing personal needs. There are accepted ages at which children are expected to demonstrate the use of various forms of communication. For example, most children understand approximately one thousand words, combine their words into simple sentences, and understand concepts related to language (e.g., on, off, later) by the time they are two years old. By the age of seven, children are expected to use culturally acceptable grammar when speaking; language at this age is much like that used by family and friends. Differences in language and communication skills are measured by performance on tests and classroom observations of student interaction. Differences in language development and communication skills are commonly observed in children of all ages. When these differences adversely affect educational performance, the individual may be entitled to special services provided for students with language impairments.

How different does language have to be before a student is considered language impaired? Many students in this category receive special services for such problems as lisping, stuttering, and mispronunciation of individual words (e.g., they say "wabbit" instead of "rabbit," "pasketti" instead of "spaghetti," or "bud" for "bird"). Some of these students have voice tones that are too low, too high, nasal, too harsh, or too hoarse. There are no absolute standards for determining when an individual's speech is "too" nasal or "too" harsh or when it will adversely affect educational performance. When speech mannerisms cause difficulties for the listener, a student may be referred for speech therapy. Some teachers are more adept than others at understanding differences in the language produced by their students. Similarly, the context in which speech occurs influences the judgments made about it. Recent government figures indicate that there are more students in this category than in any other besides learning disabilities. This is probably not surprising for a category based on differences in speech clarity or tone.

Behavioral–Emotional Reasons for Needing Special Education

Just as standards for normal intellectual performance have evolved within the educational system, standards for how students should act in school and society also have evolved. Standards for normal behavior are based more on what is judged acceptable in a specific setting than on judgments about how an individual performs on a test. Demonstrating intellectual performance that is sufficiently above or below normal is the basis for being identified as gifted or mentally retarded. Demonstrating unacceptable behavior in school is the basis for being identified with behavior disorders or emotional disturbance.

Just how different does behavior have to be before a student is considered behaviorally disordered or emotionally disturbed? Based on what you have learned about the other conditions of special education, your answer may be "behavior that is significantly different from the behavior of their peers." You are right, but you will have trouble explaining behavioral differences. There are no numerical standards for normal behavior. There are no tests to measure the normality of behavior. Classroom observations by teachers carry the most weight in identifying students with behavior disorders. Defining behavior disorders is like defining beauty—very subjective. What is acceptable behavior for one classroom may not be acceptable in another. What is acceptable behavior for one teacher is not necessarily acceptable for another.

How Many Students Receive Special Education?

Each year more than five and a half million students receive special education services in public school or private settings (Eighteenth Annual Report to

TABLE 1.4   Students Ages 3–21 Served: Number and
Percentage Change, School Years 1987–88 through 1994–95

School Year	Change in Total Number Served from Previous Year (%)	Total Served
1987-88	—	4,455,985
1988-89	1.7	4,533,793
1989-90	2.3	4,638,605
1990-91	2.5	4,756,517
1991-92	3.4	4,920,227
1992-93	3.3	5,081,023
1993-94	3.8	5,271,847
1994-95	3.2	5,439,626

Source: U.S. Department of Education, 1996.

Congress, 1996). In thinking about the number of students involved, consider that it is about the same as the total full-time undergraduate enrollment in all United States colleges and universities. The number of students who receive special education is about the same as the combined population of North Dakota, South Dakota, Montana, Nevada, Idaho, and Wyoming.

There has been a steady increase in the number of students receiving special education. From 1988 to 1995, the number of students with disabilities rose from 4,555,985 to 5,439,626; in that time span 983,641 students were added to special education enrollments (Table 1.4).

The increase in number of students enrolled in special education classes coincided with the growth in general education attendance. Other reasons for the steady rise of students identified as requiring special education include:

1. The availability of pull-out (resource room programs) for hard-to-teach students.
2. Upward swing in the poverty rate, resulting in more children coming to school with health, psychological, and intellectual difficulties.
3. More culturally and linguistically different students attend public schools.
4. A dramatic increase in the numbers of students identified as having a learning disability.

This growth has increased the need for certified special education teachers. For example, using a conservative average of fifteen students for each special class teacher, an average of 8,197 new teachers were needed each year from 1988 to 1995. The growth of special education services has also caused problems. For example, school personnel have to decide how to pay for the increasing numbers of students. Since the cost of educating students with special needs may come at the expense of educating students in general education, school personnel face hard choices when allocating funds. The growth of special education is directly attributed to passage of the Individuals with Disabilities Education Act, which mandates a "free and appropriate public education" for all students with disabling conditions.

Most school districts organize their special education programs along categorical lines. For example, your local school district may have a supervisor who is responsible for types of disabilities (e.g., emotionally disturbed, learning disabled) recognized in your state. Your local school district probably also has special classes set aside for different categories of special education students served in your state. Some states (e.g., New Jersey) are moving toward noncategorical organization. Only two states (Massachusetts and South Dakota) do not use categories as the basis for organizing their special education systems (Garret & Brazil, 1989). Until 1991, Massachusetts education regulations, for example, used the generic term "child with special needs" to refer to all students who require special education, regardless of their type of disability.

Students with Mild Disabilities

Students with mild disabilities are those typically categorized as learning disabled, mild mentally retarded, or behavior disordered. Students with language or communication impairments is another large category of mild disabilities; however, because their difficulties are treated by speech clinicians rather than teachers, we have not included information about them in this book.

The term *mild disabilities* not used to imply that these students do not have serious learning problems or that their problems are less important than those of other students. We think the term has come to be used for this group of students because many of their characteristics overlap, and they can be educated in general classrooms.

According to the definition included in the Individuals with Disabilities Education Act, 1990 (U.S. Department of Education, 1990), students with learning disabilities exhibit a disorder in one or more of the basic psychological processes involved in understanding or using spoken or written language. These may be manifested in disorders of listening, thinking, talking, reading, writing, spelling, or arithmetic. Learning disabilities include conditions that historically have been referred to as perceptual handicaps, brain injury, minimal brain dysfunction, dyslexia, and developmental aphasia. They do not include learning problems due primarily to visual, hearing, or motor handicaps, to mental retardation, emotional handicaps, or environmental disadvantages.

Students with mild mental retardation are those with impaired intellectual and adaptive behaviors and whose development reflects a reduced rate of learn-

ing. If a student's IQ score is 75–50, and the student's socializa[...]
uniformly below age expectations, an evaluation of mild mental r[...]
likely. In some school systems, students with mild mental retardatio[...]
gorized as educably mentally retarded (EMR). We will avoid that term th[...]
this text because it implies a predetermined level of ability—educable. [...]
viousness of language used to describe students with mental retardation be[...]
more evident when students with moderate mental retardation are categor[...]
as trainable (TMR), and students with severe mental retardation are categori[...]
as custodial (CMR).

Students with behavior disorders are those who exhibit persistent and con-sistent behavioral problems that disrupt their own or others' learning. Sometimes these students are referred to as emotionally disturbed. The term "behavior disordered" is more descriptive of this population of students. Using the term "emotionally disturbed" implies that we know *why* the student is unable to adapt to classroom routines—he or she has an emotional or psychological problem. In fact, this is often not the case. Many students are referred for special education because they are impulsive, distractible, or hyperactive. These behaviors can be caused by any number of factors that have no connection with a student's emotional development. Neurological factors, diet, allergies, delayed development, and ineffective teaching are some explanations for students' inability to control their behavior in a classroom.

We recognize, however, that many students with behavior disorders do, in fact, have emotional problems. There is a great deal of overlap among students identified as behavior disordered and emotionally disturbed. Even if the primary cause of a student's behavior problems is diet or allergies, the reaction of others to the disruptive behavior can affect that student's emotional development. Moreover, a student may have an emotional problem and demonstrate no overt behavior disorders. This is a particularly acute problem with adolescents who may be withdrawn or depressed but mask their emotional distress with good grades. We go into more detail about this overlap between behavior disorders and emotional disturbances in Chapter 3.

Students classified as learning disabled, mildly mentally retarded, or behavior disordered account for more than two-thirds of all students with disabilities (U.S. Department of Education, 1995), and they share many characteristics (Hallahan & Kauffman, 1977). For example, students with learning disabilities often have problems with reading comprehension, language development, interpersonal relations, and classroom behavioral control (Lerner, 1988). These same characteristics are common in teacher descriptions of students designated mild mentally retarded and behavior disordered (Coleman, 1986; Kauffman, 1985; Robinson & Robinson, 1982).

If you have observed that these characteristics can also be found in students who do not receive special education services, you are correct. It is a thin and sometimes arbitrary line that separates students with mild disabilities from other students. Many classroom problems are interactional: the result of a mismatch between teaching and learning style. The behavior, expectations, and attitude of

sroom teacher often is a key component in determining whether
rred and evaluated as having a mild disability. For example,
cs of learning disabilities, such as dyslexia (i.e., an impairment
are neurologically based; other characteristics, such as dis-
based on teacher perception of student performance. A student
will be dyslexic in every classroom; on the other hand, a student
as distractible and hyperactive in one teacher's classroom may have
difficulty attending in another classroom. How can this happen? Some teachers are more adept at engaging students in their schoolwork than others. In special education, we have learned never to underestimate the power of good teaching to "cure" a mild disability.

Whether or not it helps students with mild disabilities to be categorized as mildly mentally retarded, learning disabled, or behavior disordered is controversial. Over the years, each of these three subgroups of mild disabilities have been separated by distinct identification criteria, different teaching methods, teacher certificates linked to a single disability, and different special education placements. Each category is represented by separate professional organizations and advocacy groups. The American Association for Mental Retardation and the Association for Citizens with Learning Disabilities are two examples of category-specific organizations. Researchers develop expertise within a single category of mild disabilities and report their findings in journals that specialize in mental retardation, learning disabilities, or behavior disorders.

Yet students who are placed in different categories of mild disabilities share many common traits. Lack of interest in school and low motivation are two traits displayed by many youngsters categorized as having a mild disability. It is also clear that instructional practices proved effective for students in one category of mild disabilities can be useful with students within another category. Such instructional strategies as peer tutoring, whole language, and cooperative learning can help students learn regardless of how their mild disability is categorized.

There are advantages and disadvantages to classifying students by specific categories of mild disabilities. Special educators sometimes use the term "labeling" to describe this categorization process. Is it a good idea to label students? We will present the facts about both sides of this issue. Ultimately you will need to make your own professional decision about labeling students with such terms as mildly retarded, learning disabled, and behavior disordered. Whether or not to place a student into a mild disability category is an issue you will be faced with throughout your career as a teacher.

Labeling

Students identified as having problems in school either will meet eligibility criteria for special education services or will be unofficially labeled with such negative adjectives as "lazy," "unmotivated," "slow learner," or "behavior problem." In the latter case, neither the teacher nor the student will get help. The student will remain in general education and most likely continue to fail in school. There is an increased probability that the student will eventually drop out of school.

In most states, a student is identified as requiring special education when school evaluation data match the student with a specific disability category that is outlined by state education regulations. This classification process assumes that assigning a student a categorical name implies knowledge about the characteristics of the student's learning problem. This categorical approach to providing help has been roundly criticized by many educators who claim that labeling a student does more harm than good. What students are called determines what services they receive and where they will receive them. Because this classification process alters the school experience of many students, professionals have researched and described the advantages and disadvantages of the labeling associated with it.

Advantages of Labeling

The advantages of labeling were more obvious in the formative years of special education (mid-1940s to early 1970s) than they are now. For instance, without the category of learning disabilities, advocates for these children would have had no rallying point to promote educational programs. Imagine how ineffective scientists would be in raising money for cancer research if we had no name for it. The advantages of labeling can be summarized as follows:

1. Federal and local funding of special education programs are based on categories of disabilities.
2. Labeling enables professionals to communicate with one another because each categorical label conveys a general idea about learning characteristics.
3. The human mind requires "mental hooks" to think about problems. If present categorical labels were abolished, a new set of descriptors would evolve to take their place. There is ample evidence of this in the evolution of the term "mildly retarded," which you will read more about in Chapter 3.
4. Labeling the disability spotlights the problem for the general public. Labeling can spark social concern and aid advocacy efforts.
5. Labeling may make the nondisabled majority more tolerant of the disabled minority. In other words, the actions of a child identified as having mental retardation might be tolerated, whereas the behavior of a nondisabled child would be criticized.
6. Labeling has led to the development of specialized teaching methods, assessment approaches, and behavioral interventions that are useful for teachers of all students. (Hallahan & Kauffman, 1982)

Disadvantages of Labeling

Because of the Individuals with Disabilities Education Act, children with disabilities have made significant gains in public schools. These advances have been accompanied by problems inherent in officially designating someone abnormal. Make no mistake about it—these labels stick. Once a child is categorized as mildly retarded, behavior disordered, or learning disabled, that information will be forwarded to every new teacher in the child's cumulative folder. Along with the label comes the stigma of being deficient. For this reason alone, assigning a student to a category for special education purposes is a fateful step that should not be taken unless all other options have proved unsuccessful. The disadvantages of labeling are summarized as follows:

1. Labels shape teacher expectations. Imagine what your reaction would be if the principal informed you that the new student in your class is mildly mentally retarded. Studies on teacher expectations have demonstrated that what teachers believe about student capability is directly related to student achievement.
2. All children have some troubling behaviors. Labels can exaggerate a student's actions in the eyes of a teacher. A teacher may overreact to behavior of a labeled child that would be tolerated in another.
3. Labels send a clear message: the learning problem is with the student. Labels tend to obscure the essence of teaching and learning as a two-way street. Some students placed in a mild disability category have nothing wrong with them. They are the unfortunate recipients of ineffective schooling.
4. Labels perpetuate the notion that students with mild disabilities are qualitatively different from other children. This is not true. Students with mild disabilities go through the same developmental stages as their peers, although sometimes at a slower rate.
5. Teachers may confuse the student with the label. Labels reflect categories of disabilities. Categories are abstract, not real, concepts that are general enough to incorporate many different individuals. Almost two million students are identified as learning disabled, but as individuals, each is a unique human being. When a student is placed in a category, a teacher who knows some of the characteristics of a category may ascribe all known characteristics to each labeled child. This is stereotyping. Stereotypes handicap students when teachers rationalize low achievement by citing characteristics of the label. An example is the teacher who explains away a teaching–learning problem by stating, "We can't really expect Mary to remember too much math because she is mildly retarded."
6. Students cannot receive special education services until they are labeled. In many instances, the intervention comes too late. The need to label students before help arrives undermines a preventive approach to mild learning problems.
7. Diagnostic labels are unreliable. Educational evaluation is filled with quirks. States use different descriptive criteria for the same categories; many evaluation instruments have questionable validity and reliability; specific labels go through trends (for example, at one time learning disabilities was con-

sidered a white, middle class affliction, while African American students were overrepresented in the mild mental retardation category).

8. Labels often put the blame (and the guilt) for a student's learning problems squarely on the parents' shoulders. In many cases, this is unjustified because students may be mislabeled or teachers may not fully understand the many different causes of mild disabilities.

Focus on What to Teach Students

The purpose of the Individuals with Disabilities Education Act is to ensure that all students with special needs receive a free and appropriate education. Congress did not define what it meant by the term "appropriate." The legislators recognized that there is no one instructional approach that is best. Instead they viewed "appropriate" as a process rather than a product. Whether or not a program is appropriate is based on the ability of the school system and parents to work out a mutually acceptable individualized education program.

Individual Education Program

An individualized education program (IEP) must be written for each student receiving special education. Special education includes many services related to classroom instruction, such as transportation, occupational therapy, counseling, and adaptive equipment. Assessed instructional needs of each student determine the areas for which an IEP is developed. Each IEP must contain the following components:

1. The student's present levels of education performance, including how the student's disability affects involvement and progress in general curriculum or other appropriate activities.
2. A statement of measurable annual goals, including benchmarks or short-term objectives.
3. A statement of the special education and related services and supplementary aids and services to be provided to the student.
4. An explanation of the extent, if any, to which the child will not participate with students without disabilities in general classes.
5. A statement of any modifications in the administration of state or district assessments of student achievement that are needed for the student to participate; or, if the student will not participate, why the assessment is not appropriate and how the student be assessed.
6. The projected date for the beginning, as well as the anticipated frequency, location, and duration of services.
7. As age appropriate, a statement of the transition service needs of the student and interagency responsibilities and linkages necessary to meet them.

8. A statement of how the student's progress toward annual goals will be measured and how the student's parents will be regularly informed, at least as often as parents of students without disabilities are informed, of progress and the extent to which it is sufficient to enable the student to achieve goals by the end of the year.

Each school district may develop its own IEP format as long as the required information is included. The IEP must be developed within a meeting by participants stipulated by legislation. The IEP Team is a group of individuals composed of:

1. The student's parents or guardians.
2. At least one special education teacher (if the child is, or may be, participating in the general education environment).
3. At least one special education teacher, or where, appropriate, at least one special education provider of such child.
4. A representative of the local educational agency who is qualified to provide, or supervise the provision of, specially designed instruction to meet the unique needs individuals with disabilities; is knowledgeable about general curriculum; and is of knowledgeable about the availability of resources of the local educational agency.
5. An individual who can interpret the instructional implications of evaluation results.
6. At the discretion of the parent or the agency, other individuals who have knowledge or special expertise regarding the student, including related services personnel as appropriate.
7. Whenever appropriate, the student.

The IEP must be reviewed and revised at least once a year.

In the case of students with mild disabilities, the IEP is usually determined by the portion of the general education curriculum with which a student is having difficulty. A student with a learning disability might have an IEP that emphasizes reading and mathematics. A student with a behavior disorder would have an IEP that emphasizes self-control and adjustment to classroom routines. An adolescent with mild mental retardation might have an IEP that describes vocational goals and objectives.

Focus on Where to Teach Students

When Congress passed the Education for All Handicapped Children Act in 1975, the media hailed it as the mainstreaming law. This caused considerable concern among teachers and administrators who feared mainstreaming would lead to dumping students with disabilities into general classrooms. Newspeople inadvertently misled the public. The term "mainstreaming" is not mentioned in the law. Congress believed that students with disabilities should be educated with nondisabled students whenever feasible. The law states that students should be educated in the least restrictive environment. The intent of the least restrictive environment mandate is to assure that students are not segregated because of their disabilities and to give them every opportunity to have a normal school experience. More restrictive settings, such as self-contained special classes and residential programs, should be utilized only when a student's needs are so complex that he or she would not receive an appropriate education in a less restrictive environment. Evelyn Deno's *Cascade of Services* (Figure 1.3) provides a visual representation of the relationship between least and most restrictive settings. Level I is least restrictive. Each succeeding level establishes more distance between special and general education services.

It is the responsibility of each school system to provide a continuum of educational services ranging from least to most restrictive. We will briefly describe the types of special education services you can expect a school system to provide.

Regular Classroom Placement (Level I, Level II)

Regular placement with supportive services (e.g., materials, consultation, team teaching) is the least restrictive environment in the hierarchy of services. If a student spends less than 21 percent of the school day outside the regular classroom receiving special instruction, the federal government defines the placement as a regular classroom. Students with learning disabilities usually spend most of their day in the regular classroom. Speech clinicians, social workers, special education teachers, and school psychologists may consult with the regular classroom teacher on student needs and progress.

Resource Room Placement (Level III)

Resource rooms are commonly referred to as pull-out programs. The resource room is a special education classroom located within the student's school. A youngster goes to the resource room on a scheduled basis to receive tutorial help from a special education teacher. Students may spend from 21 to 60 percent of their school day in a resource room. Typically, resource room teachers teach fundamental skills and/or tutor students in the academic subjects that were the source of the referral. It is the resource room teacher's job to take a lead role in the development and implementation of IEPs for students placed in this setting. The majority of students who receive resource room help remain in the regular classroom for most of their school day. In 1994, 73 percent of all students with special needs received special education services in a combination of resource room and regular classroom placements (U.S. Department of Education, 1996).

Special Class Placement (Level IV)

Special classes are self-contained programs located in a public school system. They are sometimes called segregated programs because only students with disabilities are enrolled. Students are usually grouped in special classes by categories

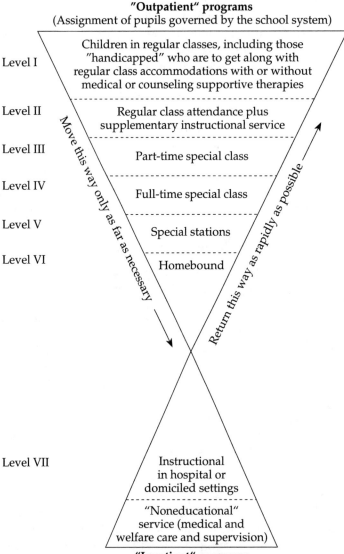

"Outpatient" programs
(Assignment of pupils governed by the school system)

Level I — Children in regular classes, including those "handicapped" who are to get along with regular class accommodations with or without medical or counseling supportive therapies

Level II — Regular class attendance plus supplementary instructional service

Level III — Part-time special class

Level IV — Full-time special class

Level V — Special stations

Level VI — Homebound

Level VII — Instructional in hospital or domiciled settings

"Noneducational" service (medical and welfare care and supervision)

Move this way only as far as necessary

Return this way as rapidly as possible

"Inpatient" programs
(Assignment of children to facilities governed by health or welfare agencies)

FIGURE 1.3 Cascade of Services

Source: "Special Education as Developmental Capitol" by E. Deno, *Exceptional Children 37*, 229–237. © 1970 by the Council for Exceptional Children. Reprinted with permission.

of disability. The special class is the most criticized of special education placements when it is used for students with mild disabilities. Although students with learning disabilities are not usually placed in special classes, students with mild mental retardation and behavior disorders are sometimes placed in these programs. Placement rates for special classes have remained at about 25 percent of the total special education population since 1975.

Special Day School Placement (Level V)

Alternative high school programs, special education early childhood programs, and private day programs are examples of special day school placements. Students are transported to these special education programs at the school system's expense. Public school systems sometimes contract with private vendors to provide special education services for students with low-incidence disabilities such as autism or multiple disabilities. In addition to the disadvantages inherent in segregation, students who attend special day school programs may spend lengthy amounts of time being transported from home to program and back home again. In 1994, 3.1 percent of students with special needs were educated in separate day facilities (U.S. Department of Education, 1996).

Homebound Programs (Level VI)

Students who are ill or require intensive medical services are educated by itinerant teachers at home. With the passage of P.L. 99–457 in 1986, incentives were created to develop individualized family service plans for infants and toddlers with disabilities at home. P.L. 99–457 (Handicapped Infant and Toddler Program, Part H) amended the Education for All Handicapped Children Act to extend special education services to preschoolers in 1991–92.

Other Domiciled Settings (Level VII)

Some hospitals have their own special education programs. Only a small percentage, less than 1 percent, of all special needs learners are restricted to hospital care (U.S. Department of Education, 1996). More than 450,000 adolescents are incarcerated in correctional facilities across the country each year (Margolis, 1988). Many of these young people are from minorities and uneducated. If a special need is identified, an incarcerated youth up to age twenty-one has the same right to special education services as students in the public school system. In their book *Special Education in the Criminal Justice System* (1987), Nelson, Rutherford, and Wolford suggest that this population is underserved and that there may be a higher prevalence of mild disabilities among prisoners than the general population. Within the past few years, some special educators have argued that an adjudication of delinquency (i.e., socially maladjusted) may be a disability in

Highlight 1.3 An Eductional Oasis on Rikers Island

In the halls of the Adolescent Reception Detention Center on Rikers Island, there are rapists and muggers, murderers and thieves awaiting judgment. But when Sharon Jones looks at the teenagers there, she sees mechanics and writers, printers and scientists. "Whatever they might be to other people, to me they're students," said Ms. Jones, principal of the Rikers Island Educational Facility, a surprising oasis of order, possibility, and education for young men who mostly never before appreciated the value of school and who mostly never before bothered to attend. Ms. Jones believes that if the offenders at Rikers Island are not educated, "you might as well set a

permanent place with them in a prison mess hall." The school has a newspaper and a literary magazine that is printed in the school's print shop. There are seven computer labs and an auto shop. And there is no violence.

" I was really into autos back at home, but I had the bad influence of my environment and I let it rule me," said Danny, awaiting trial at Rikers Island. "Then I see my teacher in here and I think, 'Oh man, I really made a mistake with my life.' But if there was no auto shop here, I don't think I would learn any lesson being incarcerated because I would have nothing to keep me interested" (Fein, 1995).

itself (Benson, Edwards, Rosell, & White, 1986). Correctional facilities include prisons, jails, and detention centers. DiGangi, Perryman, and Rutherford (1990) reported that 42 percent of offenders in a state juvenile facility required special education.

Residential Programs (Level VII)

When a student requires intensive, around-the-clock treatment, residential programs are an option. Residential placements are expensive, however, and it can cost a school system over $50,000 a year to send one student to a residential facility for a year. One program for students with severe disabilities in Providence, Rhode Island, presently costs in excess of $135,000 a year. Ironically, the funding mechanisms in some states actually create incentives for such restrictive placements by providing reimbursements that increase in proportion to time in a special education program.

Blackman reported that in Illinois "it frequently costs a school district less money to send a child to a private day, often a residential school, than educating the child within the school district" (Blackman, 1989, 461). Illinois has set aside money to fully reimburse school districts for room and board costs incurred as a result of residential placements. Despite the additional expense, residential placements cannot match the quality of public school special education programs. Private school teachers are often uncertified or inexperienced. They work longer hours (usually through the summer) and for less pay than public school teachers. Union representation, a sine qua non of public school life, is virtually nonexistent in private, residential facilities. In 1994, less than 1 percent of students with special needs were placed in residential programs (U.S. Department of Education, 1996).

Focus on How to Teach Students with Mild Disabilities

Schools can no longer ignore the individual and unique instructional needs of pupils (Lipsky & Gartner, 1989). The laws and court decisions that mandate an appropriate educational program for youth with disabilities are equally beneficial for regular education students. Working separately, general and special educators have developed instructional approaches that can benefit students both with and without disabilities. By working together, general and special educators can improve the education of all students. Some special educators have proposed a merger of general and special education. They believe that the splintering of educational services in schools has diminished efforts to help difficult-to-teach students (Stainback, Stainback, & Forest, 1989). If the ideal is the establishment of an appropriate education for students with disabilities, can this be accomplished in the general education classroom with collaborative efforts of general and special educators? The movement known as inclusion has addressed this concern and is discussed in more detail in Chapter 6, Least Restrictive Environment.

Smith-Davis put the onus of educational change on general education when she stated: "The only impediment to greater access to the [educational] mainstream by students with disabilities and other types of variance is the capacity of general education to respond with effective instruction to the diversity of needs, learning styles, and other characteristics of students who are not typical" (Smith-Davis, 1989a, 2). Both general and special educators are aware that we are in a state of transition as we conceive the best strategies for helping students with mild disabilities. Therefore, the future focus may shift from where (setting) and why (rights) students are placed in special education to a focus on *how* to educate successfully those students who are difficult to teach. Smith-Davis (1989a) defined the following factors as critical in making these decisions: (1) curriculum, (2) instruction, (3) methods, (4) materials, (5) options, (6) alternatives, and (7) instructional roles and relationships. In order to understand how these factors can make a difference in the realm of general education, it is necessary to understand the current status of the field.

Comparing General and Special Education

Because general education emphasizes a fixed, sequential curriculum, pupils with differences have been squeezed out of the system (Smith-Davis, 1989a). Many of these youth have ended up in special education, not so much to meet unique individual needs but because special education is one of the few services available to help children unable to meet the requirements of general education

TABLE 1.5   Comparisons between General and Special Education

General Education	Special Education
Cirriculum addresses group	Curriculum addresses individual
Standardizes curricula	Tailors curricula
Instruction emanates from a global view of student readiness and progress	Instruction emanates from individual assessment, diagnosis, prescription
Maintains larger class sizes; has larger pupil–teacher ratio	Maintains smaller class sizes; has smaller pupil–teacher ratio
Uses basal materials and texts; uses standard materials and texts	Uses specialized materials and texts; uses modified materials and texts
Emphasizes grades	Emphasizes meeting instructional objectives
Adheres to the learning pace of the average student	Adheres to the learning pace of individual students
Seeks help for students with academic and behavioral deviations	Specializes in students with academic and behavioral deviations
Is responsible for curriculum achievement	Is responsible for solving learning problems and helping difficult-to-teach students
Focuses on content, especially at the secondary level	Focuses on methods and student skills
Is similar to medical "general practitioner"	Is similar to the "specialist" in medicine
Does not stress early intervention	Stresses intervention at infancy or preschool age
Minimal focus on postschool transition	Significant focus on postschool transition
Involves parents peripherally	Involves parents centrally
Refers to related services	Incorporates related services

Source: Smith-Davis, 1989a.

(Sarason & Doris, 1979; Ysseldyke & Algozzine, 1982). Some of these children are not truly disabled, but in need of instructional remediation. This practice neglects preventive efforts to solve classroom problems. Often, the only way a teacher can get help for a student (or for herself) is to refer the youngster for special education evaluation. This scenario casts general and special educators in roles that make preventive collaboration difficult to achieve.

There are many differences between the two systems of general and special education. A comparative overview is shown in Table 1.5. Basically, special education is adaptive to the individual needs of students. Concepts such as individualization, specialization, heterogeneity, and lifelong learning are among those that drive practices in special education. In contrast, regular education is group-oriented, global, norm-referenced, and presents standardized curriculum.

Since 1975, special education has grown as a subsystem of general education. This growth has tended to accentuate differences between the two systems. Students have received special services, but not without cost. The stigma of being identified as deficient, along with a loss of regular classroom instructional time, has pushed students with mild disabilities further down the ladder of school success. If general and special educators can find ways to work together, the combination of knowledge and expertise will benefit all students. The following chapters will focus on the unique characteristics of students with mild disabilities. Using this knowledge as a base, in ensuing chapters we describe those strategies that can help general and special educators work more closely to assist students with mild disabilities in reaching their fullest potential.

Summary

Special education serves students with disabilities. Students with mild disabilities constitute the majority of students in special education programs. These students have problems and characteristics that make success in school difficult without special assistance. Students with a severe discrepancy between intellectual ability and performance in school are called learning disabled. Students with subaverage performance on intelligence tests and adaptive behavior problems are called mildly mentally retarded. Students with social and emotional problems that inhibit learning are called behavior disordered. These three groups of students are often referred to as mildly disabled because their problems are basically educational in nature. Today, more than two-thirds of the students served in special education programs are classified as learning disabled, mildly mentally retarded, or emotionally disordered.

Early special education programs sometimes consisted of isolated special classes or custodial placements that left much to be desired in terms of good instruction and sound educational practices. With the advent of the Individuals with Disabilities Education Act, and its subsequent supplements and amendments, special educators focused on providing appropriate education for students with mild disabilities. As a result of this monumental legislation, students who receive special services are entitled to education that is as much like normal as possible. Cooperation between general and special educators is the best strategy for ensuring the success of educational interventions for students with mild disabilities.

Activities

1. Based on what you have learned in this chapter, answer the following questions:
   a. How did schools come to deal with the disabilities, like Jake, Mary, and Felipe presented in the vignette at the beginning of this chapter?
   b. How would IEPs for Jake, Mary, and Felipe be similar?
   c. How would their IEPs be different?

2. Play the labeling game. Cut strips of tagboard that can be stapled to cloth or plastic strips and tied to one's forehead. Write labels on the strips like "cheerleader," "jock," "brain," "clown," "leader," "trouble-maker," "critic," "learning disabled," "gifted," and so on. In order to play the game, the labels are laid face down and randomly drawn by the group leader. He or she ties one to each participant's forehead without the person seeing what his or her label is before removing it. Playing this game brings about an awareness of how we label each other and how other people's reactions label us as well.

3. Simulate a planning conference between a special education teacher and a general classroom teacher. Select a hypothetical student and describe how this student functions in domains like academic achievement, language development, social skills, adaptive abilities, and so on. Have the teachers offer ideas and suggestions about remediating and accommodating the student within and between the two classrooms.

4. Visit an elementary, middle (or junior high), and high school. Arrange an interview with the principal, assistant principal, and/or guidance counselor. Ask about the special education programs at each of the schools. Which services are available? How restrictive are each of the special education settings?

5. While at the school, visit a general education classroom. Observe students while they are working. Are the students academically engaged? Is their behavior appropriate to the learning task? Can you identify any who are having learning or behavior problems?

2 Students with Mild Mental Retardation

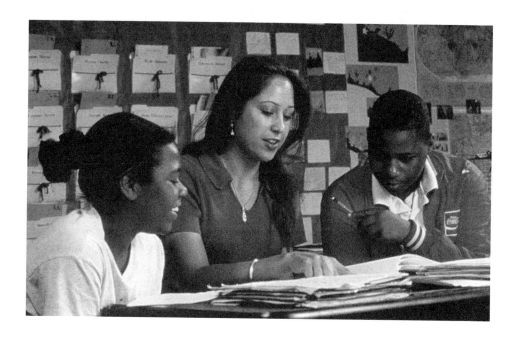

Advance Organizer

After you complete this chapter you will be able to answer the following questions.

1. How has IQ testing influenced social and education practices in the United States?
2. What is mild mental retardation?

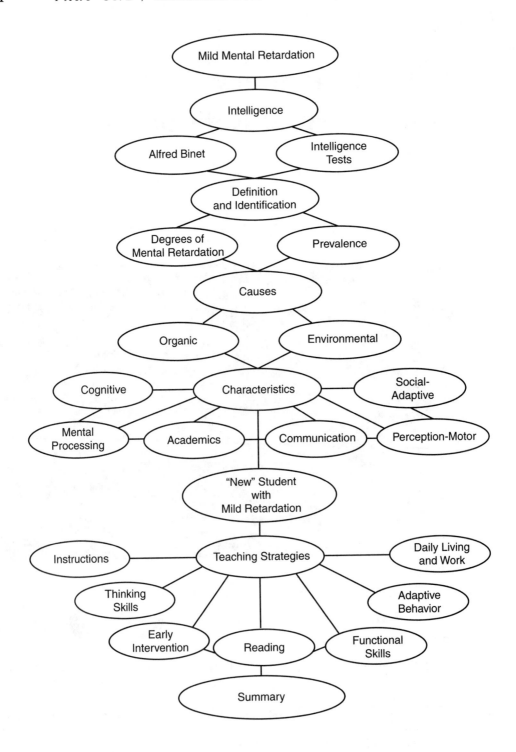

3. What are the causes of mild mental retardation?
4. Why is adaptive behavior important in defining mild mental retardation?
5. What does the "six hour retarded child" mean?
6. Why is there an over-representation of African American males in special education programs for students with mild mental retardation?
7. What are the cognitive, social, language, and academic characteristics of students with mild mental retardation?
8. How can teachers improve the functional, social, and academic skills of students with mild mental retardation?

Vignette: Larry

Larry was nine years old. Each day he boarded a yellow school bus for a half-hour journey to George Washington Elementary School. When he arrived at school, he walked past a series of cheery, primary-grade classrooms and entered a small room at the end of the hall. In this, the special education classroom, Larry struggled with reading and arithmetic. He had difficulty sitting still and attending to lessons. Because of his distractibility, he was a constant discipline problem. Despite these negatives, Larry's schooling provided him with a safe and secure routine for five hours a day.

After school, Larry returned to another world—one of disorganized squalor in a "welfare hotel." Larry, his mother, and his two-year-old sister shared a single room in the rundown tenement, which was also inhabited by drug addicts and prostitutes. Hunger, anxiety, and depression were a way of life for Larry in this bleak world, where even a trip down the hall to the communal bathroom was a hazardous journey. Larry never knew his father. His mother tried to make do on their welfare check, but it barely provided enough money to live on. She tried several times to find a full-time job, but she was handicapped by her lack of formal schooling.

Larry was one of many children who strained the resources of the city's social and educational services. His teacher described him as "depressed" and "apathetic." "Even when he smiles," she reported, "his eyes are sad." Larry was evaluated as a student with mild mental retardation soon after he began school at George Washington Elementary School six months ago. Larry's chaotic and insecure life made the prognosis bleak. His teacher felt that school could offer Larry an orderly environment, a nutritious lunch, and emotional stability. "I don't know if Larry will ever learn to read," she admitted, "he has been in three different schools in the past two years, and I doubt if he will be here much longer." This teacher's remarks underscore how unfavorable social conditions can overwhelm the best educational intentions.

Now that you have read the vignette about Larry see how many problem-solving questions you can answer. If necessary refer to other sources of information about the effects of poverty on the quality of life of children. See, for example, *Savage Inequalities* (1991) and *Amazing Grace* (1995) by Jonathan Kozol.

1. What can teachers do outside of school to promote the social welfare of young people?

2. What kind of social programs can you identify in your community that offers assistance to homeless youth?
3. What can teachers do in school with students like Larry? Is Larry's situation an isolated case?

Intelligence

In 1995, 570,865 students with mental retardation ages 6–21 participated in special education programs throughout the country (U.S. Department of Education, 1996). Most of these students, approximately 90 percent, are students with mild mental retardation. Although many students with mild mental retardation are Caucasian, minorities, especially African Americans, are over represented.

Because of their lack of success in school, students with mild retardation lose confidence in their ability to learn. Motivation is a persistent problem for teachers. Although individual students differ significantly, generally students with mild mental retardation exhibit problems in academics and social adjustment. Such specific problems as distractibility, weak verbal skills, and speech disorders are common to this population. In appearance, these students are normal. Most are not identified as having a mild disability until they enter school and begin to fall behind their age-mates in learning. After they leave school, these young people merge with the general population. In the mainstream of society, they usually leave the label "mentally retarded" behind them.

In 1968, Lloyd Dunn was president of the Council for Exceptional Children, the nation's largest professional special education organization. During a speech at the Council's annual conference, Dunn urged educators to reevaluate their view on students with mild mental retardation. He criticized special education placements that tracked students into dead-end special education programs. Dunn characterized students with mild retardation as children of poverty who were denied equal access to educational opportunity in regular classrooms. He called for the elimination of self-contained special education classes for students identified as mildly retarded. Dunn stated that the label "mildly retarded" was used by educators to explain away the school's inability to educate African Americans, Native Americans, Mexicans, Puerto Ricans, and other nonstandard-English-speaking students. Dunn was particularly forthright in his condemnation of the use of intelligence testing to categorize these hard-to-teach students.

> Again the purpose has been to find out what is wrong with the child in order to label him and thus make him eligible for special education services. In large measure this has resulted in digging the educational graves of many racial and/or economically disadvantaged children by using the WISC or Binet IQ score to justify the label "mentally retarded." This term then becomes a destructive, self-fulfilling prophecy. (Dunn, 1968, 9)

Dunn's speech alerted educators to the need to reexamine practices for diagnosing and educating students with mild retardation. The use of intelligence (IQ) tests to label students with mild retardation and the educational practices that follow are so closely knit that an understanding of one is virtually impossible without knowledge of the other (Zucker & Polloway, 1987).

Alfred Binet

In 1904, Alfred Binet and his colleague, Theodore Simon, were asked by Paris school officials to help identify students in need of special education. Binet was a fervent believer in the power of education, and he agreed to the project because he saw an opportunity to improve school services for slow learners. Previously, Binet had attempted to measure intelligence in schoolchildren by following the accepted "objective" method of calculating head size with a tape measure. He soon found that the pseudo-science of "craniometry" could not provide information to accurately select students who needed special education. The differences he found in head sizes of students designated by teachers as the smartest or dullest was insignificant.

When presented with the task of screening large numbers of Paris schoolchildren for mental retardation, Binet changed tactics and decided to follow the practical strategy of presenting youngsters with problems in abstract reasoning. He tested students on a variety of tasks, including counting money, classification, and choosing "pretty" faces drawn on cards. Binet's procedure was empirical; that is, he did not start from a theory of intelligence, rather he experimented with an array of tasks until he was satisfied that he could derive a "mental level" that would indicate a child's potential for school achievement. Because of the high priority placed by schools on verbal skills, items on Binet's original test emphasized language-based cognitive skills. This accent on language skills as a primary indicator of intelligence still persists in IQ tests today.

Intelligence Tests

The turn of the century in the United States was a time of rapid cultural and social change. Vast numbers of immigrants provided industry with cheap labor. As slums, teeming with thousands of poor immigrants, sprang up in major cities, social reform became a national necessity. While educators tried to cope with students who were different, some United States psychologists focused their attention on the relationship between intelligence and social status. In Vineland, New Jersey, Henry Goddard founded an institute to investigate the connection between heredity and intelligence. After a visit to Paris in 1907, Goddard imported Binet's intelligence scale and used it to classify the residents with mental retardation at the Vineland Training School into categories of mental deficiency. To the already existing groups of "idiot" and "imbecile," he added a new term, "moron," to describe the highest functioning level of mental retardation. It was the moron or "feebleminded" group that became the centerpiece of Goddard's research.

In 1912, Goddard set out to detect feebleminded immigrants. He selected Ellis Island as his research site. Goddard intended to use the intelligence test to detect feebleminded immigrants who would, he believed, upon entry into this country, spread pauperism and crime. Each day thousands of immigrants poured through the massive disembarkation building in New York harbor. Goddard sent two of his female associates to test immigrants as they passed through customs. Candidates for testing were selected by visual inspection. Goddard believed that an individual's posture, facial characteristics, and dress provided clues about mental ability.

Using this nonrandom selection procedure, Goddard's female associates administered intelligence tests to twenty-two Hungarians, thirty-five Jews, fifty Italians, and forty-five Russians. When the scores were tabulated Goddard found that 83 percent of Jews, 80 percent of Hungarians, 79 percent of Italians, and 87 percent of Russians were feebleminded! He dismissed language as an explanation because the Jews had been tested by a Yiddish-speaking psychologist, and their scores were as low as the other groups. Goddard did not consider testing conditions a contributing factor, rather he concluded that immigrants from southeastern Europe were genetically inferior (Gould, 1981).

Goddard's views on the genetic character of "feeblemindedness" were reinforced by his infamous Kalikak Study (1912). Goddard claimed to have traced the offspring of a Revolutionary War soldier, Martin Kalikak, to an impoverished community located in the Pine Barrens of New Jersey. He claimed that these uneducated and dirt-poor residents of this isolated area were the descendants of a sexual liaison between Kalikak and a "tavern wench." Goddard compared the intellectual abilities and economic lives of the Pine Barren residents with the legitimate descendants from Kalikak's marriage. The legitimate Kalikak clan produced lawyers, business professionals, and doctors. The illegitimate Pine Barren descendants were characterized as sexually immoral, alcoholics, and mentally retarded. Goddard's "research" provided powerful arguments for the heritability of mental retardation. Recently, Goddard's study has been "thoroughly discredited" because he failed to consider environmental factors (Taylor & Searle, 1987). Stephen Jay Gould (1981) discovered that the photographs displayed in Goddard's research had been retouched to give the Pine Barren residents a sinister and dimwitted look.

Other psychologists, including Lewis Terman, continued Goddard's work with intelligence testing and came to the same conclusions about the heritability of feeble-mindedness in such poor, ethnic groups as Mexicans and African Americans. After the publication of his "Stanford–Binet Intelligence Test," Terman, in a speech at Harvard University, made his ultimate claim for the role of intelligence testing and social engineering.

In the near future intelligence tests will bring tens of thousands of these high grade defectives under the surveillance and protection of society. This will ultimately result in curtailing the reproduction of feeblemindedness and in the elimination of an enormous amount of crime, pauperism, and industrial inefficiency.

> It is hardly necessary to emphasize that the high grade cases, of the type now so frequently overlooked, are precisely the ones whose guardianship it is most important for the State to assume. (Kamin, 1977, 47)

Politicians gave Terman's notion of guardianship a macabre twist by initiating a number of state sterilization laws. In 1907, the Indiana legislature passed a law that allowed the state to sterilize prisoners and orphans. Beginning with the preamble, "Whereas heredity plays a most important part in the transmission of crime, idiocy, and imbecility . . ." this, the first of many state sterilization laws, was passed amid high hopes of controlling the spread of mental retardation.

It was the "high grade defectives," or the feebleminded, identified through intelligence tests, that were the primary targets for sterilization. In a 1911 sterilization law, Iowa listed criminals, rapists, idiots, the feebleminded, imbeciles, lunatics, drunkards, drug fiends, epileptics, syphilitics, and moral and sexual perverts as primary targets for sterilization. Any adult who was institutionalized or any child who became a ward of the state was a potential candidate for sterilization. From 1907 to 1972, thousands of "social misfits" in state institutions throughout the country were sterilized in the name of social reform (Houts, 1977; Taylor & Searl, 1987).

By the 1930s Binet's procedure for measuring intelligence was fully Americanized and in the process distorted. Instead of a measure of school potential to identify students for special education, the U.S. IQ test was used as an "objective" measure of innate intelligence. Binet's concept of environmental stimulation to increase intelligence was turned inside out as low IQ became synonymous with intractable dullness.

Between 1928–29, 65,000 intelligence tests were administered in Los Angeles elementary schools. Youngsters whose scores ranged from 75 to 50 were placed in special classes for the "educable feebleminded" (Hendrick & MacMillan, 1987). As the use of IQ tests became common practice nationwide, immigrant and minority children were placed in segregated special classes at a higher rate than their middle-class, white peers. The tenacity with which educators cling to the IQ test as a measure of intelligence and identification of students with mild mental retardation is remarkable. When pressed, most scholars admit that IQ tests don't measure intelligence. There is no correlation, for instance, between an individual's IQ and success in life after school. But the IQ test still serves the purpose for which it was originally intended by Binet. Intelligence test scores are reasonably good predictors of school achievement, and, for this reason, until a better method is developed, IQ remains the most frequently used standard for identifying students with mental retardation.

Definition and Identification

Professionals use a number of different terms to refer to students with mental retardation: educably mentally retarded, educationally retarded, educationally handicapped, mentally handicapped, and students with significantly limited intellectual capability. Two primary characteristics are included as criteria for identifying mental retardation: significantly subaverage intellectual functioning and adaptive behavior limitations that adversely affect educational and life functioning.

Historically, several variations in the use of and emphasis on these criteria appeared in the definitions that were used for this group of students. Early definitions (before the 1970s) were based primarily on below-average IQ scores as the main indicator of mental retardation. Adaptive behavior entered the definition in 1973. Prior to that time, many psychologists (including the early researchers on feeblemindedness) used an IQ score of 85 (one standard deviation) or below as the cutoff point for retardation. The 1973 definition and criteria (cf. Grossman, 1973) operationalized "significantly subaverage" intellectual functioning by lowering the IQ cutoff point from one to two standard deviations below the mean (i.e., from 85 to 70). Today, the American Association on Mental Retardation (AAMR) definition reflects these historical traditions and providing one definition used in identifying students with mental retardation (American Association on Mental Retardation, 1992):

> Mental retardation refers to substantial limitations in present functioning. It is characterized by significantly subaverage intellectual functioning, existing concurrently with related limitations in two or more of the following applicable adaptive skill areas: communication, self-care, home living, social skills, community use, self-direction, health and safety, functional academics, leisure, and work. Mental retardation manifests before age 18.

However some states have developed their own definitions and the federal government has slightly modified the AAMR definition as well. The definition of mental retardation that appears in the Individuals with Disabilities Education Act (IDEA) reads:

> Mental Retardation means significantly subaverage general intellectual functioning existing concurrently with deficits in adaptive behavior and manifested during the developmental period, that adversely affects a child's educational performance (NICHY Fact Sheet Number 8, 1997).

State criteria for identifying mental retardation does not have to follow either the AAMR guidelines nor IDEA guidelines. However all states recognize the need to evaluate mental retardation in terms of both intellectual and social development.

Mental retardation is reflected in difficulties in learning and in performing certain daily life skills as a result of substantial limitations in conceptual, practical, and social intelligence. These limitations in intelligence—"significantly subaverage intellectual functioning"—are usually interpreted as scores of 75 to 70 or below on one or more individually administered general intelligence tests. Test scores and other information are reviewed and evaluated by teams of professionals as part of the process of diagnosing mental retardation. However, intelligence alone is an insufficient basis for identifying mental retardation—the individual also must demonstrate limited adaptive skills in key areas.

The need to ascertain a youngster's adaptive behavior outside of school before making an educational diagnosis of mild mental retardation was highlighted by the research of Jane Mercer (1973). In an eight-year study in Riverside, California, Mercer found that schools were the chief labelers of students as mildly retarded. The majority of identified youngsters were poor. When Mercer examined classification of students by race, she found a disproportionate number of Mexican Americans and African Americans placed in special classes for the mildly retarded. Mercer coined the term *six-hour retarded child* to describe the students in her research. At home and in the community, the six-hour retarded child was considered normal; in school, the same child was considered retarded. Why was there a discrepancy in views? Mercer concluded that the schools failed to take a youngster's adaptive functioning outside of school into account. In Mercer's judgment, the lack of attention to socialization skills outside of school resulted in mislabeling of many minority students. Mercer's research highlighted the need to take adaptive behavior into account before making an evaluation of mild mental retardation.

To reduce the chances of making a mistake in diagnosing mental retardation, adaptive skill limitations in more than one area must occur along with intellectual limitations. To facilitate identification practices, key skill areas central to successful life functioning and frequently related to areas of support needed by people with mental retardation are outlined in the AAMR definition. Mental retardation is a category based on differences in intelligence and adaptive behavior and their effects on learning manifested before the age when individuals are typically expected to assume adult roles (i.e., the eighteenth birthday).

Degrees of Mental Retardation

It is important to discriminate between mild mental retardation and other, more severe types of mental retardation. One demarcation point is IQ score. An IQ range from 75–50 indicates mild mental retardation. As IQ scores move below 50, the degree of mental retardation is more severe. Unlike students with mild mental retardation, students with IQs below 50 usually demonstrate observable physical and behavioral anomalies. Educators usually use the continuum "moderate to severe mental retardation" when discussing students with IQs below 50. When their disability is organic in nature (e.g., from chromosome abnormalities), students with IQ scores below 50 may be described by physicians as having clinical mental retardation.

Children with clinical mental retardation are identified at birth or soon after, because of obvious physical anomalies such as hydrocephalus (i.e., pressure on the brain from cerebrospinal fluid) or spina bifida (a defect in the bony arch of the vertebra protecting the spinal cord). There are over 350 inborn errors of metabolism that can lead to mental retardation. Students with clinical mental retardation usually have multiple disabilities—for example, communication and health impairments. Whereas students with mild mental retardation are developmentally delayed, clinically mentally retarded students are developmentally disabled. This means that their condition is chronic, and they often require lifelong rehabilitation services in such areas of functioning as independent living, employment, or mobility. Clinical mental retardation cuts across all socioeconomic levels. Prevention is the most effective strategy to reduce the incidence of clinical mental retardation in children. Genetic counseling and amniocentesis are methods of detecting clinical mental retardation.

Despite the permanent nature of their disability, students with clinical mental retardation are capable of learning and becoming useful members of society. In the past, educators placed preconceived limits on the ability of students with clinical mental retardation. For example, students with moderate (IQ 50–35) mental retardation were referred to as "trainable." Because of preconceived limits, students with clinical mental retardation were institutionalized or placed in dead-end self-contained special classes. These limits became self-fulfilling prophecies. Bereft of normal childhood experiences and maintained in caretaking facilities, children with clinical mental retardation stagnated. The deinstitutionalization movement of the 1970s combined with the passage of the Individuals with Disabilities Education Act increased their opportunities for normal learning experiences. With early intervention and well-coordinated human services, the prospects for students with clinical mental retardation have dramatically improved over the last twenty years. As a result of environmental stimulation, some students with clinical mental retardation may achieve a score in the midrange (75–50) on an IQ test. Table 2.1 contrasts students with mild mental retardation and students with clinical mental retardation

Prevalence

Of the 5,439,626 students receiving special education services during 1994–1995, 570,865 were students with mental retardation (U.S. Department of Education, 1996). This number represents 11.6 percent of all students with disabilities of ages 6–21. There is variation among the states in the numbers and percentages of the school-age population identified with mental retardation and receiving special education services. For example a survey revealed that students with mental retardation ranged from about 3 percent of students with disabilities in Alaska and New Jersey to over 20 percent in Alabama, Arkansas, Georgia, Kentucky, Massachusetts, and Ohio (Ysseldyke & Algozzine, 1995). Reasons for this variation include assignment of students with mild learning problems to categories other than mental retardation (e.g., learning disabilities), addition of the adaptive behavior criterion resulting in students being classified as mentally retarded at different rates in different states, and variations in IQ score cutoff points for mild mental retardation.

In a survey of state guidelines for identification of mental retardation, Frankenberger (1984) found that the majority of states do not adhere to commonly

TABLE 2.1   Comparison of Mild and Clinical Mental Retardation

Mild Mental Retardation	Clinical Mental Retardation
Primary cause is environmental	Primary cause is biological
Normal physical appearance	Physical anomalies
Subtle health complications	Obvious health complications
Identified after beginning school	Identified at birth or soon afterwards
IQ range 75-50	IQ range 50 and below
Developmentally delayed	Developmentally disabled
After school, able to merge into the general population	Disability is chronic and requires lifelong rehabilitative services
Higher prevalence among poor with African Americans overrepresented	Cuts across all socioeconomic and ethnic groups
Subject to misidentification	Demonstrates clearcut medical diagnostic criteria
Not recognized as a disability in all countries	Universally recognized as a disability

accepted criteria. For instance, he found, fifteen of the forty-five reporting states set no criteria for IQ cutoff. Of the thirty states that specified IQ criteria, only fifteen followed the 1973 AAMR guideline of two standard deviations below the mean (i.e., 70) as the cutoff point for mild retardation. Thirty states used some measure of adaptive behavior, yet only nine specified specific criteria for determining what adaptive behavior means. Four states indicated that a youngster's academic achievement should be considered in determining mental retardation. A follow-up study of state guidelines by Utley, Lowitzer, and Baumeister found that many states (44 percent) substituted other terms, such as "learning impaired" and "individuals with exceptional needs," for mental retardation. The researchers also found differences in IQ criteria and definitions of adaptive behavior. They summarized their findings by stating,

> inconsistencies exist not only with respect to the terminology and definitions applied, but also with respect to eligibility criteria and categorization of children identified as mentally retarded. There appears to be considerable disagreement about who is mentally retarded, what eligibility criteria should be used, and what systems of classification are most functional in the delivery of instructional services. (Utley, Lowitzer, & Baumeister, 1987, 40)

Causes of Mental Retardation

Intellectual and adaptive behavior deficits can be caused by a variety of different factors and only rarely is any one of them singled out as *the* cause of mental retardation. Typically, two sets of factors interact to cause mental retardation. These include organic problems prior to, during, and after birth, and environmental problems that result in a lack of stimulation and delays in development. A summary of organic and environmental causes is presented in Table 2.2; more detailed information is presented in the following sections.

Organic Causes

Although we describe two groups of causes, the boundary between them is not always clear. For example, because drugs have an effect on the unborn child similar to the effects of infections and genetic disorders, we have grouped them with organic causes. It could also be argued that drugs are part of serious environmental circumstances that are common for some families living in poverty and therefore should be included with other environmental causes. The edges are blurred but the problems are clear-cut.

Drugs.   From the moment of conception, a child is vulnerable to influences that can stunt normal development. A pregnant mother's health is a crucial determiner of a healthy child. Whatever a pregnant woman puts into her body will eventually be absorbed into fetal tissue. Alcohol and cocaine are especially dangerous to the fetus. Even small amounts of these drugs pose a threat to the fetal nervous system, especially during the first trimester of pregnancy.

Drug abuse cuts across all socioeconomic levels and poses an immediate threat to the nervous system of an unborn child. Because drug abusers neglect their bodies in general, the fragile nervous system of the fetus may be jeopardized by malnutrition, iron deficiency, or anoxia. Newborn infants of drug abusers often are addicted to whatever drug the mother was using. The National Institute on Alcohol Abuse and Alcoholism estimated that annually 1,500 of three million newborns will be born with fetal alcohol syndrome (FAS). Thousands of other children will have some of the characteristics of FAS, including prenatal and postnatal growth deficiencies, mental retardation, and fine-motor impairments. Low birthweight (less than 5.5 pounds) can lead to a variety of health problems, including mild retardation. Teenage pregnancies and inadequate prenatal care, for instance smoking, can cause low birth weight.

Table 2.2   Summary of Causes of Mental Retardation

Organic Causes	Environmental Causes
Drugs	Toxins
Infections	Diet
Genetics	Environmental deprivation

Infections.   Several forms of mild retardation are caused by maternal infection. Retardation can result from the mother's being infected with rubella (German measles), and can range from mild to severe. Toxoplasmosis is caused by a protozoan infection of a pregnant woman. The protozoa is sometimes found in cat litter. Toxoplasmosis can cause mild to severe mental retardation, along with a variety of health problems. Cytomegalic inclusion disease is caused by a viral infection. The child's intelligence can range from normal to severely retarded. Cytomegalic inclusion disease can also cause visual and hearing problems. Microcephaly often accompanies this disease. Kernicterus is a form of neonatal brain damage that is caused by the destruction of fetal red blood cells in utero. The principal cause of kernicterus is Rh incompatibility, but drugs, infections, and enzyme abnormalities have also been identified as etiological factors. Although mild mental retardation is sometimes present, such other symptoms as disturbed speech articulation and athetoid cerebral palsy can lead to a misdiagnosis of mild retardation in an individual with normal intelligence. Children who run high fevers for an extended period of time are also at risk of permanent brain damage that can result in mild mental retardation.

Genetics.   In the past, many pediatricians and educators assumed that children with inherited mental retardation disorders were moderately to severely retarded. Although this may sometimes be true, it is a mistake to assume that inherited mental retardation exists at any level—mild, moderate, severe, or profound. Inherited disorders are genetic in origin. Some are found in specific ethnic groups. For example, Riley–Day syndrome occurs principally within Semitic groups. Autonomic nervous system function is impaired, and children are usually small with poor coordination. Emotional problems are common, but intelligence can range from above normal to moderate mental retardation.

Down syndrome is caused by a chromosome imbalance resulting in three number 21 chromosomes instead of two. Mental retardation can range from mild to severe. Down syndrome is one of the most common forms of organic mental retardation. Since the recent institution of preschool special education programs, children with Down syndrome have demonstrated an increased ability to learn and participate in age appropriate activities. Some Down syndrome children score in the normal range on IQ tests.

Second only to Down syndrome as an inherited form of mental retardation is fragile X or Martin–Bell syndrome. Fragile X syndrome occurs in 1 of 1,000 males; however, many cases may go undiagnosed. This sex-linked disorder occurs in males four times as often as females. The name "fragile X" is derived from a break in the long arm of the X chromosome. Characteristics of fragile X syndrome may include delayed language development, hyperactivity, a long narrow face, and prominent ears. Other forms of organic, inherited mental retardation by which children may fall into the mild category include Prader–Willi syndrome, Marfan's syndrome, oral facial digital syndrome (OFD, Type I), and Klinefelter's syndrome. Each of these organic forms of mild mental retardation is complex in its educational, medical, and psychological symptoms. Seizures, behavior disorders, metabolic problems, organ dysfunctions, motor problems, speech disorders, and emotional disturbance can combine in any number of ways in specific individuals (Lemeshow, 1982).

One of the greatest difficulties for children with congenital, inherited, or organic mental retardation is overcoming the social stigma of their physical appearance. Children with Down syndrome, for instance, are sometimes placed in self-contained special classes simply based on the fact that they look "retarded." Limited expectations for success, along with isolation from nondisabled peers, can become a self-fulfilling prophecy of failure for these youngsters. Adolescence, with its emphasis on being attractive and popular, can be a particularly painful period. The aphorism "nature disables but society handicaps," aptly describes the constant struggle of these children for acceptance by their peers without disabilities.

Environmental Causes

The majority of students with mild retardation are poor and have no observable organic impairments. Poverty contributes to mild mental retardation by limiting access to experiences that lay the foundation for educational achievement and good health. Consequently, mild mental retardation is as much a social dilemma as an educational problem.

Toxins.   Lead and other heavy metals, like mercury, poison children through inhalation, ingestion, and skin contact. The toxin is absorbed by central nervous system tissue, where it can cause a variety of learning problems. Lead poisoning causes irritability, listlessness, clumsiness, and distractibility. Verbal and attending skills are most vulnerable to lead's toxic effects. A child can get lead poisoning by drinking from water pipes that are soldered with lead. Lead is found in plaster and paint. Children are exposed to lead from carbon monoxide exhaust in automobiles and factory emissions. Half of the estimated 16,000 children who are treated for lead poisoning each year develop mental retardation (Moore & Moore, 1977).

Although all children are exposed to lead in some form, poor children are most susceptible to lead poisoning. Old, dilapidated buildings and houses are often covered with lead paint. Major highways, circling over inner-city ghettos, spew hydrocarbons into the air. Eventually the lead soaks into the soil, which remains contaminated for decades. Children playing in yards or playgrounds near highways and factories are at risk of lead poisoning. Youngsters in both urban and rural areas sniff gasoline and cleaning fluid to get high.

Diet.   A proper diet is necessary for normal growth and development. Nutrition is most important during fetal, neonatal, and early life, when body cells are dividing, organs are forming, and developmental reflexes are beginning. Lack of proper nutrition in early development can contribute to growth retardation, intellectual delay, and behavior disorders. Winick (1976) found that undernutrition is a widespread problem in the United States, particularly among low-income African Americans, Native Americans, and Spanish Americans. Although research has not proved that malnourishment alone causes mild mental retardation, it is evident from studies of Third World children that there is a significant relationship between proper nutrition and normal development (Edgerton, 1979).

Deprivation.   The cultural gap between the lives of poor children and the white middle-class standards of school puts these youngsters at a disadvantage. This is particularly true in the case of minorities, especially non-English-speaking students. The increasing poverty rate of young people who live in urban areas continues to contribute to a host of health and learning problems. Students from poor families have higher rates of infant mortality, low birth weights, and childhood health problems. Poverty related conditions such as deficient maternal diet, inadequate education about prenatal care, lack of health insurance, and alcohol and drug abuse all play a role in undercutting normal child development. Most discouraging are the terrible conditions that many American youth must adapt to within areas ravaged by poverty. Consider the following description reported by Jonathan Kozol in his guided tour of East St. Louis (1991).

> East St. Louis begins at the Monsanto fence. Rain starts falling as we cross the railroad tracks, and then another set of tracks, and pass a series of dirt streets with houses that are mostly burned out shells, the lots between them piled with garbage bags and thousands of abandoned auto tires . . . . The waste water emitted from the sewage plant, according to a recent Greenpeace study, "varies in color form yellow-orange to green." The toxic substances that it contains become embedded in the soil and the marshland in which children play. Dead Creek, for example, a creek bed that received charges from the chemical and metal plants in previous years, is now a place where kids from East St. Louis ride their bikes. The creek, which smokes by day and glows on moonless nights, has gained some notoriety in recent years for instances of spontaneous combustion. . . .

> "Nobody in East St. Louis, "Ahmed says, "has ever had the clout to raise a protest. Why Americans permit this is so hard for somebody like me, who grew up in the real Third World to understand. . . ."

> "I'm from India. In Calcutta this would be explicable, perhaps. I keep thinking to myself, 'My God! This is the United States! "(p.17)

When considering the deleterious effects of poverty it is clear that mild mental retardation is as much a social as an educational problem.

Children of the poor are sometimes raised without the early childhood experiences needed for success in school. Poor children may begin school with delayed language development, inadequate reading readiness, and short attention spans. Some are latchkey children: when they finish school for the day, they return to empty homes where they must care for themselves. The gut-wrenching reality of poverty is that formal education has little meaning to a youngster whose daily existence is a struggle for survival.

In *The Longest Mile* (1969), Rene Gazaway documented the inexorable slide toward mental retardation in small Appalachian communities, or "hollows." In Duddie's Branch, Gazaway found rampant illiteracy, malnutrition, disease, and isolation. The culture was so impoverished that for some time Gazaway thought that many adults were mute. In the course of a day, a typical family exchanged no more than a half dozen words. Children under six showed little curiosity or imagination. They spent most of the day together without the benefit of adult guidance or playthings. Gazaway provided the following description of a youngster's life in Duddie's Branch:

> Hollow parents are completely indifferent to the expanding demands for more formal and informal educational experiences. Not one child from Duddie's Branch has ever seen a sandbox. None has played with finger paints, puzzles, or blocks. Their "toys" consist of broken bottles, sharp metal, discarded tin cans. Ask them about Goldilocks, and they will look at you in bewilderment—they never heard a fairy tale. I made a bean bag from an old rag and asked some of the older boys to catch it. They had difficulty. With an old string ball and a heavy stick, I tried to involve them in batting practice. I was unsuccessful. Not only do games fail to interest them, they are almost completely unable to participate in most activities. They could not be taught to whistle, or even sing a simple tune. (Edgerton, 1979, 55)

Gazaway went on to describe the inability of these children to count, draw a geometric shape, discriminate right from left, or identify pictures of common animals. In this community, characterized by disease, hunger, lack of stimulation, neglect, and minimal verbal interaction, few children could be expected to score over 70 on an IQ test. Duddie's Branchers were trapped in an unchanging cycle of mental retardation. Adults with mild mental retardation parent children who will soon become retarded themselves, and the cycle continues.

Duddie's Branch is an example of how poverty infects a community and its inhabitants. Yet one does not need to travel to Appalachia to witness the ravages of poverty. Look around your community. Are there areas where you would not walk or where you lock your car doors as you drive through? Your fear is a common reaction of many citizens to a face-to-face encounter with poverty. Yet poverty does not change with the scenery. It endures. A 1977 report to Congress, *Preventing Mental Retardation—More Can Be Done*, noted that a poor child was fifteen times more likely to be identified as mildly retarded than a child from a middle-class family.

Most poor children are not mildly retarded, but they are educationally disadvantaged. It would be a mistake to characterize all poor families as uncaring or unable to promote the development of their children. In *The Myth of the Deprived Child* (1972), Herbert Ginsburg observed that disadvantaged children are different from middle-class children. They are not deficient thinkers. The problem for many poor children, according to Ginsburg, is the mismatch between the adaptive demands of their neighborhood and school. The skills poor children acquire in order to succeed outside of school are, in many instances, different from the skills needed to succeed in school. Formal schooling demands conformity and adherence to a structured curriculum. Yet many poor children must learn at an early age to fend for themselves. The aggressive child who succeeds in the ghetto may be a discipline problem in school. Whereas school rewards such passive skills as reading and writing, success in a poor community is often the result of quick action and independent problem solving. Schools reward individual participation in academic clubs and athletic teams. Poor youngsters, who grow up in tough neighborhoods, may receive more recognition from their peers for wearing their gang "colors" than a debating club pin.

For the children of poverty, success or failure will hinge on the teacher's ability to adapt to the students' needs. This begins with an understanding of a poor youngster's life outside of school. When a student can see a connection between life in and outside of school, then there is a reason to learn. There are too many distractions on the streets for poor youngsters to sit still for eighteen years of unmeaningful formal schooling. The identification of a youngster as mildly retarded ensures the delivery of special education services. Yet provision of special education is no guarantee of success. Rather, it is the quality of these services that will make a difference. The task for both regular and special educators is to convince poor youngsters that there is a good reason to persevere in school.

Characteristics

Each person with mental retardation has a unique set of characteristics, just like each person without mental retardation. Two traits are part of this category: significantly subaverage scores on an intelligence test and limitations in adaptive behavior. Recognizing how the primary traits affect other areas of functioning will help you better meet the needs of your students with mental retardation.

The following sections describe learning characteristics of students with mild mental retardation. The sections are divided into functional domains. The first, cognitive, reviews the research on the development of thinking skills. The next section, on mental processing, describes how students with mild retardation interpret, store, and use sensory information. The section on academics explains how students with mild retardation succeed or fail in school. The communication section describes the relationship of language ability to school achievement. The perception/motor section explains how attention and memory influence learning. Finally, the section on social–adaptive skills discusses the special problems of living with the label "mildly retarded." Through a review of each of these sections you will find that students with mild retardation are more similar to than different from students without disabilities. Variations between learners with mild retar-

Highlight 2.1 A Profile of Poverty

In a large northeastern city, one elementary school encapsulated the miserable union of poverty and inadequate schooling. The neighborhood around the school resembled the aftermath of a battle scene. Shop windows were boarded, abandoned automobiles lined the streets, and the stamp of despair was etched in the faces of middle-aged men hunched in doorways. The school playground looked like a suburban landfill. Mattresses, old tires, and appliances were piled high amid broken bottles and overfilled garbage bags. Any child who played in this area risked serious injury. The outside of the school resembled a fortress with heavy metal doors and wire-mesh windows. It was a cheerless yellow building covered with graffiti.

Teachers, the majority of whom, were white, punched time cards and talked of weekends way from the chaos of the inner city. In one classroom the teacher made several tentative attempts to get his sixth-grade charges to sit down and have a group lesson. After it was clear that no one was listening, he sat down with two students in the corner of the room and helped them with some math problems. The rest of the "class" wandered around or amused themselves with solitary activity. A teenage girl doodled on the blackboard. She carefully drew an arm with a clenched fist. A hypodermic needle jutted from the bulging biceps. Another girl stared into the tiny holes of an oval pencil sharpener attached to the wall. For fifteen minutes she slowly turned the handle as she peered inside, occasionally giggling to herself. When queried about the total disorder, the teacher's response was plain, "I'm just happy they come to school, at least they are safe for a while; anything after that is a bonus."

dation and other students are differences in degree of ability rather than differences in kinds of ability.

Cognitive

What is intelligence? This is a question that continues to confound scholars in science and education. While scientists study the brain, educators study the mind. Neuroscientists calculate that the brain is composed of ten to a hundred billion neurons, with an infinite number of connections between these microscopic carriers of information. At the molecular level of brain function, thoughts are electrical impulses coursing through neural networks at the speed of light. Direct observation of brain function through such techniques as positron emission tomography (PET) scan or electroencephalogram (EEG) are incapable of distinguishing the brain of a person with mild mental retardation from that of a nondisabled person. Yet teachers in classrooms, psychologists in research laboratories, and employers in business provide ample descriptions of the different thinking abilities of individuals with mild retardation. These descriptions of different thinking skills vary depending on the point of view of the observer. For example, a teacher might describe attention problems, while a psychologist will report a subaverage mental level. An employer, meanwhile, might complain about tardiness.

Within the context of everyday life, a suitable definition of intelligence is the ability to adapt to the demands of specific settings and individuals. This social-systems view of intelligence, with its emphasis on adaptation, is different from the psychometric (i.e., IQ) concept of intelligence that prevails in schools. In the former, intelligence is a function of survival and of getting along with others; in the latter, intelligence is a score on a test.

Psychometry is the measurement of intellectual ability by mental tests. Mental tests provide an intelligence quotient (IQ) and mental age (MA) but scant information about how an individual thinks. Because the first mental tests devised by Binet and Simon were meant to screen dull students, revisions of the original IQ test continue to focus on school-related skills. For example, the Wechsler Intelligence Scales for Children–Revised (WISC-R) measures verbal and performance skills, including information questions, arithmetic, memory, and speed in putting together puzzles. To judge intellectual capacity based on performance on fourteen subtests on the WISC-R (or its latest revisions) provides a limited view of the nature of intelligence.

Sternberg (1990) described student cognitive ability in terms of thinking styles. Many learning problems could be eliminated, according to Sternberg, if teachers examined more carefully the mismatch between their teaching style and their students' thinking style. He maintained that any subject can be taught in a way that is congruent with a student's thinking style. Students who prefer what Sternberg calls the "executive" thinking style like to be told what to do and are good at recalling facts. These students make a good match with teaching methods that emphasize memorization and objective examinations. On the other hand, students who are more "legislative" in their thinking respond best to learning tasks that require imagination, planning, and creative problem solving. Teachers may confuse thinking style with quality of intelligence. When a "legislative" thinking student is taught by an "executive" style teacher, the student is at a disadvantage. According to Sternberg, teachers need to pay closer attention to the differences in how their students think.

Piaget.   The cognitive theory of Jean Piaget (1950) offers an alternative method for understanding the development of thinking. Piaget's theory describes four phases of intellectual development. Each phase is distinctively different in terms of how the individual perceives and interprets information. The *sensory–motor* stage is the initial phase of mental development. It begins at birth and typically develops through infancy. (All age indicators are only approximations. There is a good deal of variability in when individual children move onto the next stage of development.) As its title suggests, learning is linked to sensory input and evolving motor abilities. During this stage, the infant organizes and constructs a sense about how the world operates through imitation and play.

The second stage of cognitive development, the *preoperational*, begins around age two. At this point the child develops the ability to think symbolically through language, deferred imitation, games, and art. Ideas are tied to perceptions. For example, a pile of leaves that is scattered may appear to be "bigger" to a four-year-old than if the leaves were pushed close together because it covers more space. The preoperational thinker's view of the world is still characterized by the egocentrism of infancy. For example, clouds are alive because they move, and the sun sets, as a four-year-old put it, "because kids get tired."

During the primary school years (ages seven to eleven), most children are *concrete operational* thinkers. A child can mentally manipulate such symbols as numbers and words, but the child's thoughts are still tied to concrete here and now experiences. The opportunity to experiment with materials, to select topics of interest, and to investigate relationships, coupled with an increased need to share ideas verbally, characterizes thinking during this stage.

Formal operations is the final stage of cognitive development. Piaget described the onset of this stage around adolescence, although follow-up studies indicate that some college students may still be in the process of developing abstract thought (Dulit, 1972). At the formal stage, the young adult has developed the ability to reason logically, to analyze, and to search for solutions among an array of possibilities.

Unlike IQ tests, which measure *what* children think, Piaget's theory describes *how* children think. Piaget's theory of cognitive development provides the educator with insight into the student's conception of reality. The applicability of Piaget's theory in understanding the mental operations of children with mental retardation was initiated in 1943 by Piaget's colleague, Barbel Inhelder. Working with institutionalized children and adults, Inhelder (1968) concluded that individuals with mental retardation followed the same pattern of development as normal children. The difference was a slower rate of stage acquisition for individuals with a disability. Other researchers confirmed the slower cognitive development of children with mental retardation, and they discovered that mental age (MA) computed from IQ tests was a good indicator of a student's developmental level (Mannix, 1960; Marchi, 1971; Uzgiris & Hunt, 1966). For instance, a seven-year-old student with a mental age of five would probably be functioning at the preoperational stage of cognitive development rather than the concrete operational stage.

Cognitive research with individuals with mental retardation demonstrated that their reasoning abilities are better characterized as developmentally delayed than deficient (Henley, 1985). Stafford and Klein noted in their comprehensive review of Cognitive research:

> An important aspect of Piaget's orientation is that it enables one to shift from the deficit notion . . . to understanding where the retarded may be in terms of developmental structures. This positive view enables us to look at what retarded children are rather than what they are not; what they know rather than don't know. (Stafford & Klein, 1977, 308)

The major impact of Piaget's view of intelligence is that children interact and view their world in a distinctively different manner depending on their stage of cognitive development (Figure 2.1). The application of cognitive developmental theory to the instruction of learners with mild retardation requires a close look at what goes on in classrooms. Piaget described learning as interactive. Children require opportunities to learn through trial and error. They use language to compare perceptions and make adjustments to their own egocentric view of life. A teacher-directed, sit-still-and-listen classroom does not match the cognitive

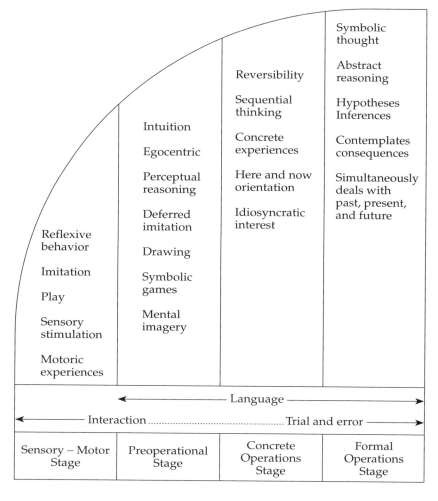

FIGURE 2.1 Cognitive Development
Source: Adapted from Wyne, M., and O'Connor, P. (1979). *Exceptional Children, a Developmental View*. Lexington, MA: D.C. Heath.

abilities of children at the sensory–motor, preoperational, or concrete stage of intellectual development.

Reid (1978) analyzed education methods from a Piagetian perspective and observed that many education techniques work in opposition to the natural abilities of students with mild disabilities. Rigidly sequenced curricula, concern for the "right" answer, drill, and memorization are formal operational strategies that overshoot the cognitive strategies of students who are at the preoperational or concrete operational stage of thinking. The neglect of educators to consider underlying developmental processes in their teaching can create a conceptual gap between the curriculum and the mediating cognitive structures of the student. The overall effect can be a loss of motivation and continued dependency on adults to provide information and solutions to problems. Educators who view the cognitive development of learners with mild retardation from a Piagetian perspective modify classroom activities to match the learning capabilities of their students.

Mental Processing

Thinking is a complex process. Suppose a stranger asks you for directions. As you picture a route in your mind, the visual center of your occipital lobe is activated. Then you mentally translate your vision into a series of steps while your left hemisphere analyzes each part of the stranger's journey. Words take shape next, and instantaneous messages flash back and forth between the parietal lobe and frontal lobe. The mouth region of the motor cortex fires signals to your tongue, jaw, and larynx. Finally, as you speak, the auditory cortex of the temporal lobe tracks your words and sentences to ensure that you are accurately describing the correct route.

This brief illustration describes the multiple tasks the brain performs in "processing" the steps of a simple communication. When a deficit exists in these processing skills, even everyday tasks can become overwhelming. Much of the pioneering research on processing skills was done using patients who had suffered head injuries. Researchers would pinpoint the damaged area of the brain, determine what processing skill was impaired, and draw a conclusion that the damaged area was responsible for that specific processing disability. With individuals who had no obvious brain damage, judgments about deficits in processing skills were hypothetical. Ellis (1963), for example, theorized that individuals with mental retardation were deficient in some processing skills and had normal abilities in others. The challenge for researchers was to determine which processing skills were intact and which were deficient.

Testing is one technique employed by educators to identify processing deficits of students with mild retardation. However, most tests that are used to measure mental processing skills have considerable validity and reliability problems. Teacher observations are the most common source of information about mental processing problems. Deficient memory skills, short attention span, distractibility, and impaired abstract thinking are commonly attributed to students with mild retardation in school. Yet teachers' observations of student actions are biased by their expectations for "normal" classroom behavior. In a teacher-directed class-room, where students spend inordinate amounts of time sitting, listening, and writing in workbooks, even small amounts of bored or distracted behavior can be misinterpreted as a problem.

Accurate identification of the processing skills needed to succeed in school is far from complete. Until the 1970s, attempts to evaluate processing skills and deficits were hindered by overreliance on the need to infer abilities from samples of behavior. Sometimes the behaviors were answers to questions on a test; at other times the behaviors were actions in the classroom. The difficulty with these indirect assessments of processing skills is that there were other factors, such as teacher bias and inadequate theory, that distorted judgments about processing skills.

With the advent of positron emission tomography (PET scans), neurosci-entists can directly observe the brain in action. Through the use of computer-enhanced imagery, physicians are able to observe the brain of a patient in the act of thinking. A radioactive tracer in the bloodstream lights the computer projection of the patient's brain in vivid colors that correspond to the part of the brain that is engaged. When the patient is talking, the left frontal lobe and motor cortex are highlighted in red. When the patient is listening, the left temporal lobe projection turns red and surrounding inactive brain tissue is colored a dim blue on the computer monitor. Although this procedure is too expensive to use in schools, the knowledge gained from PET scan research on mental processing and learning is certain to benefit future educators in their work with all students.

Academics

Traditionally, educational services for students with mild mental retardation were provided in self-contained, special classes. The curriculum was "watered down." Students were taught the regular school curriculum at a slower pace, with emphasis on drill and repetition. Students subjected to this tedious instruc-tion frequently failed to show any significant gains in academic skills.

One way to evaluate the success of school programs for students identified as having mild retardation is to examine their status after leaving school. Edgar (1987) compared the employment condition of regular education students, stu-dents with learning disabilities, and students with mild retardation. He found the group identified in school as having mild mental retardation least capable of finding adequate employment opportunities. Of 167 students with mild retar-dation who left school between 1976 and 1981 (i.e., dropouts, graduates, and age-outs) in eleven school districts in the state of Washington, just 4 percent of the group with mild mental retardation were earning more than $135.00 a week. Although 56 percent of the students were able to secure some type of employment over the five-year period, only 43 percent were still employed five years after leaving school.

In 1985, Polloway and Epstein asked sixty-seven educators of students identified as mildly retarded to prioritize the educational needs of their students. Vocational and career education was the first selection, postschool adjustment was second, and long-term effects of academic treatment programs was next. Clearly, these educators were concerned with the need of the school curriculum to enhance the lives of students after school.

Functional Curriculum.   To succeed in life, students need to apply skills learned in the classroom to the outside world. One approach is to teach functional life skills in the classroom. Instead of emphasizing arithmetic problems on worksheets, a functional curriculum would teach budgeting and shopping skills. Although reading is often treated as an isolated "subject," a functional curriculum would teach reading throughout the school day by using such everyday materials as newspapers, magazines, and job applications. Apprentice programs, where high school students spend time in the community working with "mentors" in trades and business, are examples of functional programs that integrate school with on-site job training.

A functional curriculum bridges the gap between the teaching and the application of information. It capitalizes on the cognitive abilities of students by providing learning experiences that are concrete and practical rather than abstract and hypothetical. The student can immediately see the use for new skills and have ample opportunity to evaluate personal progress. Teachers who are successful in implementing functional curricula begin by asking the question, "What do I see this student doing five years from now?"

The more severe an individual's disability, the sooner a functional curriculum should be initiated. For the learner with mild retardation, adolescence is a good starting point. This does not mean an abandonment of academic work, but a gradual emphasis on vocational skills. The dropout rate for youngsters with mild disabilities is over 30 percent in some school districts. As students approach the early teens, the best message educators can send is, "We have a reason for you to stay in school." A functional curriculum, with its emphasis on practical skills, gives students a rationale for continuing their education.

The Adult Performance Level Curriculum (APL) developed at the University of Texas is an example of a functional curriculum. It contains forty-two life skills objectives organized under five major categories: consumer economics, community resources, health, occupational knowledge, and law. The program ranges from elementary to high school and includes reading, writing, speaking, problem solving, interpersonal relationships, and computation skills. Examples of tasks in reading/consumer economics for each level are as follows: elementary—look for ads in the newspaper for toys; junior high school—read an ad for a sale and find the name of the store, location, phone number, and price of the item; high school—read and compare prices of grocery store ads. The purpose of the curriculum is to develop student competencies necessary for survival in daily life (Patton et al., 1989).

Communication

Schools are primarily verbal environments. Secondary teachers expect students to follow oral directions, recall information from lectures, locate information in textbooks, and take notes. In elementary classrooms, students are expected to listen to the teacher, answer questions correctly, read silently, and write. The one-sided emphasis on verbal skills favors the middle-class child and handicaps the poor child. Disadvantaged learners may not begin school with the middle-class language background that is a prerequisite for successful classroom partic-ipation.

Robert Ornstein, the noted neuroscientist, once observed that students are not judged on how well they use their brains, but on how well they use their mouths. Rational thought involves more than verbal abilities. The neocortex of the human brain is divided into two halves, the left and right hemispheres. For most individuals, the left hemisphere is the language center. In the left frontal, parietal, and temporal lobes of the brain, mental activity is expressed through listening and speech. The right hemisphere is the creative, intuitive part of the brain. While the left hemisphere solves problems through analysis, the right hemisphere integrates information and searches for holistic solutions. Neither half is superior to the other; both work together to produce rational thought.

The majority of school activity, including reading, speaking, and writing, requires a preponderance of left-hemisphere language skills. Therefore, a pre-school child who is not provided with such language activities as bedtime stories, listening to music, and guided conversations with adults is at a distinct disad-vantage on entering school. Because so many students with mild retardation are poor, minorities, or both, their opportunities to develop the language skills re-quired for a successful school experience may be limited.

Language Deficient versus Language Different.   Bernstein (1961) described poor children's language as a "restricted code," which was ill-suited for subtle shades of thought or meaning. Poor children, he said, were unprepared for rational thought when parents dealt with them in an authoritative, impulsive manner. Thus the disadvantaged child fails to learn such abstract concepts as causality and long-range planning. Bernstein's view of the deficient language development of poor children was used by some educators in this country to explain the inadequate school performance of poor African American children.

Bereiter and Englemann (1966) believed that a deprived environment re-tarded speech and that deficient speech led to deficient thought. School failure was the cumulative result. The "language deficient" perspective of African Amer-ican children's speech focused attention on remedial efforts to teach them "white standard English." For instance, DISTAR, a sequentially structured preschool program, was used to teach language development to poor inner-city children. The popular TV show "Sesame Street," which is designed especially with poor children in mind, adopted the deficient language hypothesis by teaching new vocabulary, labeling objects, and other basic school readiness skills.

The assumption that poverty causes deficient language, which leads to deficient thinking skills, was challenged almost immediately by researchers in the field of psycholinguistics. Robinson (1965) found that the "restricted code" hypothesis is a better description of poor children's performance than of their competence. From his studies Robinson discovered that poor children choose to speak in dialects that are accepted by their peers even when they are capable of more elaborate, middle-class speech. To test his hypothesis, Robinson asked a group of lower- and middle-class students to write a letter to a friend and to a school administrator asking for a favor. Whereas the informal letters reflected the children's social class speech patterns, the formal letter to the educator contained few elements that could be attributed to lower-class language deficiencies. Robinson concluded that when poor children chose to use more elaborate middle-class language, they can do so. More recently, Farley (1986) found that students with mild retardation were capable of age-appropriate, fluent writing.

Lobav, Cohen, and Lewis (1968) reported that poor and middle-class students are more alike than different in the way their language develops. Lobav carefully scrutinized how poor African American children learn to speak. He found that their language, which he described as "Black Standard English," progressed through a logical sequence of syntax and structure. Lobav reported that the speech of poor African American children followed a normal pattern of development. Their language was not deficient, only different from white middle-class language. The "language different" hypothesis advocated by Ginsburg (1972) highlighted the structural and functional conflicts between how poor children speak and the expectations placed on them by schools embedded in middle-class language. One example of structural conflict is the use of "White Standard English" in reading texts. A poor African American child may have difficulty because the teacher expects the child to pronounce words as they appear in the text. Functional conflicts occur when, as Robinson noted, poor children persist in using speech in school that is accepted by peers because to do otherwise would be considered unmanly.

English as a Second Language.   When English is a second language, it is difficult to determine whether mild disability exists. Language assessment of non-English-speaking or limited-English-proficient students is improving, particularly for Spanish-speaking youngsters. Still, it is difficult to identify a language deficit in a bilingual youngster. Assessment of language disorders analyzes a variety of skills, including auditory discrimination, articulation, verbal expression, and comprehension of complex relationships. According to Langdon "the purpose of testing a non-English- or limited-English-proficient student is to determine his or her proficiency in the native language and to compare it with the performance in the second language, when appropriate" (Langdon, 1983, 39). The objective is to determine whether lack of proficiency in English is due to a general language disorder or is a reflection of normal difficulties in learning a new language.

As numbers of non-English-speaking students strain the resources of public schools, determining the source of academic problems will continue

TABLE 2.3   Tests Used by School Systems that are Translated into Spanish

Bilingual Syntax Measure
Ber-Sil
Dos Amigos Verbal Language Scales
Del Rio
Leiter International Performance Scale
Language Assessment Scales
SOMPA
WISC-R
Boehm Test of Basic Concepts
Carrow Test of Auditory Comprehension of Language
Peabody Picture Vocabulary Test
Woodcock–Johnson Psychoeducational Battery
Bender–Gestalt
PEOPLE
Austin Spanish Articulation Test
Columbia Mental Maturity Test
Raven Progressive Matrices
Woodcock Language Proficiency Battery

to challenge educators. For instance, in California, there are ninety distinct language groups and nearly 400,000 limited-English-proficient students in public schools (Cegelka, Lewis, & Rodriguez, 1987). When these students fail to progress satisfactorily, standard testing procedures used to identify mild mental retardation will almost certainly indicate a disability, unless special measures are used to take language differences into account. This is because most standardized tests of intelligence primarily assess language skills. Misdiagnosis can take two forms: false positive and false negative. In the former, students are incorrectly assessed as mildly retarded, whereas in the latter situation, mild learning problems are overlooked.

To accurately assess a language disorder among non-English-speaking students, both languages are assessed by a clinician who is fluent in each. Assessment instruments are translated into the student's native language, and, if a language disorder is found, remediation begins in the student's native language (Langdon, 1983). Table 2.3 contains a list of tests that have been translated into Spanish.

The itinerant life-styles of many of non-English-speaking students make it difficult to assess mild retardation and other disabling conditions. Baca and Harris (1988) estimated approximately 80,000 migrant children in need of special education. They concluded that only 8,000, or 10 percent, of these children receive special education services. Because of limited English proficiency, poverty, and inadequate health conditions, migrant children are especially vulnerable to mild mental retardation. In a study of migrant education, Barresi (1984), found that:

1. Only 10 percent of children with mild disabilities were identified.
2. Identification occurs late in the school career.
3. Students were placed in the wrong special education programs.
4. Gaps in services existed because of different administrative procedures between school districts. (Baca & Harris, 1988)

The number of culturally and linguistically diverse students will continue to increase in our nation's schools. By the year 2,000, an estimated 40 percent of public school students will be from such ethnically diverse backgrounds as African American, Hispanic, and Asian (Ramirez, 1988). Urban schools, in particular, will be faced with increased numbers of underachieving students with cultural and language differences. Schools need to keep pace with the changing student population. If teaching techniques do not change to take into account such meaningful circumstances in children's lives as their language and culture, special education will become inundated with children identified as mildly disabled. Most of these children will not have intellectual deficiencies. Rather, they will be the product of an educational system that was unable to adjust to the changing needs of its student population.

Perception/Motor

Perception is a combination of attention, memory, and thinking. As an illustration, without looking, list the names of the authors of this textbook. Even though you look at the cover of this book on a regular basis (at least your professor hopes this is the case), you probably found naming each author a difficult task. Perception begins with selective attention. You can look at many features of your environment day after day (e.g., the color of the walls in your classrooms), but if you do not concentrate and willfully commit the sensory input to memory, your brain will not encode the information, and it will be forgotten.

Familiarity, interest, color, and movement are a few of the factors that influence perception. As infants mature, they learn to discriminate specific details from a background of competing stimuli. This figure–ground discrimination is an essential perceptual skill for successful school performance. Students with poor figure–ground discrimination skills may have trouble selecting individual letters from a line of words, become confused by oral directions, or become distracted by movement in a classroom.

According to Hebb (1966), early childhood experience plays a key role in the development of perceptual skills. Hebb theorized that environmental stimulation accelerates the growth of brain tissue and connections among neurons

in the brain. Conversely, environmental deprivation will adversely ˛
tissue development and subsequent mental processing of informatic.
years. In applying Hebb's theory to children with mild mental retardatio₁
& O'Conner noted,

> Some have argued that Hebb's theory, which stresses sheer experience to stin
> lation and variation in perceptual stimulation early in life, fails to account fo
> deviant cognitive development of disadvantaged infants who grow up in slum
> conditions, absolutely bombarded with stimulation. On the contrary, this may
> not be at all inconsistent with Hebb. Hebb's theory is built on the proposition
> that repeated stimulation is necessary for learning to occur, and that selective
> attention to those stimuli is crucial. It is now thought that some children growing
> up in such intense slum conditions may be so bombarded with stimuli of all kinds
> as to force them to tune out much of it from their awareness, and that this may
> be part of their cognitive deficit—the failure to selectively attend. What appears
> to be inattentive, off-task behavior in school aged disadvantaged children may
> have its origins in a disruptive, noisy, disorienting environment in infancy. (Wyne
> & O'Conner, 1979, 237)

Learners with mild retardation may have deficits in short- and long-term memory. Researchers use the term "rehearsal" to describe the unconscious cognitive strategies students use to remember. Rehearsal comprises various verbal strategies including repetition, rhyme, subvocal speech, and verbal self-instruction. Students with mild retardation are less likely to use spontaneous rehearsal techniques. When they are taught rehearsal strategies, short- and long-term memory improves (Scruggs & Laufenberg, 1986).

Inadequate teaching is often overlooked as a contributor to presumed deficits in attention and memory. Students who are expected to maintain attention during dull and repetitious lessons are unlikely to remember what they read or heard only moments before. Ineffective teachers use general characteristics of students with mild mental retardation as a rationale for individual learning problems. A vicious cycle of low expectations and unsuccessful learning evolves when teachers use mild mental retardation as an explanation for a student's learning difficulty. A teacher who remarks, "Well, Susan simply can't retain concepts because she's mildly retarded," is overlooking the significant role of effective teaching in helping students learn. Teaching that includes active student involvement with learning tasks, guided practice sessions, and systematic error-correction procedures will produce successful results that can overcome deficits in organizing perceptual information (Algozzine & Maheady, 1986).

The ability to coordinate perception with movement is a fundamental skill required for learning. The fact that he named the first phase of intellectual development the sensory–motor stage is a clear indication of the importance Piaget attached to early perceptual–motor experiences. Lack of perceptual–motor stimulation at a young age may delay intellectual development. The delay can be so subtle that negative consequences may be overlooked until the school years,

·ster is compared to peers in such tasks as reading, writing, and
·ion.

motor problems can manifest themselves in a variety of ways,
·rdination and inadequate fine-motor skills. Research on motor-
·nce of students with mild mental retardation consistently reports
·es with such activities as running, throwing, and jumping (Dobbins &
·ick, 1977; Holland, 1987). Poor performance in physical education classes can negatively affect student self-confidence and motivation to persevere. Conversely, physical education and recreational skills can promote student self-confidence by enhancing awareness of body coordination and performance. Such programs as Outward Bound and rope climbing increase perception and attention skills of students while providing them with challenging and successful experiences.

Social/Adaptive

Categorical labels, such as mental retardation, reinforce the tendency to classify students in terms of the single dimension ascribed by the label. The social needs of students with mild retardation may be overlooked because their "problem" is viewed in terms of subaverage intellectual functioning. Yet there is nothing retarded about the emotions of these students. Students identified with mild retardation have normal feelings. They want to be liked, accepted, and valued as human beings. Their self-esteem is strongly influenced by their status and day-to-day activities in school (Dupont, 1978).

Many students spend a significant portion of their day out of the mainstream of normal school activities. A study of students with mild retardation in northern Illinois found that more than 90 percent of the students were in regular classrooms less than half the day (Polloway et al., 1983). The stigma of spending most of the day in a special education classroom, isolated from normal school activities, can have a corrosive effect on a youngster's self-esteem. Like all other students, youngsters with mild mental retardation want to be liked and accepted, yet studies of regular education students' perceptions report nonacceptance or rejection of students identified as mildly retarded (Kuveke, 1983).

In *Childhood and Society* (1963), Erik Erikson described the beginning school years, ages seven to eleven, as crucial to a youngster's sense of competence. During these first years of school, a child seeks to master tasks that are prized by the world outside the family. Although the need to accomplish and produce is strong, there is an equal pull toward regression to the safe harbor of play and dependence of earlier years. The polar psychological demands to achieve in order to overcome feelings of inadequacy require successful school experiences for a positive outcome. Acceptance by peers plays a key role in the child's evolving self-concept. The successes or failures that a youngster experiences during these early school years will affect future endeavors throughout adolescence and adulthood.

The majority of students with mild disabilities are identified by an educational assessment after entering school. At the precise time in their young lives when they are most in need of success, these youngsters experience failure and the added indignity of being identified with such labels as learning disabled or mildly retarded. The stress of dealing with school failure, peer rejection, and segregation as a learner with mild retardation can cause students to lose faith in themselves as competent individuals. Failure in school leaves a strong impression. Educators use the term "learned helplessness" to describe student lack of confidence in their own abilities. When Reynolds and Miller (1985) compared students identified as mildly retarded with nondisabled students, they found the special-needs students showed significant signs of depression and learned helplessness. The findings suggest that students with mild retardation are vulnerable to emotional disturbance because of their failure in school and their prolonged exposure to peer disapproval (Epstein, Cullinan, & Polloway, 1986).

The "New" Student with Mild Retardation

Until the mid-1980s the category of mild mental retardation was almost exclusively the domain of disadvantaged children without obvious signs of organic retardation. In recent years, school systems have identified a "new," more organically involved student with mild mental retardation. The gradual change in characteristics used to define mild mental retardation to include more complex disabilities is due to several factors.

1. The American Association of Mental Retardation refined its definition of mental retardation in an attempt to eliminate hard-to-teach students from the classification retarded. With the decrease in "borderline" students from the category of mild mental retardation, there has been a corresponding increase of lower-functioning students included in this classification.
2. Due to the widespread implementation of special education preschool programs, students who previously might have scored in the moderate range on IQ tests are scoring in the low, mild range.
3. Since the mid-1980s, there has been an increase of children disabled in utero by drug use of pregnant women.
4. As society's expectations for children with organic disabilities improve, so does school performance. For instance, it is no longer unusual for a student with Down syndrome to score in the mild range on an IQ test.
5. In states that divide special education programs into mild and severe categories (e.g., California), parents of students with organic types of mental retardation push for classification of their youngsters in the mild category (MacMillan, 1989).

A survey of students identified as mildly retarded provides an illustration of a changing mentally retarded population. Forness and Pollaway (1987) reported that out of eighty-four students identified as mildly retarded in California, nearly 80 percent had multiple disabilities. The most frequent cited combination was intellectual, behavioral, and speech impairments.

The more disabled condition of these students raises questions regarding characteristics and educational services. For instance, will the multiple nature of these students' disabilities be used as a justification to keep students with mild mental retardation out of regular classrooms? If placed in regular classrooms, will these students' learning be disrupted by frequent "pull-outs" for such special services as speech therapy and adaptive physical education? How will nonorganically involved students feel about special instruction placements that have them sitting alongside students with obvious disabilities?

Underlying these instructional concerns is the confusing picture about how students with mild mental retardation are identified. Individual states and school systems continue to use different diagnostic criteria. A study of five Ohio cities by Smith (1984) indicated that three of four students identified as being mildly retarded were African Americans. The high percentage of African American students identified as having mild retardation in Ohio follows the historical pattern of poor and minority overrepresentation of students in special education programs. Clearly, concerns about different characteristics of students with mild retardation need to be dealt with on a person-to-person basis when deciding how to teach students with mental retardation.

Teaching Strategies

Students with mild mental retardation often need special assistance making what they are learning relevant to real-life experiences (i.e., functional skills) and adjusting how they approach learning activities (i.e., school adaptive behavior). They are students who need assistance learning the content and skills that many of their peers learn without special educational activities (Ysseldyke & Algozzine, 1995). Of course, many of their characteristics overlap with those of students with learning disabilities or emotional disturbance. Therefore, many of the approaches used to improve basic academic skills (e.g., reading, writing, and arithmetic), communication (e.g., language and speech), and behavior (e.g., attention to tasks, disruptiveness) of these other students are also useful when working with students with mild mental retardation. Effective teachers of students with mental retardation set high expectations for what they can achieve and focus their instruction on functional activities designed to promote success with real-life problems. A summary of general interventions used by teachers with students with mental retardation is presented in Table 2.4. Some general principles of effective teaching, general procedures for improving thinking skills, early intervention, and the teaching of reading and specific activities for improving functional skills, school adaptive behavior, and leisure and work skills are discussed in the following sections.

TABLE 2.4 General Interventions for Teaching Students with Mild Mental Retardation

1. Expect to see progress; mild mental retardation is not a permanent, unalterable condition.
2. Many students come to school without readiness skills: don't assume they know what you are talking about.
3. Identify a student's level of cognitive functioning (i.e., preoperational, concrete, operational), and match teaching approaches to learner's characteristics.
4. Always connect abstract ideas to student life experiences.
5. Avoid dull, repetitious work. Provide novelty in lessons.
6. Provide maximum opportunities for learning in the least restrictive environment.
7. Remember that the label "mentally retarded" is demeaning and promotes stereotyping.
8. Keep in mind that IQ tests don't measure intelligence.
9. Insist on a measure of adaptive behavior before a student is evaluated as mentally retarded.
10. Provide students with functional, career-oriented learning experiences.

Instructions

Given the array of students with different language skills and backgrounds who populate classrooms, and the amount of listening that students are expected to do, teachers face a formidable challenge when instructing their students. Teachers, however, are sometimes unclear in their lessons. An analysis of teacher talk by Nelson (1988) found that false starts, repetitions, lack of clarity, and abstract language were common aspects of teacher talk. Students with mild retardation may have attention and memory deficits that further impair their ability to understand teachers' explanations.

Robinson (1989) recommended the use of advance organizers to help alert students to important material. She proposed the following guidelines for the use of advance organizers:

1. Alert students to the transition to a new activity.
2. Identify topics or activities students will do.
3. Provide an outline or other organizational framework.
4. Clarify teacher expectations for student participation.
5. Provide background information regarding how this lesson relates to previous activities.
6. State the concepts to be learned.
7. Give examples of concepts.
8. Highlight the relevance of topic.
9. Introduce new vocabulary.
10. Specify the desired general outcomes of the activity.

These ten steps provide the student with a direct and simple framework for listening and understanding teacher expectations for successful classroom participation. They are highly effective with many students with mild retardation.

Student memory can be enhanced through the use of verbal rehearsal and self-questioning. Rehearsal requires the student to repeat directions silently several times. This strategy can help a student follow teacher directions. Self-questioning is a strategy useful for all students. After a passage is read or a lesson is taught, the student reviews key elements by asking:

What is the story (lecture) about?
Who is in the story (lecture)?
Where did the events take place?
When did they take place—in what order?
Why is this information important or useful? (Robinson, 1989, 150)

Teaching requires clarity. Many students, including those with language differences or deficits, need help in listening and remembering. The simple technique of asking students what they learned in class today can help a teacher determine what students do or do not understand.

Thinking Skills

Guided teaching of thinking skills is a general procedure used in educating students with mild retardation. Goldstein (1974) advocated the direct teaching of problem-solving skills. A major hurdle for many individuals with mild retardation is adapting to the social demands of life after school. Goldstein's Social Learning Curriculum utilizes a "logical inductive strategy" to teach students a hierarchical procedure for problem solving. Within this system, students learn to label, detail, infer, predict, verify, and generalize.

Goldstein's approach is significantly different from the traditional teacher-directed lessons so often encountered in academic programs for students with mild retardation. In a teacher-directed lesson, the teacher:

1. tells the student what is to be learned;
2. tells the student what to do;
3. calls on students to respond;
4. evaluates student answers; and
5. corrects wrong answers.

In a teacher-directed lesson, each step is controlled and monitored by the teacher. Goldstein believes that teacher-directed lessons undermine student confidence in their own thinking abilities.

The logical–inductive approach, advocated by Goldstein, encourages student input. Situations are presented to students, and the teacher guides the students' thinking by means of a series of questions. For example, the Test of Hierarchy of Inductive Knowledge (THINK) provides stimulus picture cards for classroom discussions. Students are first asked to identify details in a picture—for example, a man and boy raking a yard. Then, through a guided discussion, students attempt to analyze the problem (e.g., a boy's football is stuck in a rain gutter) and come up with solutions to solve the problem. Rather than concentrating on right and wrong answers, the teacher encourages students to share perceptions and think about what they see. The teaching of critical thinking skills to all students, both those with and without disabilities, has strong support in the educational community.

Students with mild retardation are sometimes characterized as field dependent in their thinking. This means they do not trust their own perceptions or judgments. They are easily influenced by peers and authority figures. By emphasizing individual problem solving, critical thinking programs such as Goldstein's logical–inductive strategy can help develop self-reliance and improve the reasoning abilities of students with mild retardation.

Reuven Feurenstein's Instrumental Enrichment Program teaches thinking skills by providing learners with strategies for using such cognitive skills as analysis, categorization, and inference. Students develop tool and habits of thinking that allow them to process information, see connections, visualize spatial and temporal relationships, and increase their reasoning ability (IRI/ Skylight Training and Publishing, 1997). Through a process of mediated learning teachers use paper and pencil exercises that focus on specific cognitive functions. Students receive feedback through self-correction, peer interaction, and teacher's assessment. Feurenstein's systematic method requires training in mediation practices and an introduction to cognitive and affective factors that effect student performance. Advocates of Feurensteins's methods claim that they effectively ameliorate cognitive problems experienced by students with varying disabilities including autism, mental retardation, and attention deficit disorder.

Early Intervention

Preschool programs such as Head Start provide academic interventions for children aged three to five. The ability of preschool programs to achieve positive, long-term results with students at risk of mild mental retardation was documented in *Changed Lives* (Weikert, 1984), a twenty-two-year longitudinal study of poor, African American children in Ypsilanti, Michigan. As adults, the preschoolers outdistanced peers who had no preschool experience in several criteria for success including: high school diplomas, employment, and functional skills. The number of teenage pregnancies among the preschoolers was half that of the control group and trouble with the law was reduced significantly among the preschooler group. In 1986, Congress passed P.L. 99–457 (The Infant/Toddler Program, Part H) to fund early-intervention programs for preschool children with disabilities and to offer incentives to school systems to develop programs for disabled infants and toddlers.

Successful preschool programs work with parents to continue gains made in preschool centers at home. The school–family partnership is critical because the single most reliable predictor of mild retardation is the IQ of a child's mother. Preschool programs help accelerate students at risk of school failure in cognitive, motor, language, and social–emotional development. A review of fifty-two studies of preschool programs found that 94 percent reported significant gains for children, siblings, and families of preschoolers with mild disabilities (Castro & Mastropieri, 1986). Early intervention, particularly with poor children, is one of the most effective educational strategies to ensure school achievement in later years.

For the student with mild retardation to succeed in school, the focus must be shifted from what is wrong with the student to what is right and beneficial in the curriculum. Effective teaching emphasis on thinking skills and early intervention are general procedures many teachers use to enhance the school experience of students with mental retardation.

Reading

The teaching of reading by phonics is an example of a left-hemispheric approach to language development used in schools. Phonics teaches the sounds of letters, how those sounds blend to make syllables, and the combination of syllables to make words. In the reverse procedure—decoding—students are expected to decipher new words by sounding out each letter to complete a whole word. This auditory, analytical, sequential approach to reading is fine if it takes advantage of preexisting language abilities, but what about the child who does not master the phonics approach? For students who lack good auditory and analytic abilities, phonics and eventually reading can be difficult to master.

Marie Carbo found that economically disadvantaged readers tend to be tactile–kinesthetic learners. Their approach to reading is best described as "global." These students have excellent visual and integrative skills that enable them to acquire sight vocabularies. They demonstrate an intuitive awareness of word patterns. Carbo observed that "global learners learn to read most rapidly through such activities as writing stories, reading books of their own choosing, engaging in choral reading, writing and performing in plays, and listening to tape recordings of interesting and well written books" (Carbo, 1987b, 432). The global reading style described by Carbo is an example of right-hemisphere abilities and is an apt description of the approach to learning observed by teachers of disadvantaged, underachieving students (Dennison, 1969; Kohl, 1967).

Mandelbaum (1989) reviewed best practices in teaching reading and found that a combination of functional reading lists with interesting reading material best met the needs of students with mild retardation. Several principles of effective teaching summarized by Mandelbaum are:

1. *Demonstrate Rather than Tell.* The teacher and student discuss, read, and answer questions together about a story on the student's reading level.
2. *Provide for Successful Practice.* Make sure students use reading materials that will sustain at least an 80 percent success rate.
3. *Use Direct Instruction.* Teacher-led group instruction should demonstrate the skill to be learned, provide practice with feedback, and allow for independent student practice.
4. *Plan for High Levels of Task Involvement.* Reading in unison, choral reading, and high-interest readings improve fluency and comprehension.
5. *Ignore Errors that Do Not Matter. All errors are not equal.* Every word does not have to be read correctly. Focus only on errors that change the meaning of a sentence. Provide sufficient time for a student to analyze a word and decode.
6. *Give Independent Assignments that Relate to the Lesson.* Most workbooks and dittos focus on isolated skills unrelated to stories. Avoid the drudgery of worksheets unless relevant and necessary.
7. *Integrate Subject Matter.* Use themes or webbings to cluster concepts.
8. *Measure Behavior Change.* Plot and graph reading improvement in terms of median of number of words read correctly each minute.
9. *Provide Opportunities to Learn Achievement Formats.* Formats vary widely, and students need practice with the procedures that will be used to evaluate their skills.

Functional Skills

Students with mental retardation respond to the same instructional methods as other students. They may require more time to achieve satisfactory levels of performance and typically require special instruction and extra practice to generalize what they have learned to settings other than the classroom. Sometimes they simply need to be taught how to approach academic tasks. For these students, basic academic skill instruction must go beyond basal readers and traditional worksheets. Effective teachers of these students design instructional and practice activities so that they relate to functional use in everyday life, including home and community living. Ysseldyke and Algozzine (1995) provide a detailed set of tactics for improving these functional skills; some of them are summarized with others from Smith, Finn, & Dowdy (1993) in Table 2.5.

Recall that according to a widely accepted view of intelligence, children interact differently depending on their stage of development (see Figure 2.1).

TABLE 2.5   Summary of Functional Skill Interventions

Functional Skill Area	Intervention Description
Reading	Have students use community signs, local store directories, local restaurant menus, newspapers, local street signs, yellow pages, and other everyday materials for reading practice.
Mathematics	Have students use newspaper advertisements, mail-order catalogs, menus, and other everyday materials for basic skill and problem-solving practice. Use real objects and manipulatives often when teaching math concepts.
Writing	Have students keep diaries of school events, local news stories, classroom visitors, and other everyday activities for writing practice.
Listening	Use real objects or pictures to teach sounds or names. Give students directions to follow in sentences that require movement around the room or manipulation of real objects. Read directions to students and have them make the object described in the directions.

This means that using concrete objects and manipulatives helps many children learn concepts more easily. It also means that while some students pass through the concrete stages of learning more rapidly than others, the need for these stages is extended for students with mental retardation and other developmental disabilities. Some ideas from Smith, Finn, & Dowdy (1993) for ways to extend instruction in important areas of mathematics are illustrated in Table 2.6.t

Adaptive Behavior

Adaptive behavior refers to the ability to be independent and socially responsible (Reschly, 1989). This means that students with mental retardation require a curriculum that teaches social skills, self-direction, and health and safety information. Effective teachers of these students design instructional and practice activities that they need to succeed in school and other adaptive life experiences. Most incorporate the following teaching procedures (Meese, 1994):

TABLE 2.6 Instructional Activities for Extending Learning in Mathematics

Goal: Classifying objects based on characteristics or unique features

- Have students place blocks into groups based on size, color, texture, shape, name, or other attributes.
- Have students place small toys into groups based on size, color, texture, function, or other attributes.
- Have students sort coins, paper money, school supplies, books, or other common objects.

Goal: Learning one-to-one correspondence

- Have students match sets of different objects using numbers to create sets (3 coins = 3 bottle caps).
- Have students match sets of objects with numbers used to represent them (3 coins = 3).
- Have students find as many target sets as possible in a large group of objects (all groups of 3 similar objects in a set of 100 or more).

Goal: Ordering objects on the basis of some characteristic

- Have students arrange a box of pencils from shortest to longest.
- Have students arrange coins from smallest to largest in size.
- Have students arrange sports team members from shortest to tallest.

Goal: Learning that order doesn't change relationships between objects

- Have students combine sets of items to represent relationships.

4 dimes + 3 dimes = 7 dimes	4 clips + 3 clips = 7 clips
3 dimes + 4 dimes = 7 dimes	3 clips + 4 clips = 7 clips
7 dimes – 4 dimes = 3 dimes	7 clips – 4 clips = 3 clips
7 dimes – 3 dimes = 4 dimes	7 clips – 3 clips = 4 clips

1. They carefully select skills that maximize the likelihood of a student's success.
2. They provide clear statements of the skills to be learned and reasons for learning them.
3. They demonstrate the new skills using a variety of methods (e.g., videotapes, films, live demonstrations), models (e.g., high status peers, siblings), and situations.
4. They provide plenty of examples and nonexamples of expected behaviors.

TABLE 2.7 Summary of Adaptive Behavior Interventions

Adaptive Behavior Area	Intervention Description
Social Skills	Have students take part in role-playing activities related to using appropriate social skills. Have them practice greeting friends, exchanging information, engaging in small talk, and other social and communication skills. Reward them for doing so.
Self-Direction	Teach students how to ask for help in school and community settings. Provide practice using these skills in small groups and real-life situations.
	Have students keep track of occasions in which they made a decision on their own, and discuss the outcomes of what they did. Share alternatives between and among classmates.
Health and Safety	Have students role-play emergency situations and generate, discuss, and practice alternative solutions.

5. They provide opportunities for practice under their supervision so students can receive supportive and corrective feedback and avoid practicing errors.
6. They provide recognition and rewards for successful demonstration of newly learned skills.

Some specific activities for improving adaptive behavior skills are summarized in Table 2.7.

Daily Living and Work Skills

Self-care, including activities of daily living and being successful at a job, are important adaptive behavior skills that are the focus of instruction for students with mild retardation. Self-care skills include managing personal finances, caring for personal needs, buying clothing, food, and other personal items, and getting around in the community. Job-related skills include following directions, being punctual, beginning assignments promptly, staying on task, and completing assignments; these are sometimes addressed with functional academic interventions.

Here are some ways to improve self-care skills:

1. Teach students to differentiate coins and other money.
2. Teach students to make and receive change.
3. Have students practice physical fitness activities.
4. Have students practice personal grooming skills.
5. Teach consumer economics.
6. Teach traffic and safety rules.
7. Teach students to use public transportation.

Here are some ways to improve work skills:

1. Teach students that attendance and punctuality are important.
2. Reward students for being on time and for high attendance.
3. Have students record their own attendance.
4. Reward students for completing tasks on time.
5. Have students keep records of completed assignments.
6. Have students complete job applications.
7. Provide rewards after completion of smaller tasks.
8. Set liberal standards for task completion.

Students with mild mental retardation experience difficulties in many areas of school and life functioning. There is no magic in instructional activities that work with these students. In many ways, what effective teachers do with them is just like what they do with everybody else. And, whenever necessary, they modify what they do to accommodate the special learning needs of their students. With this type of instruction, students with mild or moderate mental retardation can learn to overcome many of their problems and can be successful and productive in school and life experiences. A key here is the importance of high expectations and functional curriculum goals.

Summary

Mild mental retardation is both a social and an educational problem. The majority of children identified as mildly retarded are poor, with African Americans over-represented in many states. While many students with mild mental retardation have no identifiable organic or neurological problems, the health-threatening conditions of poverty clearly put poor children at greatest risk. The deleterious effects of such factors as low birth weight, deficient diet, and improper prenatal care can be offset by health and educational intervention for children and their families.

Characteristics of children identified with mild mental retardation can vary from one region to another. Although the American Association of Mental Retardation published guidelines for identifying mild mental retardation, individual states establish their own criteria. Consequently, the prevalence of students identified as mildly retarded varies from state to state. This means that some students who need special education services may go without, and other students without disabilities receive services.

Students with mild retardation are characterized by slower cognitive development; academic deficiencies, especially in reading; and deficits in adaptive behavior. Because success in school depends so much on verbal skills, some students—poor children and children from non-English-speaking families in particular—encounter difficulties. An individual student may demonstrate specific learning problems in mental processing, social adaption, and perception. However, students with mild retardation show a great deal of variability in learning characteristics, and generalizations about their abilities or disabilities can lead to stereotypes and negative teacher expectations.

Students with mild retardation score in a range of 75 to 50 on IQ tests, and they have deficits in social skills outside the school setting. Quality of educational programming depends on the teacher's ability to motivate students who have a history of school failure. Academic programs that emphasize functional skills provide adolescents with a reason to stay in school. Younger children learn best when teachers match instruction to their cognitive abilities. Programs that attempt to remediate specific deficiencies, such as poor memory, through drill and repetition fail to consider the point of view of the learner. Students with mild retardation need practice in developing their own thinking abilities. School programs that help students with mild retardation gain confidence in themselves as learners are most successful in helping them to adapt to life after school.

The cycle of destitution that has characterized mild mental retardation throughout the past century will be broken when disadvantaged learners graduate from school with employable skills. Education is the best offensive strategy in the war on poverty. When regular and special educators work together to keep learners in the mainstream of school life, teacher and student expectations for success are enhanced. As Lloyd Dunn eloquently pointed out, the interests of poor children are not served by labeling them retarded and relegating them to isolated special education classrooms. Ultimately it is the quality of educational programming, not the label pinned on the student, that determines success or failure.

Activities

1. Visit a special education classroom that serves students with mild retardation. Observe the students at work. How many students are in the classroom? Draw a diagram of the physical arrangement of the classroom. Observe the bulletin boards and other displays in the classroom. What topics are emphasized? Are students working in large groups, in small groups, or individually?

2. While visiting the special education classroom, ask for a private time to talk with the teacher. Try to find out what type of curriculum guide he or she uses. Which subjects are primarily taught? Is career education an integral part of the curriculum? Are social skills taught? Are functional skills included?

3. Investigate the professional organizations in the field of mental retardation. Two national organizations are the Division on Mental Retardation of the Council for Exceptional Children (1920 Association Drive, Reston, Virginia 22091) and the American Association on Mental Retardation (1719 Kalorama Road NW, Washington, D.C. 20009). Write to these organizations for their literature. Try to determine their purposes, who are their members, and what services are offered members.

4. Are there local or state branches of the national professional organizations for mental retardation? If there is a local organization, arrange to visit one of their meetings. Ask a member to visit your class and talk with students about the purpose of the organization, membership composition, and services offered members.

5. Visit the campus library. Locate the special education journals that focus on mental retardation. These journals include the *American Journal on Mental Retardation, Education and Training in Mental Retardation*, and *Mental Retardation*. Look for articles about intellectual disabilities and mental retardation in major special education journals like *Exceptional Children* and *Teaching Exceptional Children*.

CHAPTER

3 Students with Behavior Disorders

Advance Questions

Answer the following questions as you read this chapter:

1. What types of students are included in the category of behavior disorders?
2. What are some of the main components of definitions of behavior disorders?
3. How many students are included in the behavior disorders category?
4. What causes behavior disorders?

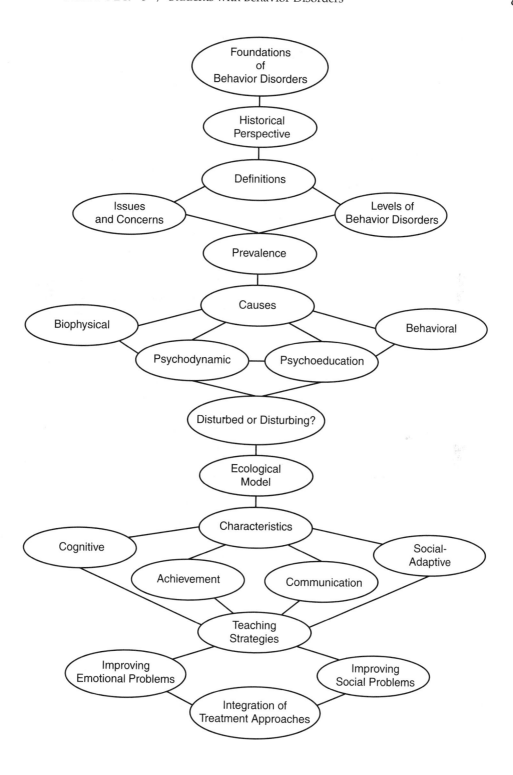

5. What are some characteristics of students with behavior disorders?
6. What instructional approaches are used by teachers of students with behavior disorders?
7. What can teachers do to improve a student's behavior?

Vignette: Fred Peterson

Fred Peterson has been a teacher for over twenty years: each of his classes has had at least one problem student. This year it was Selena. Selena could always find a way to avoid schoolwork. For example, one day Fred told the class to begin work on the math sheet he had provided each of them. "Excuse me, Mr. Peterson," said Selena. "Can I go to the bathroom?" Fred had a policy of letting students move freely throughout the school, so he let her go. About fifteen minutes later, she returned and asked if she could wash the blackboards. Fred mentioned it was probably a better idea to start on her worksheet. At this suggestion, Selena grew angry. She walked up to Fred, balled the worksheet in her fist, and threw it at Fred. "Do your own damned worksheet," she shouted, and she ran out the classroom door.

Alan is a senior in high school with decent grades. He is on the basketball team, and he has a lot of friends. Lately he and a few buddies have started smoking marijuana on the way to school in the morning. Alan maintains that after twelve years of boring classes, it's fun to go to "high" school. Ms. Hildago, his homeroom teacher, can tell when Alan has been smoking. His eyes are red and glassy. She has tried talking to Alan privately but to no avail. Alan either denies he smokes or walks away. Alan's behavior in his classes is erratic. He jokes around, makes snide comments, or just spaces out. Ms. Hildago is hesitant to discuss Alan's situation with the principal because she's afraid Alan will be expelled.

Alice has been teaching kindergarten for ten years, but she has never had a class like this one. Several youngsters have attention problems caused by alcohol use by mothers during pregnancy. Raymond, although talkative and outgoing, is unable to handle scissors or even extra fat crayons. Louis gets a sticker just for sitting still for ten minutes. He is constantly careening around the room, bumping into other children, and starting fights. Fay tries hard to do well, but she can't follow directions. She is frequently confused about what she's supposed to be doing. Alice is unable to give Fay all the individual attention she requires.

Now that you have read the vignette about some teachers of students with problem behaviors, see how may problem-solving questions you can answer. For those you cannot readily answer, try to find some additional information to use in answering them as you read the chapter. The experiences of Fred Peterson, Ms. Hildago, and Alice are typical of teachers of students with behavior disorders.

1. What should be done to help students like Selena, Alan, Raymond, Louis, or Fay?

2. Who should teach them?
3. Do all schools provide special education services for students with behavior disorders?
4. What expectations would you have for students like Selena, Alan, Raymond, Louis, or Fay if you were teaching them?
5. Should students with behavior disorders be included in classes with students without disabilities?

Experiences like these illustrate the kinds of "problems" that cause students to be identified with behavior disorders. Disturbing behaviors, noncompliance, or an inability to adjust to classroom routines are common reasons for students to be referred for special education. Each year, Phi Delta Kappa, a national education organization, commissions a Gallup Poll of the public's attitudes toward education. In most of the surveys, discipline was the number-one problem identified.

At one time or another, every teacher has a student who has conflicts with rules for proper behavior in school. The decision to evaluate a student for special education services on the basis of classroom behavior is a matter of frequency and intensity of the disturbing actions. The more "acting out" the behavior, the more likely a student will be referred for special education. The National Education Association identified the following behaviors as those most likely to attract unfavorable attention in the classroom:

1. Exhibits physical and verbal aggression toward classmates (fighting, instigation of arguments).
2. Exhibits verbal aggression toward teacher and the other authority figures (profanity, negative names).
3. Refuses to cooperate in classroom group activities.
4. Intentionally damages classroom materials.
5. Uses classroom materials to create disruptive sounds and noises. (Rivers, 1977, 9)

A student who is shy or withdrawn may have serious emotional difficulties but if she continues to follow classroom directions and completes her schoolwork, her problems may be overlooked. Depression and suicide are too common among today's schoolchildren to be ignored. Latchkey children (children who return home from school to empty houses), students with learning disabilities, and students experiencing chronic family problems are particularly vulnerable. Guetzloe summarized the causes of suicide among children:

Any problem that contributes to feelings of depression, worthlessness, helplessness, or hopelessness has the potential to trigger suicidal behavior in a vulnerable individual. Among the many factors that have been cited as contributing to youth suicide are isolation, alienation, loss, physical or psychological abuse, disturbance in peer relationships, substance abuse, rejection, incarceration, disorganization, availability of weapons, fear of punishment, fear of failure, knowledge of suicide, and humiliation. (Guetzloe, 1988, 22)

Among special educators there is concern that not enough is being done to help students with behavioral or emotional problems. This concern is equally shared by general classroom teachers who spend a large portion of their day trying to manage these youngsters behavior.

Foundations of Behavior Disorders

Hyman and D'Alessandro (1984) highlighted the complex interaction of environmental and individual factors that contribute to student behavior disorders. They found that causes often rest outside the student's ability to control.

Included among environmental causes are inadequate parenting, overcrowding, racism, lack of employment, overexposure to violence through television and other mass media, peer pressures, and specific social, political, and bureaucratic factors that ignore the needs of the young. Schools contribute to behavior problems through ineffective teaching, poor school organization, inadequate administrative leadership, inappropriate curricula, overuse of suspensions, and other punishments. Within the individual student, Hyman and D'Alessandro cited inborn traits, such as neurological impairments, that may disrupt interactions with others, ultimately causing behavior disorders. Poor self-esteem and frustration with learning are also student responses that accelerate behavior disorders. When attempting to understand students' problems, we must also take into account the troubled systems (family, school, community) that interact with and shape children's development (Apter, 1982). Placing a student in a special education program will produce minimal results if, at the end of the school day, the youngster returns home to a sexually abusive father, a tormented mother, or a neighborhood permeated with drugs and violence.

Most of us, in our own way, walk a fine line between normal and abnormal, right and wrong, mental illness and mental health. Often the force that pushes us into one or the other of these categories does not originate in our own behavior. Others with whom we interact are instrumental in shaping, defining, managing, and manipulating our feelings and behavior. This is the crux of the human dilemma. We need to interact with others to grow and learn, yet the nature of those interactions, which are often shaped by forces outside our control, help determine the kind of person we will become.

"Behavior disorders," "emotionally disturbed," "serious emotional disturbance," "mental illness," "disruptive," or "conduct problem," are all names that have been assigned to the field of study in which professionals try to explain special learning needs of students who cannot cope with the social demands of school or society. Over the years, special education has accumulated a large body of research on the causes and treatment of students with behavior and emotional difficulties. Before we discuss these different conceptual models, it would be useful to examine the historical roots of behavior disorders and their treatment.

Historical Perspective

Human history is replete with strange stories of how deviancy has been dealt with. There was a time when the treatment of insanity was worse than the condition. Early medicants believed that by boring holes in the head (a method called trephining), the devil or other evil spirits would be released and leave the body. Hippocrates first classified mental problems using mania, hebephrenia, and melancholia as terms to describe separate conditions. He also is credited with offering the first theory for the cause of mental problems, blaming an imbalance of body fluids for strange behavior (Rhodes & Tracy, 1972a,b).

Throughout the ages, theories of causation of mental illnesses or emotional disturbances ranged from witchcraft to science. One of the first environmental causes of mental illness was identified in the Middle Ages, when it was discovered that hatters were driven "mad" from the mercury they used to condition felt. When mercury use was discontinued, so was the incidence of "mad hatters." As Restak (1984) noted, "Over the centuries, schizophrenics have been burned at the stake, chained in dark dungeons, starved to death, and drowned" (p. 273). Discoveries that vitamin B6 deficiencies and syphilis caused mental illness helped move mental treatment out of the shadows and into the medical laboratory. About 1890, Kraeplin identified an advanced form of mental illness that he called "dementia praecox." This term was used to refer to adult mental illness, and the classification system surrounding it became the forerunner of the scientific classification system that is in place today (Algozzine, Serna, & Patton, 1998). After Kraeplin introduced dementia, a psychologist, DeSantis, recommended that a new term be designated for the childhood version of this mental condition. He suggested "dementia praecocissima," and the study of childhood emotional problems was given a life of its own.

Shortly thereafter, another psychologist, Heller, observed a severely debilitating, degenerative condition in infants characterized by a loss of motor and language abilities. This condition was labeled as Heller's syndrome. In 1943, Leo Kanner observed odd, stereotyped behaviors in young children. The children, although uncommunicative and aloof, appeared to have average or above average intelligence. This condition became known as early infantile autism. By 1952, the American Psychiatric Association produced a document listing the major types of mental disorders. Childhood disorders did not appear in the first *Diagnostic and Statistical Manual* (*DSM-I*), but the second edition (*DSM-II*) contained a category titled Behavior Disorders of Childhood and Adolescents. Students with behavior disorders do not exhibit the kinds of severe debilitating conditions that were first identified by early psychologists and physicians. Such disabilities as childhood schizophrenia and autism still exist; however, they are severe disabilities and are not included in our discussion of mild disabilities.

Definition and Identification

Professionals use different terms, such as emotionally disturbed, behavior disordered, and seriously emotionally disturbed, to refer to students with behavior disorders. In a few states special education services are provided to students with behavior disorders on a noncategorical basis without formally labeling them. Typically, students in this category are identified by behavior problems that interfere with productive interpersonal relations. Historically, this perspective has been reflected in the definitions used to describe and help teachers and other professionals identify these students.

Kirk (1962) suggested that a behavior deviation comprised actions that had a detrimental effect on a child's adjustment or interfered with the lives of other people. Pate (1963) stated that a child was disturbed when his behavior was so inappropriate that regular class attendance would: (1) be disrupting for the rest of the class, (2) put undue pressure on the teacher, and (3) further the disturbance of the child. Bower (1969) added several aspects to the criteria when he suggested that children with emotional disabilities exhibit one or more of the following characteristics to a marked extent over a long period of time:

1. An inability to learn that cannot be explained by intellectual, sensory, or health factors.
2. An inability to build or maintain satisfactory interpersonal relationships with peers and teachers.
3. Inappropriate types of behavior or feelings under normal conditions.
4. A general, pervasive mood of unhappiness or depression.
5. A tendency to develop physical symptoms, pains, or fears associated with school problems. (pp. 22–3)

These criteria are accepted in current federal guidelines although many professionals are not happy with them as a basis for defining the category of behavior disorders. The term "seriously emotionally disturbed" is presently used in the Individuals with Disabilities Education Act.

Issues and Concerns

Although it has the advantage of acknowledging several conceptual components of behavior disorders (e.g., emotional and social problems) and offers operational terms (such as "to a marked extent" and "over a long period of time") from which to build more specific guidelines, the current federal definition guiding identification practices does not have widespread acceptance. Unfortunately, it falls short of being a conceptually clear representation from which to develop meaningful identification procedures and treatment practices. For example, how do we identify "an inability to learn which cannot be explained by health factors," or what constitutes a "general pervasive mood of unhappiness"? And what about students who perform in school but still have emotional problems? Morse put it this way:

Note that a definition including educational performance leaves out those who have no school problems or problems that do not affect achievement, and this can be a significant number. The idea that all disturbed children must have an educational problem in behavior or achievement is a significant error. The other error lies in implying that when children have problems in school, these problems are primarily school-related. The fact is that problems are often generated outside the school environment and brought to school. (Morse, 1985, 43)

Perhaps most contentious to some special educators is the omission of "socially maladjusted students" from the ranks of students who qualify for special education services. In addressing this problem, the Executive Committee of the Council for Children with Behavioral Disorders had this to say:

This exclusion of the socially maladjusted from special education seems to be based on several assumptions. These include: (a) There is a significant population of youngsters whose antisocial behavior is more related to a general social phenomenon than a specific handicapping condition; (b) it is possible to consistently differentiate such students from those who are truly handicapped by virtue of their behavior; and (c) it is important that special education not automatically incorporate a group specified as "in trouble" by other systems, such as the juvenile justice system. (Executive Committee of the Council for Children with Behavioral Disorders, 1987)

The position of the council is that an adjudication of delinquency does not mean a disability is present. However, some students with delinquent behavior do have mild disabilities, and they have an equal right to federal services mandated by Congress for all school-aged youngsters. Indeed, comprehensive surveys of incarcerated youngsters indicate that mild disabilities are more prevalent among youthful offenders than the general population (Nelson, Rutherford, & Wolford, 1987).

The lack of clear direction in determining who receives special education services for behavioral or emotional problems is highlighted by a survey that found states use a total of 17 different terms to describe this population (Knitzer, Steinberg, and Fleisch, 1990). Most state definitions used to refer students with behavior or emotional difficulties tend to have several general similarities. They suggest that the disturbances or disorders that exist within the student's behavior patterns cause academic and social problems that in turn affect the youngster and peers. Although these state definitions help professionals to know who should be identified as requiring special education, the actual process of identification is not facilitated by any one definition in particular. Most definitions do not have clearly stated operational criteria that can be dovetailed into a special educational assessment.

Based on a historical analysis of definitions of behavior disorders/emotional disturbance, Algozzine, Schmid, and Mercer (1981) identified four operational components that should be included within any criteria for determining a behavior disorder. These include:

1. A measure of alternative placements.
2. A measure of behavioral deviation.
3. A measure of behavioral interference.
4. A measure of exclusive etiology.

Algozzine, Schmid, and Connors (1978) recommend matching their criteria with the following definition:

> [A student with behavior disorders] is one who, after receiving supportive educational services and counseling assistance available to all students, still exhibits persistent and consistent severe behavioral disabilities that consequently interfere with productive learning processes. This is the student whose inability to achieve adequate academic progress and satisfactory interpersonal relationships cannot be attributed to primarily physical, sensory, or intellectual deficits.

The operational criteria related to this definition can be applied across a variety of geographical areas and theoretical frames of reference. For example, the *alternative placement clause* ("after receiving supportive educational services and counseling assistance available to all students") may be related to and measured by the number of different activities attempted in order to alleviate the student's problems in school. Activities such as changing the student's class schedule, individual or group counseling, curriculum or teacher modifications, and outside agency intervention should be documented. The degree to which the behavioral difficulties are the result of situational factors may be measured by this process.

The *behavioral deviation clause* ("persistent and consistent severe to very severe behavioral disabilities") should be measured against predefined standards. Persistent may be defined as existing for three months or three years; consistent may be described as a marked similarity in behaviors within different school situations or as a result of similar incidents: for example, reacting consistently when faced with failure. Severe could be identified with occurrences more than twice a day, and very severe could mean occurrences of once or twice an hour. The actual interfering emotional and social behaviors must be delimited so that effective treatment strategies can be developed.

The *behavioral interference clause* ("interfere with productive learning processes") relates to the measurable results of the exhibited behavioral disabilities. It is possible to state objectively academic criteria (e.g., one standard deviation below school-district age-mates on normative tests) as well as interpersonal problems (e.g., avoided by other children, or fighting with three children in a week). If a student's "emotional problems" are thought to be caused by a lack of school or social success, that lack of progress, in addition to the behavioral problems, can be identified clearly.

The federal definition states that the student's educational performance must be "adversely affected." To what extent remains undefined.

The *exclusive etiology clause* ("not attributed primarily to physical, sensory, or intellectual deficits") enables students whose primary disability is not emotional or behavioral to receive appropriate services. It suggests that some students have a primary disability related to interfering behaviors, and these are the students who should be identified with behavior disorders.

Levels of Behavior Disorders

A systematic application of these criteria should result in the identification of two types of troubled children. The TYPE I (Student with a Behavior Disorder) is characterized by the types of behavior problems found typically in public schools. This student may be a problem in school but not at home. The behavior may be a response to an inappropriate or unmotivating school environment, and it may be responsive to positive environmental strategies. The TYPE II (Severely Disturbed Student) may be characterized by the more comprehensive form of disturbance typically not found in general classrooms. This student's behavior will be problematic at home and school, and it may exhibit itself with regularity in both favorable and unfavorable environments. The behavior will not be immediately responsive to environmental management strategies. The behavior may be traced to organic inadequacies, as in the case of youth with childhood sschizophrenia. A possible diagnostic comparison between TYPE I and TYPE II students with emotional and behavioral disorders based on the suggested operational criteria is presented in Table 3.1.

Hallahan and Kauffman (1977) suggested that the conditions referred to as learning disabilities, behavior disorders/emotional disturbance, and mild mental retardation are similar disabilities. The characteristic behaviors of each condition are also similar (Neisworth & Greer, 1975). Whereas the TYPE I behavior disordered child may be similar in many respects to students with learning disabilities and mild mental retardation, it would seem that the TYPE II child with a severe social–emotional disturbance would be unique.

TABLE 3.1 Comparison of TYPE I Behavioral and TYPE II Emotional Disturbance

TYPE I (Mild Behavior Disorders)	TYPE II (Clinical Emotional Disturbance)
General class has not been beneficial; but, placement there is a preferred goal.	General school placements have not been successful; outside placements common.
School counseling services often prove beneficial.	External counseling services are typical.
Common behavioral problems evident in assessment records.	Clinical diagnoses and problems recorded
Problems often reported in only one classroom or only at school	Problems evident at home, school, and in other environments
Evidence that interventions are effective with selected problem behaviors.	Evidence that problems are very resistant to common interventions.

Since a wide range of behaviors may be considered disturbing, the definitional criteria has the flexibility to incorporate variability. The inclusion of an "alternative placements" clause acknowledges the fact that appropriate behaviors are often socially derived. Behavior problems that are situational can sometimes be eliminated by an administrative placement change. However, the greatest advantage lies in the fact that the condition is clearly recognizable from a specific set of interfering behaviors. It is this set of behaviors that defines the condition of emotional–behavioral disturbance evident in students with mild disabilities.

Prevalence of Behavior Disorders

Short-term classroom behavior problems are common in most schools. Students in our introductory classes are surprised to learn that the prevalence of students with behavior disorders is relatively low. Of 5,439,626 students receiving special education in 1995, 428,168 were identified as seriously emotionally disturbed (U.S. Department of Education, 1996). This represents about 9 percent of the special education students and about 1 percent of the general school-age population. The overall prevalence of this group of students has been relatively constant over the last ten years (Ysseldyke & Algozzine, 1995); however, there is considerable variation from state to state in the percentage of the school-age population identified with behavior disorders. Prevalence figures can range from a high of 1.69 percent in Connecticut to a low of 0.03 percent in Mississippi.

The prevalence of students with behavior disorders tends to fluctuate considerably depending on several factors. The nature of the definition and criteria used to identify students has a major impact on the rate of identification and numbers of identified students; for example, when the Bower definition was originally used, the rate of occurrence of behavior disorders was estimated to be 10 percent (Reinert, 1976).

Rubin and Balow (1971) found that 41 percent of the students they studied had "educationally defined" behavior problems; that is, the students were identified chiefly by their inability to meet the demands of school conduct expectations. Their findings are analogous to Jane Mercer's description of the "six-hour mildly retarded student." (See Chapter Two, Students With Mild Mental Retardation). The results of the Rubin and Balow study indicated that many students may be regarded as disturbed or behavior disordered by their teachers in school. Outside of school, their behavior is adaptive to the demands of their environment.

The "six-hour" behavior disordered student, identified by Rubin and Balow, is an illustration of the widening cultural gap between poor children and the demands of school. As an illustration, consider a ten-year-old who lives in a ghetto neighborhood. What are the environmental conditions that this youth must deal with on a daily basis? The widespread reports of violence, drug use, and gang membership in poverty-stricken neighborhoods suggest that survival dictates an aggressive attitude. A ten-year-old who cannot take care of himself could quickly become prey to any passerby who fancied his sneakers, jacket, or money. In order to survive, our ten-year-old must learn to stand up for himself; he must project an image of toughness and nonchalance in the face of danger.

Now let's project this same street-wise youth into a fifth-grade classroom. His teacher has just demanded to know why he didn't complete his homework. The youth is trapped between the demands of the adult authority and the expectations of his classmates, who eagerly await his response. Our ten-year-old is no fool, he knows that his mettle is inadvertently being challenged by the teacher, so he replies, "Do your own homework." The teacher's authority has been challenged, and the teacher responds by sending the young rebel to the principal, who suspends him for the rest of the day. A cycle of hostility is now perpetuated that could lead to a special education referral because of a behavior disorder.

Prevalence rates are also affected by the instruments used to evaluate students and the individuals who are doing the evaluating. One of the earliest reported prevalence studies used teacher judgments of school-related maladjustment as the criteria; Wickman (1929) found 42 percent of the sampled students had behavior disturbing to teachers. This figure is similar to that reported by Rubin and Balow, who also sampled teachers' attitudes toward school behavior problems. In general, higher prevalence rates are reported when teachers give their opinions of disturbing behaviors rather than matching their students to specific criteria for behavior disorders.

Higher prevalence rates are reported for "mild" than for severe forms of behavior disorders. Because teacher perceptions play such a key role in determining behavior disorders, it is understandable that more students are identified as having behavior problems after they begin school and become discipline problems. Kelly, Bullock, and Dykes (1974) reported teacher-perceived prevalence rates of 12.6 for mild behavior problems, 5.6 for moderate problems, and 2.2 for students with severe behavior disorders. This general ratio has been reported elsewhere (Glidewell & Swallow, 1968). Paul and Epinchan (1991) cite more current research that indicates a prevalence rate of 11 percent of the total school population. This amounts to an estimate of six to eight million students with behavior and emotional disorders, yet in 1995 only 428,168 or 8.7 percent of all students with disabilities received special education services because of emotional disturbance (U.S. Department of Education, 1996).

Sex is an important factor in prevalence reports. In all studies of behavior and emotional disorders, boys consistently outnumber girls (Reinert, 1976; Rubin & Balow, 1971). One interpretation of this data is that girls are better adjusted than boys. It is far more likely, however, that cultural experience plays a significant role. Boys tend to develop aggressive ways of expressing emotional problems, whereas girls learn to express anger and hostility in a more covert fashion. Promiscuity, drug abuse, and depression are not the type of disturbed behaviors that teachers see, but that doesn't mean that they don't exist. The increasing pregnancy rate for teenage girls and the large numbers of babies born to cocaine and crack addicts is indirect evidence that school special education services may be overlooking females.

Between 1977 and 1995, there was a 45 percent increase in students with behavior disorders identified nationwide; more increase than any other category than learning disabilities (U.S. Department of Education, 1996). As we look toward the twenty-first century, several factors indicate that the prevalence will continue to escalate.

> Item: By the year 2000, one out of every four children will grow up in poverty. Poverty contributes to broken homes, proliferation of drugs, violence, and homelessness. Millions of American children will be required to adapt to desperate environmental demands. The same behaviors that are adaptive on the streets will be disruptive in school.
>
> Item: The incidence of infants born to mothers who are addicted to alcohol, crack, cocaine, and other drugs continues to climb. These children will present a whole new category of students with behavior disorders.
>
> Item: As we move into the twenty-first century, we are becoming a bilingual nation. While schools attempt to deal with the steady increase in non-English-speaking students, the cultural gap between home and community continues to widen. Students will be alienated from the affairs of schooling, and this alienation will be acted out in classrooms.
>
> Item: Inner-city schools continue to present the greatest challenge to educational reform. Some schools have degenerated to the point that metal detectors are placed at the schoolhouse door to screen students for weapons. The social and emotional turmoil that infects these schools requires the best teachers available. However, few young people who enter the teaching profession want to risk their psychological or physical safety teaching in ghetto schools. Without a massive infusion of educational and social support, inner-city schools will become hotbeds of chaos.
>
> Item: Violence and neglect permeate the lives of many American children. In 1987 The Wall Street Journal chronicled three months in the life of Lafayette Walton, a twelve-year-old Chicago youngster. His experience included almost daily gun and submachine gun battles in his housing project, beatings and maimings of relatives and friends, rapes, gang recruiting, cocaine-running by a nine-year-old female cousin, and several murders. (Zinmeister, 1990, 50)

The psychological and emotional fallout from poor children's violent lives presents an overwhelming challenge to American policymakers. However, there is no national agenda with the specific aim of creating safe havens for children. According to the *National Needs Analysis in Behavior Disorders* (Grosenick & Huntze, 1979), "The most glaring concern that exists in the area of behavior disorders is the staggering number of children with behavior problems who remain unserved" (Apter, 1982, 7).

To summarize, more than 400,000 students are identified as requiring special education due to behavioral or emotional disturbance. Yet many other children go unserved chiefly because their behavior is not disruptive in the classroom or their behavior does not fit categorical criteria for special education (e.g., socially maladjusted, disadvantaged, school dropouts). America's children and youth are in a state of emergency. As children become more vulnerable, the need for effective educational and community programs will continue to grow.

Causes of Behavior Disorders

The search for understanding the causes and treatment of behavior and disorders has followed many roads. Each distinctive field of knowledge—biophysical, psychodynamic, psychoeducational, and behavioral—has contributed, in a synergistic fashion, to an overall understanding of behavior disorders (see Table 3.2). During the early years of special education, theorists tended to pitch their tents in a single conceptual camp. They fortified their encampments with rigorous defenses, and with equal vigor hurled verbal assaults at each other. Thus graduate students would burn the midnight oil as they debated the relative merits of Bettelheim's psychodynamic view versus Skinner's behavior modification techniques for treating troubled children.

TABLE 3.2   Summary of Causes of Behavior Disorders

	Biophysical	Psychodynamic	Behavioral	Psycho-educational
Emphasis	Biological and physical systems	Stages of psychological development	Behavior antecedents and consequences	School adaptation and behavior change
Etiology	Genetics, nutrition, biochemistry, neurology	Conflict in development, traumatic experiences	Learning systems, conditioning, reinforcement, punishment	Conflict in development compounded by expectations
Diagnosis	Identify area(s) of biological or physical dysfunction	Identify critical phases in development or insight into origins of conflict	Identify controlling conditions within learning trials	Identify controlling influences in development
Assessment	Medical and physical exams	Psychological exams	Observations	Observations
Instruction/ Treatment	Medical and physical treatments	Psychological counseling	Behavior therapy	Reeducation
Goals	Correcting system dysfunctions	Reduction of conflict	Arranging conditions of learning	Individual and system change
Some Major Figures	Rimland Feingold	Freud Erikson Redl Bettelheim	Pavlov Skinner	Hobbs Long Morse Wood

The term "behavior disorders" is a victory of sorts for the behaviorists. Its acceptance outside the behavior modification camp indicates that psychologists and educators agree it is a faulty leap in logic to ascribe an emotional causation to all disruptive behavior. The first model we address, the biophysical, makes a clear case for understanding that behavior disorders can occur when something goes wrong with the delicate mechanism of a child's body.

Biophysical Causes

Throughout history, physical and biological factors have been identified with some of the conditions that are part of the broad classification known as behavior disorders. Researchers have linked genetics and emotional disturbance; Schwartz (1979) pointed out that evidence exists to support the role of heredity in shaping behavior and personality. This conclusion is based on findings that sex-linked differences are evident in many types of behavioral disorders. For example, hyperactivity, antisocial behaviors, and conduct disorders are more commonly identified in boys than in girls.

Thomas and Chess (1977) followed several groups from childhood to adulthood and found that their behavior patterns were relatively constant. About 40 percent were made up of the "easy child" whose characteristics included adaptability, high tolerance for frustration, and positive responses to change. The "difficult" child (about 10 percent) was characterized by irregular biological functions, negative behaviors, poor adaptability, and negativism. The "slow to warm" child was characterized by limited responsiveness, flat emotional responses, and unsatisfactory interpersonal relations. These findings were presented as support for the position that behavioral characteristics are predicated on biophysical differences among people.

The popularity of psychoactive drugs to treat behavior disorders is testimony to the widespread acceptance of the biophysical approach. Physicians prescribe drugs, and they rely on parents and others to monitor the effects those drugs have on problem behaviors. School personnel are in a crucial position to monitor a successful drug therapy program. Teachers maintain consistent contact in situations that allow for comparisons of student behavior, so observations by teachers are exceptionally valuable. The drug-monitoring process requires systematic observations and recordings of a student's behavior at various points during the school day.

Interest in using drugs is based on general knowledge about the ways chemicals influence behavior. For example, the amino acid tryptophan is converted into the neurotransmitter serotonin by chemical reactions that are regulated by enzymes (e.g., tryptophan hydroxylase); serotonin is believed to influence aggression, depression, and normal sleep patterns (Restak, 1984).

Stimulants, such as methylphenidate hydrochloride (Ritalin), dextroamphetamine sulfate (Dexadrine), and magnesium pemoline (Cylert), as well as antihistamines, such as diphenhydramine hydrochloride (Benadryl), are used to treat problem behaviors related to overactivity. Antidepressants and antianxiety drugs, such as imipramine hydrochloride (Tofranil), oxazepam (Serax), and chlorpromazine hydrochloride (Librium), are used to control problem behaviors related to mood disorders.

Experiments with lithium, a drug originally used to treat gout, indicate a calming effect with aggressive animals. In the laboratory, Siamese fighting fish, rats, and mice showed decreased hostile behavior when treated with lithium. Outside the laboratory, experiments with lithium have demonstrated interesting and controversial results with aggressive prisoners. In an experiment in the maximum security prisons at Vacaville and Sacramento, California, twenty-seven inmates were administered lithium. Although diverse in family backgrounds and personalities, the inmates were similar in their recurrent violent behavior and quick tempers. Restak described changes in both prisoner behavior and attitude after nine months:

> The results showed a decline in disciplinary action for violent behavior. Among fifteen of twenty-two subjects, the number of disciplinary acts for violent behavior were reduced. Even more interesting than the decrease in violence, however, were the reports offered by several prisoners in Dr. Tupin's study. One man stated, "Now I can think about whether to hit him or not." Another said, "I have lost my anger." Each of the Lithium dosed prisoners demonstrated an increased capacity to reflect on the consequences of his actions, a quality Dr. Tupin refers to as a "more reflective mood." (Restak, 1984, 142)

Stimulants, minor tranquilizers, and anticonvulsants commonly used for children with behavior disorders are presented in Appendix B. Each class of psychoactive medication includes generic and brand name drugs, common dosages, expected effects, and side effects. Whenever students are given drugs to treat behavior disorders, the underlying premise is that chemical body processes are being altered. Imbalances in the biochemical system are believed to be the source of the problem. Drugs are prescribed by physicians to bring abnormal body chemicals into proper levels of balance and thereby change behavior. The more disturbing the behavior, the greater the likelihood that drug treatment will be accepted as a needed procedure. In the case of students with mild behavior disorders, the use of drugs can and has created controversy.

Attention Deficit Hyperactivity Disorder. Since hyperactivity was first described in 1902 by Dr. George Still as "an abnormal defect of moral control," it has been one of the most discussed behavior disorders encountered by teachers and parents. The *Diagnostic and Statistical Manual of Mental Disorders*, or *DSM IV*, describes hyperactivity as a symptom of attention-deficit hyperactive disorder (ADHD). According to the *DSM IV*, the onset of hyperactivity occurs before age seven, persists for at least six months, and must include a subset of some of the following symptoms: fails to give close attention to details, often does not seem to listen to what is said, often fidgets with hands or feet or squirms in seat, and often talks excessively.

William Cruickshank (1986) described two types of hyperactivity: sensory hyperactivity and motor hyperactivity. Distractibility is one of the primary characteristics of sensory hyperactivity. A student with sensory hyperactivity has an exceedingly short attention span, sometimes less than a minute. The student's attention is literally tugged back and forth by the visual and auditory stimuli of classroom activity. Unable to discriminate figure–ground relationships, either visually or auditorily (i.e., separating object from background), this student encounters severe problems with the simplest task. The printed page of a book with its angled letters, spaces between letters, and pictures, is a visual mine field for a student with impaired figure–ground ability. The student is unable to stay focused on the sequential arrangement of letters and words.

According to Cruickshank, students with motor hyperactivity "seem to fall apart at the seams." They are constantly twisting, squirming, bending, and manipulating anything they can get their hands on. Hallways, playgrounds, or other open spaces, with the abundance of stimuli, cause the hyperactive student to overreact by running, yelling, and generally making a nuisance. Requesting such a student to sit still for ten minutes is asking the nearly impossible. Needless to say, a student with sensory and/or motor hyperactivity is a severe test of a teacher's patience and creativity. Cruickshank (and many other researchers) believe that hyperactivity is a neurological disorder that is outside a youngster's ability to control. With estimates of hyperactivity ranging from 3 to 10 percent of school-aged students, it is plain to see how the problem of hyperactive students would attract teachers, pediatricians, and parents to treatment with drugs.

Many hyperactive students are treated with Ritalin, a stimulant. Ritalin is a classified as a Schedule II drug, meaning that it is regarded as a drug easily abused. Its manufacture is regulated by the Drug Enforcement Administration. Kohn (1988) reported that three-quarters of a million children are receiving the drug because of ADHD. Ritalin helps some students to concentrate by activating areas of the brain that help focus attention, plan, and organize thoughts. Barkley (1977) found that approximately 75 percent of children with ADHD who take Ritalin or other psychostimulants showed short-time improvement, but found evidence still lacking to support long-term positive results. A recent synthesis of research literature by Swanson et al. (1993) sorted out expectations for effects of stimulant medication on children diagnosed with ADHD (Table 3.3).

Some possible negative effects of stimulant medication are:

1. Some students don't improve and others worsen.
2. Although concentration may improve, the linkage with improved academic achievement has not been firmly established.
3. Placebos often (up to 40 percent of the time) work as well as Ritalin.
4. Physical side-effects such as stunted growth, elevated blood pressure, facial tics, insomnia, and weight loss have been reported.

TABLE 3.3   Effects of Psychostimulant Treatment for Children with ADHD

Temporary Management of Symptoms
Decrease in overactivity
Improved attention
Decrease in impulsivity
Associated Improvements
Improvement in deportment
Improvement in social interactions
Improvement in academic productivity
Other Observations
Response to medication cannot be predicted from neurological signs, biochemical markers, or physiological measures.
Side effects are infrequent.
Higher-order thinking processes and skills show scant improvement.
There is no long-term improvement in adjustment.

Underlying the pros and cons of drug treatment for hyperactivity is the more basic question—is there a safer, more effective method for helping students control their hyperactivity? In some instances the problem may be the classroom. When students labeled as hyperactive are placed in school programs that promote movement and concrete activities, problems of hyperactivity may diminish. These classrooms utilize learning centers and small-group activities. Students with hyperactivity are able to learn because the routines of the environment allow them to move around and manipulate materials.

Other more controversial approaches to decreasing hyperactivity in students with ADHD include elimination diets to remove allergens and decrease of sugar consumption. Evidence to support diet therapy is largely anecdotal. However, widespread testimony by parents and professionals about the effect of food on behavior is difficult to ignore. Reports like the following are commonplace:

> A nurse described the effect of nitrates, a common food preservative, "I can always tell when my daughter (7-year-old) has eaten a hot dog or baloney sandwich. She is off the walls, and it takes at least an hour for her to calm down." A college professor reported the effects of sugar on his six-year-old daughter, "Forget giving her dessert before bedtime. Just peanut butter on apple slices will keep her bouncing out of her bed and awake till 10:00 P.M." (Henley, 1986; 1990)

Table 3.4 lists commercial foods that contain minimal amounts of sugar and preservatives. Many are part of dietary treatments prescribed for some children with behavior disorders.

Emotional factors can also play a role in hyperactive behavior. Life in a dysfunctional home, where a youngster is continually exposed to chaotic living situations and warped family ties, will raise a student's stress level. The normal reaction to stress is flight or fight. For a student who is experiencing chronic stress, flight in the form of hyperactive behavior may be a futile attempt to adapt to an unpredictable life style.

Psychodynamic Causes

Some educators believe that problems related to personality development are the cause of social and emotional problems of children and youth (Rhodes & Tracy, 1972a,b). Generally, these professionals have received training from psychiatrists and psychologists who believe that the inner conflict principles first developed by Sigmund Freud can be used to explain and treat behavior or emotional problems. The psychodynamic view describes the evolving personality in terms of the relationship between three strong intrapsychic forces: id, ego, and superego. The id is the pleasure seeking, impulsive force that is dominant in childhood. The superego is the conscience—it represents moral and ethical beliefs. The ego mediates between the id and the superego. The ego shapes judgments about reality. The ego guides actions by taking into account the natural consequences of behavior. The id, ego, and superego act as a system of checks and balances on individual behavior.

Consider the following illustration of the id, ego, superego relationship. A teenager walks through a shopping mall and sees a Swiss Army knife sitting on a counter. His impulse (id) is to pick the knife up and put it in his pocket. His conscience (superego) tells him it is wrong to steal, but his id is winning the battle. "I'll go to church and it will be okay," he thinks. Meanwhile his reality-testing instincts (ego) tell him to look around. He sees several mirrors arrayed along the store walls. Now the struggle is on between id and ego. The teenager walks away without the knife because he decides the knife wasn't worth the risk.

Freud described neurosis (emotional disturbance) as a conflict between the ego and the id. The person is at war with himself. The goal of psychodynamic treatment is to bring the id, ego, and superego into harmony. As Freud explained, "A man should not try to eliminate his complexes but get into accord with them; they are legitimately what direct his conduct in the world" (Seldes, 1985, 151). Over the years Freud's theory has been expanded and modified by some of the greatest thinkers in the field of psychology. A list of contributors to psychodynamic theory reads like a *Who's Who* of twentieth-century thought—Carl Jung, Alfred Adler, Erik Erikson, Anna Freud, Erich Fromm, and Bruno Bettelheim are just a sample of the writers and therapists who were heavily influenced by psychodynamic theory.

TABLE 3.4   Partial List of Foods Commonly Found in Supermarkets that are Free of Artificial Coloring, Flavoring, and Preservatives

Cereals
Cheerios
Quaker Oats, Puffed Rice, and Puffed Wheat
Post Grape Nuts
General Millis Kix
Kellogg's Raisin Bran

Crackers
Hi-Ho
Krispy Saltines
Premium Saltines
Cheese-Its
Nabisco Graham Crackers (not Honey Graham)
Pepperidge Farm Cookies

Ice Cream
Ben & Jerry's
All Natural Hendries
All Natural Breyers
All Natural Dolly Madison
All Natural Stop & Shop

Canned Juices
100% juices such as: pineapple, grapefruit, cranberry, apple, tomato. Check label to be sure that no sugar, coloring, etc., added.

Salad Dressing
Walden's

Popsicles, etc.
Hoods Orange (all natural)
Welch's Grape
York Peppermint Patty Sitcks

Frozen Waffles
Golden Harvest (at Stop & Shop and Shop Rite)

Sausage
Jones or fresh ground in butcher shop

Soda
Seven-Up
Soda water
Country Club Ginger Ale

Jelly
Smuckers
Polaner

Candy Bars
Reese's Peanut Butter Cups
Mound's
Almond Joy
York Peppermint Patties
Planter's Peanut Bars
Bit-O-Honey

Frozen Juices
Juicy Juice
Minute Maid orange juice and lemonade
Stop & Shop Lemonade
Welch's Grape Juice
Many brands orange juice—look at label

Gum
Wrigley's

Cocoa
Swiss Miss Cocoa Mix
Hershey's Pure Cocoa

Peanut Butter
Smucker's
Teddies
Fresh Ground

Mayonnaise
Cain's

Spaghetti Sauce
Prince

Sharp Cheese
"Helluva" Good Cheese

Margarine
Shedd's Willow Run
Natural food store margarine (colored with carotene, which is natural)

"Hot Dogs (without nitrates)
Wild Wind

Maple Syrup—100% Pure
Vermont Maple Orchards

Fritz Redl and David Wineman were two of the first practitioners to successfully apply psychodynamic principles to the treatment of aggressive youth. In *Children Who Hate* (1951), Redl and Wineman described how the self-control (ego development) of adolescents collapsed under the impact of specific environmental or psychological triggers. Redl and Wineman cataloged twenty-two separate self-control challenges that all children need to cope with in order to continue their emotional development. Using colorful language such as "gadgetorial seduction" and "warfare with time," Redl and Wineman presented a roadmap for identifying self-control weaknesses in specific youngsters. Their descriptions of ego functions provide classroom teachers with a clinical model for anticipating when and where a student will lose self-control (Henley, 1987).

The psychodynamic point of view underscores the need to understand *why* students are disruptive. It emphasizes the connections between how a student feels and how a student acts. The classic psychodynamic treatments are play therapy for children and individual psychotherapy for youth. For educators, who saw the value of psychodynamic principles, it was necessary to develop treatment procedures that would be useful in the classroom, where teachers must manage groups of children. Psychoeducational treatments were born out of the need to merge behavior management with psycho-dynamic theory.

Psychoeducational Causes

Proponents of the psychoeducational perspective believe that problem behaviors result from underlying psychological disturbances, and that adaptive behaviors must be learned for successful accommodation in schools. Knoblock presented a succinct description: "A psychoeducational framework assumes that behavior is caused, that there are reasons why children act as they do. Early psychoeducators like Berkowitz and Rothman believed that children's feelings were the source of observed behaviors. Now it is recognized that behaviors should be analyzed in the context of specific environments as well. . . ." (Knoblock, 1983, 107). There is a balance between concern for causes of behavior and acquisition of adaptive skills in the psychoeducational treatment model.

This integrated philosophy is illustrated in the principles of Project Re-Ed (Hobbs, 1966):

1. Students should be kept busy in school; successful completion of purposeful activities is central to reeducation.
2. Students should spend as much time as possible in positive, therapeutic environments; neighborhood schools with supportive personnel are preferred in efforts to reeducate students with behavior problems.

3. Supportive teacher–student interactions are a key to establishing academic success; teachers learn this by working with students in positive relationships.

Psychoeducators believe the student–teacher relationship is the fundamental building block for change. Out of this relationship comes mutual trust and a willingness on the part of both teacher and student to accept the needs of each other. Behavioral and emotional difficulties are viewed developmentally. Using cognitive and emotional developmental milestones as a guide, the psychoeducator attempts to identify developmental strengths and weaknesses. Classroom accommodations are made that capitalize on student abilities in order to move a youngster along the normal developmental continuum. Self-concept development, the teaching of social skills, and normalization of a youngster's school experience are all components in the psychoeducational treatment model.

Many programs for curriculum development, including *Developmental Therapy* (Wood, 1986), *Teaching Self-Control: A Curriculum for Responsible Behavior* (Henley, 1997), and *Skillstreaming* (McGinnis & Goldstein, 1990), have translated psychoeducational principles into functional systems for assessment, goal setting, teaching, and evaluation. Each of these models assumes that all students have the internal resources to change and that appropriate environmental supports can nourish and maintain student emotional growth. These treatments all assume that change begins within the individual and that the ultimate goal is to teach students to accept responsibility for their own behavior. A counterpoint to the psychoeducational treatment approach is the behaviorist model, which focuses almost exclusively on the manipulation of environmental conditions to shape student behavior.

Behavioral Causes

During the 1960s, educators and psychologists recognized the importance of behavioral principles of learning. The key points of behavioral theory and practice can be summarized as follows:

1. Behaviorists view inappropriate and appropriate behavior as learned. Behavior is a response to a person's interaction with the environment.
2. Learning occurs when environmental conditions reinforce a specific behavior. Learning takes several forms, including imitation, modeling, and operant conditioning (i.e., consequences that shape behavior).
3. Inappropriate behavior is learned through environmental conditioning and new, appropriate behaviors can be learned with proper arrangement of the conditions of learning.
4. Effective implementation of behavior treatments in classrooms requires: observable descriptions of behavior to be changed, targeting of new be-

haviors, systematic application of reinforcers, and collection of pre- and postdata to determine treatment effectiveness.

Behaviorists do not attempt to understand behavior, nor do they ascribe specific causes to behavior. Behaviorists prefer to deal with the tangible actions of students rather than theoretical explanations for disturbing behavior. The emphasis on behavior rather than causes of behavior has been the catalyst to replace the term "emotionally disturbed" with the classification "behavior disorders." Whereas the former term implies we know the reason for a behavior (i.e., disturbed emotional development), the latter designation makes no claim about causality but simply points out that there is a problem in the individual's behavior. Behavior modification is the application of behavioral theory. Operant conditioning is a form of behavior modification used to change student behavior in the classroom. Operant conditioning is based on the premise that actions are shaped or changed by their consequences. The operant is the behavior (e.g., listening, hitting, laughing), while the consequences (e.g., praising, punishing, or ignoring) either reinforce or eliminate the operant.

Examples of operant conditioning are all around us. One person can modify behavior of another; for instance, a parent who encourages a child to eat vegetables by offering ice cream for dessert. Individuals can modify their own behavior. Cooper, Heron, and Heward provide the following example of behavior, which is modified by the consequences it produces.

> When an infant moves her arms through space, setting in motion the mobile dangling in her crib, she is literally operating on her environment. The mobile's movement and sound are stimuli produced by the child's behavior, consequences of her batting at the toy with her hands. If continued observation of the baby reveals an increased rate of arm swinging when the mobile hangs in her crib, her behavior would be described as an operant. (Cooper, Heron, & Heward, 1987, 21)

Behavior can be modified spontaneously, for example, when a student invents a shortcut to solve math problems. Or behavior can be shaped systematically, for instance, when a teacher awards tokens for finishing classroom tasks. Behavior can also be modified ineffectively, as when a teacher's verbal reprimands reinforce acting out behavior. The principles of operant conditioning are always the same—the key is knowledgeable application. Many teachers, both special and regular education, use operant conditioning practices in their classrooms on a regular basis.

Schroeder and Riddle (1991) list the basic components of operant conditioning. The following is an adaptation of their definitions.

1. *Positive reinforcement*: presenting a consequence that increases the probability of a behavior in the future. Example—a student who shares toys in a play area of a classroom because of favorable reaction from other children.

2. *Punishment*: presenting or withdrawing a consequence that decreases the probability of a behavior in the future. Examples—a reprimand (i.e., presenting a stimulus) or keeping a youngster in class during recess (i.e., withdrawing a stimulus) in order to stop disruptive classroom behavior.

3. *Negative reinforcement*: increasing the probability of a behavior by avoiding an unpleasant consequence. Example—students who complete homework for five consecutive days are excused from taking a weekly math quiz. Negative reinforcement is often confused with punishment. Example—a student is sent into the hall for disrupting the class. The teacher is negatively reinforcing the misbehavior when the child continues to act up in the future in order to avoid an unpleasant classroom activity (Cooper, Heron, & Heward, 1987, 25).

4. *Extinction*: decreasing the probability of a response by withholding a previously reinforcing stimulus. Example—classmates don't laugh when a student makes a sarcastic comment in class.

5. *Differential reinforcement of other behavior (DRO)*: decreasing the probability of a response by reinforcing the omission of it; sometimes referred to as omission training. Example—a student who is disruptive is given a token for every five minutes the behavior is not emitted.

6. *Satiation*: decreasing the probability of a response by reinforcing it excessively. The reinforcer no longer maintains the behavior. Example—a teacher uses a novel reading series to encourage student effort. In a short while, student effort diminishes as the novelty wears off.

Often the above treatments are used in combination to shape behavior in the classroom; for example, a teacher might use both positive and negative reinforcement to encourage a youngster to comply with classroom rules. Positive reinforcement could take the form of verbal praise immediately following the desired behavior, and negative reinforcement would consist of a decrease in corrective comments from the teacher. A comprehensive elaboration of each component of operant conditioning is outside the scope of this book. For more details, we suggest *Applied Behavior Analysis* by Cooper, Heron, and Heward (1987), Merrill Publishing Company, and *Behavior Management: A Practical Approach for Educators* by Walker and Shea (1991), Merrill Publishing Company.

Disturbed or Disturbing?

When a student is disruptive in a classroom, does that mean that the student has a disability or are there alternative explanations? Consider the following behaviors: talking out of turn, swearing at the teacher, throwing objects, running out of the room, or refusing to do an assignment. Those behaviors are commonplace in chaotic classrooms, but they occur infrequently in classrooms where teachers demonstrate effective group management skills.

Fredric Jones (1987) studied teacher–student interactions in hundreds of elementary and secondary classrooms. Many of his observations were done in inner-city schools and alternative programs for students with behavior disorders.

One might expect Jones to report many examples of behavior disorders such as hostility, impulsiveness, or aggression. He didn't. Jones and his colleagues characterized the majority of student activity as "massive time wasting." Students walked around the room, "goofed off," and talked whenever they felt like it. In poorly managed classrooms, these behaviors occurred every twenty seconds. In well-managed classrooms, the same behaviors were noted once every two minutes. Jones found that teachers in poorly managed classrooms lost 50 percent of their instructional time dealing with disturbing behaviors (Charles, 1989). Jones concluded that many disruptive behaviors were symptomatic of mismanaged classrooms.

The classic study by Wickman (1929) is the first major investigation that attempted to identify specific behaviors that educators perceived bothersome or disturbing in their work with children. Behaviors identified were characterized as those that offended moral standards (e.g., stealing, cheating, untruthfulness) and challenged teachers' authority (e.g., defiance, impertinence). Ramsey (1981) analyzed thirty-three replications that followed this seminal study and concluded that classroom orderliness and recognition of authority are of primary importance to teachers so that they can do their job, which is to teach students.

The notion that teachers can cause behavior problems is underscored by Jacob Kounin's research. Kounin (1977) found classroom disruptions were correlated to teacher expertise. Kounin reported that the following teacher behaviors contributed to discipline problems: making verbal comments about minor disturbances such as dropping a pencil, getting sidetracked by a single student's behavior, forcing students to do boring and repetitious activities, and becoming angry or punitive when students misbehaved. Conversely, Kounin observed that teachers positively influenced appropriate classroom behavior by smooth transitions between lessons, keeping track of all student behavior in the classroom at the same time, and providing novelty in lessons. Teachers who were liked by their students had the least behavior problems.

The interactional perspective of disturbing/disturbed behaviors underscores the need to evaluate both the individual and the setting. Behavior is a function of the individual interacting within the environment. While disturbing behavior may begin with the individual student, the way in which the teacher responds is crucial in preventing further problems. Organization of classroom space, routines, and lessons influence student behavior. Imagine a seven-year-old youngster with ADHD attempting to conform to a classroom where students are expected to sit quietly at their desks and complete assignments consisting of workbooks and ditto exercises. In this classroom, the student is handicapped by her learning problem. She is unable to sit still and concentrate. Why force a student to do something that is outside her limits? Suppose we move the same student into a classroom where she can walk around and work at learning centers that feature manipulative materials. In the latter classroom, our seven-year-old is no longer restrained and she is engaged in concrete tasks that match her developmental abilities.

When a student's behavior is properly evaluated, the context within which the behavior occurs is examined. Special education has historically provided individual services for students rather than classroom support to the regular classroom teacher. The entire special education service delivery system is geared to find something wrong with the student. Yet for years special educators have recognized that disturbance is often in the eye of the beholder. In 1967, William Rhodes remarked that behavior is often more "disturbing" than "disturbed." He contended that disturbance is a function of where and with whom a student interacts (Rhodes, 1967; 1970).

School records and case histories brim with examples of the influence of adult expectations and perceptions on the lives of students classified as behaviorally disordered or emotionally disturbed. For example, Hewett and Taylor (1980) provide the following description of a "disturbed" student.

> We worked with an adolescent boy with an IQ of approximately 80. He has the misfortune to be born into a family of extremely high achievers who expected him to go to Princeton University. He was attempting an academic program in high school and failing miserably. From his father's point of view, he was just lazy. His mother babied him. His older brother teased him. His teachers criticized and demeaned him. He stayed up long hours to study but couldn't keep up. His health began to suffer. Finally, he became deeply depressed and attempted suicide. Fortunately, following this episode, a careful examination of this boy's ecosystem (home, family interactions, community, school, teacher behavior) resulted in greater understanding on the part of all parties concerned. (Apter, 1982, 72)

In analyzing this story, it is difficult to identify the source of the problem. Did the family's expectations and behaviors produce the student's problems? Did his behavior and expectations influence others' perceptions of him? Would he be a problem in another family? Would he be a problem with other teachers? The complex nature of human interactions clearly leaves the source of the disturbance unresolved in this case study. And, this is true for most students with behavior disorders as well.

The Ecological Model

When trying to understand students with behavior and emotional problems, one can get caught up in the chicken or the egg paradox. Does the behavior problem lead to negative responses from others, which ultimately result in an emotional disturbance? Or are the behavior problems caused by an emotional disturbance? Or is the student simply a disruptive individual without an emotional problem? These questions may seem to be rhetorical verbal games best suited for clever banter; but, in fact, how teachers and administrators view students and determine the answers to these questions can mean the difference between a student getting special education services, no help at all, or becoming a school dropout.

What is conspicuously absent from the general–special-education connection is a focus on prevention, which we discuss in more detail in the chapters on classroom management. More help for the classroom teacher would improve classroom management practices. Community centers would provide mental health and networking services for troubled families. More attention to the needs of children in general would produce a concentrated effort to mobilize national attention and resources to battle such childhood perils as loneliness, fear, abuse, addiction, and school failure.

The view that treatment of behavior disorders must take into account all features of a student's life (including school, family, and community) is called the ecological model. Educators who embrace the ecological perspective believe that in order to understand troubled children, we need to consider all facets of their lives.

> From this outlook emotional disturbance is not seen simply as the necessary result of intrapsychic conflict (psychodynamic model) nor as the inevitable product of inappropriate social learning (behavior modification model). Instead, according to the ecological model, disturbance resides in the interaction between a child and critical aspects of that child's surrounding environment, that is, the child's system. More specifically, ecological theorists believe that what we know as emotional disturbance or behavior disorders actually result from discrepancies between a given child's skills and abilities and the demands or expectations of that child's environment. (Apter, 1982, 2)

The ecological model emphasizes the need for comprehensive preventive systems within and outside school to make adjustments in the parts of a student's life that can cause behavior disorders. As Apter (1982) acknowledged, change strategies should be aimed at increasing competence instead of reducing deficits. Well-baby clinics, parent effectiveness training, community development programs, sex and drug education programs, and teenage counseling programs are examples of change strategies that focus on prevention while increasing the competence of young people, (Heller & Monahan, 1977).

Clearly the ecological model cannot work without community and political support. The long-range view of looking at troubled social systems requires a broad based constituency. It requires a commitment to social change and social policies that are often not shared by politicians or the populace in general. The road to social change is riddled with pitfalls.

A case study in the pitfalls of prevention is illustrated by the work of Spencer Holland, a psychologist at Morgan State University in Baltimore. Holland recommended educational intervention specifically aimed at African American male students. African American males have the highest dropout rates, get the lowest grades, and exhibit more discipline problems than any subgroup of students. Holland argued that lack of adequate male role models was a primary cause of troubles encountered by African American males.

> The most common reasons cited for the academic and social failings of young black males are that such boys come from poor, single-parent, female-headed households; that they have no positive male role models; and that they view the (school) as feminine and not relevant to their daily lives. (Chmelynski, 1990, 16)

One extension of Holland's reasoning is that referral for special services for behavior problems may be related to females teaching males. Teacher ratings of behavior are the most influential component in school evaluations of behavior disorders. Teachers rate boys as "acting out" more often than girls, and boys are more likely to be evaluated as having a behavior disorder (Algozzine, 1977). When one matches the overrepresentation of boys in the category of behavior disorders with the overrepresentation of females among teachers, a likely hypothesis is that referrals for social and emotional problems are gender related.

Some schools, influenced by Dr. Holland's work, took a hard look at gender issues in classrooms. Several school systems responded to this problem by providing African American male students with positive male role models. African American businessmen, professionals, and tradesmen volunteered as role models for students in Baltimore, Detroit, Miami, Milwaukee, San Diego, and Washington, D.C. schools. The role models tutored students, took them on field trips, and provided them with the male mentoring that was conspicuously absent in the youngsters' lives.

These volunteer programs proved so popular that school officials in Dade County, Florida, and Detroit considered starting African American male academics. The possibility of schools just for African American male students quickly produced widespread critical reactions. Specters of sexism and segregation raised by the National Organization of Women (NOW) and the National Association for the Advancement of Colored People (NAACP) caused many advocates to reconsider education programs that single out only African American boys. Proponents of the programs contended that the situation for young African American males was so dire that radical measures were in order. Holland argued that whereas African American girls have role models in their mothers and teachers, boys searching for role models in their inner-city neighborhoods find that the only successful males are drug dealers or criminals (Chmelynski, 1990). As this case study of prevention illustrates, it is easier to refer a disruptive student for special education services than it is to try to change school practices or redirect social policies.

The advantage of the ecological model is that it focuses attention on the interactional aspects of behavior disorders. David Witcher is a teacher at Batchler Middle School in Bloomington, Indiana; his comments in the August 1988 issue of the Council for Children with Behavior Disorders newsletter are revealing:

> For the past eight years, I have been a public school teacher in special education programs for so-called emotionally handicapped children and adolescents. Even after working on over a hundred cases, I still cannot tell why one student qualifies for my special services while another does not.

As long as ineffective teaching practices continue and urgent social issues are ignored, many students whose behavior problems could be prevented will be classified with behavior disorders and placed in special education programs.

One strategy for short-circuiting inappropriate referrals to special education is to differentiate those students who have behavior disorders from students whose behavior is disturbing to the classroom teacher. Henley (1986) recommends the following criteria to distinguish between students with behavior disorders and those who are disturbing. A student with behavior disorders will exhibit the following characteristics:

1. The disturbing behavior occurs in a variety of settings, not just the classroom.
2. The student is unable to develop and maintain peer relationships.
3. The student is unhappy.
4. The disturbing behavior is fixed, rigid, and predictable.
5. The disturbing behavior is self-defeating; the student shows no sign of emotional growth.
6. The disturbing behavior draws attention and emotional responses from others. (Henley, 1986, 2)

The above criteria do not focus on causes: consequently, they are as useful for identifying students whose problems are biophysically based and students whose problems result from unfortunate social–familial circumstances. They also serve as a guide to determine if the disruptive behavior is a function of the student or the classroom. If the same behavior is noted in other settings (i.e., home, community), then clearly the trouble resides within the student. However, if a student's behavior is disturbing only in the classroom, intervention strategies should be directed within the classroom setting rather than at the student. A more complete description of students with behavior disorders is presented in the following section.

Characteristics

Students with behavior disorders exhibit a wide variety of characteristics. A description of functional characteristics is somewhat hampered by the differences in professional perceptions of these youngsters. We all interpret what we see, hear, and understand in terms of the assumptions we hold about the world around us. Keep this in mind when you hear professors and teachers discussing students with behavior disorders. A professional who is solidly in the behaviorist camp does not recognize feelings as important aspects of a student's behavior. If a behaviorist were to describe the functional priorities of a youngster, feelings would be at the bottom of the list. At the same time, a professional who is devoted to the psychodynamic treatment approach would describe a youngster's functional abilities in terms of interpsychic conflicts between id, ego, and superego. The observable actions that are the foundation of the behaviorist treatment model are minimal in the psychodynamic view. A key point to remember is the power of the observer (i.e., teacher, professor, psychologist) of student's behavior to determine if a behavior is disturbing or disturbed.

Seriously emotionally disturbed students are identified by their severe deficits in perception, communication, and behavior. Such behaviors as delusions and lack of affect are marked examples of the extreme behavioral disturbances in seriously emotionally disturbed students. Students with mild behavior disorders are quite different. Before they entered school, the majority of these youngsters seemed capable of adapting to the social demands of formal education. (We hope at this point this theme sounds familiar.) Basically students with behavior disorders exhibit behaviors that interfere with productive interpersonal relationships; they are unable to adapt to classroom routines; and they cause classroom disruptions. These students have behavioral excesses or differences that make regular school progress difficult to achieve without special education.

Consider this example: Mrs. Stone, a junior high school teacher, has just passed out a sheet of math problems to be completed by each of her students. Frank's response is clearly excessive. He looks at the paper, throws down his pencil, and angrily states, "What do you think I am, a genius or something?" After this preamble, he proceeds into a harangue supported by four-letter words and no-holds-barred attacks on Mrs. Stone's professional and personal integrity. He ends up with an ultimatum suggesting that "nothing or nobody" can make him do the worksheet.

In this episode, we see grist for everybody's theoretical mill. Frank's behavior is clearly inappropriate, and a behaviorist would work to eliminate outbursts and reinforce appropriate school behaviors. The psychodynamic oriented professional examines the relationship between Frank and Mrs. Stone. Counseling might be directed at helping Frank cope with females in authority positions. From a psychoeducational point of view, Mrs. Stone is setting Frank up for failure by using typed dittos when Frank is developmentally unable to handle such abstract work. Classroom modifications that include work-related functional skills and supported employment would be directed at changing Frank's attitude toward school. The biophysical model suggests that we examine Frank's medical history. Perhaps he is allergic to ditto fluid, and the fumes set off impulsive and aggressive behavior.

In the following sections, we describe functional characteristics on which most all professionals agree regarding mild behavior disorders. The brevity of this section is testimony to the need of professionals to consolidate theoretical models in order to present a less fractured and more comprehensive description of students with behavior disorders.

Cognitive

Students classified with behavior disorders usually score in the low average range (100–75) on standardized tests of intelligence. Some professionals argue that emotional problems can cause individual students to perform poorly on intelligence tests. Anyone who is accustomed to taking standardized tests readily reports feelings of anxiety prior to and during testing. For children with minimal ability to cope with stress, an IQ test can be overwhelming. These students will give up, guess wildly at answers, or refuse to continue.

Students with behavior disorders proceed through the same stages of cognitive development as other children: sensory-motor, preoperational, concrete, and formal (see Chapter 2 for a more thorough discussion of Piagetian stages of development). Selman (1980) applied Piaget's developmental scheme to social perception, and he suggested that children go through four stages before they are fully capable of socialized thought. Paul and Epanchin summarized Selman's model:

> First, the child is in a fully egocentric state and is unable to differentiate the points of view of others. Second, the child can consider other people's ideas in a rudimentary way and realizes their thoughts can be different from his own. However, he has difficulty understanding exactly what the differences are. Third, although the child cannot consider others and his own perspectives simultaneously, he can sequentially consider first his own perspective and then another's perspective. Finally, the child is able to think about both perspectives at the same time in an integrated manner, as well as having a "third person" perspective in which he can figuratively step back from the interaction and examine both sides' point of view. (Paul & Epanchin, 1991, 195)

As children develop cognitively they are more capable of understanding a situation from another's point of view. They recognize how their behavior affects others. They are able to identify their own feelings, and they empathize with the feelings of others.

Students with behavior disorders are delayed in their social–cognitive development. They literally forget their own contributions to conflict. Their memories seem to evaporate when they are asked to recall how their actions contributed to a classroom disruption (Redl & Wineman, 1951). They seem to be able to recall only the behavior of others while they remain steadfast in their own innocence. These students cannot apply past experiences to present situations. As often as a student will experience peer retribution for teasing or belittling others the student does not change tactics that goad others into retaliation. They don't understand how their behavior affects others in a negative way. Students with social–cognitive delay are unable to learn from the experience of others, and they possess minimal strategies for solving social problems. If another youngster is disapproving, the student with emotional and social problems will maintain a fixed and predictable response such as a temper tantrum, sulking, scapegoating, or fighting.

These students need practice in developing social problem-solving skills and assessing social reality. They are unable to use their own experiences to advance their social skills in a useful manner; consequently, they remain egocentric and socially isolated from their peers with no sense of what they are doing wrong.

Academic

One characteristic of students with mild disabilities is low achievement. Most students with social and emotional difficulties don't like school. Some professionals believe these students fail because they have not developed academic survival skills (e.g., finishing tasks, following directions, adjusting to classroom routines). Other professionals maintain that emotional problems (e.g., anxiety, low self-esteem, depression) prevent students from doing well. Although researchers tend to focus on independent variables, for example, task engagement, in reality a given student could be limited by all the above characteristics.

For the classroom teacher, the main difficulty is motivation. These students have limited faith in their ability to learn. Their whole school experience has been testimony to their inadequacies. Because their behavior has been a consistent liability, they have internalized feelings of worthlessness. This makes learning a formidable task. Suppose you were on a ski slope taking your first lesson, but you were absolutely convinced you were going to fall. How far do you think you'd make it down the slope without falling? When it comes to learning, students with social and emotional difficulties are always falling down.

More than anything else these students need success in school. Learning requires risk-taking and a willingness to change; students with social–emotional problems have spent much of their lives resisting change. Sameness, even if unpleasant, provides security. For a student with behavior disorder, learning to read can be a fearful experience. Reading may mean loss of control because it is change, and if one thing about a person's life changes, what is next? Fritz Redl and David Wineman (1951) called this resistance to change "newness panic." The student is overwhelmed by apprehension when confronted with new or different experiences. This makes teaching students with behavior disorders difficult.

A secure classroom environment is the first priority. Unless psychological and physical safety is maintained, the student will be overcome by real or imagined threats. The ensuing anxiety will disrupt learning. Next, the students need to derive some personal meaning from school activities. As we discussed in the previous section, students with behavior disorders are egocentric. Schoolwork that relates to their day-to-day lives enables students to personalize their learning. Teachers can make learning relevant by emphasizing students' interests, using humor, and developing functional lessons to teach skills. Activities such as rope climbing and challenge courses help to develop risk-taking behavior and enhance self-confidence. Finally, students need reminders of their progress. Positive feedback about emerging skills helps to consolidate gains and encourages perseverance.

Think of student development as a series of upward spiraling circles. Be prepared for regression following progress. This natural cycle of growth and back-sliding is normal (Long, 1986). When teaching students who have social and emotional problems, it is easy to overlook how far they have come. Others who have a long-range view, such as administrators or counselors, can help keep intermittent reversals in perspective.

Many special education teachers are cloistered with eight to ten students in a single classroom. These teachers are expected to bring their students up to grade level, while also teaching them how to behave properly. This is a difficult task. Students are put in special education programs because they need to learn new behaviors. In a special class, there are no models for appropriate behavior. Regrettably, the reality of the situation is that the teacher is "keeping the lid on" a group of youngsters that other teachers won't tolerate in their classrooms. The burnout rate among teachers of students with behavior disorders is extremely high.

Despite the negative programmatic aspects of self-contained classrooms, these socially isolating environments serve the administrative purpose of making the problem go away. Unless the emphasis in regular classrooms changes to preventive discipline and the teaching of prosocial behaviors becomes a legitimate part of the curriculum, the label "behavior disorders" or "emotionally disturbed" will continue to be a one-way ticket into segregated, self-contained special education programs.

Communication

For students with behavior disorders, words are both sword and shield. Their verbal outbursts of hostility outrage others, while their facile excuses keep them, in their own minds, free of responsibility. The inability to communicate feelings in a socially appropriate manner results in resentment and misunderstandings between these students and others. Resentment, fear, apprehension, and other tumultuous feelings are acted out rather than discussed. At the same time, students with behavior disorders can use language in finely executed performances of manipulation. Students who are hostile know just what to say to get others to respond in kind. For example, students who whine and complain cause others to withdraw from them.

Like a crafty salesperson, troubled youngsters solicit feedback that reaffirm their position. The more angry or caustic the teacher or student response, the more secure a youngster is in the knowledge that others are indeed out to get him. The student with emotional disturbance needs negative feedback to keep his world steady and predictable. Why change one's behavior if it is clear that others are unable to change theirs? As long as teachers threaten, criticize, and shout, a student with a behavior disorder remains in control. The student pulls the strings, and the adults and peers in the classroom put on the show.

Ginott believed teachers can short-circuit this closed system of emotional turmoil through "congruent communication." Charles (1989) defined congruent communication as "a harmonious and authentic way of talking in which teacher messages to students match the students' feelings about situations and themselves" (Ginott, 1971, 57). Students need teachers to model communication methods that highlight verbal expression of feelings in appropriate ways. For example, Ginott advocated "sane messages." When addressing student disruption, sane messages describe the situation rather than criticizing the student. Sane messages give students the opportunity to assess a situation and to understand why a behavior is disruptive. Sane messages describe the area of concern rather than blaming, preaching, or criticizing students. As an illustration, two students are arguing about who is first in line; an "insane message" is, "You two are always causing trouble; both of you sit down and wait for everybody else to leave." In this situation, the students may feel attacked, and they have no opportunity to learn from the situation. A contrasting sane message would be, "When you act like that it takes longer for all of us to get to lunch; you have to take turns." The explanation provides insight into *why* the teacher is disturbed and describes a more acceptable behavior.

According to Ginott, through modeling, the teacher helps students to express their feelings and communicate their needs. "I-messages," for example, help students understand that teachers do indeed have feelings. Statements like "I am disappointed" or "I am angry" are better than "You are a nuisance" or "You ruin everything for everybody else." Teachers accept and acknowledge feelings when they avoid negative communication modes such as sarcasm and verbal insults. One of Ginott's more novel observations is the perils of praise. Praise creates a dependence on others for approval. Judgmental praise such as "You are a good girl" or "I really like the way you are acting" reinforces the need to look to others for self-worth. What of the student on the other side of the room who was equally "good?" Ginott underscores the need for teachers to understand that for every student who stands in the spotlight, twenty or so are going to feel left out. Charles (1989) has summarized Ginott's main points:

1. Good classroom discipline begins with the teacher's self-discipline.
2. Use sane messages when correcting misbehavior.
3. Teachers at their worst attack and label student characters.
4. Teachers should model the type of communication they expect from students.
5. Anger and other feelings should be expressed in sane ways.
6. Avoid sarcasm and be judicious with praise.
7. The best teachers build self-esteem and help students to trust and express their own feelings.

Social–Adaptive

A student is referred for special education services for a behavior disorder when a teacher notes frequent and chronic behavior that is markedly different from peers. Difference in behavior is based on teacher expectations and judgments. Authoritarian teachers prize student behavior that is compliant and conforming. Teachers who depend on workbooks, dittoes and other repetitious instructional materials view students who don't "stay on task" as disturbing. Teachers who encourage students to ask questions, express their opinions, and participate in group discussions would more likely view a passive and quiet student as disturbing.

Behavior should not be separated from the context in which it is viewed or judged. Apter emphasized the interactional aspect of behavior disorders when he commented that ". . . what we know as emotional disturbance or behavior disorders actually result from discrepancies between a given child's skills and abilities and the demands or expectations of that child's environment" (Apter 1982, 2). A student who is loud and aggressive may be disturbing in school, but on city streets he could be a leader. Students who are unable or unwilling to adapt to the expectations of classroom life are most likely to be referred to special education.

Achenbach and Edelbrook (1981) distinguished between internalizing and externalizing behavior problems. Internalized problems are those manifested when a student turns inward because of emotional or social conflict. Anxiety, fears, social withdrawal, and immaturity are examples of internalized problems. Aggression, noncompliance, and open hostility are examples of externalized behavior problems; they are more obvious (and get more attention) because they are disruptive.

Externalized behaviors, because they are the most difficult to deal with, are more frequently used as indicators of behavior disorders. Although all children may fight, bully, or argue, students classified with behavior disorders engage in these behaviors repeatedly. Teachers refer students because they find disciplinary measures are ineffective in controlling or minimizing externalized behaviors. Though less frequently noted, such internalized behaviors as poor self-esteem, moodiness, depression, and social withdrawal are also difficult to change. Internalized students are often overlooked in teacher's judgments about who has an emotional problem.

As children pass through developmental stages of social maturity, they acquire self-control skills that help them to restrain their impulses, assess social reality, manage group pressure, deal with stress, and solve problems in relationships. Impulse maintenance includes the ability to deal with frustration, to self-regulate behavior, and to understand that temptations are accompanied by consequences. When assessing social reality, youngsters need to be realistic about rules and routines, evaluate the effect of their behavior on others, take responsibility for their possessions, and remain reasonable about such gratifications as praise and attention. Group pressure skills include staying calm when others have lost control, managing competitive challenges, and participating in and furthering group activities. Stress management requires coping with anxiety, adjusting to new situations, separating past trauma from present events, and accepting responsibility for actions. Finally, social problem-solving skills include learning from experience, noting one's effect on others, and drawing inferences from others' experiences (Henley, 1987; Long, 1989; Redl and Wineman, 1951). (These skills are discussed in more detail in Chapter 8.)

TABLE 3.5   Suggestions for Teaching Students with Behavior Disorders

1. Recognize the differences between disturbing and disturbed behavior.
2. Look for classroom routines, lessons, and discipline practices that may contribute to behavior problems.
3. Consider diet, allergies, and other physical causes for disturbing behavior.
4. With hyperactive students, change classroom routines before going along with drug treatment.
5. Trust is the basis for social–emotional growth. Work to develop a trusting relationship with a disturbing student.
6. Use behavior modification in a systematic fashion. Don't use behavior modification as a way of rationalizing punishment.
7. Make a home and neighborhood visit of each student in your class and determine adaptive skills required for environments outside of school.
8. Present lessons in a format that connects to the personal experience of your students.
9. Assess the impact of such real-life issues as teenage pregnancy, drugs, and depression on your students.
10. Model the language and behavior that you want to foster in your students.

The less capable a student is in each self-control skill, the more likely the youngster will encounter social problems in school. Teachers who understand that the misbehavior they encounter in the classroom is based on frustration or stress are likely to demonstrate what Fritz Redl and David Wineman (1951) referred to as "symptom tolerance." Simply stated: when teachers don't personalize disruptive behavior but try to understand not only the behavior but the child as well, dealing with the behavior is easier. When teachers believe a child is intentionally being disruptive or mean or selfish, it is difficult to squelch the adult impulse to "put the kid in her place"; "show him who is boss"; or "not let the kid run all over me." No child chooses to be unhappy in school. Every child wants to be liked and admired. By working to understand the students you deal with, you will find the best way to deal with their behavior. Some general suggestions for teaching students with behavior disorders are presented in Table 3.5.

Strategies for Teaching Students with Behavior Disorders

Students with behavior disorders receive special education because they have emotional and social problems that require attention from teachers, parents, and other professionals if they are to be successful in school (Ysseldyke & Algozzine,

1995). **Emotional problems** stem from unproductive personal ways of managing stress or activities (e.g., inappropriate types of behaviors or feelings, tendency to develop physical symptoms or fears). For example, one child's response to having to wait for the school bus might be to become impatient while another's might be to become very anxious. Low self-esteem and limited self-control are common emotional problems of students with behavior disorders. **Social problems** are unproductive ways individuals respond in situations involving interactions with other people (e.g., inability to maintain satisfactory interpersonal relationships). Disruptiveness is a common social problem of students receiving special education for behavior disorders.

Effective teachers of students with behavior disorders use a variety of approaches for establishing discipline in their classrooms, managing behavior, and improving emotional and social problems. Four widely accepted discipline models, and specific activities for improving selected emotional and social problems are discussed in the following sections (see Chapters 9 and 10 for additional information on classroom management). Many of these same models, principles, and activities are also effective for improving the behavior of students with mental retardation and learning disabilities.

Discipline

Discipline is a key part of any educational program for students with behavior problems. For many people, discipline means punishment, but this is a common misconception. There are three types of discipline: (a) avoiding inappropriate behavior—preventive discipline, (b) assisting students when they first show signs of misbehavior—supportive discipline, and (c) controlling or redirecting misbehavior when it occurs—corrective discipline. For effective teachers, discipline means teaching rules or a code of conduct for appropriate behavior, practicing them, and providing recognition and reward for doing them (Meese, 1994). The underlying beliefs, primary focus, and goals for students of some widely accepted discipline programs are presented in Table 3.6. In each case, the overall goal is to teach students responsibility and respect, to develop a positive classroom environment, and to help students meet basic needs and avoid behavior problems.

Improving Emotional Problems

Students with behavior disorders respond to the same instructional methods as other students. They may exhibit more disruptive behaviors than some of their peers and, often, they need to be taught simple rules for self-control and conduct that their peers learn without instruction. Effective teachers of these students design instructional programs to include direct instruction in skills related to improving their emotional problems. Some ways to improve two common emotional problems, limited self-control and low self-esteem, are presented in Table 3.7.

TABLE 3.6 Summary of Discipline Models

Model	Characteristics
Cooperative Discipline *Albert, 1994*	Students must be valued and opportunities for behavioral responsibility must be shared.
	Keys include identifying goals of misbehavior, intervening early, building self-esteem, and involving students, colleagues, andparents.
	Goals include successful completion of school tasks and functioning as a contributing member of the school group.
Discipline with Dignity *Mendler & Curwin, 1994*	Dignity of students must be valued and improved regardless of their behavior.
	Values underlying desired behaviors are internalized through problem-solving, prevention planning, and student involvement in discipline process.
	Goals for students include believing they are capable and successful, knowing they are cared about, recognizing they can influence other people, and practicing helping others
Kids Are Worth It! *Coloroso, 1994*	Self-discipline will develop if students are treated with respect, given responsibilities and choices, and permitted to experience reasonable consequences.
	Focuses on showing students what they have done wrong, giving them ownership of the problem, and identifying ways to solve it.
	Goals include providing students with six "critical life messages" each day: I believe in you, I trust you, I know you can handle it, you are listened to, you are cared for, and you are very important to me.
Positive Classroom Discipline *Jones, 1994*	Classroom management must be positive and gentle, must set limits, and must build cooperation.
	Reducing disruptions, teaching students to internalize control, structuring classrooms,

Table 3.6   continued

Unified Discipline *White, 1997*	setting limits, using incentive systems, and managing behaviors outside the classroom are keys to effective discipline. Goals include self-regulation, cooperation with peers, and making positive contributions to the group with learning as the reward.

| | Classroom management occurs on a school-wide basis with unified attitudes, expectations, consequences, and roles serving as key implemation.

Goals include singular sets of rules across grade levels, standardized consequences for rule violations, and clearly defined responsibilities for teachers, administrators, and staff within a school. |

Improving Social Problems

Students with behavior disorders are among those many teachers least prefer to teach. This is largely because of what they do in the classroom. Disruptiveness is among their primary negative characteristics. Some specific activities for improving social problems related to disruptiveness are summarized in Table 3.8.

Integration of Treatment Approaches

When you look in special education classrooms today, you will probably see evidence of many approaches used in combination. For example, one student may be taking medication to control hyperactivity; other students may be participating in a behavior modification system designed to reinforce work completion. The teacher is likely to have the room organized in a manner that encourages student participation through learning centers or discussion groups. You may see many self-concept materials on display. One or two of the students may be in counseling either in school or after school at private agencies.

If you were to look at the teacher's lesson plans or the students' IEPs, you should see goals and objectives that center on improving interpersonal skills and reducing behavior problems. You would also see academic textbooks and other instructional materials that are the same as those used in regular classrooms. Finally, if you observed the teacher working with the students, you would see the same type of positive teaching behaviors you would expect to see in any

TABLE 3.7 Activities for Improving Emotional Problems

Goal: Improving self-control

- Prepare a chart with pockets for an index card with each student's name on it to be inserted. Hang the chart in full view of the class. When a student fails to exhibit self-control, have him or her remove his or her card and bring it to you. Note the date on the card and briefly describe the problem. Hold the card at your desk for a prespecified period of time (e.g., 2 minutes, 10 minutes, 25 minutes). Periodically check the chart and reward students whose cards are still in place with a special treat. Start each day with all cards in the chart.

- Set up contrived situations in which the goal is to exhibit self-control. Have students discuss positive and negative ways to respond to the situations. Have them talk about the likely outcomes of each different response.

- Provide students with a predetermined number of tickets each morning. Take a ticket each time the student fails to exhibit self-control. At the end of the day, collect all remaining tickets and have a drawing for a special prize.

- Select a time interval and provide tickets to students who exhibit self-control during it. Put the tickets in a "lottery box" and periodically have drawings to reward their good behavior.

- Discuss the importance of self-control with the class and provide examples of appropriate behavior. Tell students you want them to exhibit these behaviors during school and that their daily grade will depend on the number of appropriate responses they exhibit (e.g., 4=A, 3=B, 2=C). Have one student in the class be responsible for keeping track of appropriate behavior. Periodically check progress and inform students of the grades they are earning.

Goal: Improving self-esteem

- Have students write down positive thoughts and feelings about themselves each day. Work toward a goal of twenty-five "positives" in one minute. Have students chart their progress toward this goal.

- Identify a skill or activity that a student with a self-esteem problem does very well. Prepare a fifteen minute videotape of the students demonstrating the skill or activity. Periodically show the videotape to the class and make it available for individual viewing during free time.

- Take a minute several times during the day to point out positive things that have happened. Be sure each student is recognized for at least five things each day.

- Have students keep diaries or scrapbooks of their achievements.

- Have students keep charts of their performance on specific academic skills (e.g., spelling tests). Help them to show improvement on these records.

- Take some time each day to have students discuss positive qualities of their classmates. Record the comments privately and later present them to the student selected for recognition on a specific day.

Source: Responding to Individual Differences in Education (1998). Longmont, CO: Sopris West.

TABLE 3.8   Instructional Activities for Improving Social Problems

Goal: Reducing fighting and general disruptiveness

■ Briefly describe to the student that the behavior is unacceptable and discuss alternatives.

■ Move the student away from the rest of the group and tell him or her to observe how the other children are playing nicely together.

■ After a short period of time, ask the student if he or she is ready to rejoin the rest of the group. If ready, allow him or her to return to the group. If not ready, have student continue observing others. During second observation period, provide a special treat or reward for students present (i.e., not observing).

■ When the student has been returned to the group, give him or her positive attention for appropriate behavior (e.g., nonfighting behavior).

Goal: Reducing general disruptiveness

■ Set a timer to go off at irregular intervals (i.e., on one occasion, it may ring after 2 minutes; on another occasion, it may ring after 10 minutes).

■ Tell students that if they are engaged in disruptive behavior when the timer goes off, they will have missed an opportunity to earn reward points. If they are not being disruptive when the timer sounds, they will earn a reward point.

■ Total the points at the end of the day and have students exchange them for other reinforcers that are available in the classroom (e.g., supplies, activities, magazines, extra recess time).

Goal: Reducing talk-outs

■ Collect baseline data by counting the number of times a student's inappropriate talk-outs occur in a five-day period, at least one hour each day.

■ Tell the student that you will be monitoring the number of talk-outs that occur on a daily basis and, that if the numbers are low (below average for baseline), a variety of rewards will become available.

■ Randomly choose a one-hour period of time during each day. Count the number of inappropriate talk-outs that occur. Do not inform the student that the hour observations will be taken. At the end of the day, provide reward or review data with the student and develop a plan for improvement (obtaining a reward the next day).

Goal: Reducing out-of-seat behavior

■ Collect baseline data for ten days by simply counting the number of times out-of-seat behavior occurs during a designated work period.

■ After the baseline data has been collected, give each student a paper with ten boxes drawn on it. Have them place a plus sign in one of the boxes if they are in their seat and working when you give a self-monitoring signal. Have them place a minus sign in one of the boxes if they are not in their seat or working when you give a self-monitoring signal.

Table 3.8 continued

- Using a small kitchen timer, set the alarm to ring at ten randomly determined times. Reward students for appropriate behavior and improvements resulting from self-monitoring.

Goal: Reducing inappropriate noises or gestures

- Give the student a sheet of paper marked with fifteen blocks (representing fifteen two-minute intervals). Give the student a star for each two-minute block of time during which he makes either "0" or "1" inappropriate noise or gesture. If the student exceeds one disruptive behavior during an interval, begin a new interval immediately. Exchange each star for one minute of extra recess time (or one minute of any rewarding activity the student and teacher have agreed upon).

- Increase the length of the intervals and the minute value of the stars as disruptive behaviors decrease.

Source: Responding to Individual Differences in Education (1998). Longmont, CO: Sopris West.

classroom—special or regular. The differences that have come to be identified with some students are a function of assumptions people have about the nature of behavior disorders. This perspective is evident in the diversity of definitions that are used to describe troubled students in our schools.

Summary

Behavior disorders in students are one of the three prevalent mild disabilities identified in schools. Students are referred for special education programs when their behavior is perceived to be disturbed or disturbing. Teachers like Fred Peterson, Ms. Hildago, and Alice often report that these students are among the most difficult to teach. There are no absolute standards to judge the presence of normal or abnormal behavior. Frequently, judgments represent opinions about the appropriateness of behavior in a specific classroom. Normality and abnormality are relative concepts that are derived from the interaction of the actor, the observer, and the environment. Reactions to behavior vary according to the skills, expectations, and tolerance of the teacher. A signal indication of the relativity inherent in the category of behavior disorders is the variance in state prevalence figures and differences in state criteria for identifying students.

Over the years, the study of emotional and social problems has been based in four theoretical viewpoints. The biophysical perspective emphasizes the relationship between body chemistry and behavior. The psychodynamic is concerned with feelings, family history, and relationship building. The psychoeducational framework is developmental in nature. It integrates clinical insights in behavior with practical methods for managing behavior. The behaviorist position views observable behavior as the critical element. Treatment strategies are focused on modifying environmental factors that reinforce appropriate behavior.

A synthesis of these models highlights the interactional nature of behavior and emotional disorders. The ecological model promotes the notion that children are influenced by many different environments and that any attempt to help children with social or emotional problems must focus on all key elements in a youngster's life.

Activities

1. Arrange to speak with some teachers like Fred Peterson, Ms. Hildago, and Alice who work with students with behavior disorders. Ask them to describe the behaviors of the students with whom they work. How do these behaviors differ from those of general students? Ask them to talk about special interventions that might be done in general and special education classrooms. What recommendations would each of them make about teaching both social and academic skills?

2. Make a list of disruptive behaviors and ask educators at your school to rate them as disturbed or disturbing behaviors. Are some behaviors rated both disturbed and disturbing? Ask if the degree, intensity, and/or duration has an effect upon the perception of whether a particular behavior is rated as disturbed or disturbing.

3. Investigate the professional organization in the field of behavior disorders. The national organization is the Council for Children with Behavioral Disorders of the Council for Exceptional Children (1920 Association Drive, Reston, Virginia 22091). Write to this organization for its literature. Try to determine its membership and the services offered these members.

4. Find out if there are state and local branches of the national Council for Children with Behavioral Disorders. If there is a local organization, arrange to visit one of the meetings. Arrange a meeting with a member to discuss the organization's purpose, membership composition, and services.

5. Look for journals that discuss techniques for working with students with behavior disorders, like *Behavior Disorders, Programming for Adolescents with Behavioral Disorders, Behavior Therapy,* and *Journal of Emotional and Behavioral Problems.* Read several articles, from different journals if possible, and discuss techniques you find about working with students with behavior disorders in general and special education classrooms. Talk about approaches suggested for academic and social skills training. Discuss suggestions about collaboration with other educators, support personnel, and parents.

6. Read a book about individuals with emotional or behavioral problems. A list of these books would include titles such as *Dibbs, In Search of Self; I Never Promised You a Rose Garden; Lisa and David; Jordi, One Child;* and *Flowers for Algernon.* What were some aberrant behaviors and what was done to "treat" the story characters? What are some other treatment methods?

7. Observe in a general education classroom where students with behavior problems are being taught. Make a list of the behaviors that differentiate these students from others in the class. Notice how the teacher deals with them.

4 Students with Learning Disabilities

Advance Questions

Answer the following questions as you read this chapter:

1. What are the most common terms used to describe learning disabilities today?
2. Why do you think students with learning disabilities were "misclassified?"

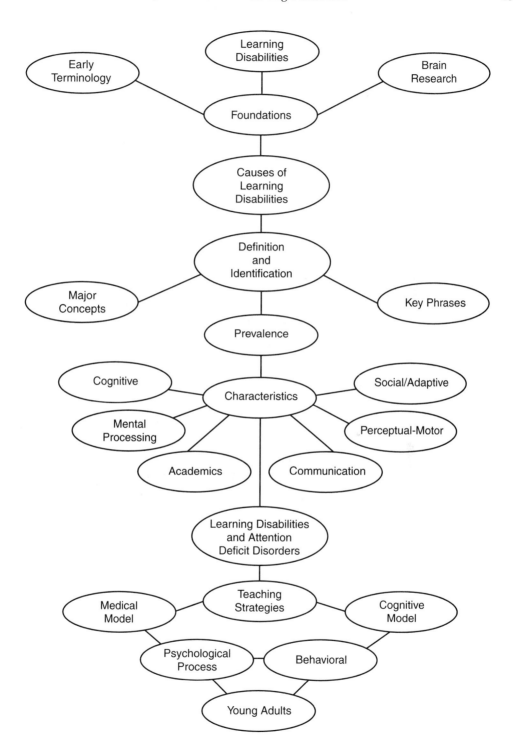

3. How has brain research contributed to our knowledge about learning disabilities?
4. What are believed to be causes of learning disabilities?
5. How is learning disabilities defined? What are some concerns about this definition?
6. What is the prevalence of learning disabilities? Can you explain the relationship between identification criteria and the numbers of students who receive special education?
7. What are the primary characteristics of students with learning disabilities?
8. What is the relationship between learning disabilities and attention deficit disorders?
9. What are the general interventions and instructional procedures used by teachers of students with learning disabilities?
10. What are some specific activities that teachers use to improve academic and interpersonal skills of students with learning disabilities?
11. What are some suggestions that might be helpful to college students with learning disabilities?
12. How can teachers and faculty assist college students with learning disabilities?

Vignette: David

David, an active and friendly child, progressed through preschool with some minor behavior problems. His year in kindergarten was without incident, and his parents recalled that he was excited and happy to be going to school. He was particularly fond of the learning games and activities that the teacher had the children play.

It was surprising then, when during first grade, David displayed ambivalence about school. Some days he seemed excited about going. On other days, he cried to stay home. David's parents talked with his teacher about his scratchy-looking printing and his problems with reading and spelling vocabulary words. The teacher always assured them that David was ahead of the class in math, and in fact, the teacher was impressed with the way in which David could add and subtract numbers in his head.

By second grade, it was apparent that David was unable to associate sounds with letters of the alphabet. The letters he wrote down for his spelling words showed little relationship to the sounds that the words made when spoken. Interestingly, David was still well ahead of his classmates in math. He did make careless mistakes aligning numbers when writing them down during seatwork. His teacher said that he needed to space his numbers more carefully so that he wouldn't make addition or subtraction errors. And if he would just try as hard in reading and spelling as he did in math, he would do fine.

Eventually, when David entered third grade, he was unable to read or spell on grade level with his classmates and was making poor grades in these subjects. He made better grades in math as long as he was careful with his written work and didn't make careless errors. His parents were disappointed with his poor report card grades in spelling and reading and tried to help him at home with his work. They noticed that if flash cards were shown David, he could remember the words better. Everyone told David to try harder.

Finally, in fourth grade, David's teacher referred him to the prereferral assistance team for prereferral interventions. The team studied David's learning capabilities and performance, and made suggestions about ways in which David could best learn. Instead of using phonics and trying to teach him sound–symbol relationships, the team recommended a sight approach. In addition, David's teacher used line cues to help him in his number spacing in math so that his numbers didn't get out-of-line and appear so confusing to him. The teacher talked with David's patents about his pattern of school problems and asked them to confirm that David's hearing was all right. These techniques seemed to help, but David needed more intense instruction using similar types of learning strategies. (Refer to Tables 4.6 and 4.7 for ideas about special instructional strategies.) Thus, David's teacher referred him for a special education evaluation.

During a multidisciplinary eligibility meeting, the school psychologist and the special education teacher explained to David's parents that the results of the intelligence test administered to David indicated above normal intelligence. The academic achievement tests showed more progress in math than in reading, as expected. A learning styles inventory revealed learning strengths in visual perception, imagery, and memory, with deficits in auditory perception that affected his encoding in spelling and decoding in reading. David also showed some mild dysgraphia spatial perception difficulties. The school psychologist told David's parents that he had a discrepancy between his ability and his achievement and concluded that David had a learning disability. The multidisciplinary team, which included David's parents, decided that David would continue to receive special interventions in the regular classroom. The special education teacher would provide both direct instruction to David and indirect consultation services about instructional interventions to David's regular classroom teacher; therefore, David would be taught in his least restrictive environment with his peers in an inclusion program placement.

Now that you have read the vignette about David, see how may problem-solving questions you can answer. For those that you cannot readily answer, think about them as you read the chapter. David's story typifies that of other youngsters with learning disabilities.

1. Why do you think that David's attitude toward school became more negative each year?
2. Why was David having difficulties with spelling and reading? Why was math a better subject area for him?
3. How was David's handwriting affecting his school work?
4. How did the prereferral assistance team assist David's teacher in working with him? How did their suggestions help?
5. Can you describe the discrepancy that David has between his ability and his achievement?
6. Do you think that placement in an inclusion program in the regular classroom is the least restrictive environment for David to be delivered special education services? Why or why not?

Foundations of Learning Disabilities

Until the mid-1960s, learning disabilities were unknown as a specific disability. Since that time, the term "learning disability" has become commonplace. Of the current disability categories named in the Individuals with Disabilities Education Act, it is the fastest growing and most controversial. (Refer to Table 4.1.) Since 1975, millions of students have been identified as "learning disabled" and treated in public schools and clinical programs by educators, psychologists, and physicians (Coles, 1989). In recent years, more than two and a half million school-aged youngsters with learning disabilities were identified and taught in the public schools (U.S. Department of Education, 1996). In almost every public school classroom, there is at least one student identified as learning disabled.

The study of learning disabilities can be traced to several diverse disciplines including psychology, medicine (i.e., ophthalmology, otology, neurology, pharmacology), linguistics, and education (Lerner, 1997). Researchers and practitioners in all of these specialized fields have made important contributions to the study of learning disabilities. Paradoxically, these diverse contributions have played a significant role in confusing our understanding of learning disabilities. Because each profession tends to view phenomena from a distinctive perspective, it is difficult to get professional agreement about what a learning disability is and how it should be treated. To a pediatrician, a learning disability is a mild neurological disorder. To an otologist, a learning disability is an auditory discrimination problem. To a teacher, a learning disability is a reading or math deficiency. To an ophthalmologist, a learning disability is a visual tracking problem. To a pharmacologist, a learning disability is a metabolic disorder. Each of these professionals will evaluate, describe, and treat learning disabilities in terms of his or her own professional point of view. Much of the confusion can be cleared up by recognizing that there are many types of learning disabilities. Throughout the past forty years, many different terms have been used to indicate a learning disability (Table 4.1).

One type of specific learning disability is dyslexia, an impairment in reading ability. A student with dyslexia may see letters backwards, reverse letters, or skip over letters while reading. Students with dyslexia have difficulty with reading comprehension. A youngster who reads "saw" for "was" *may* have dyslexia. It is important, however, not to jump to conclusions too quickly about the diagnosis of dyslexia. Children will reverse letters and numbers as their nervous systems are maturing. It is commonplace, for instance, for young children to confuse the letters "b" and "d." Many educators believe dyslexia is caused by crossed signals in the area of the brain that interprets and gives meaning to words. The term minimal brain dysfunction ascribes a neurological etiology for dyslexia. It is important to note that minimal brain dysfunction is a hypothetical explanation for dyslexia and other types of specific learning disabilities and is difficult to prove.

Terms used to identify specific learning disabilities typically begin with the prefix *dys*, which means an impairment in a particular ability, as in dysfunctional

TABLE 4.1   Terms Used to Describe Learning Disabilities Over the Past Forty Years

Attention Deficit Disorder	Perceptual Handicap
Minimal Brain Dysfunction	Behavior Disordered
Hyperactivity	Hyperkinesis
Educationally Handicapped	Impulsive
Strauss Syndrome	Strephosymbolia
Dyslexia	Word Blindness
Psycholinguistic Disorder	Multisensory Disorder
Neurologically Handicapped	Slow Learner
Reading Disability	Dyscalculia
Dysgraphia	Dysphasic
Organic Brain Dysfunction	Puzzle Children
Minimal Cerebral Palsy	Neurologically Immature
Developmentally Delayed	Mildly Handicapped
Hypoactivity	Language Disordered
Delayed Learner	Neurophrenia
Congenital Alexia	Diffuse Brain Damaged
Association Deficit Pathology	Organicity
Primary Reading Retardation	Maturation Lag

(Table 4.2). Minimal brain dysfunction cannot be proved by a standardized test. A neurological examination (including a detailed medical history, an examination of cranial nerves, an assessment of motor function, and an electroencephalogram [EEG]) *may* be able to confirm a neurological basis for a student's learning problems.

Other types of learning disabilities are more generalized in terms of behavior or cognitive difficulties. Students who are hyperactive or distractible are sometimes characterized with learning disabilities. Students who are disorganized and have difficulty following directions may be identified with learning disabilities. Poor coordination, problems with short-term memory, perceptual problems, limited concentration, speech deficits, inadequate verbal skills, and problems with becoming easily frustrated are just a sample of characteristics that have been attributed to learning disabilities.

Distinguishing the student with learning disabilities from the underachiever is a major challenge facing educators today. Resource rooms are overloaded with children who have been identified as "learning disabled" based on unreliable evaluation procedures. In recent years, almost 5 percent of the school population of students aged six to seventeen received special education services because of a presumed learning disability. Most experts agree that a range of 2 to 3 percent is a more reasonable prevalence figure for learning disabilities. Clearly, many students may be misclassified with learning disabilities.

TABLE 4.2   Specific Learning Disabilities

Each of these specific learning disabilities is generally believed to be caused by an impairment in nervous system functioning.

Dyslexia	An impairment in reading ability. The individual does not understand clearly what he or she reads.
Dysgraphia	Difficulty in writing or forming letters. Mirror writing is a severe form of this impairment.
Dysacusis	Impairment in understanding speech and deriving meaning from speech.
Dyskinesia	Clumsiness or poor coordination.
Dyscalculia	Impairment in mathematical ability.
Dyslogia	A linguistic disturbance characterized by faulty formation or expression of verbal ideas.
Dysphasia	An impairment in the ability to produce or comprehend language. It can affect either written or spoken language function.
Dysnomia	Difficulty in searching for and thinking of a word to express a thought or idea.
Dysrhythmia	Poor rhythm or the loss of ability to move with rhythm.

In a relatively brief period of time, the field of learning disabilities has emerged as a major explanation for underachievement in school. Its historical antecedents are rooted in neurological research on brain injury and brain dysfunction. Its contemporary growth has branched out into education, linguistics, psychology, and medicine. Like an apple tree, learning disabilities, with the benefit of lots of attention, has grown quickly. But the growth is wild, and the fruit is spotty. The time has arrived to do some pruning. Unless school systems become more adept at varying instruction to meet individual needs and the different learning styles of students in the regular classroom, students identified with learning disabilities will continue to fill special education classrooms. These students will overtax special education resources and make it difficult to provide adequate services to students with more severe disabilities.

Early Research on Learning Disabilities

Barsch was one of the first professionals to point out the need to look more closely at learning disabilities as a possible explanation for the failure of some children to make adequate progress in school.

> The failing learner is no longer a statistic of minor significance. Academic failure, learning inefficiency, anxiety barriers, dismissals, expulsions, dropouts, reading retardation, and a host of other problems are rampant on the educational scene. The percentages of failing students is increasing annually. . . . The problem is

immediate upon the educational terrain: the confrontation is compelling and vibrant and the pressure for action is inescapable. (Barsch, 1968, 7,10)

Barsch's remarks, which appeared in the first issues of the *Journal of Learning Disabilities*, signaled a shift toward considering the possibility that some problem learners had a learning disability. Barsch's comments linked 30 years of research with brain injured individuals to remedial services for students in public schools.

Misclassified Mentally Retarded Students.   In the 1950s, Samuel Kirk discovered that a number of persons had been misclassified as mentally retarded at the Wayne County Training School in Northville, Michigan. Kirk could not justify classifying these pupils as having mental retardation for several reasons. First, the intelligence quotient (IQ) scores of these students were too high; second, after intensive remediation in reading, they made extraordinary progress. Similar gains were rarely made by their counterparts with mental retardation.

> All of the children I taught . . . were classified as mentally retarded. In all of these cases my purpose was to show through the results of remediation that these children should have been classified as learning disabled instead of mentally retarded, since they were normal in some respects but had specific disabilities. (Kirk, 1976, 260)

Many of these individuals eventually left the institution and became self-supporting (Kirk, 1976). These misclassified individuals inspired Kirk to do further research to determine the nature of their disabilities. Kirk's findings paralleled earlier research on patients with brain injuries. In the early 1930s, Kurt Goldstein had observed perseveration, figure–ground confusion, and forced responses to stimuli in adults who had suffered brain injury (Goldstein, 1942).

Heinz Werner (1944) and Alfred Strauss and Laura Lehtinen (1947) followed similar research avenues. They identified and described exogenously brain damaged (i.e., point of origin of disability outside the body) children with mental retardation. The disabilities of these children could not be traced to genetic causes. Their behavior was characterized as perceptually disordered, impulsive, distractible, and repetitive. This condition became known as Strauss syndrome. Later, during the 1960s, William Cruickshank (1967) was instrumental in changing the focus of research from exogenous retardation to minimally brain damaged (MBD) children with normal intelligence. Cruickshank's identification of Strauss syndrome characteristics in children with average intelligence was a pivotal turning point in the study of learning disabilities (Table 4.3).

Supporters of Learning Disabilities.   The movement to gain recognition for children without mental retardation took a giant step forward in 1963 when Samuel Kirk first proposed the term "learning disability" in a speech at a special-education parents' conference. Previously, professionals had used many different terms to

TABLE 4.3   Strauss Syndrome, Characteristics of Brain Damaged Children

These are general behaviors that Strauss and Werner believed characterized brain-injured children. These characteristics influenced the later work of William Cruickshank with nonretarded children and led to treatment in classrooms that were devoid of distractions. Study carrels, which are still found in many resource rooms, are artifacts of instructional programs that were designed to focus the attention of students who exhibited Strauss syndrome characteristics.

1. Forced responsiveness to stimuli—Any noise or movement distracted the child: a pencil dropping on the floor, the sound of cars driving outside a window, a student passing by. This is different than distractibility caused by boredom.

2. Pathological fixation—The child perseverated. Once engaged in a motor task, the child repeated movements over and over. An example is a student who rubs a hole in a work sheet with an eraser. Perseveration can affect thinking, talking, or movement.

3. Disinhibition—Excessive motor activity. Now commonly referred to as hyperactivity. Strauss found that children with brain damage were attracted to specific features of objects. The "bounciness" of a ball or the "jabbiness" of a pencil would seduce the child into bouncing or jabbing.

4. Dissociation—The child was unable to integrate or see the "whole picture." For example, a student would have difficulty seeing how the parts of a puzzle fit together. The child was disorganized. This integration problem inspired Werner's famous Marble Board experiments where students were asked to repeat patterns of red and black marbles on eleven inch squares with ten lines and ten holes to each line. Children who were unable to copy the patterns were identified as dissociated in their conceptual reasoning.

Derived from Farnham-Diggory, 1978, and Bruner, Cole, and Lloyd, 1978.

identify the same children. By using the term "learning disabilities" as an umbrella concept to cover children who had been variously called minimally brain damaged, perceptually handicapped, minimally brain dysfunctional, or language delayed, advocates were able to join forces and push for federal legislation to provide remedial school services for those students.

Critics of Learning Disabilities.   The category of learning disabilities evolved as a means of addressing a condition that did not fit into preexisting classifications of exceptionality (e.g., mental retardation, emotionally disturbed). Some educators think that the label is a convenience because students with learning disabilities usually have average intelligence, no sign of emotional disturbance, and come primarily from middle class backgrounds. The critics believe that the identification of a learning disability is a way for students to get special education services without anyone being held accountable for the problem. The student is blameless because the problem is assumed to be neurological in nature. Parents are blameless because the learning problem is not caused by inadequate parenting. Finally, teachers are blameless because the students' presumed neurological impairment, rather than inadequate instruction, is the reason for school failure. According to Kronick,

> Learning disabilities is a cosmetic label which white, middleclass parents prefer because it implies that their children are not mentally retarded or disturbed, that parenting was not faulty, and that their children are not responsible for their behavior and so cannot be called "lazy" or "unmotivated." (Kronick, 1988, 33)

Coles (1989) suggested that the term learning disabilities is popular because it explains and justifies poor school performance by focusing upon presumed characteristics and attributes found within the child. Bartoli (1989) suggested that the following causal factors be considered as alternatives to neurological dysfunction: curriculum, testing, classroom dynamics, school climate, community values, teacher–parent relationships, and poverty. A comparison of Bartoli's observation with the federal definition provides a good example of how little consensus there is regarding the nature of learning disabilities.

Brain Research

The human brain weighs less than six pounds, and it can store more information than all the libraries of the world. In appearance it resembles a soft, wrinkled walnut. It communicates with itself through ten billion neurons and a hundred billion neuron connections (Restak, 1984). Neuroscientists approach the study of the brain with the same awe most of us reserve for space travel and exploration of the universe. We have much to learn about brain function, thinking, and learning disabilities. Modern technology, through the use of computerized axial tomography (CAT) scans and positron emission photography (PET) scans, can provide a detailed picture of brain function in living patients. Unfortunately, these medical techniques are far too complex and expensive to be helpful to school evaluation teams. In the future, however, we can expect that private grant and federally funded research activities will uncover more specific information about how children with learning disabilities process information and think.

Learning disabilities were first described as caused by "minimal brain damage." The disability was classified as a neurological dysfunction (Bartoli, 1989; Sigmon, 1989). The federal definition of learning disabilities states that a mental processing deficit exists, but it does not define "processing deficit." Generally, mental processing refers to thinking skills such as generalizing, abstracting, classifying, and integrating.

It is possible to detect brain anomalies in persons with severe learning disabilities. In 1861, Paul Broca, a French neuroanatomist, exhibited the brain of a deceased patient who had a severe communication impairment. His intelligence was average and he showed no indication of emotional disturbance. Broca called his patient "Tan-Tan" because those were the only words the man could utter after a stroke. Tan-Tan understood speech and communicated through gestures. Only Tan-Tan's speaking ability was impaired. The brain Broca exhibited had observable damage in a circumscribed two-inch area of the left hemisphere, including the lower portion of the frontal lobe, the lower portion of the parietal lobe, and the upper part of the temporal lobe.

Broca convinced his colleagues that Tan-Tan's speech impairment (known today as aphasia) was the result of this insult to the brain. Broca was one of the first contributors to the theory that language ability is localized in the left hemisphere of the brain (Restak, 1984).

The Russian psychologist Aleksandr Luria believed, as Broca did, that certain mental abilities were localized in specific areas of the brain. For instance, visual images are centered in the occipital lobe in the brain. Any damage to the occipital lobe will result in a visual impairment. Luria's work on memory, particularly with his most famous patient "S," documented the relationship between visual imagery and memory.

Luria's work with patients who suffered from dyscalculia (impaired ability to do arithmetic) demonstrated how defects in spatial logic, mathematical planning, and calculating could be traced to defects in specific areas of the brain. For example, Luria presented the case of an artillery commander who lost the ability to add, subtract, divide, and multiply after a bullet wound. Surrounding brain tissue was unblemished and other mathematical skills, such as counting and logic, were unaffected. In another illustration, Luria described a female patient who was unable to plan how to solve sequential problems. She became confused when given a three-part problem like: a boy is eight years old; his father is thirty years older; and the mother is ten years younger than the father—how old are they? Luria reported that this patient's thinking ability improved after surgical removal of a brain tumor (Farnham-Diggory, 1978; Restak, 1984).

It is generally accepted that specific areas of the brain control some discrete cognitive functions (Figure 4.1). Robert Sperry's (1968) work with split-brain patients detailed the different ways that the right and left hemispheres of the brain process information. Sperry studied individuals whose corpus callosums were severed by surgery in order to diminish uncontrollable seizures. The corpus callosum is the bundle of nerves that connect the left and right hemispheres of the brain. It is the line of communication that allows the hemispheres to communicate with each other. Sperry found that the left hemisphere is specialized for dealing with things in sequence; the right hemisphere deals with things all at once. The left hemisphere is often characterized as the logical, verbal, analytical half of the human brain. The right hemisphere is characterized as the intuitive, holistic, visual half of the brain.

Robert Ornstein, who studied under Sperry, found that his subjects were right- or left-hemispheric oriented; that is, they had a preferred mode of thought. Using EEG measurements of electrical activity in individuals from different occupations, Ornstein discovered that artists relied more on their right hemisphere even when the task required left hemisphere capabilities. The opposite was true

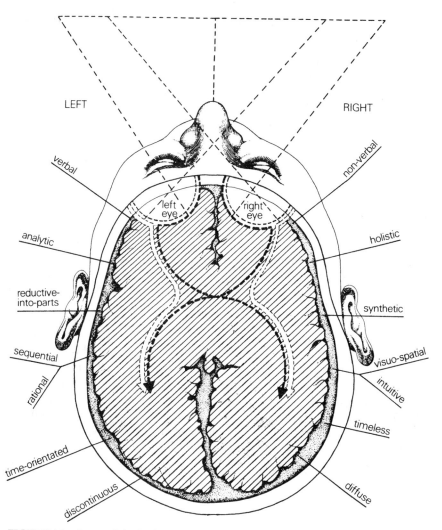

FIGURE 4.1   Areas of the Brain

Source: Charles Hamptden-Turner, *Maps of the Mind.* London: Mitchell Beazley, 1981. Reprinted with permission

of lawyers; that is, even when the task required right hemispheric thought, the lawyers tended to process the information through their left hemisphere. Ornstein concluded that the hemispheres are specialized for information processing and that individuals gradually develop a hemispheric preference.

Ornstein also found that the hemispheres of most right-handed people are specialized for specific types of thought along the lines outlined by Sperry. But, left-handed individuals, according to Ornstein, sometimes do not follow the standard left-right hemisphere localization of function. According to Ornstein,

Left-handers often show a reverse specialization, in which some information is processed in the opposite hemisphere from the one used by right-handers. Some left-handers appear to have brains organized like those of right-handers, while others show no specialization at all. Ambidextrous people seem to have the least specialization of all the groups we have tested. (Ornstein, 1978, 81)

Students with learning disabilities sometimes have a developmental history of mixed dominance (e.g., favoring neither the right nor the left hand). Perhaps the "reverse specialization" that Ornstein discovered in left-handers may provide a clue as to why left-handed children are identified with learning disabilities at a greater rate than right-handed youngsters. In applying his findings to schools Ornstein observed:

Even a casual look at the results of hemisphere research shows that the ways of thinking that seem to be primarily the province of the left hemisphere are used extensively in the basic subjects of the school curriculum. The realization that schools spend most of their time training students in what seem to be left hemisphere skills, and that most educators and taxpayers regard what seem to be right hemisphere skills as frills, has caused many people to wonder whether our educational system is unbalanced. (Ornstein, 1978, 82)

Ornstein's research indicated that there may be a mismatch between how students process information and how information is presented by teachers. If some students have a preferred mode of right hemispheric thinking, they will be at a distinct disadvantage in classrooms where the teacher relies heavily on sequenced learning, verbal skills, and analysis of problems (i.e., left hemispheric material). This supposition is supported by the work of Sally Smith (1980) at the Lab School, a special school for students with learning disabilities in Washington, D.C. Smith has found that her students respond to activities in which the arts (right hemispheric thinking) are used to teach academic skills. Smith's observation that . . . "the child with the hidden handicap of learning disability also has a hidden talent in an artistic area because he has learned unique ways of looking at things," sounds very much like Ornstein's description of individuals who prefer right hemispheric modes of thought.

A portion of the children identified with learning disabilities do have some degree of neurological dysfunction that interferes with learning and academic achievement; however, the number is far less than the two million children recently identified (Adelman, 1989; Coles, 1989). As Rourke (1989) put it, we cannot assume that brain damage or neurological dysfunction is the only plausible explanation for learning problems in students with average or above average intelligence. As long as school systems are unable to differentiate between hard-to-teach students and neurologically impaired students, these two groups will continue to be lumped together and identified with learning disabilities.

Causes of Learning Disabilities

Specific learning disabilities have been attributed primarily to neurological disorders. As we stated earlier, technology is not readily available to verify these assumptions. Thus, researchers have classified causes for the disorder in two groups: organic factors and environmental factors (Reid & Hresko, 1981; Smith, Price, & Marsh, 1986). Organically based causes are physiological in nature (i.e., endogenous), whereas environmentally based causes result from negative environmental or social factors such as inadequate diets or poor pedagogy (i.e., exogenous).

The federal law does not recognize environmental, cultural, or economic factors as primary reasons for a learning disability; however, these factors do impact upon youth and can cause subsequent disorders. For example, a child born into an impoverished environment may have parents who are economically deprived and educationally deficient. Lack of knowledge about nutrition, or the ingestion of harmful substances (e.g., paint with lead or mercury) can result in delayed development or neurological damage. Insufficient prenatal or inadequate perinatal care, as well as maltreatment of postnatal diseases or trauma (e.g., infections) are contributors to learning disorders. Thus, detrimental environmental factors and biological conditions are interrelated (Smith et al., 1986).

Many of the organic origins of mental retardation can overlap as possible contributors of specific learning disabilities and behavior disorders as well (Ramsey, Dixon, & Smith, 1986). For example, postnatal disorders of encephalitis and meningitis can result in attention disorders, behavior disorders, and mental retardation. Hyperactivity, visual impairments, and deafness can be caused by measles or whooping cough. Anoxia, or oxygen deprivation, can cause brain damage, with resulting learning or behavior disorders. Furthermore, genetic factors may precipitate learning disabilities.

Silver (1989) reported findings from a study of children with learning disabilities who were attending the TRI-Services' Center School in Chevy Chase, Maryland; the Chelsea School in Silver Springs, Maryland; and Pine Ridge School in Williston, Vermont. He calculated that the frequency of learning disabilities was 4.5 times higher among adopted children—according to his study, 17.3 percent of adopted children versus 3.9 percent of biological children. He reported that many adopted children are born out of wedlock to indigent, young women. Such mothers are likely to receive less adequate nutritional and medical care during pregnancy and insufficient emotional support. Pregnancies of young, indigent mothers are usually stressful, and Silver concluded that the mother's tension and anxiety could adversely affect the fetus. Children born to such mothers are slow to mature and sometimes develop learning disabilities.

Environmental effects take many forms and are likely contributors to learning disabilities. These effects include deprived learning experiences during infancy and preschool years. Teachers who do not have concern or tolerance for slower-maturing and -developing children or who do not adequately compensate for these learning gaps perpetuate school failure and underachievement.

Definition and Identification

Congress delayed the passage of the Individuals with Disabilities Education Act several months while it wrangled with experts and parents over a suitable definition for learning disabilities. The expression that a camel is a horse created by a committee aptly applies to the federal definition of a learning disability. It appeases everyone but pleases no one. It is extremely vague in some parts and too specific and exclusive in others. According to the latest federal guidelines being implemented under the Individuals with Disabilities Education Act, "specific learning disability" means

> a disorder in one or more of the basic psychological processes involved in understanding or in using language, spoken or written, which may manifest itself in an imperfect ability to listen, think, speak, read, write, spell, or do mathematical calculations

The term includes such conditions as perceptual handicaps, brain injury, minimal brain dysfunction, dyslexia, and developmental aphasia. The term does not include children who have learning problems that are primarily the result of visual, hearing, or motor handicaps, of mental retardation, of emotional disturbance, or of environmental, cultural, or economic disadvantages.

Highlight 4.1 What Is a Learning Disability?

In order to help you understand the difficulty in defining a learning disability, we are going to give you a brief quiz. First question—what is a table? Nice going—you figured that out without much trouble. When you can see, feel, and eat off something, it's not hard to define. Let's try another. What is the wind? That's a little harder. You can't see the wind, and you don't use it very often (except for some kite flying or sailing if you're fortunate); but you can feel the wind, and it's

a common part of life. But did you give a specfic definition or did you just describe what it means to you? The more abstract a concept, the further removed from direct experiences (our senses), the harder it is to come up with one definition. Let's extend this thinking to one more question. What is eternity? Now there's an abstract concept. We'll have to accept a lot of different views on this one. We have the same problem with the term "learning disabilities." It is a very abstract idea, and it is interpreted in many different ways.

Major Concepts and Key Phrases

The federal definition for learning disabilities has been criticized because it is broad-based and includes undefined terminology. It is helpful to understand the thoughts and concerns that existed when the major concepts and key phrases were first proposed and put into practice in 1975.

Basic Psychological Processes.   This phrase has yet to be specifically defined but refers to the processing functions that any learner must have intact in order to receive, integrate (i.e., organize, associate, store, retrieve), or express information. It infers that learning problems of students in this category are of a neurological nature and that development is uneven due to subtle disorders of mental processing. Chalfant and Scheffelin (1969) describe "mental processes" as sensing information by listening, looking, or touching; integrating sensations through such cognitive functions as attention, discrimination, memory, integration, concept formation, and problem solving; and responding through speech or body movements.

Language-Based.   The federal definition states that the disorder is language-based and occurs inlearning situations that involve oral language, listening comprehension, written composition, writing, spelling, reading (e.g., vocabulary, word-attack skills, decoding, comprehension), or arithmetic (e.g., calculation, reasoning, general problem solving). Due to each student's specific processing deficit, uneven abilities are manifested in these language-based areas highlighted in academic tasks.

Inclusion Clause.   The federal definition specifically includes examples of presumed central nervous system deficits like perceptual handicaps, brain injury, minimal brain dysfunction, dyslexia, and developmental aphasia. These deficits are representative of more severe disabilities, and are not typically identified during educational assessment of students with mild learning disabilities.

Exclusion Clause. The federal definition excludes mental retardation, emotional disturbance, visual impairments, organic hearing dysfunctions, and motor disabilities as primary causes of learning disabilities, even though these conditions can coexist with learning disabilities. According to the definition, a learning disability cannot be attributed to conditions such as environmental, cultural, or economic disadvantage. This part of the exclusion clause is particularly perplexing because it is difficult to determine whether a student's underachievement is due to a subtle central nervous system disorder, delayed developmental growth, inadequate teaching, or a lack of environmental opportunities.

Because the federal definition is ambiguous, criteria were established to complement and to spell out a *functional* method for determining whether a student has a learning disability. Consider the following:

a. A multidisciplinary team may determine that a child has a specific learning disability if:
   1. The child does not achieve commensurate with his or her age and ability levels in one or more of the areas listed in paragraph (a) (2) of this section, when provided with learning experiences appropriate for the child's age and ability levels, and
   2. The team finds that a child has a severe discrepancy between achievement and intellectual ability in one or more of the following areas:
      i. Oral expression;
      ii. Listening comprehension;
      iii. Written expression;
      iv. Basic reading skill;
      v. Reading comprehension;
      vi. Mathematics calculation; or
      vii. Mathematics reasoning.
b. The team may not identify a child as having a specific learning disability if the severe discrepancy between ability and achievement is primarily the result of:
   1. A visual, hearing, or motor handicap;
   2. Mental retardation;
   3. Emotional disturbance; or
   4. Environmental, cultural, or economic disadvantage. (U.S. Office of Education, 1977, pp. 65081–65085)

These criteria are referred to as the discrepancy formula because they focus attention on the gap between a youngster's academic achievement and intellectual ability. They are more useful for educators because they provide functional guidelines. Simply stated, the criteria hypothesize that a severe discrepancy between intelligence and achievement indicates a learning disability. Because both intelligence and achievement can be measured by testing, the discrepancy formula has been widely accepted. All states include discrepancy in their identification procedures for learning disabilities (Smith, 1991). This nationwide acceptance has not solved all the problems in identifying students with learning disabilities. Two key aspects of discrepancies require closer inspection.

Intellectual Ability.   For many years, William Cruickshank, a pioneer in the field of learning disabilities, argued against assuming that only children with average or above average intelligence have learning disabilities. The way the present discrepancy formula is written, it appears as though students with mental retardation or other disabilities cannot have learning disabilities. It is not uncommon to hear teachers define a student with learning disabilities as a youngster with *average* intelligence who is underachieving. This is misleading, and the results show up in educational programming. As an illustration, a child with Down syndrome has a clear neurological impairment, but rarely does one hear learning disabilities discussed as an explanation for academic problems. Any learning problems a student with Down syndrome has with reading or math are attributed to mental retardation. The possibility that the student might have dyslexia or some other specific learning disability can be overlooked.

Discrepancy between Achievement and Intellectual Ability

As Farnham-Diggory (1978, 5) pointed out, "A learning disabled child is presumably not up to a 'grade level' that can be specified in terms of test scores. Grade-level work is what 50 percent of the children in a particular grade are doing." If grade-level measures are accurate, half the class will always have a discrepancy between their ability and achievement. This leaves us to ponder what a *severe* discrepancy is. According to Smith (1991), 57 percent of the states provide guidelines on how to quantify severe discrepancy. Two or more years below grade level is common. Some states use three or more years below grade level. In almost half of the states, the meaning of "severe discrepancy" is left in the hands of local school systems.

Too many referrals to special education programs are a major problem that has evolved from the discrepancy notion. Many students are under grade level. If teachers take "below grade level" to mean that students need special education, referrals are quick to follow.

Public Law 94–142 was originally titled the Education for All Handicapped Children Act (EHA)—*not* the Education for All Slow Learners Act. Emphasis on the purpose of Public Law 94–142, to serve students with disabilities, was further supported through renaming the law Individuals with Disabilities Education Act (IDEA). Yet throughout the country, a domino effect is taking place. Slow or unmotivated learners are overcrowding special education programs, and students with real learning disabilities are not getting the help that they have a legal right to expect. These students have intellectual and learning potential and need special help for deficits that hinder their learning abilities.

Prevalence of Learning Disabilities

About 5 percent of the school population received special education services under the category of specific learning disabilities in recent years (U.S. Department of Education, 1996). This is a large group (about 1 or 2 in every class of 25–35) of students. Of the 4.9 million students who received special education in recent years, slightly over 50 percent (51.1 percent or 2.5 million students) were included in the specific learning disabilities category. This is the largest group of students currently being identified and provided special education services. Most students with learning disabilities are served in general education settings (39.3 percent), where they spend less than 21 percent of the school day outside their regular classroom, or resource rooms (41 percent), where they spend up to 60 percent of the school day outside their regular classroom. Of the remainder, 18.8 percent are taught in separate classes, and less then 1 percent (0.8) in separate schools, residential facilities, or by homebound/hospital instruction.

There are more students with learning disabilities reported each year than any other special education category (Algozzine & Ysseldyke, 1986; U.S.. Department of Education, 1996). Biklen and Zollers (1986) noted that youngsters identified by schools as learning disabled constitute over 40 percent of students placed in special education services. The U.S. Department of Education (1996) provides another frame of reference in Table 4.1. The disability category of Specific Learning Disabilities reports a 17.3 percent increase of school-aged students served in special education in this category between 1990–91 and 1994–95.

Prevalence of learning disabilities depends upon multiple factors. Because of this, reliable figures are difficult to obtain. Only generalities about the numbers of students identified and served can be accurately stated. Numbers of students depend upon methods and criteria used for identification and classification (Lerner, 1997). As a result, the number of students classified as learning disabled varies from state to state (Algozzine & Korinek, 1985). Much of this variation is a result of the discrepancies in the eligibility guidelines used by states (Algozzine & Ysseldyke, 1987). The more stringent the criteria, the fewer students with learning disabilities are identified. Therefore, a student determined eligible for services in one school district or state may not meet requirements in another.

Data reporting the numbers and percentages of children and youth receiving special education and related services have been published by the U.S. Department of Education since school year 1976–77. These statistics are based upon student-count data submitted by states and territories. A continued trend of increases to the category of learning disabilities is attributed to:

1. The vagueness of the federal definition for learning disabilities.
2. Social acceptance and preference for the learning disabilities classification (rather than mental retardation or behavior disorders).
3. Differing criteria used by states for qualification for services. (Sigmon, 1989)

It appears there is much truth in the statement made by Ysseldyke, Algozzine, and Thurlow that "learning disabilities is whatever society wants it to be" (1983, 145).

Characteristics

Each student with learning disabilities has unique characteristics, just as does each student with any other disability and as do students without learning disabilities. Student characteristics can be categorized within functional domains. These domains include cognitive abilities, processing skills, academic achievement, communication development, perceptual–motor skills, and social-adaptive skills. All domains interact; no functioning areas operate independently.

Each student needs to be viewed holistically. If one part of an auto malfunctions, the rest of the vehicle will not function properly. Compensations can be made, but the malfunctioning part affects the overall service the

TABLE 4.4 Teaching Students with Learning Disabilities

	Cognitive	Academic	Adaptive	Social	Perceptual/ Perceptual Motor	Language
Learner Characteristics	Normal or above average intelligence.	Uneven pattern of academic performance.	Some degree of field dependency.	Susceptible to distraction. Social imperception.	Difficulties with learning modalities and eye–hand coordination. Inadequate gross or fine motor skills.	Difficulty in reading or language skills.
Instructional Intervention	Adapt instruction to individual cognitive abilities.	Identify entry-level skills for each academic area.	Emphasize independent strategies for learning.	Teach self-management skills. Make social skills training situational	Adjust instruction to individual learning styles and physical capabilities.	Provide opportunities for language stimulation activities.

car gives; for example, have you ever tried to go somewhere only to find that your car would not start because the battery was dead? You quickly learned that the best-performing engine will not function at all because the starter would not turn over. You may have used a jumper cable to start your car—which means you were able to temporarily bypass the main problem. But sooner or later, the battery had to be replaced. People with learning disabilities are a heterogeneous group of individuals who have deficits in one or more of the functional domains. The problem can be bypassed or overlooked for a period of time—but sooner or later, the specific disorder has to be addressed.

Students with learning disabilities do not have an easily identifiable problem. We cannot assume that the problem simply resides within the student. We have to look at all of the interactive components within the child's learning environment; for example, what task is the child being required to perform? If it is above his or her functioning level or if instruction is inappropriate, the student may fail. Curricular and task components should be analyzed as assiduously as learner behavior. Learner characteristics by functional domains are presented in Table 4.4, along with general instructional interventions for students with learning disabilities. We will have more to say about teaching in sections that follow.

Cognitive

The existence of a learning disability is often detected in a particular academic area, such as reading, or a mental process like attention or memory. If the student displays deficiencies across several academic areas and has adaptive and/or social problems, the individual is showing characteristics more like those of a child with mild mental retardation.

There is overlap between cognitive functioning, intellect, and processing of information. Cognitive refers to a wide spectrum of thinking skills (e.g., memory, analysis, deduction). Jacobs (1984) defines cognition as the active process of mental awareness and thinking. Some of these skills are sampled by an intelligence test.

Children without disabilities approach learning by asking themselves questions, organizing information, and using environmental cues. This process of thought is called metacognition (Ryan, Short, & Weed, 1986). Students with a learning disability typically do not acquire the skills of learning how to think through problems naturally. These students can be taught how to organize their thoughts through metacognitive training.

Students who don't utilize metacognitive strategies while learning may appear to be apathetic or passive. Torgesen (1977) reported that teachers described students with learning disabilities as dependent, lazy, impulsive, and disorganized. A negative cycle occurs when a student's academic progress is limited by his or her inadequate learning strategies. The person becomes soured toward learning, and teachers come to expect the student to be a passive learner. This cycle of failure can be changed if students are taught learning strategies.

Metacognitive training emphasizes teaching students *how* to learn rather than teaching them specific content (Tarver, 1986). Deshler et al. (1983) suggested teaching students study skills like scanning, outlining, note taking, time management, and questioning. Tarver (1986) stated that metacognitive training includes instruction in various (1) self-monitoring strategies (e.g., self-questioning, self-interrogatives, self-checking); (2) self-instructional strategies; and (3) executive strategies (e.g., selecting the strategy most appropriate to the task or problem at hand).

Lloyd (1980) emphasized the positive benefits of using self-instructional training, sometimes called academic attack strategy training. This involves training in use of self-verbalization to apply academic strategies. The student is taught to ask himself or herself: "Am I paying attention?" "What is the problem asking me to do?" "What is my plan for solving this problem?"

Deshler, Schumaker, and Lenz (1984) look at cognitive skills as highly interactive with academic achievement, and contend that students with learning disabilities are deficient in both. Their view is supported by factors such as the high number of students with learning disabilities who (1) reach an academic plateau of fourth- or fifth-grade level in the tenth grade, (2) have not passed minimal competency tests, and (3) are school dropouts. Most of these students are unable to generalize what they have learned across subjects or settings. The fact that these students are reported to be less satisfied with their personal social lives and continue to live with parents after secondary school years supports the contention that they need to acquire the cognitive tools necessary for life after school.

Mental Processing

Students with learning disabilities may experience problems when attempting to process knowledge and information. Learning problems can occur during any step of the processing sequence: receiving information through the senses (e.g., visual, auditory, haptic); using integrative skills to organize, store, react to, or retrieve acquired information; and responding through movement or speech. According to the definition in Public Law 94–142 (EHA, 1975) and its amendments, Public Law 101–476 (IDEA, 1990) and Public Law 105–17(Amendment to IDEA, 1997), specific learning disability means "a disorder in one or more of the basic psychological processes involved in understanding or in using language, spoken or written." As we have pointed out, the specific disorder is assumed to be neurological in origin, but cannot be identified (or even proved to be the cause) due to lack of access to technological procedures that can pinpoint the specific spot in the brain where a neurological dysfunction is located. Perceptual–motor deficiencies and disorders in listening, thinking, speaking, reading, writing, spelling, or mathematical calculations are typically the means by which educators or clinicians infer mental processing problems. The assumption is that some type of "blockage" (or "mis-signaling") is occurring along the perceptual neuro-pathways that transmit and integrate information within the brain during the act of thinking (Ramsey, 1995).

Processing skills relate directly to cognitive skills. As noted, a problem may occur in one or more of the perceptual neuro-pathways activated during learning. In school, these perceptual neuro-pathways are primarily visual or auditory. Educators use terms such as visual or auditory discrimination, visual or auditory memory, visual or auditory closure, visual or auditory sequencing, and visual or auditory blending to describe the interplay between perception and mental processing. Difficulties can occur at any point along the perceptual processing continuum: reception (input), integration (association), or expression (output).

The receptive process utilizes subskills that are essential to learning. These include attending to task, and being able to discriminate what is heard or seen (Ramsey, 1995a). Attending relates to one's knowing what to pay attention to and what to ignore (Tarver, 1986). Distractibility is sometimes confused with attending, as the student may be thought to be not attending when he or she is actually attending to the distraction. Learners must enhance appropriate attending skills in order to be proficient in the classroom (Tarver, 1986).

Discrimination refers to the ability to differentiate one thing from another (e.g., an object, an item, a sound). When asked to identify the letters "m" and "n," the child must visually perceive that there are two humps in "m" and only one in "n." Children learn to discriminate by color, shape, pattern, size, position, and brightness. Eventually students must be able to visually discriminate letters and words to learn to read. This requires more intricate visual processing skills than some students with learning disabilities may have.

Subskills directly related to the auditory receptive process include auditory attending, auditory awareness, and auditory discrimination. Sometimes it is necessary for the teacher to eliminate auditory distractions within the classroom. In order to read, a child must be able to perceive individual phoneme sounds and to correspond these sounds with correct letter symbols. These skills are necessary for decoding written (and spoken) languages (Ramsey, 1995a).

Academics

The continued decline over the school years of the academic attainment of students with learning disabilities has been the focal point of much research (Deshler, 1978; Koppitz, 1972–1973). The impact that delayed developmental cognitive functioning has on academic progress was addressed in a study by Speece, McKinney, and Appelbaum (1986). They concluded that students with learning disabilities, even though they showed average intelligence on tests, did not catch up with their peers after three to four years of remedial services.

The disparity between academic performance and intellectual ability characterizes students with learning disabilities. The federal definition specifies academic areas in which learning disorders are manifested during school experiences. Reading, mathematics, spelling, and writing are listed. For students

Table: 4.5   Typical Reading and Spelling Patterns of Students with Visual Processing Difficulties

- Confuse letters that differ in directionality (b-d, p-q)
- Confuse with words that can be reversed (was-saw)
- Limited sight vocabulary; unrecognizable from word configuration
- Lose place reading, especially when moving gaze from the end of the line on the right side to the beginning of the next line on the left side
- Omit letters and words because they were not visually noted
- Insert and substitute letters erroneously as well as omit them
- Have difficulty learning irregular words that cannot be sounded out phonetically
- May find it easier to read words when learn to spell them first
- Sometimes experience difficulty recalling the shape of letters when writing them
- Spell phonetically but inaccurately (cof-cough; bisnis-business)
- Can spell difficult phonetic words but not simple irregular phonetically spelled words

with learning disabilities, regular classrooms with consultant or inclusion programs and resource rooms serve as primary settings in which specific academic problems are addressed by special educators.

Instructional procedures must match the learning style of students in order for them to achieve success in learning to read (Ratekin, 1979). Since reading skills are necessary in every subject area (e.g., science, history, geography), Wong (1985) suggests that learning strategies be combined with teaching school subjects. Palinesar (1982) suggested, for example, that reading comprehension can be improved by teaching students self-monitoring strategies, such as reciprocal questioning and summarization skills (i.e., metacognition). However, to use self-questioning skills, a student must have an adequate knowledge base in the particular subject matter. The acquisition of knowledge may be hampered due to inattention, decoding problems, vocabulary deficiencies, poor reading comprehension skills, and inadequate instruction in content areas (Wong, 1985). It is essential that passive or inactive adolescents learn effective thinking and studying strategies, such as the cognitive strategy approach proposed by Alley and Deshler (1979).

Edge and Burton (1986) cite studies in which many students with learning disabilities are able to perform such computational skills as adding, subtracting, multiplying, and dividing, but they lack the ability to use these computational skills in problem-solving situations. These authors further point out that students need to know how to apply computational skills to financial situations that occur in everyday life.

Spelling problems are sometimes the initial reason for student referrals. In some instances, the teaching of spelling has been integrated into a broader language arts curriculum (Reid & Hresko, 1981b). This tends to make the spelling task easier for students with learning disabilities. Spelling and other language-related disorders have been studied by a number of researchers. A major type of difficulty that has been pinpointed in students with learning disabilities is the incorrect utilization of standard rules in a phonics approach to spelling. Boder and Jarrico (1982) refer to these errors as phonetically inaccurate (PI). PI spelling errors contain inaccurate phoneme-grapheme (i.e., sound-symbol) correspondences. Letters of the alphabet (i.e., symbols) that correspond with phonemic sounds are not used in the spelling of words. Cicci (1983) concluded that these errors must reflect an underlying language disorder. Horn, O'Donnell, and Leicht (1988) determined that an excessive number of PI disorders is characteristic of persons with learning disabilities; however, other factors, such as inattention and carelessness, might also contribute to this problem. Eighteen percent of the young adult sample population with learning disabilities in this study were characterized by PI spelling and deficient speech sound perception.

Communication

Language progresses through stages of development. These stages begin with early responses to and imitations of sound, continue with one to several word

Table 4.6   Typical Reading and Spelling Patterns of Students with Auditory Processing Difficulties

- Lack ability to analyze the sequence of sounds and syllables in words; often the sounds become reversed in words
- May misunderstand phrases in songs and rhymes like "Hosé can you see?" for the first line of our national anthem
- Poor ability to remember individual sounds or sequences of sounds
- Difficulty blending individual sounds into words
- Difficulty substituting sounds in one word for sounds in another word, whether in initial, final, or medial position (e.g., man-fan; cat-cut; tan-tag)
- Experience problems remembering sounds of individual letters and sounds represented by regular and irregular letter combinations
- Unable to quickly retrieve letter sounds while analyzing words so that the beginning sound of a word is forgotten by the time the individual recalls the last letter of the word (naming problem)
- Limited sight vocabulary because the student has difficulty memorizing words without being able to use phonetic cues
- Guesses at unfamiliar words rather than using word-analysis skills
- Spelling attempted more by sight than by ear
- Correct spellings occur primarily with words that the individual can visualize
- Bizarre spellings occur, because phonetic patterns cannot be applied
- Extraneous letters and omitted syllables occur when spelling

sentences, go through grammatical refinement, and extend into abstract realms. Children with mild disabilities typically lag behind in language and communication skills, whereas children who excel in intellectual ability are observed to progress more rapidly through the stages.

Youngsters with learning disabilities may have specific disorders related to the general processing of language-based information (Ramsey, 1995a). Like any type of processing skill, language disabilities can occur anywhere along the cognitive continuum (i.e., reception, integration, expression). Language disorders usually interfere with academic achievement, not only in subject areas like reading, spelling, language arts, and mathematics, but also in listening, thinking, and expression. Recall that language is identified as the broad-based disorder in learning disabilities in the federal definition:

> Specific learning disability means a disorder in one or more of the basic psychological processes involved in understanding or in using language spoken or written, which may manifest itself in an imperfect ability to listen, think, speak, read, write, spell, or to do mathematical calculations. (U.S. Office of Education, 1977, pp. 65082–65085)

Language is a complex phenomenon. It refers to the ways in which a person receives, comprehends, and transfers thoughts to another person and to oneself. Five components are traditionally identified in the study of language: phonology, morphology, syntax, semantics, and pragmatics. Youth with learning disabilities may have difficulties with basic speech sounds (phonemes), units of meaning (morphemes), sentence structure (syntax), relationships between words, grammatical forms, and underlying meaning (semantics), and everyday context usage (pragmatics).

In the receptive channel, phonology refers to how well a person can discriminate speech sounds. Quite often, proficiency, or lack of it, is observed as a child attempts to form letter–sound associations. In the expressive channel, phonology refers to the production or articulation of speech sounds. Misarticulation is a major problem area in verbal expression for many children (Bryen, 1982; Lund & Duchan, 1988). Morphology refers to the linguistic structure of words and how word units (i.e., prefixes, suffixes, tense, and comparative endings) change the meaning of the word. Syntax includes grammatical usage of word classes, word order, and transformational rules for the variance of word order. In other words, syntax refers to the arrangement of words within sentences. Semantics relates to the understanding and use of word meanings and vocabulary, respectively, when viewed in terms of receptive (listening and reading) and expressive (speaking and writing) abilities. Receptive and expressive skills in semantic functioning include vocabulary, categorization, ability to define, identification of synonyms and antonyms, and detection of ambiguity or absurdity. One's listening vocabulary and level of spoken vocabulary may be determined by assessment of semantic receptive and expressive skills (Bryen, 1982; Lund & Duchan, 1988). Pragmatics is the practical application of language. It is concerned with the way language is used to communicate rather than with its structure.

Perceptual–Motor

The ability to process (or use) information received through the sense organs of the body is necessary for learning. Deficits within this functioning domain may stem from the perceptual realm and underlie cognitive and motoric functions. For example, a child may incorrectly copy simple geometric designs. If she cannot "see" her errors, a problem might exist in her perceptual (input) mechanism, whereas a child who can acknowledge her errors but cannot correct them may have a deficiency in her motoric (output) mechanism. Likewise, a child who is unable to "write" on a paper at his desk what he "sees" on the chalkboard or in a textbook may be experiencing cross-modal difficulties. The difficulty rests in the ability to transfer from one modality to another (e.g., visual to motor, auditory to expressive). Keep in mind that the perceptual–motor hypothesis described above is only one of the several possible explanations for a child's behavior.

According to Jacobs (1984), perception, memory, and attention are integrative processes and are used collectively to obtain information from the environment and make it meaningful. Perception is the differentiation of distinctive features with filtering of irrelevant information. Attention is affected by a person's capacity to organize and make sense of information (Reid & Hresko, 1981). Memory is dependent upon attention and how well information has been received and associated with experience. Perception, attention, and memory are necessary prerequisites for learning. Jacob suggests that each individual uses unconscious metacognition strategies to organize and remember new information.

Some students with learning disabilities have coordination problems. They may appear awkward or clumsy when attempting ordinary childhood activities like riding a bicycle, skipping, and jumping rope. Children with learning disabilities frequently develop these skills, but later than their age-mates. Problems with fine motor skills may become apparent when these children are cutting with scissors and manipulating small objects. Motor problems are most evident in school during physical education and during handwriting and art activities (Lewis & Doorlag, 1987).

Dysgraphia is a term that describes the impaired handwriting skills some children demonstrate when attempting to form letters of the alphabet. The child can see accurately what to write but cannot manage correct writing movements (Bush & Waugh, 1982). An example is mirror writing. Each letter is symmetrical but backwards. This condition is not to be confused with children who have poor handwriting skills of a temporary nature due to late maturation or those who write poorly due to carelessness or lack of practice.

During the formative years of learning disabilities research (1950s–1960s), perceptual–motor differences in underachieving children with average intelligence were considered indicators of a minimal brain dysfunction. When hard-to-teach children were unable to match peers in such tasks as copying geometric shapes, researchers believed that a learning disability represented by perceptual–motor processing difficulties was present. Treatment programs were developed based on the premise that the presumed perceptual–motor dysfunction would be remediated by having students practice such worksheet tasks as connecting dots, tracing lines, and finding hidden objects in pictures. Perceptual–motor training declined in the early 1970s when basic assumptions of this approach were unsupported by research. Perceptual–motor training failed to improve academic skills, and tests used to identify perceptual–motor dysfunction were found to be unreliable.

Social/Adaptive

Contrary to definitions of mental retardation and behavior disorders, there is no mention of adaptive behavior in the definition for learning disabilities. This omission is noted by experts in the field of learning disabilities (Mercer, 1973; Strawser & Weller, 1985; Weller, Strawser, & Buchanan, 1985). The researchers contend that failure to consider social skills difficulties as a trait of learning disabilities contributes to mistaken placements of students with learning disabilities in programs for students with mild mental retardation or behavior disorders.

Social skills underlie one's ability to adapt to the environment. Students with learning disabilities demonstrate adaptive behavior problems through such difficulties in school performance as lack of self-control, poor self-esteem, and inadequate interpersonal relationships. Adaptive behavior skills shape friendships, communication, and vocational choices (Weller et al., 1985). Social competence has been operationally defined as the ability to act appropriately in social situations. This is an area in which youngsters with learning disabilities may exhibit difficulties (Bryan, 1978; Carlson, 1987; McConaughy, 1986). Social competence comprises an umbrella of social skills that one needs in order to be accepted in social situations (Hops, 1983; McFall, 1982). A socially adept person selects appropriate skills in particular circumstances and uses social skills in ways that lead to positive outcomes (Deshler & Schumaker, 1983; Larson & Gerber, 1987). Taking appropriate actions and making appropriate responses in social situations requires the use of adequate social perception, social knowledge, and social performance. Some individuals with learning disabilities lack the ability to perceive social situations correctly, show deficiencies in social "know-how" skills, and fail to act appropriately. These students require instruction in the use of social skills (Wojnilower & Gross, 1988).

Several factors have been suggested as contributors to social problems of children with learning disabilities. Carlson (1987) reported studies that showed those with learning disabilities have processing deficits in social comprehension and misinterpret social situations. Specific cognitive functions may be affected in some persons with learning disabilities that cause an impaired ability to understand or empathize with another person's feelings, make inferences about social cues, or predict and evaluate consequences for social behavior (Schumaker & Hazel, 1984). Margalit and Shulman (1986) concluded that individuals with learning disabilities exhibit anxious behavior due to dependency needs. They sometimes misinterpret information from their environment and misperceive social cues (Fine, 1987). Both are problem areas related to perceptual and cognitive deficiencies. Such students adopt an egocentric perspective and exhibit an inability to shift the focus away from themselves (Derr, 1986). An overwhelming number of studies indicate problems including social competence, personal failure in social interaction (Bryan, Donahue, & Pearl, 1981) and peer relationships (Bruininks, 1978; Bryan, 1974).

Researchers report that delinquent behaviors and antisocial acts characterize a significant number of adolescents with learning disabilities (Bryan, Werner, & Pearl, 1982; Larson & Gerber, 1987; McConaughy, 1986). Even as children, these youngsters evidently lack the skills and inner control to handle age-appropriate tasks and to manage their own behavior (McWhirter, McWhirter, & McWhirter, 1985). Because of this, they may receive negative feedback from family and neighbors. Messages like this lessen feelings of self-worth (McConaughy, 1986). Thus, by adolescence, it is not surprising when students with learning disabilities exhibit behaviors that are out of step with prevailing values.

Zigmond, Levin, and Laurie (1985) reported tardiness, absenteeism, and off-task behavior by high school students with learning disabilities. Ysseldyke and his colleagues (1982) observed no differences in the classroom behaviors of elementary nonlearning-disabled children and those with learning disabilities. Contrary to this finding, other researchers found that children with learning disabilities, when compared to nonlearning-disabled elementary students, spend more time off-task (McKinney, McClure, & Feagans, 1982) and engage in more non-task-related behaviors (Sherry, 1982).

Learning Disabilities and Attention Deficit Disorder

Much professional and parental attention has been focused on problems associated with inattention and hyperactivity in children. The American Psychiatric Association now describes a condition, Attention Deficit Disorder or Attention Deficit Hyperactivity Disorder (a condition we introduced in Chapter 3) in which children show developmentally inappropriate degrees of inattention, impulsiveness, and hyperactivity. Associated features include low self-esteem, mood instability, low frustration tolerance, academic underachievement, problems with social relationships, and temper tantrums. The problems are common, conservatively estimated as occurring in as many as 3 to 6 percent of children not currently classified and receiving special education.

Attentional problems usually begin in early childhood or in the elementary school years. They continue into adolescence and adulthood and can last a lifetime. They can be difficult to recognize, for the symptoms frequently appear to be emotional problems, learning disabilities, inconsistent parenting, inflexible teachers, or stressful environments. Each child or adolescent with an attention disorder manifests difficulties in an individual manner, although a core of behaviors indicative of attentional disorders has been identified.

In the fall of 1990, Congress inquired of the public whether or not to add Attention Deficit Disorders as a special education exceptionality category. In early 1991, it was decided not to do so, for several reasons. First, many of these students were already meeting eligibility criteria for specific learning disabilities, emotional behavioral disorders, or other health impairments. Second, there is no neurological test that will conclusively confirm the condition of ADD (or ADHD); therefore, testing for the disorder is an ambiguous endeavor.

Since that time, many students have been accommodated in the general classroom without having been declared eligible for any exceptionality category. Legal experts have used the terminology "students with disabilities" stated in Public Law 93–112, Section 504 (Rehabilitation Act of 1973), since Attention Deficit Disorders is not specifically named as a category in Public Law 101–476 (Individuals with Disabilities Education Act of 1990). The school must receive documented evidence (e.g., a letter from the physician treating the youngster) that the student has the disorder and needs reasonable accommodations in order to learn in the general classroom. A 504 Plan must be developed by the general education teacher that specifies which reasonable accommodations the youngster needs, and how they will be provided.

Attention disorders have existed for many years. The most widely accepted definitions have appeared in the Diagnostic and Statistical Manual of Mental Disorders (DSM) of the American Psychiatric Association (APA). Names have been given to this disorder like Minimal Brain Dysfunction, Hyperkinesis, Attention Deficit Disorder With and Without Hyperactivity, Attentional Deficit Hyperactivity Disorder, and undifferentiated Attention Deficit Disorder. Characteristics associated with ADD and ADHD are similar to those associated with learning disabilities. For example, inattention, hyperactivity, and impulsivity are key behavioral characteristics associated with learning disabilities and "clinically significant distress or impairment in academic functioning" is an analogous phrase for "significant discrepancy between ability and achievement." Moreover, interventions prescribed for students with ADD and ADHD are often used with students with learning and behavior disorders (e.g., training or shaping appropriate behaviors, reducing inappropriate behaviors, creating stimulating learning tasks, and using varied instructional activities) (Ramsey, 1995a).

To be diagnosed as having an attentional deficit, or ADHD, a child, adolescent, or adult must demonstrate eight of the following symptoms and they must have occurred before the age of seven:

1. Often fidgits with hands or feet or squirms in seat.
2. Has difficulty remaining seated when required to do so.
3. Is easily distracted by extraneous stimuli.
4. Has difficulty awaiting turn in games or group situations.
5. Often blurts out answers to questions before they have been completed.
6. Has difficulty following through on instructions from others (not due to oppositional behavior or failure of comprehension), e.g., fails to finish tasks or chores.
7. Has difficulty sustaining attention in tasks or play activities.
8. Often shifts from one uncompleted activity to another.
9. Has difficulty playing quietly.
10. Often talks excessively.
11. Often interrupts or intrudes on others, e.g., butts into other children's games.
12. Often does not seem to listen to what is being said about him or her.
13. Often loses things necessary for talks or activities at school or at home (e.g., toys, books, assignments).
14. Often engages in physically dangerous activities without considering possible consequences (not for the purpose of thrill-seeking), e.g., runs into street without looking. (American Psychiatric Association, 1994)

Professionals concerned with students with attention deficit disorders offer the following "principles of remediation" for improving inattention, excessive activity, and impulsivity:

Inattention

- Decrease length of required assignments and tasks.

- Break assignments into smaller parts to be completed at different times.
- Give a preferred task to be completed after a less preferred task.
- Give fewer spelling words, math problems.
- Use fewer words in explaining assignments or expectations (concise and global verbal directions).
- Use distributed practice, rather than mass practice.

- Make assignments and school tasks interesting.
  - Allow work with partners, in small groups, in centers.
  - Alternate high- and low-interest tasks.
  - Use overhead projector when lecturing.
  - Allow child to sit closer to the teacher.

- Increase novelty especially into later time periods of longer tasks.
  - Make a game out of checking work.
  - Use games to over-learn rote material.

Excessive Activity

- Channel anxiety into acceptable and productive behavior.
  - Encourage directed movement in classrooms that is not disruptive.
  - Allow standing, especially during end of assignments.

- Use activity as reward.
  - Provide activity rewards (errand, clean board, organize teacher's desk, arrange chairs) for improvement.

- Use active responses in instruction.
  - Use teaching activities that encourage active responding (talking, moving, organizing, working at the board).
  - Encourage daily writing, painting, etc.
  - Teach child to ask questions that are on-topic.

Impulsivity

- Give the child substitute verbal or motor responses to make while waiting and where possible encourage day-dreaming or planning in the interim.
- Instruct the child on how to continue on easier parts of task (or do a substitute task) while waiting for teacher's help.
- Have the child underline or rewrite directions before beginning or give magic markers or colored pencils for child to underline directions or relevant information.
- Encourage doodling or play with clay, paper clips, pipe cleaners while waiting or listening to instruction.
- Encourage note taking (even just cue words).

If you teach, you are likely to have at least one student whose behavior is characterized by symptoms associated with inattention, hyperactivity, or impulsivity. Sometimes the student(s) will be identified with specific learning disabilities and sometimes with some other condition (e.g., ADD, ADHD). Sometimes the student will not be classified at all. Paying attention, listening, following directions, sitting still, playing quietly, waiting, concentrating, and remembering are difficult for many students, especially when what they are being asked to do competes with other more interesting things to do (as far as they are concerned). Take heart, for while there's plenty of interest and attention provided these students and their problems, there's not much mystery here. Good teaching is good teaching and stimulating, active lessons often go a long way in focusing the attention and controlling the activity of *many* of these students.

Strategies for Teaching Students with Learning Disabilities

Students with learning disabilities are those with performance in school that is not up to what is expected and for whom no other cause of this low achievement is evident. Students with school achievement problems have been around for a long time and a variety of teaching strategies have been proposed. Contemporary intervention practices stem from four major theoretical models: the medical model, the psychological process model, the behavioral model, and the cognitive/learning strategies model (Poplin, 1989). In general, treatment models evolve in response to how the problem of learning disabilities is conceptualized. Authorities within each model highlight different student characteristics. Early conceptualizations and corresponding treatment practices were based on the assumption that underlying causes of learning failure were neurological.

Then the behaviorists brought in the environmental perspective. They believed behaviors were learned and those behaviors could be altered through operant conditioning. More recent practices reflect an interrelated view. Regardless of whether the cause is neurological (e.g., intrinsic disorders, developmental lag), school-based (e.g., ineffective teaching), or environmental (e.g., "learned helplessness"), the student can be taught to be a more self-sufficient, independent learner.

Medical Model

During the late 1940s and 1950s, the medical model developed with an emphasis upon diagnosis and treatment of neurological symptoms. Diagnosis included: (1) thorough reviews of case histories, (2) extensive anecdotal records, (3) tests of neurological functioning (involuntary motor reflexes), (4) lists of characteristic symptoms, (5) intelligence tests, (6) electroencephalogram (EEG) tests, and, often, (7) the administration of medication. Students typically attended private facilities or institutions where they were taught in a structured, stimuli-free environment. These early programs misclassified students with learning disabilities as mentally

TABLE 4.7   Medical Interventions for Students with Learning Disabilities

Common Medications

Ritalin	Generic name is Methylphenidate. Intended effects include improved academic and behavorial performance, heightened ability to focus, increased attention span. Potential side effects include tolerance over a period of time, flushed face, dry mouth, nausea, and drowsiness.
Dexedrine	Generic name is Dextroamphetamine. Intended effects include less classroom restlessness, increased attention span and focusing capabilities, improved academic and behavorial performance. Potential side effects include loss of appetite, loss of sleep, headaches, stomachaches, dizziness, and apathy.
Cylert	Generic name is Pemoline. Intended effects include improved classroom behavior, improved academic performance, and increased attention span and focusing capabilities. Potential side effects include tolerance over a period of time, loss of sleep, flushed face, dry mouth, apathy, and drowsiness.

Dietary Programs

Elimination Diet	Controls food additives such as artificial flavors, preservatives, and coloring, thought to be responsible for hyperactivity and other behavior problems.
Sugar Control	Without dietary control, blood-sugar and energy levels drop after eating, creating problems in learning. Eating patterns are controlled to reduce effects of low blood-sugar levels.
Megavitamins	High dosages of vitamins are prescribed as a way to improve and control body chemisty.
Allergy Control	Removal of allergens in attempt to bring about changes in behavior that result from them.

retarded or brain-damaged (Wiederholt, 1974). The specific category of learning disabilities was unknown to these early researchers.

Interventions based on the medical model focus on correcting or compensating for physical or neurological problems. In the area of learning disabilities, this is evident primarily in the use of psychoactive medication and dietary control programs to improve students' behaviors in the classroom (see Table 4.8). Teachers' responsibilities in these programs are primarily evaluative. If a student in your room is on medication or a special diet to control his or her behavior, you should find out as much as possible about the expected effects and potential side effects of the treatment. You should provide frequent feedback to parents and physicians regarding changes in the student's behavior. You should also check with your principal and school nurse to determine whether any special procedures are required or guidelines available for teachers with students on medication or special diets.

Psychological Process Model

In the 1960s, emphasis shifted from the medical realm to the educational arena. This was due to three primary factors: (1) the recognition of the existence of students with disabling conditions within the public schools, (2) insufficient evidence that neurological examinations could reliably differentiate neurologically impaired youth from the normal population, and (3) a lack of evidence that neurological interventions alleviate school learning problems (Coles, 1989; Poplin, 1989). Treatment, however, continued to be given in controlled and structured pull-out programs or special classes. Emphasis was placed upon remediation of perceptual skills. Teachers were trained in methods for educating students with minimal brain dysfunction. They focused on changing behaviors described by such terms as distractibility, inadequate figure–ground discrimination, and impulsivity. Psychological process tests and remediation materials proliferated. In 1971, Newell C. Kephart described the student with perceptual disabilities in the preface of his book, *Slow Learner in the Classroom.*

> He does not see what we think we show him; he sees something different. He does not hear what we think we are saying to him. He does not make the connections as we do between bits of information which we think we are presenting in such a beautifully organized fashion. His central nervous system is treating these items in a different way.

Regular classroom teachers sometimes referred to these students as "lazy," "unwilling to try," and "inattentive"! Kephart attempted to dispel such negative references and to help teachers understand how these students perceive things in a different way. The shift in perspective from apathetic student to different type of learner advocated by Kephart was a major contribution to educating the public about learning disabilities.

Helmer Myklebust was recognized for his work in determining a relationship between neurological disorders and language development. He coined the term "psychoneurological learning disorders." This term refers to students with reading and other language impairments. He maintained that if the central nervous system is dysfunctioning, there may be a learning disorder of one or more of the following types (Myklebust, 1964; classroom problems by the authors).

1. Perceptual disturbance: Inability to identify, discriminate, and interpret stimuli. (Classroom problem: Poor recognition of everyday sensory experiences [e.g., reading letters, following directions].)
2. Disturbance of imagery: Inability to recollect common experiences although they have been perceived. (Classroom problem: Deficiencies in recalling words and other information provided.)
3. Disorders of symbolic processes: Inability to express experiences symbolically. (Classroom problem: Children with aphasia, dyslexia, dysgraphia, dyscalculia, and language disorders have difficulty using letters and numerals.)
4. Conceptualizing disturbances: Inability to generalize and categorize experiences. (Classroom problem: Problems classifying ideas.)

Teaching methods that evolved from this orientation emphasized three primary approaches to correcting processing problems (Lerner, 1985): (1) Strengthening the areas of processing deficits (e.g., students with visual processing problems were provided exercises designed to improve visual processing skills); (2) Using processing strengths to overcome problems (e.g., students with auditory processing problems were taught using primarily visual approaches); or (3) Strengthening weak areas and using strong areas simultaneously.

Behavioral Model

In the 1970s educators became disillusioned after seeing slight progress being made by students who were assessed and taught by psychological process model methods. Test results were unsuccessful in differentiating students with learning disabilities from their low-achieving peers, and psycholinguistic and perceptual process training models were unable to provide evidence of improved ability to perform academic tasks. The behavioral model emerged from a need for social skills training coupled with a general lack of academic achievement in regular classrooms.

Proponents of the behavioral model proposed direct instruction of academic and social skills. Prerequisite processing abilities were minimized in delivery of special education services. The remediation of inadequate sensory processes was replaced by a functional approach to teaching. The discrepancy clause written into the Individuals with Disabilities Education Act made processing tests less important in assessment. The discrepancy clause states that there must be a significant difference between potential and achievement. This is determined by administering tests of intelligence and tests of academic achievement and then comparing results between these two types of tests. Programmed texts, short-term objectives, task analysis, and criterion-referenced tests were developed as educational materials during this decade (Poplin, 1989). The purpose of these materials was to provide the classroom teacher with a functional, sequenced approach to academics.

Improving Behavior.   Norris G. Haring, while director of the Children's Rehabilitation Unit at the University of Kansas Medical Center, argued for the use of
behavior modification because it deals with observable behaviors and deempha-
sizes mental types of remediation. According to Haring, achievement oriented
behaviors increased when events (i.e., reinforcers) were arranged to follow targeted behaviors (Haring & Phillips, 1962). Careful arrangement of reinforcers,
Haring maintained, was a more practical way to teach students with learning
disabilities.

Ogden Lindsley taught the use of "precision teaching" in instructional settings while at the University of Kansas. According to Lindsley (1964), precision
teaching is a type of instruction that directly measures student performance on
a daily basis. Students are administered probes (i.e., skill samples) each day that
correspond to their instructional objectives. These frequent measurements provide a systematic method for planning instruction. In addition, Lindsley encouraged the use of contingency management, which is similar to behavior
modification. Contingency management is an "if–then" type of arrangement that
incorporates carefully selected reinforcers to follow specified target behaviors.

Behavior modification, precision teaching, and contingency management
were transferred from the laboratory setting into the classroom in an effort to
identify observable and measurable student behaviors. The goal was to teach by
contingency (i.e., an "if–then" type of reinforcement) rather than concentrating
upon undetectable neurological causes. By looking at task requirements, adding
contingencies, and observing the learners' responses, behaviorists believed that
students could be more effectively taught. Observable behaviors related to learning (such as staying on-task, being in seat, or raising one's hand to talk) were
targeted for reinforcement.

Improving Academic Achievement.   During the 1970s, studies of brain functioning, which were characteristic of the medical model, were replaced by measurements of academic achievement. Persons attempting to instruct students with
learning disabilities were teachers, not clinicians. Academic achievement was the
primary concern of educators. Further support for the academic point of view
was provided by the development and early utilization of standardized tests
which, though imperfect, could measure academic skills (e.g., KeyMath Diagnostic Arithmetic Test [1971], Gates–MacGinitie Reading Tests [1972]). The academic model rejected the concept of mastering mental processing skills as
prerequisites to academic achievement. Many of the instruments developed to
measure mental processing abilities were proved inadequate (Myers & Hammill,
1982). The academic achievement camp remained the primary force in teaching
students with learning disabilities in the 1980s. The notion that instruction for
students with learning disabilities should focus upon acquisition of academic
skills and the application of these skills into everyday functioning skills became
widely accepted among special educators. Still, the academic remediation approach had its limitations. It was characterized by critics as teacher-directed and
student-passive. Critics maintained that behavioral treatments bred student de-

pendency. Poplin (1989), for instance, felt that students should develop autonomous ways of learning in order to adequately prepare for self-sufficiency after school.

Cognitive Model

Teaching students how to learn, how to manage their own behaviors in the learning environment, and how to generalize information from one setting to another is a present-day emphasis in learning disabilities. Initiated in the early 1970s, this approach is called *metacognition*. The metacognition movement was derived from previous research in psychological processing dysfunctions, information processing, cognitive psychology, metacognitive theory, tenets of general education, and self-reinforcement principles in behaviorism. Metacognition ties together the past with the present. Cognitive strategists recommend that students be taught "strategy behaviors" necessary to perform academic tasks.

Cognitive strategists emphasize a self-monitoring approach to learning. Self-questioning, self-checking, self-correcting, self-evaluating, and self-reinforcing are components of cognitive strategies. Students are taught such learning skills as outlining, organizing time, memorizing, studying, and generalizing conceptual information from one setting to another. Teaching students "how" to learn is paramount (Reid & Hresko, 1981). Presently, two cognitive/learning strategy models predominate: cognitive behavior modification and the cognitive strategy model.

Cognitive Behavior Modification. Donald Meichenbaum at the University of Waterloo in Ontario, Canada, is a primary contributor to the cognitive behavior modification (CBM) approach. Meichenbaum (1977) emphasized teaching students a variety of self-instructional strategies (e.g., self-questioning, self-checking), a variety of self-guidance strategies (e.g., "What do I have to do? I have to find the main idea in this paragraph."), and a variety of executive strategies (e.g., reflection about one's own array of strategies and selecting the strategy most appropriate to the task at hand). The goal is to train students to use verbal statements and images that prompt, direct, and maintain their behaviors (Lovitt, 1989).

In Meichenbaum's "What's my problem? What's my plan?" problem-solving program, students are taught to verbalize statements of self-correction, self-evaluation, and self-reinforcement (Meichenbaum & Goodman, 1971). Hallahan and Kauffman (1982) outlined Meichenbaum's self-instructional procedure:

1. *Cognitive modeling.* The adult model performs a task while verbally instructing himself.
2. *Overt, self-guidance.* The student performs the same task by imitating instructions spoken by the model.
3. *Faded overt self-guidance.* The student softly repeats the instructions spoken by the model.

4. *Covert self-instruction.* The student performs the task while silently instructing himself.

Tarver (1986) theorizes that gradual fading of speech from overt (outward) to covert (inward) will change the student's spoken language into the inner language that typically regulates thought. According to cognitive behavior modification advocates, modeling and imitations of inner language improve thinking skills.

Cognitive Strategies. Another type of metacognitive approach teaches such study skills techniques as scanning, outlining, taking notes, and time management. The model is derived from cognitive psychology and information processing literature. The cognitive strategy model incorporates theories based on student learning styles, cognitive styles, thinking skills, and cognitive behavior modification research. Torgesen (1977) hypothesized that passive learning is a characteristic of many students with learning disabilities. Thus, cognitive strategy researchers addressed how students approach learning.

A descriptive scheme was devised by Kinsbourne and Caplan (1979) for distinguishing between learning disorders of cognitive "style" and those of cognitive "power." The first, those of cognitive style, refer to children characterized as having attention deficits. These students exhibit difficulties with impulsivity, distractibility, and other symptomatic behaviors of inattention. In contrast, students who display disorders of cognitive power experience difficulty grasping particular types of concepts or remembering certain kinds of information. Examples of cognitive "power" problems include dyslexia (reading disability), dyscalculia (mathematical disability), and perceptual–motor impairment (Bohline, 1985).

Knowing how one knows, metacognition, is also stressed in the cognitive strategy model (Wong, 1979). Brown (1978) summarized metacognitive processes as including the identification and analysis of the task at hand, the reflection on what one does and does not know about the situation that may be necessary for solving the problem, the designing of a plan for dealing with the problem, and the monitoring of one's progress toward solving the problem. Other assumptions in the cognitive strategy model are: (1) the learning strategies students need are relatively stable across learners and tasks, (2) the act of verbalizing a strategy assists learning, and (3) knowing how one learns is advantageous to further learning (Poplin, 1989). The following guidelines detail Meichenbaum's (1985) techniques for teaching metacognitive strategies:

1. Teachers need to adopt metacognitive outlooks. They should have the attitude that self-instructional thinking skills exist and can be taught.
2. It is important that teachers be aware of their own metacognitive skills and make students aware of these. Teachers let students down when they fail to assist them in developing the metacognitive skills that they themselves find effective.

3. Teachers need to conduct a task analysis of the skills to be taught. This requires reducing the desired metacognitive skills into a series of simpler subskills.
4. Teachers must be aware that generalization of the learned metacognitive skills will not simply occur; learning opportunities that cut across various settings (e.g., home, community, work) must be employed.

A major criticism of strategies for teaching students with learning disabilities (Table 4.10) has been the lack of generalization and maintenance skills (Lovitt, 1989; Poplin, 1989). What is taught in one training site or classroom has not been proved to carry over or generalize sufficiently to other settings or circumstances. When skills do not carry over, maintenance, or sustained use of them diminishes. Some suggestions for assuring generalization include tasks that place responsibility for learning on the student. These include (1) student self-instruction, (2) student self-rehearsal, (3) practice in multiple settings, (4) dividing skills into manageable portions, (5) student self-monitoring, (6) teacher feedback about performance, (7) skills taught to mastery level, and (8) teacher reinforcement of skill acquisition.

Contemporary thinking about best practices for teaching students with learning disabilities combines academics with cognitive learning strategies. In other words, it is important that teachers focus upon academic skills; however, this can be effectively accomplished through teaching students how to learn, how to manage their own behaviors in school, and how to generalize information

TABLE 4.8   Suggestions for Teaching Students with Learning Disabilities

1. Teach the student to organize materials and assignments. Use lists to establish work priorities. Teach study skills.
2. Help the student to think through steps in completing a task. Use questions such as the following as a guide: "How much time do I have to complete a task? What materials will I need? Who can I ask for help?"
3. Overlook such minor errors in written work as spelling and handwriting. Emphasize quality of ideas and perseverance.
4. Provide right hemispheric activities such as art, drama, and images to represent ideas. Don't overemphasize such left hemispheric functions as verbal reasoning, logic, and sequential arrangement of ideas.
5. Provide emotional support to help ease the frustration of a learning disability.
6. Provide options during tests such as untimed or oral exams. List answers to multiple-choice questions vertically rather than horizontally.
7. Give clear and concrete directions. Have the student repeat instructions back to you.
8. Link new ideas to the student's experience.
9. Use multisensory materials. Repeat concepts, but use novel presentations rather than drill.
10. Collaborate with parents.

from one setting to another. Some suggestions for teaching students with learning disabilities are presented in Table 4.8.

Young Adults

It was once thought that the problems encountered by children with learning disabilities ended upon reaching adulthood. It has become evident that a learning disability persists as individual lives evolve.

Up until 1960 there was little research, limited personnel, and few teacher training programs specifically for youngsters with learning disabilities in the public schools. But, due to parent advocacy groups, the Association for Children with Learning Disabilities was formed. This eventually led to the Specific Learning Disabilities Act of 1969, which authorized teacher training and research. Finally, in 1975, the passage of Public Law 94–142 occurred, which federally mandated special services for learning disabled studuents (Smith, 1983).

It was not until the 1970s that the need for providing college programs for students with learning disabilities was recognized. Gertrude Webb at Curry College in Milton, Massachusetts, was one of the first to develop college services for those with learning disabilities. Her pioneer efforts and the development of the Program of Assistance in Learning at Curry College inspired other colleges and universities to develop similar programs (Mangrum & Strichart, 1984).

For many students who manage to survive high school academics, college is increasingly becoming a goal (Osman, 1979; Ramsey, 1996; Treible, 1996). As stated previously, the belief at the onset of the learning disabilities era was that these children would eventually outgrow their disability. As it became obvious that this condition was ongoing, more pressure was put on colleges to serve their needs.

Section 504 of the Rehabilitation Act of 1973 (P.L. 93–112) has had vast importance for college learning disabilities programs. The requirement states that colleges receiving federal assistance may not discriminate against any qualified individual.

> No otherwise qualified handicapped individual in the United States, shall solely by reason of handicap, be excluded from participation in, be denied the benefits of, or be subjected to discrimination under any program or activity receiving federal financial assistance.

The Americans with Disabilities Act (P.L. 101–336) extended these provisions into publicly supported, as well as private, schools.

Characteristics

The characteristics and special needs of learning disabled young adults in college differ little from the characteristics and needs they had when much younger.

The domains discussed in this section include: cognitive, language, perceptual motor, academic, work/study habits, and social/affective.

Cognitive.   The college student with learning disabilities may have difficulties with sequencing, understanding abstract concepts, reasoning, short- and long-term memory, organization, and generalizing (Mangrum & Strichart, 1984). Difficulties are often experienced in processing information. These can occur in the receptive, associative, or expressive learning modalities (Ramsey, 1995).

Language.   The weaknesses children with learning disabilities experience in receiving, processing, and acquiring language skills continues to be a problem (Smith, 1983). The young adult may have trouble grasping what is spoken, expressing appropriate vocabulary, understanding words in context, clear and precise written expression, sentence structure, punctuation, and written composition (Mangrum & Strichart, 1984).

Perceptual Motor.   Educators working with students with learning disabilities at colleges report that perceptual motor problems continue. These students may have trouble locating information and performing tasks that require motor coordination. One particular problem they may encounter is the form in which tests may be given. For example, tests that require students to fill in circles or to grid in answers may penalize students who actually know the information that is being tested but cannot perform the fine motor tasks required to show evidence of their knowledge (Hobbs, 1982).

Academic.   Because of deficits in basic skill areas, the student with learning disabilities may have difficulties reading required material, spelling, handwriting, and math (Mangrum & Strichart, 1984).

Work and Study Habits.   Smith (1979) reports that the college student with learning disabilities may continue to have problems organizing and budgeting time, completing work and getting work started, and establishing long- and short-term goals. This student may also suffer from test anxiety (Mangrurn & Strichart, 1984). Note taking may present a serious problem as well (Roberts, 1983).

Social and Affective.   The social difficulties experienced by youngsters with learning disabilities continue to follow them into adulthood. They have difficulties establishing good relationships with others, reading body language, expressing their own feelings, and relating to authority figures (Mangrum & Strichart, 1984). Social implications of behavior problems extend beyond academic programs. A national survey revealed that 44 percent of incarcerated adolescents had a history of learning disabilities (McConaughty, 1985).

Likewise, young people with learning disabilities frequently suffer from poor self-concepts and tend to feel insecure and frustrated with life. They may have difficulties meeting responsibilities, curbing impulsive behavior, and maintaining motivation (Mangrum & Strichart, 1984).

Alternative Strategies

Mandates of the Rehabilitation Act of 1973 prohibit colleges from requiring that students disclose disabilities. But students with learning disabilities are encouraged to bring their learning problems to the attention of college officials in order to receive appropriate services. Some of the services offered students with learning disabilities include:

1. Assessing students to determine deficit areas, in order to provide appropriate services.
2. Using tape recorders for lectures.
3. Providing students with an outline as an aid for organizing content.
4. Photocopying class notes.
5. Allowing testing modifications (e.g., administered orally, additional time, less items).
6. Purchasing textbooks in advance so they can begin reading earlier.
7. Using taped textbooks.
8. Securing tutors to help students understand and master the content of subject areas.
9. Having another student take notes.
10. Offering special courses to students according to their needs. These might include writing courses, typing, study skills, or instruction in college survival.
11. Using microcomputers with word processing programs. Some also have word-check programs, which would help with spelling errors when writing research papers and other composition projects. (Ramsey, 1995b, 1997)

Looking to the Future

There needs to be an ongoing effort to provide services within colleges to young adults with learning disabilities. These services need to be focused upon helping them cope more effectively with academic learning and study techniques, as well as vocational preparation concerns. Social skills interventions need to emphasize interactions with instructors, peers, and personal development. Maintaining effective communication is essential (Ramsey, 1997)

Summary

The search for appropriate terminology that would identify learning disabilities continues to challenge educators. The first terms used to describe this population

Table 4.9   Suggestions for Faculty Who Teach Students with Learning Disabilities

1. Provide students with a detailed course syllabus the first week of class.
2. Clearly spell out expectations before the course begins (e.g., grading, material to be covered, due dates).
3. Start each lecture with an outline of material to be covered that period. At the conclusion of class, briefly summarize key points.
4. Speak directly to students, and use gestures and natural expressions to convey further meaning.
5. Present new or technical vocabulary on the chalkboard or use a student handout. Terms should be used in context to convey greater meaning.
6. Add stories and examples to illustrate or provide examples to information being taught.
7. Role play, act out, draw, or utilize some other media or activity to build meaning to conceptual material.
8. Give assignments BOTH orally and in written form to avoid confusion.
9. Announce reading assignments well in advance for students who are using taped materials.
10. Help students find community resources, like The Talking Book Center (affiliated with the National Organization for the Blind) where they can get tape-recorded reading materials (e.g., textbooks, newspapers, magazines).
11. Facilitate use of tape recorders for notetaking by allowing students to tape lectures.
12. Provide study questions for exams that demonstrate the format, as well as the content, of the test. Explain what constitutes a good answer and why.
13. If necessary, allow students with learning disabilities to demonstrate mastery of course material using alternative methods (e.g., extended time limits for testing, oral exams, taped exams, individually proctored exams in a separate room).
14. Let students use a simple calculator, scratch paper, a thesaurus, and/or a speller's dictionary during exams and formal writing exercises.
15. Provide adequate opportunities for questions and answers, including review sessions.
16. Modify the amount of practice work required when needed.
17. Be sure students are being taught by you, or by someone else at the college, skills relating to how they can more efficiently and effectively:
    (1) study,
    (2) manage time,
    (3) take notes,
    (4) proofread their work,
    (5) take a multiple-choice, true-false, or essay test,
    (6) cope with stress, and
    (7) engage in decision-making and problem-solving.
18. Encourage (or require) students to use campus support services (e.g., pre-registration, assistance in ordering taped textbooks, alternative testing arrangements, specialized study aids, peer support groups, diagnostic consultation, study skills training, and academic tutorial assistance.

emphasized medical and neurological processing deficits. The most popular and widely accepted name was "minimal brain dysfunction," or "MBD."

In 1962, Kirk suggested the name "learning disabilities." This new classification was intended to distinguish persons with learning disorders and average intelligence from other exceptionality categories, especially mental retardation.

Table 4.10 Suggestions for College Students with Learning Disabilities

1. If you know that you have a learning disability, or if you think that you may have a specific learning disability, but aren't sure, contact the student support services office on campus. Get information about evaluation services and procedures.
2. If you know that you have a learning disability, talk with your instructors before the academic term begins.
3. Set realistic goals and priorities for coursework.
4. Keep ONE calendar with all relevant dates, assignments, and appointments.
5. Use a tape recorder during lectures. Selectively tape-record key points using the pause" switch.
6. Listen to the tape as soon after class as possible to refresh your memory, then reorganize and if necessary, rewrite sections of your notes.
7. Make notes of any questions you might have so that they can be answered before the next exam,
8. Sit toward the front of the classroom to maximize your eye contact and to reduce distractions.
9. Estimate how long a given class assignment will take, generally planning on two hours outside of class for every hour in class. Build in study breaks to prevent fatigue
10. Seek campus support help early in the academic term in order to stay on track in your classes.
11. Prepare for tests and quizzes with a study buddy or form a small group for study.
12. Take advantage of the tutorial services offered on your campus.
13. Go to study sessions if they are offered.
14. Utilize talking books and audiotapes of books, class discussions, and lectures.

Many students were identified as mentally retarded during the 1940s and 1950s, because the category "learning disabilities" didn't exist. The classification was adopted following Kirk's use of the term to link together students with average intelligence and presumed mild neurological disorders.

The current federal definition of learning disabilities was formulated in 1968 by the National Advisory Committee on Handicapped Children. This definition served as the basis for the Learning Disabilities Act of 1969, and was subsequently included in the Individuals with Disabilities Education Act. Thus, this definition is widely used in providing appropriate public education to students who are eligible for services because of a learning disability. The operational part of the federal definition is referred to as the discrepancy clause.

The prevalence of learning disabilities is reported by states to be between 2 and 5 percent of the school-aged population. The number of existing cases eludes accuracy because methods and criteria used for identification differ from state to state. In lieu of data reported by respective states showing otherwise, federal estimates have remained at 2 percent.

The etiology of learning disabilities has been classified into two groups: organic and environmental. The majority of students identified as having learning disabilities have no demonstrable organic problem, thus their causes are assumed to be environmentally based. These cases result from inadequate or negative environmental factors, including poor instruction and a schooling system that makes few allowances for developmental differences within like age-groups of children. The case for organic-based learning disabilities is much stronger for students with specific, localized conditions such as dyslexia, dysgraphia, and dysnomia. These conditions are more universally known, described, and documented.

Characteristics of students with learning disabilities are classified by developmental domains of functioning. These functioning domains include cognitive skills, academic achievement, language and communication development, perceptual and perceptual–motor skills, and social–adaptive skills. Students with learning disabilities demonstrate learning difficulties in at least one of these functioning domains.

From the 1940s to the 1990s, treatment models evolved in response to theories about the causes of learning disabilities. For example, the medical approach of the 1940s and 1950s advocated the use of heavily structured and controlled learning environments to offset presumed neurological deficits. Programs were developed during the 1960s that attempted to ameliorate perceptual deficits. This approach is called the psychological process approach. Interaction between the learner and the environment was the major emphasis during the 1970s. This is the behavioral approach. Arranging the environment, reinforcing appropriate behavior, and using systematic instructional approaches in the teaching of academic skills are components of this model. Contemporary thinking, brought over from the 1980s into the 1990s, states that it is important to teach academics, but it is also necessary to teach students how to learn, how to manage their own behaviors in school, and how to generalize information from one setting to another. Cognitive/learning strategies models emphasize the need to produce self-sufficient, independent learners for a lifetime.

Activities

1. What are some teaching strategies that David's fourth grade teacher used to help accomodate his learning? Why were these helpful? What other interventions could she have used?

2. Examine typical reading and spelling patterns of students with visual or auditory processing difficulties listed in Tables 4.6 and 4.7. Do you reconize any of David's learning problems? Are there other processing patterns that David's teacher might find helpful to identify?

3. Arrange to speak to several special educators who work with students with learning disabilities. Ask them to describe the ways in which a learning disability is manifested by their students. How do they function in school compared to regular grade-level peers?

4. Ask the educators in the second activitiy to discuss strategies and instructional approaches that they use with students who have learning disabilities? Ask the educators to talk about special interventions that they would recommend for these students in general and special education classrooms. What recommendations would each of them make about teaching social, academic, and study skills?

5. As an extension to activities two and three, ask the special educators to describe ways in which each of them works with other educators, support personnel, and parents. How do they collaborate effectively with general classroom teachers and support personnel like guidance counselors, social workers, school nurses, and building principals? What things do they do to build relationships with parents?

6. Look for journals that discuss techniques for working with students with learning disabilities, like the *Journal of Learning Disabilities, Learning Disabilities Quarterly, Learning Disability Focus,* and *Remedial and Special Education.* Read several articles from different journals if possible, and discuss techniques about working with students with learning disabilities in general and special education classrooms. Talk about approaches suggested for academic and social skils training. Discuss suggestions about collaboration with other educators, support personnel, and parents.

7. There are two major professional organizations as well as a major parent-professional organization in the field of learning disabilities: The Division for Learning Disabilities of the Council for Exceptional Children (1920 Association Drive, Reston, Virginia, 22091); the Council for Learning Disabilities (P.O. Box 40303, Overland Park, Kansas 66204); and the Learning Disabilities Association (4156 Library Road, Pittsburgh, Pennsylvania, 15234). Write to these organizations for their directories and literature. Determine the purposes, membership, and services offered by these organizations.

8. Find out if there are active state and local branches of these national organizatons in your area. If there is a local organization, arrange to visit one of those meetings. Try to determine concerns that the group is currently addressing in your community. Ask a representative from the group to visit you class and speak about the organizations's purpose, membership composition, and service.

9. Join the Student Council for Exceptional Children. Find out when and where the annual state CEC conference is going to be held, and suggest that the local chapter send representatives. Volunteer to attend as a representative, and while at the conference, attend the meeting for the Division for Learning Disabilities.

10. Write a proposal to give a presentation at the state CEC conference. Share teaching aids that you have made in your methods course, or student teaching. Practicing teachers and other teachers-in-training enjoy seeing and hearing about new ideas. Remember that this gives you a "foot in the door" for an interview for a teaching position upon graduating, as many people within your state will remember you. It also gives you something of a professional nature that you have done to list on your resume or vita!

5 Overview of Students with Mild Disabilities

Advance Questions

Answer the following questions as you read this chapter:

1. What is the difference between noncategorical and cross-categrorical identification of students with mild disabilities?
2. Students with mild disabilities have which generalities in common?

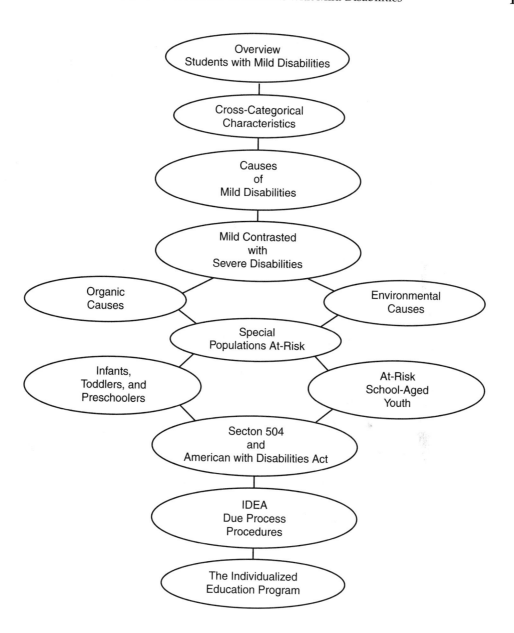

3. How do the learning and behavioral disabilities of students considered mild versus severe compare?

4. How does serving students in special education under IDEA compare with providing protections given by Section 504 of the Rehabilitation Act and the Americans with Disabilities Act for students with disabilities who are not eligible for special education?

5. What are organic and what are environmental causes of mild learning and behavioral disabilities?

6. Who is served under Part B of the Individual with Disabilities Education Act? Who receives Public Law 99–457, Part H services?

7. Who are the special populations at-risk of educational and school failure? Describe these two main groups of students.

8. In which instructional settings are students with mild intellectual, learning, and behavioral disabilities primarily taught?

9. Where might a teacher or parent locate social programs for students at-risk?

10. Explain the due process procedure that must be followed when making decisions abut who will receive services in special education?

11. List student behaviors required for success in the general education classroom.

12. What are some effective strategies for modifying classroom instruction?

Students with mild disabilities are those who are served in special education in the categories of learning disabilities, mild mental retardation, or behavior disorders. These students are referred to as having a mild disability because many of their special learning needs and characteristics go undetected until they reach school age. The majority are enrolled full time within regular education classrooms or receive special services in a resource room one to several periods a day. Whether you are a general or special education teacher, you will have these students in your classroom.

Tale of Three Students: Vignettes

Karim's third-grade teacher reported that his academic abilities were significantly delayed. In reading, Karim had difficulty blending letter sounds and recalling content from reading and listening. Mathematics was also a problem for Karim, although he experienced some success with basic facts. He did have, however, difficulty mastering reasoning and problem-solving skills. His teacher estimated that he was two to three years behind his classmates in academics. Karim's teacher also reported that he had poor social skills. Working cooperatively with classmates and controlling impulses were two areas in which Karim experienced difficulty. His teacher stated that Karim's "immaturity" and social withdrawal were a source of frustration to her. His IQ was sixty-nine. Karim has been identified as a student with mild mental retardation.

Jack was in constant trouble because he did not turn in assignments or complete work in class. His fifth-grade teacher reported that his academic performance suffered due to his incomplete work. Jack was a source of frustration to his teacher and family. Although she tried to handle most discipline problems herself, his teacher sent Jack to the principal's office an average of three times per week. His teacher described Jack as "sullen and hostile." When he was in these moods, he talked out in class, refused to work, and became disruptive. Jack had been involved in several fights in school and on the bus; one was enough to get him suspended from school. Jack was identified as a student with a behavior disorder.

José was eight years old. His IQ was 110. His teacher reported that José had average intelligence and a good understanding of spoken language. He was extremely verbal and often engaged in long conversations on a variety of topics; however, José's performance in spelling and written language was comparable to students who were three years younger than he. He was unable to reproduce letters legibly. Although he readily recognized each letter of the alphabet, he had difficulty both remembering what the letters looked like and executing the motor patterns necessary to form each letter. When José was given a set of letters to copy, his written product was often illegible. José's fine motor coordination and memory difficulties extended into the area of arithmetic. He understood mathematical concepts but had difficulty reproducing numbers and remembering basic facts. His academic performance in math was approximately two years below his peers. José has been identified as a student with learning disability.

Answer the following problem-solving questions about the three students in the vignettes, Karim, Jack, and José.

1. Can you identify differences between the three students?
2. What are the social and adaptive differences shown by Karim, Jack, and José?
3. How could these learning and behavior differences influence decisions regarding the least restrictive environment and an appropriate educational plan?
4. Are Karim, José, and Jack more similar or different in terms of their educational needs?

Cross-Categorical Characteristics of Students

Special education labors under the weight of two contradictory beliefs. The first is that each student is unique in his or her individual learning needs. That is why all students are required by law to have an individual education program. The second belief is that there are homogeneous groups of mild disabilities that can be described, classified, and remediated. This typology assumption led to the formulation and separation of mild mental retardation, behavior disorders, and learning disabilities into distinct categories of mild disabilities. We can see the results of this bipolar perspective in the debate over whether students with mild special needs are best served in special education or general education programs.

TABLE 5.1   Generally Accepted Categorical Descriptions of Students with Mild Disabilities

	Mildly Retarded	Emotionally Disturbed (ED) Behavioral Disordered (BD)	Learning Disabled
Cognitive	Subaverage intellectually. Eligibility criteria/2 SDs below the mean (50–75 IQ); often demonstrate short memory span, difficulty transferring learning, inability to project beyond the present situation, poor reasoning skills, poor abstract thinking, attention deficits.	Average to low-average intelligence scores; behavior interfaces with test scores.	Average or above average intellectually. Mental processing dysfunctions affect thinking and learning abilities.
Academic	Delayed academically. Demonstrates expectancy of failure, has slow learning rate, repeats unsuccessful strategies or behaviors, does not attempt new tasks.	Behavior interfaces with school achievement. Weak, average, or superior academic performance.	Have processing deficits. Lack generalization skills, demonstrate learned helplessness, work slowly on tasks, may or may not have developed coping skills.
Adaptive	Eligibility criteria specifies poor adaptive skills. Hyperactive, low tolerance/frustration, easily fatigued, moral judgement comparable to mental age. Delayed community-family adaptive skills.	Discipline problem. May have anxiety, fears, physical pain. May be unhappy or depressed.	Learn to compensate for deficiencies. Dependency needs. Outer-directed.

TABLE 5.1   continued

Social	Socially and emotionally immature. Unfavorable self-concept. Lacking in self-esteem. Susceptible to peer influences.	Poor peer relations. Disruptive behavior/conduct problems. May be shy/withdrawn or aggressive. Disturbing behavior demonstrated in various settings. Often elicit emotional responses in others.	Lack social insightfulness. Poor self-esteem. Susceptible to peer influences. Often feel inferior but want acceptance.
Perceptual-Motor	Delayed developmental skills affect perception and motor abilities.	Intact perceptual and motor skills generally.	Impaired perceptual and motor abilities. Eye–hand coordination problems. Awkward. May lack orientation skills.
Language	Speech/language delayed or deficient. Poor social communication.	Spoken content problems (e.g., profane, argumentative, disrespectful language).	Receptive, integrative, and expressive language difficulties. Deficient processing abilities. Poor social communication.
General Characteristics	Manifest problems adapting to the environment. Lag behind in most academic areas. Perform best physical/motoric skills.	Display behavior that is persistent and incompatible with cultural norms to a significant extent. May have concomitant academic deficits.	Manifest specific learning problems in one or two academic areas. May have concomitant negative behavioral manifestations.

Note: These characteristics have historically been attributed to each category. Individual students' profiles will vary considerably.

Numerous leaders in the field have suggested that we use noncategorical and cross-categorical placement options for students with mild disabilities (Reynolds and Balow, 1971). The two terms are similar, but there are also differences. Noncategorical refers to generic or broad-based special education programs (e.g., student with special needs). No categorical assignment is made. Cross-categorical means that a student may have been found eligible for special services because of any one of the three mild disabilities—mild mental retardation, learning disabilities, or behavior disorders. Because their educational needs are similar, these students are not separated from each other for purposes of special education instruction. In this book we explain the characteristics of each category of mild disability, but you will note that all chapters discuss educational interventions that are cross-categorical.

The use of noncategorical and cross-categorical references to students with mild disabilities is based on the belief that utilizing such terms as "student with special needs" or "student with mild disability" reduces the stigma associated with such terms as "mild mental retardation" or "behavior disorder." Historically, certain characteristics have been attributed to students with mild disabilities. Table 5.1 shows generally accepted categorical descriptions of students with mild disabilities. In reality these generalized characteristics are not descriptive of any individual student. They are general characteristics that are representative of *all* individuals identified as having a mild intellectual, learning, or behavioral disability.

It's reasonable to categorize students with developmental disabilities (e.g., autism) because at the more severe level, learning and behavioral characteristics, etiological roots, and instructional approaches are more readily identifiable. But at the mild level, there is overlap between learning and behavioral characteristics of students.

Gallagher (1972) contends that there is a price that must be paid when we label a student mildly disabled, but without the label, we will never know what would have happened to the individual in the absence of special education services. Of course, placement may or may not lead to effective treatment. Another thought expressed by Gallagher that finds truth in contemporary practices is that special education placement may occur as an "exclusionary process masquerading as a remedial process." There are those general classroom teachers who refer their most troublesome cases to special education and ask that they be given no further responsibility for these youngsters.

Domains of functioning for any child during school include cognitive, academic, social, and language skills. Table 5.2 identifies instructional strategies for students with mild disabilities across the three high prevalence categories of mild retardation, emotional disturbance, and learning disabilities. This categorical view of students with mild disabilities begins to unravel when researchers investigate what happens after special education placement.

Hallahan and Kauffman (1982) state that categorically differentiated instruction matched to characteristics is largely nonexistent. The authors give an example:

TABLE 5.2   Summary of Instructional Strategies by Functional Domains

	Mild Mental Retardation	Learning Disability	Behavior Disorder
Cognitive	Identify stage of cognitive development. Match teaching style to student level of development and learning style.	Teach metacognitive, "how to learn" skills. Teach study skills.	Provide decentering activities to teach students to share perceptions of others.
Academic	Provide early childhood education. Teach thinking/problem solving skills. Teach functional/career skills.	Teach students self-monitoring strategies. Analyze products and performance for learning disability clues.	Focus on enhancing motivation to learn. Provide emotional support Build on student experiences.
Language	Emphasize intuitive skills and high interest in reading. Use systematic analysis of skills and progress. Respect cultural differences.	Utilize alternatives to phonics such as whole language and right hemispheric activities. Identify specific language processing deficits and teach coping skills.	Emphasize congruent communication: "sane" and "I" messages. Accept student feelings; promote expression of feelings.
Social	Emphasize activities to build confidence and self-esteem. Teach social skills.	Teach social perception skills. Teach social behavioral skills.	Establish a systematic behavior management program. Teach self-control skills.

Anyone, who happens to look in on each of three special classes or resource rooms for mildly disturbed, mildly retarded, or learning disabled children is not likely to see very different teaching techniques being used. . . .The appropriate teaching strategies and the materials used are very nearly the same for each of the three areas. (Hallahan & Kauffman, 1982, 435)

Similarly, Ysseldyke et al. (1982) suggest that a student diagnosed as having a learning disability may *not* require instructional treatment different from that of youngsters with diagnoses of mild mental retardation or behavior disorders. They also state that many students without disabilities can benefit from specialized instruction designed for students with mild disabilities.

Miller and Davis (1982) suggest ways in which alterations of present categorical arrangements could occur. They recommend: (1) redefining existing exceptionality categories, (2) creating novel structures in which existing categories could be expanded or limited, or (3) establishing a category-free approach. Most advocates of a noncategorical approach have *not* suggested that *all* classification systems be rejected because without classification systems, it is difficult to distinguish students with mild learning disorders from hard-to-teach, unmotivated, or underachieving students. In order to receive special education services a student should have an identifiable disability.

Massachusetts is one state that instituted a noncategorical approach to identifying students with special needs. The result was rampant referrals and the highest percentage of students with special needs in the nation (U.S. Department of Education, 1990). During the mid 1980s in some urban areas, over 20 percent of the entire Massachusetts school population received special education. In 1992 Massachusetts regulations were changed to require school systems identify a specific disability before a student receives special education. The challenge for educators is to accurately identify students with mild disabilities and ensure that students are placed in programs that enhance rather than stifle learning.

Some generalities can be made about students with mild learning disorders—who they are and who they are not.

Students with mild mental retardation, learning disabilities, and behavior disorders are the largest subgroup of students receiving special education services.

Student counts are taken annually in each state across the nation, and these data are reported to the Department of Education as FTE (Full Time Equivalence) statements. States can identify and serve up to 12 percent of their school-age (5 to 17 years old) population in special education. This cap is stated in IDEA (Rothstein, 1995). Figure 5.1 illustrates placements of students with disabilities between 1989–90 and 1993–94.

Since 1976, a prevalence figure of 11 to 12 percent for special education students out of a possible 100 percent of the total school population has been adhered to by the U.S. Department of Education. We estimate that of the number of students identified, those with mild disabilities are approximately 75 to 90 percent of the total special education population. The population of students with mild disabilities receiving special education constitutes approximately 9 percent of the total school population.

Students with mild disabilities are served during the school-aged years.

FIGURE 5.1   Percentage of All Students with Disabilities Ages 6–21 Served in Different Educational Environments: 1989–90 to 1993–94

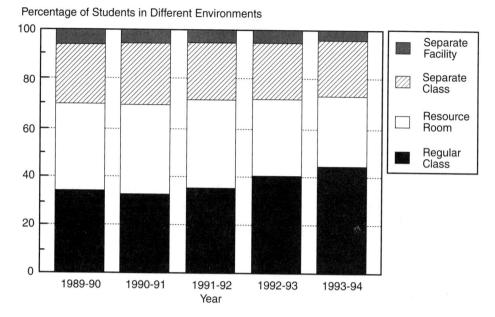

Source: U.S. Department of Education, Office of Special Education Programs, Data Analysis System (DANS).

Mild disabilities are unrecognizable before entering and after exiting school. The physical appearance of these students is like that of students without disabilities. There are no differences in facial features or body dimensions. Students with mild disabilities are, in almost all respects, normal children who have encountered learning problems. Consequently, they remain unidentified until entry into public school and they mesh into the mainstream of society upon leaving school. Acquaintances and employers usually don't make a connection between social and work difficulties and the fact that at one time, an individual received special education services. After all, most people exhibit some minor skill deficits in particular situations and under certain circumstances.

The categories mild retardation, behavior disordered, and learning disabled are unreliable.

Education is not precise in pinpointing students with mild disabilities. Consider a scenario in which a virus would be identified by different criteria in the various states. An infected child traveling cross-country would be diagnosed as sick in one state and healthy in the next. Despite the difference in diagnosis the child would still be ill.

This is the problem with mild disabilities. Because there are no consistent state criteria, some students are accurately diagnosed while others are misevaluated as false positives or false negatives. A false positive means that some students are incorrectly identified as having a mild disability, whereas, with a false negative, some students who have a mild disability are overlooked.

Unreliable evaluations are complicated by the diversity of behaviors that are subsumed under the category learning disabled. Everybody has trouble in school at one time or another. As James Ysseldyke, an authority on special education assessment practices, has pointed out, at one time or another eighty percent of all American schoolchildren could be identified as having a learning disability!

Similar troublesome problems are observed across these categories when we must determine which mild disability category fits a student. An analogy could be that of a preschool child attempting to put geometric shapes into the right holes of a container. When the particular objects do not fit into any of the holes, he just pounds on them or pushes harder to make them go in. Perhaps a hypothetical student with mild disabilities is like a square shape (Figure 5.2). We

*"Oh dear, some of these kids don't **fit** into the categories."*
"No problem——we'll just stuff 'em in."

FIGURE 5.2 School Category Machine

Illustration by Lois Creech

try to shove her into the circle representative of mild mental retardation, or, seeing at least two straight sides, we try to push her into the triangle representative of learning disabilities. If that does not work, then we try the behavior rectangle because, even though it does not have all sides equal, it does have four sides like a square. The child may not have the exact dimensions of the category, but she is similar enough to all three that we figure if we just try hard enough, she can make a fit with one of them.

This analogy is much like the example given by Blackman in his assessment of "negative school labels." On the television news program *60 Minutes* a local sheriff was questioned about the probable guilt of a particular individual (the accused allegedly had been observed in a criminal act by several people). Said the sheriff: "Hey, man, if it looks like a duck, flies like a duck, flaps like a duck, eats like a duck, walks like a duck, tends to like the company of other ducks . . . hey, I think you got yourself a duck!" (Blackman, 1989, 460).

Common characteristics of students with mild disabilities are listed in clusters in Table 5.3. These clusters contain characteristics representative of psychological, educational, and social behaviors, in particular.

For example, the psychological cluster is characterized by items that make reference to the fact that the disability is difficult to detect. Typically, a mild disability remains undetected until the child begins school. The condition surfaces when learning demands are placed upon the individual and the person is unable to produce accordingly. The physical appearance of the student is the same as that of students in full-time regular education, and the cause of the mild disability is usually unknown. A poor self-concept often results.

As we said, the problem first becomes apparent in the educational setting. Thus, characteristics reflective of educational behaviors are fairly common. The child is a low achiever and exhibits an obvious lack of interest in schoolwork. The preference for concrete rather than abstract lessons reflects his or her need for better understanding of what is being taught. These students respond better to active rather than passive learning tasks. Teachers often observe weak listening skills and limited verbal and/or writing skills. Many students are distractible. Unfortunately, teachers sometimes overlook talents and abilities that many of these students possess. These students are often self-conscious and prefer to receive special help in their regular classroom. They require modifications in classroom instruction in order for learning to occur. Due to the difficulties these students experience in school, they often have a higher dropout rate than regular education students.

Socially, students with mild disabilities sometimes experience friction when interacting with others and demonstrate problem behaviors in the classroom. They show a need for adult approval and are often stereotyped by others. During school years most function better outside of school than in school; however, following school years, many experience difficulties finding and maintaining employment.

TABLE 5.3   Common Characteristics of Students with Mild Disabilities

The following characteristics will vary from one student to another but are generally the same across the categories of mild mental retardation, behavior disorders, and learning disabilities. They are clustered under psychological, educational, and social characteristics.

Psychological Characteristics

- Mild disability undetected until beginning school years
- Cause of mild disability is difficult to detect
- Physical appearance the same as students in full-time regular education
- Poor self-concept

Educational Characteristics

- Lack of interest in school work
- Prefer concrete rather than abstract lessons
- Weak listening skills
- Low achievement
- Limited verbal and/or writing skills
- Right hemisphere preference in learning activities
- Respond better to active rather than passive learning tasks
- Have areas of talent or ability that are overlooked by teachers
- Prefer to receive special help in regular classroom
- Higher dropout rate than regular education students
- Achieve in accordance with teacher expectations
- Require modifications in classroom instruction
- Distractible

Social Characteristics

- Experience friction when interacting with others
- Function better outside of school than in school
- Need adult approval
- Have difficulties finding and maintaining employment after school
- Stereotyped by others
- Behavior problems exhibited

Students with mild disabilities are those who are most likely to be taught in general education classroom inclusion program or for one or several periods a day in the resource room.

Special education services for students with mild disabilities are delivered in the general classroom and/or in the special education resource room. For these students, the issue is the effectiveness of the education they are receiving in both types of classrooms.

For every study that presents gains by students with mild intellectual, behavioral, or learning disorders in general education classrooms, there is a contradictory study that demonstrates gains through services from placement in resource rooms (Fuchs & Fuchs, 1986; Glavin et al., 1971; Marston, 1988). Proponents of inclusion are now showing positive results from keeping students with mild disabilities in general classroom placement. Educators are attempting to refocus this murky picture by shifting the viewfinder from where students are educated to what teaching methods work best. In subsequent chapters, you will find that many strategies that work well with students in general education are just as useful for teaching students with mild learning disorders, and vice versa. Good teaching is a constant that cuts across both special and general education.

The concern about quality and benefits of special education services has more recently surfaced in the professional literature about inclusion. With inclusion, the special education teacher often coteaches in the general classroom or serves as a consultant to general education teachers of students with mild disabilities who remain full time in their classrooms. Regardless of placement, federal law requires appropriate education in the least restrictive environment.

Causes of Mild Disabilities

Causes for mild disabilities are subdivided into two categories: organic (biological) and environmental (Figure 5.3).

Under the category of organic, we will discuss pre-, peri-, and postnatal factors, genetic factors, biochemical factors, and maturational lag. These are contributors that originate within the body (i.e., endogenous). We include under environmental reasons for mild learning and behavior disabilities discussions about factors relating to poverty, nutrition, toxins, language differences, sensory deprivation, emotional problems, and inadequate education. Although some environmental factors (e.g., toxins) cause organic dysfunction, the point of origin is outside the body (i.e., exogenous).

Mild Contrasted with Severe Disabilities

The more severe the disability, the sooner the problem is identified. In fact, it is not unusual for a parent of a child with mental retardation to learn of this at birth. The appearance of the infant may differ from that of normal babies, with enlarged head circumference, tell-tale facial features, or inadequate response to visual or auditory stimuli. Several medical tests are now in use with expectant

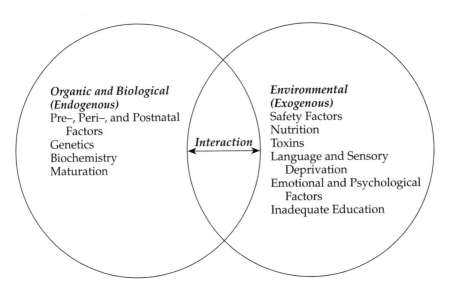

FIGURE 5.3   **Common Causes of Mild Disabilities**

mothers to provide information about possible abnormalities in their unborn fetus. These include ultrasound scans (the recording of tissue densities by sound waves), amniocentesis (examination of amniotic fluid and culturing of fetal cells), chorionic villus biopsy (examination of fetal cells in placental tissue), fetoscopy (the surgical placement of an endoscope into the uterus), and blood analysis (analyses of embryonic cells that migrate from the fetus into the mother's bloodstream).

As mentioned earlier, however, mild learning and behavior difficulties are usually not discovered until children enter school. This is because, in classrooms, teachers are able to detect intellectual, learning, and behavioral problems that can go unnoticed in less formal settings. The schedule and routines of classroom life serve as a backdrop to compare children's ability to cope with various academic and social demands. Such mild learning problems as distractibility or delayed social development become apparent when students are unable to sit for variable periods of time or follow prescribed classroom routines.

As a teacher of students who have learning or behavioral difficulties, you may never know for sure the origin of their learning problems. Attention deficit disorder with hyperactivity (ADD-H), for example, has been attributed primarily to minimal brain dysfunction; but allergies, developmental lag, emotional problems, and lead poisoning can also cause attention difficulties and hyperactivity. For individual students, the cause may be any one of the above or a combination of agents.

Fortunately, educational intervention is not contingent on identifying and curing the cause of a problem. Educational intervention begins with the identification of a student's strengths and weaknesses in thinking, behaving, concentrating, using language, and functioning in other areas. Once an educational assessment profile of an individual student is compiled, teachers can select any one of numerous educational strategies to enhance learning. No one plan works for all students even though their functional problem may be the same. For example, one student who is identified as hyperactive may respond to a behavioral intervention program that uses positive reinforcement or encouragement to extend the student's ability to concentrate. Another student with hyperactivity may flourish in a classroom that provides indirect instructional methods, such as learning centers and peer tutoring.

An informed understanding of causal agents can prove beneficial in the identification of students who are at risk for developing learning or behavioral difficulties. For instance, students who live near toxic waste discharge run a high risk of developing a mild disability. Better knowledge about etiology provides educational programs with information to prevent learning problems. An example is the Head Start preschool program aimed at ameliorating the effects of poverty, such as inadequate nutrition and lead poisoning.

Determination of causes can also:

- Provide a better understanding of the child for family members and educators.
- Provide justification for government programs aimed at preventing disabilities.
- Enable better communication among various human service agencies.
- Suggest a particular treatment approach (e.g., diet instead of behavior modification).
- Provide information that may facilitate referrals outside the educational system.
- Enable more accurate prognosis. (Smith, Price, & Marsh, 1986, 58)

Organic Causes

Pre-, Peri-, and Postnatal Factors. Mild learning, intellectual, and behavioral problems may be the result of prenatal, perinatal, and postnatal problems. Learning problems have been traced to the following prenatal conditions:

- Maternal endocrine disorders (e.g., hypothyroidism, diabetes)
- Maternal–fetal blood type incompatibilities (i.e., Rh factor)
- Maternal age, reproductive readiness, and efficiency
- Maternal cigarette smoking
- Maternal drug and alcohol abuse
- Rubella

- Radiation exposure
- Anoxia
- Accidents (Pasamanick & Knoblock, 1973)

Maternal health, diet, and lifestyle are important factors that affect fetal developmental deficits. Recently, educators have become alarmed at the increasing number of children who are born with disabilities as the result of maternal cocaine addiction. The appeal of crack, a cheap, smokable form of cocaine, has tragically increased the number of children afflicted with learning disorders. Although crack passes through the mother's system in a few days, it remains in the uterus for eighteen to twenty days. Cocaine restricts the oxygen supply to the infant by constricting blood vessels in the placenta. Neurological damage, respiratory ailments, social–emotional disturbances, and physical impairments are possible effects of crack usage on the newborn infants. Extreme hyperactivity, irritability, unresponsiveness, learning disabilities, and mental retardation are some of the problems educators are encountering in children born to crack users.

Infants born of mothers who have consumed alcohol during pregnancy may develop fetal alcohol syndrome. This disability is characterized by mental retardation and other serious learning problems. Prenatal and postnatal growth deficiencies are present in approximately 50 percent of babies born to mothers classified as severely and chronically alcoholic, with an unknown number of babies affected by a lesser degree of alcohol abuse during pregnancy and nursing (Smith, Price, & Marsh, 1986; Umbreit & Ostrow, 1980). *Abstinence from alcohol consumption during pregnancy is recommended by obstetricians, as the amount that can be consumed without ill effects currently is unknown.*

Researchers have attributed various pre- and postnatal factors to mild disabilities. Maternal malnutrition can harm the development of the fetus's central nervous system and modify the growth and biochemical maturation of the brain (Hallahan & Cruickshank, 1973; Silver, 1989). Secondary cigarette smoke and substance abuse by nursing mothers have been reported as cumulative, postnatal toxins (Silver, 1989; Smith-Davis, 1989a,b).

Genetics.   There is some evidence that dyslexia, a type of learning disability that impairs a student's ability to read, occurs in family lineages. Schizophrenia, a severe emotional disturbance, also appears to have, in some instances, a genetic component. Some forms of mental retardation leave unmistakable genetic tracers. Riley–Day syndrome is an inherited form of mental retardation that occurs principally among people with Jewish backgrounds. Marfan's syndrome is a rare, inherited disorder that causes visual impairments and mild mental retardation.

Until recently, the best way to determine a genetic factor in learning disorders was to count cases in a particular family or in a specific ethnic group. This approach is relatively clear-cut when tracking obvious developmental disabilities such as Riley–Day syndrome. The presence of such anomalies as small stature, spinal curvature, insensitivity to pain, and behavior problems allow for construction of a clinical profile that is both observable and measurable. Because students with mild learning disorders are normal in appearance and have no obvious medical complications, conclusions about the relative importance of genetic factors are tentative. The history of mild mental retardation, in particular, is replete with assertions and counterassertions about genetic versus environmental factors.

As neuroscientists and geneticists become more adept at chromosome and gene identification, they will unravel the mystery of why some individuals develop learning disabilities and other mild learning disorders. In the meantime, the code word is caution when making assertions about an individual's innate, inherited characteristics. When any disorder appears with regularity in different generations of the same family, environmental influence cannot be dismissed as a causal factor. Home life, readiness for school, adequacy of teaching, motivation, and attitude toward learning are the deciding factors in a large number of cases of students with mild learning disorders.

Biochemistry.   Despite its durability, the human body is a delicately balanced organism. The way our body functions depends on how well approximately 100,000 different chemicals work together. In order for the body and mind to function in unison, these chemicals must mesh in rhythmic patterns that assure optimum performance of all body organs. An imbalance in one area, such as glucose metabolism, will adversely affect mood, perception, and thinking. In the flurry of educational evaluations that precede a determination of special education services, physiological reasons for a learning problem are often overlooked. Alan C. Levin, Director of the New York Institute for Child Development, reported that 75 percent of the students referred for learning or behavior problems had a physical or biochemical problem that contributed to their difficulties (Brickland, 1976). Vitamin deficiencies, allergic reactions, and abnormal mineral levels (e.g., iron deficiency) are just a sample of biochemical explanations for why students fail to develop normal learning and socialization skills.

It is also possible that many behaviors that are considered disturbing in school are stress related. Hans Seyle (1975) defines stress as the nonspecific response of the body to a demand. By this he means that regardless of the type of stressor experienced, the biochemical reactions of the body are the same. The student who views reading as a threatening activity or who perceives the teacher as hostile may instinctively resort to a flight or fight response. Withdrawal, apathy, resentment, moodiness, and anger are nonverbal responses to stress that are common both inside and outside the classroom. The ability of the teacher to identify physical signs of a youngster in distress (e.g., eyes with dilated pupils or increased muscle tone of the body) is important because many students do not have the verbal facility to describe feelings like panic, tension, and anxiety. Students with behavior disorders, in particular, are apt to act these feelings out rather than communicate them verbally.

Educators, both general and special, have been reluctant to accept biochemical explanations for learning problems. There are two reasons for their indisposition. First, possible biochemical causes for learning problems are difficult to track down. Hair analysis, for example, can pinpoint mineral deficiencies, but the procedure requires expertise that is outside the range of most family physicians. The oral glucose tolerance test can evaluate hypoglycemia (low blood sugar), but it requires six hours of medical attention and frequent blood samples. The cost, time, and complications of these evaluation procedures are discouraging. Second, educators, in general, simply do not accept biochemical explanations for learning problems because the evidence is largely anecdotal. For example, while Feingold's (1975) and Crook's (1980) research on how specific foods can cause allergic reactions and learning problems caught on with parents, educators remained unimpressed. School menus, which weekly offer schoolchildren large doses of preservative-laden and chemically treated foods, graphically illustrate a lack of concern about biochemical contributors to learning problems.

Maturation. Although it is common knowledge that children physically develop at different rates, parents and educators sometimes overlook the fact that children's nervous systems follow the same idiosyncratic pattern as height and weight. Differences in development are not uniformly equal. Small children in a classroom may have quick reflexes, while larger children may lag behind others in the ability to coordinate movement. This developmental lag is normal and, eventually, as the students' nervous systems mature, they will be on an equal physical footing with others in the class. Developmental delay is more serious with some children, presumably because there is an irregularity in the physical development of their nervous system.

Developmental delay is a characteristic of mental retardation. Moreover, Bender (1968) and de Hirsch (1965) suggest a relationship between the immaturity evident in some youth with learning disabilities and a lag in the maturation of some central nervous system components. Immaturity can also be an individual trait and, given time, corrected on its own.

Much is being written about developmental lag and mild learning and behavior disorders in relationship to recent brain research. Within the brain, some reasoning abilities are localized in specific areas. For instance, in most individuals the language center of the brain is in the left frontal and temporal lobe of the neo-cortex. A slight anomaly to a small area of the brain can be responsible for problems in such abstract skills as calculating and reading. Often these problems are detectable only in a formal learning environment, such as a classroom.

Hynd and Hynd contend that developmental anomalies exist in all brains. Not all brains develop in the same way (e.g., time stages, growth sections), and not all parts of the brain develop uniformly within a single individual. These researchers contend:

> While it is easy for psychologists and educators to conceive of separate distributions for IQ, reading achievement, math achievement, personality, and so on, it seems almost impossible for these same professionals to conceive of a separate distribution of neurological development. It is almost as if an assumption is made

that everyone was born with a perfect unblemished cerebral cortex. (Hynd & Hynd, 1984, 491)

This statement has several implications. First, rather than assuming that students with mild disabilities have organic deficits, consider the possibility of developmental lag that, given time, can "catch up." Second, educational modifications can stimulate development in schoolchildren while maturation proceeds. Third, if all brains are "blemished" in some fashion, learning disabilities may be contextual. In school the context is verbal skills. Thus students with language-based learning disabilities stand out, while students with deficits in musical or artistic abilities would be overlooked.

Environmental Causes

Environmental factors can enhance a child's learning potential or retard progress. The most rapid developmental growth in physiological, intellectual, emotional, motor, and linguistic functioning domains occurs during preschool years.

Safety Factors.   Physical safety is necessary for the healthy growth and development of any child. A complicated delivery, early injury, illness, or falls and accidents can be traumatic and show their effects as the child develops learning readiness. Harmful events can occur even under well-supervised medical and familial conditions. Nevertheless, accidents frequently occur during times of inadequate supervision at home, on the playground, and even in school.

Nutrition.   Adequate nutrition of mothers prior to and during pregnancy and of children during growing years is necessary for normal development (Peterson, 1987; Smith & Patton, 1989). Nutrition can affect learning potential and has been identified as a contributing factor in mild mental retardation, learning disabilities, and some forms of disturbed behavior (Smith et al., 1986). Nutritional intake has been studied extensively and has contributed to the enactment of federal programs such as Head Start; the Woman, Infant, and Children Program (WIC); Home Start; and subsidized school lunches and breakfasts, along with grant approvals for parent education programs.

Many different children are at risk of learning problems as a result of poor nutrition. Poor children, children of teenagers, migrant children, and children in rural areas are most likely to develop learning and behavior problems as the result of poor nutrition. Some of the symptoms of a lack of a proper diet are listlessness, irritability, fatigue, and inability to concentrate. Although poor nutrition slows metabolism and restricts the functioning of the central nervous system, the effects are reversible. The most prevalent nutritional disorder in the United States today is iron deficiency. Mothers of iron-deficient children tend to be younger, less educated, poor, and depressed. Iron-deficient children have short attention spans and behavior problems. Drinking cow's milk rather than mother's milk or formula can harm infants. Uneducated families who are unable to afford formula sometimes feed their infants cow's milk or sweetened beverages such as carbonated colas.

Feingold (1975) proposed the elimination of food additives and natural substances called salicylates by adherence to a special diet called the Kaiser–Permanente (KP) Diet. Though unproved in curbing hyperactivity and learning disabilities in controlled studies, parents and teachers have attested to beneficial effects from use of the elimination diet with children with learning and behavior problems (Mayron, 1979). Allergies, which come about as abnormal responses to substances within the environment (e.g., food, chemicals, inhalants, dust, mold, selective foliage), have been associated with learning and behavior problems. It is estimated that 60 to 80 percent of this nation's population has suffered an allergic reaction to food at some time during their lives (Mayron, 1979). Cott (1972) supported megavitamin therapy (i.e., massive use of vitamins to eliminate deficiencies associated with learning and behavior problems); however, success in using large doses of vitamins to treat learning and behavior problems has not been substantiated in independent studies (Silver, 1975). Other dietary deficiencies correlated with learning and behavior disorders include deficiencies in protein, zinc, magnesium, and calcium (Mayron, 1979).

The cumulative aspect of nutritional effects is most aptly illustrated and summarized by Crook (1980):

> If you don't use the right kind of fuel in your automobile, it won't run properly. It may sputter, jump, jerk, and knock. Similarly, the poor performance of the inattentive, overactive child is often caused by improper "fuel": too much sugar and other junk food and insufficient amounts of essential nutrients, including complex carbohydrates, essential fatty acids, vitamins, and minerals.

The impact of maternal substance abuse, malnutrition during pregnancy, and poor medical care of mother and child is discussed under prenatal, perinatal, and postnatal delivery factors.

Toxins. Environmental pollution is a contributory source for mild disabling conditions. Toxins found in the environment that have a strong likelihood for causing intellectual, learning, and behavioral problems include hydrocarbon (from coal, petroleum, and natural gas) (Mayron, 1979), lead (from such sources as paint, plaster, automobile exhausts) (Smith & Patton, 1989), and mercury (from factory contaminated waterways) (Peterson, 1987). Contamination from toxic waste sites and landfills that burn lead batteries contribute to learning problems as well. A follow-up study of 425 children treated for lead poisoning in the Chicago inner-city area reported 39 percent with neurological damage, 54 percent with recurrent seizures, 38 percent with mental retardation, and 13 percent with cerebral palsy (Wallace, 1972). Oil and chemical spills continue to be studied for negative effects on development and learning (Figure 5.4).

Although high doses of radiation are known to be deadly, effects from low-level radiation are not so easily determined. Pregnant mothers, however, are

FIGURE 5.4   Cars and Kids Don't Run on Bad Fuel

Illustration by Lois Creech.

advised to avoid unnecessary dental, chest, and other body X-rays because of possible damage to the developing fetus. Electromagnetic radiation in radio frequency wavelengths has been implicated as a possible cause of hyperactivity and underachievement (Mayron, 1979). And, though not well understood, evidence has linked radiation from fluorescent lights and televisions to learning and behavior problems (Smith, Price, & Marsh, 1986). In addition, the pollution of air, soil, and water has resulted in the contamination of many foods. Animal products are especially apt to contain insecticides and other toxic substances. These toxic substances may place a further burden on a child's developing immune and nervous systems.

Language and Sensory Deprivation.   Intellectual learning and behavioral development is retarded by the absence of sensory, linguistic, and cognitive stimulation. Children learn through interaction within their environment (Piaget, 1950). During infant and preschool years, overlooked health problems such as ear infections can hinder involvement in activities that are important to the development of academic readiness. Regular trips to the pediatrician or family physician are necessary to detect subtle hearing and visual difficulties. Unfortunately, many poor or uneducated parents are unable to provide preventive health attention for their children.

Children can develop verbal language problems when adequate models are unavailable to them during early years while speech is forming (Smith & Patton, 1989). Deficits occur in homes where there is language deprivation. For example, if a primary caregiver does not initiate speech or respond to a youngster's speech efforts, the child's language will suffer. A blaring television prevents active language interaction and makes discrimination of unique sounds impossible. Sometimes bilingual confusion exists. Adverse effects in the academic setting may be countered in classrooms where respect for diverse language forms (e.g., bilingual, African American and Anglo-Saxon derivatives) is shown, while instruction continues in standard English (Bryen, 1982).

Emotional and Psychological Factors.   Many children with mild learning, intellectual, and emotional disorders exhibit lack of self-esteem, insecurity, low frustration tolerance, and impulsive behavior. Home life that at an early age is unstable, abusive, or psychologically stressful, contributes to poor emotional and social development of the young. Furthermore, some children are slow to respond to maternal bonding and nurturing. Sometimes these children will not allow themselves to be comforted during stressful times.

Mary Ainsworth (1978) studied infant–mother bonding at twelve months of age. Ainsworth found that infants respond differently to their mothers. In an experiment called the "strange situation," Ainsworth analyzed infant reaction when the mother left them in an observation room. Securely attached infants cried when the mother left and greeted the returning mother with pleasure. Avoidant infants gave the impression of independence and did not seem to be affected by the mother leaving or returning. Insecurely attached infants clung to mother and cried profusely when mother left. However, upon return of the mother, insecure infants resisted all attempts to be soothed and would angrily arch away from mother's comforting embrace.

The infant behavior influenced the mother's response. Attached mothers were more responsive to feeding signals and crying of infants. These mothers readily returned smiles. Mothers of avoidant and insecurely attached infants were unresponsive or rejecting. Without intervention, these attachment patterns persisted. Insecure and avoidant infants often become problem children. At age two, they tend to lack self-reliance and show little enthusiasm for problem solving. From three to five, they have poor peer relations and little resilience. At six, insecure and avoidant children are apathetic and unmotivated. Ainsworth has found that teachers tend to treat securely attached children in age-appropriate ways. Teachers tend to excuse and infantilize insecurely attached children. With avoidant children, Ainsworth found, teachers are controlling.

Ainsworth's research is valuable because it highlights the interactional aspect of social–emotional growth. Significant adults in a child's life, whether they are parents or teachers, help mold a youngster's personality by the way they respond to his or her behavior. A teacher who ignores a child because "she just wants attention" or gets angry at a child who is "immature" is unwittingly contributing to the development of the offensive behaviors. Child abuse, inconsistent nurturing, neglect, and poverty all play a role in contributing to the development of avoidant and insecure children. The effect of an early unnurturing or depriving living environment may result in youth who lack motivation for learning and are unconcerned about others. Further unacceptance may be shown by teachers who have a differing value system coupled with intolerance for youth who are disturbing in the classroom.

Inadequate Education.   Negative expectations for students with mild learning and behavior problems are handicapping factors in the classroom. Poor instructional programming, disorganized teaching practices, and low expectations for educational outcomes of children with mild disabling conditions contribute to learning difficulties. Hallahan and Kauffman (1994) include the following teacher behaviors as contributors to school failure: insensitivity to individuality, requirement of conformity to rules and routines, inappropriate and inconsistent disciplinary practices, reinforcement of inappropriate behaviors, and emphasis upon student inadequacies.

Insufficient development of prerequisite readiness skills occur both in home and school environments. The absence of intellectually stimulating experiences and lack of exposure to materials that will be used in school contribute to academic delay (Smith & Patton, 1989). Lack of readiness for school coupled with desultory teaching in school almost guarantees school failure.

Special Populations At Risk

Infants, Toddlers, Preschoolers

When the Individuals with Disabilities Education Act (IDEA) was written. Congress understood that early intervention is effective for young children with disabilities, and through IDEA authorized several programs to establish a coordinated service delivery system for children with disabilities form birth through age 5. The Early Intervention Program for Infants and Toddlers with Disabilities (Part H) promotes a comprehensive approach to meet the needs of children with disabilities from birth through age 2 (Goldberg, 1997). A variety of discretionary programs support projects that finance activities such as personnel preparation and research endeavors. An example is the Early Education Program for Children with Disabilities (EEPCD, Section 623 or Part C). The Preschool Grants Program is authorized under Section 619 of Part B. This program requires that the states and outlying areas provide services to children with disabilities ages 3 to 5.

The Early Intervention Program. (hereafter called Part H) was created by the passage of Public Law 99–457, the Education of the Handicapped Act Amendments of 1986, and was amended in 1992 by Public Law 102–119. Part H provides funds to states and outlying areas to address the needs of children with disabilities form birth through age 2 and their families through "a statewide system of coordinated, comprehensive, multidisciplinary, interagency programs providing appropriate early intervention services to all infants and toddlers with disabilities and their families, including Indian infants and toddlers with disabilities on reservations" (U.S. Department of Education, 1996, 31). Through this program, but at each state's option, services may be provided to infants and toddlers who are at-risk of having a substantial developmental delay if they do not receive appropriate early intervention services.

The settings in which infants and toddlers with disabilities and their families are served. The number of infants and toddlers and their families receiving early intervention services in accord with Part H as recorded on December 1, 1993.

The Preschool Grants Program.   A free appropriate public education (FAPE) is made available to all eligible children with disabilities ages 3 to 5 through the Preschool Grants Program. Data from the 18th Annual Report to Congress shows that ten states and outlying areas provide FAPE form birth, while Virginia does so at age 2. FAPE is assured by all other states and outlying areas at age 3.

Pre-School Children Served

Special education and related services were received by more the 524,000 preschool children during the school year 1994–95. Of this number, 45.8 percent were five-year-olds, 34.3 percent were four-year–olds, 19.9 percent were three-year-olds, (U.S. Department of Education, 1996). Under Public Law 99–457, at the state's discretion, infants and toddlers, ages birth to 2, are eligible for early intervention services if they are currently experiencing developmental delays or ate at–risk of having such developmental delays. Preschoolers, children aged 3 to 5, are entitled to special education at the state's discretion if they have developmental delays in physical, cognitive, communication, social, emotional, or adaptive development. In 1992, all states reported having mandates in place in order to provide a free appropriate public education (FAPE) to all three- through five-year-old children with disabilities.

The definition for children with disabilities is also used to identify these youth. IDEA defines children with disabilities as those

> with mental retardation, hearing impairments including deafness, speech or language impairments, visual impairments including blindness, serious emotional disturbance, orthopedic impairments, autism, traumatic brain injury, other health impairments, or specific learning disabilities . . . who, by reason thereof, need special education and related services.

Two significant developments outside of IDEA have begun to impact on the way in which preschool services are provided. One of these is the Americans with Disabilities Act (ADA) and the other is the concept of "developmentally appropriate practice." The ADA mandates that preschoolers with disabilities can no longer be excluded from a public day care or kindergarten facility due to their disability, and that reasonable accommodations are to be given children with disabilities according to need. The ADA became effective in 1992. It is predicted that this Act will lead to an increased number of community preschool settings accessible to children with disabilities. If special education provisions are incorporated, more children with disabilities will have an opportunity to receive educational services in mainstreamed settings. The ADA is discussed later in this section as we talk about school-aged children with disabilities.

The developmentally appropriate practice is built around the premise that different types of practices are appropriate for children of different ages and for individual children. This means that developmental needs are to be recognized in relation to age appropriateness as well as what is appropriate for the individual (U.S. Department of Education, 1993). Unstructured learning through play, child-initiated activities, individualization, and active engagement are some of the practices that are being discussed as options for these programs.

At-Risk School-Aged Youth

School efforts to help at-risk students have focused almost exclusively on children and youth from low socioeconomic backgrounds. The term *compensatory education* is used to describe federal programs that are targeted for disadvantaged children who are at risk of academic failure.

About 25 percent of school-age youth needs significant assistance to benefit from education, but only about half or 12 percent of these fit the IDEA definition (Rothstein, 1995). Two criteria must be met in order to qualify for special education. A youngster must:

1. qualify for one of the disability categories listed in the law.

2. must also need special education and related services because of a disability. The presence of a disability does not necessarily mean that special education assistance is needed.

The half (again about 12 to 13 percent) reported by Rothstein as requiring significant assistance in order to benefit from education and who do not qualify for special education are considered "at risk." Some receive reading and math assistance from compensatory education programs—like Title 1.(See Chapter 1.) Some are referred to as "slow learners" or "underachievers." Others are chronic discipline problems or frequent truants. All have a high probability of becoming school dropouts.

Students at-risk is a generic term that describes a range of problems of school-aged youth. Low achievement, retention in grade, truancy, and behavior problems are indicators that a student may be at risk of school failure. Approximately 15 percent of all high school students leave school before their graduation date; thus, after infants, the most vulnerable at-risk population is adolescents. A student is at-risk when failure is likely to occur—either in school or in life. Whether or not a youth is at-risk is a function of the family and community as much as school actors. Problems linked to family and society include drug abuse, deficient school readiness skills, emotional problems, absenteeism, and family turmoil. Retention, low achievement, behavior problems, and absenteeism are school variables that are characteristics of students at-risk.

School Drop Outs

The annual drop out rate for students with disabilities ages 14 to 21 is 5.1 percent. Students with behavior disorders have a higher rate than any other type of disability. Older secondary students are more likely to drop out than younger secondary students, although the latter group have a sizable proportion of students who also dropped out of school. Students with disabilities who drop out are less likely than those without disabilities to eventually earn a high school diploma.

Warner (1991) studied factors that influence retention. Schools and communities can apply some of these findings to assist at-risk students who might be potential dropouts.

- Students who received individual attention such as tutoring or counseling were more likely to remain in school.
- Smaller classes, tutoring, and other services increased the chances that students would succeed in general classes.
- Students in general classes were less likely to have high absenteeism or to be retained in grade if classes were small or if they had help from an instructional aide.
- Students who received job-specific vocational education performed better in school and at work than those who did not, had significantly lower

Highlight 5.1

Jerome is sixteen years old. He has barely scraped through school. His reading and calculating skills are on par with those of an average ten-year-old. Each year his teachers promote him, hoping that their successor will have more luck in teaching Jerome. Jerome's poor academic skills are counterbalanced by his leadership ability. The other students look up to him because he is tough but kind. In the inner-city school Jerome attends, this is a charismatic combination. When Jerome leaves school at the end of the day, he walks home through a maze of drug dealers, winos, and storefronts girded with iron gates. His mother would like to move Jerome and his two sisters to a nicer neighborhood, but her salary as a fast food restaurant worker barely provides the family with rent and food money. Jerome is street-wise, and lately he has begun to make extra money by selling crack. All his teachers agree that Jerome is a good kid, who, with a few opportunities, could be a success; but, in educational jargon, he is a functional illiterate. Jerome is at risk of graduating from high school unable to read a newspaper.

absenteeism, and were significantly less likely to fail a course, miss school, or drop out.

- Students who socialized with other students outside of school and were involved in extracurricular activities were less likely to fail a course, miss school, or drop out.

When a student is identified as at-risk of education failure the educational response has often been to place the student in a special education program rather than a compensatory education program. For instance, since the passage of the Individuals with Disabilities Education Act, the number of all learning-disabled students has increased beyond all reasonable expectations. However, as Slavin (1989b) points out, labelling students "learning disabled" is no guarantee that their problems will be remediated.

This increase (in learning disabled students) represents the entry into the special education system of low achievers who would not have been served in special education in the past. In other words, special education has assumed a substantial burden in trying to meet the needs of students at-risk of school failure. Yet research comparing students with mild handicaps in special education to similar students left in regular classrooms finds few if any benefits for this expensive service. (Slavin, 1989b, 15)

A better response to at-risk students is to identify effective teaching practices from all sectors (general, compensatory, and special education) and use these methods with all students receiving education in the mainstream (for example, cooperative learning based on planned student groupings, and peer tutoring work with students who are accelerated, average, at-risk, and have mild disabilities). Unsuccessful teachers need to be retrained in effective teaching practices. Teachers must be willing to work with a broad spectrum of students, including those identified as at-risk or with a mild disability. The gray area between students with mild disabilities and at-risk students may have been expanded by 1997 changers to IDEA, which permit states to use "developmental delay" as eligibility criteria through age nine, rather than a specific disability category (Huemann and Hehir, 1997). Experience with noncategorical criteria suggests that absent the accountability of having to substantiate a specific mild disability the numbers of students placed in special education, particularly "slow learners" will increase.

Perhaps the most difficult challenge is to convince teachers that their responsibilities to youth do not end at the schoolhouse door. Most of the problems of at-risk students begin in the home and community. Teachers who make home visits and who value parental participation in school activities are capable of understanding the needs of at-risk students more clearly than teachers who have little interest in their students' lives outside of school.

Section 504 of the Rehabilitation Act and the Americans with Disabilities Act

Unreported in the special education data are the at-risk students who are called "slow learners," and who may or may not have received some type of compensatory education.

Slow learners is the name reserved for students who fall through the cracks between special education and general education. Unless a student is found eligible under IDEA for learning disabilities, behavior disorders, or mental retardation (or other exceptionality listed in IDEA), the youngster is not required to have an individualized educational program. The educational needs of "slow learners" are rarely met, because general education is geared toward the average student. Moreover, with disagreement among professionals about the definition for learning disabilities, many remain unclassified. Some youngsters who are slow learners have a learning disability, but they have not been provided with special education because they are not identified.

Several categories of children with disabilities are at-risk. Even though they have a condition or a documented disability, they may not be eligible for special education as defined in IDEA. For instance, a child with an emotional disorder may not meet the federal criteria for "intensity and degree." Others have medical conditions, but these conditions are not listed as disabilities in IDEA. An example is a child with AIDS whose condition is not listed under "Other Health Impairments" in IDEA.

Many students are protected under Section 504 of the Rehabilitation Act and the Americans with Disabilities Act (ADA). However, they are not covered by the stringent procedural safeguards available under IDEA. The safeguards include the right to remain in the current placement, nondiscriminatory evaluation, an individualized educational plan, an impartial determination as to the appropriate placement and other due process protections (Rothstein, 1995).

Youth with social maladjustments (e.g., incarcerated youth) do not qualify for special education under IDEA unless an emotional–behavioral disorder is documented. There is disagreement over whether to identify or even attempt to separate youth with social maladjustments from other youth who meet the federal definition of "serious emotional disturbance." Unlike slow learners, some of whom may qualify for Title I services, incarcerated or delinquent youngsters have no federal safety net of services.

Another category of children who require significant assistance in schools, but for whom there is no category in special education, are those with attention deficit disorders (ADD). In order to assess public opinion about whether ADD should be a separate special education disability, the 1990 amendments to IDEA required that the Department of Education solicit comments about the issue. It was decided that this condition would not become a separate disability category under IDEA. Several reasons were given, including the fact that many youngsters with ADD qualify for special education services as learning disabled and behavior disordered. Many youngsters with ADD and ADHD have received special education services under the category, "Other Health Impairments."

Youth who are addicted to drugs and alcohol are protected under IDEA only if they qualify for special education and related services under one of the disability categories. These students, like other categories described, are at risk and while they do not qualify for special education under IDEA, they are entitled to protection under Section 504 of the Rehabilitation Act or the Americans with Disabilities Act, referred to as ADA. Only the slow learner is not protected under IDEA, Section 504, or the ADA.

What determines whether a person is entitled to protection under Section 504? The individual must meet the definition of a person with a disability, which is

> any person who (i) has a physical or mental impairment which substantially limits one or more of such person's major life activities, (ii) has a record of such an impairment, or (iii) is regarded as having such an impairment.

The individual must also be "otherwise qualified." This means that the person must be able to meet the requirements of a particular program in spite of his or her disability (Rothstein, 1995). If the person meets the definition of a person with a disability under Section 504, "reasonable accommodations" that be made by recipients of federal financial assistance. Public school systems receive this assistance, so teachers must make accommodations that are educationally beneficial for these students. The usual remedy when a violation of Section 504 is proved is the termination of federal assistance, which means loss of federal funding to the school system.

In 1990, Congress passed Public Law 101–336, the Americans with Disabilities Act (ADA). The ADA is similar to Section 504 of the Rehabilitation Act, except ADA does not require entities to be recipients of federal financial assistance. Whereas protection under Section 504 includes public schools, protection under ADA extends into private schools. The ADA is similar to Section 504 because it requires schools not to discriminate and to provide reasonable accommodations in its educational policies, practices, and procedures (Rothstein, 1995; U.S. Department of Education, 1996). Interestingly, the mandate for implementing reasonable accommodations where appropriate for a youngster with a disability, but who does not meet the eligibility criteria for a special education category, seems to be drawing general classroom and special educators closer together with the use of effective teaching practices that benefit all students, including those we have mentioned as at-risk and slow learners.

Identification of Learning Problems

The following is a description of a typical chain of events outlined in Figure 5.5. Identification of a student's learning problem occurs when comparisons are made within the general peer population about a student's academic or behavioral characteristics. Teachers hold expectations for student behaviors, and those who exhibit behaviors that differ significantly are singled out. Salend and Lutz (1984) identified student behaviors required for success in the regular classroom. These behaviors are grouped into the following major areas:

1. Interact positively with other students.
   Work well with others.
   Respect feelings of others.
   Play cooperatively.
   Share materials and property.
   Avoid fights.
   Refrain from stealing.

2. Follow class rules.
   Remain quiet while others are talking.
   Use appropriate language.
   Tell the truth.
   Keep hands and feet to self.
   Use time wisely.

3. Display proper work habits.
   Follow directions.

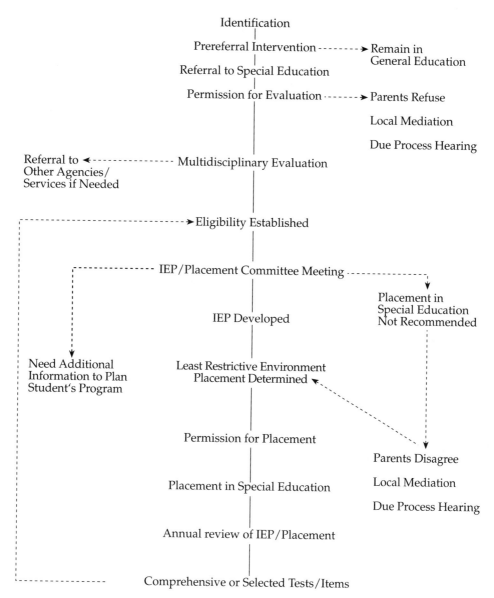

FIGURE 5.5 Due Process Procedures

Source: Georgia Department of Education

Seek assistance when appropriate.
Initiate assignments independently.
Attend to task.
Persist at difficult tasks.

Attend regularly.

Have materials ready.

Students with mild disabilities are identifiable by academic and social behaviors that deviate from those of their classmates; however, these students are not always so obvious. Imagine a continuum of children working on an assigned worksheet. On the far left side of the continuum, students are working on task, appearing to be concentrating on what they are doing, and are busily writing answers on a worksheet. As you look a bit further toward the center, you can see that these students are working on task, concentrating, and recording answers about 50 percent of the time. Now, as you move past the center toward the right of the continuum, notice that students are off task, staring into space, or jesting with each other while they ignore worksheets on their desks.

Students at the far right end of the continuum are displaying disturbing academic and social behaviors at a high rate, duration, or intensity; these students are easily identified by their nonconforming behaviors. It would make things simpler if a certain portion of the continuum could be designated as representative of the characteristics and traits of students who are special education candidates. Unfortunately, identification of students with mild disabilities is not this simple. Imagine that some of the students at the left side of the continuum appear to be working appropriately, but closer inspection shows no rhyme or reason for the answers they are writing. Others appear to be working on task, but are drawing doodles on their worksheets.

These students often fall further and further behind. Their learning problems are not as noticeable, and they are tolerated by the teacher. Students like these are often told to pay attention, listen, and try harder. Because they have no obvious disability, they are mistaken for being lazy or apathetic. These children are at risk because if they are not identified as deviating from the norm in their learning, they are likely to fall increasingly further behind age-mates in school.

Prereferral Intervention

Once a student is identified as being at risk academically or socially, remedial interventions are attempted within the general classroom. Federal legislation requires that sincere efforts be made to help the child learn in the general classroom. The concept of general education intervention is based on a redistribution of the resources of special education toward more immediate problem solving in general education (Pugach & Johnson, 1989b). This preventive approach to learning problems is discussed in more detail in Chapters 6 and 9 (Least Restrictive Environment and Classroom Management).

In some states, school-based teams of educators are formed to solve learning and behavior problems in the regular classroom. These informal problem-solving teams have a variety of names that include concepts of support (school support teams, student support teams), assistance (teacher assistance teams, school assistance teams, or building assistance teams), and appraisal (school appraisal teams) (Pugach & Johnson, 1989b).

Regardless of what the teams are called, their purpose is similar. Teacher assistance teams are created to make professional suggestions about curricular alternatives and instructional modifications. These teams may be composed of a variety of participants, including regular education teachers, building administrator, guidance counselor, special education teacher, and the student's parent(s). The team composition varies based on the type of referral, the needs of the student, the availability of educational personnel, and state requirements.

Modifications are tried in an attempt to accommodate the student in the general classroom. Modifications are based on the presumption that learning problems can occur because of a mismatch between teaching and learning style. Students have different learning styles (see Chapter 7, Learning and Teaching). Whereas one student might benefit from phonics instruction, another student could be baffled by the system of blending sounds to make words. The second student might excel at a reading approach that emphasizes children's literature rather than phonics-oriented basal readers. Effective instruction recognizes differences in how students learn. The strategies shown in Table 5.4 for modifying regular classroom instruction are effective with students at-risk, students with mild disabilities, and students without learning problems.

Implementation and results of any intervention that is tailored to meet the unique needs of a student should be documented. Anecdotal records, test results, and samples of work help team members assess progress during regularly scheduled meetings. Thus, appropriate changes within the classroom environment and teaching approaches are attempted prior to or in lieu of special education referral. At this time, focus remains on what can be done in the regular classroom to assist the student. Special education labels are not considered—only modifications that might help the student to progress in the general classroom.

Referral to Special Education

Referral is the process through which a teacher, a parent, or some other person formally requests an evaluation of a student to determine eligibility for special education services. Ramsey (1995a) lists six factors that may influence a decision to refer. The factors are: (a) student characteristics, such as the abilities, behaviors, or skills that students exhibit (or the lack of them); (b) individual differences among teachers in their beliefs, expectations, or skill in dealing with specific kinds of problems; (c) expectations for special education assistance with a student who is exhibiting academic or behavioral learning problems; (d) availability of specific special education programs; (e) parents' demand for referral or opposition to referral; and (f) institutional factors that may facilitate or constrain teachers in making referral decisions.

Fewer students are referred when school districts have complex procedures for referral, lengthy paperwork is required, special education classes are filled to capacity, psychological assessments are backlogged for months, or building principals and other site administrators do not fully recognize the importance of special education services.

TABLE 5.4   **Strategies for Modifying General Classroom Instruction**

Strategy 1	Provide active learning experiences to teach concepts. Student motivation is increased when students can manipulate, weigh, measure, read, or write using materials and skills that relate to their daily lives.
Strategy 2	Provide ample opportunities for guided practice of new skills. Frequent feedback on performance is essential to overcome student feelings of inadequacy. Peer tutoring and cooperative projects provide nonthreatening practice opportunities. Individual student conferences, curriculum-based tests, and small group discussions are three useful methods for checking progress.
Strategy 3	Provide multisensory learning experiences. Students with learning problems sometimes have sensory processing difficulties; for instance, an auditory discrimination problem may cause misunderstanding about teacher expectations. Lessons and directions that include visual, auditory, tactile, and kinesthetic modes are preferable to a single sensory approach.
Strategy 4	Present information in a manner that is relevant to the student. Particular attention to this strategy is needed when there is a cultural or economic gap between the lives of teachers and students. Relate instruction to a youngster's daily experience and interests.
Strategy 5	Provide students with concrete illustrations of their progress. Students with learning problems need frequent reinforcement for their efforts. Charts, graphs, and checksheets provide tangible markers of student achievement.

It is important that referral procedures be clearly understood and coordinated among all school personnel. All educators need to be able to identify characteristics typically exhibited by students who have mild learning disabilities. Also, the restrictiveness of special service settings must be known and the appropriateness of each clearly understood. The more restrictive special education programs tend to group students with similar behaviors and learning problems for instruction.

Multidisciplinary Evaluation and Eligibility

If instructional modifications in the regular classroom have not proved successful, a student may be referred for multidisciplinary evaluation. The evaluation is comprehensive and includes norm- and criterion-referenced tests (e.g., IQ and diagnostic tests), curriculum-based assessment, systematic teacher observations (e.g., behavior frequency checklist), samples of student work, and parent interviews. The results of the evaluation are twofold: to determine eligibility for special education services and to identify a student's strengths and weaknesses in order to plan an individual education program.

Eligibility is based on criteria defined in federal law or state regulations. Identification of a mild disability occurs in many states when a student's evaluation results correspond with established eligibility criteria for learning disabilities, mild mental retardation, or behavior disorders. As mentioned previously, there is variation in state eligibility criteria.

Evaluation by a multidisciplinary team is the means by which eligibility criteria is determined. A variety of professionals including a speech-language pathologist, school psychologist, special education teacher, and guidance counselor can be involved in the multidisciplinary evaluation. The wording in federal law is very explicit about the manner in which evaluations must be conducted and about the existence of due process procedures that protect against bias and discrimination. Provisions stated in the law include:

1. Testing of children in their native or primary language unless it is clearly not feasible to do so.
2. Use of evaluation procedures selected and administered to prevent cultural or ethnic discrimination.
3. Use of assessment tools validated for the purpose for which they are being used (e.g., achievement levels, IQ scores, adaptive skills).
4. Assessment by a multidisciplinary team utilizing several pieces of information to formulate a placement decision.

According to the law, parents *must:*

1. Be notified before initial evaluation or any change in placement by a written notice in their primary language describing the proposed school action, the reasons for it, and the available educational opportunities.
2. Consent, in writing, before the child is initially evaluated.
3. Consent, in writing, to classification and placement in least restrictive environment.

Parents *may:*

4. Request an independent educational evaluation if they feel the school's evaluation is inappropriate.
5. Request an evaluation at public expense if a due process hearing decision is that the public agency's evaluation was inappropriate.
6. Participate on the committee that considers the evaluation, placement, and programming of the student.

All students referred for evaluation for special education should have on file the results of a relatively current vision and hearing screening. This will determine the adequacy of sensory acuity and ensure that learning problems are not due to a vision and/or hearing problem.

Evaluation methods correspond with criteria for special education disabilities. For example, a multidisciplinary evaluation for a student being evaluated for mild mental retardation would include the individual's intellectual functioning, adaptive behavior, and achievement levels. Other tests are based on developmental characteristics exhibited (e.g., social, language, and motor).

A student evaluated for learning disabilities is given reading, math, and/or spelling achievement tests, an intelligence test to confirm average or above average cognitive capabilities, and tests of written and oral language ability. Classroom observations and samples of student work (such as impaired reading ability or impaired writing ability) also provide valuable indicators of possible learning disabilities.

Eligibility for services in behavior disorders requires documented evidence of social deficiencies or learning deficits that are not due to intellectual, sensory, or physical conditions. Therefore, any student undergoing multidisciplinary evaluation for this categorical service is usually given an intelligence test, diagnostic achievement tests, and social and/or adaptive inventories. Results of behavior frequency lists, direct observations, and anecdotal records collected over an extended period of time often accompany test results.

Additional information frequently used when making decisions about a child's eligibility for special education include:

- Developmental history
- Past academic performance
- Medical history or records
- Neurological reports
- Classroom observations
- Speech and language evaluations
- Personality assessment
- Discipline reports
- Home visits
- Parent interviews
- Samples of student work

If considered eligible for special education services, the child's disability should be documented in a written report stating specific reasons for the classification decision.

Once very three years, reevaluations of a student's progress are required by law and serve the purpose of determining the growth and changing needs of the student. During the reevaluation, continued eligibility for services in special education must be assessed, using a range of evaluation tools similar to those used during the initial evaluation. All relevant information about the student is considered when making a decision about continued eligibility.

The Individualized Education Program (IEP)

Once a student has been found eligible for special education, the next step is the development of an individualized education program (IEP). The IEP is written during a meeting of the IEP team. The reauthorization of IDEA, signed into law on June 4, 1997, expands the number of members required to serve on an IEP team. According to the June 1997 issue of *CEC Today*, the team will now consist of

> . . . a special and, where appropriate, a general education teacher; an individual who can interpret the instructional implications of evaluation results; the student's patents; a special education administrator; and, at the discretion of the parent or the school, other individuals who have knowledge or special expertise regarding the student (9).

There are instances when the parents do not attend and IEP meeting. The local education agency (LEA) must document its attempts to ensure parental involvement. This documentation includes records of telephone calls, copies of correspondence, and attempts at face-to face contact.

When it is completed, the IEP must include the following:

1. a statement of the youth's present level of educational performance;
2. a statement of annual goals and short-term objectives, and criteria for a determining whether objectives have been met;
3. a description of specific services and programs to be provided;
4. the extent of participation in the regular education program;
5. a statement of services to help a student make the transition from school to the community (mandated for students from 14 to 21);
6. the projected dates and duration of special education services.

Parental consent must be given in order to implement the program once the IEP has been completed. Assessment of whether educational goals and objectives have been met must be completed annually.

Under the 1997 Amendment, a new section of IDEA outlines what the IEP team should consider when developing a student's IEP. These are listed (*CEC Today*, June 1997, 9).

1. The strengths of the child, the parents' concerns for their child's education, and the results of the child's most recent evaluation.
2. If a student's behavior has impeded his or her learning or that of others, the strategies, including positive behavioral interventions, and supports needed to address that behavior.
3. If the student has limited English proficiency, the language needs of the student as they relate to the IEP.
4. If the student is blind or visually imparied, provision of instruction in Braille and the use of Braille.
5. The student's communication needs.
6. Whether the student requires assistive technology devices.

Parent's Participation in Placement. Another new IDEA provision concerns the involvement of parents. This provision clarifies that each state or local education agency shall ensure the parents of each student with a disability that they, the parents, are members of any group that makes decisions about the educational placement of their child.

Placement for Special Education Services.   By law, placement for special education services must be made in the student's least restrictive environment. In actuality, the placement site at which the youngster's goals and objectives in the IEP can best be met is considered to be his or her "least restrictive environment." For students with mild disabilities, this generally is the regular classroom with or without consultative or direct services from a special educator and sometimes services in the resource room. The inclusion of students receiving special education in the general classroom is a placement option in the least restrictive environment continuum of services and is discussed in Chapter 6.

Summary

Students with mild disabilities are those who receive services in special education for learning disabilities, behavior disorders, and mild mental retardation. As a general classroom teacher, or as a special education teacher or consultant, you work with these children and youth every day. If you are or will be a general classroom teacher, these are the students whom you teach full-time or who go to the special education resource room for one to several periods each day. If you are, or are training to be, a special education teacher, these are the students who either appear at your classroom door at a regularly scheduled time each day, or they are those to whom you provide services in the general classroom. You may teach them on the elementary level in an academic content area like mathematics, reading, or spelling, while simultaneously integrating social skills training into scholastic studies. If you are a special teacher of secondary level students, you may also teach prevocational or life career skills, along with content in subject areas like history, geometry, English, and so on.

Regardless of the category in which they are receiving services, these students have similar learning needs. In fact, unless you are informed about each one's specific exceptionality classification, you may not know whether a particular student is labeled mild mentally retarded, learning disabled, or behavior disordered. Because of this, states now deliver services under noncategorical and cross-categorical systems. *Students with mild disabilities are generally more alike than different.*

Generalities can be made about mild disabilities. First, students with mild mental retardation, learning disabilities, and behavior disorders are the largest subgroup of students receiving special education services. In fact, the total group of students with mild mental retardation, behavior disorders, and learning disabilities comprise more than half of the total special education population. Second, they are served primarily during their school-aged years. Mild disabilities are often unrecognized before and after school years. Third, the categories for mild mental retardation, behavior disorders, and learning disabilities are unreliable. Many psychological, educational, and social characteristics overlap. No nationally accepted criteria exist. Although many students with mild disabilities receive special education services, there are some who are incorrectly identified as having a mild disability and others who have a mild disability but are overlooked. Finally, students with mild disabilities are most likely to be placed in the general classroom and in resource services. Effective collaboration between general and special education teachers is vital.

Causes for mild disabilities can primarily be subdivided into two major categories: organic (biological) and environmental. The organic category includes prenatal, perinatal, and postnatal factors, genetic factors, biochemical factors, and maturational lag. Environmental reasons address factors relating to poverty, nutrition, toxins, safety, language differences, sensory deprivation, emotional problems, and inadequate education. In most cases, it is difficult to trace mild disabilities to their origins, and mild learning and behavior difficulties usually remain undetected until children enter school.

Particularly vulnerable populations of at-risk students are identified: infants, preschoolers, and adolescents. Existing and new compensatory education and special incentive programs can offset school failure. School-age students who are not eligible for special education under IDEA are protected from discrimination through Section 504 and the Americans with Disabilities Act. These two Acts also state that reasonable accommodations should be made when needed to benefit educationally students with disabilities who are not eligible for special education. The inability of some students to keep up and make successful progress within our educational system results in an increased number of school dropouts on the secondary level. Failure in school and failure in life is highly predictable.

More effective teaching practices need to be directed toward at-risk students throughout their school careers. More effective collaboration needs to occur between general education, compensatory education, and special education. Likewise, these same efforts must be made among educators and other professionals, parents, and community service personnel.

A series of mandated steps must occur before a student can be delivered services in special education. The full sequence of procedural steps includes: identification of learning problem, prereferral intervention, referral, evaluation, eligibility and classification, development of an individualized education program, placement, and reevaluation. Identification is made from comparisons of academic and behavioral characteristics with those of age-mates. Interventions are modifications that are tried to help the child learn in the regular classroom. The special education referral process is initiated when the student is unable to progress satisfactorily following interventions in the regular education classroom setting. An evaluation is conducted by a multidisciplinary team. If the student meets criteria set forth by the law or other governing regulations, he or she is determined eligible and assigned to a special education category or classification. An individual education plan (IEP) is developed and the student is placed in a special education class that the multidisciplinary team agrees is the individual's least restrictive environment. Every three years, evaluations are required by law in order to determine the growth and changing needs of the student.

Activities

1. Visit a school and observe students with mild learning, intellectual, and behavioral disabilities. Interview the teacher about the characteristics you identify after having read this chapter. Compare your findings about these students with those of Karim, Jack and José in the vignettes.

2. Invite a Head Start or a teacher from an early intervention program to visit your class. Prepare questions about the identification and services for at-risk infants, toddlers, and preschoolers.

3. Have a panel discussion about pros and cons of categorical understanding of students with mild disabilities versus a cross-categorical perspective.

4. Inquire about services on your college/university campus for students with mild disabilities. Which students have services and how are the services provided? Are there students with disabilities who do not have services?

5. Invite a regular education teacher and special education teacher to come to one of your classes. Ask them to comment on categorical versus cross-categorical approaches to teaching students with mild disabilities.

6. Conduct a campus survey. What are students' attitudes about persons with learning disabilities, persons with mild mental retardation, and persons with emotional/behavioral problems?

PART TWO

Teaching Students with Mild Disabilities

6 Least Restrictive Environment

Advance Questions

Answer the following questions as you read this chapter.

1. What comparisons can you make between least restrictive environment, mainstreaming, and inclusion?
2. What problems identified by Madeline Will led educators to develop inclusion programs?

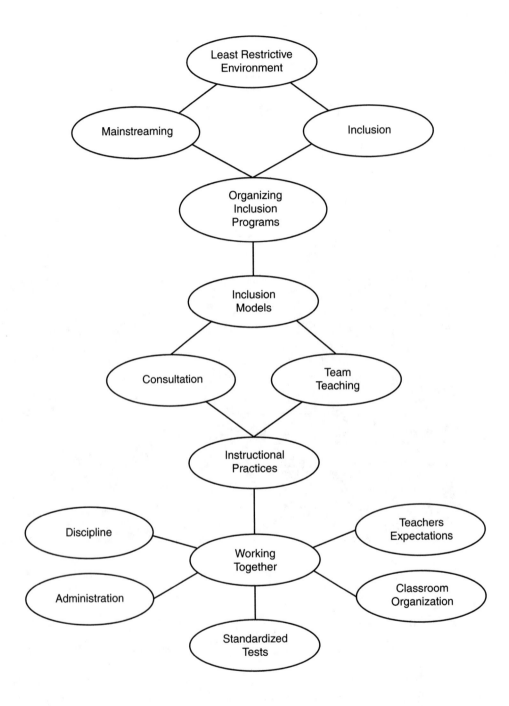

3. What are five steps for setting-up an inclusion program.
4. How does consultation and team teaching support inclusion?
5. How would you organize a peer tutoring program?
6. What is cooperative learning and how would you use cooperative learning in the classroom?
7. What is the whole language approach to reading? How does it differ from phonics approach to teaching reading?
8. How does career education support inclusion?
9. What is open Education?
10. What are the benefits of using computers in the classroom?
11. What are five key issues that both general and special educators are concerned with?

Vignette: Luis, Pablo, and Karim

Luis Lopez could name the exact day he decided to quit teaching students with mild disabilities. It wasn't that he didn't like teaching his special class at Gerena Elementary School. For the first time in their lives, Luis' students enjoyed school. They were learning new skills and gaining confidence in themselves. By all measures Luis was a success. His special class for students with learning and emotional disabilities had received accolades from numerous professionals, including education professors from the nearby university. Luis seemed to be doing all the right things, but it all ended abruptly for him on Tuesday, January 27.

It was an ordinary morning, but Luis knew there was going to be trouble when Karim climbed off his school bus and stormed into the classroom. "They called me retarded," Karim said as he slammed his books on his desk. Pablo filed in next. "The kids on the corner say we ride the 'retard bus'." Pablo's face was red and he appeared ready to explode. The boys' anger set off a chain reaction among Luis' other students as they described the humiliation of riding a special education bus to school.

That afternoon while Luis was driving home, he came to a simple but powerful conclusion. Any success he had as a teacher would never offset the stigma his students felt because of their placement in a special class. The neighborhood kids were wrong; his students were not retarded. But what difference did the label make? The fact remained that his students wanted to be accepted as normal kids. This was more important to them than reading, math, or a high school diploma. Luis' world was turned topsy-turvy when the magnitude of his situation sunk in. By developing a model special education program, Luis was contributing to the segregation of his students. Sure he was planning to mainstream some of them soon, but Luis knew that as soon as a few moved out, the school system would quickly replace them with others. As the weeks passed, Luis realized he could no longer teach special education students in a self-contained, special education program. At the end of the year, Luis resigned and entered graduate school.

Luis, like many other good special education teachers, was caught in a catch-22 situation. If he continued to develop an exemplary special class program, he would get more referrals and placements. As his reputation grew, it would be easier for his school system administrators to convince parents that a special class was the best choice for their children; yet Luis' goal was to return his students into general education classrooms. He was enough of a realist to understand that special education classes were dead-end solutions. The longer a student stayed in a special class, the less likely he or she would be ever to return to a general education program. As Luis saw it, the cards were stacked against kids who didn't fit into the system. It was ironic, he thought, that the better he became as a special educator, the more he would contribute to limiting his students' opportunities.

1. Do you think Luis' problem is a fair representation of how special education teachers feel about their work?
2. Did Luis overreact?
3. What other options did Luis have beside quitting?
4. Did Luis let his students down by leaving?
5. Is it common place for students to be stigmatized because they are placed in self-contained special education classrooms?

Luis' story illustrates a basic principle of human nature. Each of us wants to be viewed as normal. When students are categorized and shipped into self-contained special classrooms, they are viewed as deviants by their peers and eventually by themselves. During the civil rights struggle of the 1960s and 1970s, many people fought, and some died, in order that others could be integrated into mainstream society. Today individuals with disabilities are fighting those same battles and the stakes are just as high. In 1954, the Supreme Court ruled in *Brown v. The Topeka Board of Education* that separate but equal was unconstitutional. Yet separation of disabled and nondisabled is a commonplace occurrence in public schools.

The integration of students from special education into general education is called mainstreaming. It is one of the most discussed and least understood concepts in special education. When the Individuals with Disabilities Education Act (IDEA) was passed in 1975, the media dubbed it the "mainstreaming law." Many educators believed mainstreaming meant that students with mild to severe disabilities would be placed in regular classrooms.

The worst fears of educators who viewed the federal law as an intrusion into the regular classroom never materialized. Rather, an opposite trend began to build—the movement of students out of general education into special education programs. In 1977, 3,708,601 students received special education services; ten years later 4,421,601 students were identified as disabled and receiving special education services (Jordan, 1989). While the total special education population grew by 700,000, the number of students with mild disabilities skyrocketed. For example, in 1977 there were 797,226 students with learning disabilities identified in the public schools. By 1995, the number of students with a learning disability increased to 2,513,977 (U.S. Department of Education, 1996).

Rather than more special education students put in general classrooms, we witnessed a reverse trend—more general education students were placed in special education programs. We estimate that approximately 15,000 students are referred each week for special education services. In Massachusetts for instance almost seventeen percent of the student population is receiving special education. Where did all these special education students come from? Were they sitting undetected in general education classrooms, or have special education mandates provided a fast track out of general education for problem learners? (Massachusetts Department of Education, 1996)

Least Restrictive Environment

The term mainstreaming does not appear in federal legislation; rather, the mandate for keeping special education students in general education comes from the "least restrictive environment" provision of the law. When students are educated in the least restrictive environment, they are taught in classrooms that most closely approximate a normal learning situation. For many students with mild disabilities, the least restrictive environment is full-time placement in a general education classroom. For students who require more intensive remedial help, the least restrictive environment would be part-time resource room instruction with the majority of their school day spent in the general classroom. When students with special needs are segregated in full-time special classes or alternative special education programs, they are in the *most* restrictive environment. Their opportunities to associate with nonspecial-needs children are severely limited.

When a student with a mild disabling condition is placed in a special education program, there is a presumption that it is a temporary situation. Placement in a special education program is no badge of distinction for child or parent. Indeed, if parents suspected that, once identified as having a special need, their youngster would be permanently tracked in special education, it is unlikely that they would be so cooperative and eager to have their child receive special education services.

When Gartner and Lipsky requested data from the federal government on numbers of special education students who return full-time to regular education, they received the following reply.

> Thank you for your letter in which you ask about data concerning children who had been certified as handicapped and have returned to regular education. While these are certainly very interesting data you request, these data are not required in State Plans nor has the Office for Special Education Programs collected them in any other survey. (Gartner & Lipsky, 1987, 367)

The absence of data on the success rate of students returned to regular education raises questions about program efficacy and the ability of special education services to remediate learning difficulties.

Least Restrictive

```
↑   I     1. Full-time general class/
|   N        room placement with
|   T        support services. (Inclusion)
|   E
|   G     2. Resource room (pull-out)
|   R        program for part of the
|   A        day, and general education
|   T        placement without special
|   E        education services the rest
|   D        of the day (Mainstreaming)

|   S     3. Full-time placement in
|   E        self-contained special
|   G        classroom in regular
|   R        school.
|   E     4. Special day or alternative
|   G        school program outside
|   A        of regular school.
|   T     5. Homebound/Hospital.
|   E     6. Residential facility.
↓   D     7. Correctional facility.
```

Most Restrictive

FIGURE 6.1 Continuum of Special Education Placements

In a study of three American cities—Milwaukee, Wisconsin; Charlotte, North Carolina; and Rochester, New York—researchers found that over a two-year period 17 percent of youngsters with special needs terminated special education services and returned full time to the general classroom. The remaining 83 percent of students remained in special education (Walker et al., 1988). The majority of the students in the study were identified as speech impaired, mentally retarded, learning disabled, and behavior disordered. Students identified as speech impaired (33 percent) were most likely to return to general education. Children identified as learning disabled had the next highest return rate (14.9 percent). Students with behavioral disorders were more likely to be reclassified than returned full time to general education classrooms. Two years after initial placement, less than one in ten students with behavior disorders returned to regular education.

When students with disabilities are kept out of the mainstream of normal school life, it underscores the differences between them and students without disabilities. Indeed many separate special education programs are classified by such categories of disabilities as emotionally disturbed, mentally retarded, or behavior disordered. When a student is grouped with eight to ten other "behavior disordered" students, taught in a program by a teacher who is trained in "emotional disturbance," and isolated in a special classroom that is located in a secluded area of the school, it is unlikely that the student will either feel or act "normal."

The intent of the least restrictive environment provision of the law is to assure that a student's special education program is as normal as possible. Each school system is required to provide a continuum of special education placements. Figure 6.1 lists special education programs for learners with special needs ranging from least to most restrictive environments. Once the bold line is crossed, a student is out of the mainstream, and the prospects for return to a normal school experience are bleak. (This might be a good time to return to Chapter 1 and review the descriptions of each type of special education placement.)

Mainstreaming

Mainstreaming means returning students to general education classrooms without special education services. Many articles and essays describe the advantages of mainstreaming; for example, students with mild disabilities develop better academic and socialization skills when they are educated in well-organized mainstreamed classrooms (Guralnick & Groom, 1988; Wang & Baker, 1986). Yet there are reports about failed mainstreaming and teacher concerns for students who are "over their heads" or "lost" in general classrooms. As Susan Ohanian states, it takes more than good intentions and administrative fiat to make mainstreaming work. In the following excerpt from "P.L. 94–142: Mainstream or Quicksand," she highlights the folly of unplanned mainstreaming endeavors.

> When following the mandates of P.L. 94–142 we need to figure out just what it means to mainstream children "to the maximum extent appropriate to their needs." Many school districts lump all children with learning problems together in a sort of academic twilight zone. The educable mentally retarded [i.e., students with mild mental retardation], the low normal, the learning disabled (whatever that means this week), and the emotionally disturbed are all sent off to regular English, science, social studies, and mathematics classes—until the situation becomes too traumatic either for the child or for the teacher. I always figured my district had to see blood before it would demainstream a child. (Ohanian, 1991, 219)

Mainstreaming works if benefits are accrued by students with special needs, general education students, and their teachers. A general education teacher who is asked to take a youngster with a mild disability into her classroom might legitimately ask, "What's in it for me and my students?" After all, is it fair to ask general educators to teach special education students at the expense of the other students? The answer is unequivocal—no. An educational program that does not have something for everybody is headed for failure. Teachers, administrators, and parents will not tolerate the education of a minority of students if it takes away from the learning of the majority.

Wang and Baker's (1986) meta-analysis of eleven empirical studies on mainstreaming indicated that mainstreamed students consistently achieved better than nonmainstreamed students with comparable disabilities. The paradox of students with special needs doing better in general rather than special education programs can be explained by several factors.

1. The research on the ineffectiveness of tracking students by ability groups demonstrates that students perform better academically in heterogeneous groups than in homogeneous groups (Lewis, 1990; Massachusetts Department of Education, 1991).
2. Modeling enhances learning. Students naturally imitate their peers. Good peer models provide teachers with success examples that can help encourage students with learning problems to strive harder.
3. Teacher expectations for success go up in relationship to perception of a student's capability. Mainstreamed students may benefit from increased teacher expectations because the student is perceived to be ready to succeed in the regular classroom.
4. Teachers who were used as mainstreaming research subjects may try harder to succeed with their students. The "Hawthorne Effect" (i.e., trying harder to excel because of the perceived special status of being a research subject) is well-documented in research annals.
5. How students feel about their abilities has a lot to do with success. Students in special education programs may feel stigmatized. This can affect motivation and perseverance, two crucial elements in school success.
6. Teachers who agree to accept mainstreamed students may be more skilled than their colleagues.

Inclusion

Inclusion is a movement designed to bring special education services into the general classroom. This is a significant change from the traditional practice of having students receive special services in resource rooms or self-contained special education classrooms and then return to general education classrooms without special education support (i.e., mainstreaming). See Table 6.1.

In 1986, Madeline Will, the Assistant Secretary for Special Education and Rehabilitative Services, reported on the status of educational programming for hard-to-teach students. She noted that despite intensive efforts to remediate learning difficulties through remedial education, Title 1, bilingual education, migrant education, and special education students were still dropping out of school at a 25 percent rate per year. She also noted that 30 percent of high school graduates were functionally illiterate. Will concluded that a merger of special education

TABLE 6.1 Key Definitions

Least restrictive environment: Students with disabilities must be placed in appropriate education programs to meet their individual needs. Every effort should be made to place students with special needs in general education programs. Parents and the school system together select from a continuum of special education placements to determine what is the least restrictive setting for a student.

Mainstreaming: Students with disabilities placed in general education classrooms either full or part-time without special education support.

Inclusion: Students with disabilities placed in general education classrooms full-time with special education support services provided.

---

and general education services would enhance the ability of the public schools to educate students at risk of school failure.

According to Will, four obstacles to effective educational progress are unintentional by-products of special education services.

1. *Fragmented instruction.* Students who do not meet eligibility criteria for specific remedial programs "fall through the cracks" and receive no special help. Financial incentives determine program choices. School systems "put the child where the money is with too little regard for educational need." Many who receive special services are put in "pull-out programs," others in self-contained classrooms. Meanwhile, there is a lack of coordination between general and special educators. Consequently remedial and special education students fall further behind in their studies. Each minute they spend in a special program, students miss a minute of regular classroom instruction. Likewise, students who could use extra help are overlooked because their learning problems are not severe enough to qualify for remedial or special education. The present system of general education emphasizes remediation rather than prevention of learning problems.

2. *Dual systems.* Special and general education have separate administrative structures, distinct budgets, and separate training for teachers. The duality of these systems creates a gap between the general and special educator. Building principals do not feel ownership of special programs because of separate financial, administrative, and decision-making procedures. Special education teachers feel estranged from general teachers because they tutor students in resource rooms or teach small groups of students in self-contained classrooms. The physical isolation of special education classrooms minimizes contact, communication, and mutual problem solving. With these constraints it is difficult to foster a sense of shared responsibility for the instructional needs of special learners. Learning becomes jeopardized when special and regular instruction do not complement each other.

3. *Stigmatization of students.* Schools are social environments. Isolation of students from their peers decreases self-esteem and increases negative attitudes about school. All children want to be accepted and feel they belong. Low expectations for success, failure to persist on tasks, learned helplessness, and continued school failure are some of the negative consequences of separating students into categories of "special needs."

4. *Placement decision as battleground.* The Individuals with Disabilities Education Act is based on the premise that parents have much to contribute in making school-based decisions. Requirements for special programs can place teachers and parents in opposing positions. Parents get stereotyped as "pushy" if they fight to get a youngster into special education and "uncaring" if they don't attend school meetings. The cumulative effects of these misunderstandings are "a series of adversarial, hit-and-run encounters" between parents and educators.

Will summarized her position on the need for coordination between special and general education by pointing out that the "major flaw" in school practice is the belief that improvement in student performance is dependent upon the creation of new educational environments. Instead of viewing a learning problem as a deficiency in the student, Will recommended a reevaluation of the classroom setting where the learning problem is first observed and a reallocation of resources to maintain students in the general classroom.

The strategy of merging general education with special education and other remedial programs appeared to be an idea whose time had arrived. Criticisms of special education programs for students with mild disabilities had mounted over the preceding years. Hobbs's (1975) position that classifying students by disabling conditions was "a major barrier to efficient and effective delivery of services" seemed more valid than ever. Wang, Reynolds, and Walberg (1986) reported that only twenty percent of special education students were classified according to rigorous physical and physiological measures. Will (1986) pointed out that the proliferation of "pull-out" programs had created a fragmented approach to educational intervention that failed to meet the educational needs of learners with mild disabilities. Stainback and Stainback (1984) recommended a unitary system of education to replace the splintered approach of providing help through regular, special, remedial, migrant, bilingual, and Title 1 education programs.

Inclusion eliminates pull-out programs for remedial populations. Within the inclusion model personnel, money, and material resources are reallocated for use in the general education classroom. General education teachers, with support, take on greater responsibility for the education of special populations. One of the major rationales for inclusion is that it provides a better academic environment for students with mild disabilities than either pull-out (resource room) programs or separate special education classes.

Organizing Inclusion Programs

Careful planning precedes the implementation of successful inclusion programs. Inclusion will not work if teachers are coerced to comply or if special and regular educators are not given ample time to plan together. Students cannot be included with the expectation that simply seating students with mild disabilities next to other youngsters in a general classroom is a formula for success. There are five basic strategies that help ensure an inclusion program will work for both teachers and students. By following the guidelines of establishing entrance criteria, communicating with parents, understanding student needs, preparing for a change, and evaluating progress, teachers will increase the probability of a successful inclusion program.

Establish Entrance Criteria. Full-time placement in the general classroom begins with identification of criteria for inclusion. Criteria might include such classroom behaviors as "follows directions" and "works independently." When regular and special educators work together to develop criteria for a particular classroom or school, an inclusion program has the best chance for success (Morsink, Thomas, & Correa, 1991).

Although some educators recommend academic criteria for inclusion, this approach should be used cautiously. For the majority of youngsters with mild disabilities, it was lack of academic skills that prompted their removal from regular classes in the first place. Strict academic criteria for inclusion, such as reading at grade level, may in fact act as a screening system to keep students out of the regular classroom. The notion of grade level as an academic goal is misleading because the statistical concept is based on 50 percent of a student population reading below the standard set for grade level!

Communicate with Parents. Parents play a vital role in student achievement. Parents of students with mild disabilities attend individual education program conferences, participate in decisions regarding type of special services, and approve placement changes. Lack of communication between teachers and parents can foster misunderstandings and adversarial positions. Parents are concerned about their youngster's progress in school. They want to be kept informed and need to know that the teacher respects their views.

Often the only time parents hear from the teacher is when something is wrong. A weekly note indicating classroom successes, a home visit, or a monthly phone call to review student progress can bridge the communication gap between home and school. Parents can provide information on a student's interests, likes, dislikes, and time spent outside of school. When parents feel that the teacher values their input, crossover learning between school and the family is more likely to occur. A productive teacher–parent partnership can be a powerful alliance for change and growth in a youngster's life.

Understand Student Needs.   Full-time entry into a general classroom can be an anxiety provoking experience for a student. Special education programs provide a safe haven from the demands of normal school routines, and special education students may experience "newness panic" (Red and Wineman, 1951). Some students withdraw, while others act out in uncharacteristic ways. It is not unusual for a recently included student to regress to disruptive behaviors that the special education teacher thought were eliminated. The first few weeks is not the time to evaluate the viability of the inclusion decision. The included student needs reassurance that a few bumps in the road will be tolerated.

When a student is identified as having a mild disability, it is sometimes difficult to remember that the student has the same developmental needs of other children. Students with mild disabilities are more alike than different from nondisabled students. A student with dyslexia has difficulty reading, but this academic activity is a small slice of a youngster's daily experience. Students with dyslexia play Little League, get into trouble, and sing in church choirs, just like other children. All adolescents share a common need for group approval and independence from authority. These developmental needs are just as immediate in a youngster with an emotional or behavior disorder as with other adolescents. Interpreting a youngster's behavior from a developmental perspective rather than an assigned school label provides a clearer picture of a youngster's actions.

Prepare for a Change.   General and special education classrooms differ in many respects (Deno, Maruyama, Espin, & Cohen, 1990). A self-contained special class, for instance, ranges from eight to twelve students. In the special class, a youngster has an individualized academic program and constant adult attention. General classrooms, on the other hand, contain large groups of twenty to thirty-five students. In the general classroom, students must follow directions, wait for teacher assistance, and concentrate on learning tasks with minimum adult supervision. Before initiating inclusion it makes sense to begin a transition program to help prepare the student for the upcoming change.

Because educational materials, routines, and behavioral expectations are different in the general classroom, the student can begin adapting while still in the special education program. The special educator can teach classroom routines. For example, the general classroom teacher might require note-taking or homework. The use of textbooks and completion of general classroom assignments can begin in the special education program. The student needs success with new routines and activities in the secure confines of the special program in order to build confidence for general classroom performance.

Adequate preparation requires communication and planning between special and regular educators (Schulte, Osborne, & McKinney, 1990; Zigmond & Baker, 1990). Meetings between teachers provide a basis for problem solving, goal-setting, and evaluation of student progress. As an illustration, teachers might decide to begin inclusion gradually. Students could begin by spending forty-five minutes a day in the general classroom for the first month. The teachers decide to pick a high interest time, such as science, where the special education students would work on a small group project with new classmates. This plan would decrease student anxieties about academics, while providing an opportunity to make friends. During the initial month, the special and general educators evaluate progress and make adjustments in classroom routines.

Inclusion places an additional burden on the general classroom teacher. Before inclusion the classroom teacher, special education teacher, and building level administrator need a plan to provide support for the general classroom teacher. Support could include additional planning time, consultation, team teaching, new instructional materials, or a teacher aide.

Evaluate Progress.   Enormous amounts of time and money are spent by school systems to assess the educational status of children referred for special education. Norm-referenced tests measure how they compare in academics to their peers. Criterion-referenced tests pinpoint specific strengths and weaknesses in academics. Psychological tests attempt to determine whether a student has mild mental retardation, a learning disability, or an emotional disturbance. Observations detail learning styles and student ability to adapt to classroom routines. These are the most common evaluation procedures used to identify and place youngsters in special programs.

Once students have moved full time into the general classroom, the need to evaluate progress does not diminish. However, evaluation methods shift to curriculum-based assessment. Samples of student work, observations of student interaction, and charting of student progress provide detailed evaluative information. Students' individual education programs are reviewed to match learning objectives with classroom work. Evaluation also includes assessment of teaching behavior. Does the teacher provide enough time for the student to answer questions? Are classroom materials adapted to meet student needs? Is the student seated in an area of the room that makes it easier to concentrate and follow teacher directions? Is the teacher providing enough hands-on activities to help students master specific skills? These are a sample of questions that could guide observations of teaching methods in an inclusion program.

Court Cases

When making the decision to put a student in an inclusive setting two legal principles included in IDEA need to be balanced—least restrictive environment and appropriate educational placement. A series of court cases during the 1980s and 1990s provide legal precedents for how school systems and parents work together to determine the best placement for a youngster. In *Roncker v. Walker* (U.S 6th Cir., 1983) the court established the "feasibility" principle.

> In a case where the segregrated facility is considered superior, the court should determine whether the services which make the placement superior could be

feasibly (emphasis added) provided in a non-segregated setting. If they can, the placement in the segregated school would be inappropriate under the Act. (cited *CEC Today*, p. 4, 1996).

Roncker v. Walker was influential in highlighting the need for a full continuum of services for students and confirmed that for some students a segregated special education program was a better placement than an inclusive general education classroom.

In *Daniel R.R. v. State Board of Education* (U.S. 5th Cir., 1989) the court moved in the opposite direction and stated that Roncker placed too much emphasis on educational benefit. This ruling broke new ground by deciding that the nonacademic benefits of general education classrooms also need to be taken into account. *Daniel R.R.* established a two-part test for inclusion. First, the court asked if the addition of supplemental aids and services will help a student achieve satisfactory progress in the general education classroom. If the answer is "no", the second test is whether the school has included the student with special needs in general curriculum activities to the maximum extent appropriate. By placing more responsibility on school systems to justify why a student is not included in general education classrooms, *Daniel R.R.* gave inclusion a legal boost that led to a large increase of students with special needs placed within inclusive classrooms. An often overlooked side note to the *Daniel R.R.* decision was that the court stated that the effect of inclusion on general education students should also be taken into consideration.

A U.S. Ninth Circuit court case *Sacramento City Unified School District, Board of Education v. Rachel Holland*, simplified previous decisions by establishing four criteria for determining if an inclusive setting is appropriate: academic benefits of general education, nonacademic benefits of general education, effects of a student with a disability on other students, and the cost of inclusion. The school system argued the student could not be maintained in the general education classroom without first having provided supplemetary services and assistance within the general education classroom. The court decided that a segreagated special placement was inappropriate and directed that Rachel be placed in an inclusive classroom.

Each of these court cases will continue to be refined by others, however it is clear that the mandate for an appropriate education requires that a continuum of educational placements must be made available to students with special needs. If parents opt for an inclusion program for their youngster, and the school system disagrees, it is incumbent on the school system to explain why the general education classroom cannot be modified to accommodate the special needs student.

Inclusion Models

Every profession has models for putting theories to work. Economists have supply-and-demand models for explaining changes in financial trends. Psychologists use developmental models to explain human behavior. Like a blueprint, a model provides a set of instructions for the application of an idea. Education has many models. There are instructional models, assessment models, and discipline models. In education, a model is judged in terms of its usefulness. An elaborate model of instruction may be well researched in terms of how children learn, but if it requires too much teacher time or is too expensive to implement, teachers will look someplace else for ideas. Teachers like practical ideas that increase student competence. A good idea for one teacher may seem esoteric or nonfunctional to another. Teachers adopt models that match their professional philosophy and personal values.

A set of guidelines for inclusion qualifies as a model when it has proved effective in a variety of educational programs. This is no easy task because circumstances vary so much from region to region, system to system, and from school to school. The following two topics; consultation and instructional practices, describe inclusion models that have proved useful in many classrooms.

Each approach can stand on its own or be combined with other models and strategies. Ultimately, the choice of an inclusion model depends on how well it matches the needs of students, teachers, and parents.

Consultation

One of the most often cited criticisms of the teaching profession is the lack of career options for those who are not inclined toward administration. Teachers can spend thirty years in a classroom with few opportunities to share their wisdom or expertise. The consulting teacher is a role that can enhance teacher effectiveness by replacing direct special instruction of students with collaboration between special and general education. Consultation enables teachers with diverse expertise to generate creative solutions to mutually defined problems.

The consulting teacher model is an alternative to the pull-out approach to special education services (Phillips & McCullough, 1990). Instead of working directly with special needs students (for example, in a resource room), the consulting teacher plans with the general classroom teacher to facilitate inclusion. Some of the responsibilities of the consulting teacher include observing in the general classroom, sharing materials with the general classroom teacher, demonstrating instructional techniques, coordinating programs, and presenting in-service workshops for general educators.

The consulting teacher provides intervention at the site of the learning problem. Both the student with the learning problem and the instructor with the teaching problem can be helped within the general classroom. Consultation can remedy such disadvantages of pull-out programs as fragmentation of instruction and stigmatization of students. It provides a viable means for educators to jointly own the problem of a difficult learner. Through a process of shared problem solving, collaborative consultation crosses over boundaries that have traditionally separated general and special educators.

In Winooski, Vermont, special education professionals provided services by team teaching with general classroom teachers. In Montlake, a Seattle elementary school, pull-out programs were eliminated. The general and general education teachers team taught multi-age reading and math groups. No distinction, in either of these two programs, was made between special and general students (Villa & Thousand, 1988).

When Jenkins and Heinen (1989) asked remedial and special education students if they preferred help from their general classroom teacher or a resource room teacher the students chose their general teacher. An interesting footnote to the student preference study was their choice of resource room services over special education instruction in the general classroom. It seems that leaving the classroom for remediation is less embarrassing than having a specialist work directly with the student in the general classroom. This is an important piece of information for educators who favor direct special services (e.g., one-to-one aides) to students in the general classroom. It is clear from this study that students do not wish to draw attention to their learning problems, and, given the choice, they would choose the less stigmatizing alternative of leaving the classroom for remedial help.

The consulting teacher concept seems to offer clear advantages to both teachers and students. It consolidates services, provides expertise in hard to reach rural areas, and can save school districts money while improving educational services to students. Yet the consulting model presents its own set of problems that must be addressed in order to gain the desired results.

Consulting requires careful scheduling and administrative support. Consulting is ineffective if the classroom teacher and consulting teacher do not have adequate time to plan. The building principal controls each classroom teacher's schedule. Administrative support in terms of release time and a nonjudgmental view toward teachers who are working with a consultant are two prerequisites for successful implementation of this model.

Consulting requires diplomatic communication skills on the part of the consultant and a readiness to cooperate on the part of the consultee. Any "helper" has a power advantage over the person who is being helped. The need for consultation, if not handled properly, can imply weaknesses in the ability of the recipient. Imagine the following scenario. A twenty-four-year-old special education teacher has just completed graduate training as a teacher consultant, and her first assignment is a teacher who is a twenty-year veteran of the public schools. The teacher was selected by her principal because she has a higher than average referral rate for special education services, and the principal wants to establish an inclusion model. It is clear, without drawing out this illustration any further, that a successful outcome is problematic. How will the general classroom teacher feel about this "youngster" observing in her classroom and offering suggestions for changes in instruction? How will the consultant deal with the general classroom teacher's attitude toward outside help? Can consulting work when the general classroom teacher has not directly requested outside assistance?

Consulting works when there is genuine collaboration among all parties (e.g., general classroom teacher, consultant, special services teachers). There are superb and mediocre teachers in both special and general education. For the consulting teacher model to be useful, there needs to be a commitment to sharing of expertise and resources on both sides of the fence (Pugach & Johnson, 1989a). Trust must precede collaborative problem solving. Consultant teachers should be selected from the ranks of the most experienced and respected teachers in a school system. Pinning the title "consultant" on a teacher who lacks the expertise or interpersonal skills to work with classroom teachers will disrupt rather than facilitate mainstreaming efforts.

The consultant teacher model seems well-suited to facilitate the inclusion of students with mild disabilities. It is designed to provide services to both students and teacher in the general classroom. Through consulting, special educators can advance the integration of both their students and themselves. It is a holistic approach to what has become a very fragmented instructional pattern in public schools—the removal of hard-to-teach students from their normal classroom setting. Ultimately, the success of the consulting teacher model depends on a mutual sharing of ideas, methods, and responsibilities between regular and special educators.

Team Teaching

Team teaching means that both the special and general education teacher work together full time in the general classroom. There are several advantages to this approach:

1. Instead of working in isolation the teachers work as partners and share planning and instructional responsibilities.
2. There is an emphasis on prevention because both teachers are able to intervene to alleviate learning problems as they are developing.
3. Communication with parents is enhanced.
4. Students get help from both teachers without being stigmatized.
5. Special education materials and other resources such as instructional aides are used in the general classroom.
6. Responsibility for the learning of all students is equally shared between general and special educators.

Sometimes team teaching programs are set up as multigrade classrooms. For example, a third- and fourth-grade class might be combined with two general education teachers and one special education teacher. Selling this idea to parents can be problematic because of concerns about quality of instruction when two grade curriculums are covered simultaneously. Parents of the fourth-grade students might feel their children are getting a watered down curriculum, while the parents of the third-grade children might be concerned that the curriculum is too advanced for their youngsters.

Of course team teaching also presents all the problems inherent in cooperative work. Teachers are used to being independent and difficulties can arise around instructional approaches, discipline, and sharing of preparation. Inevitably there are personality conflicts when teachers are not involved in the decision about who will work together. Team teaching arrangements, especially multiage classrooms, need careful planning. It is best to run a pilot program in a school before beginning a team teaching program that will involve several classrooms.

Instructional Practices

Teachers never cease to puzzle about how to teach students with varying abilities. Students are so different in personality, motivation, work habits, and interests that even the best teachers are challenged to keep all their students involved in learning. The selection of the following instructional practices is based on the flexibility each provides for teaching students who are different. These are a sample of worthwhile instructional practices for maintaining students with mild disabilities in the general classroom.

Peer Tutoring.   One of the best ways to learn something is to teach it to someone else. Cloward (1967) reported that high school students in a New York City antipoverty program gained nearly five months on grade level for each month they tutored another student. Peer tutoring can be equally effective for students with and without mild disabilities. For example, Maheady, Sacca, & Harper (1988) established a classwide peer tutoring program for fifty tenth-grade social studies students. The students ranged in age from fifteen to seventeen years. Weekly study guides developed by regular and special education teachers were used as the basis for half-hour tutoring periods, three times a week. Progress was measured by weekly quizzes. The researchers reported that the implementation of CWPT (classwide peer tutoring) resulted in an increase in test scores for both special and regular education students.

Peer tutoring places the responsibility for learning on the student. This is a potent change for students with mild disabilities who are often passive learners. With a tutor, students accustomed to sitting alone at their desks waiting for the teacher are directly involved in their learning. Peer tutoring provides individualized instruction. The nonthreatening aspect of peer tutoring encourages students to admit a lack of understanding without concern about adult evaluation. Working with another student provides a youngster with opportunities to discuss, question, practice, and evaluate learning with immediate feedback. Jenkins and Jenkins (1981) described seven steps to implement a peer tutoring program.

1. *Determine which children are to be tutored.* Start small. Begin with four or five students who like to work with other children. Slow development of a tutoring program gives the teacher opportunities to restructure tutoring sessions as needed. Tutoring is not for everyone. Students who are serious behavior problems may not respond well to working with fellow students.

2. *Prepare the school for tutoring.* The principal and teachers who are involved in the program must be convinced that a tutoring program will not disrupt regular school activities. A written proposal outlining scheduling and monitoring procedures will ensure that all participants are clear about each person's role. Accountability is a major issue in schools. The tutoring program developer should reassure the other teachers that time used for tutoring will not detract from the tutor's classroom performance.

3. *Determine a time for tutoring.* Daily sessions of one half-hour produce the best peer tutoring results. Peer tutoring within the classroom does not present the scheduling difficulties that occur when two separate classes are involved. Working out a program between classrooms requires careful negotiation of time and space—two valuable commodities in schools. Establish a set time each day for tutoring sessions. When a program is initiated, adjustments in plans are almost always required. This is a normal consequence of implementing a novel idea. Build in a first week evaluation, with the expectation that adjustments in schedules will be needed.

4. *Inform parents about the program.* Parents are always curious about school programs that vary from traditional teacher instruction. In public schools, even minor changes can have a ripple effect. Some teachers, particularly those who are not involved in the program, may be suspicious of its value. It is best that parents receive written notice about peer tutoring rather than hearing about it from their children or other parents. Such a letter would contain a brief description of the program skills that students will learn, program supervision methods, and evaluation procedures. Invite parents to school to observe the tutoring program in action.

5. *Design lessons and a measurement system.* Decide what content tutors are to teach; then specifically detail tutoring methods. For example, a reading lesson might involve five minutes of listening to oral reading followed by the tutee writing a list of words she found difficult. Then the tutee could write a sentence containing each word. Tutors need clear guidelines for their work. Avoid unstructured tutoring sessions where the students are not sure of their responsibilities. Detailing student progress on daily charts is a recommended procedure for keeping track of program effectiveness.

6. *Conduct tutor training.* Although tutorial skills will vary with age and content, there are some general training needs applicable to all tutors. Each tutor should be clear about punctuality, confidentiality, and positive regard for the tutee. Schoolwork needs to be evaluated in a systematic manner. The tutor will need to understand how progress is measured. Daily charts, percentage of correct answers, or random samples of behavior are examples of data that tutors commonly are asked to maintain.

The tutor will require training. A natural tendency to prompt or do the work for a tutee can be addressed by the teacher modeling proper instructional behavior. The tutor is a helper. This requires the ability to interact in a positive manner. Some key interpersonal skills are active listening and praising good effort. Change behaviors that intimidate or cause the tutee to feel incompetent. Model error correction behaviors that encourage sustained effort.

7. *Maintain tutor's involvement and interest.* Frequent reminders of the tutor's positive contributions can be gleaned from tutee progress charts. Special recognition at assemblies or through the awarding of certificates will serve the dual purpose of rewarding tutors and encouraging other students to be involved with the program. Teaching is no less a difficult endeavor for a youngster than it is for an adult. Periodic group meetings with tutors can provide the program developer with opportunities for refining the program and boosting morale.

Peer tutoring is cost effective, and it provides a student with individual attention. If conducted in a thoughtful and systematic manner, peer tutoring can increase school achievement and motivation of both students.

Cooperative Learning. According to William Glasser (Gough, 1987), when students lack control over their learning, motivation to persevere is undermined. Glasser contends that student cooperation and motivation demonstrated in extracurricular activities can be transferred into the classroom. Cooperative learning is a method of structuring small groups of nondisabled and disabled students so that all the individuals achieve a learning goal through mutual planning and decision making.

Cooperative learning can be used with all age groups to teach any part of the curriculum. Putnam and her colleagues (1989) compared fifty studies of cooperative, competitive, and individualistic learning situations. Cooperative learning produced more instances of positive relationships between students with and without disabilities. Benefits from cooperative learning include: increased student motivation, higher test scores, and enhanced social skills (Johnson & Johnson, 1986; Putnam et al., 1989; Slavin, Madden, & Leavey, 1984; Smith, 1987).

There are four steps to establishing cooperative learning groups in the classroom:

1. *The teacher selects members of each learning group.* Cooperative learning groups are heterogeneous in composition with a balance between males and females, high and low achievers, and active and passive students. A typical group would include three to six students with no more than one student with a mild disability. The balance of the groups is crucial to ensure that each group has strengths to offset individual academic or social weaknesses.

2. *The teacher directly teaches cooperative group skills.* Most students are conditioned to earn grades based on individual work, often in competition with other students. Such familiar refrains in classrooms as, "Pay attention to your own work," or "no talking while we are working" are antithetical to cooperative learning. The teacher who uses cooperative learning wants students to talk and work with each other. Cooperative learning requires such interpersonal skills as the ability to trust and work with others; good listening skills; acceptance and support of others; and the ability to resolve conflicts constructively (Johnson & Johnson, 1990).

Some students may have difficulty making the transition from passive, teacher directed learning to cooperative learning activities. Roy Smith (1987) found he needed to teach his junior high school students how to work cooperatively. He described six steps for teaching cooperative skills:

a. Identify the specific skills group members will need to demonstrate; for instance, listening or providing information.
b. Help students become aware of the need for cooperative skills.
c. Help students gain a clear understanding of each skill.
d. Provide students with situations in which to practice cooperative skills.
e. Give students descriptive feedback on their performance of each skill.
f. Persevere in practicing the skill. Role playing, group discussions, brainstorming sessions, and observer feedback of group activities are samples of classroom methods that help students acquire and reinforce cooperative group skills.

3. *The teacher assigns cooperative group activities.* There is a difference between small group work and cooperative learning. In typical small group activities, students are given an assignment with little attention paid to how they will work together. A common complaint about small group activities is that a few students do all the work. In cooperative group activities students work together toward a common goal, and the group tasks are equally divided among group members. One approach to subdividing group participation is the "jigsaw" strategy. The group is given an assignment, and each member has part of the materials needed to complete the task; for instance, the assignment could be a group report on drugs. Each student would have a different source of information, such as a medical reference book, newspaper clippings, magazine articles, and an encyclopedia.

Another approach for beginning cooperative groups is to assign each member a specific role to facilitate the group work. One student would be responsible for reviewing suggestions, another would question individual members to elicit their ideas, while a third group member could be responsible for keeping the group on track. When students are experienced in cooperative learning, it is possible to turn virtually any part of the school curriculum into a collaborative learning experience.

4. *The teacher evaluates group efforts.* In cooperative groups, students learn that they sink or swim together. There are two levels of group assessment:

    a. Did the group accomplish its goal?
    b. How well did the group work together?

Products such as a classroom presentation or tests where individual scores are averaged to give a group score are examples of ways teachers have evaluated group goals. Self reporting by groups or observer feedback on group dynamics can provide information on group interaction. Group evaluation should be criterion-referenced. Before the group work begins, the teacher should clearly outline the criteria used for group evaluation. For example, a cooperative group activity on drug abuse could conclude by members summarizing each other's contributions.

Tateyama-Sniezek (1990) cautions against investing too much enthusiasm in cooperative learning as a tool to increase academic achievement of students with mild disabilities. She points out that more studies need to be undertaken that include students with mild disabilities in cooperative learning groups. Stephens and Slavin (1991) took issue with Tanteyama-Sniezek's findings. They pointed out that when group rewards and individual accountability are both included in cooperative learning activities, the outcomes for students with and without disabilities are positive.

Both peer tutoring and cooperative learning groups capitalize on students as classroom resources. The active involvement of students in their own learning enhances mainstreaming efforts by fostering social relationships between students, increasing student motivation, and supporting the acquisition of skills. A poster in the classroom of a teacher who used cooperative learning activities summarizes the impact of collaborative learning strategies. It simply states, "None of us is smarter than all of us" (Smith, 1987, 664).

The Whole Language Approach to Reading.   The National Assessment of Educational Progress (NAEP) noted an improvement in reading ability of students between 1971 and 1984, yet there are still many students, particularly economically disadvantaged youngsters, who struggle over the printed word. The NAEP data for 1984 indicated that 40 percent of thirteen-year-olds could not read or understand their textbook with ease. About two-thirds of the nine-year-old students interviewed in the National Assessment of Educational Progress reported that their teachers did most of the reading for them. Teachers pointed out the hard words, read parts of stories aloud, and told them how to find the main idea before they read the story (Lapointe, 1986).

The whole language approach remediates reading deficiencies by integrating reading with writing. The achievement data presented by the NAEP supports the premise that reading and writing skills are tied together. Better readers are better writers. In whole language classrooms, reading and writing are not taught as separate subjects. Students improve their skills in both areas by engaging in holistic activities like journal writing and choral reading. Students are enveloped in reading materials. Emphasis is placed on children's literature along with basal reading texts. Whole language teachers have found that such authors as Maurice Sendak, Chris Van Alsburg, Jane Yolen, and Mercer Mayer create stories that enchant young readers and instill the desire to read. Creative writing is encouraged in whole language. Priority is given to student imagination and expression rather than such editorial skills as spelling and punctuation.

Whole language offers an alternative to the lock-step phonetic approach common in many classrooms. Phonics are not eliminated, but the teacher recognizes that endless drills like "the fat cat sat on the tan hat" do not enliven a child's desire to read. More attention is paid to the quality of children's literature, discussion of stories, and student initiated reading-writing activities. Intuition, visual imagery, and spontaneous learning all play a part in whole language instruction. Students are encouraged to describe their experiences, write them down, and read them to others. Whole language increases student motivation by linking reading to real life experiences.

Career Education.   One of the most perplexing problems facing educators today is how to keep students from dropping out of school. One out of four students who begins high school does not graduate with his or her senior class. Students who experience school failure through elementary and junior high school are prime dropout candidates by their sixteenth birthday. Slavin (1989b) noted that by the time a student has reached third grade, reliable predictions can be made about who will drop out and who will remain in school. Moreover, one-half of all high school graduates, over twenty million students, will not attend college. For these students, "the forgotten half," many school reforms (such as higher academic standards) inhibit rather than facilitate their adjustment from school to employment (The William T. Grant Foundation Commission on Work, Family, and Citizenship, 1988).

Career education attempts to provide a meaningful school experience for students by bridging the gap between the curriculum and work. Students are taught employable skills while in school. The most effective career education programs are those that either simulate real life experiences or place a student in direct, supervised work experience. One approach is to assign students to work with "mentors" in community businesses. A student might attend academic courses in the morning, spend three afternoons in vocational skills classes learning such trades as carpentry and plumbing, and spend two afternoons working with an experienced craftsman at a local building site.

Career education differs from vocational education by providing career counseling and teaching work habits that will enhance a student's marketability. Promptness, appearance, ability to follow directions, and perseverance are a few of the attributes employers value in their employees. Data from a detailed assessment of a student's abilities in school subjects, leisure activities, occupational preferences, and personal characteristics can help instructor and student choose an appropriate educational plan to prepare a youngster for life after school.

Open Education.   The goal of the open education method is to teach students to take responsibility for their own learning. Open education was spawned as part of the counter-establishment movement in the late 1960s and early 1970s. It has roots in the Progressive movement of the 1930s and the British informal school system. Each of these educational practices viewed teaching and learning as a process that linked student experience to activity-based instruction. Student initiation and discussion of classroom events are valued; rote learning, drill, and such passive learning materials as worksheets and dittos are used sparingly.

Although open classrooms are not as numerous as in the past, open education methods are still prevalent. Peer tutoring, cooperative learning, activity centers, and discovery learning are a few examples of open education methods used in classrooms throughout the country. With its emphasis on student participation and the classroom as a "community," open education methods provide a good foundation for inclusion efforts. The problems of overactive and restless students are diminished, for example, when they have opportunities to move about the room while working at learning centers. Students who have difficulty remaining quiet will not become disruptive in open classrooms where students are encouraged to exchange ideas. Barnes and Knoblock (1973) observed that the open classroom, with its emphasis on democratic group procedures, is particularly well-suited to respond to the needs of students who have conflicts with authority, problems in establishing relationships, and feelings of loss of control over their feelings and behavior.

One of the primary criticisms of open education is the difficulty in measuring student learning. Standardized achievement tests are geared more to teacher-directed methods than student-centered techniques. When students are allowed to follow their interests in reading, math, or writing, their learning will not coincide with tests matched to curriculum guides. As a result, the beneficial effects of open education methods on student achievement are difficult to prove (Slavin, 1989a). However, increased student motivation and greater attention to student feelings are a few of the unmeasurable benefits attested to by teachers, students, and parents who have been exposed to open classroom practices

Computer Assisted Instruction.   The history of education is replete with examples of technological innovations that never fulfilled their original promise. Television, for instance, was expected to revolutionize education by hooking students up to a worldwide network of experts in every discipline. When personal computers were first introduced in schools in the early 1980s, gloomy tales of machines replacing humans in the classroom became a staple for teacher-lounge debates. The computer literacy movement helped dispel the darker images of how computers would subvert education. Rather than replacing teachers, many school computers are underutilized.

Computers can fill an important niche within inclusive classrooms by providing students with a tool for expression and learning. For a student with handwriting, reading, or spelling problems, word processing is an excellent alternative to labored composition efforts. Seeing one's ideas printed cleanly and concisely can provide a student with the incentive to persevere with creative writing. Interactive software can promote both reading and problem-solving skills. Hypertext provides students with access to supplementary information by layering pages on the computer screen. Placed on the perimeter of a classroom as a learning center, a computer can prove a valuable resource for a teacher who follows a few simple guidelines for computer application in the classroom:

1. Think of a computer as a stereo. The machine is useless if you don't select software (i.e., music) that you like and need.
2. It's unnecessary to know how to program in order to use a computer. The basic computer skill is typing.
3. Different computers run different software. Be certain the machine you select for your classroom can accommodate the software you want.
4. There are many adaptive devices available that make a computer accessible to students with physical, visual, and auditory disabilities.
5. Talk with other teachers who use computers in the classroom. New software and computer applications are continually being developed.

Good teaching is the selection of an instructional practice that best suits the needs of students. Effective teachers use a variety of instructional practices in their classrooms. When students are having difficulty learning, it makes more sense to vary the teaching approach than to assume there is something wrong with the learner. Each instructional practice offers an alternative method for helping hard-to-teach students in the regular classroom. No one approach is best for all students and teachers. Used in combination, these practices can match the diverse needs of an inclusive classroom.

Working Together

Schools must change in order to meet the demands of the future. As Demographic trends indicate increased poverty among students. A growing proportion of students are nonwhite and non-English-speaking, and there is an increase of students from single-parent families. If the schools of the future are to meet the growing demands of hard-to-teach students, changes must occur in present school practices that serve to separate students (and teachers) into groups of "haves" and "have nots."

General and special educators can work together to teach all children. There are contact points where key issues faced by regular and special educators rub together. All educators, whether special or regular, must deal with problems of teacher expectations, standardized tests, classroom organization, discipline, and dual systems of administration. The ability of educators to meet these challenges and solve them together will set the course for an improved educational system for the students of the twenty-first century.

Teacher Expectations

Research on effective instruction indicates the powerful effect of teacher expectations, both positive and negative, on student performance. When students are labeled as deficient and put in "special" programs, the message is clear—there is something intrinsically wrong with this student. Labels like mentally retarded and learning disabled become explanations for why a student is difficult to teach. Students are then grouped with other "deficient" learners, and teacher expectations for the group decline. Conversely, when teachers believe that learning problems are temporary hurdles that can be overcome by adapting teaching methods, there is an expectation that success will come with hard work. When teachers have high expectations, the performance of students is enhanced.

But what about teacher expectations of themselves? Two Rand Corporation studies found that positive teacher opinions of their own ability had a beneficial effect on students' learning (Armor et al., 1976; Berman et al., 1977). McDaniel and DiBella-McCarthy described the teaching style of these confident teachers.

> High efficacy teachers maintained high academic standards, had clear expectations for students, concentrated on academic instruction, maintained on-task behavior, and demonstrated "withitness." They combined a secure classroom environment with a strong academic orientation.... High-efficacy teachers allocated twice as much time to whole group instruction as did low-efficacy teachers. (McDaniel & DiBella-McCarthy, 1989, 35)

Teachers who believe in their own ability have good group management skills. They encourage student participation and have less discipline problems. Perhaps most important, high-efficacy teachers are problem solvers. They view a student's learning difficulties as a temporary problem, and they try different teaching approaches until they get results. Teacher preparation programs that concentrate on developing high-efficacy skills will provide young teachers with the tools needed to help all learners in the regular classroom.

Classroom Organization

Between kindergarten and twelfth grade a student will spend more than 11,000 hours in school. How much of this time is actually spent learning? According to researchers who have studied life in schools, only a fraction of a school day is allocated to instruction, and students spend even less time engaged in learning activities. Out of a typical 390-minute school day, teachers spend less than half that time teaching. In their survey of second-, third-, and fourth-grade classrooms, Ysseldyke and Algozzine (1984) found that students have few opportunities to do independent work, and they spend a lot of time in such passive activities as listening and waiting.

Students spend as little as 12 percent of their school day questioning, reading, writing, or engaged in some other activity that reflects active learning. Goodlad (1984) reported that a good deal of what goes on in schools is like painting by numbers. The teacher gives directions, and students follow them in robotlike fashion. He described the emotional tone of these classrooms as flat. The climate of these rooms lacked joy and warmth. Goodlad noted that although teachers verbalize the need for students to become independent thinkers, many teachers exhibit a need to control student decision making.

More attention needs to be directed toward how classrooms are organized. When the teacher controls every action, from distribution of materials to collecting lunch money, precious instructional time is wasted. Students must be actively involved in their learning to succeed. Such active teaching strategies as cooperative learning projects, learning centers, and peer tutoring allow teachers to move about the room and guide student learning. By shifting the classroom instructional norm from "frontal teaching" to student-centered activities, teachers can increase instructional time and allow learning to proceed at the student's pace.

Standardized Tests

For many years, U.S. education has heavily favored standardized tests. Perhaps this is rooted in our competitive spirit or the mistaken belief that standardized tests provide a true "objective" measure of achievement. Standardized tests are used to compare achievement between school districts, and they are used to compare the gains made by individual students. Each year fifty million schoolchildren take standardized tests. In some classrooms around the country, instruction is test-driven. In these classrooms, teachers teach to the test, and a student's learning is summarized by a single number at the end of the year.

The billion-dollar-a-year testing industry is unregulated. There are no consistent criteria for who takes the test. In some school systems, all children are evaluated, whereas in other systems, students who receive special instruction are excluded. Some critics of current testing procedures have pointed out that a school superintendent can increase district test scores by placing students in special education programs, and only administering tests to general education students. Chester Finn, past assistant U.S. Secretary of Education in charge of research, characterized standardized testing in America as the "Lake Wobegon" effect. He observed that in the mythical Minnesota town popularized by the humorist Garrison Keillor, all the children are "above average." Finn's comment was prompted by national achievement scores that each year showed a rise in average test scores for all schoolchildren. In their zeal to demonstrate how much their school systems have improved, this statistical paradox has been conveniently ignored by many educators (Fiske, 1988).

Neill and Medina summarized the case against standardized tests.

At best, standardized testing is hopelessly inadequate for promoting school reform. At worst, such testing will preclude reform. In either case, the continued domination of testing will mean that millions of students—primarily those most in need of improved education—will be dumped into dead-end tracks and pushed out of school. (Neill & Medina, 1989, 695)

Alternatives to standardized tests are available to teachers. Curriculum-based assessment, classroom observations, and student portfolios provide more detail about student learning than standardized tests. Evaluation of student performance can improve when assessment paints a picture of a student as learner rather than student as test-taker.

Discipline

What type of classroom behavior would you find disruptive? Some teachers are disturbed by a student who constantly needs structure and direction. Other teachers resent students who don't sit still and have difficulty waiting. Which is the best student behavior—quiet, outspoken, compliant, or nonconformist? There are as many views on proper student behavior as there are teachers.

Because teachers organize their classroom routines to match their own likes and dislikes, there is no standard for determining "normal" classroom behavior. Jacob Kounin (1977) reported that some teachers create discipline problems in their classrooms, for example, by switching topics without a smooth transition or abruptly ending a lesson.

The Phi Delta Kappa Commission on Discipline (1982) did a national survey of schools with successful discipline policies. The commission found these schools were student-oriented. Schools with good discipline concentrated on the cause of discipline problems rather than adopting isolated practices to punish wrong-doers. Routine discipline problems were handled in the classroom. When serious infractions occurred, such due process procedures as student hearings were established to give students an opportunity to present their side of an issue. Schools with good discipline emphasized positive behaviors and implemented preventive measures instead of punitive actions to improve discipline. Awards, honor days, and positive communications with parents are a few strategies used to reward well-mannered behavior.

The schools surveyed by Phi Delta Kappa were not soft on discipline; in fact, several schools had strict behavior codes. The factor that distinguished exemplary schools was their emphasis on teaching prosocial behaviors. For example, the Beta School for underachieving students in New York City reinforced positive behaviors by issuing "Commendation Cards" to selected students. The Rocky Mountain School in Marietta, Georgia, used social studies as a forum to help students learn human relations skills in the classroom.

Working and getting along with others is a basic prerequisite for a successful career after school. When teachers and administrators value the feelings of students and model effective interpersonal skills, students learn to be more responsive to the needs of others. When teachers and administrators dictate and punish, students learn the wrong lesson—might makes right. As adults we look at repressive governments and cheer on populations who fight for self-determination. Why then should we be surprised to discover that repressive school policies contribute to student discipline problems?

Each year, throughout the country, over an estimated two million students are administered corporal punishment. A long list of research studies illustrates that physical reaction to disruptive behavior rarely yields effective results—yet corporal punishment continues in many public schools, particularly in the Southeast (Hyman & D'Allesandro, 1984). If corporal punishment is prohibited by state law, then it cannot be used as a discipline procedure for special education students. However, when state law allows corporal punishment, there is no exception for special education students unless specified in a student's individual education program. Emotionally disturbed, neglected, and sexually abused students can be further traumatized by onerous discipline procedures. Teachers and parents need to work together to ensure that school discipline procedures do not duplicate conditions that have led to an emotional problem. Although the National Education Association passed a resolution against corporal punishment, it is legal in many states, and the Supreme Court has repeatedly upheld the right of teachers to "paddle."

School-aged youngsters are deluged with T.V. shows and movies that romanticize violence. Drug abuse is a national tragedy, and 50 percent of all students will experience the hardship of divorce. Teachers and parents cannot ignore the sad truth that the "mean streets" of America also include the hallways of many schools. When metal detectors are needed to keep out weapons in some urban schools, it is clear that students are frightened and need help. By providing the students with humane and fair discipline practices, teachers can instill in young people the moral values and social skills they will need to successfully cope with life after school.

Administration

The purpose of administration is to develop policies and procedures that make schools better places to teach and learn. Principals, superintendents, and special education directors can work together so schools will meet the needs of disabled and nondisabled students. A dual system of regular and special education administration makes mutual problem solving and planning difficult, if not impossible.

Virtually all aspects of special education programming are in the hands of special education administrators. This means that although special education programs are located in their buildings, school principals are administratively disconnected from their operation. Regular and special education have separate budgets, separate administrators, and separate teacher certification procedures. As might be expected, this dual system of education creates and sustains separate priorities. When the entire special education system is set up on a separate administrative track, there are few built-in incentives to teach youngsters with mild disabilities in the regular classroom.

Title 1, bilingual education, migrant programs, and special education services are administered separately. The net result is a jumble of overlapping programs designed to provide remedial education. Guidelines for each type of remedial program, including eligibility criteria and evaluation of student progress, are imprecise and often confusing. Some of the more common educator complaints are:

1. Some students are placed in the wrong program.
2. Turf issues about educational resources put program directors in competition with each other.
3. Students who don't match eligibility criteria fall between the cracks and receive no help.
4. The pull-out system of delivering remedial services causes students to fall further behind their classmates because they miss too much regular classroom instruction.

The underlying assumption of pull-out programs for remedial services is that differences between each subgroup of students requires specialized instructional techniques. Yet the meager research base for successfully matching specific instructional approaches to distinctive learner characteristics fails to justify the dollars spent to maintain specialized pull-out programs.

Summary

Inclusion means educating students with disabilities in the general classroom with special education support. The legal mandate for inclusion is based on the least restrictive environment provision, reaffirmed in the Individuals with Disabilities Education Act. However, as Luis Lopez discovered in the account cited at the beginning of this chapter, least restrictive environment is more than a legal concept. Each student wants to be viewed as normal by peers and teachers. When students are pulled out of their classroom for special instruction or placed in segregated "special" programs, it creates an artificial division between them and their peers.

Inclusion can be an effective educational intervention. A well-planned inclusion program helps develop both academic and social skills as well or better than pull-out or self-contained special education programs. Planning an inclusion program includes establishing entrance criteria, communicating with parents, understanding student needs, preparing students for a change, and evaluating student progress.

Sound general educational practices work equally well with students with mild disabilities. Cooperative, peer tutoring, whole language, open education, career education, and computer-assisted instruction are examples of instructional methods that help all students learn. Consultation strategies offer teachers and students alternative strategies to achieve inclusion programs.

The educational tradition of viewing learning difficulties as defects in the student has created and sustained a dual system of public education in this country. One brand of education, "general," is for students without learning problems, and another brand of education, "special," is for students with learning problems. Each year the numbers of students placed in some sort of "special" program increases.

Both special and general educators have a stake in realigning their efforts to teach students with mild disabilities. The inclusion movement breathed new life into mainstreaming efforts by focusing attention on the benefits of merging special and regular education efforts for hard-to-teach students. It is clear by now that uninspired teaching does as much to create learning problems as do the characteristics of individual students. By focusing attention on ways of enhancing classroom learning environments, educators can best serve the needs of all students.

Activities

1. Arrange to meet with several general classroom and special education teachers of students with mild disabilities. Ask them questions about how inclusion works for them. What special needs do students with mild disabilities have in their general and resource classrooms? Are their needs similar? Do the teachers collaborate with each other as they plan for the students' instruction? Do both participate in developing the students' individual education programs?

2. Visit the campus library. Locate major journals in special education. Look for articles on mainstreaming and inclusion. In particular, look for inclusion models and ways in which inclusion concerns have been resolved. Identify articles that present effective ideas about adapting and modifying instruction in the regular classroom.

3. While visiting your campus library, look through journals that publish articles about special education teachers who function as consultants. What would the role of the special education teacher be like in this capacity as compared to functioning in a direct service delivery role? How would a special education consultant deliver indirect services to general classroom teachers?

4. Working in small groups, write scripts showing effective and ineffective interactions between general classroom and special education teachers as they plan for students with mild disabilities. Which responsibilities would the general classroom teacher assume? Which responsibilities would be assumed by the special education teacher?

5. Visit nearby schools with inclustion programs. Note adaptations in general education curriculum.

CHAPTER

7 Learning and Teaching

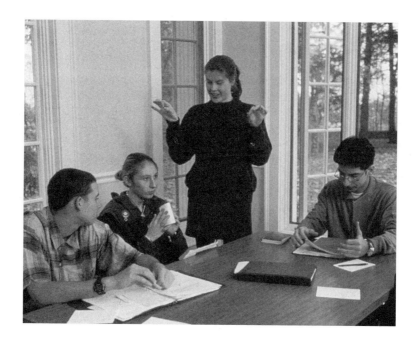

Advance Questions

Answer the following questions as you read this chapter.

1. How does student perception influence attitudes about school?
2. How does a developmental perspective help teachers understand their students?
3. What is the hidden curriculum?

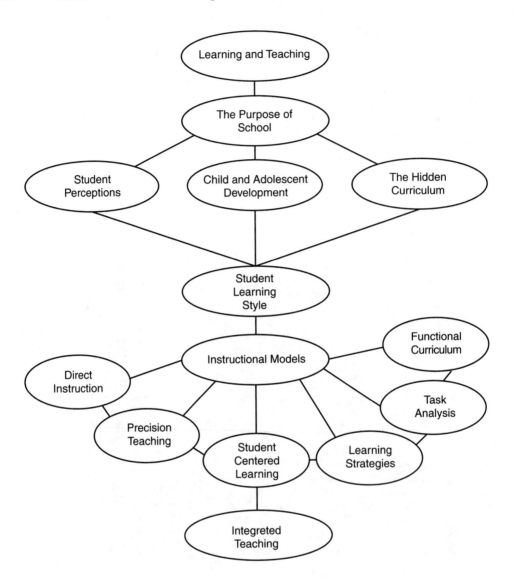

4. What is the connection between direct instruction and the effective school research?
5. What is the purpose of precision teaching?
6. What is the connection between the work of William Glasser and student-centered learning?
7. What is the purpose of teaching students learning strategies?
8. How could task analysis be used to teach multiplication of two digit numbers?
9. What is functional curriculum?
10. How can information about a student's learning style enhance instruction?
11. What is "integrated teaching"?

Vignette

Each morning, forty-eight million youngsters troop off to school. They arrive on foot, in cars, and in an armada of yellow school buses. Bells ring; children file into classrooms; the teacher closes the classroom door, calls for attention, and another school day begins. What happens next? Other than sleeping and watching television, no activity demands as much of a youngster's time as school. Even though teachers and students spend almost a thousand hours together each year, our knowledge about what transpires inside classroom walls is fragmentary.

Public school classrooms are oxymorons. They are actually private places. The teacher works alone. The students are there, but they are quiet consumers. Students rarely complain about bad teachers. To whom would they address their complaints? And what would be the purpose? The next day the same teacher would be standing in front of them. This is because teachers, once they have achieved tenure, have almost total job security. Barring an economic downturn that can lead to layoffs, teachers have the assurance of continuing their profession, with minimum outside interference, until retirement.

Teachers do their best or worst work in virtual isolation from their peers. The act of one teacher observing another teacher in the classroom is so unique that when it happens it is labeled an innovation. Occasionally the seclusion of classroom life is pierced by researchers, and the insights gleaned are informative.

Some teacher spend most of their day standing or sitting in the front of the classroom. Their primary teaching tools are lecture, texts, workbooks, and worksheets. Other teachers appreciate the need for students to be active learners. These teachers mix student-centered learning with direct instruction. They are flexible and are more adept than "frontal teachers" at modifying their instruction to meet the needs of individual students. Teachers who vary their teaching methods are more successful than those who depend on one or two "tried and true" ways of teaching.

Problem Solving Questions

1. Can you recall an elementary school teacher who did most of his or her teaching from the front of the room? Looking back on that classroom experience how successful was that teacher with students with learning problems?

2. Would you rather be a student in a classroom that featured "frontal teaching" or a classroom that featured student-centered learning? Why?
3. Can you name some specific instructional approaches for individualizing the curriculum for students with learning problems?
4. How do students that you work with in your field-based courses feel about school? Do a survey of elementary and secondary students and compare their perceptions of life in classrooms.

What Are Schools For?

Ask any teacher what schools are for, and you are likely to get a variety of answers ranging from the basic—"Schools are to teach skills for life," to the enthusiastic—"Schools are to help kids learn about themselves and the world around them." But what about the consumers? What do the students who, from age five to seventeen, spend 12,000 hours in classrooms think about school?

Student Perceptions of School

Noyes and McAndrew (1971) interviewed students throughout the country and asked them, "What are schools for?" A typical response was:

> We go to school because it is the law. They make you stay until you are sixteen, and by then you may as well go on since you probably only have another year or two anyway. The point of it, I guess, is to get a diploma so you can go to college. (Noyes & McAndrew, 1971, 321)

The overall impression made by the students in this study was that the purpose of school was preparation for college. Students did not view school as a place that would meet their personal needs. They gave different versions of the same theme—figure out a way to get through school with the least resistance.

Mallery (1971) interviewed students from eight high schools. The purpose of his study was to examine the effects of the school experience on student values. When students made spontaneous references to curriculum, they talked about the need to get good grades. Virtually all students wanted to find some purpose in their schoolwork. They singled out for praise courses that allowed active participation. They emphasized teacher personality. They respected teachers who provided opportunities to build self-confidence, independent thinking, and personal expression. According to these students, competition for grades and the pressure to be admitted to college increased as they advanced from ninth to twelfth grade.

In elementary school, White found that student and teacher perceptions about the purpose of school differ. Whereas teachers value the content of the curriculum, students pay more attention to teacher judgments of their work. In the words of one student:

> . . . you have to have a half-inch margin on your papers . . . you put the headings on the right not on the left, and line it up . . . the cover should be felt if you want an A . . . you can't hand in papers that aren't neat, she'll really mark you down . . . you have to write out "remainder" or it's wrong. . . . (White, 1971, 341)

Students measured their progress by grades rather than what they learned. When he was a special education teacher, one of the authors of this volume had a straightforward reminder regarding the importance of grades to students:

> The director of our program had accepted the teachers' recommendation that we substitute descriptive evaluations for grades. The students participated in assessing their learning. Students met with the teachers to determine if their work in each subject showed improvement. Peter and I had a conference at my desk about his progress. "Do you think your reading has improved?" I asked him. "What do you mean?" he replied. "You know, are you getting better at reading?" I asked. "How should I know," Peter said, "you're the teacher. It's your job to give me a grade so I'll know if I've learned anything."

Peter's comment illustrates the distance between teacher and student perspectives about school. Students are not connected to their learning in the ways adults imagine. They learn the rules of school and how to get by, but curriculum as adults understand it does not have the same meaning to students. Whereas teachers want students to learn, students want to get the teacher's approval, receive good grades, and enjoy the company of their friends. Sometimes they are excited about learning, and sometimes they are bored. At all times, students realize that their fate is essentially in the hands of the teacher. Some students cope with the inequality of power and perform at a level that will satisfy both teacher and parents. Others fall by the wayside. These failures are eventually classified as students at-risk, school dropouts, or students with mild disabilities.

What are the characteristics of classroom life that create such a discrepancy between how teachers and students view learning? It should come as no surprise that students view grades as the Holy Grail of their school experience. From the time they receive their first report card until they take the Scholastic Aptitude Test (SAT) in high school, students are continually reminded of the importance of grades. Tests are as indigenous to life in schools as chalk, blackboards, and textbooks.

Some teachers' efforts are best characterized as test- rather than curriculum-driven. These teachers teach to improve test scores rather than to stimulate a love of learning. As long as school-based quizzes and national achievement tests continue as the key measure of success in school, students will concentrate on grades as their most important goal.

Child and Adolescent Development

"What did you do in school today?" When a father asked his six-year-old daughter Margaret this question, she answered, "Well, we had lunch in the cafeteria, we lined up for the bus, and we had folder work on Thursday and we had fun together, me, Brian, all my friends." She added, "That's not all but I forget the rest."

Margaret's response illustrates another major difference between the way in which teachers and students view school. When she thinks about school, Margaret considers its most gratifying aspects—lunch, friends, and a side reference to her studies—"folder work." Children are not miniature adults. There are significant developmental differences between teachers and their students. One developmental distinction is in perceptions of goals.

While adults take the long view, students look at the future from short range. Teachers are concerned with distant goals; students are concerned with here and now. For a five-year-old, twenty minutes is an endless wait. Summer for a twelve-year-old seems to extend into the distance, an uninterrupted progression of sunny days and steamy nights. To the freshman and sophomore, high school appears as if it will never end. Time limits have slight meaning to teenagers who perceive themselves as immortal.

Within this context of time without end, parents and adults pound away at such themes in high school as "You need to learn math in order to get a good job," or they tell primary-grade children, "If you finish your work in twenty minutes, you will get free time at the end of the week." Each of these messages leaves a faint impression on students who are unable to fathom the mystery of work today for tomorrow's reward. Child and adolescent development lend weight to Einstein's view that time is relative. Discipline, grades, and learning are fundamental classroom issues that teachers approach as long-range preparation for work or college, while youngsters jolt forward one day at a time with eyes cast on more substantial concerns, such as watching the clock hands on the wall slowly creep toward dismissal.

Developmental differences between students and teachers are accepted and valued in many early childhood programs, but teachers and administrators sometimes lose track of child and adolescent development. This neglect by school personnel creates a gulf between teachers and students that can have dire consequences. To paraphrase Robert Sternberg (1990), we ignore students' developmental differences at our peril—and theirs.

Part of growing up is learning to take on the perspective of those who are older. Primary-school-aged children learn to be less egocentric as they acquire the ability to perceive a situation from another's point of view. Students in elementary school are here-and-now oriented. It isn't until adolescence that students can begin to think about future goals. Each of these developmental changes occurs through a process that Piaget characterized as assimilation–accommodation. This means that changes in student perceptions occur gradually, with a good deal of regression intermingled with advancement.

Developmental needs dictate priorities to students, and these priorities can put a student in conflict with adults. For the teenager, relationships, intimacy, and getting a driver's license are major concerns. Adolescence is a time of "grandiose ascension." Teenagers fly high above the mundane matters of the everyday world as they experience new mental and physical abilities they never imagined they would possess (Bly, 1990). Many teenagers perceive parents as "old fashioned" and too strict. When bad things happen, teenagers are reluctant to face them head-on. Denial is a useful defense mechanism for skipping over the hardships of a family's divorce, a mother's addiction, or a father's neglect. This is why depression and drug abuse are such developmental hazards for adolescents. Adolescents are more likely to act out their emotional struggles than to reflect or talk to others.

In high school, acceptance by one's peer group can be more pressing than getting homework done. The teenager confronts the social dilemma of breaking free from the bonds of adult authority at precisely the same time that parents and teachers are demanding "responsible behavior." This pulling in opposite directions usually leaves both adults and adolescents perplexed. Even though developmental changes are at times baffling, these changes help explain why the meaning of school is interpreted differently by teachers and students.

The Hidden Curriculum

Much of what transpires in school is dictated by what Phillip Jackson (1968) described as "the hidden curriculum." Whereas the visible academic curriculum channels schedules and routines, the hidden curriculum—comprising praise, power, and crowds—more subtly exerts its influence. In classrooms, students must learn to accommodate themselves to the hidden curriculum. A student's ability to adapt to these three unpublicized features of classroom life will, just as surely as achievement test scores, determine school success or failure.

Praise. Learning to live in a classroom requires learning to perform successfully under constant adult supervision. Students must elicit praise from teachers. They must learn to sit still, wait their turn, follow directions, and do well on tests. Successful students learn to please their teachers. Although teachers may be disappointed by errors in academics, students soon learn that it is violation of classroom rules for behavior that causes teachers the greatest aggravation. Students receive praise based on their ability to follow the organizational guidelines laid down by their teachers. Students who garner reproof rather than praise in their attempts to adapt to the norms of classroom life may eventually find themselves referred for special education.

Power. The evaluative norms in classrooms contribute to an unequal balance of power. Children are accustomed to bending to the authority of parents, but school presents a different situation. The intimacy and duration of contact that is characteristic of parent–child relationships is absent in school. As Jackson (1968) put it, "For the first time in the child's life, power that has personal consequences for the child himself is wielded by a complete stranger." At the precise time in their lives that they are developmentally ready to take on the world and demonstrate their capacity for mastery, five-year-old children are sent to school and placed under the authority of a "teacher" (Erikson,

1963). In developmentally based classrooms, students are given time and opportunity to explore their personal abilities. In teacher-centered, curriculum-based classrooms, students are immediately pressed into compliance. In the latter settings, students are expected to follow directions, get the "right" answers, and master the curriculum.

The contrast between student compliance and teacher power is subdued in democratic, student-centered classrooms, but the essential institutional power of schools is invariant. Students must go to school. They must listen to the teacher. Their lives are regulated by bells, schedules, and routines. They cannot decide when they will eat lunch. They cannot decide when it's time to stop their studies. They cannot go to the bathroom without permission.

This is not a criticism of schools; rather, it is a description of institutional life. Schools manage large numbers of children with limited space and resources. Student behaviors such as tractability, obedience, and conformity are prized by administrators. Nonconforming behaviors, rebelliousness, or lack of attention are dealt with swiftly and surely. It is no wonder that "good students" seek to create a favorable impression on teachers.

One approach is to curry favor. The extreme example is the apple polisher who realizes that teacher evaluations can be enhanced by anticipating and fulfilling teacher expectations. This ability to appraise social reality is a valuable skill in the workplace as well. However it is conspicuously absent in students with mild disabilities, who are not as adept at deciphering social cues as students without mild disabilities.

John Holt, in his book *How Children Fail* (1977), catalogued the many strategies students devise to avoid teacher disapproval. Holt observed that students display remarkable ingenuity and cunning in bluffing teachers. According to Holt, teachers unconsciously give children clues about correct answers through eye movement and by body language. By watching these nonverbal signs, students can make a good guess at the right answer. While teaching in a special education program, one of the authors discovered how students go about the business of faking.

> One day I was doing a math drill with a small group of five students with learning disabilities. I showed them a flash card and one after another they came up with the right multiplication answer. I felt great. I thought I was finally making progress. At recess I took Timmy aside and told him how pleased I was with his multiplication work. He looked at me sheepishly and said, "We didn't really know the answers; you were sitting with your back to the window, and we could read the answers on the other side of the cards each time you held one up."

The students' insouciance was unnerving. It was as if every student in the group, without any prior discussion, was in on a secret plan. Clearly students do a great deal of thinking in school as they try to tip the scales of power in their direction.

Crowds. The third aspect of the hidden curriculum is crowds. Classrooms are crowded places where, for the most part, students work alone. Additionally, students must adapt to delays, interruptions, and waiting. According to Jackson (1968), the typical elementary school teacher engages in 1,000 interactions a day. When researchers have cataloged how teachers and students utilize their time together, the results have been astonishing. For example, Ysseldyke and Algozzine (1990) reported that out of 390 minutes in an elementary school day, 170 minutes was time lost to lunch, recess, physical education, and similar activities. Of the remaining 220 minutes, forty minutes was spent in free time, lunch counts, roll call, and other "housekeeping" activities. Eighteen minutes was spent in "fetch and put away" activities. Out of the entire school day, a student averaged two minutes of individual time with the teacher. Students and teachers spend large chunks of time together, but the crowded conditions of schools and the ensuing artifacts of organizational life play havoc with instruction and learning. Educational researchers are beginning to appreciate that time management is a critical element of effective classroom instruction (Berliner, 1979, 1988; Good & Brophy, 1986; Rosenshine, 1979).

Student Learning Styles

Just as there is no one best way to teach, there is not a best way to learn. Students who are primarily verbal learners generally do well in school. They follow verbal directions; they listen; they participate in class discussions; and they have good reading comprehension skills. Some educators have pointed out that school work is primarily left hemispheric oriented. The right and left hemispheres of the neocortex process experience and information in different ways: the left hemisphere is the verbal, logical, abstract side of the neocortex; the right hemisphere is visual, intuitive, holistic, and insightful in the way it handles information. Students whose learning style is left hemispheric oriented have an advantage, while students who are right hemispheric oriented are at a disadvantage in school. If the school curriculum emphasized creative activities like art, drama, and spatial reasoning, students who were right hemispheric oriented might excel. (See Figure 4.1.)

In the Lab School, Washington, D.C., teachers use art to develop organizational skills, strengthen memory, and promote academic readiness. Art activities provide Lab School teachers with opportunities to observe a student interacting with many different mediums of expression (1980). This provides teachers with insights about educational needs and information about how a child learns most effectively. Experimental programs in New Baskerville City, Oakland, California, and Columbus, Ohio, resulted in higher standardized test scores in reading and math when teachers incorporated both right and left hemispheric activities in their lessons (Grady & Luecke, 1978).

Marie Carbo reported that the phonics method of learning to read is unsuitable for some children. Phonics is a left hemispheric oriented instructional strategy. It requires sequential processing and reproducing of sounds. Students must learn to sound out individual letters and then analyze how each sound combines to make a complete word. For a youngster who is right hemispheric oriented, this predominant left hemispheric strategy is burdensome and could lead to reading failure. Carbo states that "... many global/visual students derive little, if any, benefit from phonics instruction because their strong intuitive abilities enable them to perceive the patterns of entire words or phrases with relative ease" (Carbo, 1987a, 56). Notice that Carbo does not describe global/visual (right hemispheric) students as deficient. Their learning style is different. When teachers use only phonics instruction to teach reading, global/visual learners encounter difficulties. It is the mismatch between instructional strategy and learning style that gives the appearance of student inadequacy. Carbo describes global/visual learners as students who do well when: reading books of their own choosing, participating in choral readings, writing their own stories to read, and listening to tape recordings of interesting books. Drill and repetition of such reading skills as decoding bore these children. They perform better with whole language reading instruction.

In the formative years of special education (1950–75), a variety of tactile–kinesthetic approaches to reading were designed for students identified as having learning disabilities. Grace Fernald's multisensory approach to reading continues to be widely used in resource rooms. The Fernald approach requires the student to look at a word as it is pronounced by the teacher; say the word while tracing it; copy the word while saying it; and write the word from memory. The teacher reinforces word knowledge by using the rehearsed word frequently during reading instruction. The Fernald approach was based on the premise that the student had a learning disability, probably neurological in origin, that impaired ability to read through conventional instruction (usually phonics). It is important to note that in most instances it was impossible to verify the neurological impairment; instead, the impairment was inferred.

Although it is clear that some students do have a subtle neurological impairment and a learning disability, it is also evident that many students are misidentified as learning disabled. The problem is not within the student but is caused by the overreliance on a single instructional strategy that creates a mismatch between student learning style and teacher methods. This sort of standoff is no contest; the student will be placed in special education and the teacher will continue blithely on her way heedless to her lack of instructional flexibility. The most effective teachers are able to match instructional approaches to learning styles. This coupling of instruction and student, however, can present a confusing array of approaches because of the myriad ways that learning styles are described in the research literature.

Research in learning (also called cognitive) styles has been going on for forty years. Convergent and divergent thinkers; field-dependent and field-independent learners; analytic and thematic styles; legislative, judicial, and executive styles are just a sample of the diverse terminology used to explain preferred learning styles of students. In order to assist teachers sort through various options, Charles (1976) synthesized the research on learning styles. He described three types of learners: adventurers, ponderers, and drifters. He suggested that each style requires a different approach to teaching. An adventurer is a divergent thinker. This student moves quickly through materials and ideas. The adventurer is right hemispheric oriented. Learning is intuitive, creative, and spontaneous. The adventurer is tolerant of ambiguity and not so concerned with finding the "right" or "wrong" answer. Teacher latitude in structure works best for the adventurer who feels hemmed in by too much teacher control. This individual responds best to student-centered learning that provides opportunities for discovery and experience activities. The adventurer needs flexibility and encouraging feedback.

The ponderer is reflective and analytical (left hemispheric preference). This student looks for details and "correct" answers. The ponderer likes facts and generally does well with standardized achievement tests. A student with these qualities learns best when expectations are clear and direct. The ponderer works well with teacher-directed activities and responds to praise. The ponderer conforms well to classroom rules and expectations for behavior. This student is a convergent thinker. Using art as a metaphor, the adventurer could be compared to the many spontaneous hues used by an impressionist, while the ponderer reflects the clear, crisp lines of an Andrew Wyeth painting.

The drifter is an uncertain learner. The drifter does not display the self-confidence or initiative of the adventurer and ponderer. This student requires more attention from the teacher. Assignments often go unfinished. Without teacher encouragement and intervention, the drifter loses interest in schoolwork. The drifter leans on adult authority to overcome feelings of learned helplessness. Andy Warhol, with his ironic view of modern pop culture, symbolizes the drifter. This individual is an oxymoron—a pupil who is out of place in school. Even though surrounded by the security of a predictable learning environment, the drifter is befuddled. Each learning task is approached with apprehension and a sense of foreboding. Bereft of the tools for classroom success, the drifter approaches schoolwork in an aimless and lackluster manner.

Each of these learning styles suggests a need to modify instructional strategies. The adventurer learns best in an environment that offers latitude and the opportunity to have some control over activities. Cooperative learning and activity centers are examples of student-centered instructional strategies that would respond to the learning needs of the adventurer. The ponderer would do well with the clear-cut structure of teacher-directed instruction. Hunter's model (ITIP) or other strategies that provide sequential steps to skill development give the ponderer a predictable path to success. The drifter needs encouragement and support. This student requires immediate feedback about classroom performance. Precision teaching and learning strategy techniques would match the needs of the drifter.

Identifying students' learning style is a good beginning for instruction, but teaching is not a mechanical one-to-one correspondence activity. We cannot fit students to instruction like so many eggs nestled in a carton. To some extent all students need control over their environment, as well as teacher-directed group instruction and assistance in how to learn.

Rather than emphasizing the "right" way to teach, learning style literature underscores the fact that students are different. Student learning style is a unique blend of individual development and life experience. Teachers who understand learning styles respect the capabilities of their charges. The literature on learning styles provides a sharp contrast to the traditional school norm of student conformity to a single standard of instruction or behavior. As John Holt remarked, "Children are not only extremely good at learning, they are much better at it than we adults are. As a teacher it took me a very long time to find this out" (Holt, 1977, 232). By utilizing an array of instructional models, the teacher builds a bridge between the student and the curriculum. Research on instructional models and learning styles helps us to grasp the complexity of learning and to appreciate the need for teachers to remain flexible when deciding how to teach individual students.

Instructional Models

Trying to find the best way to teach is a major goal for educators. Educational journals brim with debates about which system of instruction is most effective for teaching reading, math, writing, and appropriate behavior.

As the pendulum of educational reform swings from left to right, priorities change and so do instructional approaches. The late 1960s and early 1970s were a time of widespread social change. The "establishment" was challenged through civil disobedience, antiwar protests, and folk-rock music. Student-centered learning, with the counterculture theme of "freedom to learn," flourished during this period. The name given to educational reform during this period—"open education"— underscored the goal of flexibility in classroom instruction. Later, during the more conservative 1980s, direct instruction and the effective schools research emphasized basic skills and testing for student mastery. The 1990s witnessed a plethora of education reform movements, which for the most part were fragmented and politically driven.

The search for the best way to teach is tied to many factors. Among these are local leadership, politics, economics, and public support. Education is more like law than like medicine. Absolute cures for educational ills are almost nonexistent. Rather, like law, education must change and adapt to the needs of society; for example, educational policy is shaped at the local level by superintendents, who are hired by school committees. School committees are elected by voters in the community. Consequently, introduction of educational change, along with the necessary budgetary adjustments, must eventually have public support.

Each of the following instructional models has been used successfully with students with mild disabilities and nondisabled students. None is foolproof. The selection of a specific instructional model should come after a careful review of educational goals, schoolwide resources, and student need.

Direct Instruction

Direct instruction, also referred to as mastery learning, refers to a variety of carefully sequenced, teacher-directed methods. The term was originally used to describe *DISTAR*, a teaching guide for reading and mathematics. More recently the term "direct instruction" has been used by researchers to describe a set of procedures derived from the effective schools research of Rosenshine and Stevens (1984). Their research indicated that when teachers followed a hierarchy of instructional steps in their lessons, low-achieving students demonstrated increased academic achievement in basic skills.

Direct instruction encourages the use of teacher demonstration, guided practice, and feedback. According to Larivee (1988), "Design components of direct instruction include mastery learning, carefully designed sequential instruction, flexible skill-level grouping, adequate opportunity for practice, and periodic review of previously learned concepts" (307). A teacher would utilize direct instruction by:

1. *Teacher demonstration*—Provide clear, controlled presentations of new material. Model each step of the material to be learned.
2. *Guided practice*—Follow the demonstration, ask questions, and check student understanding of material.
3. *Feedback*—Circulate among students as they work on independent activities related to the new material. Provide corrective feedback on their work. Use frequent cumulative review.

The work of Madeline Hunter and her Instructional Theory into Practice (ITIP) instructional model is an example of a direct instruction program that has been implemented in thousands of schools throughout the country. Hunter stated that teachers were first and foremost decision makers, and teaching decisions should be informed by educational research. Hunter's ITIP system divided teaching into practical lists and sublists that teachers could follow as they made decisions regarding how and what to teach; for example, she organized the teaching act into seven components:

1. Knowledge of human growth and development
2. Content
3. Classroom management
4. Materials
5. Planning
6. Human relations
7. Instructional skills

These components identify the kinds of decisions a teacher makes minute-by-minute in the classroom. Hunter wanted teachers to understand how cause and effect influenced learning within each component. She encouraged teachers to use data from learning situations to augment teaching decisions and increase student mastery of content. Hunter summarized her approach in an interview with Mark Goldberg, "... all of the 5,000 decisions a teacher makes every day fall neatly into three categories: what you are going to teach, which we call a content category; what the students are going to do to learn it and to let you know that they've learned it, which we call learning behavior category; and what you as the teacher will do to facilitate and escalate that learning, which is called a teaching behavior category" (Goldberg, 1990, 41).

In their summary of direct instruction for students with mild disabilities, Bickel and Bickel (1986) noted, "Effective teachers take an active role in creating a positive, expectant, and orderly classroom environment in which learning takes place." Teachers' control time management, signal when academic work will begin, maintain a group focus, expect students to be accountable, and provide a variety of instructional tasks. Direct instruction is based on teacher control of instruction and close supervision of student work. It has produced good results in teaching basic skills, particularly with low achievers. Critics maintain that direct instruction stifles student initiative and that it doesn't teach higher-level thinking skills. Critics also express concern that direct instruction undercuts motivation by reinforcing student dependence on the teacher (Knap, Turnbull, & Shields, 1990).

Precision Teaching

Jamie is a fifth-grade student at Somewhere Elementary School, U.S.A. Five days a week, Monday through Friday, Jamie reads aloud, answers math problems, and spells words dictated by her teacher. Each of these tasks is timed, and Jamie plots her own scores on separate graphs for reading, math, and spelling. A line is extended from the points where other scores have been plotted (Figure 7.1). This procedure enables her teacher to visually track Jamie's learning rate. Jamie and her classmates are participating in precision teaching. Their teacher is measuring their learning performance daily. By seeing the changes in students' learning each day, Jamie's teacher, and others who utilize precision teaching, can adjust their instructional plans as needed (White, 1986).

Ogden Lindsley observed that learning can be enhanced by frequent, self-recorded responses on standardized charts. He encouraged teachers to concentrate on rate of responses instead of percentages of correct responses. Lindsley recommended that teachers teach their students to record their own rate of learning on standardized charts (Lindsley, 1990).

Lindsley designed precision teaching around a framework of behavior modification developed by B.F. Skinner. This framework consists of six basic components:

1. By assessing daily performance, teachers can directly measure performance and monitor learning.
2. Calculating rate of response (i.e., the number of correct responses per minute) establishes a consistent measure of behavior.
3. A standard chart format provides a visual display of performance patterns.
4. Definitions of behavior are descriptive and functional.
5. Analysis of instruction is ongoing.
6. The emphasis is on building appropriate and useful behavior, rather than focusing on doing away with undesired or inappropriate behavior.

FIGURE 7.1 Precision Learning Chart
Contributed by William Wolking.

When students like Jamie are assessed daily, their changes in performance from one timed assessment to the next guide instruction. The more frequently the timed assessments are made, the more often decisions can be made about the effectiveness of instruction for an individual student. Timings are done each day, thus students have sufficient opportunities to demonstrate skills.

Educators traditionally look for accuracy in student responses. Daily timed assessments provide the data to measure both the accuracy and the rate of learning. Wolking (1991) provided the following description of Jamie.

> At the beginning of this unit of study, Jamie answered 20 subtraction fact problems in a minute. She got 13 correct and made 7 errors. Twelve school days later she answered 47 subtraction facts in a minute. On this timing, she got 45 correct and made 2 errors. The learning line for her correct responses showed that she was improving at a rate of 65% per week. The learning line for her error responses showed she was reducing her errors at a rate of about 70% per week. Overall, Jamie's correct responding has improved by 246% (from 13 to 45 per minute correct), and her error responses have decreased by 250% (from 7 to 2 errors per minute) in just twelve school days.

Precision teaching requires plotting scores on a chart so that changes in student learning can be tracked. This chart is a ratio or logarithmic scale, and referred to as the "standard celeration chart." The logarithmic scale displays performance values that are recorded as number of responses per minute. When scores are plotted, an individual's pattern of learning can be seen by drawing a line through the dots. This line of connected points is called a learning line. Generally, the steeper the learning line, the faster learning is occurring. Conversely, the more horizontal or flatter the learning line, the slower the rate of learning. The chart is called a standard or celeration chart because the same rate of learning is always displayed by the same slope.

Student-Centered Learning

In his widely acclaimed book *A Place Called School,* John Goodlad (1984) laments the lack of vigor in United States classrooms. He describes some teachers as "frontal" in their style. By this he meant they seemed rooted to the front of the room, where, like ship captains, they oversee all classroom activity. In describing the culture of school, Goodlad characterizes the teacher a virtually autonomous person who controls almost every aspect of classroom life. Many students labor alone, solitary figures in groups, with little to say about how they spend their days. Many students, Goodlad said, engage in a narrow range of passive behaviors such as listening to the teacher, writing answers to questions, and taking tests or quizzes. Goodlad was not the first educator to describe public schools as havens of autocracy that demand conformity. Demands for changing schools to be more student-centered seem to follow every reform movement that insist teachers get back to the basics. For every point about empowering teachers, such as Hunter's direct instruction model, there is the inevitable counterpoint to empower students.

Glasser (1985) argued that schools should become more responsive to student needs. According to Glasser, student apathy and unwillingness to participate in classroom activities is a direct response to student impotence. As an illustration, Glasser pointed out that no one has to coerce students to work hard at extracurricular activities. Yearbooks, science fairs, athletics, and debate clubs represent a few manifestations of activities that students engage in with enthusiasm. Glasser maintained that the opportunity to exercise control of extracurricular activities increases motivation and involvement. He articulated four student needs that schools should strive to fulfill in the classroom:

1. Students need to belong. They need to feel a part of a larger community and to feel that they are valued by the group.
2. Students need power. They need to make decisions and have responsibilities.
3. Students need freedom. They need to feel self-reliant and in control of their own destiny.
4. Students need fun. They need to have joy and humor, and they want to work for personal satisfaction.

Notice that none of these needs relates to specific parts of the academic curriculum; rather Glasser is focusing on deeper, developmental needs. It's at the developmental level where student-directed and teacher-directed advocates split. Teachers who formalize student-directed learning in their classrooms assume a developmental view of education. Preschool education is the only sector of public education that holds to a strong developmental outlook. Once students begin first grade and continue through middle and high school, developmental views on how young people learn and what their psychological needs are get mired in a curriculum logjam (Elkind, 1986). Teachers wilt under the pressure to get a student "ready" for the next grade. Achievement, tests, basal readers, spelling tests, and an endless array of workbooks provide the grist that students must grind their way through in traditional, curriculum-centered classrooms. In high school, the winds of curriculum pick up pace as teachers bend to pressure to prepare students for graduation and college entrance requirements.

In a student-centered classroom, it is unlikely that students would select the same topics mandated by the school system for each grade. Here lies the dilemma for the student centered teacher. What is the priority: specific curriculum requirements that are best taught through teacher-directed lessons, or student-centered activities that may overlook content measured in standard tests of achievement? A negotiated solution is workable. Teachers can merge both approaches. Direct instruction on the periodic table is more likely to grab a student's attention after a few experiments in a chemistry laboratory. Classroom discussions about the pros and cons of abortion can provide the same insight into the judicial system of our country as that covered by a mundane chapter in a social studies text. Cooperative learning projects can cover the same content as a lecture on algebraic equations.

Student-centered classrooms look different than teacher-directed classrooms. Furniture is arranged to enhance student conversation in small groups; cooperative learning and peer tutoring are commonplace. Myriad objects for concrete learning experiences are arranged on tables. While students work, the teacher moves about the room encouraging, providing feedback, and giving directions. Some students are engaged in small groups; others work independently. Work schedules are arranged to allow students to study different topics at the same time. Rote learning, drills, and passive materials such as worksheets and dittos are shunned.

A common misconception of student-centered classrooms is that they are unstructured. A visitor to a student-centered fourth grade might observe the following scene. Adults and students are scattered throughout the room. In one corner, a parent volunteer is listening to three students take turns reading. Along the perimeter of the room, students in pairs are working at several tables that are labeled "math center," "science center," "art center," and "writing center." In another corner of the room, a student is playing a math game at a computer. Two students are cleaning the gerbil cage. Four students are sitting on pillows and reading library books in the "quiet corner." A student teacher is standing in front of the blackboard reviewing fractions with a group of five students. Finally, the visitor spots the teacher in another corner. Around her is a group of seven students. She is doing a phonics lesson. The room is a beehive of activity. People are talking and walking about. Everybody is busy.

To the untrained eye, the scene may appear disorganized, but there is a complex structure that holds everything together. A student-centered classroom requires a well-thought-out plan for moving students from one center to another; materials and themes at the centers need continual refurbishing; volunteers need direction; student progress must be monitored; and the daily schedule must ensure that all students have a blend of direct and indirect learning experiences. A teacher in a student-directed classroom must be capable of supervising several simultaneous activities.

As long as teachers view direct instruction and student-centered learning as philosophical opposites, the debate about which is the best way to teach will continue indefinitely. A ten-minute slide show on the history of U.S. education would resemble a dance with strobe lights. Following every slide of students frozen in their seats listening to the instructor, there would be a slide picturing students spread around the room involved in different activities. Since the early 1900s the educational pendulum has traced a well-worn track back and forth between direct and student-centered instruction. Teachers who are capable of integrating both approaches into their lessons on a daily basis can attend to the demands of curriculum without forsaking the developmental needs of their young charges.

Learning Strategies

A twelve-year-old given the task of remembering a list of objects (e.g., milk, bread, soda, candy) might repeat the words several times in order to commit them to memory. Learning strategies (also referred to as cognitive strategy, cognitive behavior modification, and metacognitive skills) are mental schemes for memorizing, solving problems, planning, or organizing (Pressley & Harris, 1990). Many individuals independently learn these strategies in the normal course of development; others never acquire these strategies on their own. The lack of learning strategy development may be the basis for many of the learning problems encountered by students with mild disabilities.

Alley and Deshler, practitioners in the field of special education, identified learning strategies as "... techniques, principles, or rules that will facilitate the acquisition, manipulation, integration, storage, and retrieval of information across situations and settings" (Alley & Deshler, 1979, 13). These authors support the need to teach students how to use learning strategies to improve comprehension and retention of classroom content. Equally important is teaching students how to generalize learning strategies outside of school.

> The adage "Give me a fish, and I can eat for a day. Teach me to fish, and I can eat for a lifetime" summarizes the goal of this approach. The intent is to teach students skills that will allow them not only to meet immediate requirements successfully but also to generalize these skills to other situations over time. (Alley & Deshler, 1979, 13)

Learning strategies help students learn to cope with mild disabilities by providing them with a set of directions for improving their ability to learn. Pressley and Harris present the following guidelines for using learning strategies to improve reading comprehension:

1. Summarize the story. Dialogues and classroom discussions enhance memory of plot and characters.
2. Construct an internal visual representation of the story. This procedure can be enhanced through art activities.
3. Relate student experience to a story.
4. Make up questions about the story while reading. (Pressley & Harris, 1990, 32)

The teaching of learning strategies begins with the teacher modeling the strategy. Students might be assigned an essay, for example, and the teacher would begin by demonstrating how to write an intuitive outline (see Figure 7.2). The purpose of the intuitive outline is to get ideas out before listing them in a sequential outline. An intuitive outline is completed by a student brainstorming by herself. She begins by placing the theme or main idea in an oval, and then writes each idea associated with the main thought on lines that branch out from

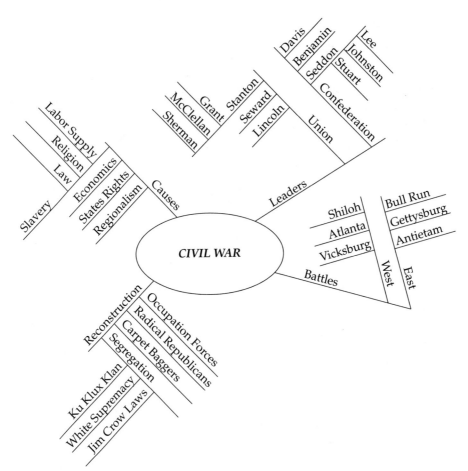

FIGURE 7.2   Intuitive Outline

the center. As a new idea comes to mind, it is added to an existing branch or a new branch is started. Just as a tree branches out spontaneously in different directions, the intuitive outline grows to accommodate the natural progression of ideas. This learning strategy (sometimes called webbing) can help solve common problems such as "writer's block" or test anxiety.

Another example of a learning strategy is mnemonics, a system of memory training that helps students remember important concepts by associating ideas to visual stimuli. A student might remember key principles of the U.S. Constitution, for instance, by going for a memory walk down his street and mentally "picking up" due process from the delicatessen, freedom of the press from the newspaper machine, and the right to bear arms from the department store mannequin.

Mann and Sabatino (1985) recommend the following steps for incorporating a learning strategies approach in the classroom:

1. Describe the strategies needed to solve a classroom problem. (One way to do this is through task analysis—break the solution down into specific steps.)
2. Measure a student's use or nonuse of strategies.
3. Help students implement selected strategies and adjust and revise as needed.
4. Monitor how well the strategy is working.
5. Motivate students to use the strategy. (Scott, 1988, 33)

Selecting the best strategy is a key element in utilizing the learning strategy approach. Scott (1988) recommends teaching problem-solving skills demonstrated by successful students. She identified concentration, independence, reflection, self-direction, active learning, and persistence as core learning strategies students with mild disabilities could learn to improve their classroom performance. Scott presented a variety of activities to teach each learning strategy to a student. For instance, concentration can be taught by playing chess or other games. Reflection could be taught by having students count to ten before they give an answer.

Learning strategies teach students how to learn by helping students to organize their thinking and teaching them thinking skills they will use throughout their lives. However, one should be cautious about jumping too quickly on the learning strategies bandwagon. Much of the seminal work in this area has been conducted under experimental conditions that are unlike classroom conditions. Further research will provide insight into: how to teach learning strategies that students can use in different settings; how to integrate learning strategies into the curriculum; and how to design texts to support strategy instruction (Harris & Pressley, 1991).

Task Analysis

Task analysis is the process of breaking a learning task down into its component parts and teaching each part as a distinct skill. It is often used by sports instructors in teaching such activities as tennis, golf, and skiing. The premise that a hierarchy of subskills underlies mastery of a learning task (e.g., to win a tennis match, to shoot par on a golf course, to ski expert slopes) is the pedagogical foundation of task analysis. By arranging skills in a hierarchy, each skill builds on the next. Task analysis is a sequenced, systematic approach to teaching, which provides opportunities for evaluation of each subskill. When using task analysis the teacher will need to:

1. write a behavioral statement about the learning task (e.g., to be able to divide three-digit numbers with 90% accuracy),
2. design an outline of the learning task broken down into a hierarchy of subskills,

3. evaluate student abilities in relationship to each of the subskills before instruction,
4. select materials and procedures for teaching each subskill,
5. provide feedback to students about subskill development,
6. evaluate acquisition of each subskill through systematic monitoring.

Students generally have some prior knowledge and skills when they begin instruction. Teachers who use task analysis define the task that the student will perform, state the conditions under which the task will occur and show the criterion measurement required for mastery. Task analysis identifies a sequence of skills needed to perform a task successfully; criterion measurements identify whether the student possesses the necessary skills or knowledge for that task. The level of performance that is acceptable is the "criterion level," and it is often specified on the student's individualized education plan (IEP).

Through task analysis, the teacher can plan learning activities in the order in which they need to be learned to reach mastery as indicated on the student's IEP. (See Chapter 8 for a description of IEP development). The criterion set for determining mastery of the behavioral objective can be measured by using criterion-referenced testing, or some other informal, curriculum-based type of assessment.

Functional Curriculum

If students with mild disabilities are not anticipating pursuing a postsecondary education, a more practical, applied curriculum may be needed (Polloway et al., 1989). A functional curriculum includes life skills and teaches them both in the classroom and in the community. When using this approach, basic academic skills are reinforced in a practical manner. For example, math could include paying bills, budgeting, and balancing a checkbook. Reading can be related to assembling appliances, cooking, or home repair. Community-based instruction takes students beyond their traditional textbooks and classroom instruction into the community where they learn skills firsthand and have the opportunity to apply those skills in real life situations. Generally, as students with mild disabilities reach middle and high school years their needs must be evaluated and their curriculum planned accordingly. Polloway and his colleagues (1989) offer the following suggestions for curricula planning for students with learning problems:

1. *Adult-referenced.* The content should be based on a top-down focus, reflecting curricula alternatives based on successful community adjustment rather than from a elementary-oriented focus upward.

2. *Comprehensive.* Curricula offered to students should include a broad range of topics—generally, a combination of academics, vocational training, social skill development, and life skills preparation.

3. *Relevant.* Students at the secondary level need meaningful programs. A student who can relate academic concepts to his or her own experiences is more apt to understand and then apply the concept.

4. *Empirically and socially valid.* Students must acquire skills that are valuable to them personally, appropriate for the communities in which they live, and meaningful to other members of that community.

5. *Flexible.* Curricula must be flexible enough to accommodate a wide variety of diverse student needs as well as the uniquenesses of different community settings.

6. *Community-based.* Much of the training should occur out of the classroom and in actual community settings to increase the probability that skills will generalize across settings and conditions.

Everyone must ultimately function in a community setting regardless of the level of schooling pursued or accomplished. This means that life skills preparation is important for all students at all levels of schooling. Many students figure out skills they need as adults through experience. Students with mild disabilities do not have the ability to problem-solve or learn accidentally; therefore, they need to be taught more directly and purposefully (Brolin, 1989; Kokaska & Brolin, 1985; Patton et al., 1989) (Figure 7.3).

Integrated Teaching

Instructional strategies are like tools in a mechanic's kit. Just as a mechanic will select an adjustable wrench for a particular problem and then move on to other tools, a teacher can select direct instruction to teach specific concepts and then follow up with student-centered activities or learning strategies. The more tools in the instructional kit, the better equipped a teacher is to choose the best instructional strategy for a given situation.

Glickman (1987) draws a distinction between "effective" schools and "good" schools. Effective schools sponsor teacher-directed learning. They narrow the academic focus. Students are taught in large groups from prescribed instructional objectives. Reviewing, demonstration, checking for student understanding, and frequent tests are standard procedures. Glickman asks the question: Should there be more to school than Scholastic Achievement Test (SAT) scores? And, if a school is effective, does that necessarily mean it's a good school? To illustrate his point Glickman relates the following story.

A special education teacher recently told me that she had asked her supervisor for permission to take her students on a five-minute walk to a grocery store to observe transactions at the check-out counter. The supervisor immediately asked, "Which specific objectives will this walk accomplish?" The teacher replied, "I

	Consumer Economics	Occupational Knowledge	Health	Community Resources	Government and Law
Reading	Read an ad for a sale, locating name of store, location, phone number, and price of item	Read a job description	Locate poison control numbers in phone book	Use phone book to locate recreational program in community	Locate and read list of state and U.S. congressmen
Writing	Fill out a magazine order form completely	Practice writing abbreviations for words	Write a menu for a balanced diet	Write letter to TV station about a program they just cancelled	Fill out voter registration form
Speaking, Writing, Viewing	Discuss saving versus spending money	Discuss reasons why people work	Listen to positive and negative feedback on personal appearance	Call library to find out if they have a certain book	Discuss why we need to vote
Problem Solving	Use $10 for the evening, which activity would you choose: movies, bowling, or pizza	Decide on job environment: inside, outside, desk, travel, etc.	Role play appropriate behavior for various places (movies, church, restaurant)	Locate the skating rink on a city map and decide the best way to get there	Decide what items have state and/or local tax
Interpersonal Relations	Ask salesperson for help in purchasing jeans	List questions they would ask in job interview	Discuss honesty, trust, and promise; define each	Call skating rink to inquire about hours	Call to find out what precinct you live in
Computation	Compute the sales tax on a pair of jeans	Compute net income	Calculate and compare the prices of hair washing products	Calculate bus fare to and from the teen center	Calculate the cost of getting a driver's license (fee, gas)

FIGURE 7.3   APL Model of Functional Competency: Examples of Tasks (Junior High School)

don't know. I simply want my students to see transactions involving real money. Besides getting out of the classroom for a while would be fun." Responded the supervisor, "I'm sorry. If it's not one of our curriculum objectives, we don't do it!" (p. 623)

Glickman's point is well made. His concern about the overemphasis of one instructional strategy to the exclusion of others is shared by many educators and researchers. Moreover, Ronald Brandt (1990) observes that teachers have difficulty making changes in their teaching style "like so many compliant windmills on a Kansas prairie." A more comprehensive view of instructional strategies is needed to help teachers integrate seemingly disparate teaching methods.

Harris and Pressley (1991) point out that student-centered and teacher-directed strategies are false dichotomies. Students do indeed need opportunities to construct their own knowledge (i.e., student-directed), but that does not obviate teacher-directed lessons. As Harris and Pressley point out, students will direct their own thinking even when exposed to direct instruction.

> . . . children engaged in the rehearsal of mathematics operations may construct new procedural forms, such as arithmetic shortcuts, while practicing. As students develop skill and proficiency, they do not do exactly what they have been taught. This construction of personalized learning has been well recognized among (learning) strategy researchers. (Harris & Pressley, 1991)

Another element in the discussion of the merits of direct and indirect instruction is the uneasy hypothesis that teachers gravitate toward instructional strategies that reflect their personalities. Claudia Cornett observes that teachers tend to choose instructional strategies based on their personal educational philosophies (Cornett, 1983). The research in this area is thin, but there is ample anecdotal evidence that authoritarian teachers prefer teacher-directed strategies, while student-centered strategies are preferred by teachers who have a developmental view on teaching and learning. More research in this area might produce some uncomfortable insights. While researchers labor to determine the effectiveness of specific strategies and college professors promote strategies based on their utility, it may be that teachers select instructional strategies based on conscious or unconscious personal preferences!

Strong and a small group of colleagues (1990) created a framework to integrate five different instructional strategies: ITIP (Hunter's model of direct instruction), learning strategies, student learning styles, cooperative learning, and reading and writing in content areas. Each member of the group identified a basic operating principle that represented the core premise of an instructional strategy. They called these core principles their "declaration of interdependence." From teacher-directed ITIP, they derived the principle that teachers' decisions should be based on verified educational research. From the learning strategy approach, they highlighted the need for teachers to incorporate reasoning skills in lesson designs. From the research on student learning style, they emphasized flexibility in using a range of instructional strategies. Cooperative learning underscored the social dimension of learning; that is, the sum total of learning in a small group will surpass the learning each student could accomplish working alone. Finally, from the reading and writing across the curriculum literature, they highlighted the need to appreciate the artfulness of teaching.

In order to make use of Strong's integrative model, teachers need to understand how each system works, have knowledge of the learning characteristics of students, and have administrative support for experimentation. Any time a teacher tries something different in a classroom, there is an element of risk. Change is anxiety provoking, and schools are organizations (some would say bureaucracies) that have many built-in mechanisms that resist change. Schedules must be adhered to; school norms must be followed; and principals have most of the power. In a school where teacher-directed learning is the norm, the teacher who attempts to set up student-centered activities is risking failure and ridicule. Without administrative support, teachers must struggle in isolation against the odds. Only in schools where innovation and experimentation are valued will teachers succeed in providing the best of all worlds for their students.

The notion that there is one best way to teach is naive and limiting. Voluminous research that documents that students have different ways of learning should give any teacher reason to pause before wholeheartedly adopting one method of classroom instruction to the exclusion of others.

Summary

Teachers and students sometimes differ in how they view school. While teachers are concerned with long-range successes, students are more concerned about the here-and-now. As children become adolescents, they are often more concerned about peer acceptance than about adult approval. Too often, we ignore developmental differences between students and adults. Teachers like students to adapt to the often unstated norms of public school life; therefore, students with mild disabilities need to learn the hidden curriculum.

Effective teachers are able to use a variety of instructional approaches. In recent years, teachers have found that students with mild disabilities share many of the same learning problems, and that many of the same instructional models are shared by teachers of students with and without disabilities. Educators are realizing that instructional models like precision teaching, direct instruction, student-centered learning, learning strategies, task analysis, and functional skills hold promise for all students. Rather than matching instructional approaches to types of disabilities, teachers are encouraged to match general curriculum strategies to the characteristics, needs, and learning styles of individual students.

Activities

1. Prepare a short survey that can be used to obtain perceptions about schools and their purposes. Use it to interview public school students, regular classroom teachers, and special education teachers about their perceptions.

2. Divide into small groups. Each group will be assigned a skill to be taught to pupils. Outline a task analysis for your particular skill.

3. Arrange to speak to several people who work at various jobs in the community. Ask them about specific tasks and responsibilities that the pupils begin acquiring in school (e.g., being on time to school, must be on time to work; being

polite and pleasant, customers expect to be talked to politely; and so on). The goal is to help make learning meaningful.

4. Select a theme (e.g., racism), a skill (mathematical), or a concept (science) for a lesson. In cooperative groups design a lesson using each of the following teaching approaches: direct instruction, precision teaching, student-centered learning, learning strategies, and task analysis.

5. Define your personal learning style. Provide three examples to demonstrate why you matched yourself with ponderer, drifter, or adventurer. What are other ways of describing learning style? What is the connection between different learning styles and special education referrals?

8 Instructional Modifications

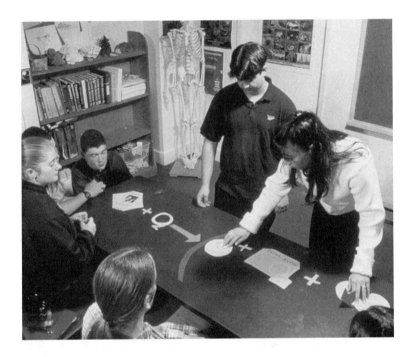

Advance Questions

Answer the following questions as you read this chapter.

1. How do instructional techniques and modifications for students with mild disabilities compare with those used with general education students?
2. How does classroom time management affect learning? What is the difference between allocated time, engaged time, and academic learning time?
3. What are some alternative testing and grading systems?

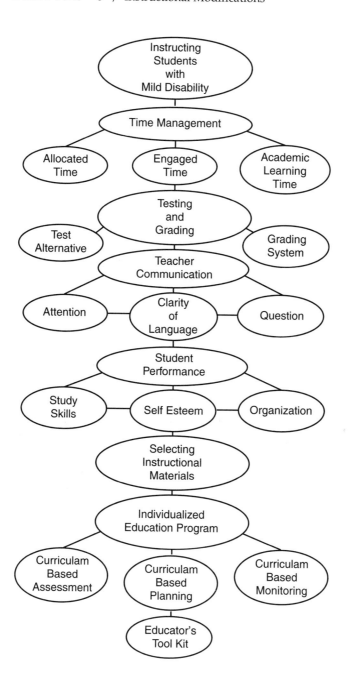

4. How does good communication between teacher and students contribute to effective teaching?
5. What are some practical suggestions for modifying classroom practices in order to meet the needs of students with mild disabilities?
6. When can curriculum-based instruction be used effectively?
7. What are some guidelines for writing individual education programs?

Vignette: Shirley Allen

It was three A.M. and Shirley Allen was tossing and turning. Instead of sleeping she was worrying about the conversation she had with Mr. Kane that afternoon. After two years of successful fourth grade teaching, her principal had asked her to participate in an inclusion program beginning the new fall term. Shirley considered all the additional responsibilities she would be taking on. Her head buzzed with questions. How could she adapt the curriculum to meet the needs of her special education students? What changes would she make in how she used instructional time? How about grading and homework, should she be consistent with all students the same or make adjustments for the special needs students? She was going to be responsible for helping develop IEP—how was she going to do that? Fortunately she had listened to old professor Moriarty's warning at the end of her undergraduate course in mild disabilities. "Don't sell your text back to the bookstore at the end of the semester," he said, "someday you are going to need it." Well the time had come. Shirley got up and rummaged through cartons she stashed in the back of her closet. After fifteen frantic minutes she found the text. She breathed a sigh of relief and slowly turned the pages—ah, so many fond memories, the yellow highlighting provided iridescent testimony to her hard earned A in the course. She found the chapter on instructional modifications and began reading. The guidelines for dealing with classroom organization, grading, homework, and IEPs were clear and practical. Half-an-hour later she closed the book with a smile. Apprehension was replaced with excitement over the challenge of setting up her inclusion program. 'I can do this', she thought as she wearily padded back to bed and dozed off.

Think about the challenges of teaching students with mild disabilities. Use the following questions as a guide.

1. Was Shirley overreacting to her new challenge?
2. How can teachers modify instructional approaches for students with mild disabilities?
3. Should grading and homework assignments be the same or different for students with and without disabilities?
4. What are some main features of IEP development?

Instructing Students with Mild Disabilities

There is a common perception that students with mild disabilities require instructional strategies that are distinctive from effective regular education teaching methods. This assumption is based on the "medical model" perspective that characterized the formative years of special education. Just as medicine is geared toward treating diagnosed disorders, the medical model applied to special education was oriented toward matching an educational treatment to specific types of mild disabilities. Students were placed in special education programs based on the assumption that there was something intrinsically wrong with them and that special education instruction would help remediate learning problems symptomatic of specific disabling conditions.

While some mild disabilities, such as dyslexia, are individually based, many mild disabilities are the result of a variety of overlapping issues that are interactional in nature. Poverty, lack of school readiness skills (e.g., mild mental retardation), disorganized classrooms, dysfunctional families (e.g., behavior disorders), and mismatch between instruction and student learning style (e.g., learning disabilities) all contribute to a cycle of school failure that can result in a special education placement.

Jenkins, Pious, and Peterson (1988) wanted to determine whether students with mild disabilities were different from other students. The researchers analyzed differences between students identified as learning disabled and students identified as underachievers. They compared the instructional levels, learning rates, and learning styles of each group. They found more similarities than differences between the two groups of students. Students with and without disabilities had identical achievement levels. Individual students in each group demonstrated considerable overlap in learning rate and instructional level.

> There are not two discrete sets of instructional methods—one set for use with "special" students and another set for use with "regular" students. As used here, instructional methods refer to basic instructional processes, such as the development of behavioral objectives, curricular-based assessment procedures, task analysis, the arrangement of antecedents and consequences, and open education/discovery learning methods. While some methods need to be tailored to individual characteristics and needs, few, if any, can be clearly dichotomized into those applicable only for special students or only for regular students. (Stainback & Stainback, 1984, 103)

Best teaching practices for general education students are also best teaching practices for students with mild disabilities. Teachers in both general and special education have at their disposal instructional strategies to facilitate the learning of students with mild disabilities.

When we talk about students with mild disabilities, underachievers, and other hard-to-teach students, qualitative distinctions among groups are difficult to detect. The challenge for educators is to implement instructional strategies that can change school failure to success for all students.

Time Management

Data about time management are based primarily on research in general education classrooms. Researchers are interested in finding out how learning is influenced by teachers' use of time. Rich and Ross (1989) found that teachers are allocated approximately 55 percent of the classroom day for instruction, but only half of that time, or 25 percent of the entire day, is utilized by students engaged in learning tasks. How is it that out of an entire school day only one-fourth of the time is spent learning?

Jacob Kounin's (1977) research on classroom organization in elementary and secondary schools bears testimony to how time is wasted in classrooms. Kounin found that many teaching behaviors disrupt lessons. He used such terms as "thrusts," "dangles," "truncations," and "flip-flops" to describe common time wasters. "Thrusts" refers to intrusions in lessons. Principal announcements over the loudspeaker are an example of "thrusts" that interrupt lessons and make it difficult for teachers to get back on track. One inner-city school teacher was so distracted by PA announcements that his first action of the new school year was to disconnect the speaker from his classroom wall! This minor act of rebellion nearly cost him his job.

"Dangles" occur when a teacher leaves a lesson in midair, for example, when a visitor comes to the classroom door. Students may be left with a per-functory remark like, "I'll be out in the hall for a minute. Turn to page 36 in your workbooks and complete the problems." It is the rare group of students who would not take a teacher's momentary absence as an invitation to relax and catch up on some classroom gossip. The ensuing reprimand upon the teacher's return usually wastes more time and creates an unpleasant mood. After such an incident teacher and students are hard pressed to rejoin the lesson with their original enthusiasm.

Teachers "flip-flop" when they reverse directions in a lesson. Flip-flops may be fostered by strategically minded students who would rather hear how Mrs. Jones spent her summer vacation on Cape Cod than hear a lecture on the "mollusk family." Teacher anecdotes turn into tangents and digressions, which entertain both teacher and students while instructional time is sliced into smaller pieces. When teachers flip-flop, students with mild disabilities become confused and dispirited. The teacher who begins a lesson on multiplication of fractions and then realizes that some review in fractions is needed may move back and forth too abruptly for students to keep track of the central ideas. Students with weak listening or attending skills will give up and lose the teacher's train of thought.

"Truncations" occur when a teacher abruptly ends a lesson and moves on to something else without alerting students to the change. The conclusion of a lesson and transition to the next topic is one of the most critical parts of instruc-tional time. Many behavior problems occur because of disorganized transitions. Dealing with classroom disruptions is a major time-waster. By moving smoothly from one lesson to the next, the teacher diminishes management problems and focus students' attention on the next lesson.

Kounin found that teachers who were able to maintain a group focus were most successful in using instructional time. These teachers were able to monitor the entire class without being distracted by minor incidents that could cause the entire class to become diverted, like stopping a class discussion because there is a piece of paper on the floor or because someone isn't paying attention. Such teachers demonstrate "withitness" and "overlapping." They are able to work with an individual student without losing track of the rest of the group. Students describe a teacher who demonstrates "withitness" as having "eyes in the back of her head."

Allocated Time

Allocated time refers to the amount of time scheduled for a specific subject. State and school districts generally mandate a minimum number of minutes per day or hours per week for curriculum topics, such as reading and mathematics. The actual time teachers spend on subject matter within these allocated blocks of time varies. Different beliefs about what is important for students to learn, along with teachers' likes and dislikes for teaching specific subjects, shapes how time is allocated in classrooms. A teacher's enthusiasm for a subject is often an indicator of how much time will be allocated for covering that curriculum area.

Good time management begins with measurements of time allocation. A colleague observing in the classroom can help determine the average number of minutes allocated to each subject or topic. From a qualitative perspective, colleague observation can target such instructional interferences as thrusts, dangles, and truncations. This feedback can help a teacher make necessary adjustments in order to increase allocated time.

Engaged Time

Engaged time refers to the amount of time that a student is working. Engaged time is a significant indicator of achievement (Berliner, 1988). Engaged time can reflect whole group involvement, or the time a student is working alone. Time measures begin from the time students initiate an activity up until they finish. Engaged time depends upon such variables as a teacher's classroom management and organizational ability, how effectively the teacher matches instruction to student learning styles, and how well students understand what is expected of them. Students can be wasting time and give the appearance of being engaged in their work.

How many times have you had the experience of reading twenty pages of text only to realize after you close the book that you don't remember anything! Engagement requires active involvement with learning materials. When students are doing something—moving, talking, writing, counting, measuring, questioning, drawing—their level of engagement is heightened. When students are required to be passive—listening, reading, completing workbook pages—their level of engagement is questionable. Students may look like they are engaged in the learning task, but, as we all know, looks can be deceiving.

Students with mild disabilities, in particular, have difficulties with engaged time. They often lose track of teacher directions or misunderstand an assignment. They might be anxious about something that happened at home. Such students are feeling distress. The biophysical distress reaction is fight or flight. Since there is no way to fight frustration, and fleeing from the classroom is a last resort, students with mild disabilities will withdraw into the false antidote of daydreams. On the outside they may seem a model of classroom decorum as they quietly turn pages or scribble notations on their worksheets. Yet their minds can be light-years away from the task.

Academic Learning Time

Berliner defines academic learning time (ALT) as "time engaged with materials or activities related to the outcome measure being used (e.g., an achievement test), during which a student experiences a high success rate" (Berliner, 1988, 15). When teachers evaluate students specifically on subjects in which students were engaged, academic learning time will improve. If this sounds confusing, let's look at it from a different point of view.

Suppose a sixth-grade teacher allocates sixty minutes a day to whole language instruction of reading. She has selected this teaching method because she gets high student involvement. At the end of the year, the school system administers a standardized reading achievement test. There is a vocabulary section where students are required to give the meaning of solitary words. Also included are timed reading comprehension sections, which include paragraphs of increasing complexity. As the teacher reviews the test, she feels an icy tingle down her spine. The test clearly favors students with strong phonetic skills! Her students are going to do poorly on this test because it is measuring a different set of skills than they were taught. If academic learning time is to improve, curriculum, instruction, learning, and evaluative measures must mesh. The amount of time a student spends demonstrating a specific skill is important to school success. Teachers who are able to monitor student progress through observation, pre- and posttesting, informal testing, and student portfolios are most effective in enhancing academic learning time. This procedure is called curriculum-based assessment.

Materials that are too difficult impede academic learning time. This is a particularly nettlesome problem for teachers of students with mild disabilities. What do you give a fifteen-year-old, street-wise, inner-city youth, who is on a first-grade reading level, to read? How do you reteach fundamental math concepts to eighteen-year-olds who need manipulative materials? One solution is high-interest library books (perhaps with brown paper on the covers) for reading and functional lessons (measuring, check writing, grocery budgets) for mathematics. Students who have failed with the traditional basal texts are not going to improve through drill and repetition with similar materials.

To improve academic learning time, students require opportunities to practice skills in novel situations. They need to see how skills can be generalized, and they need to demonstrate skills in different settings. It doesn't help to teach students to read if they are never going to pick up a book to read for enjoyment or if they don't know how to read the classified section of the newspaper. Berliner illustrates the interrelationship between allocated time, engaged time, and academic *learning time.*

> If 50 minutes of reading instruction per day is allocated to a student who pays attention about one-third of the time (engaged learning) and only one-fourth of the student's reading time is a high level of success, the student will experience only about four minutes of ALT—engaged reading time at a high success level. Similarly, if 100 minutes per day is allocated for reading for a student who pays attention 85 percent of the time and is at a high level of success for almost two-thirds of the time that student will experience about 52 minutes of ALT (academic learning time). (Berliner, 1988, 17)

There are many reasons why students experience lesser amounts of academic learning time. Distractibility, inadequate study skills, emotional problems, disorderly classrooms, and disorganized instruction are samples of the reasons ALT is minimal for students. Students with mild disabilities are placed in double jeopardy when they are pulled out of their classroom for special education services. Unless the resource room teacher is duplicating materials and instructional strategies utilized in the regular classroom at the time of the student's absence, academic learning time will be lost day after day, week after week, month after month. This is a strong argument for mainstreaming or inclusion. (See Table 8.1 for commonly used methods of assisting students.)

Testing and Grading

Tests are administered by teachers to find out what students have learned. This in turn helps teachers to know how effective their instruction has been. It is characteristic of students with mild disabilities to function academically at levels lower than their grade placement. Because of this, both testing and grading systems may require modifications.

Testing Alternatives

Methods for testing students with mild disabilities vary in type, structure, and level of response. Students can be asked to respond to tests and quizzes with written answers, verbal responses, or by demonstration. Learner characteristics often dictate the amount that can be tested at one sitting, the time needed for completion, and whether the testing results can best be achieved by giving group or individually administered tests. Responses should be monitored and expanded from simple recognition and recall to higher-level thinking skills, like inference, analysis, synthesis, evaluation, and appreciation.

When administering a test, sufficient time be given students so that they can complete it without rushing. Students with mild disabilities may have short attention spans; therefore, schedule intermittent breaks. Read test directions orally and give an example of the expected correct response. Remind students to review

TABLE 8.1 Instructional Accommodations

Textual

- Give students an advance organizer, which can also be fused for review or for homework.
- Preteach students vocabulary words in the context in which they will read
- Tape record the text. Recorded text segments should be clear and short. You may want to provide an overview of the selection. Also, give the reader page numbers, and summarize important information periodically.
- Teach textbook structure (headings, subheadings, different print, introductory and summary paragraphs).
- Teach active reading. The student reads a paragraph, covers it, and recites the main point and/or important information in his or her own words.
- Highlight important information.
- Give students a partial outline of important information, to be completed while reading.
- Pair question numbers from a study guide with page numbers on which the information can be found.

Sequencing or Assignment Completion

- Break up tasks into workable and obtainable steps and include due dates.
- Provide examples and specific steps to accomplish the task.
- List and/or post requirements necessary to complete each assignment.
- Check assignments frequently.
- Arrange for the student to have a "study buddy" in each subject area.
- Define all requirements of a completed activity (e.g., your math is complete when all five problems are corrected).

Test-Taking Skills

- Allow extra time for testing
- Teach test-taking skills and strategies.
- Give alternate forms of the test: oral, essay, short answer, multiple choice, fill in the blank.
- Use clear, readable, and uncluttered test forms.
- Provide a scribe.
- Allow students to take tests on computers.
- Give students the opportunity to practice with the accommodations before the test.

Source: CEC Today, 4(3), September 1997, p. 15.

their tests, complete any unanswered questions, and make corrections where needed. For students who have difficulty with traditional tests, alternatives suggested by Bauer and Shea include projects, checklists, discussions, student–teacher interviews, and student-developed portfolios designed to demonstrate student knowledge and understanding of content. Finally, giving brief, frequent tests increases students' opportunities for success.

Grading

Much debate has centered around how the performance of students with mild disabilities should be graded. Carpenter (1985) suggests using the following questions to guide grading decisions: "On what criteria are grades based? What type of medium (e.g., letter grades, pass–fail) should be used? Who should participate in the grading process? How frequently should grades be given?"

Teachers generally include class participation, seat work, tests (e.g., daily, weekly, unit), homework, and special projects in student evaluations. More than one grade could be given to reflect other student attributes, such as effort, attitude, or study skills. Supplement number or letter grades with oral and written information.

A major dilemma for teachers is how to grade work that is completed on the student's functioning level in the general classroom, but not at his or her grade level placement. It is generally agreed that student work that is performed satisfactorily should be reinforced if it is at the student's functioning level and not his or her grade level. One practice is to link grades to the goals and objectives in a student's IEP (Brantlinger & Guskin, 1988). Schultz, Carpenter, and Turnbull (1991) suggest using a criterion-referenced skill list so that specific objectives can be checked as "mastered" or "needs improvement."

Another means of assigning grades is to reward students with the grades earned but coded with actual functioning levels. For example, a fourth-grade student with mild learning disabilities earns an "A" in reading at the second-grade level (the student's actual functioning level in that subject)—thus an "A2" appears on the student's report card as his grade in that subject.

Special educators are encouraged to meet with general teachers on a regular basis to discuss student progress and achievement. Meetings provide the opportunity to convey to the classroom teacher a clear description of a student's strengths, weaknesses, capabilities, and needs. By doing so, additional data by which to determine grades are provided to the general classroom teacher. Perhaps most important is the inclusion of the general classroom teacher in IEP meetings and decisions. Whenever possible, engage in cooperative grading arrangements so that both general classroom and resource room performances are evaluated. Charting student progress can help illustrate student gains that might otherwise be overlooked. It may help to involve students in their own grading when possible.

Co-grading often occurs when students with disabilities are taught in general education classrooms. The special educator may make modifications and adaptations to daily work, tests, and homework assignments. Vaughn et al. (1997) suggest that grading procedures and guidelines be discussed and agreed upon during the development of the individualized education plan. They also remind teachers that different grading standards may exist between elementary and secondary level classes. For example, whereas at the elementary level, teachers can consider students' ability and progress, at the secondary level, grading is often done on the basis of established standards.

Special educators are encouraged to meet with general teachers on a regular basis to discuss student progress and achievement. Meetings provide the opportunity to convey the classroom teacher a clear description of a student's strengths, weaknesses capabilities, and needs. By doing some additional data by which to determine grades are provided to the regular classroom teacher. Teachers need to engage in cooperative grading arrangements so that encouragement and reinforcement for work and effort is given through reasonable accommodations in assessment and grading.

Teacher Communication

Effective teaching depends upon good communication between teacher and students (Johnson, 1972; Jones & Jones, 1986). Participants in communication are actively involved as senders and receivers. The sender is the person who communicates the message, verbally or nonverbally; the receiver is the person who ultimately responds to the message. The communication process may break down if the message cannot be heard, understood, or is misinterpreted. When any of these happen, communication exchanges usually cease.

By using good communication skills, a teacher has more assurance that the intended message is getting across to the students. By being a model of a good listener, a teacher can help students learn to listen and respond appropriately to others. Attention is the prerequisite to listening.

Attention

For some students, special techniques are employed to gain and hold attention (Morsink, 1984; Jones & Jones, 1981; Ramsey, Dixon, & Smith, 1986; Stephens, 1977). For instance, the teacher might first call the student by name when asking a question to assure attending by that individual, conversely the teacher can ask the question before calling the name of a student to create greater interest or anticipation from members of the group. Selecting students at random to answer questions helps to keep everybody alert and listening. Enthusiasm and keeping lessons short and interactive assists in maintaining the attention of those students with attending problems. Some students may be better able to focus their attention when environmental distractions are eliminated or at least reduced, and nonverbal signals can be used to draw students' attention to the task. Attending skills can be taught through games that encourage active listening. Arranging the classroom so that all students can see the teacher helps direct attention to the appropriate location. Finally, by paying close attention when students speak, teachers become good models for attending skills.

Clarity of Language

There are many ways in which teachers can improve the clarity of their communication (Gloeckler & Simpson, 1988; Lewis & Doorlag, 1987). One is to give clear, precise directions. Teachers can simplify verbal directions by using shorter sentences, familiar words, and relevant explanations. Asking a student to repeat directions or to demonstrate understanding of them by carrying out the instructions is an effective way of monitoring clarity of expression. In addition, clarification can be achieved by the use of concrete objects and multidimensional teaching aids, and by modeling (i.e., demonstrating) what should be done in a practice situation.

Finally, a teacher can clarify communications by using a variety of vocal inflections. The use of intonation (i.e., stresses on certain words or sounds), and juncture (i.e., spacing of words) can add clarity to a message. For example, pausing before stating key words or stressing those that convey particular meanings helps students.

In situations involving behavior and feelings, the more immediate the feedback, the more helpful it is. Disturbing situations should be discussed as they occur.

> Buddy's father is a salesman and travels during the week. One Sunday evening, he told Buddy all the things that had bothered him during the weekend. His dad did not feel that Buddy had been glad to see him on Friday evening, and he thought that Buddy spent too much time with his friends instead of with him on Saturday and Sunday. Buddy felt that he was being "dumped on" and that his good traits were overlooked, so he withdrew and pouted. Communication ended and nothing was really resolved between Buddy and his dad.

Had Buddy's father talked with him throughout the weekend as things occurred, perhaps his feelings of being left out of his son's life could have been resolved. Had Buddy known how his father felt earlier, he could have reassured him by doing something special with him.

Johnson (1972) gives several suggestions that teachers can use when providing feedback. First, give a student only the amount of feedback that he or she can understand at that time. Overloading a student with feedback reduces chances that the feedback will be used. Second, describe what happened rather than making judgmental evaluations about the situation. For instance, "You need to be sure to pronounce clearly the words at the end of your sentences," rather than, "You don't make a good public speaker." Last, give objective feedback—avoid moralizing. Do not make personal judgments about statements made by the students or their behavior. Instead, give the students descriptive feedback; for example, "Johnny, the rule says you need your pencil and paper ready to begin work," rather than, "You always forget your notebook!"

Questioning

Berliner (1979) found that the cognitive thinking level of the questions that teachers ask is typically low rather than high. For example, a lower-level question asks for a literal answer, like "Who was the first astronaunt?" A higher-level question requires a student to apply knowledge, analyze and synthesize information, or make evaluations and interpretations. For instance, "Why do astronauts weigh less in space than on earth?" requires students to apply their knowledge of gravity. Both lower- and higher-level cognitive questions are relevant and are needed in classroom learning; however, teachers may need to focus on asking more higher-level questions.

Asking lower-level questions encourages student participation and builds factual knowledge. From these bases of knowledge, higher-order questions stimulate and facilitate the development of more sophisticated thinking—like analyzing or evaluating an idea. In the long run, students achieve considerably more when their thinking is heightened and expanded.

Regardless of the level of a question, Belch (1975) suggests strategies for improving teachers' questioning skills.

1. Ask questions that require more than a yes or no response.
2. Allow sufficient time for students to deliberate the question.
3. Reword or restate questions when students fail to respond or respond incorrectly.
4. Challenge student responses in a professional way. Avoid giving "put-downs" or other belittling responses.
5. Direct questions to all students and not just to volunteers or the brighter ones.
6. Try to sequence your questions. Encourage students to use logical thinking and build one question on another, or build one question on the answer given to a previous question.

Student Performance

Self-Esteem

Teachers may have sterotyped perceptions of students with mild disabilities; likewise, expectations of these students may be less than what is expected of other students (Coleman, 1985; Siperstein & Goding, 1985). Students often pick up on their teachers' perceptions and develop similar negative stereotypes toward classmates with mild disabilities.

Teachers can serve as positive role models—that is, model positive reactions toward students with mild disabilities in order to create an environment of acceptance and support. Teachers do this by conveying that they want to work with the students and by supporting students' efforts.

Sara and Juanita have low self-esteem due to their learning problems. Both girls are in their early teens, come from middle-class backgrounds, and are popular with their peers. Sara experiences difficulty comprehending what she has read. Even though she rereads a passage several times, she still has problems answering questions about what she has read. Juanita, on the other hand, has difficulty with written expression. She reads assigned subject content with ease and can tell you what she has read, but cannot write legible responses to short answer or essay type questions. Sara has withdrawn and become quiet in class; whereas Juanita acts belligerent and sassy.

Both of these students would benefit from successes in the areas in which they are experiencing difficulties. By following a few practical suggestions, a classroom teacher can help students such as Sarah and Juanita.

First, assign tasks in which the students can succeed, and make certain that the assignments are understood so they can be carried out successfully. Point out something favorable about each student's daily work, and praise efforts, even if progress is small. Whenever offering constructive criticism, recognize the effort that was made and explain the desired outcome rather than just calling attention to shortcomings.

Much of a youngster's self-esteem is tied to social acceptance. Students can make contributions to class discussions by explaining a concept or discussing a topic with which they are familiar. Simulations and role play activities help students to rehearse social responses; cooperative learning provides opportunities to learn with other students. Peer tutoring develops feelings of satisfaction in helping other persons. Grouping students with low self-esteem with classmates who have similar interests enhances social conversation so they can more easily work together on class projects. Providing time for students to share positive accomplishments with classmates and to write daily happenings in a private journal also builds self-confidence.

Encourage students to use word processors so that writing can more easily be edited. Word processing encourages trial, error, and practice. Mark and give credit for students' correct and acceptable work, not just their mistakes and errors (e.g., circle or put checks by correct responses, indicate number correct with a plus symbol).

Study Skills

Knowing how to study is essential to successful performance in school. Students with mild disabilities demonstrate poor study skills (Polloway et al., 1989; Reid & Hresko, 1980). Many teachers are either unaware that study skills must be taught to these students or do not know how to teach these kinds of skills (Scruggs & Mastropieri, 1986).

R.J., a sixth grader, exemplifies this problem. During early elementary school years, R.J. had no problem reading assigned stories, doing basic math operations, and spelling weekly spelling words. Therefore, R.J.'s parents were perplexed when he began bringing home low grades in science and social studies. There was no doubt that R.J. was reading the assigned chapters in his science and social studies textbooks—but he made failing test scores in these subjects. His parents and teacher discovered that R.J.'s lack of effective study skills left him ill-prepared for tests in these classes.

One way to find out if students need to improve their study skills is to ask them questions about their study habits. Stephens, Blackhurst, and Magliocca (1988) recommend using a checklist for this purpose. See Table 8.2 for the Study Habits Checklist.

Often, students like R.J. read the pages but don't comprehend what the written passages mean. The SQ3R method of study is effective in helping students to better comprehend what they are reading (Cheek & Cheek, 1983; Mercer & Mercer, 1985; Wallace & Kauffman, 1986). The SQ3R study skill teaches students to:

- survey or scan the material: read the title, first paragraph, subheadings, last paragraph;
- develop questions: change the title and subheadings into questions;
- read the material: find answers to the questions;
- recite both the questions and answers;
- review the material: recite questions and answers daily.

The SQ3R method can be modified and used to help students better understand math problems (Georgia Department of Education, 1989). The student procedure is as follows:

- survey or scan the whole problem to determine what needs to be done;
- change the math problem into a series of questions;
- determine the facts that need to be answered;
- determine processes needed to answer the facts;
- perform computation to solve the problems;
- question the answer by checking the computation.

Reading comprehension is enhanced when students can relate their personal experiences to what they are reading. Since each reader's background will vary, involve students in firsthand experiences (e.g., field trips) when possible. Another method is to stimulate students' thinking about a topic before oral or silent reading begins (Wilson, 1983). Polloway and colleagues (1989, 229) suggest having the teacher introduce a reading selection by saying, "As you read, think about what you would do if you were caught in a flood as Van is in this story." This helps a student personalize a story.

Active reading is encouraged when a teacher initiates a discussion related to the selection the students are about to read. For example, encourage students to comment on a passage by giving their opinions or by having students read a passage and justify or change their original opinions (Polloway et al., 1989). When

TABLE 8.2   Study Habits Checklist

—— Do you have a regular place where you study?

—— Do you keep a chart that shows the time you spend studying?

—— Do you have a regular time to study?

—— Do you keep a homework assignment book?

—— Do you keep a calendar of tests, reports, and projects?

—— Do you keep a notebook or folder for each subject?

—— Do you take class notes?

—— Do you make notes or highlight material while reading?

—— Do you review class notes and reading notes regularly?

—— Do you outline or summarize what you read?

—— Do you make note of and look up new words?

—— Do you keep for review all returned papers and tests?

—— Do you visit and use the library regularly?

Adapted from: Stephens, Blackhurst, and Magliocca, 1988, pp. 160–161.

students make predictions about the story and generate their own questions, their comprehension is improved.

Students with mild disabilities frequently feel overwhelmed with the amount of material they are expected to learn. The teacher can reduce the amount of written work that is presented or assigned (Carbo, Dunn, & Dunn, 1986; Schulz, Carpenter, & Turnbull, 1991). Students can demonstrate mastery of learning material through projects (Lewis & Doorlag, 1987). For example, students can track the position of planets in relation to the sun by constructing a mobile on which styrofoam balls representing the planets are scaled in size and distance from a sun. Projects enhance interest in learning.

Organizational Skills

Organization is important for success in the general classroom. Students with mild disabilities often have organization problems. Particular areas in which organization assistance might be needed include: (a) keeping track of materials and assignments, (b) following directions, (c) completing class assignments, and (d) completing homework assignments.

Keeping Track of Materials and Assignments.   Roberto, a fifth grader, has a problem keeping track of his materials and homework assignments. One day his English teacher gave him a slip of paper that excused him from that evening's homework in her class. He had earned this waiver by receiving good grades on a specified number of prior homework assignments. When handed this paper, Roberto jammed it into one of his pants pockets. The next day, his teacher asked the students to turn in either their homework assignment or their homework waiver. Roberto suddenly realized that he had neither the excuse nor the homework.

What can be done in the classroom to help students like Roberto learn responsibility? He could keep all of his schoolwork in a large loose-leaf notebook and not in single folders that could be lost. Students with mild disabilities may not have the materials and supplies necessary to begin their classwork. This is especially a problem when students move from one classroom to another for different subjects. These students need to be shown how to organize and plan ahead for classroom needs. One way to help students develop judgment and planning skills is to teach them strategy games like Monopoly, checkers, or chess. Mnemonic devices and lists help students organize priorities (McCoy & Prehm, 1987).

Following Directions.   *Maria has problems following classroom directions. Invariably, Maria answers the wrong set of questions, uses the wrong type of paper, or in some way, exhibits difficulties following directions.*

Before giving directions to students like Maria, have them clear their desks of distracting objects. A cleared desk helps students to focus attention, as does maintaining eye contact while stating directions. Break directions into parts one, two, and three. Provide visual cues. For example, write key words or steps on the chalkboard or on a large chart. Ask students to restate the directions as they understand them. If directions are written, underline or circle directional words. Gloecker and Simpson (1988) caution against giving directions to a group several times. Students may "tune out" the initial instructions because they have learned that the directions will be repeated. In addition, the instructions may be reworded the second time, and thus become confusing. Encourage students to ask for clarifications if part of the directions are missed or misunderstood.

Students sometimes experience problems in proper sequencing. To assist with this difficulty, keep the number of directions in a sequence to a minimum. Check to see if the student understands the order in which the directions were given. This can be done by listening to him or her repeat the directions in sequence (Gloeckler & Simpson, 1988).

Completing Class Assignments.   *"Class, you have ten more minutes to finish your assignment," said Mrs. Green. Even that won't help Janice, she thought, as she walked by the girl's desk. Look at her paper—she hasn't even written six math problems on it! I wish I knew what I could do to get her to finish her class assignments!*

Some students, like Janice, have difficulty completing class assignments on time. Before looking for strategies that might be helpful with particular students, teachers might analyze how they are going about assigning work. First, is adequate time being given to finish assigned tasks? Not everyone works at the same pace, and some students require more time than others. Therefore, as in Janice's case, Mrs. Green could assist her in pacing her work. After advising students of exactly how much time is being allowed, Mrs. Green could help Janice set a kitchen timer on her desk that shows her just how much time she has spent on a particular assignment, and how much time is left. Or Janice could be given an assignment sheet with two blank clocks, one for the teacher or student to fill in hands to signify time to begin and one for drawing hands to end that task. With either of these time reminders, a reward system for completed work would help reinforce student efforts.

There are several other strategies that help students with mild disabilities complete work. Students need to know exactly when assignments must be turned in. Mini-deadlines set throughout the day alert students periodically to work that is due. Scheduling a brief free-time period before work is due allows some catch-up time if needed.

Completing Homework Assignments.   *Completing homework assignments is a problem for Sheriffo, a fourth grader. It's not that Sheriffo won't do the work—he does what he can. His problem is that the homework assignments given by his teacher cover new concepts he has yet to master. So why don't his parents help him? Well, his father is a sales representative and travels during most week days. His mother works part-time as a nurse at one of the nearby hospitals. The family with whom Sheriffo stays during the evenings while his mom works is so busy with their own activities that no help is possible there.*

The tasks assigned by Sheriffo's teacher are in the category of new tasks—not practice tasks. Because her teacher is overlooking this basic principle, she is handicapping Sheriffo. Students should be assigned only homework that they are capable of completing successfully. Tasks that are too difficult instill feelings of frustration and hopelessness in students.

Cooper (1989a, 7) defines homework as "tasks assigned to students by school teachers that are meant to be carried out during nonschool hours." He states that homework helps students to understand academic work and to remember what they have learned (Cooper, 1989b). More indirectly, homework helps in the improvement of: students' study skills, attitudes toward school, and an awareness that learning occurs in other places than school. Other nonacademic benefits, named by Cooper, include the fostering of independence and responsibility. Homework involves parents in the school process, makes them more aware of what their child is studying, and signals support of their child's education.

There can be a negative side to homework. For example, too much work on the same topic leads to boredom. Homework should not deprive a youngster of recreational activities. If parents try to assist their child with homework, their use of different methods from that of the child's teacher can cause confusion. Not understanding what or how to do a homework assignment can result in copying or cheating.

Homework too often accentuates inequities in home environments. For instance, some children do not have quiet, well-lighted places to do their homework; some do not have the necessary materials; and some, like Sheriffo, do not have someone to answer their questions or monitor them.

So what can be done to reap the benefits of homework yet make sure individual student abilities and home situations are considered? First, remember that only practice tasks should be given as homework. Second, when deciding upon the amount of homework, the objective is for the student to practice things learned at school; thus, too much homework, especially if practiced with errors, can be harmful.

England and Flatley (1985) encourage teachers to talk with their students when homework problems arise. They suggest that teachers ask their students whether they need help or if they are confused about a homework assignment. There may be legitimate reasons that preclude completing a particular homework assignment.

Some homework do's and don't's listed by England and Flatley (1985, 36–37) are given in Table 8.3.

Coordinate homework with parents. One way to do this is to have students keep a special notebook or folder in which homework assignments are recorded. Such a log would include type of assignment, specific instructions, when it was taken home, and when it was completed. Parents might sign the page on which the day's homework assignments are recorded. Keeping a homework log would ensure that parents know each day what their child is assigned for homework. An alternative is to ask parents to sign the actual homework papers, either before they are turned in or after they have been graded and returned to the youngster. Encourage parents to reward successful completion of homework assignments.

Selecting Instructional Materials

Teachers are faced with difficult decisions about which instructional materials to select for students, especially those with mild disabilities. When given the choice, Ramsey (1988, 1995a) discovered that teachers most often select materials they (a) are most familiar with, (b) have been trained to use, (c) can find available, and (d) can identify with their teaching style.

Smith (1983) maintains that the most appropriate materials for a teacher to use with students who have learning problems are those which:

- have a logical, hierarchical sequence of instructional objectives,
- are adaptable to a variety of learning styles (e.g., adventurer, ponderer, drifter),
- cover the same objectives in multiple ways,

TABLE 8.3   Do's and Dont's of Homework

Do try to make homework interesting. For example, practice math by calculating areas of living room, bedroom, and kitchen, rather than solving problems on a drill worksheet.

Do explain the specific reason for homework assignments.

Do listen to what students have to say about specific homework assignments.

Do solicit parent feedback about homework. Remember that parents have to enforce homework and may spend time helping with assignments.

Don't use homework as punishment.

Don't make up spur-of-the-moment homework assignments.

Don't assume that because there are no questions asked about a homework assignment that students understand it.

Don't expect students (even your best students) always to have their homework assignments completed.

Don't give a homework assignment on a topic unless it has been taught in class.

- pretest to determine where teaching should begin,
- have a built-in evaluation mechanism for determining mastery of instructional objectives,
- allow students to proceed at their own rate and even skip objectives they have already mastered,
- have reinforcement activities.

To this list, Ramsey (1995a) adds a few additional criteria for the selection of instructional materials. Stories should contain characters who are the same age, gender, and race as the readers. Young readers will be more interested in reading stories when they see pictures and other illustrations that are representative of themselves, their friends, and their families. Likewise, content and vocabulary need to be at their reading levels. Finally, instructional materials should meet the learning needs of students, as noted on their IEPs.

Modification of Materials

Students with mild disabilities sometimes require modifications in materials. One type of modification that is often needed is a reduced number of problems for classroom seat work. For instance, why have Johnny, who works at a pace much slower than his classmates, work out twenty long division problems when he can show he knows how to do the mathematical operations by answering five of these problems correctly? And when Caitlin experiences difficulties with division, why not use error analysis? That is, pinpoint what she is doing procedurally that is causing the same error to occur in several problems. When error analysis is applied, the student has only one calculation error to correct.

Another type of modification is to alter questions. For example, the usual way that teachers give spelling tests is by pronouncing words orally and having students write them. Instead, the teacher could give students word choices that are similar and have them underline or circle the correct spelling of words from a multiple-choice format. Or use the cloze procedure where the teacher deletes selected letters which must then be filled in by students. Similarly, the teacher can alter the instruction by having students work at learning centers and use picture directions rather than written sentences. Or use a buddy system whereby one student reads the instructions, and the other performs the tasks.

In order to present content at secondary students' reading and comprehension levels, a teacher might write information presented in textbooks, develop chapter outlines, code paragraphs to chapter questions, and so forth. This is done using magic markers to highlight the main idea, topic, and specific vocabulary words or letters. Discarded books and workbooks can be put together and reassembled in ways that meet specific instructional needs of students.

Individualized Education Program

In order to qualify for federal funding under IDEA, each state must develop a policy that "assures all children with disabilities the right to a free appropriate public education." The development of a program of *appropriate* special education and related services occurs through the mechanism of an individualized education plan. The curriculum specified in this program must be tailored to meet the needs of the individual student.

The program (i.e., IEP) includes a written statement about a youngster's present education performance, the annual goals and short-term goals to be achieved, a statement of specific services to be performed, dates for initiation and duration of services, and criteria, procedures, and schedules for evaluating whether the objectives are being achieved (Table 8.4). The IEP is developed at a meeting in which the following people are present: the local education agency representative who is qualified to provide or to supervise the provision of special education, the child's teacher, the parents, and the child, if appropriate. Other persons may be included at the discretion of either the parents or the education agency. If this is the first time the child has been evaluated, the evaluator or an individual qualified to address the evaluation must be present (Rothstein, 1995). A sample IEP with statements corresponding to required components is shown as Figure 8.1.

The first step in developing an individual program for a specific child is to *assess*. Due to the medical connotation, the term "evaluation" rather than "diagnosis" is used when examining the assessment data that is collected from testing and other informational sources. Testing and other forms of assessment, however, generally occur on a regular basis for each student. Teachers monitor daily growth

TABLE 8.4 Essentials of the Individualized Education Program (IEP)

- **Present level of performance**—This statement describes what the student can or cannot do at the present time. This description comes from test results, school records, special evaluations, and the observations of parents, teachers, and the student's multidisciplinary evaluation team. This includes information about the student's efforts to learn and his behavior.
- **Annual goals**—Statements that describe what the student should be able to do at the time of the annual review.
- **Short-term objectives**—These are the behavioral objectives that state what the student must do to reach annual goals. Teachers use these objectives to write the student's lesson plans.
- **Special education and related services**—These are people, programs, and special resources the student needs in order to learn and reach his goals.
- **When and where the special education services will be provided**—This explains how long a student will spend in a special education setting. It also states how long the student will spend in a regular classroom setting with nondisabled students.
- **Who will work with the student and keep track of his progress**—This is generally the student's teacher. Other resource and support personnel may be included.
- **Beginning and ending of the special education services**—This describes when the IEP starts and when the next review will take place.
- **Evaluation**—This is completed ongoing until the end of the IEP period. It notes the student's progress and success in meeting his goals. It is the basis for developing the next IEP, if there is one.
- **Signatures**—Parents and teachers involved in developing the IEP may sign their names on the form. The IEP form is a plan for the student's education and is not a binding contract between the educators and the parents. The signatures are documentation of involvement.

by informal tests, observations, and other forms of curriculum-based assessment. According to the law, the educational program for each student receiving special education is revised at least once a year. Yearly standardized tests are given to determine progress in content areas taught. The law further requires that each student in special education be reassessed at least every three years. (See Appendix D for a list of frequently used tests.)

Curriculum-Based Assessment

Standardized assessment practices are often criticized for their lack of relevance to instruction. Assessment procedures linked to what is taught in school have reemerged as promising alternatives to standardized assessment (Blankenship, 1985; Deno, 1985, 1986, 1989; Tucker, 1985; Wesson, 1991; Ysseldyke & Algozzine, 1982).

Advocates of curriculum-based assessment point out the need to target evaluation procedures on content that is taught in the classroom (Algozzine, Ruhl, & Ramsey, 1991). Standardized achievement tests comprise a limited sample of questions that the test-makers believe reflect the classroom's curriculum. If

Page 1 of 2   Special Education Department   Type of Staffing

                           Individualized Education Program (IEP)   Initial _____

                                                                                   Review _____

Student: <u>Jerry Smith</u>   B'date <u>5/15/86</u>   School/Grade <u>Lake Park/3</u>   Date <u>2/23/95</u>

Student Attendance # _____   Parent/Guardian <u>Janet Smith</u>   Work Phone <u>324-1168</u>

Date of Original Program Entry <u>2/23/94</u>   Address <u>1421 McGill Street</u>   Home Phone <u>322-7722</u>

I. Present Level of Performance
   Test results indicate average intelligence. Academic performance in reading vocabulary, and comprehension
   below second grade expectancy levels. Parents describe Jerry as well-meaning, but overactive and immature.

II. Prioritized Annual Goals (see attached page(s) for short-term objectives)
   1. Jerry will increase his reading comprehension to 2nd grade level, as measured by the Woodcock Reading
      Mastery Tests–Revised.
   2. Jerry will increase his word recognition skills from 2nd to 3rd grade level, as measured by the Woodcock
      Reading Mastery Tests–Revised.

III. Recommended Special Education and/or Related Services

	Implementation		Anticipated	
<u>Service/Program</u>	<u>Date (Projected)</u>	<u>Hours/Week</u>	<u>Duration</u>	<u>Review Date</u>
<u>Resource Room</u>	<u>2/30/95</u>	<u>5 hrs</u>	<u>One school year</u>	<u>2/23/96</u>

Regular Class Placement: <u>25</u> Hours/Week   Transportation: ___Yes <u>x</u> No   Documentation of Attempts to

Adaptive Physical Education ___Yes <u>x</u> No   Involve Parent/Guardian

Committee Members Present: This is to certify that I was invited to   Date   Comment
_____Chairperson   participate in the writing of this IEP & that I   1/10/95   note sent home
_____   understand its contents. Due process rights   1/30/95   phone call
_____   & procedures have been explained & I have   _____   _____
_____   been provided a copy of these rights. I   _____   _____
_____   understand that a copy of this IEP will be
                                     given to me upon my request.

                                                                                   Date   <u>2/23/95</u>

                      _____
                      Parent/Guardian Signature

FIGURE 8.1   Sample IEP Form

Page 2 of 2

Individualized Education Program (IEP)

Short-Term Objectives

(Complete at least one objective for each goal)

Student: Jerry Smith   B'date 5/15/86   Program: LD Resource   Date 2/23/95

Person to Provide Service Nora Clark

Annual Goal: Jerry will increase his reading

comprehension to 2nd grade level, as measured by the Woodcock Reading Mastery Tests-Revised

Short-Term Instructional Objectives	Criteria for Mastery	Date Reviewed	Method of Evaluation	Mastery Yes	No
1. Given a selected 2nd grade reading passage, Jerry will verbally answer literal and inferential comprehension questions about the content.	80% accuracy	3/15/95	Teacher prepared list of literal and inferential comprehension questions drawn from a reading passage	Yes	
2. Given a selected story from a 2nd grade reading book, Jerry will write correct answers to 8 of the 10 questions.	80% accuracy				

Annual Goal: Jerry will increase his word recognition skills from 2nd to 3rd grade level, as measured by the

Woodcock Reading Mastery Tests-Revised.

3. Jerry will use the context of sentences from a 2nd grade reading passage to identify unknown words.	85% accuracy	4/15/95	Teacher observation	Yes	
4. Given a list of 20 vocabulary words from a selected 3rd grade reading story, Jerry will read 18 correctly.	90% accuracy				

FIGURE 8.1   cont'd.

the standardized test-makers are wrong in their hypotheses, the student is evaluated on content she or he was never taught. Curriculum-based assessment is defined as "the practice of obtaining direct and frequent measures of a student's performance on a series of sequentially arranged objectives derived from the curriculum used in the classroom" (Blankenship, 1985, 234).

An illustration of curriculum-based assessment follows:

> Carol, a kindergarten teacher, decided to teach her students a unit on frogs. Before beginning her lessons she asked her students a series of questions about the amphibians. She tabulated their responses. After the unit, she again quizzed her young charges. She found that they could answer 75% more questions about frogs after the unit than before. By evaluating student progress based on their ability to learn the classroom curriculum, Carol was practicing curriculum-based assessment.

Curriculum-based assessment involves repeated measurement of a student's performance on a sequenced curriculum (Research Brief for Teachers, 1988). Counting and graphing are the best means of tracking student progress. For example, a teacher could ask a student to read a passage from a story that seems to match his present reading level. Each incorrectly read word is marked. A final tally reveals that the student knew two-thirds of the words in the story. This 66 percent figure provides baseline data to measure future progress. Every few days, after instruction, the student's progress in reading is again measured. Graphing the results of each measurement provides a visual means of efficiently marking progress.

Curriculum-based data is collected "prior to instruction, immediately following instruction, and throughout the year to assess long-term retention" (Blankenship, 1985, 238). Assessment of student progress in relationship to the classroom curriculum has several uses:

1. Various instructional procedures are evaluated and, if necessary, changed.
2. The data can provide information to support special education referrals.
3. Current performance, goals, and objectives for individual education plans (IEPs) are written in a straightforward language; this enhances communication between parents and administrators.

Curriculum-Based Planning

All students with mild disabilities must have an individual education program (IEP) to document student current performance and instructional goals. Fuchs and Shinn (1989) identified two categories of problems associated with using non-curriculum-based assessment methods to write IEPs. First, IEP goals are typically vague and global (e.g., ... will improve one year in reading) or overly specific, covering small details. Second, without curriculum-based assessment, IEP goals are written so that substantive and procedural compliance with federal requirements related to multidisciplinary evaluation procedures are inadequate. Fuchs and Shinn (1989) suggest that instructional planning can be improved by writing curriculum-based IEP objectives.

Deno (1986) described a three-step process for formulating curriculum-based IEP objectives. First, current performance data are collected. Next, a level of the curriculum is specified (e.g., employment skills for a secondary student), conditions and behavior are identified, and a date for review of progress is established. Finally, a criterion for success is specified based on curriculum standards or individual performance records. Having done this, the process of actually writing objectives is straightforward.

Curriculum-Based Monitoring

Some educators express concern that much of traditional special education practice represents a "refer, classify, place, and forget" to students with special learning needs (Algozzine & Ysseldyke, 1983, 1986; Ysseldyke & Algozzine, 1982, 1984, 1990). Curriculum-based assessment practices offer considerable promise for improving periodic and annual reviews used to decide whether to continue or terminate special education services (Allen, 1989; Marston & Magnusson, 1988; Shinn, 1986). Assessment activities for periodic and annual reviews are similar; annual reviews tend to be more thorough and typically are documented with a formal written report (Allen, 1989). The focus of these activities is assessing the general benefits of special education services and deciding whether to continue or modify current levels of service to meet special learning needs.

In determining benefits of special education, teachers make curriculum-based comparisons of student performances before and after entering special programs. Comparisons of special education and general education progress are used in deciding when to terminate special programs. If a student's performance falls within the average range of performance for grade-level peers (e.g., within one standard deviation above or below their mean), return to regular class placement would seem appropriate (Allen, 1989), but as Marston (1978) points out a grade-level standard is too strict a criterion for mainstreaming. Performance of other low-achieving students may be a more appropriate standard (Allen, 1989; Salvia & Ysselkdyke, 1998).

Curriculum-based assessment is not a panacea for all problems with assessment. However, it does offer a number of advantages over traditional psychometric practices. First, gathering performance indicators in classroom-based curriculum materials and comparing them to similar scores obtained by peers clearly goes a long way in making assessment relevant for instruction. Too often, skills measured by items on standardized tests bear little relation to daily classroom activities (Good & Salvia, 1987; Jenkins & Pany, 1978; Salvia & Ysseldyke, 1998).

Long-Range Goals and Short-Term Objectives.   In education, curriculum-based objectives are developed following assessment. The intent of educational prescription is to *prescribe* or develop an individualized education program consisting of long-range goals and short-term objectives with time lines, assigned responsibilities, and accountable criteria for accomplishing the plan.

The initial plan is based on the assessment that was performed in order to make multidisciplinary decisions about eligibility and program planning. Specific goals are selected in accordance with assessment results which in turn are described in the IEP as present levels of functioning. At least two objectives are developed as a means of reaching each goal.

Goals.   Goals are projections of how much a student should be able to progress in a subject or behavior in a year. They are referred to as "long range" because of the year's time span.

Objectives.   Objectives are "short term" means for reaching each goal. They are similar to the behavioral objectives outlined in a task analysis. The similarity to task analysis is that the objectives lead, in succession, to obtainment of the goal. The objectives are broken into shorter steps than the overall goal, thus, each is attainable in a shorter period of time.

Like behavioral objectives, short-term objectives begin with a verb that states what the student should be able to do in order to demonstrate whether or not he or she has learned what you wanted him or her to learn. The verbs must be observable and measurable, and specific to attainment of the goal for which they are written. Table 8.5 lists verbs that meet these criteria along with a sampling of some which do not meet the criteria.

Objectives specify (1) the conditions under which performance is obtained, (2) the learning behavior being performed, and (3) the criterion for success (Mager, 1962). Rather than stating that Alex will decode words at the second-grade level, which is really a global objective or goal, each objective describes specifically one discrete skill that will move Alex closer to the goal. Consider the following example:

Given a written list of one syllable words, Alex will sound each out with 80 percent accuracy.

The condition (i.e., Given a list of one syllable words) describes the context for observing Alex. The behavior (i.e., will sound each out) describes the action Alex is expected to perform, and the criteria (i.e., with 80 percent accuracy) identifies how Alex's skill will be evaluated. A list of four to five such objectives would be arranged in a hierarchical fashion, culminating with the stated goal of improving Alex's phonetic decoding skills. Teacher accountability, student progress, and program effectiveness can be scrutinized on a more professional level when instructional objectives are stated in a clear, observable, and lucid fashion. Other examples include:

TABLE 8.5   Verbs for Behavioral Objectives

Verbs that are observable and measurable

name	contrast
write	analyze
demonstrate	synthesize
solve	label
recite	read
identify	transcribe
differentiate	translate
construct	run
list	spell
enumerate	summarize
compare	participate

Verbs that are not observable and measurable

know	have faith in
understand	inculcate
appreciate	foster
develop an appreciation for	instill
grasp the significance of	show respect for
enjoy	have a positive attitude toward
believe	comprehend

Conditions

1. Given a list of twenty spelling problems. . . . . . .
2. Given ten math division facts on a worksheet. . . . . .
3. Given a list of fifteen vocabulary words. . . .
4. Without access to. . .
5. Without the aid of. . .

Criteria

1. With 90% accuracy. . . . .
2. Not more than 5 errors. . . . .
3. At least 3 out of 5 times. . . . .
4. With 80% correctness. . . . .

To summarize, a short-term objective

1. states in shorter steps the means by which a goal will be accomplished;
2. begins with a verb that states the specific behavior to be performed;
3. describes conditions under which behavior is expected to occur;
4. indicates a criterion level for acceptable performance.

The next step in IEP is to *implement* the instruction. Implementation occurs through use of instructional models. We discuss instructional models in Chapter 7. In this chapter, we describe a number of instructional adaptations that have components which make them appropriate for planning and implementing instruction for students with mild disabilities.

Once the program has been implemented, teachers and other support personnel then *reassess.* There are several reasons for reassessing a student following implementation of instruction. Reassessment occurs so that some determination can be made about the amount of progress a student has made in reaching long-range goals and short-term objectives. Reassessment also occurs so that adjustments can be made in the uses of instructional models if necessary. Actually, it is important that assessment occur ongoing and accompany daily implementation of instructional programming. Table 8.6 lists methods of assessing student progress.

The Educator's Kit of Tools

Many professionals carry tool kits. Carpenters and repair persons have a collection of tools that enable them to perform carpentry and various types of repair work. Lawyers and business people carry their tools of trade in an attache case. Physicians used to carry a medicine bag when making house calls. We used the tools that mechanics carry in an earlier example when discussing integrative teaching.

One of the authors encourages students in her "methods for learners with mild disabilities" course to construct an educational kit. Many special education teachers now go into the general education classroom to teach students with special learning needs. Others travel from school to school or from room to room in order to teach these students; still others remain in a resource or self-contained classroom of their own. The tools each teacher-in-training makes and places into this kit help that person to be ready with accessible "tools of the trade" to teach students with mild disabilities. The curriculum with which these tools will be used includes mathematics, reading, spelling, and social skills. With the tools assembled, teachers are equipped and prepared to provide meaningful learning experiences for their students.

Each educational kit contains:

Reading

1. A scope-and-sequence or skills hierarchy.
2. A set of basic sight words (e.g., Dolch Word List, survival words).

TABLE 8.6   Methods of Assessing Student Progress

Types of Modification	Procedures
Verbal Tests	Test administered verbally by the teacher, paraprofessional, peer, or another to permit student to complete similar requirements.
Shortened Test	Reduce the number of test items on a scale to permit additional time.
Level of Questions	Use different level of questions for different students—similar to shortened tests but the items are written at a more concrete level.
Length of Time for Completion	Increase the amount of time a student has to complete a test to allow for slower writing, reading, comprehension, or performance speed. This is important with many students.
Frequency of Tests	Utilize short written, verbal, or performance measures given on a frequent basis—daily or weekly—to assess student progress. This allows for more feedback on student progress.
Types of Responses	Provide for short answer or simple marking of correct response by the student. Measure should be matched to student's response strengths.
Verbal Review of Information	Use verbal review of information rather than testing. Have student review the course or unit content with teacher, paraprofessional, peer, or resource teacher. This permits the student to present what he or she has learned and does not require that the student be tested via traditional test items.
Peer Tutoring	Include peer tutoring for testing purposes. This permits the student to learn from peers. The peer tutor should receive some basic training.
Development of Instruction Packet	Have student develop a packet of materials to show knowledge and understanding of content of the unit. This shows what the student believes is important.
Checklists	Use developmental checklists to permit the observation of student learning in a sequential and organized way that shows student progress. Checklists are good in vocational courses. They permit the teacher to limit the number of formal tests.
Class Interaction	Assess student participation in discussion that indicates student mastery of content

Source: Robinson, G.A., Patton, J.R., Polloway, E.A., & Sargent, L.R., 1989, p. 387

3. A teacher-made gameboard that provides practice and reinforcement for many skills.

Mathematics

1. A scope-and-sequence or hierarchy of skills.
2. Teacher-made number lines, multiplication table charts (wall or student desk size), and an abacus.
3. A teacher-made gameboard that provides practice and reinforcement for many math skills.

Social Skills

1. A set of classroom rules, few in number and positively directed (wall or student desk size).
2. A teacher-made social skills activity that provides role play or simulation opportunities for practicing and reinforcing many social skills.

The construction of tools encourages teachers to accommodate students' learning needs. Commercial materials will not always provide the means for teaching a particular skill to a student; therefore, some teaching aids will need to be tailored and adapted to meet special learning or behavioral needs of many students. This activity not only prepares teachers by having educational tools ready for use with students, but it requires them to give thought beforehand about what they perceive they will be doing in the way of instruction with their students.

Summary

Effective teachers are able to use a variety of instructional models. In recent years, special educators have found that students with mild disabilities share many of the same learning problems. There is a growing sentiment that matching specific instructional approaches to student learning characteristics is the best course to take.

Research has addressed students who have low self-esteem, poor study skills, and weak organizational skills perhaps more than other learning problems. These difficulties can be found on a day-to-day basis within most classrooms with students who have learning disabilities, mild mental retardation, and behavior disorders. These particular problems are also identifiable with low achieving and at-risk learners, as well as other nondisabled youngsters. Practical strategies for dealing with these difficulties include affirmation, successful experiences, and direct teaching of organizational skills.

Numerous studies have also noted the importance of time management, allocated time, engaged time, and academic learning time. Teachers are effective when they make appropriate modifications in testing and grading practices. Modified tests more accurately assess the achievement of learners with mild disabilities. Student grades should accurately reflect individual progress, even if in small increments.

Effective teaching also depends upon good communication between teacher and students. It is important that student attention be directed toward the instruction being given, that teachers be clear in their instructions and explanations, that teacher feedback be appropriate to the purpose, and that questioning skills reflect good instructional techniques.

Activities

1. Discuss a curriculum-based assessment procedure for this course. See how many variations you can develop. Compare curriculum-based assessment for a college course, with curriculum-based assessment in public school.
2. Visit a public school classroom. Observe for an hour and chart how much time is allocated, engaged, and academic learning time.
3. Survey public school students regarding their views on homework. Do they think homework serves a useful purpose? Where do they do their homework? Who helps them? Research the attitude toward homework in Asian countries. Are there similarities? Are there differences?
4. Write a mock IEP on yourself. Discuss the difficulties. Do a survey of special educators. Ask them what they think of IEPs. What are the advantages; what are the drawbacks?

9 Classroom Management

Advance Questions

Answer the following questions as you read this chapter:

1. What effects do teacher attitudes have on classroom management?
2. What is preventive discipline?
3. What are some commonly used classroom discipline methods?
4. What are some key features of life space interviews?

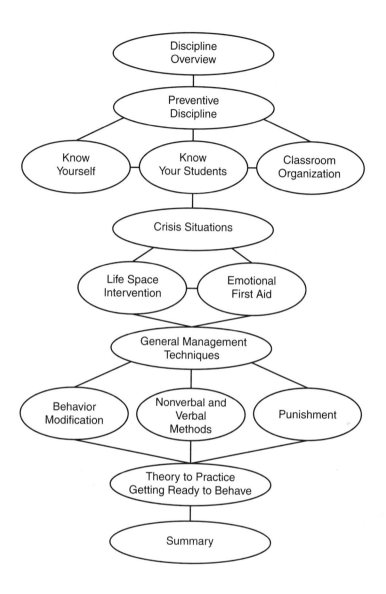

5. What are some common behavior modification strategies?
6. What is the difference between verbal and nonverbal classroom interventions?
7. How does classroom organization influence classroom management?
8. What are some advantages and disadvantages of using punishment to control behavior?

Vignette: Mr. Mellon

Mr. Mellon has been a principal for 15 years. Each year his teachers have requested "inservice" on classroom management. Over the years, he has provided workshops on discipline, behavior modification, assertive discipline, discipline with dignity, positive classroom discipline, unified discipline, and a mix of other classroom management methods. If you walked into his school on any day in any year, you would observe teachers using a mixture of these methods to manage the complex range of behaviors presented by students with mild disabilities and their classroom peers. You might also observe two teachers implementing the same model, but doing it very differently. If you looked at office referrals for Mr. Mellon's school, you would notice that students in some teachers' rooms are referred more often than students in other teachers' rooms. If you questioned the teachers about these differences, some would argue that some students are more difficult to teach than others. The characteristics of classroom management that are prevalent in Mr. Mellon's school are common in many elementary, middle, and high schools across the country.

Now that you have read the vignette about classroom management systems and discipline, see how many problem-solving questions you can answer. For those you cannot readily answer, try to find some additional information to use in answering them as you read the chapter. The experiences at Mr. Mellon's school are typical of those of many teachers working with students with mild disabilities.

1. Why should teachers be concerned about classroom management?
2. Should teachers teach students how to behave or just teach them academics?
3. Are all models of classroom management equally suited for all teachers?
4. How should a principal or teacher select classroom management strategies to use in a school or an individual classroom within it?
5. Should different methods of classroom management be used with students with different types of mild disabilities?

Classroom management is the essential teaching skill. The most elegant lesson will fall apart if the teacher is unable to maintain a sense of order and purpose in the classroom. The first signal that a new teacher is experiencing difficulty is usually problems with discipline. Przychodin (1981) notes, "No teacher can teach a class that is out of control, and once it is reported that the teacher cannot control the classroom his reputation in the public eye begins to decline."

Many special needs programs are populated with youngsters who were referred for discipline problems. Disruptive behavior in the regular classroom is the fast track to special education services. Although classroom teachers may have tolerance for weak academic skills, deficiencies in self-control quickly strain teacher patience. Since 1977 there has been a steady increase in students identified as having some type of behavior or emotional disorder. These students constitute the highest proportion of special needs students in the 12–21 age bracket.

Educators have a penchant for labeling behavior problems, and those labels have a way of intimidating even the most sanguine teacher. Such terms as emotionally disturbed, attention deficit disorder, hyperactive, and conduct disordered have a common theme—the youngster needs help with discipline. How is a teacher to manage a classroom with youngsters such as these? The answer actually is quite simple—look behind the label for the child. Labels are deceptive. They obscure the truth by implying that a student is qualitatively different from others. All students, with and without educational labels, have similar needs. Every student needs attention; every student needs success; every student needs recognition.

This chapter will describe behavior management practices that have proved useful with all students. Many of the strategies were designed specifically for youngsters with behavior and emotional disorders. Other strategies were developed within general education. This blend of general and special education discipline practices will provide you with a functional guide for teaching students with mild disabilities.

It takes more than one tool to tune a car, and it takes more than one approach to effectively manage a classroom. Our design is eclectic and practical. Theory is embedded in practice. Our goal is to help you, the classroom teacher, create an environment that is supportive of pluralism. Our schools are populated by many different students—different cultures, different languages, and different motivation to learn. The teacher who says, "I treat all students the same," and then proceeds to try to get them to conform to a rigid set of behavioral expectations will be continually frustrated. Like Sisyphus, the mythical king whose eternal punishment was to roll a rock to the top of the hill only to have it roll back down again, the educator who presses for obedience will put much effort into a futile task. Young people are resilient and resourceful. They may bend to a heavy hand, but they will end up resenting any system of discipline that overlooks their culture, their personal needs, or their integrity.

Discipline—An Overview

All students, at some time, present behavioral challenges to teachers. Incidents can range from a few cases of noncompliance to serious emotional problems. All teachers, whether general or special education, need a diverse array of classroom management skills to facilitate learning. Baker (1985) reported a strong relationship between good grades and acceptable school behavior. He found that "a student whose grades were mostly Ds was nine times as likely as a student whose grades were As to have had trouble with the law, twenty four times less likely to have done homework assignments, and about three times more likely to have cut classes" (483).

Students are not the only casualties of classroom discipline problems. In their survey of teacher burnout, Feiter and Tokar (1982) reported 58 percent of teachers polled said that student misbehavior was the primary cause of their job-related stress (Baker, 1985, 484). The following remarks by Amanda, a graduate student working toward her M.Ed. in education, illustrate the psychological impact of discipline problems on a beginning teacher.

> At the breakfast table last week, I was talking incessantly about how well I was doing in my courses at the college and about how all of the information I was getting about teaching was finally coming together. I was sure that I was soon going to be an English teacher extraordinaire, just like Robin Williams' character in the film *Dead Poet's Society*. My husband was staring at me with his cold, calculating eyes and I knew what was coming; we had this conversation before. "What will you do when some kid acts up in your first class?" he asked, a knowing smile on his lips. "Well that's easy," I said, "I will handle it in as mature and responsible a way as you would expect from someone of my obvious mental stature." And I smiled, but my husband did not. "You'll cry," he said, and then he smiled. (Leverault, 1990)

Every teacher would like a class full of motivated, well-adjusted young scholars. But as Amanda's breakfast conversation with her husband indicates, the more realistic expectation is that public school teaching requires intestinal fortitude as well as good teaching skills.

Students are impressionable human beings with complex life histories. Some inner-city schools have set up metal detectors to stop students from carrying weapons. But there is no method for screening such emotional baggage as hostility or despair. These burdens cannot be checked at the schoolhouse door. Poverty undermines hope. Drug abuse scorches intellectual ability. Dysfunctional families thwart personal development (Menacker, Weldon, & Hurwitz, 1989). Even students who are raised in the best conditions by loving parents experience emotional ups and downs.

There is no easy life. All young people must grapple with the distress that accompanies growth. The metaphor "growing pains" refers to more than pinched toes from tight fitting shoes. Personal growth requires persistence, mentoring, and opportunity. It is hard work for both student and teacher. Growth is first an emotional and second an intellectual experience. Before students can learn, they need an emotional base of security, trust, and self-confidence. It is the classroom teacher's responsibility to nurture these feelings in some students and teach them to others.

Preventive Discipline

Many discussions about school discipline begin with what the teacher should do after a student is disruptive. Preventive discipline focuses on teacher actions that will decrease classroom disruptions. Preventive discipline is defined as a classroom management system designed to promote student self-control by focusing teacher intervention at the cause of discipline problems and by teaching prosocial skills. Preventive discipline requires self-knowledge and knowledge of student strengths and weaknesses.

Know Yourself

Kohn (1991) points out that what a teacher believes about the nature of his or her students can have a profound effect on how classroom management is handled. The teacher who believes students need to be taught obedience will emphasize teacher control of student behavior. Many teachers use rewards and punishment as external motivators to encourage conformity. In such classrooms the teacher makes the rules, determines sanctions, and doles out justice. Student behavior is controlled by teacher power.

The authoritarian approach to discipline is commonplace in schools and widely accepted. Some parents select schools based on the premise that their children will get "old fashioned discipline." Although authoritarian tactics have admirers and detractors, the use of such teaching practices is rarely controversial. The case of Joe Clark is a notable exception.

Joe Clark was the principal of Eastside High School in Eastside, New Jersey. Each day he patrolled the halls of Eastside with a bullhorn. His motto, "There's only one way—my way," hung on his office door as a stern reminder that Joe Clark was a tough disciplinarian. Before Joe Clark came to Eastside, the school was in chaos. Fights and drug deals were routine in the halls of this inner-city school. Learning was almost nonexistent. Each year Eastside students tallied pathetically low on standardized tests of achievement.

After his arrival, Clark, a retired Army sergeant, quickly took charge. In one incident, he suspended sixty students without notifying the school board. He locked school doors—a fire code violation—to bar intruders. As a result of Clark's tough tactics, 1,900 students either dropped out or were expelled from Eastside. To some, including former Secretary of Education William Bennett, Joe Clark was a hero—an example of a no-nonsense disciplinarian in action. The remaining students at Eastside walked the school hallways without fear, and their standardized test scores improved. Other educators argued that Joe Clark did not solve problems; he merely transferred them from the halls of his school to the streets of his community. After a deluge of positive and negative media attention, Joe Clark resigned. He was commended by President Reagan and a movie was made of his exploits as principal of Eastside. Is Joe Clark a pedagogical hero or villain? He got results, but did the end justify his means?

Albert Shanker, past president of the American Federation of Teachers, believed Joe Clark created more problems than he solved. According to Shanker, punishments, suspensions, and expulsions become necessary when schoolwork ceases to be relevant for students. When students are made to sit still and listen quietly for four to six hours every day, when they are hopelessly behind the rest of the class with no chance to catch up, classroom disruptions are inevitable. Shanker believed many classroom disruptions can be traced to student apathy, student frustration, and lack of student control over daily events. Shanker's wry comment that teachers are the most powerful people in the world "because who else can tell 200 people exactly when they can go to the bathroom?" succinctly captures the essence of discipline codes in some classrooms.

Classroom management practices are saturated in values (Morse, 1987). Each time a teacher reacts to a classroom disruption, a hidden message is embedded in the teacher's action. Sometimes the message is autocratic, 'You need to behave because I say so.' With other teachers, the message is humanistic, 'I expect you to be responsible for your actions.' When teachers act in anger, the hidden message is, 'I can't control myself either.' This is the most unsettling message of all because students first and foremost need the security of knowing the teacher is in control. When teachers punish students, the embedded message is, "You can't control your behavior, so I must do it for you." Punishment accompanied with anger creates stress among students, and increases the likelihood of further discipline problems (Kohn, 1991; Kounin, 1977).

When adults feel secure, they are more capable of responding to the different developmental needs of youngsters. Conversely, insecure adults may feel threatened by disturbing student behavior that is developmentally normal. Rezmierski explains:

> . . . adults who are still struggling to develop a sense of power or autonomy are likely to have difficulty dealing with adolescent children for whom this is a natural developmental struggle as well. Such adults may even have difficulty dealing with their two-year-olds who display what some have called the first round of adolescence. . . . (Rezmierski, 1987, 6)

Discipline practices that take developmental phases of youngsters into account emphasize the needs of the students. Some teachers are predisposed toward authority (i.e., power) practices; others are predisposed toward democratic (i.e., cooperation) practices (Lasley, 1989). Before establishing a classroom management system, teachers should understand their own psychological needs. This requires reflection and honesty. Effective discipline is emotionally disengaged from student behavior. Teachers who respond to individual discipline problems with anger, defensiveness, or hostility create stress among all the students in the classroom. This "ripple effect" will either lead to more discipline problems (Kounin, 1977) or produce a group of obedient but frightened learners.

All teachers have pet peeves. Some dislike tattling; others can't tolerate name calling. Fighting is the worst offense in many teachers' minds. *The key action is not the student transgression, but the teacher intervention.* Teachers who know themselves are more effective disciplinarians because they don't take misbehavior personally. Such teachers realize that students need to be taught what is expected of them. Canter (1989) says:

> Teachers too often assume that students know how they are expected to behave. Teachers first need to establish specific directions for each activity during the day—lectures, small group work, transitions between activities, and so forth. For each situation, teachers must determine the exact behaviors they expect from them. . . . [Teachers] must teach the students how to follow directions. . . . They must model the behaviors, ask the students to restate the directions, question the students to make sure they understand the directions, and immediately engage the students in the activity to make sure that they understand the directions. (p. 59)

The aim of discipline is to teach students how to behave in a socially responsible manner. Sometimes compliance or noncompliance to classroom routines obscures the real issue. When ten-year-old Jorge consistently argues with his classmates, he is disturbing the classroom, but there is a deeper, more fundamental concern—Jorge lacks the ability to maintain relationships with his peers. Classroom discipline procedures aimed solely at stopping him from arguing in school miss the point. Jorge needs to learn how to socialize with others both in and out of school. In the later sections, we will describe strategies that help teachers manage behavior problems while promoting the development of prosocial skills.

Know Your Students

The Phi Delta Kappa Commission on Discipline (1982) had this to say about good discipline practices:

> Educators in well-disciplined schools know that behavior is caused. When misbehavior occurred, the principal and faculty tended to go beyond merely punishing students for the misbehavior. They searched for probable causes and they addressed them. They improved discipline in their schools by taking steps to remove those causes and by establishing activities within their school and community that would result in good behavior. (p. 12)

Discipline is a double-edged sword, and it cuts both ways. Students have an obligation to cooperate and to allow others to learn. Teachers and administrators have a duty to understand their students and to deal with disruptions in a fair and equitable manner. Teachers who believe students need to learn to be responsible for their own behavior work to help students to develop inner controls. These classrooms are characterized by a respect for student differences. Discipline is approached as a process rather than an end in itself (Henley, 1987). In this context, students are encouraged to develop social skills that will help them to adapt not only to the classroom, but also to the world at large. Cooperation, decision making, and accountability for behavior are skills emphasized by teachers who believe discipline should be a learning experience.

Developmental Differences.   Knowledge of child and adolescent development enhance understanding about why students behave as they do. Such giants in the field of psychology as Jean Piaget (1950), Erik Erikson (1963), and Lawrence Kohlberg (1973) have described significant differences in how children think and feel.

These researchers have described stages of cognitive, social–emotional, and moral development. As a youngster grows and matures, each stage is characteristically different from preceding stages. The domains of development are interactive. Progress in cognitive development affects moral reasoning. Social–emotional development influences and in turn is influenced by cognitive and moral acquisitions. The construction of "models" of development within specific developmental domains tends to obscure the synergistic power of human growth.

"Experts" in one area of development can be woefully naive about other areas. Consider a school psychologist who recommends placing a seven-year-old student in a special class for students with mild retardation based on a finding of "delayed cognitive" development. Cognitive development is not the only issue in this youngster's life. At the age of seven, the student is at the stage that Erik Erikson characterizes as industry versus inferiority. The child's ability to master the world outside of home is a central challenge during this period, and relationships with peers provide the impetus for meeting this challenge. From a developmental perspective, the psychologist's recommendation has created a dilemma for the student. A self-contained special class placement is stigmatizing. At the precise time in the youngster's social–emotional development when success with peers is central to further growth, the student is relegated to a special classroom for students with mental retardation.

One Teacher's Experience.   Herbert Kohl took his first public school teaching assignment in an inner-city sixth grade. His thirty-six students were academic failures who saw no connection between their lives on the streets of Harlem and the pristine view of America depicted in their textbooks. Over time, Kohl came to recognize that effective discipline began with understanding how his students felt about school and life.

> Each day there were incidents, and ultimately I accepted them as inevitable and impersonal. Alvin's malaise or John's refusal to work were natural responses to an unpleasant environment; not merely my class but a cumulative school environment which meant nothing more to most of the children than white-adult ignorance and authority. There was no simple solution to such discipline problems, and sometimes it seemed necessary to learn to be patient and indulgent with a child who won't behave or refuses to work. A teacher must believe that such problems exist in his classroom because he hasn't found the right words or the right thing, and not that they lie in the heart of the child. (Kohl, 1967, 29)

In Kohl's view, discipline begins with understanding and respect. There is always a reason for misbehavior. Boredom leads to distractibility and inattentiveness. Vandalism is anger erupting in mindless destruction. Impulsivity can signal a learning disability. Teachers who try to understand their students look for the causes of classroom disruptions. They recognize that students are complex human beings with developmental needs that can overshadow reading, writing, and calculating. By looking beyond misbehavior and trying to understand why a student is a discipline problem, a teacher can gain insight into the causes of disruptive behavior (Phi Delta Kappa Commission on Discipline, 1982).

Classroom Organization

A well-organized classroom deters discipline problems. Organization includes the total school attitude toward discipline. The principal takes the lead in establishing an atmosphere of trust and respect. Within the classroom, teachers need to manage individual student behavior in group situations. Groups influence individual behavior, and individual behavior shapes group actions. The manner in which a teacher responds to the group dynamics of a classroom can contribute to or prevent discipline problems.

Effective classroom management requires attention to teacher behaviors that minimize behavior problems. Jacob Kounin (1977) and other researchers have found that teachers prevent discipline problems through their ability to monitor the entire group without becoming distracted by minor incidents that cause the entire class to become diverted. Such teachers demonstrate "withitness" and "overlapping."

"Withitness." "Withitness" is a keen sense of what is happening throughout the classroom (DeLuke & Knoblock, 1987). Two features of "withitness" reduce misbehavior:

1. Select the right student for a desist. When a teacher reprimands the wrong student, the rest of the class assumes she does not know what is going on. Kounin found this "ripple effect" can work to the teacher's disadvantage, as in the above example. Clarity in identifying the correct student and clearly explaining the preferred behavior increases conformity among the rest of the class. Kounin also found that anger, sarcasm, or other roughness in the teacher's reproach upset younger children. The "ripple" effect is most pronounced at the beginning of the school year, and it loses its impact as the year goes on.

2. Attend to the more serious infraction when two problems develop at the same time (Charles, 1989). Taking steps to stop a misbehavior before it "sets off" other students is characteristic of "withit" teachers. These teachers have the ability to judge the "contagibility" of student behavior, and they respond accordingly. For example, Eileen is gazing off into space. The "withit" teacher takes note of her inattention but does not disrupt the smooth work flow of the rest of the class. Planned ignoring or proximity control work best. However, when a serious disruption occurs, verbal desist is warranted.

"Overlapping."   "Overlapping" is closely aligned to "withitness." It refers to the ability to monitor two situations simultaneously. Suppose the teacher is working with a small reading group of seven students, and she lost track of events around the rest of the classroom. This absence of "overlapping" would almost assuredly result in misbehavior. Students with their hands up would be ignored; students who are done with their work would start looking for something else to do; and a mischievous student would have an opportunity to cause a disturbance. The "overlapping" teacher keeps the small group on task while at the same time managing the flow of activity throughout the rest of the classroom.

Maintain a Group Focus.   Virtually all of a teacher's day is spent managing students in groups. Kounin reported that the manner in which teachers conduct their group lessons had a significant impact on discipline problems. Teachers maintain a group focus by encouraging cooperation. For example, during a presentation one student demonstrates at the blackboard, and students in their seats offer suggestions and comments. Students are encouraged to listen, help others, share ideas, and work toward group goals. Well-managed groups have a high rate of student work involvement. Student boredom and indifference to work assignments is a main cause of discipline problems. Tasks that are repetitious and require minimal thought invite discipline problems. As Morse observes:

> If school is not inviting, if the tasks are not clear, interesting, and at an appropriate level, how can we expect students to be on task? Adverse student reactions should be expected when classes are dull, teaching is uninspired, and failure is built in. Their oppositional behavior is a sign of personal growth and integrity. (Morse, 1987, 6)

Teachers who find ways to relate learning to student interests and lives outside of school help students to see value in their lessons. When students understand the purpose of tasks, they can make a connection between teacher expectations and their personal needs; this increases group harmony and minimizes classroom disruptions.

Crisis Situations

While all students have "good" and "bad" days, some students have persistent problems in adapting to school expectations and routines. The intensity and duration of student disruptions will determine the severity of the problem. An emotional disturbance can cause a student to act out feelings of anger, hostiligy, or isolation. For instance, students who engage in attention-getting behaviors don't know how to relate in socially acceptable ways. Many students who receive special education services for behavior problems are identified as emotionally disturbed.

Most of the causes for emotional problems are outside the classroom teacher's reach. Time is a factor no one can overcome. A student's aggressive behavior may be caused by sexual abuse that happened several years earlier. Childhood difficulties, such as separation of parents or death of a loved one, may be overcome in a positive manner by one student or thrust another student into the depths of depression. What then is a teacher to do when confronted with the awesome obstacles presented by a student's troubled life history?

Although a teacher cannot (and should not) pretend to be a therapist, the teacher can utilize therapeutic strategies that have proved useful with students who have an emotional disturbance. One such strategy is the life space intervention (Redl, 1971; Wood & Long, 1991).

Life Space Intervention

The life space intervention (LSI) is a technique for turning listening into a plan for student behavior change. If a teacher wants to understand why a student behaves a certain way, the best source of information is the student. The LSI uses crisis situations to move a youngster toward more constructive behavior. The following five-step procedure summarizes key points of the life space intervention. For a more thorough analysis see *Life Space Intervention* by Mary Wood and Nicholas Long (1991).

Step 1. Ventilate Feelings.   The LSI is a conversation between student and teacher. Unlike most such conversations, in the first phase the student does most of the talking and the teacher listens. The LSI is initiated by the teacher after a specific incident. It requires some privacy. A quiet corner of a classroom might work or if the student is out of control, he or she should be removed from the classroom for the interview.

The teacher begins by allowing the student to ventilate feelings. No moral implications are attached to what is said. The teacher is nonjudgmental and supportive of the student's feelings. Such statements as, "I can see you are angry," or "When Alex said that you must have felt hurt," emphasize empathy and communicate that feelings, even negative ones, are important. During Step 1 of the LSI, the teacher is accepting. This builds trust and helps the teacher to understand the student perspective.

The student may swear, whine, or blame others. It may seem strange not to correct these "inappropriate" comments. Some youngsters lack the verbal skills to express strong feelings in a socially acceptable manner. Strong language is a symptom of frustration. The intention at this stage is to build trust. The subsequent steps aim at behavior change.

Step 2. Clarify the Incident.   Physical signs that the student is beginning to unwind (e.g., relaxed muscle tone; steady, calm breath) will become evident. At this point, the incident that prompted the LSI is ready to be clarified in two stages.

First, ask the student to explain what happened. The student is likely to place blame on you, other students, other adults, anyone but himself or herself. This is to be expected. The purpose of the LSI is to help a student learn to accept responsibility for individual behavior. If the student was in the habit of "owning up" to disturbing action, you wouldn't need the life space intervention.

The student's view is significant data. Action is guided by perception. Attempting to correct the student version would eliminate an important source of information. Right or wrong, distorted or clear, the student perspective is a crucial clue in understanding behavior.

Next, the incident is reviewed again, except this time the teacher assists the student to paint a reality-based picture of the crisis situation. The student is prompted to describe the physical scene and chronological time frame. Comments such as, "Where were you standing when Cole threw the eraser?" or, "What happened next?" help the student to recall events. You want to find the central issue. A gentle reminder interjected at this point about how the adult saw events unfold can be helpful, but caution is advised because too much "reality rub" will place teacher and student at odds. The student is reflecting, an unaccustomed practice, and he or she will jump at an opportunity to argue over details, and thus derail the LSI.

Step 3. Look for Patterns. Once the central issue is identified, use questions such as, "Has this happened before?" or gentle reminders such as, "Last week it seemed you had the same problem with Sally," to help students gain insight into their own behavior. Many times students with emotional problems will deny their experience. They literally forget past episodes, or they may be unable to learn from experience. The student may be "stuck" in behavior patterns, continually repeating the mistakes of the past.

Up to this point, the LSI has focused on affective fallout from the incident. Looking for patterns switches emphasis to the cognitive domain. The student may be well-equipped to deny a history of problems related to the incident. Projection (i.e., finding one's own faults in someone else) and rationalization (i.e., explaining away behavior) are well entrenched defenses against change. Initially it is enough at this stage to get agreement that there does seem to be a problem. Future interviews can continue to explore disturbed behavior patterns.

Step 4. Implement a Plan. The purpose of the life space intervention is to help a student assume personal responsibility. When a persistent pattern is identified by both teacher and student, the next logical step is to consider alternative ways to deal with the problem. Questions such as "What could you have done rather than knock all of your books off the desk?" or, "Are there any signals we could arrange for the next time you are feeling frustrated?" move the discussion into the problem-solving stage. While the teacher provides supportive or clarifying questions, it is up to the student to do the problem solving. The student needs to "own" the behavior and the solution.

Of course, reality rules of the school and common sense also come into play. A student may be overly zealous in terms of self-imposed consequence. Neither punishment or 'consequences' are part of the solution. The plan is preventive. 'Each time I feel frustrated with my work, I'll close my book and count to ten slowly.' 'Every time I lose my temper I'll put a check in my self-monitoring log.' 'If I get angry I'll blow off steam by walking around the room.'

The intent of the planning stage is to get students thinking and working on their emotional or behavior problems. Student plans are not usually characterized by their elegance. It may be tempting to step in and offer a more reasonable alternative. The student may need to be reminded about such reality concerns as the implausibility of leaving the room when upset. The initial plan might require multiple adjustments, but that is the nature of personal growth. Changing habitual behavior patterns is a difficult endeavor. Whether or not the mechanics of the plan achieves the objective is secondary. The student is learning to take responsibility for behavior. In the long run, there is no more important goal. The final act of the LSI is for the teacher and student to write the plan and sign it. The "contract" increases commitment and provides a basis for future life space interventions (Fagen, 1986).

Step 5. Transition Back to Classroom Activity. A smooth transition back to classroom activities helps the student save face and establishes a routine for further life space interventions. Wood and Long (1991) suggest preparing the student with the following questions:

> "What is your group doing now?"
> "When you left the group they were writing news reports. Do you think they are still at it?"
> "When you go back to your room, what will they be doing?" (p. 148)

Keep in mind that being removed from the classroom during a crisis situation can be embarrassing. Hard-won gains made during the life space intervention can dissipate if the student or classmates are unable to return to a normal routine. Getting a student returned to work gives the life space intervention a successful closure. Table 9.1 summarizes the key points of the life space intervention.

Emotional First Aid

Sometimes the situation calls for a less intensive investigation into the student's behavior and reasoning. An abbreviated version of the LSI can be used to provide emotional first aid. Just as a doctor tends to temporary physical bumps, bruises, and fractures, the teacher who uses emotional first aid tends to such temporary feelings as anger, rejection, or hostility. According to Long, emotional first aid provides support for students "when their defenses become ineffective and they

TABLE 9.1   Life-Space Intervention

Purpose: To Defuse Crisis Situation and Seek Solutions

Step 1. Ventilation of Feelings

Teacher behavior: Listens.
Teacher attitude: Accepting, nonjudgmental; allows for ventilation of feelings.
Student behavior: Talks, expresses strong feelings such as anger, hostility, or frustration.

Step 2. Clarify the Incident

Teacher behavior: Asks questions, probes for details of incident.
Teacher attitude: Tries to help student see his or her contribution to the crisis incident.
Student behavior: Attempts to reconstruct a time-line of events that culminated in crisis incident.

Step 3. Look for Patterns

Teacher behavior: Within dialogue helps student to remember similar situations.
Teacher attitude: Problem solving.
Student behavior: Attempts to relate present crisis incident to past problems with adults or peers.

Step 4. Implement a Plan

Teacher behavior: Supports student in searching for alternative ways of handling crisis situations.
Teacher attitude: Helps student take responsibility for actions.
Student behavior: Develops a written contract that describes student solutions.

Step 5. Transition Back to Classroom Activity

Teacher behavior: Discusses what student needs to do in order to rejoin group.
Teacher attitude: Student may need face-saving options or reminder of consequences.
Student behavior: Calmed down and, with support, ready to resume activities.

find themselves overwhelmed by reality demands and/or internal conflicts" (Long, 1990, 11). The following illustration describes the use of emotional first aid.

Andy has just stalked out of Ms. Halpin's special class. She catches up with him in the hall. He is leaning against the wall ten feet from the classroom door. As she walks nearer it is clear he is near tears. When she tries to speak to him he covers his ears and says, "Leave me alone." Ms. Halpin knows that Andy's characteristic defense from stress is flight. Andy is eight years old. He is overweight and more immature than the other preadolescents in her special class for students with behavior disorders. Andy is often scapegoated by the other students, and he plays right into their manipulations each time he cries and runs away.

"I know it hurts when the others tease you," Ms. Halpin says. "I hate them," is his immediate retort. "I will give you the stopwatch," Ms. Halpin tells him. "After five minutes come back into class, and you can clean the gerbil cage." She hands Andy her stopwatch and goes back into the classroom. After four minutes he returns and walks over to the gerbil cage to begin one of his favorite activities.

Long (1990) describes five uses of emotional first aid: to drain off frustration, to support the management of strong feelings, to maintain communication during stress, to regulate social and behavioral traffic, and to provide umpire service. In this brief episode, Ms. Halpin managed all five. She allowed Andy time and space to ventilate his anger. She helped him deal with his anger by her supportive comments. Instead of punishing him for leaving the room, she maintained communication by remaining nonjudgmental and concerned about his feelings. She emphasized social regulations by giving him five minutes to return to the classroom, and she emphasized his accountability by handing him the stopwatch. Finally, she recognized that she could not solve Andy's problem for him. Like a good umpire, she remained neutral while requiring Andy to return to the classroom.

Both the life space intervention and emotional first aid are directed at helping students make good choices. Each technique takes into account the student's point of view and feelings. Each provides support and ultimately points the student in the direction of personal accountability. Each also adheres to the principle that behavior management should be nonjudgmental and nonpunitive. They emphasize therapeutic approaches to the management of discipline problems by helping students to manage their feelings while working toward solutions to behavior problems. The life space crisis interview is a long-range technique for helping students learn new behaviors. Emotional aid provides "hurdle help" for students who are distressed.

Students need leeway to learn how to behave and work with each other. Minor arguments, testiness, and bad moods are all part and parcel of the human experience. In a well-managed classroom, the teacher respects each student's right to have a "bad day." A student's momentary loss of temper or stubbornness will soon pass if tolerated, but can be blown out of proportion if a teacher overreacts.

Much of the behavior encountered by teachers reflects the social–emotional development of students. There are developmental differences between students which need to be accounted for when managing behavior. Young students are naturally egocentric. Arguing is one of the ways they learn to take on the perspective of others. Adolescents are searching for their identity. Their burgeoning sense of independence may run counter to an adult need for obedience. As youngsters seesaw their way through emotional growth, conflicts with authority figures are inevitable. Students need some latitude as they grope their way along the difficult passage to adulthood. Appreciating developmental struggles of students helps to depersonalize the inevitable conflicts that occur when children and adults occupy the same space for five hours a day, 180 days a year.

Managing Student Behavior

Once there was a school administrator who believed he had hit on the perfect plan for classroom discipline. With the assistance of his daughter, who was a graduate student in special education, he embarked on a systematic collection of interventions matched to problem behaviors. His goal was to develop an index card system, compact enough to fit into the top drawer of a teacher's desk. The cards would alphabetically list student discipline problems and briefly explain the correct intervention; for instance, if a student refused to obey, the teacher would flip through the cards, pull out the 3" X 5" labeled "disobedience" and read what to do. His approach was well-meaning, but hopelessly naive. Student behavior cannot be matched to interventions like dominoes. Every student is different, and every situation unique. Therefore, teachers need an array of interventions to meet the changing needs of the classroom. Each of the following strategies is research-based (Cooper, Heron, & Heward, 1987; Dreikurs, Grunwald, & Pepper, 1982; Ginott, 1971; Jones, 1987; Redl & Wineman, 1957). Each is useful for eliminating problem behaviors, but none is teacher-proof. Professional judgment determines the best intervention to use at any given time. Classroom interventions anticipate student disruptions and nullify potential discipline problems. Each category of interventions—behavior modification, nonverbal interventions, and verbal interventions—prevents disruptive behavior while maintaining a sense of mutual respect between teacher and student. None will work all the time. Good classroom management requires the ability to select an appropriate strategy from an array of alternatives.

Behavior Modification

Behavior modification is regularly used to teach prosocial behavior to students with mild disabilities (Ager & Cole, 1991). Behavior modification programs are data-based. Target behaviors (i.e., behaviors to be eliminated or shaped) are observed and measured. Prior to initiating a program, the target behavior is described in precise, behaviorally concrete terms. Vague behavior descriptors such as "immature," "aggressive," or "cooperative" are replaced with such target behaviors as "whines," "hits other students," and "shares toys." Baseline data on the frequency of the target behavior are collected for at least a week prior to beginning the program. These data serve as a comparison for determining progress at a later date. Once a target behavior has been selected and counted, the most appropriate consequence is determined (e.g., reinforcement, token economy, extinction, etc.). Next, a schedule to administer consequences is developed (e.g., reinforcement in the form of verbal praise will follow each time a student raises her hand).

The following systems: token economies, contingency contracts, timeout, and cognitive-behavior intervention are well-established in the behavior modification literature and in special education programs.

Token Economies. A token is a general conditioned reinforcer. Tokens are paired with backup reinforcers such as special privileges or toys from a "class store." A token is given to a student to reinforce a target behavior. At a later time in the day or week, the student can exchange accumulated tokens for the backup reinforcer. The value of tokens is derived from the student desirability for backup reinforcers. For example, without goods to purchase (backup reinforcers), money (tokens) would be useless. Cooper, Heron, and Heward (1987) provide the following guidelines for implementing a token economy:

1. Select a token that is durable and cheap (e.g., rubber stamp, chips, pennies, Pogs).
2. Be clear about rules and behavior(s) for earning tokens.
3. Whenever possible, use regularly occurring events or privileges for backup reinforcers.
4. Guard against bootlegging of tokens. Hoarding of tokens is often a signal that students don't understand the token's value.
5. Establish a rate of exchange; begin with a low ratio of token to backup reinforcer and increase the ratio as the program becomes successful.
6. Decide in advance how to remove the system.

The efficiency and immediacy of token economies make them an attractive motivation.

Contingency Contracts. A contingency contract is a written agreement between a teacher and student. The contract serves as a positive reinforcer to shape a target behavior. A contingency contract specifies the responsibilities (i.e., the behaviors) of each party and the consequences associated with compliance. Schroeder and Riddle (1991) list five key elements of a contingency contract: detailed privileges and obligations, observable behaviors, sanctions for failure, bonus clauses for consistent compliance, and clear description of methods for administering reinforcers. Contingency contracts are a way of concretely emphasizing student responsibility for behavior. Salend (1987) suggests that responsible behavior can be increased by involving students in making such contractual decisions as determining the target behavior, selecting reinforcers, and evaluating systems.

Timeout. Cooper, Heron, and Heward (1987) describe two types of timeout: nonexclusionary and exclusionary timeout. Nonexclusionary timeout consists of planned ignoring, withdrawal of a specific reinforcer, contingent observation, and the timeout ribbon. Planned ignoring is the removal of such social reinforcers as attention, praise, or verbal comments. Withdrawal of specific reinforcer means that an identified positive stimulus is removed when an undesirable behavior occurs. In one study, researchers turned off classroom music each time students left their seats, thus significantly reducing out-of-seat behavior (Ritschl, Mongrella, & Presbie, 1972). Contingent observation is the change of seating of a student for a specified period of time following a classroom infraction. During the contingent observation time period, the student is able to observe the activity of the rest of the group, but may not participate. The timeout ribbon is a paired reinforcer. When a youngster wears the ribbon, it is a signal that there are opportunities to receive positive reinforcers. When the ribbon is removed, no reinforcers can be gained.

Exclusionary timeout is the removal of a student to a room outside the classroom for a specified period of time. Release from timeout is contingent on cessation of disturbing behavior. While an effective intervention if used sparingly, exclusionary timeout can be misused and even abused. Procedures for using exclusionary timeout must be spelled out clearly to both students and parents. Exclusionary timeouts are documented with a timeout log. Such data collection protects against abuse and provides information to determine the effectiveness of exclusionary timeout as a means of extinguishing disruptive behavior.

The aim of timeout is to institute a brief, 5–10 minute isolation of a student from classroom activities because of disruptive behavior. Longer periods of timeout are not recommended for several reasons. Instructional time is lost. The student may prefer the timeout, thus it becomes a positive reinforcer. Removing a student from the classroom may be more disturbing than the behavior that prompted the timeout. Finally, timeout can be unnecessarily punitive (Cuenin & Harris, 1986).

Cognitive-Behavior Intervention.   The purpose of cognitive-behavior intervention is to teach youngsters social skills. According to Ager and Cole (1991), cognitive-behavioral interventions influence the cognitive processes of participants in order to bring about behavior change.

Deluke and Knoblock (1987) point out that thinking is a buffer between feelings and behavior. Strategies such as coaching, modeling, self-instruction, self-talk, and social problem-solving activities teach youngers to think before they act. Despite the widespread acceptance of cognitive-behavior interventions, Gresham (1989) reported scant evidence that cognitive-behavior techniques fostered more significant changes in behavior than more traditional behavior modification procedures. In their meta-analysis of 22 studies of cognitive-behavior training, Ager and Cole (1991) found that a lack of description of treatment procedures by researchers made replication and verification of behavior change claims difficult to achieve. Despite the methodological shortcomings, cognitive-behavior treatment continues to have strong support among researchers and practitioners.

The goals of behavior modification are to increase appropriate or adaptive behavior and to decrease inappropriate or maladaptive behavior. As Casey, Skiba, and Algozzine (1988) indicated, three primary approaches have been used to manage classroom behavior: redirecting teachers toward positive rather than negative behaviors, providing tangible rewards for positive behaviors, and providing negative consequences for inappropriate behavior.

Behavior modification has a certain intuitive appeal. After all, it's common parenting and teaching practice to reward "good" behavior and punish the "bad." Schools are awash in everyday practices that reflect behavior modification. Students who learn their lessons get good grades. Teachers use stickers and progress charts to encourage students to work harder. Detentions, staying after school, and suspensions are everyday procedures for dealing with students who don't abide by school expectations for proper behavior.

When the normal corrective procedures don't seem to work for a student, it's common for a teacher to step up the reward and punishment cycle through the application of a homespun behavior modification program. Some teachers do this without training in specific techniques. Consequently, errors in treatment undercut the effectiveness of the program and add to the unfortunate judgment that it's the student who is at fault. When teachers begin a behavior modification program, they should keep the seven guidelines listed in Table 9.2 in mind.

Some illustrations of behavior modification methods for improving the behavior of students are presented in Table 9.3. Rewards and creating a positive atmosphere in the classroom are a big part of this approach. The following program, "One-Minute Behavior Management," is a quick and efficient approach for using behavior modification with an entire class, rather than with specific individual students.

One-Minute Behavior Management. Effective teachers recognize the importance of general classroom management methods to productive classroom in-

---

TABLE 9.2 Guidelines for Behavior Modification Programs

---

1. Describe and count the frequency of the disturbing behavior to be changed before beginning the program.
2. Identify the target behavior, if possible with student input.
3. Select a reinforcer that is meaningful to the student.
4. Avoid using sugar foods as reinforcers (e.g., cookies, candy, raisins).
5. Don't take away reinforcers for punishment.
6. Do a postfrequency count of the target behavior after a specified period of time to determine the program's effectiveness.
7. If the program isn't working, don't blame the student; change the plan.

TABLE 9.3 Illustrations of Behavior Modification

Tactic	Illustration
Reward students for reducing out-of-seat behavior	Gather data on the number of times the student is out of his or her seat for ten class periods. Provide a sticker, star, or other token for each class period that the student is out of seat less than average during the data collection phase. Keep track of improvements and discuss them with the student.
Reward appropriate classroom behavior	Provide your class with an opportunity to earn free time based on their behavior. Start a stopwatch at the beginning of a class period. Each time misbehavior occurs, stop the watch and announce to the class that it will start again when appropriate behavior resumes. At the end of the class period, determine the amount of free time that was earned and allow students to select activities for that time period.
Reward appropriate behavior in other students	Look for opportunities to reward other students for appropriate behavior. For example, if a student fails to comply with a request you have made, turn to another student and make a similar request. When the other student complies, provide a reward or special attention for the appropriate behavior.
Ignore inappropriate behavior	The process of withholding attention or reward from previously rewarded behavior is referred to as putting the behavior on extinction. As a general rule, extinction is used for behaviors that are minimally disruptive, attention-seeking types of problems. Often, simply ignoring these behaviors decreases them.
Use contracts to control behavior	Help students set goals for appropriate behavior and then design contracts that detail expectations and rewards for meeting the terms of the agreement

struction. The One Minute Behavior Management System for Teachers (Algozzine, 1997) was inspired by the bestselling book, *The One Minute Manager* by Kenneth Blanchard and Spencer Johnson. The philosophy guiding One Minute Behavior Management for teachers is simple:

Students who feel good about themselves produce good results.

Three processes lead to successful One Minute Behavior Management in the classroom. They are: **one minute goal setting, one minute praisings, and one minute reprimands.** One minute goal setting involves teachers making sure that students know what they're being held accountable for and what good performance looks like. Teachers then try to catch students doing something right so they can give students one minute praisings. One minute reprimands are given only when teachers are sure students understand how to behave correctly and make a mistake. Feedback in the one minute reprimand is immediate and never attacks a student's worth or value as a person.

One Minute Goal Setting. At the beginning of the year, or at the beginning of a new task, activity, or responsibility, the One Minute Behavior Management teacher takes time for one minute goal setting. The teacher makes it clear to students what their responsibilities are and what they will be held accountable for in the system (i.e., this is what we believe is important—these are our goals).

Goals formulated during one minute goal setting by the teacher, students, or a particular student should be written down (e.g., goals for the year should be posted in the classroom) and reviewed frequently. Goals for a field trip can be written on the chalkboard before leaving. Individual student goals can be written on a sheet of paper and kept in a notebook or classwork folder.). They should be stated in behavioral terms (e.g., We will walk in the hall at all times. At the end of our field trip, we will thank our guide for her time and effort.). One Minute Behavior Management teachers review goals frequently with students to ensure that they know what is expected and can actually do it.

One Minute Praising. The philosophy guiding one minute praisings is this:

Help students reach their full potential—catch them doing something right!

Teachers in classrooms practicing One Minute Behavior Management tell their students that they are going to monitor their behavior. They observe their students carefully and try to catch them doing something right relative to agreed upon classroom goals.

When a teacher catches a student doing something right, the teacher immediately gives the student a one minute praising. The teacher makes eye contact, or if the teacher thinks it appropriate, puts a hand on the student's shoulder or touches the student in a friendly way. The contact is brief but lets the student know that the teacher is on his or her side. After that, the teacher looks the student right in the eye and tells the student exactly what he or she did right. Then the teacher shares how good he or she feels about what the student did (Grumpy, you're doing a good job raising your hand during our group discussions. I care about you and seeing you be successful with this goal really makes me happy.) and pauses for "a minute" to let the praise "sink in."

One minute praisings are especially important at the beginning of the year, or at the beginning of a new task, activity, or responsibility. After consistent and frequent use of one minute praising, many students catch themselves doing something right and praise themselves. Also, students are always wondering when the teacher will praise them again and that keeps them going. You don't have to praise someone for very long for them to notice that you notice and you care.

One Minute Reprimands.   One minute reprimands are given only if students have been working with the same goals for some time and teachers are sure that students can meet the performance standards set to achieve these goals. If this is the case, and a student makes a mistake, the teacher is quick to respond. For example, at the end of September, Louis has received much praise because he has successfully refrained from laughing out loud during quiet work times for ten days in a row. He has received several rewards for successfully meeting his goal of remaining quiet during quiet work times. However, on the first Monday in October, Antonio makes a face at Louis while he is working on his math worksheet and Louis laughs so hard, he disturbs all the other students and falls out of his chair. Louis's teacher recognizes the occasion for a one minute reprimand.

As soon as a teacher observes a mistake, she meets with the student and confirms the facts. Then she may put a hand on the student's shoulder or come around to the student's side of the desk. She does not smile, but looks the student straight in the eye and tells him precisely what he did wrong ("Louis, laughing out loud like that is not one of your goals. I care about you and want you to be successful and learn in this class. I am disappointed because you were doing so well controlling this. Please don't do it again.").

One minute manager teachers let each student know what he or she is doing and why. They know that not doing this often leads to failing with students. Sometimes teachers have to care enough to be tough. Teachers remember to be tough on behavior, not the student. A saying that reminds teachers how the one minute goals and the consequences (the praisings and the reprimands) affect people's behavior is this: "Goals begin behaviors. Consequences maintain behaviors."

Nonverbal and Verbal Methods

An orderly classroom climate is widely acknowledged as a key component of effective instruction. Classroom disruptions are among the greatest obstacles to creating and maintaining a calm and productive classroom environment. A variety of general nonverbal and verbal intreventions are available for managing classroom disruptions.

Nonverbal interventions have several advantages over verbal interventions. Silence does not draw attention to the student or inadvertently reinforce the behavior. Classroom activities proceed without interruption when the teacher manages classroom behavior unobtrusively (McDaniel, 1986). Lastly, nonverbal interventions help teachers avoid "power struggles" with students.

Body Carriage. Frederic Jones (1987) observed teachers in hundreds of secondary and elementary classrooms. He found that teachers conveyed leadership through body language. Posture, eye contact, facial expressions, and gestures conveyed confidence or uncertainty. Students observe teacher body language and make judgments about what they see. Charles summarizes Jones's findings:

> Good posture and confident carriage suggest strong leadership; a drooping posture and lethargic movements suggest resignation or fearfulness. Effective teachers even when tired or troubled tend to hold themselves erect and move with a measure of vigor. (Charles, 1989, 92)

Teachers who convey authority naturally through body language encounter half the behavior problems of teachers in "loud, unruly" classrooms (Charles, 1989, 90).

Planned Ignoring. Sometimes disruptive student behaviors are intended to attract the attention of the teacher and other students. When teachers ignore attention-seeking behaviors, the audience is eliminated. Planned ignoring works best for minor classroom disturbances. The teacher who interrupts group lessons or activities with a continual stream of admonitions such as "sit still," or "pick up that piece of paper" disrupts learning while drawing attention to the misbehavior. Paradoxically, this "negative" attention can reinforce behavior problems.

Signal Interference. Every adult has memories of childhood teachers who could quell minor disturbances with a flick of a light switch or a finger raised to the lips. There are numerous nonverbal signals for quieting a class: eye contact, snapping fingers, a frown, shaking the head, or a quieting gesture with the hand. Visual signals do not disturb students and emphasize the teacher's awareness of all activity in the room.

Proximity Control. Teachers who stand or sit as if rooted to the front of the room are compelled to issue verbal directions in order to deal with disruptions. Teachers who move around the room merely need to stand near a student or gently place a hand on a student's shoulder to stop a disturbing behavior. Teaching while moving has several advantages: rather than being a separate, remote entity, the teacher becomes physically a part of the group; the teacher is able to monitor students more easily; the teacher projects more of a presence because students can't predict where the teacher will be standing at any given moment; finally, standing nearby also reassures students that the teacher is in control.

Removal of Seductive Objects. Manipulation is a strong channel for learning, and in most instances should be encouraged. However, some students become distracted by objects. Fritz Redl and David Wineman (1951) indicated that the ability to control the impulse to handle, grab, or steal seductive objects was a basic component in the development of self-control. When teachers leave valuables or students leave toys around, youngsters who are prone to "gadgetorial seduction," the objects might disappear. Removing seductive objects decreases the pressure on a youngster's burgeoning self-control system.

Verbal Interventions

Because nonverbal interventions are the least intrusive, they are preferred. Verbal interventions are useful after it is clear that nonverbal interventions have been unsuccessful in desisting a disruptive behavior.

Humor. It may sound strange to use humor to calm a disruptive student, but it is a very useful technique. Almost every school has a teacher who is capable of defusing discipline problems with a quip or easy comment. Humor is a basic human need. People watch T.V., go to the movies, and pay to watch live performances just to laugh. The teacher who smiles and jokes in the face of adversity sets a strong model for students. A word of caution, however: avoid sarcasm, cynicism, or teasing. Rather than lightening a moment, sarcasm increases tension and creates resentment. Cynicism and teasing breed resentment.

Sane Messages. When teachers respond to disruptive behavior with anger, they add to student anxiety, which increases the likelihood of further behavior problems (Kounin, 1977). "I" messages let students know how the teacher feels. Such statements as, "I am frustrated because you keep interrupting this lesson," or "I am disappointed because you didn't maintain control when I left the room," describe the situation rather than attacking a student's character (Charles, 1989, 59). Sane messages are descriptive and model appropriate behavior (Ginott, 1971). Sane messages help students understand how their behavior affects others. They are a direct appeal to change behavior. "Bev, when you talk during silent reading, it disturbs everyone in your group," is an example of a sane message. "Bev, keep quiet," is an example of what Ginott calls an insane message. In the first instance, the reason for a change in behavior is explained to the student. In the second instance, the "insane message," the student feels personally attacked. Such a directive as "keep quiet" or "shut up" may get the intended results, but if the model for expressing needs is abrupt and callous, students will take the same approach in their own conversations.

Restructuring. Restructuring means changing a lesson or activity that is floundering. When confronted with student disinterest, the best option may be to move onto another activity. Restructuring is part of the decision-making powers of a teacher. One inner-city sixth-grade teacher gave a spelling test every time the class seemed restless and difficult to manage. "It was amazing," he reported;

"one minute they are ready to climb the walls, and the next minute they were quietly and dutifully folding their papers and numbering lines from 1 to 20!"

Hypodermic Affection.   Each student from time to time needs a shot of caring. Hypodermic affection lets students know that they are valued human beings. Students get frustrated, discouraged, and anxious in school. Students with mild disabilities, in particular, need encouragement to persevere with tasks at which they have failed in the past. Sometimes a smile, a pat on the back, or a kind word can help a student over a psychological hurdle. Showing interest in a student's life outside of school, and plainly communicating concern are ways of building trust. A trusting relationship between student and teacher is the key to solving all discipline problems.

Praise.   Verbal praise is frequently used to reinforce positive classroom behavior. The aphorism "Catch them being good" describes the most useful approach to praise. For example, some students need attention. Praising their behavior when they are not seeking attention while ignoring disruptive behavior is a useful way to use praise in the classroom. Too much praise can undercut impact; too little praise communicates indifference. Effective praise is directed at student behavior rather than the student personally. "You really are trying hard" encourages student effort. It is a descriptive statement that gives the student guidance in terms of the type of behavior the teacher expects to see.

Ginott pointed out the "perils of praise" (Charles, 1989). Praise directed at a student personally is condescending and manipulative. A statement such as, "You are a good person to have in my class," implies the teacher is making such judgments about all the students. What about the students who don't get the same compliment? Remember there is always a "ripple effect" in the classroom. Everyone wants to be liked by the teacher. Judgmental praise may make one student feel good, while another may feel rejected. Praise works best when it evaluates behavior instead of the student.

Alerting.   Imagine a group of students during recess playing kickball. They are hot, sweaty, and thoroughly enjoying themselves. All the running around has them excited, and they are eager to continue the game. The teacher looks at her watch and realizes she should have had them back into the classroom five minutes ago. What does she do? One approach is to abruptly end the game and rush the entire group back to class. Abrupt changes will almost assuredly result in behavior problems.

In his extensive research on classroom discipline, Kounin (1977) found the manner in which teachers handled transitions to be a key element in effective discipline. Charles succinctly summarized Kounin's findings: "Teachers' ability to manage smooth transitions and maintain momentum was more important to work involvement and classroom control than any other behavior management technique" (Charles, 1981, 33).

Alerting helps students to make smooth transitions by giving them time to make emotional adjustments to change. This is particularly true for impulsive students or students who are easily frustrated. Alerting takes many forms. One method is to count down the number of minutes before a change will take place. Usually two warnings in five-minute increments is sufficient. Alerting is useful when moving from a high student preference activity (e.g., recess) to a low student preference activity (e.g., grammar lesson).

Accepting Student Feelings. A student walks into class in the morning radiant with the news that the family will be visiting Disneyland. The teacher is pleased to have such a happy youngster in class for the day. It is a pleasure to accept positive feelings and reaffirm their expression. The next day the same youngster walks into class furious. Her dad has been laid off his job, and the trip to Disneyland is canceled. The student is angry and frustrated. She hates her dad; she hates the teacher; and she hates her schoolwork. These feelings are not so easy to accept and reaffirm. Teachers, who have a one-sided view of student feelings, allow for the expression of positive feelings but are reluctant to accept feelings of distress.

Students need to learn how to express such feelings as anger, frustration, and impatience. Students act out these feelings when they lack appropriate verbal skills. The teacher who attempts to put a lid on student behavior that is embedded in anger or frustration is sowing the seeds of further discontent. Distressful feelings cannot be made to disappear. Suppressed feelings will resurface. By providing opportunities for students to express all types of feelings, teachers reaffirm students. Role playing, class discussions, life space interventions, and journal writing are samples of classroom methods that help students channel difficult feelings into constructive outlets.

Punishment

Punishment is one of the most misunderstood and attitude-laden reactions to student actions. Punishment stops behavior through force—either physical or psychological. In the attempt to get students to toe the line, punishment communicates the message that might makes right. One of the factors that makes punitive approaches so appealing is that in terms of short-term goals, they appear to work. Such punishments as checks on a blackboard, "timeout," calls to home, or trips to the principal's office may halt disruptions, but too frequently the gains are temporary. Punishment does not change behavior nor does it teach new behaviors (Hyman & D'Allesandro, 1984; Kohn, 1991; Morse, 1987).

In Pell City, Alabama, a mother was sentenced to a reduced penalty of six months in prison for assaulting a school principal. The attack was provoked by the three paddlings the principal had given the woman's seven-year-old son. In sentencing the mother to jail, the judge said, "We have to set an example for others so that they not perform the same act you did. I sentence you to five years" (Smothers, 1987). This bizarre incident serves as a dramatic reminder that in many states corporal punishment is an acceptable means of disciplining students. As the father of two students in Huffman, Alabama, told to a *New York Times* reporter, "If the student needs a paddling, he ought to get a butt busting" ("Classroom Discipline and Lessons," 1990, p. A15). Instruments of physical punishment in schools include doubled-over belts, lacrosse sticks, baseball bats, arrows, electrical cords, and wooden drawer dividers. A Chicago principal used a penknife to drill a hole in a student's fingernail (Hyman & D'Allesandro, 1984, 42).

Sometimes it's difficult to determine where treatment for disruptive behavior ends and abuse begins. This is particularly true when punishment is couched in scientific jargon. For example the term "negative aversives" is used in special education to label such tactics as blasts of cold water in the face from an atomizer or pinching to thwart disruptive behavior. Whether or not negative aversives are a euphemism for punishment is a matter of some dispute. In Rhode Island, parents of children attending the Behavioral Research Institute defended the use of negative aversives. The Behavior Research Institute served diverse types of behavior disorders from juvenile delinquency to autism. "Negative aversives" ranged from pinches and hot sauces placed in the mouth to blasts of pressurized air on the side of the face, and, ultimately, restraints where a youngster was spread-eagled against a wall face first and held fast by strong cloth bands.

When punishment is used, it should be guided by school policy. Braaten, Simpson, Rosell, and Reilly recommend seven procedural elements to guide the use of punishment in schools:

1. Information about the use and abuse of punishment should be provided to teachers.
2. Teachers should be trained in the use of punishment.
3. Punishment procedures should be approved by the school board and be disseminated to teachers, parents, and students.
4. Records of punishment usage should be maintained.
5. Complaint and appeal procedures should be established.
6. Infractions that warrant punishment should be explained to all students and teachers.
7. Procedures for periodic review of punishment procedures should be implemented. (Braaten, Simpson, Rosell, & Riley, 1988, 80)

Punishment is commonplace and controversial. Some teachers use it first; others as the last resort. Punishment is effective when used sparingly. Reserve punishment for events or actions that cause physical or psychological harm to students or teacher. Remember if punishment and its antecedent—threats—are used as a primary discipline tactic, there is nothing left to fall back on when those methods fail to achieve the desired results.

Getting Rudy to Behave: Putting Theory Into Practice

Rudy is a sixth-grade student. He has been diagnosed as having attention deficit disorder with hyperactivity. He takes medication for his condition three times a day: before, during, and after school. Rudy also meets with the school adjustment counselor for an hour once a week.

Rudy's school behavior is impulsive. He runs in hallways. He often jumps and hits door frames with his right hand like he's dunking a basketball. He is unable to resist misusing such objects as pens, pencils, and paper clips by taking them apart or using them as "weapons." Rudy is also disorganized and frequently fails to complete assignments.

Transition times are difficult for Rudy, especially unstructured times, such as finishing an assignment and getting ready for lunch. When the class makes the transition from lecture to independent work, it takes Rudy several minutes to settle down and begin the task at hand. Often Rudy will get sidetracked into some other type of activity like cleaning his desk.

Socially Rudy cannot work with other students in such activities as group work or cooperative learning. He tends to be disruptive in his group and prevents the other children from completing assignments. Rudy does not anticipate consequences and seems not to care about the effects of his actions on others.

Rudy's problem is twofold: his behavior is disruptive and his social skills are weak. We further discuss social skills and how to help students learn social skills in the following chapter. For now we will concentrate on Rudy's behavior and what to do about his classroom disruptions.

The prevailing expert opinion indicates that Rudy's disorder, attention deficit with hyperactivity (ADHD), is neurologically based. This means that Rudy is not intentionally causing behavior problems. His medication may need to be increased, because his teacher does not report any behavior gains despite two dosages each day. On the other hand, Rudy may be one of those youngsters who does not respond to medication and another treatment may be preferred (see information on diet in Chapter 3, Students with Behavior Disorders).

Remember the school administrator who wanted to develop an index card system matched to each type of behavior problem? He believed there was one solution to each classroom discipline problem. In fact any number of combinations of interventions may fit the problem. Finding what works best with Rudy is trial and error. Try one approach, see how it works, and build on it or try another.

Each time Rudy disrupts the class, the teacher will take him into a corner of the room, which she has set up with a divider to provide some privacy. She will have independent work assignments ready for the rest of the class so she and Rudy can have a few private minutes together. She will provide *emotional first aid* and highlight the effect of Rudy's behavior using *sane messages*. She will encourage Rudy to describe what happened and she will *accept his feelings*. Her goal for these sessions is to maintain communication during stress and to regulate behavior by reminding Rudy in a nonjudgmental fashion that her job is to protect the ongoing classroom programming by using timeout if necessary.

In order to help prevent Rudy's disruptions she will use *alerting* to help him get ready for transitions and she will use several nonverbal interventions such as *proximity control*, *signal interference*, and *removal of seductive objects* to provide support without drawing attention to his behavior.

His teacher also understands that Rudy needs a more intensive plan to help him learn to control his behavior throughout the day. She will institute a *behavior modification program*. She will do a behavior frequency count of his most disturbing behavior—running through the halls. After gathering this data she finds that three out of every four times the class moves from one area of the building to another she has to correct Rudy's behavior. She will set up a *token economy* with Rudy. Each time he walks through the halls in an appropriate manner she will give him a ticket that he can exchange for a baseball card (baseball is one of his favorite sports) at the end of the day. The use of this *positive reinforcement* will be discussed with the class before. This will alleviate negative student feelings about being left out of the reward system. Additionally, for every ten baseball cards Rudy earns, the class will have ten extra minutes of recess. This should help everyone pull for Rudy to succeed. After a month, Rudy's teacher will do another behavior frequency count to see if the positive reinforcement program is taking hold.

The success of the interventions for Rudy will be based on several factors including administrative and parental support. No guarantees go with this behavior plan for Rudy, but the teacher's knowledge of an array of behavior strategies plus her understanding that all behavior interventions require timely adjustments is movement in the right direction.

Summary

Well-managed classrooms facilitate learning. No one can learn in a class that is constantly disrupted by behavior problems. Discipline problems cause stress in both teachers and students. For the novice teacher, classroom management is a major concern. At one time or another all students present discipline problems. While authoritarian discipline tactics hold some appeal, promoting student participation in discipline policies increases their sense of personal responsibility and helps to prevent future behavior problems.

Preventive discipline is based on the premise that many classroom disruptions can be avoided. Teachers who use preventive discipline techniques strive to intervene before a disturbance turns into a full-blown discipline problem. Such teachers are skilled in an array of behavior management tools including behavior modification, nonverbal, and verbal interventions.

Activities

1. Arrange to speak with a principal like Mr. Mellon, one who has been working in schools for 10 to 15 years. Ask him or her to describe the classroom management models being used in his or her school. Ask if there are differences in how teachers implement the model(s) and in how effective the model(s) is (are) in maintaining order in the school. share the results of your experience with another student in your class or another teacher in your school.

2. Observe an elementary or secondary class. Count the nonverbal interventions the teacher uses in a half-hour. Count the verbal interventions the teacher uses in a half-hour. Analyze the data. Look for classroom rules and other signs of teacher management style. Does the teacher style more closely approximate Canter or Glasser?

3. Watch the video *Lean on Me,* about Joe Clark. Have a class debate; was he a hero or villain?

4. Role play a crisis situation using the Life Space Intervention. Discuss the usefulness of LSI. Ask classroom teachers if they have heard of LSI; if so, do they use it?

5. Visit a public school classroom. Look for signs of behavior modification practices. Do you think they work?

CHAPTER

10 Teaching Social Skills

Advance Organizer

When you complete this chapter you will be able to answer the following questions:

1. Why is social skill instruction needed in some classrooms?
2. What is the difference between autocratic, permissive, and democratic classrooms?

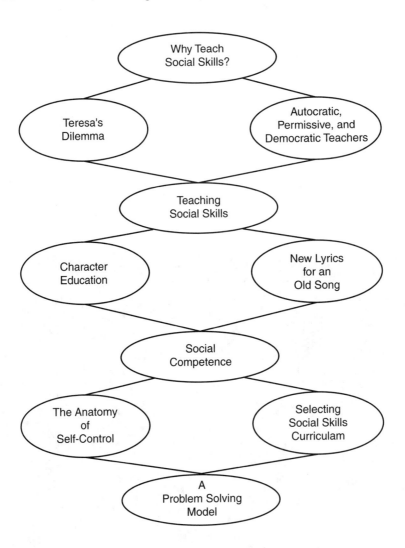

3. What does "character education" mean?
4. How does values clarification fit into a classroom curriculum?
5. What are some specific social skills that comprise self-control?
6. What problem solving steps would you follow to develop a social skills program for a specific student?

Vignette: Debbie

Debbie is eleven years old and in the fifth grade. Her teacher is concerned about Debbie's behavior. She seems less mature than the other students. Debbie is overactice and has difficulty following class rules. She gets out of her seat often and always seems to have an excuse to leave the room. In the hallways, cafeteria and library she often acts up. In the classroom she has difficulty waiting for teacher help. Her teacher believes Debbie needs an evaluation for ADHD and is planning on talking to the principal about it.

Although Debbie likes other students she spends a lot of time alone on the playground. Her classmates shy away from her because she tries to relate to them by gossiping, teasing or doing favors. She enjoys reading and math and her grades would be much better if she could stay focused on her classwork. Her teacher is fairly traditional, which means she does a lot of frontal teaching. Much of Debbie's school work consists of textbook reading, worksheets, and other 'seatwork.'

Problem solving questions:

1. What social skills is Debbie lacking?
2. Do you think Debbie should be removed from her classroom and placed in a self-contained special education class for students with behavior disorders?
3. What could Debbie's classroom teacher do to help Debbie learn the social skills she lacks?

Consider the challenge of classroom management. The typical classroom teacher engages in 1,000 interactions a day (Jackson, 1968). Less than half of these interpersonal exchanges relate to teaching. The majority of time is spent trying to keep the classroom running smoothly. Maintaining a group focus, minimizing disruptions, and encouraging student participation require the organizational skills of the "one minute manager" and the human relations skills of a Dale Carnegie. Each student is a unique human being with likes, dislikes, strengths, and weaknesses. Regardless of ability or personality of individual students, the classroom teacher is expected to bring each "up to grade level." The public school classroom is one of the best examples of our democratic tradition. Public education is based on the common school principle that all students should have an equal opportunity to succeed in life. Yet all students do not start out equal. The inequity of student life experiences and student ability imposes the greatest challenge on public school teachers.

Why Teach Social Skills?

Many with mild disabilities come to school bereft of the social skills needed for success. It would be unfair to punish a student with low frustration-tolerance for being restless. Such a practice is tantamount to forcing a student with cerebral palsy to run a fifty-yard dash! Students with emotional and behavioral disorders have not developed their condition due to a lack of sanctions in their lives; in fact, many case histories reveal numerous scrapes with authority. Teachers who have students with mild disabilities in their classrooms soon learn the meaning of "dis-ability." It is a lack of ability, a condition that a student can't overcome without help.

Behavioral and emotional difficulties are not visible like physical disabilities, but they are no less debilitating. Limiting disruptive behavior is not enough. Students need opportunities to learn socially acceptable behavior. Parents send their children to school because they believe it is a safe and orderly environment. Good classroom management requires a blend of humane practices that combine high expectations for success with a willingness to organize a classroom to maximize the learning of both academic and social skills.

Teresa's Dilemma

When Teresa, a beginning third-grade teacher, arrived for the first day of work she was confronted with a variety of organizational tasks. Housekeeping duties such as attendance and lunch count were outlined by the principal. The first hours alone in the classroom were spent inspecting textbooks, reviewing curriculum guides, and arranging furniture. The maintenance person dropped by to give some not so subtle tips about how he likes to find the room at the end of the day. Colleagues offered helpful advice about how to get along with the administration. It was an exciting time, and Teresa eagerly anticipated the arrival of her young charges.

Yet one nagging thought remained: "Can I maintain discipline?" The new teacher was fully aware that everybody would be watching to see if she could handle her students. Teresa's apprehension about discipline is a normal reaction to the often unstated, but nevertheless powerful norm of public school teaching—teachers who can control their classrooms succeed, and teachers who cannot control their classrooms fail. Such suggestions as "Keep a tight rein," and "Don't smile until Christmas," when given by experienced teachers, usually add to, rather than subtract from, the novice's anxieties. Advice steeped in repressive or authoritarian tactics presents an unsettling picture of students. A new teacher such as Teresa might begin to wonder if her first students are an undisciplined bunch that must be tamed before they can be taught.

Teresa is at a crossroads. Discipline styles are established during the first days of school (Strother, 1985). The manner in which discipline is approached the first day will set the pattern for the rest of the year (Charles, 1983, 9). Teresa wants to start off on the right foot, but which foot is that? Like many other young teachers she wonders if she should "come down hard" on her students so they learn "who is boss." Or should she try to be a friend and try to help teach her students self-control?

Teresa went to the library that evening. She looked up classroom discipline and found a bewildering array of "discipline models." Some discussed consequences for behavior and positive reinforcement. Others described caring and trust as important prerequisites to classroom control. Ideas from one model sometimes contradicted ideas from another. More recent texts noted concerns about violence in schools. Some detailed the importance of teaching students such social skills as conflict resolution and stress management. It became evident to Teresa that some students would enter her classroom handicapped by an inability to get along with others. Matters were further complicated when Teresa read that attempts to make students comply with classroom rules through rewards and punishments sometimes backfire. Some students learn to manipulate reward systems while others grow hostile, resentful, and apathetic when exposed to so-called "obedience models," which relied principally on the carrot-and-stick philosophy. In total, most of the arguments about the best way to manage classrooms seemed too abstract, while her apprehensions about her first day were very real.

Then Teresa read a passage from Charles's book *Elementary Classroom Management:*

> . . . on the first day the teacher should go over with the students exactly what the basic rules for student behavior will be. Four to six rules are considered sufficient, and most teachers have these rules fairly well in mind although they wisely allow students to give input, discuss, and have at least some say in deciding how the rules will be enforced. When students participate in making such decisions, they become more likely to abide by them, see them as fair, and recognize the necessity for rules in helping learning occur better for all. (Charles, 1983, 10)

This seemed sound advice. Take charge the first day, but give students input into decisions about discipline. Teresa liked this cooperative approach to classroom management. It matched her intuitive belief that teaching and learning can be fun when teacher and students work together. Teresa resolved to work *with* her students.

Autocratic, Permissive, and Democratic Classrooms

Dreikurs classified teachers into three types: autocratic, permissive, and democratic (Charles, 1989). Autocratic teachers rule by will. They believe all power and control should rest with the teacher. Permissive teachers do not provide guidance or leadership. They are unsure of themselves and are easily frustrated with administrators or other teachers who "don't understand." Democratic teachers maintain discipline through student participation. They understand that authority is a natural by-product of their teaching position. Democratic teachers expect students to become disciplined by acquiring inner controls. Autocratic, permissive, and democratic teachers approach their classes in very different ways. Each acts in accordance with a set of distinctive beliefs about what students need.

Autocratic teachers believe power is the teacher's best tool for managing student behavior. Such teachers believe students are unable to control themselves. Often students will react to autocratic teachers in a manner that supports this Hobbesian view of nature. (Thomas Hobbes, a seventeenth century English philosopher, believed that the natural passions of people ran counter to such virtues as justice and equity. According to Hobbes, only power, exercised by an outside authority, motivates people to behave in a benevolent manner.) Students have an uncanny way of living up to teacher expectations. When teachers expect the worst, that's usually what they get. Negative student behavior confirms the teacher's basic assumptions about the need to control students through power and authority. The result is classroom management by fiat. The teacher makes the rules, rewards the "good," and punishes the "bad." Autocratic discipline strategies are teacher-directed, with minimal student participation.

Permissive teachers are confused. They believe child development theory supports giving children choices, and they naively anticipate that, left to their own devices, students will follow the right course. Permissive teachers want to be democratic, but they are unable to organize classroom practices (e.g., class discussions, cooperative learning) to support democratic procedures. They abdicate their natural authority as adults in the misguided view that they are creating an environment that will allow the natural goodness of children to emerge. This lack of leadership soon leads to chaos. They want their students to like them and will attempt to win students over by favors, shortcutting rules, and making deals. Permissive teachers don't stay in the profession for long. Although there is a high tolerance for autocratic classroom practices in public schools, the chaotic classrooms of permissive teachers are usually short-lived. Permissive teachers either burn out quickly or are asked to leave. Ironically, permissive teachers rarely see themselves that way. They consider themselves democratic or "therapeutic."

Democratic teachers believe that students need to share power with the teacher in order to learn how to behave responsibly. Democratic teacher strategies are cooperative. The teacher assumes the role of leader rather than ruler. Democratic teachers know their authority is a natural by-product of being a teacher. It isn't necessary to keep reminding students who is in charge. Democratic teachers combine teacher-directed lessons and student-centered activities. Such classroom practices as cooperative learning, classroom discussions, and peer tutoring are featured in democratic classrooms.

In a democratic classroom, students are asked to help frame rules for the year. This opening gambit establishes the climate for approaching discipline as a cooperative venture. The democratic teacher has two clear goals for her students. First is the development of good interpersonal relationships. Students and teacher alike need to be treated with respect and compassion. Such human relations skills as listening, courtesy, and a sense of humor foster student self-esteem and provide a comfortable climate for learning. Second, the democratic teacher wants to see the class evolve into a cohesive group. There is a continual focus on group management. Students work in groups, talk in groups, and play in groups. The democratic teacher strives to create a group identity in the classroom. Students in a democratic classroom share a sense of togetherness not found in autocratic or permissive classrooms. Democratic classrooms provide students with many opportunities to develop and enhance a variety of social skills including personal responsibility, group participation, and individual decision making.

Teaching Social Skills

Many general and special educators agree that social skills instruction has a legitimate place in the classroom. Participation in our changing society requires adaptability and human relations skills. Through most of the twentieth century, students graduated from high school found employment in manufacturing. Factory workers needed to follow directions, tend to repetitious work, and accept company rules. The workplace required obedience and conformity. A worker's value was judged on the ability to complete an honest day's labor. However, the blue collar world of work is slowly disappearing from the American scene.

The United States is evolving into a service economy. Many new jobs in the twenty-first century require the ability to handle people instead of machines. Employers want employees who can cooperate with others, solve social problems, and resolve conflicts. Historically, the teaching of these skills was assumed by the family and church. But the changing demographics of U.S. society indicate that traditional means of training children in social abilities need support from the schools.

London (1987) characterizes today's children as potential victims of a "psychosocial epidemic." He states that millions of American children are at risk because of rents in the social fabric of childhood. London provides the following statistics: 715,000 children are born to unwed mothers; over a million nonsexual cases of child abuse are reported each year; three million fourteen- to seventeen-year-olds may have a drinking problem; half a million children attempt suicide each year, and six thousand die by suicide. Students need help in managing their lives. They need to understand how to make good choices. They need to learn to view problems from the other person's point of view. They need assistance in coping with feelings that drive them to drugs and sex.

Character Education

Schools are the only places where children are assured constant adult supervision. If today's youngster is to successfully navigate the social storms that await outside school, they will need adult help. Social skills education in the curriculum can provide a lifeline. Character education (Kohn, 1991; Lickona, 1988; London, 1987) is a term that best seems to suit the evolving notion about what a social curriculum would encompass. Proponents of character education stress the teaching of co-operation and mutual respect. Moral development, with its attendant emphasis on caring for others, is emphasized in character education, as is reflection and commitment to moral principles. London lists two primary components of character education: (1) education in civic virtue and in the qualities that teach children the forms and rules of citizenship in a just society, and (2) education in personal adjustment, chiefly in the qualities that enable children to become productive and dependable citizens (London, 1987).

The Child Development Project (Kohn, 1991), begun in 1982 in the San Ramon Valley (California) Unified School District, is an example of a character education curriculum. In the CDP program, children participate in decisions about how classes can become "caring communities." Classroom management practices are directed toward teaching prosocial skills. Classroom meetings, co-operative learning, and warm student–teacher relationships are highlighted. A literature-based reading program encourages students to reflect on personal values while learning to read. The CDP program, which was adopted by the Hayward, California, school district, has as its overall goal—teaching children to develop self-control. According to Marilyn Watson, an educator in CDP, teachers have learned that you don't need punishment and rewards to have a well-managed classroom. The core of classroom discipline, according to Ms. Watson, "lies in teachers developing positive relationships with their students and helping them to understand the reasons behind the rules."

Character education can be included in any lesson. Lickona describes how a second-grade teacher merged character education with a science lesson. For a science project, the class was incubating twenty chicken eggs. The teacher suggested that the students might want to open one egg to observe embryonic development. Later that day, Nathaniel, seven years old, expressed reservations, "Mrs. Williams, I've been thinking about this for a long time. It's just too *cruel* to open an egg and kill the chick inside!" Mrs. Williams listened and decided to bring the topic up for a class discussion. Some students agreed with Nathaniel; others wondered how you could kill a chick if it hadn't been born yet. Mrs. Williams gave her students the night to think it over. The next day, the majority decided not to open the egg (Lickona, 1988, 422). This brief episode illustrates a common strategy in character education—values clarification.

Values Clarification.   Moral reflection requires understanding one's values. Lickona describes moral reflection in the following way:

> The word reflection refers to a wide range of intellectual activities, including reading, thinking, debating moral questions, listening to explanations by the teacher (e.g., why is it wrong to make fun of a handicapped child), and conducting firsthand investigations to increase children's awareness of the complex social system to which they belong. (Lickona, 1987, 422)

When using values clarification in the classroom, the teacher encourages reflection. The purpose is to guide students in exploring personal values. The teacher does not attempt to impose his or her own value system; rather, opportunities are arranged for students to examine their own values, consider alternatives, and make future choices. Teachers who use values clarification assume that with guidance and freedom, students will identify personal values that reflect the common good. Values clarification can be a proscribed lesson (e.g., class discussion on whether or not to open an egg), or it can be embedded in the flux of daily classroom life. Students are constantly reflecting their values in unconscious ways. Examples of these are:

> Attitudes: "I feel that . . ." "I don't like . . ."
>
> Aspirations: "One day I'm going to . . ."
>
> Purposes: "I plan to make a . . ."
>
> Interests: "I like to . . ." "I enjoy . . ."
>
> Activities: "After school I'm going to . . ."

Essential to values clarification is questioning. By formulating questions, the teacher can assist the student to understand personal values. Values clarification probes would include questions such as the following:

1. Choosing Freely
   Where do you suppose you first got that idea?
   How long have you felt that way?
   What will you do if you don't succeed?
2. Choosing from Alternatives
   What else did you consider before you picked this?
   How long did you look around before you decided?
3. Reflective Choosing
   What would be the consequences of your choice?
   How much thought have you put into this choice?
   What is good about this choice?
4. Prizing and Cherishing
   Are you glad you feel that way?
   What good is it?
   What do you want?
5. Affirming
   Would you tell the class the way you feel?
   Do people know you feel that way?
6. Acting on Choices
   What is a plan of action?
   Where will this lead you?
7. Repeating
   What are your plans for doing more?

Has it been worth the time and effort?

Values clarification is aimed at helping students learn how to think through their choices. Caution is advised about making direct statements under the guise of questioning. For example, "You don't really think that is proper behavior, do you?" is a veiled attempt to have a student conform to the teacher's values.

Goals of Character Education.   Character educators are proactive in terms of teaching students specific values. For example, Lickona (1987) cites the following goals for character education:

1. To promote movement away from individualism toward cooperative relationships and mutual respect.
2. To foster the growth of moral agency—the capacity to think, feel, and act morally.
3. To develop in the classroom and in the school a moral community based on fairness, caring, and participation—such a community being a moral end in itself, as well as a support system for the character development of each individual student.

Several variations on the above themes appear in other character education models. Edwards (1991) emphasizes a modified version of the 1921 Dalton Plan, where students determine their own schedules from subject lab alternatives. The purpose of the Dalton Plan is to teach students to assume responsibility for their own learning in a noncompetitive atmosphere. Kohn (1991) stresses a caring curriculum. He encourages teachers to develop empathetic relationships with their students; to promote cooperation over competition; and to allow students to participate in the governing of the classroom. Each of these conditions, Kohn maintains, increases academic skills by investing students in their day-to-day learning.

New Lyrics for an Old Song

The notion of teaching values, moral development, or social skills in the classroom is not a novel idea. Moral development is a cornerstone of Western philosophy. The eighteenth century philosopher, Immanuel Kant, believed that moral behavior was directed by reason. He provided the following "categorical imperative" to guide reason and actions, "Act only on that maxim through which you can at the same time will that it should become a universal law" (Seldes, 1985, 223). According to the categorical imperative, the rightness of behavior depended on the reasoning behind the act, not the consequences (Benniga, 1988). This focus on the internalization of judgment is what sets advocates of character education apart from teachers who believe students are best trained through external manipulation.

No educator in the twentieth century was a more ardent advocate of character education than John Dewey. In 1909 Dewey published *Moral Principles in Education* in which he advocated the teaching of initiative, courage, judgment, and persistence. He maintained that external control of students instills dependence on the judgment of authority figures. Dewey believed that the purpose of education was to help students develop social consciousness. According to Dewey, concern for the social good required nurturing. Students needed opportunities to help their classmates, participate in classroom decisions, and discuss moral questions.

Classrooms don't have to be inclined toward character education to teach values. All classrooms are saturated in values. Either covertly or overtly, American students for generations have been instilled with values educators believed crucial to success. Consider the following excerpt from *McGuffey's Fourth Eclectic Reader* (1920):

Lazy Ned

"'Tis royal fun," cried lazy Ned,
"To coast upon my fine, new sled,
And beat the other boys;
But then, I can not bear to climb
The tiresome hill, for every time
It more and more annoys."
So while his schoolmates glided by,
And gladly tugged uphill, to try
Another merry race;
Too indolent to share their plays,
Ned was compelled to stand and gaze,
While shivering in his place.
Thus, he would never take the pains
To seek the prize that labor gains,
Until the time had passed;
For, all his life, he dreaded still
The silly bugbear of uphill,
And died a dunce at last. (cited in Benniga, 416)

Unobtrusive artifacts of values permeate life in classrooms. For example, tests promote competition, while stringent behavior codes demand conformity. Benniga provides insight on the pervasiveness of covert moral education. "Whether or not they offer specific programs, schools provide moral education. In many schools and districts the curriculum in morality is informal and unwritten. It pervades the school and classroom rules (Benniga, 1988). As an illustration, consider the recent change in how scholars depict Christopher Columbus. For years Columbus was portrayed in American textbooks as a prototype of American values. Against all odds, the story goes, he altered our conception of the world and discovered America. He brought Christianity to the native "Indians" and opened the gates to a "new world." So esteemed was Columbus that the Knights of Columbus promoted him for sainthood.

Now compare this traditional tale of Columbus with the view held by some Native Americans. According to Russell Means of the American Indian Movement, Columbus practiced genocide with the fervor of a despot. Under Columbus's administration, Indians living in what is now the Dominican Republic were shipped to Europe as slaves; thousands of others were raped, tortured, and murdered. Recent disclosures of Columbus's misadventures prompted the United Nations to cancel a celebration of his quincentenary. The National Council of Churches stated that the 500th anniversary of Columbus's discovery should be a time of penitence instead of jubilation. Cultural values are shaped by textbook writers and teachers. In the case of Columbus, the atrocities committed against Native Americans were paved over by historians eager to promote Columbus as an icon of American values.

Moral education is as basic to schools as mathematics and reading. What type of moral education do we want to pass on to our students? Advocates of character education believe school should emphasize prosocial skills. These educators prefer cooperation to competition, altruism to individualism, and empathy to egocentrism.

The teaching of prosocial skills is especially relevant for students with mild disabilities. Students with mild mental retardation are characterized by deficits in adaptive behavior; students with learning disabilities have difficulty deciphering social cues; and students with emotional or behavioral disorders act out their emotions in disruptive ways. Teaching students with mild disabilities how to regulate their behavior in socially acceptable ways is a goal for educators and parents.

Social Competence

Cox and Gunn (1980) list three reasons why students have difficulty adjusting to social situations:

1. The student does not know what are appropriate behaviors.
2. The student may have knowledge of appropriate behavior but may lack practice.
3. Student emotional reactions to situations may inhibit performance of the desired behavior. (cited in McGinnis & Goldstein, 1984, 4)

Lack of social competence is one of the primary reasons that students with mild disabilities have difficulty in regular classrooms (Nelson, 1988). More than one special educator has been chagrined at how a student with mild disabilities seemed to "fall apart" when transferred from a special education program to a full-time regular classroom placement. Advocates of direct teaching of prosocial skills develop curricula to enable transition from the security of special education programs to the demands of normal school routines. Such programs as *Skillstreaming the Elementary School Child* (McGinnis & Goldstein, 1984), *Developmental Therapy* (Wood, 1986), and *Teaching Self-Control: A Curriculum for Responsible Behavior* (Henley, 1997) provide goals, instructional objectives, learning activities, and consulting guidelines. The aim of each program is to teach social skills that can be generalized beyond the secure confines of special education programs.

Each of these programs is based on the premise that social skills training of students with special needs requires cooperation between general and special educators. Students cannot be "fixed" in self-contained special education programs and then shipped as finished products into general classrooms. (See Chapter 6 for guidelines about inclusion.) In order to develop appropriate social skills, students with mild disabilities need time to learn with and from nondisabled students. Social skills training requires agreement by general and special educators on specific areas of competence to be developed.

Developmental skills, those that cut across many settings, are preferred to context specific skills. Youngsters must be able to cope with social demands in many different environments. Training a youngster with low frustration tolerance to complete three worksheets is a school context skill. Teaching the same youngster to verbalize rather than act out feelings of frustration is a developmental skill that is useful in many settings (Fagen & Hill, 1987). While following directions, completing assignments, taking notes and other "school survival skills" (Silverman, Zigmond, & Sansone, 1981) are important, unless these skills are embedded in a more comprehensive framework students will leave school without the tools to manage the broader social demands of work, family, and the community (Figure 10.1).

The Anatomy of Self-Control

Fagen and Long (1975) define self-control as the ability to direct and regulate personal behavior flexibly and realistically in a given situation. The work of Redl and Wineman (1951) presents a structural model for describing a self-control curriculum. In their quest to unveil the "anatomy of self-control," Redl and Wineman detail a list of specific self-control skills that children normally develop as they learn to restrain their impulses and relate to the world at large. Redl and Wineman's detailed descriptions provide the classroom teacher with a paradigm of self-control (Henley, 1987). As children mature, they must learn to control their impulses, assess social reality, manage group pressure, deal with stress, and solve social problems (Henley, 1994).

What follows is a brief description of the social skills entailed in each of the above areas (see Table 10.1). The items describe self-control developmental milestones. The descriptions can help the classroom teacher in the following ways:

1. To identify individual student self-control strengths and weaknesses.

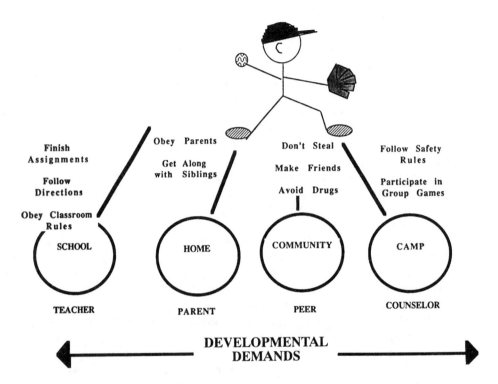

FIGURE 10.1   Developmental Demands

2. To anticipate situations when a student might lose control.
3. To establish goals and objectives for a prosocial curriculum.

Impulse Control.   Impulses are powerful psychological motivators. A student may have an impulse to hit another student or an impulse to throw a textbook in frustration. Impulses are derived from an infant's need for immediate gratification. As children grow and mature, they learn to delay gratification. A student with self-control is capable of restraining impulses. Situations or conditions can strain the impulse control abilities of students and cause classroom disruptions. The following self-control skills are a subset of impulse control:

1. *Resisting Temptation.* As they grow and mature socially, students learn to control the impulses brought on by tempting situations or objects. A student who sees an examination lying on the teacher's desk and resists the urge to pick it up to survey the questions is practicing self-control. Schools are filled with

TABLE 10.1 Self-Control Skills

Impulse Control
Resisting Temptation
Using Materials Properly
Spontaneously Establishing Self-Control
Tolerating Frustration

Assessment of Social Reality
Anticipating Consequences
Evaluating the Effect of Behavior on Others
Appreciating Feelings
Accepting Praise and Affection
Taking Care of Personal Possessions

Manage Group Pressure
Resisting Group Contagion
Maintaining Control Under Impact of Peer Pressure
Adapting to Competitive Challenge
Participating in Group Activities

Stress Management
Coping with Anxiety
Controlling the Floodgates of the Past
Adapting to New Situations
Relaxing

Solve Social Problems
Recalling Disruptive Actions
Learning from Experience
Drawing Inferences from Others' Experiences
Resolving Conflicts

Adapted from Redl and Wineman, 1951; Fagen, Long and Stevens, 1975; and Henley, 1984. Preventive Discipline Project, Westfield State College, 1988–1992.

alluring objects. Equipment, toys, and learning materials can present strong temptations to students who lack temptation resistance. Students with emotional problems sometimes steal with no idea about what to do with the object once it is in their possession. One youngster in a program for students with emotional problems was literally seduced by gadgets of any sort. He was so predictable that the teaching staff always knew to go to Peter's "treasure hole" under the school-yard fence to check for missing items.

Space has its own attraction. Open spaces invite running. Enclosed spaces invite yelling. Field trips, in particular, offer myriad possibilities for disruptive behavior for a youngster who has difficulty curbing impulses.

2. *Using Materials Properly.* Most students understand the purpose of class-room materials. Books are for reading. Erasers are for cleaning blackboards. Clay is for modeling. Chisels are for scraping wood. Other students use classroom materials as props to act out feelings. An impulsive toss of an eraser across the room at an offensive peer or jabbing an adjacent student with a pencil illustrate how students misuse materials. These students are unable to restrain the impulse to "send a message" with the closest object available. Care should be taken to keep a close watch on materials that could be used to injure another student in a sudden outburst of anger or frustration.

3. *Spontaneously Establishing Self-Control.* Many a substitute teacher has been greeted by a spontaneous, "Oh boy, a sub"; or in other words, "Let the fun and games commence." The substitute teacher scenario is an example of how in certain situations even well-mannered students can fail to spontaneously establish self-control. Controlling one's own behavior when there is no authority figure around to monitor is a sign of maturity and emotional development. Conversely, the absence of spontaneous self-control skills indicates that a youngster is motivated by impulses rather than a sense of social responsibility. Organized classroom activities and routines support the student in maintaining self-control. When schedules indicate a change in routine, particularly from structured to open-ended activities, the impulsive youngster does not have the inner resources to substitute internal for external controls. Transition times, in particular, challenge the impulse control system of the students.

4. *Tolerating Frustration.* Frustration can be overwhelming for a youngster who lacks impulse control. Such a mundane obligation as waiting for help with a classroom assignment can culminate in a display of anger. When a four-year-old child cries because she loses in a game, that is acceptable. When an unhappy nine-year-old throws a board game aside, sending everyone's pieces flying be-cause someone else bought "Boardwalk," there is a problem. It is quite remarkable to behold how children learn to accept minor frustrations and persevere as they mature. Learning to swim, ride a bike, and play a musical instrument are all building blocks toward perseverance, an essential quality for success in life.

For many children, frustration-tolerance happens naturally and gracefully. Others need to be taught how to handle frustration. Usually low self-esteem exemplified by an "I can't do it" attitude is characteristic of students with low frustration-tolerance.

Assessment of Social Reality. All students learn to take measure of social situations. For instance, behavior that is accepted by one teacher may be forbidden by another. Developing children are remarkably adaptable, and their insight into behaviors that are acceptable and unacceptable is a determinant of how they are accepted by others. Well-adjusted children are capable of maintaining relationships. They interpret social cues and make adjustments in their behavior based on what a situation demands. Deficiencies in their assessment of social reality will result in persistent conflicts with peers or adults.

1. *Anticipating Consequences.* In the classroom, as elsewhere, rules and routines organize activity and keep harmony. Students may not like rules, but they understand why rules are necessary. They know there are consequences for breaking rules. In society, norms substitute for rules, and laws are legislated codes of behavior. Social consequences follow violation of norms, and legal action is the consequence for breaking the law. Students who have an unrealistic notion of rules, norms, and laws interpret them as personal affronts to their integrity or well-being. They resent consequences. Such students, when confronted with consequences for their behavior, may become hostile.

2. *Evaluating the Effect of Behavior on Others.* Youngsters learn that their actions stir up corresponding reactions in others. Without this insight, a student will fail to recognize how personal behavior shapes the way that others act. A youngster who is "mean" to another may show remorse or at least understand why a friend has decided to leave. Some students with behavioral or emotional difficulties are unable to untrack their self-centered thinking. To such a student interpersonal problems are always the fault of others.

3. *Appreciating Feelings.* Students with emotional problems have difficulty accepting the feelings of others. This is not surprising because their own feelings are such a mystery to them. Their ability to identify and describe feelings in themselves and others is deficient. Low self-esteem coupled with a naive grasp of the significance of feelings leaves a student with emotional disturbance at a loss to contemplate his or her own life experience.

4. *Accepting Praise and Affection.* Trust is a basic requirement for social exchange between teacher and student. A student who has difficulty trusting adults will have difficulty forming attachments to others. Expression of care and interest may be reciprocated by hostility or resentment. Many students with emotional problems have well-entrenched defenses against what they consider a hostile world. Such youngsters need to learn to accept and give affection.

5. *Taking Care of Personal Possessions.* A bike that is left unlocked may get stolen. Carelessness in keeping track of assignments can mean coming to school unprepared. Personal responsibility in managing day to day activities is important for school success. Students who can manage their daily lives do well in

school. Other students need to learn how to organize themselves. They are undermined by their own unintentional carelessness.

Manage Group Pressure.   Virtually everything in a classroom happens in a group situation. Group dynamics have a powerful impact on young people both in and out of school. The need to belong and the need to socialize with like-minded people are strong forces that can impel a youngster to make good or bad choices. Why does one youngster join Boy Scouts, while another joins a gang? Why does one youngster look for mystical experience with drugs, and another choose religion? In many cases the answer is the power of peer pressure to shape young people's choices. The ability to handle group pressure is a hallmark of self-control. Students who are overly influenced by peer groups give up control of their lives. These students need to learn how to manage group pressure.

   1. *Resisting Group Contagion.* Excitability is contagious. When a class is "out of control," one or more students set off others with their disruptive behavior. Overstimulated students become leaders in pandemonium, and the teacher is hard pressed to restore order. Some students have the internal strength to maintain internal control while others around them are out of control. Meanwhile, other students are swept away by the excitement. Such students need to learn how to appraise situations reasonably and to strengthen their sense of themselves as agents of their own control.

   2. *Maintaining Control under Impact of Peer Pressure.* For young people, particularly adolescents, peer pressure is a powerful shaper of attitude and behavior. When confronted with peer pressure, students may be hard pressed to make the types of decisions that adults would advocate. Self-control within groups means being able to steer an individual course of action, even though it may be the opposite of group expectations. By helping students learn to make prosocial decisions despite group pressure, teachers not only enhance classroom management but also provide students with the tools to deal with myriad group pressures outside of school.

   3. *Adapting to Competitive Challenge.* Competition is a basic fact of life in our society. Keeping a balanced perspective about winning and losing is necessary to productivity both in and out of school. Winning and losing gracefully require self-control and positive self-regard. Competition in school, both obvious (e.g., tests) and unobtrusive (e.g., art displays), are factors that all students must learn to accept. Resilience, perseverance, and task commitment are basic to success. Students who avoid competition or think of themselves as "losers" need help in learning how to handle competitive challenge.

   4. *Participating in Group Activities.* Cooperative group work is prevalent in all levels of society. Learning to help others, resolve conflicts, and share resources are signs of personal growth. Each of these skills requires the ability to "decenter," that is, to consider the other person's perspective. Although these skills develop naturally in some students, others become fixated on their own point of view. This impedes their ability to cooperate and maintain group harmony. Such students need opportunities to learn to set aside their own personal agendas and focus on the concerns of the group.

Stress Management.   Stress is the electricity of life. Through a combination of perception and biochemical reactions, stress energizes us to action. Schultz and Heuchen (1983) succinctly state, "All life events carry the potential for introducing stress into a person's life" (cited in Knoblock, 1987, 216). Hans Seyle (1975) defines stress as the nonspecific response of the body to any demand, pleasant or unpleasant. For a student, a pleasant prospect, such as anticipating a field trip to the zoo, causes stress just as surely as the unpleasant prospect of going to school without assigned homework.

Learning to manage stress is an important adaptive and survival skill. Perception plays a key role in inducing a stress reaction of fight or flight. Students with emotional disabilities often misinterpret social cues. Overreaction to mild stressors is commonplace with these students. An ordinary task, such as reading aloud in class, can bring on a temper tantrum (i.e., fight) or refusal to perform (i.e., flight). Learning to adapt to stressful classroom situations can help prepare students for life outside of school. Essentially there are four characteristic stressful conditions that challenge the self-control abilities of students.

1. *Coping with Anxiety.* Some students are so ridden with anxiety (painful apprehension or sense of foreboding) that they are unable to decipher reality-based threats from normal expressions of feeling. Their reaction may be to strike out or verbally assault the perceived protagonist. Many teachers have difficulty understanding that overreaction to routine situations, brought on by a student's inability to cope with anxiety, is a symptom of his or her disability. In the section on the life space interview, we emphasized the value of gathering information on how a youngster perceives events in the classroom. Through the use of LSI and other active listening techniques, it is possible to identify specific stressors that set a youngster off into a fight or flight reaction.

2. *Controlling the Floodgates of the Past.* Fortunately most students have the capacity to separate present events from past unpleasant situations. For example, a student will attempt to persevere in a mathematics assignment despite past difficulties with arithmetic. Given this situation, even a well-adjusted youngster will need support and will at times get frustrated. Students with behavioral disorders have life histories replete with failure or trauma. A minor dose of recall is all that is needed to set off a severe stress reaction.

3. *Adapting to New Situations.* Learning to adjust to unfamiliar situations or people is an essential adaptive skill. Adaptive responses to stress caused by new situations include questions, verbalization of apprehensions, and caution. When students have not learned these adaptive skills, their reactions can be disturbing. Pretenses of familiarity, avoidant behaviors, and unwarranted hostility are samples of how students overreact to new situations or people.

4. *Relaxing.* After a hard day at school, a youngster might look forward to going home and playing with friends. On a rainy day, such a child might pick up a favorite book or get back to completing a model. Relaxation reduces stress. Relaxation is an emotional and biochemical state. Numerous body signs indicate an individual is relaxed: the pulse rate goes down, skin temperature is warm to the touch, breathing is paced and easy. Chronic stress disables the immune system; chronic stress can cause disease. Students with emotional difficulties are rarely able to achieve a prolonged state of relaxation. Even games dissolve into a series of petty disputes. Alone, they have difficulty sustaining solitary activity. Television, alcohol, and drugs are pastimes of youth that are nonadaptive attempts to relax.

Solve Social Problems.   Interpersonal problems are difficult to solve. The negotiating of relationships requires the ability to reflect on one's own behavior. One must be able to apply the lessons of the past to present situations. Once a problem is identified, it is necessary to consider various options and eventually choose a course of action. Ultimately, social problem solving requires evaluation of goals and the means to achieve those goals. A student must be able to apply these skills in both individual and group situations. The final achievement is measured by a student's ability to develop and maintain relationships. When a youngster lacks these skills, interpersonal conflicts are frequent, and a youngster becomes isolated by his own futile social gestures.

1. *Recalling Disruptive Actions.* Every teacher and parent is familiar with the refrain, "It wasn't my fault." Denial of personal culpability is normal in young children. As students develop better insight into their own behavior, they begin to accept responsibility for their actions. Students with emotional problems sometimes literally "forget" their own behavior. Redl and Wineman (1951) called this forgetfulness "evaporation of self-contributed links to the causal chain." The youngster is unable to perceive how his or her actions culminated in a classroom disturbance. This lack of recall should not be confused with lying to avoid punishment. Rather the deficiency rests in the inability to perceive personal feelings or behavior clear enough to review a series of events.

2. *Learning from Experience.* Students should be able to apply past experiences to present situations. Learning from past mistakes is a basic strategy for solving social problems. Natural consequences play a significant role in social maturity and development. Children learn to modify their behavior based on reactions from peers: teasing is returned in kind; selfishness keeps others away. Students with behavior or emotional problems may persist in the same social errors regardless of the consequences. Even positive social experiences provide few clues for future behaviors. These students seem unable to learn from their experiences in order to piece together the behavioral steps needed to work out social problems to their advantage.

3. *Drawing Inference from Others' Experiences.* Some students learn and profit from other students' mistakes or successes. This modeling is a basic style of learning for young people. Adults count on the fact that one youngster may be an example to others. This is the premise behind severe punishment (e.g., expulsions), and it is a premise behind awards and honors. Many youngsters do in fact learn from others and use the experience so gained to guide future actions. A student who cannot learn from the mistakes and successes of others is handicapped by shortsightedness. Adults cringe when they hear a youngster say, "It can't happen to me." The ever increasing numbers of pregnant teenagers and drug dependent youngsters are stern reminders that a key social problem-solving skill is drawing inference from what happens to others.

4. *Resolving Conflicts.* You don't change a lightbulb with a hammer, and you don't solve social problems with aggressive behavior. Many youngsters need to learn conflict resolution, negotiation, and cooperation as social tools. The need for students to be able to appraise social situations and develop peaceful strategies for solving problems has never been greater. Racism and teen violence are commonplace in today's society. Every classroom discipline system should help provide students with the human relations tools needed for functioning as a productive member of a democratic society.

Selecting a Social Skills Curriculum.

Teachers who practice preventive discipline realize that youngsters need to be taught skills that enhance social adaptability. The Redl and Wineman model identifies specific self-control skills that students need in order to function as mature and responsible members of a classroom community. A sound social skills curriculum is research-based. It is derived from a theory or model of human development. It substitutes adaptive skills for nonconstructive behavior both in and out of school. A social curriculum begins with general goals and then delineates observable student behaviors matched to goal statements. Specific objectives provide a basis for evaluation of student growth and program accountability. See Table 10.2 for a list of some frequently used social skill programs.

All social curricula emphasize one key point—scheduling time to teach social skills is a legitimate educational activity. If students are going to change their behavior, they require opportunities to learn new behaviors in an organized and relevant manner. Wood states, "A (social skills) program must have relevance to the student's world beyond the special classroom, and the skills learned in the program must produce satisfying results in personal, real life situations" (Wood, 1986, 12).

TABLE 10.2   Social Skill Programs

Teaching Self-Control: A Curriculum for Responsible Behavior, 1997 by Henley, National Educational Service.

Curriculum Strategies: Social Skills Interventions for Young African-American Males, 1997 by Taylor, Praeger Publications.

The Equip Program: Teaching Youth to Think and Act Responsibly Through a Peer-Helping Approach, 1995 by Gibbs, Potter and Glodstein, Research Press.

Getting Along with Others: Teaching Social Effectiveness to Children: Skill Lessons and Activities, 1983 by Jackson, Jackson and Monroe, Research Press.

Tribes, A New Way of Learning and Being Together, 1995 by Gibbs, Center Source Publications.

Second Step: A Violence Prevention Cirriculum, Grades 1–3, 1992 by the Committee for Children, Seattle Washington.

Skillstreaming the Elementary School Child: A Guide for Teaching Pro Social Skills, 1984 by McGinnis and Goldstein, Research Press.

Social Skills Activities for Special Children, 1993 by Mannix, Prentice-Hall Trade Books.

Back Off, Cool Down, Try Again: Teaching Students How to Control Agressive Behavior, 1995 by Rockwell, Council for Exceptional Children.

Improving Social Competence: A Resource for Elementary School Teachers, 1994 by Campbell and Siperstein, Allyn and Bacon.

Schumaker et al. (1983) pose five questions to serve as a guide in selecting a social skills curriculum:

1. Does the curriculum promote social competence?
2. Does the curriculum accommodate the learning characteristics of the students for whom it is to be applied?
3. Does the curriculum target the social skills deficits of the students for whom it is to be applied?
4. Does the curriculum provide training in situations as well as skills?
5. Does the curriculum include instructional methodologies found to be effective with the population of students for whom it is to be applied? (cited in Walker & Shea, 1991)

Social skills can be taught directly or indirectly. Direct instruction begins with the identification of a specific skill—for example, the social problem-solving skill of learning from experience. For a lesson, a teacher could select a contemporary problem—how to increase drug awareness among schoolchildren. The class is divided into small groups comprised of four students. Each group is given art materials, reference materials, and recent newspaper articles. The students must brainstorm five ways of increasing drug awareness and present their findings to the entire class.

Social skills also can be taught indirectly. Peer tutoring, cooperative learning, classroom discussions, and role playing are just a sampling of ways to teach academic topics while cultivating social abilities. Peer tutoring can be useful for any academic subject. Cooperative learning could produce a single-act play. Classroom discussions could highlight the role of different cultures in American history. Role playing such protagonists as Thomas Henry Huxley and Bishop Wilberforce of Oxford in their famous confrontation about evolution could help students gain insight into how discourse shapes science.

Educators are coming to the realization that intervening to eliminate disruptive behavior is not enough. Teaching social skills is a legitimate use of classroom time. Students can learn no more valuable skill than how to get along with others. Values clarification, character education, and social skills curriculums help students to cope with life both in and out of school.

A Problem-Solving Model

Teachers in general and special education classrooms are confronted with a variety of behavior problems. Some students, often those with more intense emotional or behavioral problems, require an organized intervention plan. Dealing with chronic disruptive behaviors requires a systematic problem-solving method. The following procedure is a model for responding to persistent classroom disturbances.

1. *Describe Student Behavior.* Disturbing behavior should be described, not evaluated. Avoid clinical-sounding terms that interpret behavior. Rather than saying that a student is "distractible," describe his behavior; for example, "Steven typically sits still for about five minutes, then he starts sliding books around on his desk, dropping pencils, and talking to other students." Common evaluative comments to be avoided are: hyperactive, immature, aggressive, noncompliant, attention-seeker, and withdrawn. Evaluative terms are too abstract to clearly communicate a problem. A behavior that is "aggressive" to one teacher may be "assertive" to another teacher and "immature" to a third teacher.

Description enhances communication among teacher, parents, and student. It ensures that everybody is talking about the same behavior, and it prevents the misunderstandings that arise when behavior is labeled. Moreover, descriptions of behavior can be counted. Interpretations cannot. You cannot observe "hyperactivity," but you can see and count how many times a youngster gets up from his desk.

2. *Count Behavior.* Educators use a tool called a behavior frequency chart to count behavior (Figure 10.2). Disturbing behaviors are listed next to a series of boxes for each day of the week. Each time a student demonstrates a disturbing behavior, the time is written in the appropriate box. This checklist can be located on the teacher's desk or some other convenient spot in the classroom.

The purpose of the behavior frequency chart is to provide a data base for determining the severity of a classroom problem. The more frequent the disturbing behavior, the more likely it is a disturbance in the classroom. The chart gives the teacher an objective way of calculating frequency of the behavior. The data can provide other important information. Perhaps many of the disruptions occur during a specific time of the day; this could provide some insight into cause. Knowing when a disturbing behavior occurs helps the teacher determine antecedents. For example, the student might be most disturbing after transitions from preferred to nonpreferred activities. Finally, no program can be properly evaluated without initial baseline data. In a few months, do another count to determine whether the intervention program is working.

3. *Empathize with the Student.* All behavior occurs for a reason. Put yourself in the student's shoes. What does he or she feel? A life space intervention would be helpful at this juncture to elicit the student's perspective.

Consider physiological causes first. Is the student getting enough sleep? How about diet? The average American teenager eats a 120 pounds of refined sugar a year. What is your student eating? Is lead poisoning a possiblity? When was the last time the student's vision and hearing were checked? Some attention problems are traced to hearing impairments.

What about the student's family? Are there problems at home? Does the student have a home? For that matter does the student have a family? Don't forget drug and alcohol abuse. Does the student come to school with frequent bruises? Emotional neglect is more difficult to determine than physical abuse, but no less important. Talking to students provides useful information about his or her family and life after school.

Empathizing means trying to understand the problem from the student's point of view. Disturbing behavior in class, if it's serious enough to require a specific plan, will show up outside of school too. Enlist the aid of family members. Empathy alone will not solve the problem, but it will change your perspective. Judgments of the student change from a classroom nuisance, to a real person with a complicated life. Empathizing helps the teacher to depersonalize the classroom disruptions. Approaching the issue with professional detachment ensures that an intervention plan is professionally prepared, without anger or resentment.

4. *A Twofold Plan: Interventions and Teaching Social Skills.* After describing, charting, and counting the disturbing behavior, the next step is to determine the best intervention to curb the disturbing behavior, and to identify a prosocial skill to replace the disturbing behavior.

Remember Teresa? When we left her at the beginning of this chapter, she was ready to begin her first week of teaching. Teresa has completed a behavior frequency chart on a female student, Sylvia (see Figure 10.2). Sylvia is 12 years old. She is verbal, bright, and impulsive. Sylvia's quick tongue is matched by her fast mood changes. Teresa has counted Sylvia's verbal taunts and sarcastic remarks. They are usually directed at Teresa; and when Sylvia launches these verbal missiles, everything in the classroom stops. Watching Teresa and Sylvia match wits has become a great source of entertainment for the rest of the class.

Through her charting, Teresa sees that Sylvia starts her day out well, then, around 10:00 A.M., she warms to her task of harassing the teacher. By lunch time, Sylvia has made on average five unprovoked and disturbing remarks aimed at Teresa and other students. Sylvia also moves about the room without permission. Empathizing with Sylvia, Teresa considered the possibility that Sylvia might resent her; but why? A conversation in the teacher's lounge with some of the faculty reveals that Sylvia formed a close attachment to Ms. Collins, her fifth grade teacher. Sylvia asked Ms. Collins to fail her so she could spend another year with her.

Teresa decided to adopt a couple of interventions. First, she would restructure Sylvia's morning. Teresa worked out an arrangement for Sylvia to do peer tutoring each morning in a third grade classroom from 9:45 to 10:15. Sylvia had no problem with academics, and she had a sensitive side that Teresa hoped could be capitalized on to nurture younger children. Second, Teresa determined to bolster her relationship with Sylvia through hypodermic affection and sane messages. She wanted Sylvia to learn that she was a valued classroom member, but

Student: __Sylvia__   Week: __September 7 - 14__

Describe Behaviors	Mon.	Tue.	Wed.	Thu.	Fri.
Verbal taunts directed at teacher	10:00 10:07 10:08 11:15 1:05	9:45 12:57 2:10 2:19	10:12 10:13 10:23 2:19	11:45 11:47 2:29	10:28 10:51 11:12 11:13 11:17
Verbal taunts directed at other students	9:13 12:19 12:20	None	None	11:46 11:51 11:58	None
Moving around the room without permission	10:01 10:08 11:17	2:11 2:21	None	11:45 11:47	10:27 10:53

Comments:

FIGURE 10.2 Behavior Frequency Chart

at the same time Teresa knew it was important for Sylvia to understand the effect of her taunts.

Teresa decided to direct her social skills activities toward helping Sylvia assess social reality. Sylvia needed help specifically in evaluating the effect of her behavior on others. The more she thought about it, the more Teresa realized that the other students could learn about how their behavior affects people. Teresa determined to develop a unit for the entire class. She would do values clarification, role playing, cooperative learning activities, and more peer tutoring.

5. *Evaluate the Plan.* How many times do teachers settle on a system for changing student behavior without ever evaluating the plan? In our experience this happens far too often. W. H. Auden had this to say about changing human behavior,

> *We would rather be ruined than changed*
> *We would rather live in our dread*
> *Than climb the cross of the moment,*
> *And let our illusions die. (Seldes, 1985, 23)*

Changing behavior is a difficult enterprise. A behavior change plan that is elegant on paper can mislead a teacher into overlooking periodic evaluations. Every behavior intervention plan should be evaluated on a regular basis. Three months is a reasonable amount of time to look for some change. Another evaluation requires another behavior frequency count. If there is no decrease in disturbing behaviors, a new plan may be needed. Go back and review the steps outlined in this chapter. Did you miss anything in terms of empathizing with the student? Did you, for instance, fail to talk with family members? Perhaps you need to try some different interventions. If the problem is more serious you might consider life space interventions.

If you are seeing a change in behavior, you hit the mark on your first try. That is a good start. Success in working with a youngster to learn socially adept skills is well worth the effort. Twenty years from now, your students may have forgotten how to multiply mixed numbers; but if they can listen to another person's point of view, you will have left them a valuable legacy.

Summary

Students with behavior problems are handicapped by their lack of social skills. Often these youngsters have been identified by the school system as having a mild disability, sometimes the student is viewed simply as a chronic discipline problem. Regardless of the label, disruptive classroom behavior has a profound negative effect on both teacher and students. Social skills instruction is an educational strategy for helping students with persistent behavior problems learn more appropriate ways of interacting with others both in and out of school.

The notion of teaching social skills has a long history in American education. Character education and values clarification are two social skills approaches that have been utilized in classrooms for many years in the attempt to shape student attitudes and behavior. When applied to students with behavior problems, social skills instruction is often combined with behavior interventions. The application of a problem-solving approach in order to select specific social skills and behavior interventions helps teachers respond to persistent classroom disturbances in a systematic fashion.

Activities

1. Recall your favorite class in elementary or high school. What social skills did your teacher expect you to demonstrate? Did you meet those expectations? What social skills did you develop outside the classroom?

2. In a cooperative learning group, brainstorm ten social skills you think students should learn. Give a rationale for each. Present the results to the class. Discuss similarities and differences in perspective.

3. Have a classroom debate on the question: Is social skill instruction a legitimate part of the curriculum?

4. Research old public school textbooks—history, reading, and health would be good choices. Look for values that were highlighted in these texts (e.g., typical American family had mother taking care of children and father working, while Spot just romped around).

5. Review the Redl & Wineman social skills list. Select three skills and develop a lesson plan for each.

11 Building Family Partnerships

Advance Organizer

When you complete this chapter, you will be able to answer the folowing questions:

1. How do social and economic conditions effect the quality of life of children in the United States?
2. What are some barriers to family-school communication?

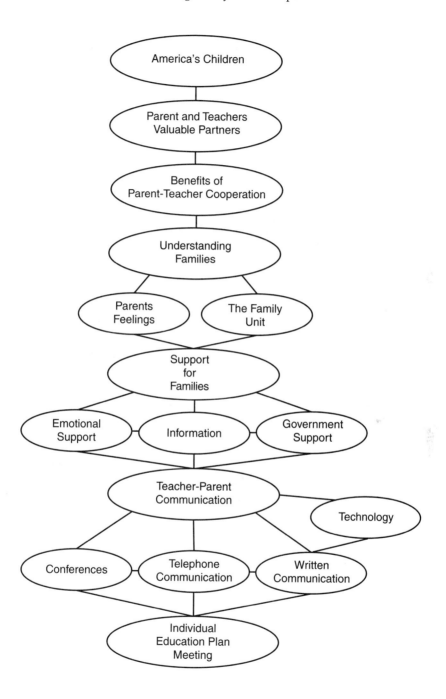

3. What are some ways that schools have overcome communication barriers that impede parental participation in their youngsters schooling?
4. What is the emotional impact on family members of having a youngster with a mild disability?
5. What are some ways that parents can gain more information about their role in their youngsters schooling?
6. How do government funded programs enhance opportunities for youth?
7. What are some due process rights of parents when a youngster is placed in a special education program?

Vignette: Eileen

Eileen slowly climbed the steps of the run-down, two-family house. She felt apprehensive in this poor neighborhood where every house seemed to need a new coat of paint. As she reached for the doorbell, Eileen reviewed why she was here.

Her student, Alexis, a pretty twelve-year-old, seemed to be compensating for her weak academic skills by playing the role of class clown. Every time Eileen gave an assignment, Alexis had a comment. "You never showed us how to do this," or "This is stupid, why do we have to do it?" were typical of the disturbing remarks Alexis directed at Eileen on a regular basis.

Perhaps this home visit would help. After a moment's hesitation, Eileen knocked on the front door. Within a few seconds the door swung open. Alexis stood in the doorway. She was dressed in her best Sunday dress. "Hi, Mrs. Morrison; my mother is in the living room." Alexis led Eileen into a sunny room with blue muslin curtains. Standing with teapot in hand was Alexis's mother. "I'm Mrs. Taylor; I'm pleased you could visit us; Alexis tells me so many wonderful things about you." Eileen glanced at Alexis whose face had suddenly turned three shades brighter. "Please sit down and have some tea," invited Mrs. Taylor. She turned to Alexis, and said, "Go into the kitchen and get some oatmeal cookies for your teacher." "Yes, momma," was the quick reply, and Alexis breezed into the other room. Eileen watched in astonishment. "Is this the same child who has been carrying out a single-handed verbal assault on me in class?" she wondered.

Mrs. Taylor smiled, "It's been difficult for Alexis ever since her daddy died, but she tries hard and she's a good girl." "I'm sorry, Mrs. Taylor. I didn't realize your husband had passed away," responded Eileen. Mrs. Taylor's smile slowly melted away. "Alexis needs help with her schoolwork, I know; but trying to raise her and her younger brother and sister on my waitress salary has been difficult for all of us," said Mrs. Taylor. "Tell me, what can I do at home to help Alexis with her reading? I didn't get past eighth grade, and I want Alexis to earn her high school diploma," continued Mrs. Taylor. Eileen sat down and the two women spent the next hour discussing how together they could help Alexis improve her schoolwork.

As Eileen drove home, she reviewed her home visit. Alexis comes home from school and makes dinner for her seven-year-old brother and nine-year-old sister. Her mother is trying to raise three children on a waitress' salary. They can't afford a car. And most surprising of all, Alexis is not the disruptive child at home that she appears to be in the classroom. Eileen smiled to herself. She knew that her classroom strategy for handling Alexis would change. The insights she gained from this visit would help her to better manage Alexis's attention-seeking behavior in school. As she drove toward her condominium in the suburbs, Eileen vowed to make more home visits. An hour in a student's home, she realized, could eliminate countless hours of misunderstanding in school.

After reading the above vignette answer the following questions.

1. Do you think Eileen's apprehension about visiting homes in a low income neighborhood is shared by other teachers?
2. Why don't more teachers visit with their students families?
3. Do you think school systems should require home visits?
4. What are some reasons for making home visits? What are some reasons for not making home visits?

Eileen's home visit highlights a little-appreciated fact—students' lives do not begin and end at the schoolhouse door. From kindergarten to senior year in high school, students spend only one-eighth of their time in school. Student experiences outside school have a profound influence on student behavior in the classroom. If a student is having difficulty in school, a home visit can provide a teacher with useful insights into how to handle the problem. In today's public schools there are many communication gaps between students and teachers. Language, cultural, and ethnic differences lead to misunderstandings. Communication is a vital link to bridge this gap. Families are the best source of information about a student's likes and dislikes, emotional peaks and valleys, motivation, and activities outside of school.

America's Children—A Threatened Species

Children, James Coleman noted, require "social capital" in order to grow, learn, and prosper. Social capital refers to the social networks and adult relationships that nurture children during their development. Coleman found, for instance, a lower dropout rate among students in Catholic schools (3.4 percent) than among students in public schools (14.3 percent). He explained the discrepancy in terms of social capital in the Catholic schools. The community of school and church helped families keep students in school. Because of the additional adult support outside the family the students attending Catholic schools had a strong incentive to stay in school. Coleman highlighted the bonding together of adults through shared goals and beliefs as a primary source of social capital.

Social capital has steadily eroded since the turn of the century. In early-twentieth-century agricultural society, children were mentored by extended families, neighbors, and community members. Informal relationships between adults outside the family were commonplace. The transformation to an industrial society disconnected children from the lives of adults. Fathers returned home from factories tired from hours of mindnumbing toil on assembly lines. Soon mothers followed fathers into the workplace. The family unit as a source of social capital began to unravel as the pressure to maintain a decent standard of living increased each year. With more time spent in work, adults had less time to spend in community activities such as parent–teacher organizations (PTOs) and Scouting (Coleman, 1987). The overall effect has been an alienation of children from basic nurturing elements in society that were common throughout history.

The U.S. Census Bureau reported that in 1995, twenty percent of children under 18 lived in poverty. From 1979 to 1994 the number of children living in poverty increased from 3.5 million to 6 million. Infant mortality for children born into poverty is more than 50 percent higher than for children above the poverty line (i.e., $16,050.00, 1997 annual income for a family of four living in the 48 contiguous states). African American children have almost twice the infant mortality rate of white children—16.5 deaths per 1,000 live births compared to 6.8 deaths per 1,000 live births. Poverty is the single most crucial factor in determining quality of life for children. Tragically, government assistance for poor children in the United States falls far behind that provided by other countries. (See Table

TABLE 11.1   Child Poverty in 17 Developed Countries Before and After Goverment Assistance

Country	Year	Before Assistance	After Assistance	Percent of Children Lifted Out of Poverty by Government Assistance
United States	1991	26%	22%	17%
Austrailia	1989	20%	14%	29%
Canada	1991	23%	14%	40%
Ireland	1987	30%	12%	60%
Isreal	1986	24%	11%	54%
United Kingdom	1991	30%	10%	67%
Italy	1991	12%	10%	17%
Germany	1989	9%	7%	24%
France	1984	25%	7%	74%
Netherlands	1991	14%	6%	55%
Norway	1991	13%	5%	64%
Luxemburg	1985	12%	4%	77%
Belgium	1992	16%	4%	77%
Denmark	1992	16%	4%	77%
Switzerland	1982	5%	3%	35%
Sweden	1992	19%	3%	86%
Finland	1991	12%	3%	78%

Source: Rainwater, Lee, and Timothy M. Smeeding, 1995, "Doing Poorly: The Real Income of American Children in a Comparative Perspective," Working Paper No. 127, Luxemborg Income Study, Maxwell School of Citizenship and Public Affairs, Syracuse University, Syracuse, New York.,

11.1 for a comparison of the United States and other countries' poverty rate before and after government assistance.) (U.S. Bureau of the Census, 1995.)

A University of Maryland School of Medicine study reported that of 168 teenagers who visited an inner-city clinic for routine medical care, 24 percent had witnessed a murder and 72 percent knew someone who had been shot. One of every ten girls who visited the Baltimore clinic had been raped (Zinmeister, 1990). The violence children are exposed to is impulsive and random. Children have killed other children for sneakers, college jackets, and professional ball team hats (Telander, 1990).

Most parents care deeply about their children. A few parents are indifferent and, unfortunately, a small minority of parents actually harm their children. Neglect and abuse are a sad reality in some homes. The Children's Defense Fund estimated in 1997 that every 47 seconds, a child is abused or neglected—a total of 675,000 a year. Table 11.2 lists the daily state of affairs for children of the United States.

Early medical and educational intervention for youth should be a national priority. As a society, we are at risk of squandering our most precious national resource—our children. Without a major shift in our national priorities, many youngsters will mature without hope for success in life. Drugs, crime, violence, and despair will be their legacy to future generations.

Parents and Teachers: Valuable Partners

Home visits, teacher–parent meetings, and school socials were once common aspects of life in the United States. James Comer's memories of his neighborhood recall a time when the authority of parents was transferred to teachers through proximity.

> When I went into the grocery store with my mother and father in the 1940s, it was a rare day that we did not encounter someone from my elementary school— the custodian, the principal, the secretary, or a teacher. There would always be an exchange of pleasantries and sometimes an exchange about my school behavior or achievement. The knowledge that my parents knew and appeared to like and respect the people at my school had a profound impact on my behavior. (Comer, 1986, 442)

During the era of the neighborhood school, indirect involvement of parents in school activity was underscored at each chance meeting of teachers and parents at the grocery store, bus stop, park, or library. Trust and mutual respect between school and home was a by-product of close-knit communities. The separation of school and community began in the 1960s with the advent of racial integration through busing. The process of neighborhood-school detachment continued in the 1970s with the middle-class exodus to the suburbs and subsequent region-alization of small town schools. Today, separation of school and family is a

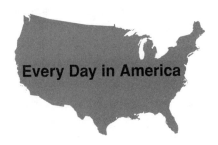

TABLE 11.2   Every Day in America

For all U.S. children

Every Day in America

1 mother dies in childbirth

3 people under 25 die from HIV

6 children and youths commit suicide

13 children and youths are murdered

16 children and youths are killed by firearms

36 children and youths die from accidents

81 babies die

144 babies are born at very low birthweight

311 children are arrested for alcohol offenses

316 children are arrested for violent crimes

403 children are arrested for drug offenses

443 babies are born to mothers who received late or no prenatal care

781 babies are born at low birthweight

1,403 babies are born to mothers younger than 20

2,377 babies are born to mothers who are not high school graduates

2,556 babies are born into poverty

2,658 public school students are corporally punished

3,356 high school students drop out*

3,436 babies are born to unmarried mothers

5,500 high school graduates do not go on to college*

5,702 children are arrested

10,684 babies are born

17,152 public school students are suspended*

(Most recent available data as of July 10, 1997)
*Every school day

Source: Children's Defense Fund

pervasive condition in United States education. Sometimes the only time a parent has direct contact with the school is when there is a problem. While such measures as school open houses provide some assurance that teachers and parents get an opportunity for personal meetings, these are usually large group activities that preclude personal conversation between parents and teacher.

A common teacher complaint when parents are missing conferences or open houses is that parents "don't care." There are many explanations for parents not attending school functions. Their own education may have left them with negative feelings about school. Perhaps the parent is illiterate or a school dropout. Parents may not have a phone or transportation. There may be a language barrier or a communication problem (the message doesn't reach the parent). A parent might miss a meeting or school function due to an inability to obtain child care. When schools provide child care, parental attendance increases. Parents may be working when meetings are held. Many IEP meetings, for example, are held during the day without regard for parental work schedules.

In most instances, it is the teacher who makes the initial contact to arrange a meeting. Teachers need adequate administrative support to organize and follow through on parent–teacher contacts. They need time during the school day to make arrangements, and they need adequate space to hold meetings. Teachers need access to a telephone. Providing preparation time for teachers is the best way a principal can enhance parent–teacher communication. Attempts to improve parent–teacher contacts sometimes meet resistance. When teachers in Rochester, New York, were required to make home visits as part of a nationally proclaimed reform model that included higher wages, some reneged on their commitment, claiming they did not have the necessary "social worker skills." In some school systems, it is a violation of the union–management contract for teachers to make home visits!

The isolation of school and family continues at the same time that schools and teachers are being asked to take on responsibilities that used to be the sole domain of the family. Fear of AIDS, teenage pregnancies, and drug abuse have reordered curriculum priorities. Sex and drug education have become major concerns in schools. In many urban and suburban school districts, Johnny can't read because he's too "high" to care. When schools find ways to work with parents on problems of youth, the results are impressive.

Benefits of Parent–Teacher Cooperation

The National Committee for Citizens in Education (NCCE) found that when teachers maintain frequent contact with parents, students profit. Parent–teacher partnerships produce measurable gains in student achievement. "Some of the major benefits of parent involvement include higher grades and test scores, better long-term academic achievement, positive attitudes and behavior, more successful programs, and more effective schools" (Henderson, 1987, 149). The greater the degree of parental involvement, the greater the likelihood that students will succeed in school. In a review of 53 studies that measured the impact of parent–teacher partnerships, the NCCE did not find a single negative report. The evidence also indicated that students who were at risk for educational failure gained the most from parent–teacher collaboration.

At-risk students include the disadvantaged, the students with mild disabilities, and underachievers. These students are frequently absent from school. Some are behavior problems. Almost all lack the motivation to persevere. By age 16, the at-risk student is a prime dropout candidate. Research on students at-risk indicated that "by the time students are in the third grade we can fairly reliably predict which students will drop out and which will complete their schooling" (Slavin, 1989b, 5). The early onset of school failure underscores the need for close school–family partnerships at the beginning of formal schooling. Successful preschool programs, such as Head Start, place a premium on parent involvement. Disadvantaged students who participate in preschool programs with strong parent involvement components outperform their peers through high school. Despite the documented benefits of parent participation in preschools, the carryover of parent participation into general education is at best uneven. Some educators believe the best place for parents is at a bake sale or car wash. Williams (1988) reported that principals and teachers preferred that parent involvement be limited to extracurricular activities. The educators in Williams's study did not view parent involvement in educational decisions as either useful or appropriate.

Leitch and Tangri (1988) investigated barriers to school–family partnerships in two poor, inner-city, Washington, D.C., junior high schools. Twenty-nine teachers and sixty families participated in the study. The researchers found that a parent from a single-family household was less likely to be involved than one from a two-parent household. The larger the family (six members or more), the more likely the involvement. Extended families, both single- and two-parent, were the most involved. Members of foster families were highly involved. Employment made it difficult for almost half the parents to get to school functions. Among the unemployed, poor health was the most frequent reason for lack of participation. Education did not seem to be a factor; parents who finished and those who did not finish high school were involved on an equal basis.

From the teachers' perspective, their own family responsibilities were factors that impeded setting aside time for parents. Teachers who enjoyed their work tended to value parent involvement more than teachers who were unhappy or disgruntled. Almost half the teachers surveyed blamed parents. Some parental attributes listed by discontented teachers were: unrealistic expectations about the school's role; parental jealousy of teacher's upward mobility; poor parental attitudes about school; large families (although the data showed large families participated more frequently); and lack of parental skills to help with schoolwork. Other teachers listed the following school barriers to parental involvement: absence of school activities; teachers' suspicions of parents; and teacher apathy. All the teachers recognized that changes in society had diminished the parental role. They felt that the schools needed to change to meet the changing social fabric of families and the community.

Leitch and Tangri (1988) reported that parents believed teachers looked down on them. "One parent said that teachers have the attitude, 'I got mine, and you got yours to get'" (Leitch and Tangri, 74). Parents characterized school attempts to get them involved as meager. Parent–teacher organization meetings were the most commonly reported school invitation, although many parents said they never received such notices. The same small group of parents seemed to control most parental activities. Despite the negative attitudes attributed to both teachers and parents, Leitch and Tangri summarized their report by stating that a lack of specific planning about how to organize and utilize parent resources was the major barrier to school–home collaboration.

When administrators and teachers make a commitment to parent involvement, results have followed. In many schools, parents volunteer in classrooms. They sponsor orientation programs, conduct alcohol education classes, welcome new families, arrange for guest speakers, provide library assistance, and much more. The principal is the catalyst in these ventures. The principal allocates resources, persists in parent recruiting efforts, and establishes a school-wide norm that parents are welcome. In order for parent–school partnerships to flourish, parents need to make decisions about school policies. Treating parents as teacher aides and doling out menial tasks works against collaboration. It's not how much time parents spend in school that counts, it's the responsibilities they assume (Sandford, 1987). A well-planned and comprehensive parent–school partnership can have a positive impact on both individual students and the school (Henderson, 1987).

In 1968, the School Development Program initiated a pilot program to promote parent participation in the New Haven schools. The first project school initially ranked thirty-second out of thirty-three city public schools on standardized achievement scores. Fourth grade students were nineteen months below grade level in reading and eighteen months below grade level in mathematics. Behavior problems were rampant. The school climate was permeated with a sense of despair. Staff rivaled students in absences. Working with the principal, a group of parents and teachers developed a master plan for school improvement. They formed a School Advisory Committee. The group set goals for academics, staff development, and school spirit.

Parents were soon involved in almost every aspect of educational programming. They worked in classrooms as teacher aides. Parents tutored students in "therapeutic activity groups" that integrated academics with the arts and social skills. A revised social calendar lured parents to school functions. Activities included a Welcome Back to School dinner for orientation and recruitment of new parents. A February "blues" party boosted school spirit. A parent involvement handbook informed mothers and fathers about opportunities for participation in school activities. The handbook outlined parental roles and responsibilities. Each year, new parents were recruited to ensure that participation would continue after students graduated. Attendance at school functions increased from twenty to four hundred parents. By 1984, the School Development

Program had: raised student achievement scores seven months above grade level; increased student attendance to number one in the city four out of five years; eliminated many discipline problems. The results of the School Development Program project bear testimony to the benefits of school–parent cooperation.

James Comer continued his work with approximately 100 urban schools throughout the country. His goal was to create school management teams comprising parents, teachers, and mental health professionals. These schools enhance teachers' knowledge of their students, draw parents into the educational process, especially governance and management, and combine school and community services (Reed & Sauter, 1990). In 1991, The School Development Program merged with the school of the 21st century to form CoZi, a family support model that enhances families' efforts to participate in their children's schooling (Comer, Zigler, and Stern, 1997). Other such programs throughout the country bear witness to the ability of teachers and parents to work together to improve schools.

In San Francisco and Redwood City, California, Henry Levine's accelerated schools model established specific achievement goals for all elementary-school children. Parents as educational decision makers is a key component in this program. Joyce Epstein developed other parent involvement models, which emphasize reciprocal relationships—the parents within the school and the school within the community. Parent involvement projects share the following values: no child is labeled a potential failure because of social or economic factors; social and physical development of children is as important as academic and cognitive gains; children's development is a shared obligation of school, family, and community. These principles are exemplified in the work of the League of Schools Reaching Out, a confederation of forty-one urban schools that span thirteen states and Puerto Rico (Davies, 1991).

The League takes an enlarged view on the meaning of parent involvement. The term "parent" is broadened to "family," which may include grandparents, uncles, aunts, and other significant adults in a youngster's life. The League advocates coordinating with social agencies that provide assistance and support to families—for example, agencies that administer housing, mental health, and public health services. Hard-to-reach families are targeted. Included in this group are the non-English-speaking, the unemployed, and the indigent. League members recognize that the families that are least responsive are precisely the ones that most need to get involved with educational affairs. The League of Schools Reaching Out is attempting to revitalize Coleman's concept of social capital by abandoning the deficiency view of urban life and identifying strengths in families. Cultural diversity is prized and families are encouraged to establish their own priorities for school–community partnerships (Davies, 1991).

Just as Eileen's home visit deepened her insight into Alexis and her school behavior, educators throughout the country are learning that families are a teacher's best source of information about students. Families can provide information on developmental, social, and academic problems. Student attitudes toward school are shaped in the home. When families value the educational process, students succeed. If teacher and family are at odds, students are left without direction. But when teachers and families cooperate, they are able to help a student focus on productive goals. Each year teachers begin anew the hope of helping their students grow and learn. Building parental partnerships has proved to be one of the most effective means of turning this hope into reality.

The greater the risk of school failure, the more crucial the need for family involvement. When a student has a learning, behavior, or emotional problem, the need for family–teacher cooperation intensifies. An appropriate education for students with mild disabilities is based upon school–family cooperation. According to federal and state laws, parents must participate in decisions regarding their youngster's special education services, educational placement, and individual education plan. This built-in mechanism for teacher–parent collaboration does not guarantee successful outcomes. Success or failure depends on trust, mutual respect, and cooperation.

Understanding Families

Cooperation begins with understanding. How does it feel to have a child identified as disabled? What is the impact of a child with special needs on the family? What type of support is available to parents of students with mild disabilities? Parenting is complex and difficult. Parents of children with disabilities must deal with all the tensions and pressures familiar to other families, plus the extra stress of raising a child with special needs.

Parent Feelings

Few children with mild disabilities are identified as requiring special services until they enter school and begin to encounter academic or discipline problems. Suddenly, parents are faced with an array of demands as they attempt to cope with the burden imposed by their child's inability to fit into the normal routine of school life. Excerpts from Connie and Ralph Floord's (1989) diary help to convey the feelings experienced by parents whose child became a school "problem."

> September, 1985. David began school today. The house seemed so quiet when the three left. David was so happy when he got home. Bubbling away about how much fun it is to ride the bus, and have "lots of kids to play with."
>
> October, 1985. David's teacher told us that David has no self control. He has been having a lot of trouble getting along with the kids in his class. We spoke to him, but he says it is all the other kids' fault.
>
> May, 1986. The complaints about David in school never stop. His teacher says she doesn't know what to do with him. Maybe adjustment to school was just difficult. Maybe first grade will be better.

January, 1988. The school called work today and left a message with the switchboard that they need to set up a conference about David's problem behavior. This is just great. Now people at work also know that something is wrong.

November, 1988. We just came from talking with the [school] psychologist. He thinks David would be better off if we let him enter a special class. David seems smarter than that, but something has to change. He will be starting in the next few weeks, if some [school] committee says that's what should be done.

December, 1988. The meeting of the Committee on Special Education was like the Inquisition. We got there and had to face seven school people. It seemed like they wanted to know everything. The meeting better be confidential and we hope we don't have to go through that again. David is going to the special class in a couple of days. We hope this is the answer, but what does emotionally disturbed mean? What did we do wrong? How can we tell the family about this?

When dealing with "experts," parents often report feeling overwhelmed with the trappings of authority. Betty Lou Kratoville's description of her meeting with a counselor provides a glimpse into the inner world of one parent's feelings during a meeting with a counselor.

As a parent, my attitude toward all the professional men and women I went to in search of diagnosis and remediation for Matthew was one of absolute humility. In retrospect, my reverence may have, at times, been misplaced. I neglected to remember that counselors are, first and foremost, human beings. That they too laugh and cry and make mistakes and that they are not, really, larger than life. At the time they somehow seemed invincible, ten feet tall, with desks the size of battleships, their offices guarded by iron-spined sentinels who always seemed to be popping in with terse announcements, "Your next appointment is waiting." I, lily livered and abject, would slink from the office, reeling under the impact of cool professionalism and a hundred unanswered questions. (Buscaglia, 1975, 133)

Guilt, denial, anger, and despair are frequently mentioned in professional literature as parental reactions to a child with a disability. The extent to which a parent will experience these feelings is contingent on many factors, including finances, the severity of the disability, the age of the child, availability of child care, and support from family and professionals.

Miller (1968) reported that parents of students with special needs go through a cycle of disintegration, adjustment, and reintegration. The first stage, after the child is diagnosed as having a disability, is characterized by shock, grief, and guilt. In the second stage, parents alternatively accept and deny their child's disability. Finally, parents begin to accommodate to their child's special needs by supporting each other and dealing with issues as they arise. This best-case scenario depends on the family's, particularly the father's and mother's, ability to adapt to the stress of managing life when a child has a disability.

Ferguson and Ferguson (1987) stated that guilt has been overemphasized by professionals who studied parental feelings. They said that such interpretations as parental "guilt reaction" can lead professionals to conflicting conclusions. Solnit and Stark (1961), for example, viewed parent activism as a method for coping with guilt, while MacKeith (1973) reported that parental guilt led to apathy and depression. Analyzing parents' behavior in terms of guilt reactions is based on psychodynamic investigations of the "typical" parent of a child with a disability. Although there is some benefit derived from research that seeks to understand and explain parental reactions to a child's disability, the "typical" parent exists only in normative studies, not in reality. Terms like "typical" and "average" are artifacts of quantitative studies that provide a teacher with limited information about the parent sitting with her at a meeting.

Parents need to be treated as individuals. Each parent has a unique view of his or her child's disability. In order to work effectively, educators need to understand the parent's perspective. This is difficult to do if the parent is pitied or patronized. Trust and respect are essential for communication between parent and teacher. Federal law has made parents key decision makers in determining the type of educational services that will best suit their youngster.

The Family Unit

The universal role of the family is to nurture the young child. Within the family milieu, the child learns the social and intellectual competencies needed to succeed in society. When a family has a child with a special need, all family members are affected. Mother, father, and siblings must learn to cope with the unique stress of living with their child. A child with a disability imposes demands that strain the family's ability to function. Families must cope with several critical periods in the life of a child with a disability (Gloecker & Simpson, 1988):

1. Birth, when parents, usually of children with moderate to severe disabilities, first realize their child is disabled.
2. When the disability is first diagnosed and treatment begins. For parents of children with mild disabilities, this is usually the beginning school years.
3. When the child is placed in a special education program. Placement in segregated special class, pull-out program, or mainstreamed regular classroom can influence parental perceptions about the severity of their child's disability.
4. When the child reaches adolescence, peer acceptance or rejection becomes a central concern.
5. As the child nears the end of the public school years, parents must make transitional plans for their child's future.
6. If by adulthood the son or daughter has not been able to live independently, parents begin worrying about what will happen when their child outlives them.

The family's ability to manage these stress points depends on the severity of the disability, their emotional resources, and the type of support the family receives.

Sometimes the stress can be too much. For example, studies have found that parents of children with mental retardation have higher suicide and divorce rates than families without disabled children (Price-Bonham & Addison, 1978). It also appears that children with disabilities are at greater risk of child abuse (Embry, 1980). In some instances, child abuse or neglect is the cause of the disability. Other problems encountered by families include increased financial burdens, isolation, chronic fatigue, and emotional problems (Gallagher, Beckman, & Cross, 1983).

Coping with the demands of raising a child with a mild disability begins with the husband–wife relationship. Friedrich (1979) found that marital satisfaction is the single best predictor of a family's ability to rear a child with a disability. When husband and wife share the nurturance and physical care of a son or daughter, their marriage can become stronger.

Rick Bennion's comments about his child with mental retardation highlights the need for fathers and mothers to support each other during difficult times.

> Finding out you have a retarded child is somewhat analogous to walking through a mine field. You remain in constant shock and fear as you grope along an uncharted course. The next step is always tenuous, and the lack of a clear-cut path adds to an incessant mental fatigue. For us the initial reactions were, I suppose, rather the norm: Why us? How about a second diagnosis? Is there a miracle cure lurking on the horizon? In the midst of continuous anguish, much solace can be derived from a few words of compassion from friends, loved ones, and particularly each other. No matter how trying, an ongoing dialogue between husband and wife is a must to breach the abyss of despair that envelops your being. (Bennion, 1983, 39)

Gallagher, Cross, and Schartman (1981) studied families who made a successful adjustment to having a child with a disability. Their data suggested that the quality of the husband–wife relationship was an instrumental factor in helping the family cope with stress. Two personal characteristics that the researchers found associated with adjustment were the mother's self-confidence and a "set of supporting values" (e.g., strong religious beliefs).

Working Parents.   The majority of U.S. women are now part of the work force. This shift in family dynamics presents problems to husbands and wives in their roles as parents. Among some of the problems facing working parents are day care, after-school care, and job responsibilities. Employer sensitivity to the needs of parents is a key factor in how involved they will become in school activities, conferences, or parent organizations. Keep in mind that some parents work evenings and others may work two jobs. Employers who provide employees with flexible short-term leave help promote school–parent relationships. Without an employee leave arrangement, a parent has to choose between attending a teacher conference and losing a day's pay!

Child care is a pressing problem. Particularly difficult is obtaining child care for older youngsters. Espinoza (1988) reported that in a sample of seventy-nine children aged eight to thirteen years, 42 percent were latchkey children.

They were left to care for themselves after school. Parents were anxious about their children returning from school to a home with no adult supervision. An additional 20 percent of the youngsters were supervised by an older sibling, many of whom were just a year or so older. Schools can support working parents by providing after-school child care; arranging evening IEP conferences, and providing an evening telephone service for parent questions regarding homework and other school issues.

Single Parents. Kathleen McCoy, author of *Solo Parenting: Your Essential Guide* (1987), calls single parenting the toughest job in the world. The demographics on single parents indicate that it may be not only the toughest job, but the lowest paying as well. According to the Census Bureau, two-thirds of female-headed families with children under eighteen received some sort of welfare benefits (Zinmeister, 1990). Some researchers and policymakers have dubbed this phenomenon "the feminization of poverty."

African Americans have been most affected by this change in the family structure. An estimated three out of four African American children will spend at least part of their life in a single-parent family. Each day 343 African American babies are born to mothers younger than twenty (Children's Defense Fund, 1997). Two out of every five U.S. teenagers (of all races) get pregnant, and one in every five gives birth to a child before the age of twenty (Children's Defense Fund, 1997). The overwhelming majority of "kids having kids" are unmarried.

Mothers who care for their children alone struggle to make ends meet. Shelter, food, clothing, medical care, and child care are top priorities. Most single mothers work. Two-thirds of mothers with school-aged children and one-half of mothers of preschool-age children are employed. Wikler (1979) surveyed mothers of children with disabilities and found that their greatest need was respite or child care; next was financial assistance; and the third greatest need was moral support. The U.S. Department of Agriculture found that almost 10 percent of the average single mother's income goes for child care. Although day care is a necessity for all working mothers, mothers of children with a disability have the combined problem of finding a safe place for their child while they work, and locating someone to provide respite care. The more severe a child's disability, the greater the need for respite. Wikler noted that 73 percent of mothers with children who have special needs received some type of social welfare support, but respite care was not included (Vadasy, 1986).

Single parents of either sex experience more stress than married couples (Beckman, 1983). Daily chores such as shopping and doing laundry are compounded by nonstop parenting duties. Social isolation, particularly when a child with special needs is involved, increases the loneliness of a single parent. The most obvious impact of single parenting is financial hardship. Parents who must work full time have less time to spend with their children. These families are buffeted by the constant strain of struggling to make ends meet. Older children get recruited as surrogate parents as mothers try to balance impossible schedules. Latchkey children are common in single-parent families. Without a partner to provide emotional support, the parent may be less capable of providing nurturance to a difficult-to-care-for child. This means that normal developmental milestones, such as "the terrible twos" and adolescent rebelliousness, can become the source of severe stress in the single-parent family.

Single parents may cope with their loneliness by relating to their child as an adult friend. Elkind (1982) discovered that single parents are more likely than married couples to treat their children as confidants. Strong emotional bonds can develop between parent and child when that child becomes decision maker, friend, and helper. Children in single-parent families grow up faster than children in two-parent families. Weintraub and Wolf (1984) reported that single mothers of preschool children treated their children more maturely than married mothers.

There are also negative consequences from relating to a child as an adult friend. The child may be unable to cope with the responsibility of providing emotional support. The parent may become possessive of the child and restrict opportunities for independence. Outside support from friends and other family members can lessen a parent's dependence on his or her child to fulfill the need for companionship.

Many separated or divorced couples continue to share parenting responsibilities. Splitting child-raising schedules is a common practice that ensures that a child will continue to get parenting from both father and mother. The manner in which each parent is able to make the transition from married to separate life while continuing the respective parenting role is a key variable in the emotional development of a child.

Support for Families

Help for families who have a child with a disability can be broadly divided into three categories: emotional support, information, and federal government programs. Emotional support for parents of children with mild disabilities begins with the immediate family, branches out to grandparents and other relatives, and continues with friends and neighbors. Professional support agencies complement "grass root" networks by providing information and services that train families to help themselves. The stronger their support system, the more capable the family will be in coping with the daily stresses of raising a child with a disability.

Federal programs are primarily targeted for low-income families. Poverty continues to play a significant role in the development of mild disabilities, particularly mild mental retardation and behavior disorders. Children without adequate nutrition and health care are at-risk populations. Environmental threats to normal development include heavy-metal poisoning, child abuse, child neglect, community violence, lack of proper educational experiences at home, and drug abuse. Government programs, when funded properly, can prevent and/or remediate medical and environmental conditions that contribute to mild disabilities.

Emotional Support

Parents of children with disabilities often feel alone. Featherstone (1980) reported that "a special loneliness is the most pervasive theme in the stories told by parents of disabled children. This loneliness is nourished from within and without. . . . The two most prominent ingredients of a parent's loneliness are difference—his own and the child's—and isolation" (cited in Stagg & Catron, 1986, 283).

Support groups help parents cope with isolation. When parents have an opportunity to discuss their problems with other parents of children with disabilities, they learn they are not alone. Over the years many self-help, support groups for parents have sprung up in local communities. Sometimes leadership for these groups comes from local professionals; more often parents themselves are the organizers.

Support groups provide parents with an emotional lifeline as they discover that others share their experiences (Spriggs and Daniels, 1997). When parents talk to parents, a sense of comradeship supplants feelings of loneliness and isolation. The Federation of Families for Children's Mental Health, for example, has assisted many family-run organizations in getting started (Huff, 1997). Support groups also help parents learn how to use their influence to get the best educational services for their children. Many school systems have parent advisory councils. These advocacy groups are comprised of parents with disabled children and representatives from the local educational agency. They meet on a regular basis to discuss issues pertaining to delivery of special education services in their community. How much influence a parent advisory council has is largely determined by the political activism of member parents. Some typical activities of a parent advisory council include regular review of special education policy in their school system, dissemination of information to parents of special needs children, and the writing of grants to improve educational services for children with disabilities.

Information

Recent federal legislation has enabled parent-organized groups to develop a national networking system. The Education of the Handicapped Act Amendments of 1983, P.L. 98–199, authorized a grant program to support organized parent efforts to provide information and training through the Technical Assistance for Parents Program (TAPP). The purpose of TAPP is to provide a system of peer support that allows experienced parent centers and new parent centers to learn from each other and professional experts. TAPP is coordinated by the Federation for Children with Special Needs, a parent center in Boston, Massachusetts.

Four regional parent center's constitute TAPP (see Table 11.3). Each of these parent-information centers is committed to improving public perceptions of children with disabling conditions. Their goal is to enhance educational and vocational opportunities for children with special needs.

TABLE 11.3   List of TAPP Locations

The Tapp Central Office is run by:

The Federation for Children with Special Needs
95 Berkeley Street, Suite 104
Boston, MA 02116
(617) 482-2915 (Voice and TDD)
(617) 695-2939
www.fcsn.org/tapp

Martha Ziegler, Project Director

MIDWEST
PACER Center, Inc.
4826 Chicago Avenue South
Minneapolis, MN 55417-1098
(612) 827-2966 (Voice/TDD)
(612) 827-3065 Fax
mnfolger@gte.edu.net
800-537-2237 in Minnesota
Regional Director: Paula Goldberg
TA Facilitator: Susan Folger

Area Served: *Colorado, Illinois, Iowa, Indiana, Kansas, Kentucky, Michigan, Minnesota, Missouri, Nebraska, North Dakota, Ohio, South Dakota, and Wisconsin.*

NORTHEAST
Parent Information Center
P.O. Box 2405
Concord, NH 03302-2405
(603) 224-7005 (Voice &TDD)
(603) 224-4365
picnh@aol.com
800-947-7005 (New Hampshire only)
Regional TA Director: Judith Raskin

Area Served: *Connecticut, Delaware, Maine, Maryland, Massachusetts, New Hampshire, New Jersey, New York, Pennsylvania, Puerto Rico, Rhode Island, Vermont, the District of Columbia, and the Virgin Islands.*

SOUTH
Exceptional Children's Assistance Center, Inc.
P.O. Box 16
Davidson, NC 28036
(704) 892-1321
(704) 892-5028 (Call first to dedicate line)
800-962-6817, North Carolina only
Regional TA Director: Connie Hawkins

Area Served: *Alabama, Arkansas, Florida, Georgia, Louisiana, Mississippi, North Carolina, Oklahoma, South Carolina, Tennessee, Virginia, and West Virginia.*

WEST
Washington PAVE
6316 South 12th
Tacoma, WA 98465-1900
(206) 565-2266 (Voice &TDD)
(206) 566-8052 Fax
wapave@nwrain.com
800-572-7368 in Washington
Regional Director: Joanne Butts
TA Facilitator: William Habermann

Area Served: Alaska, Arizona, California, Hawaii, Idaho, Montana, Nevada, New Mexico, Oregon, Texas, Utah, Washington, Wyoming, American Jurisdictions, and the Department of Defense Dependent Schools.

The National Information Center for Children and Youth with Handicaps (NICHY) provides educational information and technical assistance to parents, advocates, and professionals. NICHY maintains a collection of resource publications and fact sheets that help parents locate assistance in their local communities. Since 1922, the Council for Exceptional Children (CEC) has provided both parents and professionals with support services, including national and regional conferences, journals, and political activism on behalf of children with disabilities. While CEC provides support activities for all types of disabling conditions, other national organizations provide support services for families of children with specific disabilities. The Association for Children and Adults with Learning Disabilities and The National Association of Retarded Citizens have state and local chapters throughout the country. These organizations provide parents with information on recent developments in research and teaching children with specific impairments. Parents or educators who wish to contact any of these organizations can get the necessary information from state department of education offices.

There are many organizations and agencies eager to help support families. (See Table 11.4 for a list of Internet addresses). Yet each year countless parents struggle alone, unaware of the support network that is available to help them. By providing parents with a list of local and regional support agencies, teachers can help ensure that their classroom efforts are complemented by help outside of school. Mild disabilities are more than just a school problem. Learning disabilities, mild mental retardation, and behavior disorders are family problems. When families are supported at home, children with special needs have a better opportunity to overcome their impairments in school and in the community.

Several federal programs provide funds to support parent training and participation in their children's education. Typically these programs follow three-year funding cycles. The largest programs are funded by the Office of Elementary and Secondary Schools (OESE). Two such programs are Even Start and Parental Assistance. Even Start is targeted for disadvantaged families. In 1997, $95,523,000.00 was appropriated to support local family literacy projects that integrate early childhood education, adult literacy, and parenting education in both urban and rural settings. Parental Assistance provides funds to establish parent information and resource centers to help parents better understand their children's educational needs. From 1996 through 1998 appropriations for Parental Assistance was $50,000,000.00. Non-profit organizations that work in cooperation with local education agencies are eligible to apply for grants to coordinate existing parent support programs, develop resource materials for parents, and support promising models of parent participation in schooling. Parental Assistance focuses on serving parents who are low-income, minority, and have limited English proficiency.

The Office of Bilingual Education and Minority Language Affairs allocated $82,079,000.00 in 1998 for discretionary grants for school-wide bilingual education or English-as-a-second-language programs. Grants could be used for family ed-

TABLE 11.4   Agencies and Organizations that Support Families

American Association of Mental Retardation
www.aamr.org

American Council of the Blind
www. acb.org/

American Speech and Hearing Association
www.asha.org/asha/

Autism Society of America
www.syr.edu~jmwobus/autism/

Children and Adults with Attention Deficit
Disorder (CHADD)
www.chadd.org/

Children's Defense Fund–Parent Resource
Network
www.childrendefense.org/prn.html

Council for Exceptional Children
www.cec.sped.org/home.htm

Federation for Children with Special Needs
www. fcsn.org/

Genetic Disorders Hotline
www. geneletter.org

Internet Resource for Special Children
www.irsc.org/disability.htm

Learning Disabilities Associations
www.Ldonline.org/

National Clearinghouse on Instructional
Practice
www.edc.org/fsc/ncip

National Educational Service (at-risk and
behavior disorders)
www.nes.org/

National Information Center for Children and
Youth with Disabilities (NICHY)
www.nichy.org

National Information Center on Deafness
www.gallaudet.edu:80~/ncd

Office of Special Education and Rehabilitation
Services
www.ed.gov/offices/OSERS

U.S Department of Education
www.ed.gov/

Complied by Linda Nober, Education Department, Westfield State College.

ucation, parent outreach, and a variety of instructional services to improve the education of limited English proficient students. Additionally, the Individuals with Disabilities Education Act mandated funds for parent training and information centers. Educational agencies and nonprofit organizations that provide families with training and information to enable them to participate more effectively in meeting the educational needs of students with disabilities are eligible to apply for funding. In 1997, $13,535,000 was appropriated to fund the Parent Training and Information Centers grant.

Because federal grant funding is cyclical and subject to legislative approval changes in funding priorities and appropriations are frequent. Updated information regarding federal assistance to enhance families involvement in schooling can be obtained through the Department of Education website—www.ed.gov/.

WIC. The Special Supplemental Food Program for Women, Infants, and Children (WIC) is a federal program that attempts to reduce infant mortality and the numbers of low-birthweight babies. WIC provides nutritional help for children from birth to age five by providing mothers with vouchers with which to buy cheese, milk, orange juice, cereal, and infant formula. As of September, 1996, an average of 7,193,381 women received WIC benefits every month (Federal Domestic Assistance Catalog, 1997).

EPSDT. Medicaid and Early Periodic Screening, Diagnosis and Treatment (EPSDT) services make some health care services available to families who are unable to afford health insurance. Prenatal care, increased birthweight, decreased neonatal deaths, and fewer abnormalities are some of the benefits of EPSDT for poor children. By the end of 1989, only 15 states met federal guidelines for provision of health services to poor families. Childhood immunization programs, which prevent measles, rubella, mumps, polio, diphtheria, tetanus, and pertussis, are successful but underfunded. "American one-year-olds have lower immunization rates against polio than one-year-olds in 14 other countries. Polio immunization rates for nonwhite babies in the United States rank behind 48 other countries, including Botswana, Sri Lanka, Albania, Colombia, and Jamaica" (Children's Defense Fund, 1990, 5). As a result of EPSDT, in 1997, an estimated 37,177,000 recipients including low income persons over 65, disabled, low income children, and pregnant women received medical assistance (Federal Domestic Assitance Catalog, 1997).

Head Start. Head Start is a federally funded program that provides preschoolers with a range of crucial services. The Head Start educational programs help youngsters learn school readiness skills, thus increasing their chances for academic success when they enter public school. Nutrition and medical screening, including EPSDT and dental checkups, are components of Head Start. Parent involvement is built into every Head Start program. Parents are encouraged to attend parenting workshops on such topics as nutrition and developmental play at home. Some Head Start programs are home-based. Head Start teachers visit youngsters' homes and demonstrate early childhood activities for parents. In 1996, 752,077 children enrolled in Head Start. Children with disabilities comprise 13 percent of the Head Start enrollment (Federal Domestic Assistance Catalog, 1997).

The most notable accomplishment of a Head Start preschool was attributed to the Perry Preschool Program in Ypsilanti, Michigan. By age 19, students who had attended the Perry program "were more likely to have finished high school, were dramatically less likely to have committed a crime, were less likely to be on welfare, and were earning more money" when compared to peers who had not attended the Perry program (Stein, Leinhardt, & Bickel, 1989, 149).

Federal programs make significant contributions to strengthening the ability of parents to improve the health and education of their children. Only the federal government has the financial and political leadership required to make children a national priority. In order to provide for the needs of youth, a new vision of community is needed. A community is a network of people working together toward common goals. This new vision would promote community organizations as extended families. Services such as youth clubs, athletic organizations, schools, mental health clinics, and parent resource centers can help parents and children. All of these ventures are woefully underfunded.

Although we can't turn back the clock to the neighborhood school memories of James Comer, there are many paths to the goal of providing for our nation's children. WIC and EPSDT are based on the premise that children need to be healthy to learn. Head Start integrates health services, parent involvement, and education to help at-risk children succeed in school. Innovative programs and parent involvement provide a decision-making role for parents in schools, establish support for parents to assist children to learn at home, and enhance parent–teacher communication.

Teacher–Parent Communication

Effective teacher–parent communication is essential in order to provide students with mild disabilities an appropriate education. Good communication with parents serves three useful purposes. First, it provides teachers with information about their students and parental expectations for school. Second, parents get reliable and up-to-date information to help them make decisions about their child's special education. Finally, when parents and teachers communicate and work together, they develop trust and a sense of shared commitment (Cattermole & Robinson, 1985). Trust helps the school and family support each other and share expectations for student achievement. This is the type of social capital that can make a significant difference in a youngster's life.

Communication means more than simply relaying information. The medium of exchange tells parents how the school system feels about them. Schools and teachers who seek minimum parent involvement do the least to attract a parent's attention to important issues. For instance, one school system was obligated by state special education regulations to form a special needs parent advisory board. Instead of sending letters of invitation to parents describing the need for parent participation, the superintendent and special education director squeezed the message on the back of the weekly school lunch menu. As expected, there was minimal parent response. Did this mean that the parents in this school system were apathetic? Of course not, but judgments about parent behavior are sometimes based on such transactions.

Each parent is a unique person with his or her own interests, needs, and concerns. Understanding parents of children with mild disabilities requires treating each parent as an individual. Teachers who communicate through words and actions their respect for parents are most successful at forming cooperative parent–teacher partnerships. One strategy to establish a basis for trust and mutual respect is to make telephone calls to parents notifying them of their child's positive classroom contributions. This offsets the parental expectation that the only time they will hear from school is when there is a problem.

The following description of an exceptional teacher by a parent highlights the anxiety and hope that parents harbor when they first meet their child's teacher.

> I just met a talented and gifted teacher, and I'm still tingling with joy. He invited the parents to a meeting, before the beginning of school, to introduce himself and to discuss the year. I wouldn't have missed it for the world, but I went with fear. What if I didn't like the man? Within half an hour, however, I felt the tension drain from my body to be replaced with excitement. Before me was a talented and gifted teacher. I knew other exceptional teachers before, and this time I could identify the qualities they had in common. (Williams, 1988, 61)

Linda Williams (1988), parent, goes on to describe a teacher who loves to learn, is not afraid to take risks, believes teaching is helping children to learn, conveys the message that parents are important, and respects children. She might also have added that this teacher was capable of communicating his enthusiasm to parents. Parents need to know what kind of person is teaching their child. A parent's usual main source of information about a teacher is the child. Face-to-face, telephone, and written communications help parents better understand the teacher as a person.

Conferences.   When parents and professionals meet to discuss a child, parents need to feel that they are valued participants. Teachers who treat parents with respect, rather than judging their feelings or behavior, create the best climate for a cooperative partnership. It wasn't long ago that professionals placed the majority of the blame for a child's learning problem on inferior parenting skills. Professionals viewed parents as part of the problem rather than part of the solution. The one-sided view that says, "It's all the parents fault," bred a condescending attitude toward parents of children with disabilities (Gallagher, Beckman, & Cross, 1983). In order to avoid barriers to effective communication, teachers should keep in mind the following pointers outlined by Gloeckler and Simpson (1988).

1. *Parents of exceptional children are more like parents of nondisabled children than they are different.* There are no generalizations about families of children with mild disabilities that hold true in all cases. Each situation is unique. The majority of special needs children come from families where other children do not have learning problems.

2. *Parents of children with mild disabilities, in general, are not the cause of their children's disabilities.* The causes of mild disabilities have been traced to many sources, including poor instruction, faulty assessment practices, neurological impairments, and poverty. To view parents as the single contributor to a child's disability is misleading and unfair. Teachers may encounter some parents who are inadequate. These individuals need support and help, rather than condemnation.

3. *Parents are interested in their child's welfare and will react positively to those they believe are genuinely interested in their children.* No teacher behavior demonstrates understanding more than listening. Parents need someone to listen more than someone to tell them what to do. Listening indicates concern and interest in each individual situation. Listening helps professionals to problem-solve with parents. When parents feel their point of view is respected, they are more likely to be open and honest in their conversations.

4. *The family is a social unit.* When something happens to one member of a family, all members are affected. When a child is identified as having a learning disability, mild mental retardation, or emotional disturbance, each member of the family—mother, father, siblings, and relatives—will have individual reactions. The interrelationship among family members will have an impact on how a student behaves in school.

5. *Parents have the greatest impact on their own children.* Parents are the most influential adults in a child's life. No matter how many professionals are involved with a youngster, the specialist is still the parent. Parents need accurate and full knowledge of their child's status in school. Explanations of classroom actions, test results, and professional judgments should be honest and direct. Often students behave differently at school than at home. Describing student actions in descriptive, nontechnical language helps the parent to understand discrepancies between home and school behavior.

An initial parent–teacher conference is more than a meeting about a child. It sets the tone for all future teacher–parent contacts. In order to prepare for a conference, imagine how the parent feels driving or walking to the conference. What will be on his or her mind? Think about feelings that precede a visit to a doctor, dentist, lawyer, or professor. A common concern is that something is wrong. Some parents, particularly those of children with mild disabilities, approach a conference with apprehension. They might be concerned that they appear to be "bad" parents, or they hope the teacher has some magic up his or her sleeve that is going to turn things around for their child. Their schooling may have been a negative experience, so the simple task of walking into a classroom and sitting down with a teacher can be anxiety provoking.

The first step to a productive parent–teacher conference is preparation. The following are some practical suggestions for parent–teacher meetings.

1. *Physical preparation.* Physical preparation means attending to the accoutrements of the conference. Don't sit behind a desk. If you are an early childhood teacher, provide adult-sized chairs. Have concrete samples of student work available to highlight topics you want to cover. Sit at a table that is wide enough to display student work. Have all your materials ready; it is important for a parent to view you as an organized person.

2. *Mental preparation.* Have a mental or written checklist of specific items you want to review. Avoid using materials, such as test profiles, that require turgid educational jargon to explain. Remember, you want to talk in plain language. If the parent is non-English-speaking, make an attempt to communicate in a way that will help set the person at ease. If a translator is necessary, a smile and cheery "Buenas tardes," for example, can go a long way toward helping a Spanish-speaking parent to relax.

3. *Establish a mood.* Begin a conference with good news. This will set a positive tone and help smooth the waters for any trouble spots that need to be reviewed. Be candid and direct with parents. Honesty helps establish trust. Don't dominate the conference. At least 50 percent of the talk should come from parents. Remember that the purpose of the conference is for both of you to learn about each other. Use active listening skills. Encourage parents to give examples of their concerns by talking about what happens at home. Remember that you are probably the only other adult outside the family that a parent can confide in about his or her child. This is an opportunity for parents, but they need your nonjudgmental support in order to express their concerns. Finally, don't be defensive. If a parent makes what appears to be a negative remark about your teaching or the curriculum, listen to what they have to say. They may have a point. In any case, by listening to them, you demonstrate respect.

4. *Carryover.* Teachers can use a parent conference to assist parents with their children at home. Many parents would like to do more but they need guidance. Table 11.5 offers ideas for parents to improve their children's school performance. Follow-up is sometimes necessary. For example, you could give a parent a reading list of children's books, or you might refer a parent to another resource such as the WIC program or Head Start. A teacher's credibility rides on follow-up. After the conference is over, make a careful written record of the conversation. Include suggestions and questions that were discussed, and the type of follow-up you agreed on (Bjorklund & Burger, 1987).

Telephone Communication. School systems that make creative use of telephones can extend educational services to families. For example, the San Diego County Office of Education installed an EdInfo service. It offered seventy-five prerecorded messages twenty-four hours a day in English and Spanish. Funded through a grant from the Wells Fargo Bank Foundation, EdInfo provided families with information on such topics as parents and teachers, tests and testing, drug and alcohol abuse, and special programs (Chrispeels, 1991).

Within the Indianapolis school system, Dial-A-Teacher gave families assistance with homework. This direct access line was staffed by two teams of teacher specialists Mondays through Thursdays from 5 P.M. to 8 P.M. Each five-member

Table 11.5   Helping Parents Help Their Children

1. You Can Help Your Child Mentally by
–praising your child for work well done and for good effort.
–eliminating comparisons of your child to another child.
–showing confidence in your child's abilities.
–being realistic in your expectations of your child.

2. You Can Help Your Child Physically by
–seeing that your child gets adequate sleep.
–providing a schedule or fixed routine for your child to follow during school days.
–seeing that your child has an appropriate diet with limitations on the amount of "junk food" consumed.
–encouraging your child to exercise regularly.
–seeing that your child visits his/her dentist and doctor on a regular basis.
–showing your child a lot of love.

3. You Can Help Your Child Academically by
–talking with your child. Have your child talk about the day's activities or future plans for the weekend or any other subject of interest.
–listening to your child. Responding to questions encourages curiosity and motivation in a child.
–reading to your child and having your child read to you.
–seeing that your child does assigned homework.
–establishing a regular time and place for your child to study.
–providing materials to use while studying (e.g., pencils, paper, dictionary, etc.)
–providing materials to use while studying (e.g., pencils, paper, dictionary, etc.)
–allowing your child to do his/her own work, but being available to provide assistance if needed.
–taking your child to the library often.
–playing vocabulary games with your child, such as naming common objects around the house and their uses; going to the grocery store and naming fruits and vegetables.

–playing question games with your child. Ask your child questions that begin "What if" or "How will."
–having your child memorize some vital pieces of information, such as a family telephone number, home address, your place of employment, the police emergency number, and other information needed for your child's safety and well-being.
–serving as a positive role model for your child by reading, using appropriate speech, writing notes or letters, watching educational television programs.

4. You Can Help Your Child in Test-Taking by
–ensuring your child gets a good night of sleep so as to be alert during the next day.
–seeing that your child eats breakfast.
–seeing that your child dresses appropriately for outside weather conditions.
–getting your child to school on time (so there will be no last minute problems).
–encouraging your child to do his or her best on the test, but not placing undue pressure on your child.
–demonstrating verbally and nonverbally that you have confidence in your child's abilities to perform well on the test.

5. You Can Help Your Child in Other Ways by
–seeing that your child turns in assigned homework.
–keeping up-to-date on your child's progress in school.
–getting to know your child's teacher(s).
–volunteering to work in a school classroom or making materials for use in the classroom.
–participating in school-sponsored activities.
–reviewing your child's work folder as it is sent home from school.
–supporting the parent-teacher organization of the school that your child attends.

Source: Whiting, J. (Child Service Coordinator), and Aultman, S. L. (Georgia Learning Resources System Center Director), 1990.

team comprised teachers with expertise in specific academic subjects. The specialist teams help parents and students solve difficulties with specific homework assignments.

The "Homework Hotline" was a live, call-in television show carried by two Indianapolis cable systems. The purpose of the call-in show was to provide assistance in mathematics for students in grades one to six. When parents or students made their calls, they talked to teachers who used chalkboards to go over and, if necessary, reteach math concepts.

The Parent Line/Communicator was a computerized telephone message service in Indianapolis that provides families with information on approximately 140 different topics such as parenting skills, adult education, and magnet schools. Fifty messages featured information on drug and alcohol abuse. The line was open twenty-four hours a day. As many as 3,000 calls were made by families each month (Warner, 1991). These innovative programs, sponsored by the Indianapolis School System, illustrate that with a little bit of imagination (and some funding) the telephone can provide families with immediate access to school services.

Recently, a teacher of students with mild disabilities described how he had to confront another teacher about interrupting his classes. The other teacher, who is in an adjacent classroom, would barge into his class two or three times a day to use the telephone affixed to his classroom wall. Her explanation was that she needed to use a phone to contact parents and mentors in her work–study program, and the only telephone that was accessible was in his classroom. Although he sympathized with her plight, the special education teacher pointed out that she was constantly disrupting his classes. She apologized, and they both tried to figure out a way to get the school administration to give her a phone line. Unfortunately, this scenario is all too common. Teachers need administrative support and the necessary funding to make use of a telephone. As Ron Davies points out, "A telephone is a low-cost but crucial piece of equipment to encourage school/family/community connections" (1991, 379).

Written Communication

Written communication is the most frequent method of school to home communication (Cattermole & Robinson, 1985). Newsletters, parent handbooks, and bulletins provide families with information regarding their rights and obligations under the Individuals with Disabilities Education Act. Teachers and administrators usually assume that parents understand this information. Given the importance of parental involvement in special education decisions, it is clearly in the school's best interests to disseminate readable information to parents.

In order to fulfill their obligations, parents need a working knowledge of special education law and regulations. They should understand notification, evaluation, and placement procedures. Parents also must be aware of due process procedures established to protect their rights. Parents should know how to utilize parent advocates. Finally, parents need to understand their role in developing and implementing the individualized education program.

Roit and Pfohl (1984) assessed the readability of written information disseminated to parents regarding their involvement in special education meetings. The readability study was prompted by widespread concern about passive parents. The researchers hypothesized that parents did not clearly understand information presented in school information materials. Their supposition had particular significance for parents of students with mild mental retardation and behavior disorders because a disproportionate percentage of these children come from either non-English-speaking or culturally different families. Additionally, Educational Testing Service data on adult literacy indicated that between eighteen and twenty-three million adults cannot read a daily newspaper.

The results of the readability study indicated that large pages filled with small print made reading overwhelming and unappealing. The use of examples, samples, charts, and pictures enhanced the readability of printed materials. Additionally, glossaries and questions were found to be helpful aides to parent understanding. The researchers found that bold headings and outlines did not communicate information as effectively as paragraphs that related concepts to specific situations. Such common words as "plan" and "right" needed to be explained when they were used to denote both educational and legal usage. Finally, Roit and Pfohl recommended organizing the content of printed material into five broad categories: (a) disabling conditions (e.g., what is a learning disability and how does it affect a youngster developmentally, socially, and academically?); (b) normal child development; (c) legal issues and trends in litigation; (d) assessment and placement procedures; (e) the role of parents in the educational process.

Although parent conferences, the telephone, and newsletters represent the traditional approach to school–family communication, educators are beginning to realize that the electronic media has tremendous potential for interconnecting families and teachers, especially in isolated rural areas.

Technology

In Westfield, Massachusetts, the superintendent had a weekly television show on the local cable public access station. During this show he explained such issues as why school buses ran late and how two new schools would be funded. He interviewed principals and teachers and explained to viewers how public schools compete with other city agencies for shrinking dollars. Television offers educators tremendous opportunities for making contact and educating parents and students alike. Yet television is just one piece in a panoply of electronic devices that present themselves as solutions awaiting someone clever enough to devise the problems. For example, unless someone envisions expert teachers talking with students in far-flung areas, the problem of how they will communicate does not exist and the solution—distance learning—remains dormant. Or, it takes an appreciation of computer technology to wonder if it would be possible for an expert on student learning styles to design a program to diagnose learning problems of students suspected of having mild disabilities. The technology is available, but it begs for a question to spur the hunt for a solution (Levinson, 1990).

Like the T.V. show "Jeopardy," technology anticipates our questions. CD-ROM technology is the answer. What is the question? (How can we make the vast information of libraries and museums accessible to the average classroom?) Let's try another. The answer is satellite transmissions. The question is, How can an educational institution (school, college, university) make the talents of one gifted teacher available to thousands of students and parents? Such information systems as the internet, CD-ROM, cassette tapes, satellite T.V., interactive computing (i.e., electronic bulletin boards, electronic mail), and teleconferencing are powerful, virtually untapped resources for connecting teachers, schools, and home.

The Internet home shopping networks, C-Span, public access cable, and CNN news beam immediate and interactive information into millions of U.S. homes. It appears that the dream of educators—lifelong learning—is about to be fulfilled, but in ways hardly imagined even ten years ago. The classroom has expanded into the living rooms of the United States. Televised college study through distance learning is available in many areas—and can be validated through supervised examinations offered in regional centers or over the Internet.

The tools are available for educators to expand the notion of social capital into social electronic capital. As an illustration, US Vidotel in Houston, Dallas, and Ft. Worth offers terminal users a combination of interactive math games, *Grolier's Encyclopedia,* and a directory that lists information about local school systems and educational services. The Internet can provide multiple options for parent involvement. Parents can communicate with teachers and each other via teleconferences. School web pages provide access to school menus, activities, and volunteer schedules. Interactive web pages provide tutoring for homework assignments. These electronic systems are not a substitute for face-to-face contact, but they do provide a valuable new link between home and school (Grunwald, 1990). While teachers scramble to find an available telephone (see section on telephone communication), the communication industries are devising new, more profitable ways of bringing electronic communication into U.S. homes. The Internet puts the world at the fingertips of every school child. The U.S. Department of Education provides an array of technology information to assist teachers, parents, and students in using the Internet and other electronic technologies. The Network of Regional Technology Consortia (R*TEC) program is one example. Six regional offices have been established to disseminate information for the effective use of technology in education. Special emphasis is placed on fostering regional cooperation and resource sharing. Table 11.6 lists each regional center. The use of high tech information systems to facilitate school–home communication will require a commitment in dollars that does not presently exist within either state or federal budgets. It remains to be seen whether educators can turn Internet possibilities into a future partnership between schools and families.

TABLE 11.6   Technology in Education Consortia

Northwest Educational Technology Consortium (NETC)

URL: http://www.netc.org/   Toll free: 1-800-211-9435
E-mail: netc@nwrel.org   (voice mail)
                                Phone: 503-275-0658
                                Fax: 503-275-0449

Pacific and Southwest Regional Technology in Education Consortium (PSR*TEC)

URL: http://   Phone: 562-985-5806
psrtec.clmer.csulb.edu/   Fax: 562-985-4528
E-mail: clmer@csulb.edu

North Central Regional Technology in Education Consortium (NCRTEC)

URL: http://www.ncrtec.org/   Phone: 630-571-4710
E-mail: ncrtec@ncrel.org   Fax: 630-218-4989

South Central Regional Technology in Education Consortium (SCR*TEC)

URL: http://scrtec.org/   Toll free: 1-888-TEC-2001
E-mail: info@scrtec.org   Fax: 913-864-0704

Northeast Regional Technology in Education Consortia (NetTech)

URL: http://www.nettech.org/   Phone: 212-541-0972
E-mail: debs@enc.org   Fax: 614-292-2066

Southeast and Islands Regional Technology in Education Consortium (SEIR*TEC)

URL: http://www.serve.org/   Toll free: 1-800-659-3204
seir-tec/   Phone: 404-893-0100
E-mail: seirtec@serve.org   Fax: 404-577-7812

The Individual Education Program Meeting

One of the remarkable aspects of the Individuals with Disabilities Education Act is that parents are required to collaborate with educators to determine the appropriateness of their youngster's individual education program (IEP). The law requires parental involvement in deciding:

1. Type of special services required (e.g., speech therapy, counseling)
2. Educational placement (e.g., full-time regular class with support, resource room, special class).
3. Makeup of the individual education program (e.g., annual goals and objectives).

Students with mild disabilities cannot be evaluated or placed in a special education program without parental consent. If parents do not agree with educational decisions about their youngster, they have the due process right to mediation and appeal. Table 11.7 lists parental due process rights. The fact that several parent–school disagreements about special education services have reached the Supreme Court highlights the importance of parent–school cooperation.

The IEP begins with the initial referral and concludes with the parents agreeing to special education services outlined in the program. The IEP is a management tool designed to ensure that special education services match a

TABLE 11.7 Parents' Due Process Rights

1. The right to examine all school records.
2. The right to request a special education evaluation.
3. The right to refuse the school permission to do a special education evaluation.
4. The right of child to remain in a regular classroom until parents agree to special education services.
5. The right to request an independent educational evaluation paid for by the school system.
6. The right to bring an advocate to all meetings.
7. The right to participate in the development of an individual education program (IEP).
8. The right to disagree with the IEP.
9. The right to appeal all decisions made by the school system regarding special education services.
10. The right to review and amend the IEP each year.
11. The right to expect full cooperation from the school system in all matters concerning special education.
12. The right to have a child educated in the least restrictive environment.

TABLE 11.8   Components of an Individual Education Program

An individual education program (IEP) is a written plan provision of special education services for a student who is disabled:

Each IEP must contain:
1. A statement of the child's present level of educational performance
2. A statement of annual goals, including short-term instructional objectives.
3. A statement of the specific special educational and related services to be provided the child, and the extent to which the child will be able to participate in regular educational programs.
4. The projected dates for initiation of services and the anticipated duration of the services.
5. Appropropriate objective criteria and evaulation procedures and schedules for determining, on at least an annual basis, whether the short term instructional objectives are being met.

student's individual needs and that special education services are monitored. It contains annual goals and objectives, a statement about a student's educational strengths and weaknesses, and a description of special education and related services. Table 11.8 lists the basic components of the IEP. The individual education program must be approved by parents before a student can be placed in a special education program.

The purpose of the IEP planning meeting is for educators and parents to discuss their views about a student's special education needs. The participants in the meeting include, but are not limited to, the student's teacher (both general and special education), the student's parents or guardians, a representative of the local education agency (public or private), and a member of the assessment team. Some state guidelines provide for student participation. In Massachusetts, for example, a student fourteen years or older has the right to participate in an IEP meeting. The Individuals with Disabilities Education Act also gives parents the right to bring an advocate with them. There is no stipulation about an advocate's qualifications. An advocate is someone who can help the parent sort through the often bewildering array of decisions they are confronted with during an IEP planning meeting.

In theory, the IEP meeting is democratic and provides for maximum parental input into a child's special education program. Unfortunately, the reality is quite different. Often, parents do not view themselves and are not viewed by educators as colleagues at the meeting. Parent participation at IEP meetings is minimal. A survey of several hundred families (Lynch & Stein, 1987) reported that 50 percent of parents did not feel they were active participants and only 34 percent of parents made suggestions during the meeting. Sometimes, because of time conflicts, transportation problems, child care needs, or work commitments, parents are unable to attend the meeting. When parents are absent, the IEP is usually mailed to them for their signature.

When parents attend the IEP meeting, a variety of group dynamic factors impede participation. Consider the following scene. A group of professionals are sitting around a table facing the parents. Each professional takes a turn reporting on the educational failure of their child. The parents are deluged with educational jargon like "subaverage IQ," "deficient adaptive behavior skills," "dyslexic," and "behavior disordered." Education jargon places the parents at a serious disadvantage as they try to follow what is being said. Without an advocate to help the parents sort out what is happening, the parents are in jeopardy of consenting to an IEP that is unclear.

All IEP meetings are not as muddled for parents as the one just described. When educators are sensitive to parents' feelings and take the time to explain what they are talking about, parents have an opportunity to be involved. Educators need to remember that it takes a good deal of resolve for a parent to participate in a meeting that is intended to analyze what is wrong with his or her child. One parent expressed her feelings this way.

> The IEP process was something that was really hard for me to accept and get into, because I'm not by nature an assertive person. In a group I don't speak up that much, but as a parent in an IEP conference, I have to. I have to be totally prepared. I may have a lot of confidence in the staff that's working with him; they're all great people. But I have to know what each is doing with Geoff and where they're headed with him. I need to review my concerns when I go to the conference, to speak up, and really be his advocate. I have to do that. I think the parent is the one who has the best whole concept of the child, with regard to where he's been and where he's going. And the parent has a lot to offer the staff members knowledge and understanding of the child. (Roberts, 1986, 206)

The IEP planning meeting is an important event in a parent's life. By following a few basic guidelines, educators can ensure that the meeting enhances rather than diminishes parent–teacher communication.

1. Before the meeting, give parents basic information on how the meeting will be conducted, who will be attending, and what they can do to be effective participants.

2. Arrange seating so parents are not sitting on one side of a table, "squared off" against the professionals.

3. Avoid general negative statements like "Harry is eight but has a mental age of five." There is enough valid criticism of educational assessment procedures to warrant tempering of professional enthusiasm for the accuracy of test results.

4. Encourage parent questions after each professional makes a contribution.

5. Be conscious of the group dynamics. Is one person dominating? Are there hidden agendas? Are the professionals communicating their views in plain language? Are parents giving off distress signals with body language? Most important, are parents being given ample opportunity to verbally participate?

6. When the meeting is over, summarize the group's conclusions and indicate one professional that the parents can contact to answer questions that may occur to them on the way home.

In order to ensure an appropriate education for students with disabilities, Congress mandated parent participation in IEP meetings. By encouraging active parental participation, educators not only fulfill their legal responsibilities, they also provide students with their best opportunity for success.

Summary

Teachers and families share a common vision. Both want children to develop the social and intellectual skills needed to function as contributing citizens. Homes, schools, and communities are besieged by the ravages of poverty, drugs, and alcohol. Schools and families need each other. When educators reach out to families and seek their involvement, schools improve, students achieve, and communities grow closer together.

As we survey the state of our schools and our youth, it appears that we are losing more student minds than we are gaining. The number of school failures seems to grow steadily each year. The numbers of learning disabled students, for instance, has increased by over 100 percent since incidence figures were first reported in 1976. As poverty grows in this country, so will the numbers of students with mild disabilities. Adolescents with behavior disorders are the fastest-growing population of students with mild disabilities. Educators cannot stem this tide without parental help. Congress recognized the need for school–family cooperation by mandating parent participation in special education programming. The Supreme Court has upheld, and in some instances broadened, the role of parents in securing an appropriate education for their children with disabilities. Before the implementation of the Individuals with Disabilities Education Act, educators often perceived parents as the problem. Today, parents are an integral part of the solution.

Parents of children with mild disabilities need support and understanding as they deal with the daily stresses of modern life. When a child is evaluated by the school as having a mild disability, it affects all members of the family. This ripple effect in turn influences the family's ability to cope with the demands of parenting and education. There are many organizations that support families. Yet most families struggle on in isolation, unaware of the network of help that is available to help them. Parents need opportunities to communicate with others who share their problems. Parents need information about their rights and responsibilities as co-determiners of their child's appropriate education. Successful experiences with the schools are needed in order for parents to believe in their ability to promote their child's education. Most of all, parents need teachers who respect them and value their role in shaping the education of their children.

Activities

1. Organize a mock school meeting to which parents have been invited. The purpose of the meeting is to inform parents of students with mild disabilities about the due process guidelines mandated by Public Law 94–142. Half of the class members should act as parents and the other half as school personnel. School personnel can be the building principal, guidance counselor, special education teachers, support teachers (art, music, physical education), and so on. The school personnel should present the guidelines, and then answer any questions the parents might have. Both groups should formulate guidelines they will present and questions they might ask.

2. Divide into teams of four to six students. Each group should simulate two teacher–parent conferences. The first simulation might show ineffective things a teacher might do, such as exhibiting poor planning, having a negative attitude, and so on. The second simulation might show things a teacher can do to have an effective conference with parents. One of the team members could serve as a narrator and describe the things the teacher is doing that lead to an ineffective and then an effective teacher–parent conference. Either the teacher or another student might videotape the conferences for later review and discussion.

3. Divide into "family" groups. Each group will be the parents, siblings, or grandparents of one of the following:

    a. an infant with an intellectual disability.
    b. an infant with a physical disability.
    c. a school-age child with a learning disability.
    d. a school-age child with an intellectual disability.
    e. a school-age child with a behavior disorder.
    f. a school-age child with gifted abilities.
    g. an adolescent with an intellectual disability.
    h. an adolescent with a learning disability.
    i. an adolescent with a behavior disorder.
    j. an adolescent with gifted abilities.

Discuss your feelings about various school transitions (e.g., entering school, transferring to junior high, graduating).

APPENDIX A

A Chronology

Date	Mental Retardation	Behavior Disorders	Learning Disabilities	Generic to General and Special Education
1799		Jean Itard's attempts to train Victor, the Wild Boy of Aveyron (France). Treatment centered around sensory stimulation exercises coupled with systematic teaching procedures.		
1792		Philippe Pinel appointed head of Bicêtre Hospital of mentally ill in Paris, France. Pinel influenced humane treatment.		
1802			Franz Joseph Gall speculated that specific regions of the brain control certain mental activities.	
1817				Thomas Gallaudet became principal of the first residential school for the deaf and mute persons in Hartford, CT.
1820s	Almshouses erected in America for the destitute, originally designed to provide humane and moral care for the poor; became catchalls for the retarded, insane, ill, and other afflicted.			

404

Date	Mental Retardation	Behavior Disorders	Learning Disabilities	Generic to General and Special Education
1828		Horace Mann influenced authorization of funds for state hospitals for the insane in Massachusetts.		
1831				Samuel Howe became director of the Perkins School, Formerly called the New England Asylum for the Blind.
1834				Louis Braille publishers the first Braille code.
1830s & 1840		Conditions in state hospitals were little better than almshouses. Other forms of treatment included public auctions, selling of chattel slaves, and abandonment.		Horace Mann set economic and legal foundations of American public education, while Secretary of Massachusetts Board of Education (1837-1848) wrote bills which became national standard (e.g., lengths of school year, tax base for financial support of schools, standardized teacher training, standardized school curriculum, political selection of school superintendent, and so on). Established first state normal (teacher training) school (1839).

Date	Mental Retardation	Behavior Disorders	Learning Disabilities	Generic to General and Special Education
1837	Samuel Howe began a class for training retarded children at Perkins Institute in Boston, Massachusetts.			
1839				The first state normal school opens in Massachusetts. Elementary level teachers receive 11 weeks to one year of preparation.
1842	Edward Sequin was instrumental in founding the first school for care and education of mentally retarded (MR) students in Paris, France.			
1843		Dorthea Dix reported cruel and inhumane treatment to the Massachusetts Legislature (e.g., chains, locks, cages, bloodletting practices). Influenced construction of special asylums— some improvement over prisons and poorhouses. Nonexistent rehabilitation and education programs.		

Date	Mental Retardation	Behavior Disorders	Learning Disabilities	Generic to General and Special Education
1846		First educational facility (Westborough, Massachusetts) for socially maladjusted youth. Established with reformatory and educational goals in mind; thus called a "reform school."		
1848	Massachusetts was the first to support state schools for the mentally retarded in the United States.			Depression brought financial strains. Dorthea Dix reveals shocking conditions in asylums.
1850s		Overcrowding doubled clientele of reform school. Custodial rather than instructional services rendered.		
1851	Harvey Willus was the first state-supported school for MR in New York (transferred from Albany to Syracuse in 1855). Other such schools followed in the northeastern and New England states: Ohio (1857); Connecticut (1858); Pennsylvania (1859); Kentucky (1860); Illinois (1865).			

Date	Mental Retardation	Behavior Disorders	Learning Disabilities	Generic to General and Special Education
1850s	Edward Sequin believed retardation to be treatable and curable. Environmental factors (e.g., health, diet) considered important.		Pierre Paul Broca Demonstrated that speech disorders were the result of damage to the frontal convolutions of the brain. He proposed that the functions of the brain's left and right hemispheres were different	
1860s		Prevailing belief that social deviance was inevitable product of immigrant population, largely poor and uneducated		
Mid-1860s	Rise of Darwinist thought. Environmental view gave way to emphasis on innate deficiencies. Mood of pessimism became dominant. State institutions became more custodial. Samuel Howe was discouraged with the results of the Perkins Institute.			National Deaf-Mute College opened, later renamed Galludet College.
1866		Samuel Howe became discouraged by increased size and bureaucratization of mental hospitals and reform schools.		

Date	Mental Retardation	Behavior Disorders	Learning Disabilities	Generic to General and Special Education
1870s		Establishment of "ungraded schools" for mischievous and disruptive children in: New Haven, Connecticut (1871); New York City (1874); Cleveland, Ohio (1875).		
1870-1890	Herbert Spencer Britain) developed a "philosophy of natural selection" (weaker members of society pose threat to future of mankind, thus only the most fit of human species be allowed to survive).			
1875–1900		Classes for socially maladjusted children grew rapidly.		
1887				Anne Sullivan begins work with Helen Keller.
1890s	Increased advocacy efforts for special classes or schools for recalcitrant or mentally deficient children.			More stringent administration of compulsory attendance laws. Educational Commission of the City of Chicago (Hapur Report) urged the establishment of ungraded classes for unmanageable children.

Date	Mental Retardation	Behavior Disorders	Learning Disabilities	Generic to General and Special Education
Late 1800s	First public school programs for the MR in: Providence, Rhode Island (1896); Springfield, Massachusetts (1897); Chicago, Illinois (1898); Boston, Massachusetts (1899); New York City (1900). Called class for "backward" children.			
1896		First U.S. psychological clinic for children opened at the U. of PA by Lightner Witmer.		
1897				National Education Association (NEA) approves the Department of Special Education.
1898				Alexander Graham Bell states that children with handicaps have a right to education in the public schools.
Turn of Century		Establishment of special classes to cope with children who presented problems for regular classrooms.		Anti-immigrant attitude perpetuated Social Darwinism.

Date	Mental Retardation	Behavior Disorders	Learning Disabilities	Generic to General and Special Education
1900				Special class programs for gifted begun in NYC and Worcester, Mass.
Early 1900s	MR children frequently assigned to foreign-speaking "steamer" classes; many normal foreign children placed in classes for the mentally deficient.			Day classes are provided children with blindness in Chicago. The first electrical amplifying device is developed for persons with hearing impairments. Term "special education" used by Alexander Graham Bell at the NEA convention.
1902	Ungraded classes in New Haven, Connecticut reported to serve three distinct types of children grouped together: Incorrigible boys, mentally defective children, and non-English-speaking youth.			
1904	Alfred Binet creates the first paper and intelligence test.	G. Stanley Hall, founder of the American Psychological Assocation, originator of child-study movement. Published *Adolescence*, a two-volume study of youth development and adaptation to the environment.		Preparatory schools opened for gifted students in Worchester, Mass. New Jersey's Vineland Training School held summer classes for teachers of students with M.R. Public Law 58-171, promoted circulation of reading materials for persons with blindness.

Date	Mental Retardation	Behavior Disorders	Learning Disabilities	Generic to General and Special Education
1905				Maximillian P.E. Groszman became the founder and director of the National Association for the Study and Education of Exceptional Children; was first to use term "exceptional." E. L. Thorndike planned a scale to measure educational achievement.
1907	Indiana passed first sterilization law for mental defectives.			
1908	Henry G. Goddard, while Director of Research at the Training School in Vineland, New Jersey, translated the Binet intelligence scales into English and made adaptations for their use in the United States.	Clifford Beers, published personal experiences in mental institutions for a depressive mental disorder. Exposed inhumane and inadequate treatment.		
1909		Elizabeth Farrell helped establish the first special education class in New York City.		

Date	Mental Retardation	Behavior Disorders	Learning Disabilities	Generic to General and Special Education
1911	Goddard published own version of the Binet-Simon Test. New Jersey was the first state to pass legislation concerning the education of MR children in the public schools. Defined MR as "three or more years retarded in mental development."			
1911	New Jersey mandated special classes when number of students with MR in district totaled 10 or more.			
1912	Devereau School Founded in Philadelphia for treating youth with mental retardation and emotional disturbance.			
1912	Publication of "The Kallikak Family," which gave fuel to the prevailing eugenics theory. Portrayed the "feebleminded" as a menace to society and to the future of the human race. Proposed that social undesirables (e.g., criminals, paupers, drunkards) arose from the genetic stock of mentally deficient.			

Date	Mental Retardation	Behavior Disorders	Learning Disabilities	Generic to General and Special Education
1914	Charles Scott Berry set up the first teacher training program in special education at a residential school for MR in Michigan			
	St. Louis, Missouri public school system adopted eligibility standards for special schools for the severely MR and ungraded classes for borderline and backward students.			
1915				Connecticut Board of Education hired Arnold Gessell as first official school psychologist to examine slow-learning children, and to devise better methods for their school instruction.
1915				*Laggards in Our Schools,* by Leonard P. Ayres, used as one of first special education texts.
1916	Lewis Terman produced the Stanford-Binet Scale of Intelligence.			

Date	Mental Retardation	Behavior Disorders	Learning Disabilities	Generic to General and Special Education
1917			James Hinshelwood, a French physician, defined "word blindness" as a condition in which an individual with normal vision is unable to interpret written or printed language. Hinshelwood theorized that this difficulty is caused by a defect in the left hemisphere of the brain, the portion that stores memories of words and letters.	
Between 1852 and 1918				Compulsory school attendance required in all states of the Union, beginning with Massachusetts (1852) and ending with Mississippi (1918).
1918	Wyoming appointed State Director of Special Education responsible for MR, crippled, and speech defective children.			
1919	St. Louis eligibility standards of 1914 were adopted statewide, and subsequently adopted by other states.			

Date	Mental Retardation	Behavior Disorders	Learning Disabilities	Generic to General and Special Education
Years prior to 1920	Relatively small number of teachers trained to work with mentally or socially handicapped. Most facilities were residential with staff members trained on the premises. Technology was not yet developed for assessing individual differences, and special education was not included in curricula at teacher colleges.			
1920s		August Aichhorn, student of Sigmund Freud, developed residential facility for aggressive, delinquent boys.		Columbia University Teachers College prepared teachers of the gifted.
1922	W.E. Fernald persuaded Mass. to set up statewide system of mental clinics for diagnosing children with M.R.			The Internatinal Council for the Education of Exceptional Childeren (CEC) founded with Eliz. Farrell as first president in N.Y.C. Original purposes for establishing the CEC organization included: 1) To emphasize the education of the special child rather than his identification or classification. 2) To establish professional standards for teachers in the field of special education. 3) To unite those interested in the problem of the special child.

Date	Mental Retardation	Behavior Disorders	Learning Disabilities	Generic to General and Special Education
1922	Council for Exceptional Children (CEC) founded with Elizabeth Farrell as first president. Original purposes of establishing the CEC organization included: 1) To emphasize the education of the special child rather than his identification or classification. 2) To establish professional standards for teachers in the field of special education. 3) To unite those interested in the problem of the special child.			
1924	Estimated 43,000 persons with M.R. reside in institutions; 40 state institutions nationwide in existence.	American Orthopsychiatric Association founded. Concerned with early prevention and correction of children's behavior disorders.		Classificaion of exceptionalities published by John Lewis Horn in the Education of Exceptional Children.
1925			Samuel Orton coined the word strephosymbolia (twisted symbols).	
1926			Sir Henry Head theorized that disorders in language could not be dichotomized as sensory or motor.	Hollingsworth implemented enrichment programs for the gifted in New York public schools.
1922–1932	MR enrollment in separate facilities within public school systems more than tripled.	Growth of separate facilities within public school systems for deviant children.		

Date	Mental Retardation	Behavior Disorders	Learning Disabilities	Generic to General and Special Education
1928				Seeing eye dogs for the blind are introduced in the US. Courses in special education offered at 43 teacher training institutions.
1929		Special classes for socially maladjusted frequently called "disciplinary classes." Employed strong arm rather than education or rehabilitation approach.	Samuel T. Orton speculated that one side of the brain dominated the language processes; therefore, he concluded that disabled children who had no demonstrable brain injury had failed to establish hemispheric dominance.	
By 1930	Sixteen states passed legislation regarding education of the mentally handicapped.			U.S. Office of Education established a section of Exceptional Children and Youth administered by Elise Martens.
Early 1930s			Kurt Goldstein observed meticulosity, perseveration, figure-ground configuration, forced responses to stimuli, and catastrophic reaction in adult, brain-injured patients.	
The 1930s	Decrease in special programs for MR and socially deviant youth due to: 1) Less money for special programs; and 2) Dissatisfaction with the quality of education in special classes.			

Date	Mental Retardation	Behavior Disorders	Learning Disabilities	Generic to General and Special Education
	Public schools more likely to provide separate facilities for MR children than for any other exceptionality group, especially the Northeast and north central states.	Establishment of disciplinary classes for truant and incorrigible youth in the schools.		
	Building principals often experienced difficulty in distinguishing between pupils who were "fit subjects" for disciplinary classes and those who were mentally retarded.			
1932				Thirteen states established a state director in charge of administrative special education services.
1933				The first teaching certificates for special education are issued (Mental Retardation, Deaf, Speech Defective, Partially Sighted, Blind, and Crippled).
				The International Council for the Education of Exceptional Children was shortened to the International Council for the Exceptional Children (ICEC).

Date	Mental Retardation	Behavior Disorders	Learning Disabilities	Generic to General and Special Education
1934				The Board of Education of Cleveland Heights v. State ex rel Goldman ruled that the exclusion of a child with low mental functioning, on the basis of tests prescribed by the State Department of Education, was unauthorized.
1934				Certification guidelines are established by the American Association of Instructors of the Blind.
				Talking books on phonograph records are produced.
1935	Edgar Arnold Doll publishes the Vineland Social Maturity Scale.			
1935	New York was the first state to certify school psychologists. Roles consisted largely of evaluating and making recommendations for placement in special services of children viewed as "backward" or MR.			

Date	Mental Retardation	Behavior Disorders	Learning Disabilities	Generic to General and Special Education
Late 1930s and Early 1940s			Alfred A. Strauss and Heinz Werner investigated brain-injured, mentally retarded children. Findings led to the identification of the exogenous subgroup of retarded children (externally brain-injured).	
1943			Grace Fernald used the VAKT (visual-auditory-kinesthetic-tactile) approach in the development of remedial reading programs.	
1944		The Sonja Shankman Orthogenic School opened in Chicago under Bruno Bettelheim for children with emotional disturbance		
The 1940s-W.W.II years	Use of handicapped (including MR) in many jobs due to able-bodied men being away at war.		Laura Lehtinen collaborated with Strauss to develop teaching procedures. Strauss and Lehtinen coauthored *Psychopathy and Education of the Brain-Injured Child* (1947) in which two interventions were suggested: 1) Manipulation and controlling the environment, and 2) Teaching the child voluntary control.	World War II years necessitated man power.

Date	Mental Retardation	Behavior Disorders	Learning Disabilities	Generic to General and Special Education
1946		Division of Child Welfare in NYC organized "600 schools" for children viewed as emotionally disturbed or socially maladjusted. Despite therapeutic intent, these schools were operated as warehouses for uncontrollable boys and were custodial in nature.		
		Fritz Redl and David Wineman opened Pioneer House, a residential treatment center for severely aggressive adolescents. Developed the Life Space Interview intervention.		
Until Early 1950s	Nearly all schools had policies which excluded children with I.Q.s below the mild range. Parents of these children were expected to educate them at home, or place them in state or private residential facilities.	Pearl Berkowitz and Esther Rothman extended psychotherapy into the classroom at Bellevue Hospital in N.Y.		
Early 1950s	Federal funding for teacher preparation in M.R. enacted.	William Morse designed mental-health milieu in camp setting.		

Date	Mental Retardation	Behavior Disorders	Learning Disabilities	Generic to General and Special Education
1948 to1952 to1958	Number of children enrolled in special public school programs increased from 87,000 to 113,000 to over 213,000.			
1950	National Association for Retarded Citizens (NARC) first organized in Minneapolis, Minnesota. This organization was considered the primary source of help to families with retarded children, as well as a major information disseminating and legislative lobbying force.			
The 1950s			William M. Cruikshank facilitated the transfer of brain-injured research from exogenous retarded children to children with normal intelligence. Cruiskshank conducted the Montgomery County Project in Maryland.	
1951		Fritz Redl and David Wineman publish *Children Who Hate*.		

Date	Mental Retardation	Behavior Disorders	Learning Disabilities	Generic to General and Special Education
1953	P.L. 83—531 Cooperative Research Act. Funds earmarked for research with students with M.R.	B.F. Skinner published *Science and Human Behavior.* Proposed operant conditioning as treatment model for B.D.		
1954				Cooperative Research Act of 1954 (P.L. 85-531) authorized support for cooperative research in education; funding was granted for this in 1957.
1955			Helmer R. Mycklebust defined language as symbolic behavior (i.e., using words as symbols for expressing ideas and feelings and labeling objects). Strauss and Newell C. Kephart coauthored Vol. II of *Psychopathology* ... in which comparisons were made of research on brain-injured children of normal intelligence with research on mentally retarded brain-injured children.	

Date	Mental Retardation	Behavior Disorders	Learning Disabilities	Generic to General and Special Education
1956			Spaulding presented an approach to written language disability called Unified Phonics Methods. Words are pronounced and component sounds are written in accordance with the rules of English spelling. Jerome Bruner coauthored *A Study of Thinking* (Bruner, Goodnow, & Austin) which stressed the importance of studying covert cognitive processes.	All 48 states had established legal provisions for some sort of state assistance, advisory and/or financial, to local special education programs. The degree of involvement and support varied from state to state, and the growth of special education services has not been at the same rate for all types of exceptional programs.
1957				Public attitude toward education for all children was spurred by general concern of the populace for American education after the Russian launching of Sputnik.
1958 & 1959	P.L. 85-926 and P.L. 86-158 authorized fellowship awards for graduate students intent on careers as teacher-trainers or administrators of the mentally retarded:		Noam Chomsky gave support to "inner thinking processes."	

Date	Mental Retardation	Behavior Disorders	Learning Disabilities	Generic to General and Special Education
1950s and 1960s	Improved education and training of MR occurred under the Kennedy administration.			
1960s		Edward L. Thorndike, called the "father of reinforcement theory," believed the connection between stimulus and response represented all learning.	J.M. Wepman postulated that the language "transmission" process is divided into receptive and expressive modes. "Integration" provides for the decoding and encoding of previously learned patters to give meaning to the stimulus. Emphasized role of recall, transmission (receptive and expressive modes), and integration (the decoding and encoding of previously learned language patterns). Beginnings of educational focus on children with learning difficulties. Ogden R. Lindsley developed a comprehensive set of measuring procedures, called "precision teaching," which includes pinpointing behavior, counting and charting	

Date	Mental Retardation	Behavior Disorders	Learning Disabilities	Generic to General and Special Education
1960s continued			performance, and making instructional decisions based on performance data.	
Early to Mid-1960s		Norris Haring and E. Lakin Phillips combined Cruickshank's structured environment classroom and B. F. Skinner's operant conditioning to develop educational programs for emotionally disturbed children.		
1962		The Council for Children with Behavioral Disorders (CCBD) was founded as a division of CEC. Nicholas Long became Director of Hillcrest		
1962		Children's Center, Washington D.C. (residential school for B.D.). Long trained teachers in psycho-educational principles. Norris Haring and E. Lakin Phillips applied behaviorism in their Arlington Project for educating students with behavior disorders..		

Date	Mental Retardation	Behavior Disorders	Learning Disabilities	Generic to General and Special Education
1963	Passage of P.L. 88-164 increased support for training of personnel and extended support for professional training to severe areas of childhood exceptionality, including mental retardation and emotional disturbance; authorized use of funds for research and demonstration projects in field of handicapped education.		Term "learning disabilities" was introduced by Samuel Kirk at a national conference of parent organizations and subsequently adopted. Association for Children with Learning Disabilities (ACLD) was formed as a parent, teacher, professional interest group.	
Mid-1960s			Department of Health, Education, and Welfare sponsored several task forces to study brain-injured children with learning problems. Term "minimal brain dysfunction" (MBD) was introduced.	Host of domestic legislation was enacted at the federal level, aimed at launching "War on Poverty" and achieving the "Great Society."
1964		Council for Children with Behavior Disorders established as a division under CEC.		
	P.L. 89-313 encouraged programs to educate children with disabilities residing in institutions and other state-supported residential facilities.			

Date	Mental Retardation	Behavior Disorders	Learning Disabilities	Generic to General and Special Education
1965	P.L. 89-105, added to P.L. 88-164, permitted the construction and operation of research facilities and related programs, including the training of special personnel.	National Society for Autistic Children (NSAC) was founded. Was one of the first major parent-interest groups devoted to concerns of the emotionally disturbed child. Organization has sought public school involvement for autistic children and has opposed their placement in private or residential facilities.		P.L. 89-10, Elementary and Secondary Education Act, Title VI (ESEA) provided assistance to children in "disadvantaged" areas (including handicapped children). Act was called the "Great Society's" legislative package and was considered a significant effort to alleviate poverty through schooling. Eleven colleges and universities received funding by the U.S. Office of Education to help support training of personnel in this field. Office of Economic Opportunity (OEO) established to aid the culturally disadvantaged or deprived child.
1965				Head Start, an OEO-funded project, along with remedial reading, counseling and tutorial services was begun.

Date	Mental Retardation	Behavior Disorders	Learning Disabilities	Generic to General and Special Education
				Student Council for Exceptional Children (SCEC) is organized.
1960			Richard Whelan used token reinforcement methods at the Children's Rehabilitation Unit. Association for the Advancement of Behavior Therapy founded.	CEC publishes first set of professional standards for special education. U.S. Office of Education funds grant for CEC to operate the ERIC Clearinghouse on Exceptional Children. Federal Bureau of Education for the Handicapped (BEH) formed. Encouraged training, research, demonstration, etc.
1965	Burton Blatt publishes expose on institutions "Christmas in Purgatory"			
1967	Hobson v. Hanson litigation resulted in finding the "tracking" system in Washington, D.C. to be unconstitutional. Based on standardized test results, children were placed in honors, general, or special programs. Relying on Brown v. Board of			A separate Bureau for the Education of the Handicapped (BEH) was creates within the U.S. Office of Education .Special Education was included in the top policy-making levels for the first time.

Date	Mental Retardation	Behavior Disorders	Learning Disabilities	Generic to General and Special Education
1967 continued	Education, the court held that assessment measures were culturally biased and sustained an unjustifiable racial separation of students. A disproportionate number of African-American children were enrolled in special classes.			
1968	Lloyd Dunn questioned the wisdom of special self-contained class placement for students with MR.	Joint Commission on Mental Health of children estimated at least 100,000 children were in residential treatment institutions for B.D., and 1.5 million children and youth were in need of psychiatric services.	The Division for Children with Learning Disabilities (DCLD)(now Council for Learning Disabilities) was organized as a professional division within the CEC	P.L. 90-538 authorized the negotiation of grants and contracts with both private and public agencies to establish experimental preschool- and early education programs for special needs students.
		Frank M. Hewett designed the "engineered" classroom using developmental sequence of educational goals known as the Santa Monica Project.	The National Advisory Committee of Handicapped Children (NACHC) was formed to develop a definition for learning disabilities. *Journal of Learning Disabilities* was published.	P.L./90-583, (Handicapped Children's Early Education Assistance Act), established experimental demonstration centers for the education of preschool children with disabilities.

Date	Mental Retardation	Behavior Disorders	Learning Disabilities	Generic to General and Special Education
1969			P.L. 91-230, the Specific Learning Disabilities Act of 1969, was passed along with all of the categories of programs and services for educating children with special needs who receive federal assistance. The definition developed by the NACHC under Kirk's leadership was used in this act.	P.L. 91-61, provided the authority to the secretary of health, education, and welfare to contract a university to develop, construct, and operate a national center of educational media and materials for persons with disabilities.
Late 1960s and 1970s	Skinner defined two types of learned behavior: respondent (involuntary) and operant (voluntary). Transferred work with animals in the laboratory (1950s) to observable, measurable events in the educational arena (1960s and 1970s).			"Right to fair classification" cases filed as class action suits. Parents and other interested parties argued that the labeling and placement procedure by which children are processed into special education is culturally discriminatory and a violation of the 14th Amendment's Constitutional guarantee for due process and equal protection under the law.

Date	Mental Retardation	Behavior Disorders	Learning Disabilities	Generic to General and Special Education
Early 1970s				Jean Piaget's developmental theory suggested that instruction should recognize maturational growth and not require students to perform skills for which they are not ready.
The 1970s	NARC organized effective lobbying forces and succeeded in bringing about massive increases in school services for children previously thought to be "unteachable."	Juvenile justice system dealt with 900,000 youth ages 10 to 17, which was 3 percent of this age group.		
1971	Pennsylvania Association for Retarded Children alleged violations of due process and equal protection under the 14th Amendment of the U.S. Constitution regarding barring of low I.Q children from public schools in that state. Similar "right-to-education" suits initiated in other states.			The optacon, and optical scan of a printed page, generates a tactile impression of letters for persons with blindness.

Date	Mental Retardation	Behavior Disorders	Learning Disabilities	Generic to General and Special Education
1971	Larry P. v. Riles was filed as a class action suit in California on behalf of several Black children who had been placed and retained in EMR classes. Plaintiffs alleged use of racially and culturally biased testing procedures, which violated the Civil Rights Act of 1871 and the right to equal protection under the California Constitution and the 14th Amendment of the U.S. Constitution.			
1972	A preliminary injunction was issued by the court halting the use of I.Q. tests in the state of California for placing Black children in classes for the EMR.			P.L. 92-424, mandated a minimum of 10 percent of the enrollment slots in Head Start programs be made available to students with disabilities. Mills v. the Board of Education mandated the District of Columbia serve all students with disabilities.
1973		Peter Knoblock promotes open education for disturbed children.		P.L. 93-112, Section 504, specified that no individual with a disability should be excluded from the participation in, be denied benefits

Date	Mental Retardation	Behavior Disorders	Learning Disabilities	Generic to General and Special Education
1973 continued				of, or subjected to discrimination under any program or activity receiving federal financial assistance.
1974	Carl Fenichel developed the League School in Brooklyn (first day school for psychotic children). Enlisted parents as partners.			P.L. 93-380, Title VI, extended the Education of Handicapped Act. Required states to locate and serve all children with handicaps. Assured an education with one's peers, if possible, and mandated nondiscriminatory evaluation materials. Included in law was Family Educational Rights and Privacy Act of 1974, referred to as Buckley Act. This Act protects the confidentiality of school records and provides procedures to challenge questionable information in student records.

Date	Mental Retardation	Behavior Disorders	Learning Disabilities	Generic to General and Special Education
1975		U.S. Senate report (sub-committee to Investigate Juvenile Delinquency, 1975) documented growth of violence and crime in schools.		Public Law 94-142 (Education for All Handicapped Children Act) (EHA) provided for a free, appropriate public education for all handicapped children, and defined special education and related services. Mandated that an individualized education plan (IEP) or an individualized family services plan (IFSP) be developed for every child found eligible for special education or early intervention.
1975	P.L. 94-142, The Education for Handicapped Childrens Act is enacted into Federal Law			CEC revised Professional Standards and Guidelines in Special Education.
1976				The Kurzweil Reader, a prototype translator of printed text into speech for readers with blindness, is invented.
1978				Gifted and Talented Children's Act (Title IX-A), provides funds to state and local

Date	Mental Retardation	Behavior Disorders	Learning Disabilities	Generic to General and Special Education
1978 continued				education agencies and public and private agencies to meet the needs of gifted and talented students.
1978			Formation of the National Joint Commission for Learning Disabilities (NJCLD).	
Late 1970s				The Reagan Administration attempted to deregulate and decentralize all phases of public education; however, most categorical services and mandates regulating special education survived this initiative. Department of Education established by Congress.
1980		U.S. Dept. Of Health and Human Services reported 15,000 children ages 14 and under admitted to inpatient facilities and over a quarter million seen in outpatient psychiatric clinics.		A separate U.S. Department of Education established, removing responsibilities form the Department of Health, Education, and Welfare.

Date	Mental Retardation	Behavior Disorders	Learning Disabilities	Generic to General and Special Education
1981				S-1 v. Turlington rules that complete cessation of services for students with disabilities is not allowed; expulsion is allowable under some circumstances.
1982				The DCLD membership voted to withdraw from CEC and form an independent organization, the Council for Learning Disabilities (CLD). A cadre of former DCLD members began a new CEC division called the Division for Learning Disabilities (DLD).
1983				Office of Special Education and Rehabilitative Services (OSERS) created under the newly established Department of Education.
				Public Law 98-199 (EHA Amendments) passed. Reaffirmed the federal role in special education by expanding P.L. 94-142 with

Date	Mental Retardation	Behavior Disorders	Learning Disabilities	Generic to General and Special Education
				supported preschool, secondary, and post secondary programs for the handicapped, and support for special education teacher preparation, early childhood education, parent training, and information dissemination.
1985				Children "at risk"—poor, nonwhite, disabled, and female become the focus of education reform.
1986				Public Law 99-457 (EHA Amendments) reauthorized existing EHA, amended PL 94-142 to include financial incentives for states to educate children ages 3 to 5 by the 1990-91 school year, and established incentive grants to promote programs serving handicapped infants (birth to age 2).

Date	Mental Retardation	Behavior Disorders	Learning Disabilities	Generic to General and Special Education
1988				The Gifted and Talented Students Education Act of 1988 authorized funding of a National Research Center and demonstration programs to build the nationwide capability to meet the needs of gifted and talented students, especially those from traditionally underserved populations.
1989				Academic standards take the spotlight. The National Council of Teachers of Mathematics is the first to state its curriculum standards.
1990				P.L. 101-336 (Americans with Disabilities Act) (ADA) gives civil rights protection to individuals with disabilities in private sector employment, all public services,

Date	Mental Retardation	Behavior Disorders	Learning Disabilities	Generic to General and Special Education
1990 continued				public accommodations, transportation, and telecommunications. Patterned after (and extends) Section 504 of the Rehabilitation Act of 1973. Prohibits discrimination on the basis of disability and requires agencies to provide "reasonable accommodations."
				P.L. 101-392 (Carl D. Perkins Vocational and Technology Education Act) provides resources to improve educational programs needed in order to work in a technologically advanced society.
				Guarantees full vocational, educational opportunities for all special needs populations.

Date	Mental Retardation	Behavior Disorders	Learning Disabilities	Generic to General and Special Education
1990 to 1991			The U.S. House of Representatives opened for citizen comment the issue of a separate exceptionality category for students with attention deficit disorders. The issue died without legislative action.	Public Law 101-476 (Individuals with Disabilities Education Act) (IDEA) reauthorized and renamed existing EHA. This amendment tto EHA changed the term "handicap" to "disability," expanded related services, and required individual education programs (IEPs) to contain transitional goals and objectives for adolescents (ages 16 and above, special situations age 14.) The exceptionality categories of autism and traumatic brain injury were added.
1991				National Education Goals 2000 are adopted. Encourages involvement of reform-minded communities, national examinations, and parental choices including private schools.

Date	Mental Retardation	Behavior Disorders	Learning Disabilities	Generic to General and Special Education
1992				Rehabilitation Act Amendments establish the presumption that anyone can be employed and increase the focus on vocational rehabilitation services for minorities.
1994				P.L. 103-239 (School to Work Opportunities Act) promotes collaboration and problem solving by the Department of Education and Labor. Encourages partnership models between school-based and employment-based sites at the local level. Promotes interagency agreements, technical assistance, and services to employers, educators, case managers, and others.
1995				CEC published its third set of standards for the preparation and certification of special education teachers.

Date	Mental Retardation	Behavior Disorders	Learning Disabilities	Generic to General and Special Education
1997				P.L. 105-17 (Amendment to and reauthorization of IDEA) adds general education curriculum to student's IEP, modifies alternative placement options pending discipline determinations, and modifies transition requirements.

Bibliography

Cullinan, D., Epstein, M.H., & Lloyd, J.W. (1983). *Behavior disorders of children and adolescents*. Englewood Cliffs, NJ: Prentice-Hall, Inc.

Gearheart, B.R. (1974). *Organization and administration of educational programs for exceptional children*. Springfield, IL: Charles C. Thomas, Publisher.

Rhodes, W.C., & Tracy, M.L. (1966). *A study of child variance: Conceptual models* (Vols. 1 & 2). Ann Arbor, MI: University of Michigan.

The Council for Exceptional Children. (1997, May & June). *Teaching Exceptional Children*, 29(5), 5–49.

Commonly Used
Psychoactive Medications*

Stimulants

Expected Classroom Effects

Stimulants are the most widely used drugs in the treatment of students with mild disabilities. Their intended effects are to make the students more ready to learn rather than to make the students learn. They have their so-called "paradoxical effect" of decreasing symptoms by increasing behaviors that inhibit hyperactivity, distractbility, and inattention which often interfere with a readiness to learn.

Stimulants Commonly Used With Students With Mild Disabilities

Dextroamphetamine sulfate.   (Dexedrine) is usually administered in 5 milligram dosages (daily at 8 am and 12 noon). Less classroom restlessness, increased attention span, and improvements in social and emotional behavior patterns are the expected effects. Most common side effects are loss of appetite and loss of sleep; less common are headaches with blurred vision, apathy, stupor, tiredness, dry mouth, and drug tolerance over long periods of use.

Methylphenidate hydrochloride.   (Ritalin) is usually administered in a single 20 milligram dose in the morning or in two 10 milligram doses in the morning and afternoon; it is generally taken before a meal. Less classroom restlessness, increased attention span, and improvements in social and emotional behavior patterns are the expected effects. Most common side effects are loss of sleep; less common are headaches with blurred vision, apathy, stupor, tiredness, dry mouth, and drug tolerance over long periods of use. Ritalin does not suppress appetite as much as Dexedrine.

Magnesium pemoline.   (Cylert) is usually administered once a day in a 37.5 milligram dosage and is considered slower acting than other stimulants. Less

---

* *Source:* B. Algozzine, Behavior Problem Management: Educatior's Resource Service. Rockville, MD: Aspen Publishers, 1997.

classroom restlessness, increased attention span, and improvements in social and emotional behavior patterns are the expected effects. Most common side effects are loss of appetite and loss of sleep; less common are headaches with blurred vision, apathy, stupor, tiredness, dry mouth, and drug tolerance over long periods of use. Cylert is preferred over Dexedrine because it does not suppress most children's appetites as much.

Minor tranquilizers

Expected Classroom Effects

Minor tranquilizers are the second most commonly used drugs in the treatment of students with mild disabilities. Their intended effects are to reduce anxiety and agitation associated with some emotional and learning problems. The goal again is to help students become more receptive to instruction.

Minor Tranquilizers Commonly Used With Students With Mild Disabilities

Amitriptyline hydrochloride. (Elavil) is usually administered in varying dosages according to level of problems, but is not recommended for students under 12. Expected effects include antidepressant and sedative action. Most common side effects are sleepiness, dry mouth, blurred vision, nightmares, dizziness when first standing up, and weight gain.

Maprotilene hydrochloride. (Ludiomil) is usually administered in initial dosage of 75 milligrams daily which can be divided; dosages of as low as 25 milligrams are recommended for some. It is indicated for treatment of depressive illness and relief of anxiety associated with depression. Expected effects include antidepressant and sedative action. Most common side effects are sleepiness, dry mouthy, blurred vision, nightmares, dizziness when first standing up, and weight gain.

Imapramine hydrochloride. (Tofranil) is usually administered in one 10–25 milligram dose an hour before bed to control enuresis or 75 milligrams once a day for more serious problem behaviors. It is the most widely recognized and recommended antidepressant for children under 12 years of age; there can be as much as a three-week lag before effects are noticed. Controlled bed-wetting and improved emotional and social patterns result in children who are depressed or overly anxious. Most common side effects are dry mouth, urinary retention, blurred vision, tremors, drowsiness, sweating, and some postural rigidity.

Chlordiazepoxide hydrochloride. (Librium) is usually administered in divided doses up to 30 milligrams a day; it is not recommended for children under six. Expected effects include reduction in anxiety, general relaxation, sense of well-being, and general drowsiness. Most common side effects are confusion, skin eruptions, edema, gastrointestinal symptoms, unwanted drowsiness, jaundice, and some changes in electroencephalogram patterns.

Hydroxine hydrochloride. (Atarax) is usually administered in varying doses according to the level of the individual's problems. Expected effects include reduction in anxiety, aggressiveness and hyperactivity. Most common side effects are tolerance, dependence, and dry mouth.

Meprobamate. (Equanil) is usually administered 2 or 3 times a day in 100–200 milligram dosages. Expected effects include reduction in anxiety; it is used for its sedative effects. Most common side effects are unwanted drowsiness, dependency, and hematologic disorders.

Deanol acetamid obenzoate. (Deaner) is usually administered in one 100 milligram dose in the morning. Improved emotional and social patterns result in children who are immature or anxious. Most common side effects are headaches, constipation, insomnia, and skin rashes.

Major Tranquilizers

Expected Classroom Effects

Major tranquilizers are less commonly used than stimulants and minor tranquilizers in the treatment of students with mild disabilities. Their intended effects are to reduce symptoms associated with more severe disabilities, including depression, psychotic behavior, and delusions associated with clinical forms of emotional disturbance. The reduction in symptoms is associated with a more favorable clinical receptiveness for behavioral intervention.

Major Tranquilizers Commonly Used With Students With Mild Disabilities

Haloperidol. (Haldol) is usually administered in 1 milligram dosages several times a day; it is not recommended for children. Haldol is used to treat mania, paranoia, social withdrawal, and aggressive problems associated with schizophrenia. Most common side effects are skin reactions, jaundice, and impaired vision.

Chlorpromazine hydrochloride. (Thorazine) is usually administered in 10–24 milligram dosages two or three times a day; it can be increased to 50 milligrams for adolescents. Expected effects include reduction in activity and general reduction in aggressive, negative symptoms commonly seen in seriously disturbed individuals. Most common side effects are skin reactions, impaired vision, and weight gain.

Thioridiazine hydrochloride. (Mellaril) is usually administered in 10 milligram dosages three or four times a day for preschoolers and in 25 milligram dosages three or four times a day for older children. Expected effects include antidepressive symptoms, reduced anxiety, aggression reduction, and less overall activity. Most common side effects are sexual dysfunction in males, disturbed color vision, and weight gain.

Anticonvulsants

Expected Classroom Effects

Anticonvulsants are commonly used in the treatment of students with sudden, brief, localized seizures or widespread convulsive seizures associates with epilepsy and some types of mild disabilities. Therapeutic effects do not cure convulsive disorders, but do not control seizures without altering other functions of the Central Nervous System.

Anticonvulsants Commonly Used With Students With Mild Disabilities

Phenobarbital. (Luminal) is usually administered in 100 milligram dosages and may require as long as 15 minutes to take effect. Expected effects include control of grand mal seizures. Most common side effects are sedation, rashes, slurred speech.

Diphenylhydantoin. (Dilantin) is usually administered in varying milligram dosages dependent on age of individual, ranging from 50 milligrams for 1–2 year olds to 300–400 milligrams for adolescents. Expected effects include control of grand mal seizures; generally considered drug of choice for most forms of epilepsy (except petit mal seizures). Most common side effects are ataxia, nystagmus, vertigo, blurred vision, confusion, hallucinations, nausea, and urinary incontinence.

Ethosuximide. (Zarontin) is usually administered in 0.5–1.0 milligram dosages two or three times a day. Expected effects include control of petit mal seizures; generally considered drug of choice for this form of seizures. Most common side effects are gastric distress, nausea, vomiting, anorexia, headaches, fatigue, dizziness, and blood disorders.

Carbamazepine.   (Tegretol) is usually administered in varying dosages relative to diagnosis and age. Expected effects include reduction of psychomotor and grand mal seizures. Most common side effects are drowsiness, double vision, uncoordination, rapid eye movement, nausea, and skin rashes.

Ethosuximide.   (Zarontin) is usually administered in 0.5-1.0 milligram dosages two or three times a day. Expected effects include contol of petit mal seizures; generally considered drug of choice for this form of seizures. Most common side effects are gastric distress, nausea, vomiting, anorexia, headaches, fatigue, dizziness, and blood disorders.

APPENDIX C

Genetic, Pre-, Peri, and Postnatal Disorders

A. Genetic Disorders

Occur at the time of conception within the fetus's genetic code. Some common genetic disorders are:

1. Cystic fibrosis: severe health impairment of the lungs, causing ill health and eventual death.
2. Muscular dystrophy: a wasting disease of the muscles, causing gradual weakness and inability to walk.
3. Diabetes: caused by lack of insulin output by the pancreas; usually controllable.
4. Asthma: a breathing disorder that frequently limits physical activity; often controllable.
5. Inherited personality characteristics and abilities: sometimes precipitate behavior disorders or learning disabilities.
6. Phenylketonuria (PKU): defect in metabolism of proteins; can result in retardation if not controlled with diet from birth.
7. Galactosemia: defect in metabolism of carbohydrates; can result in retardation if not controlled with diet from birth.
8. Tay-Sachs Disease: a defect in metabolism of fats; most prevalent in Jewish families; usually causes paralysis, blindness, convulsions, and death by the age of 3.
9. Arthogryphosis: characterized by stiff joints and weak muscles, and missing or smaller than normal limbs; crippling but not progressive.
10. Osteogenesis imperfecta: Brittle Bone Disease; bones break very easily; causes crippling and deafness or hearing impairment.
11. Spinal muscular atrophy: progressive degeneration of motor nerve cells; results in clumsiness to paralysis, depending on degree of severity.
12. Congenital blindness.
13. Congenital deafness.

Source: Eyes on the Special Education: Professional Knowledge Teachers Competency Test by R.S. Ramsey, M. J. Dixon, and G.G. B. Smith, with publication assistance from S.L. Aultman (Director), Albany GA: Southwest Georgia Learning Resources System Center, 1986

14. Tuberous sclerosis: a biochemical disorder causing the growth of tumors on the brain, face, eyes, and internal organs; can result in retardation, blindness, disfigurement, and death.
15. Down syndrome: an abnormal number of chromosomes; more common in children of mothers over 40; often results in retardation and is accompanied by physical problems, particularly heart problems.
16. Cretinism: lack of the thyroid hormone; almost always causes retardation.
17. Fragile X syndrome–defect on the tip of the X chromosome causing some hormonal difficulties.

B. Prenatal Disorders

Occur during the time of intrauterine development before birth. The most frequently encountered prenatal disorders are:

1. Clubfoot: one foot turned down or turned in; results in physical impairment.
2. Spina Bifida: a congenital defect resulting when the bones of the spine fail to grow together; occurs during the first 30 days of pregnancy; can result in paralysis, mental retardation, and early death, depending on the degree of involvement, but does not necessarily cause retardation or death.
3. Scoliosis (curvature of the spine), lordosis (swayback), and kyphosis (humpback): can cause physical deformities and difficulty in ambulation.
4. Phocomelia (missing or stunted limbs): affect motor activities and/or ambulation, depending on affected limbs; caused by maternal infection, such as Rubella, early in pregnancy, or by the taking of medications such as Thalidomide or other drugs.
5. Deafness or blindness: can result from maternal illnesses such as rubella early in pregnancy.
6. Hydrocephalus: an excess of cerebrospinal fluid, causing enlargement of the skull and increased pressure on the brain, resulting in retardation.
7. Fetal alcohol syndrome: results in microcephaly, retardation, and stunted growth and other physical abnormalities, including curved spine caused by excessive consumption of alcohol by the mother during pregnancy.
8. Drug dependency at birth: results from the mother using drugs during pregnancy, also often causes retardation.
9. Cleft lip and palate: incomplete fusion of the upper lip and/or palate, which even if surgically repaired can result in nasality and other speech problems.
10. Rh incompatibility: caused by an incompatibility in the Rh factors in the blood of an Rh- mother and an Rh+ fetus; can result in tissue damage and retardation.
11. Prematurity and/or low birthweight: can be caused by cigarette smoking or drug use during pregnancy, also common in teenage pregnancies.

C. Perinatal Disorders

Occur during or shortly after birth. The most common causes of perinatal disorders are:

1. Anoxia, or oxygen deprivation: can cause brain damage and cerebral palsy (with resulting paralysis, blindness, and learning or behavior disorders); epilepsy (seizures); and cerebral palsy (resulting in gross- and fine-motor impairment and speech defects).
2. Maternal infections, such as AIDS, syphilis, and herpes simplex, which can infect the child before or during birth, resulting in brain damage and retardation.

D. Postnatal Disorders

Occur after birth. They include:

1. Encephalitis and meningitis: can result in mental retardation, behavior disorders, or attention disorders.
2. Measles, whooping cough: can result in visual impairment, deafness, hyperactivity, disorders of attention, mental retardation, and behavior disorders.
3. Stroke or brain injury: can result in aphasia and paralysis.
4. Spinal cord injuries; paralysis.
5. Polio: paralysis or muscle weakness.
6. Amputation: due to injury or disease, the effect depends on the limb involved.
7. Retrolental fibroplasia: blindness resulting from excessive oxygen being given to premature infants in incubators.
8. Lead poisoning: can result in retardation; other learning and behavior disorders.
9. Brain tumors: can cause blindness, deafness, gross or fine motor impairment, or retardation.
10. Extreme malnutrition: can stunt growth, cause cretinism, or cause retardation.
11. Immune disorders such as rheumatoid arthritis, which causes joint pain and impairs gross and fine motor ability.
12. Leukemia and other childhood cancers: affects the child's general health; treatments often produce weakness and nausea.

Tests

Frequently Used Achievement Tests

Test	Major Areas	Type of Test		Standardization		Administration	
Name	Tested	Formal	Informal	Norm-Referenced	Criterion-Referenced	Individual	Group
Brigance-R Diagnostic Inventories	reading, writing, spelling, mathematics, language, motor skills		×		×	×	
Diagnostic Achievement Battery (DAB)	listening, speaking, reading, writing, mathematics	×		×		×	
Kaufman Test of Educational Achievement (KTEA)	reading, spelling, mathematics	×		×		×	
Peabody Individual Achievement Test-Revised (PIAT-R)	mathematics, reading, spelling, general information	×		×		×	
Wide Range Achievement Test-Revised (WRAT-R)	reading, spelling, arithmetic	×		×		×	
Gilmore Oral Reading Test (GORT)	oral reading	×		×		×	
Durrell Analysis of Reading Difficulty	oral & silent reading, listening, comprehension, word analysis, spelling, handwriting	×		×		×	

Test	Major Areas	Type of Test		Standardization		Administration	
Name	*Tested*	*Formal*	*Informal*	*Norm-Referenced*	*Criterion-Referenced*	*Individual*	*Group*
Gates-Mac-Ginitie Reading Tests	silent reading, vocabulary, & comprehension	X		X			X
Gray Oral Reading Tests-Revised (GORT-R)	oral reading	X		X		X	
Slosson Oral Reading Test	word reading	X		X		X	
Test of Reading Comprehension (TORC)	reading comprehension	X		X		X	
Woodcock Reading Mastery Tests-Revised (WRMT-R)	reading	X		X		X	
The Boder Test of Reading-Spelling Patterns	reading, spelling		X			X	
Test of Written Language (TOWL)	written language	X		X		X	X
Larsen-Hammill Test of Written Spelling (TWS-2)	written spelling	X		X		X	X
Enright R Diagnostic Inventory of Basic Arithmetic Skills	math computation	X			X	X	X
Key Math-Revised	mathematics	X			X	X	

Frequently Used Intelligence Tests

Test	Major Areas	Type of Test		Standardization		Administration	
		Formal	Informal	Norm-Referenced	Criterion-Referenced	Individual	Group
Name	_Tested_						
Coloured Progressive Matrices (CPM)	visual perception & analogous reasoning	×		×		×	
Denver Developmental Screening Test-Revised (DDST)	social, fine motor, gross motor, & language skills	×				×	
Detroit Tests of Learning Aptitude-Revised (DTLA-2)	vocabulary sequencing, detail recognition, and memory	×		×		×	
Detroit Tests of Learning Aptitude-Primary (DTLA-P)	verbal & nonverbal aptitudes, structural & conceptual aptitudes, memory & motor skills	×		×		×	
Goodenough-Harris Drawing Test	conceptual & intellectual maturity & personality characteristics	×				×	×
Kaufman Assessment Battery for Children (K-ABC)	cognitive ability & achievement	×		×		×	
McCarthy Scales of Children's Abilities (MSCA)	general intellectual abiliity	×		×		×	
Slosson Intelligence Test for Children and Adults (SIT)	mental ability	×		×		×	

Test	Major Areas	Type of Test		Standardization		Administration	
Name	Tested	Formal	Informal	Norm-Referenced	Criterion-Referenced	Individual	Group
Stanford Binet Intelligence Scale (4th ed.) (SB)	verbal reasoning, quantitative reasoning, abstract/reasoning, short-term memory	×		×		×	
System of Multicultural Pluristic Assessment (SOMPA)	cognitive abilities, sensory-motor skills, & adaptive behavior	×		×		×	
Wechsler Intelligence Scale for Children-Revised (WISC-R)	general intelligence	×		×		×	
Woodcock-Johnson Psycho-Educational Battery-Revised (WJ-R)	cognitive ability and academic skills in reading, writing, mathematics, & general knowledge	×		×		×	

Frequently Used Language Tests

Test	Major Areas	Type of Test		Standardization		Administration	
Name	Tested	Formal	Informal	Norm-Referenced	Criterion-Referenced	Individual	Group
The Goldman-Fristoe Test of Articulation (GIFTA)	articulation	×			×	×	
Auditory-Visual Single Word Picture Vocabulary Test-Adolescent (VSWPVT-A)	receptive picture vocabulary		×			×	×
Boehm Test of Basic Concepts-Revised (BTBC-R)	basic relational and space, quantity, & time concepts	×				×	×
Clinical Evaluation of Language Fundamentals Revised (CELF-R)	word meaning; word & sentence structure; recall and retrieval	×		×		×	
Expressive One-Word Picture Vocabulary Test (EOWPVT)	expressive vocabulary	×		×		×	
Expressive One-Word Picture Vocabulary Test-Upper Extension (EOWPVT-UE)	expressive vocabulary	×		×		×	
Peabody Picture Vocabulary Test-Revised (PPVT-R)	receptive single-word vocabulary	×		×		×	
Preschool Language Scale (PLS)	receptive & expressive language; articulation	×			×	×	
Test of Adolescent Language (TOAL-2)	receptive & expressive language, spoken & written	×		×		×	×

| Test | Major Areas | Type of Test | | Standardization | | Administration | |
| | | | | Norm- | Criterion- | | |
Name	Tested	Formal	Informal	Referenced	Referenced	Individual	Group
Test of Language Development-2-Primary (TOLD-2-P)	receptive & expressive language	×		×		×	
Test of Language Development-2 Intermediate (TOLD-2-I)	receptive & expressive language	×		×		×	
Test of Word Finding (TWF)	accuracy & speed of naming	×		×		×	
The Word Test	expressive language	×		×		×	

Frequently Used Perceptual/Perceptual-Motor Tests

Test	Major Areas	Type of Test		Standardization		Administration	
Name	Tested	Formal	Informal	Norm-Referenced	Criterion-Referenced	Individual	Group
Test of Visual Motor Skills (TVMS)	visual perception & eye-motor coordination	X		X		X	X
Test of Visual-Perceptual Skills (Non-Motor)	visual- perception (all types)	X				X	
Bruininks-Oseretsky Test of Motor Proficiency	motor proficiency, gross & fine motor skills	X				X	
Miller Assessment for Preschoolers (MAP)	sensory and motor abilities; verbal & nonverbal cognitive abilities	X		X		X	
Peabody Developmental Motor Scales (PDMS)	gross & fine motor skills	X				X	X
Marianne Frostig Developmental Test of Visual Perception (DTVP)	visual perception	X				X	X
Purdue Perceptual-Motor Survey	laterality, directionality, perceptual-motor skills	X			X	X	
Wepman Auditory Discrimination Test	auditory discrimination	X				X	

REFERENCES

Abeson, A., & Weintraub, F. (1973). The law and that other minority. In N. Kreinberg & S. H. L. Chow (Ed.), *Configurations of change: The integration of mildly handicapped children into the regular classroom.* California: National Institute of Education, 12–44.

Achenbach, T. M., & Edelbrook, C. S. (1981). Behavioral problems and competencies reported by parents of normal and disturbed children aged 4 through 16. *Monographs of the Society for Research in Child Development, 46,* (Serial No. 188).

Adelman, H. S. (1989). Beyond the learning mystique: An interactional perspective on learning disabilities. *Journal of Learning Disabilities, 22*(5), 301–304, 328.

Ager, C. L., & Cole, C. L. (1991). A review of cognitive-behavioral interventions for children and adolescents with behavioral disorders. *Behavioral Disorders, 16*(4), 260–275.

Ainsworth, M. D. S. (1978). *Patterns of attachment.* Hillside, NJ: Lawrence Erlbaum Associates.

Albert, L. (1994). Cooperative discipline. *Teaching Kids Responsibility, 1*(1), 1.

Alberto, P. A., & Troutman, A. C. (1982). *Applied behavior analysis for teachers.* Columbus, OH: Merrill Publishing.

Algozzine, B. (1977). The emotionally disturbed child: Disturbed or disturbing? *Journal of Abnormal Child Psychology, 5,* 205–211.

Algozzine, B. (1990). *Behavior problem management. Educator's resource service.* Gaithersburg, MD: Aspen Publishers.

Algozzine, B., Christenson, S., & Ysseldyke, J. E. (1982). Probabilities associated with the referral to placement process. *Teacher Education and Special Education, 5,* 19–23.

Algozzine, B., & Korinek, L. (1985). Where is special education for students with high prevalence handicaps going? *Exceptional Children, 51,* 388–394.

Algozzine, B., & Maheady, L. (1986). When all else fails, teach. *Exceptional Children, 52*(6), 287–300.

Algozzine, B., Morsink, C. V., & Algozzine, K. M. (1988). What's happening in self-contained special education classrooms? *Exceptional Children, 55,* 259–265.

Algozzine, B., Ruhl, K., & Ramsey, R. (1991). *Behaviorally disordered? Assessment for identification and instruction.* CEC Mini-library. Reston, VA: The Council for Exceptional Children.

Algozzine, B., Schmid, R. E., & Connors, R. (1978). Toward an acceptable definition of emotional disturbance. *Behavioral Disorders, 4,* 48–52.

Algozzine, B., Schmid, R., & Mercer, C. D. (1981). *Childhood behavior disorders: Applied research and education practice.* Rockville, MD: Aspen.

Algozzine, B., Serna, L., & Patton, J. (1998). *Childhood behavior disorders: Applied research and practice.* Austin, TX. Pro-Ed.

Algozzine, B., & Ysseldyke, J. E. (1983). Learning disabilities as a subset of school failure: The oversophistication of a concept. *Exceptional Children, 50,* 242–246.

Algozzine, B., & Ysseldyke, J. E. (1986). The future of the LD field: Screening and diagnosis. *Journal of Learning Disabilities, 19,* 394–398.

Algozzine, B., & Ysseldyke, J. E. (1987). Questioning discrepancies: Retaking the first step 20 years later. *Learning Disabilities Quarterly, 10,* 301–312.

Algozzine, K. (1997). One minute behavior management. In B. Algozzine (Ed.) *Problem Behavior Management: Educator's resource service* (pp 11:36–11:40). Gaithersberg, MD: Aspen Publishers.

Allen, D. (1989). Evaluating solutions, monitoring progress, and revising intervention plans. In M. R. Shinn (Ed.), *Curriculum based measurement: Assessing special students*. New York: Guilford Press.

Allen, L. D., Gottselig, M., & Boyland, S. (1982). A practical mechanism for using free time as a reinforcer in the classroom. *Education and Treatment of Children, 5*(4), 245–253.

Alley, G., & Deshler, D. (1979). *Teaching learning disabled adolescent: Strategies and methods*. Denver, CO: Love Publishing.

American Association on Mental Retardation. (1992). *Mental retardation: Definition, classification, and systems of support—Workbook*. Washington, DC: Author.

American Psychiatric Association. (1994). *Diagnostic and statistical manual of mental disorders* (4th ed.). Washington, DC: Author.

American Psychiatric Association. (1987). *Diagnostic and statistical manual of mental disorders* (3rd ed. rev.). Washington, DC: Author.

American Psychiatric Association. (1993). *Diagnostic and statistical manual of mental disorders* (4th ed.) (DSM–IV). Washington, DC: Author.

Apter, S. J. (1982). *Troubled children, troubled systems*. New York: Pergamon.

Armor, D., Conry-Oseguera, P., Cox, M., King, N., McDonnell, L., Pascal, A., Pualy, E., & Zellman, G. (1976). *Analysis of the school preferred reading program in selected Los Angeles minority schools*. (Report No. R–2007–LAUSFD). Santa Monica, CA: The Rand Corporation. (ERIC Document Reproduction No. ED 130–243).

Association for Supervision and Curriculum Development (1994). *Curriculum update*. Alexandria, VA: Author.

Baca, L., & Harris, K. D. (1988). Teaching migrant exceptional students. *Teaching Exceptional Children, 24*(4), 32–35.

Baker, K. (1985). Research evidence of a school discipline problem. *Phi Delta Kappan, 66*(7), 482–488.

Bane, M. J., & Ellwood, D. T. (1984a). *The dynamics of children's living arrangements*. Cambridge, MA: Harvard University. (Contract No. HHS-S2A–82). Washington, DC: U.S. Department of Health and Human Services.

Bane, M. J., & Ellwood, D. T. (1984b). *Single mothers and their living arrangements*. Cambridge, MA: Harvard University. (Contract No. HHS–100–82–0038). Washington, DC: U.S. Department of Health and Human Services.

Banks, J. (1993). Multicultural education: Development, dimensions, and challenges. *Phi Delta Kappan, 75*(1), 22–28.

Barkley, R. A. (1977). A review of stimulant drug research with hyperactive children. *Journal of Child Psychology and Psychiatry, 18,* 137–165.

Barnes, E., & Knoblock, P. (1973). Openness and advocacy: Teacher attributes for mainstreaming children with special needs. In N. Keinberg, & S. L. Chow (Eds.), *Configurations of change*. San Francisco, CA: Far West Laboratory for Educational Research and Development.

Barresi, J. (1984). Interstate migrant council. National policy workshop on special education needs of migrant handicapped students. *Proceedings Report*. Denver, CO: Education Commission of the States.

Barsch, R. H. (1968). *Perspectives on learning disabilities: The vectors of a new convergence*.

Bartoli, J. S. (1989). An ecological response to Cole's interactivity alternative. *Journal of Learning Disabilities, 22*(5), 292–297.

Bateman, B. D. (1974). Educational implications of minimal brain dysfunction. *Reading Teacher, 27,* 662–668.

Bauer, A. M., & Shea, T. M. (1989). *Teaching exceptional students in your classroom*. Boston: Allyn and Bacon.

Bauwens, J., & Hourcade, J. (1995). *Cooperative teaching: Rebuilding the school house for all students.* Austin: Pro-Ed.

Bauwens J., Hourcade, J., & Friend, M. (1989). Cooperative teaching: A model for general and special education integration. *Remedial and Special Education, 10* (2), 17-21.

Beckman, P. J. (1983). Influence of selected child characteristics on stress in the family of handicapped infants. *American Journal of Medical Deficiency, 88,* 150–156.

Belch, P. (1975). The question of teachers' questions. *Teaching Exceptional Children, 1,* 46–47.

Bender, L. (1968). Neuropsychiatric disturbances. In A. H. Kenney & V. T. Keeney (Eds.), *Dyslexia.* St. Louis, MO: Mosby.

Bender, W. N., & Golden, L. B. (1988). Adaptive behavior of learning disabled and non-learning disabled children. *Learning Disability Quarterly, 11,* 55–61.

Benniga, J. S. (1988). An emerging synthesis in moral education. *Phi Delta Kappan, 69*(6), 415–418.

Beninghof, A.M. (1993). *Ideas for inclusion.* Longmont, CO: Sopris West.

Bennion, R. (1983). Why us? In Dougan, Isbell and Vayas Associates (Ed.), *We Have Been There.* Nashville, TN: Abington, 32–40.

Benson, D., Edwards, L., Rosell, J., & White, M. (1986). Inclusion of socially maladjusted children and youth in the legal definition of the behaviorally disordered population: A debate. *Behavioral Disorders, 11*(3), 213–222.

Bereiter, C., & Englemann, S. (1966). *Teaching disadvantaged children in the Preschool.* Englewood Cliffs, NJ: Prentice Hall.

Berliner, D. C. (1979). Tempus Educare. In P. L. Peterson & H. J. Walberg (Eds.), *Research on teaching: Concepts findings and implications.* Berkeley, CA: McCutchan Publishing.

Berliner, D. C. (1988). The half-full glass: A review of research on teaching. In E. L. Meyen, G. A. Vergason, & R. J. Whelan (Eds.), *Effective instructional strategies for exceptional children.* Denver, CO: Love Publishing.

Berman, P., McLaughlin, M., Bass, G., Pauly, E., & Zelman, G. (1977). Federal programs supporting educational change. Vol. 7: Factors affecting the implementation and continuation. Santa Monica, CA: The Rand Corporation. (ERIC Document Reproduction Service No. ED 140 432).

Bernstein, B. (1961). Social class and linguistic development: A theory of social learning. In A. H. Halsey, J. Flored, & C. A. Anderson (Eds.), *Education, economy and society.* New York: Free Press.

Bernstein, D. K. & Tiegerman, E. (1989). *Language and communication disorders in children.* Columbus, OH: Merrill Publishing Company.

Berres, M. S., & Knoblock, P. (Eds.) (1987). *Program models for mainstreaming: Integrating students with moderate to severe disabilities.* Rockville, MD: Aspen Systems.

Bickel, W. E., & Bickel, D. P. (1986). Effective schools, classrooms, and instruction: Implications for special education. *Exceptional Children, 52*(6), 489–499.

Biklen, D., & Zollers, N. (1986). The focus of advocacy in the LD field. *Journal of Learning Disabilities, 19,* 579–586.

Bjorklund, G., & Burger, C. (1987, January). Making conferences work for parents, teachers and children. *Young Children,* 26–31.

Blackman, H. P. (1989). Special education placement: Is it what you know or where you live? *Exceptional Children, 55,* 459–462.

Blankenship, C. (1985). Using curriculum based assessment data to make instructional decisions. *Exceptional Children, 52*(3), 233–238.

Bly, R. (1990). *Iron John: A book about men.* Reading, MA: Addison-Wesley Publishing.

Boder, E., & Jarrico, S. (1982). *The Boder Test of Reading-Spelling Patterns*. New York: Grune & Stratton.

Boeckx, R. L., Postl, B., & Coodin, F. J. (1977). Gasoline sniffing and tetraethyl lead poisoning in children. *Pediatrics, 60*, 140–145.

Bohline, D. S. (1985). Intellectual and affective characteristics of attention deficit disordered children. *Journal of Learning Disabilities, 18*, (10), 604–608.

Bower, E. M. (1969). *Early identification of emotionally handicapped children* (2nd ed.). Springfield, IL: Charles C. Thomas.

Bracey, G. W. (1991). Why can't they be like we were? *Phi Delta Kappan, 73*(3), 104–117.

Bradley, B. (1988, March). School: The parent factor. *Parents, 88*, 111–114.

Brady, P. M., Manni, J. L., & Winikur, D. W. (1983). Implications of ethnic disproportion in programs for the educable mentally retarded. *The Journal of Special Education, 3*, 295–302.

Brandt, R. (1989). On parents and schools: A conversation with Joyce Epstein. *Educational Leadership, 47*(2), 24–27.

Brandt, R. (1990). Overview: Making connections. *Exceptional Leadership, 47*(5), 3.

Brantlinger, E. A., & Guskin, S. L. (1988). Implications of social and cultural differences for special education. In Meyen, E. L., Vergason, G. A., & Whelan, R. J. *Effective instructional strategies for exceptional children*. Denver, CO: Love Publishing.

Braaten, S., Simpson, R., Rosell, J., & Reilly, T. (1988). Using punishment with exceptional children. *Teaching Exceptional Children, 20*(2), 79–81.

Brickland, M. (1976). *Natural healing*. Emmas, PA: Rodale Press.

Brolin, D. E. (Ed.) (1989). *Life centered career education: A competency based approach*. Reston, VA: The Council for Exceptional Children.

Brown, A. (1978). Knowing when, where, and how to remember: A problem of meta-cognition. In R. Glasser (Ed.), *Advances in instructional Psychology*. Hillsdale, NJ: Lawrence Erlbaum Associates.

Brown v. Topeka, Kansas Board of Education (1954). 347 U.S. 483, 745. Ct. 98 L. Ed.

Bruininks, V. L. (1978). Actual and perceived peer status of disabled students in mainstream programs. *The Journal of Emotional Special Education, 12*, 51–58.

Bruner, J., Cole, M., & Lloyd, B. (1978). *The developing child series*. In S. Farnham-Diggory. (1978) *Learning disabilities: A Psychological Perspective*. Cambridge: Harvard University Press.

Bryan, T. H. (1974). Peer popularity of learning disabled children. *Journal of Learning Disabilities, 7*, 621–625.

Bryan, T. H. (1978). Social relationships and verbal interactions of learning disabled children. *Journal of Learning Disabilities, 11*, 107–115.

Bryan, T., Bay, M., & Donohue, M. (1988). Implications of the learning disabilities definition for the regular education initiative. *Journal of Learning Disabilities, 21*(1), 23–28.

Bryan, T., Donohue, M., & Pearl, R. (1981). Studies of learning disabled children's pragmatic competence. *Topics in Learning and Learning Disabilities, 1*, 29–39.

Bryan, T., Werner, M., & Pearl, R. (1982). Learning disabled students conformity responses to prosocial and antisocial situations. *Learning Disability Quarterly, 5*, 344–352.

Bryen, D. N. (1982). *Injuries into child language*. Boston: Allyn and Bacon.

Buber, M. (1965). *Between man and man*. New York: Macmillan.

Burgan, T. S. (1974). Peer popularity of learning disabled children. *Journal of Learning Disabilities, 7*(7), 621–625.

Buscaglia, L. (1975). *The disabled and their parents: A counseling challenge*. Thorofare, NJ: Leo F. Buscaglia.

Bush, W. I., & Waugh, K. W. (1982). *Diagnosing learning problems* (3rd ed.). Columbus, OH: Charles E. Merrill.

Canter, L. (1976). *Assertive discipline: A take charge approach for today's educator.* Seal Beach, CA: Canter and Associates.

Canter, L. (1978). Be an assertive teacher. *Instructor, 88,* 60.

Canter, L. (1989). Assertive discipline: More than names on the board and marbles in a jar. *Phi Delta Kappan, 71*(1), 57–60.

Carbo, M. (1987a). Matching reading styles: Correcting ineffective instruction. *Educational Leadership, 45,* 55–62.

Carbo, M. (1987b). Reading styles research: What works isn't always phonics. *Phi Delta Kappan, 68*(6), 431–435.

Carbo, M., Dunn, R., & Dunn, K. (1986). *Teaching students to read through their individual learning styles.* Englewood Cliffs, NJ: Prentice Hall.

Carlson, C. I. (1987). Social interaction goals and strategies of children with learning disabilities. *Journal of Learning Disabilities, 20*(5), 306–311.

Carpenter, D. (1985). Grading handicapped pupils: Review and position statement. *Remedial and Special Education, 6*(4), 54–59.

Casey, A., Skiba, R., & Algozzine, B. (1988). Developing effective behavioral interventions. In J. L. Graden, J. E. Zins, & M. J. Curtis (Eds.), *Alternative educational delivery systems: Enhancing instructional options for all students.* Washington, DC: National Association of School Psychologists.

Castro, G., & Mastropieri, M. (1986). The efficacy of early intervention programs: A meta-analysis. *Exceptional Children, 5,* 417–424.

Cattermole, J., & Robinson, N. (1985). Effective home school communication—from the parents perspective. *Phi Delta Kappan, 67*(1), 48–50.

Cawley, J. F., Fitzmaurice, A. M., Shaw, R. Kahn, H., and Bates, H. III. (1979). LD youth and mathematics: A review of characteristics. *Learning Disability Quarterly,* 29–44.

CEC Staff. (March 1997). CEC testifies before Congress, calls for quick IDEA reauthorization. *CEC Today, 3* (8) 1, 7, 9.

CEC Staff. (June 1997). IDEA sails through Congress. *CEC Today, 3* (10), 1, 9, 15.

Cegelka, P., Lewis, R., & Rodriguez, A. (1987). Status of educational services to handicapped students with limited English proficiency: Report of a statewide study in California. *Exceptional Children, 54*(3), 220–227.

Chalfant, J. C. (1985). Identifying learning disabled students: A summary of the National Task Force Report. *Learning Disabilities Focus, 1,* 9–20.

Chalfant, J. C., Pysh, M. V. D., and Moultrie, R. (1979). Teacher assistance teams: A model for within—building problem solving. *Learning Disability Quarterly, 2,* 85–96.

Chalfant, J. C., & Scheffelin, M. A. (1969). *Central processing dysfunction in children: A review of the research.* National Institute of Neurological Diseases and Stroke, Monograph #9. Bethesda, MD: U.S. Department of Health, Education, and Welfare.

Charles, C. M. (1976). *Individualizing instruction.* St. Louis: C. V. Mosby.

Charles, C. M. (1983). *Elementary Classroom management.* New York: Longman.

Charles, C. M. (1989). *Building classroom discipline: From models to practice* (3rd ed.). New York: Longman.

Cheek, E. H., & Cheek, M. C. (1983). *Reading instruction through content teaching.* Columbus, OH: Merrill Publishing.

Chernow, F. B., & Chernow, C. (1981). *Classroom discipline and control: 101 practical techniques.* West Nyack, NY: Parker.

Children's Defense Fund (1971). *The way we go to school: The exclusion in Boston.* Boston: Beacon Press.

Children's Defense Fund (1990). *Children 1990: A report card, briefing book and action primer.* Washington, DC: U.S. Government Printing Office.

Chmelynski, C. (1990). All-Black, all-male classes. *The Educator, 12*(10), 16–18.

Chrispeels, J. H. (1991). District leadership in parent involvement—Policies and actions in San Diego. *Phi Delta Kappan, 72,* 367–371.

Cicci, R. (1983). Disorders of written language. In H. R. Myklebust (Ed.), *Progress in learning disabilities.* New York: Grune & Stratton.

Classroom discipline and lessons in social values. (1990, January 31). *New York Times,* p. 87.

Cleveland, D. W., & Miller, N. B. (1977). Attitudes and life commitments of older siblings of mentally retarded adults: An exploratory study. *Mental Retardation, 15,* 38–41.

Cloward, R. D. (1967). Teenagers as tutors of low achieving children: Impact on tutors and tutees. In V. Allen (Ed.), *Children as teachers: Theory and research in tutoring.* New York: Academic Press.

Coleman, J. M. (1985). Achievement level, social class, and the self-concepts of mildly handicapped children. *Journal of Learning Disabilities, 18*(1), 26–30.

Coleman, J. (1987, August/September). Families and schools. *Educational Researchers,* 31–38.

Coleman, M. (1986). *Behavior disorders: Theory and practice.* Englewood Cliffs, NJ: Prentice Hall.

Coles, G. S. (1989). Excerpts from *The learning mystique: A critical look at "Learning Disabilities". Journal of Learning Disabilities, 22*(5), 267–273, 277–278.

Coloroso, B. (1994). Kids are worth it. *Teaching Kids Responsibility, 1*(1), 1.

Comer, J. P. (1986). Parent participation in the schools. *Phi Delta Kappan, 67*(6), 442–446.

Comer, J.P., Zigler, E.F. and Stern, B.M. (1997). Supporting today's families in the elementary school. *Reaching Today's Youth: The Community Circle of Caring Journal,* 1 (3), 37–43.

Compton, C. (1990). A guide to 85 tests for special education. Belmont, CA: Fearon/Janus/ Quercus. Simon & Schuster Education Group.

Cook, L., & Friend, M. (1995). Co-teaching: Guidelines for creative effective practices. *Focus on Exceptional Children, 28* (3), 3–15.

Cooper, H. M. (1989a). *Homework.* White Plains, NY: Longman.

Cooper, H. M. (Nov. 1989b). Synthesis of research on homework. *Educational Leadership, 47*(3), 85–91.

Cooper, J. O., Heron, T. E., & Heward, W. L. (1987). *Applied behavior analysis.* Columbus, OH: Merrill Publishing.

Cordin, F. S. (1982). Lasting effects of early learners and education: A report from the consortium for longitudinal studies. In Heller, Holtzman, & Messick (Eds.), *What research and experience say to the teacher of exceptional children: The reasoning ability of mildly retarded learners.* Reston, VA: The Council for Exceptional Children.

Cornett, C. E. (1983). *What you should know about teaching and learning styles.* Bloomington: Phi Delta Kappan. (Phi Delta Kappa Fastback Series #191).

Costello, M. (1994). *Confessions of a special Eddie.* Whitestone, NY: Wizard Press.

Cott, A. (1972). Megavitamins: The orthomolecular approach to behavioral disorders and learning disabilities. *Academic Therapy, 7,* 245–257.

Council for Exceptional Children. (May, June 1997). *Teaching Exceptional Children, 29* (5), 5–49.

Council for Exceptional Children. (1994, January). Statistical profile of special education in the United States, 1994. *Teaching Exceptional Children, 26*(3), 1–4.

Cox, R. D., & Gunn, W. B. (1980). Interpersonal skills in the schools: Assessment and curriculum development. In D. P. Rathjier & J. P. Foreyt (Eds.), *Social competence: Interventions for children and adults.* New York: Pergamon Press.

Cremin, L, (1961). *The transformation of the school.* New York: Vintage Books.

Crnic, K. A., & Leconte, J. M. (1986). Understanding sibling needs and influences. In R. Fewell & P. Vadasy (Eds.), *Families of handicapped children: Needs and supports across the life span.* Austin, TX: Pro-Ed, 75–90.

Crocker, A. C. (1981). The involvement of siblings of children with handicaps. In A. Milunsky (Ed.), *Coping with crisis and handicap.* New York: Plenum.

Crook, W. G. (1980). Can what a child eats make him dull, stupid, or hyperactive? *Journal of Learning Disabilities, 13,* 53–58.

Crook, W. G. (1989). Dr. Crook discusses hypoglycemia. *Complex carbohydrates promote good health.* Jackson, TN: Professional Books.

Cruickshank, W. M. (1967). *The brain injured child in home, school, and community.* Syracuse: Syracuse University Press.

Cruickshank, W. M. (1981). *Learning-disabled children and neurological impairment.* Keynote address to the Association of the New York State Educators of the Emotionally Disturbed, Syracuse, NY.

Cruickshank, W. M. (Spring, 1986). The learning disabled hyperactive child. *Perceptions, 1,* 7–9.

Cruickshank, W. M., Bentzen, F. A., Ratezelburg, F. H., & Tannhouser, M. T. (1961). A teaching method for brain injured and hyperactive children: A demonstration-pilot study. In W. M. Cruickshank (Ed.), *Syracuse University special education and rehabilitation.* (Monograph Series 6). Syracuse, NY: Syracuse University Press.

Cuenin, L. H., & Harris, K. R. (1986). Planning, implementing, and evaluating time out interventions with exceptional students. *Teaching Exceptional Children, 18*(4), 272–276.

Cullinan, D., Epstein, M.H., & Lloyd, J.W. (1983). *Behavior disorders of children and of adolescents.* Englewood Cliffs, N.J.: Prentice-Hall, Inc.

Cummings, S. T. (1976). The impact of the child's deficiency on the father: A study of the mentally retarded and the chronically ill children. *American Journal of Orthopsychiatry, 46,* 246–255.

D'Angelo, D., & Adler, R. C. (1991). Chapter 1. A catalyst for improving parent involvement. *Phi Delta Kappan, 72,* 350–354.

Danielson, L. C., & Bellamy, T. C. (1989). State variations in placement of children with handicaps in segregated environments. *Exceptional Children, 55*(5), 448–455.

Davies, R. (1991). Schools reaching out. *Phi Delta Kappan, 72*(5), 376–382.

Debor, M. (1975). What is to become of Katherine? *Exceptional Children, 41,* 517–518.

Decker, T. W., & Polloway, E. A. (1989). Written language. In G. A. Robinson, J. R. Patton, E. A. Polloway, & L. R. Sargent (Eds.), *Best Practices in Mild Mental Retardation.* Reston, VA: The Division of Mental Retardation Council for Exceptional Children.

de Hirsch, K. (1965). Plasticity and learning disabilities. In J. Hellmuth (Ed.), *Learning disorders* (Vol. 1). Seattle, WA: Special Child Publications.

DeLuke, S. V., & Knoblock, P. (1987). Teacher behavior as preventive discipline. *Teaching Exceptional Children, 19,* 18–24.

Dennison, G. (1969). *The lives of children: The Story of the first street school.* New York: Random House.

Deno, E. (1970). Special Education and Development Capital. *Exceptional Children, 37,* 229–237.

Deno, S. L. (1985). Curriculum-based measurement: The emerging alternative. *Exceptional Children, 52*(3), 219–232.

Deno, S. L. (1986). Formative evaluation of individual student programs: A new role for school psychologists. *School Psychology Review, 15*(3), 358–374.

Deno, S. (1989). Curriculum-based measurement and special education services: A fundamental and direct relationship. In M. Shinn (Ed.), *Curriculum-based measurement: Assessing special children.* New York: Guilford Press.

Deno, S., Maruyama, G., Espin, C., & Cohen, C. (1990). Educating students with mild disabilities in general education classrooms: Minnesota alternatives. *Exceptional Children, 57*(2), 157–161.

Deno, S. L., & Mirkin, P. K. (1977). *Data-based program modification: A manual.* Reston, VA: Council for Exceptional Children.

Derr, A. M. (1986). How learning disabled adolescent boys make moral judgments. *Journal, 19*(3), 160–164.

Desanctis, S. (1906). On varieties of dementia praecox. *Rivista Sperimentale diFrenlatria, 32,* 141–165.

Deshler, D. D. (1978). Psychoeducational aspects of learning disabled adolescents. In L. Mann, L. Goodman, & J. L. Wiederholt (Eds.), *Teaching the learning disabled adolescent.* Boston, MA: Houghton Mifflin.

Deshler, D. D., & Schumaker, J. B. (1983). Social skills of learning disabled adolescents: Characteristics and intervention. *Topics in Learning Disabilities, 3,* 15–23.

Deshler, D. D., Schumaker, J. B., & Lenz, B. K. (1984). Academic and cognitive interventions for LD adolescents: Part 1. *Journal of Learning Disabilities, 17*(2), 108–117.

Deshler, D. D., Warner, M. M., Schumaker, J. B., & Alley, G. R. (1983). Learning strategies intervention model: Key components and current status. In J. D. McKinney & L. Feagans (Eds.), *Current topics in learning disabilities.* Norwood, NJ: Ablex.

Dewey, J. (1909). *Moral principles in education.* Boston: Houghton Mifflin.

Diana v. California State Board of Education, Civil No. 70–37 R.F.P. (N.D. Cal, January, 1970).

DiGangi, S. A., Perryman, P., & Rutherford, R. B., Jr. (1990). Juvenile offenders in the 90's: A descriptive analysis. *Perceptions, 25*(4), 5–8.

Dobbins, D. A., & Rarick, G. L. (1977). The performance of intellectually normal and educable mentally retarded boys on throwing accuracy. *Journal of Motor Behavior, 9,* 23–28.

Dougan, T., Isbell, L., & Vegan, P. (Eds.) (1983). *We have been there.* Nashville, Abingdon Press.

Dreikurs, R., Grunwald, B., & Pepper, F. (1982). *Maintaining sanity in the classroom.* New York: Harper & Row.

Dunn, L. (1968). Special education for the mildly retarded—is much of it justifiable? *Exceptional Children, 35,* 5–22.

Dupont, H. (1978). *Counseling and Human Development.* Denver, CO: Love Publishing.

Edgar, E. (1987). Secondary programs in special education: Are many of them justifiable? *Exceptional Children, 53,* 555–561.

Edge, D., & Burton, G. (1986). Helping learning disabled middle school students learn about money. *Journal of Learning Disabilities, 19*(1), 46–51.

Edgerton, R. B. (1979). *Mental retardation.* Cambridge, MA: Harvard University Press.

Edmonds, R. (1979, September). Effective schools for the urban poor. *Educational Leadership, 37,* 15–27.

Edwards, J. (1991). To teach responsibility, bring back the Dalton Plan. *Phi Delta Kappan, 72*(5), 398–401.

Elkind, D. (1982). Parental stresses: Their detrimental effects on the emotional well-being of children. *International Journal of Sociology of the Family, 12,* 275–283.

Elkind, D. (1986). Formal education and early childhood education: An essential difference. *Phi Delta Kappan, 67*(9), 631–637.

Ellis, N. R. (1963). The stimulus trace and behavioral inadequacy. In N. Ellis (Ed.), *Handbook of Mental Deficiency.* New York: McGraw-Hill.

Embry, L. H. (1980). Family support for handicapped preschool children at risk for abuse. *New Directions for Exceptional Children, 4,* 29–57.

England, D. A., & Flatley, J. K. (1985). *Homework—Any why.* Bloomington, IN: Phi Delta Kappa Educational Foundation (Monograph, Fastback 218).

Epstein, M. H., Cullinan, D., & Polloway, E. A. (1986). Patterns of maladjustment among mentally retarded children and youth. *American Journal of Mental Deficiency, 2*(2), 127–134.

Epstein, M. H., Patton, J. R., Polloway, E. A., & Foley, R. (1989). Mild retardation: Student characteristics and services. *Education and Training of the Mentally Retarded, 24,* 7–16.

Erikson, E. (1963). *Childhood and society* (2nd ed.). New York: W. W. Norton.

Espinoza, R. (1988). Working parents, employees, and schools. *Educational Horizons.* Winter, 62–65.

Executive Committee of the Council for Children with Behavioral Disorders (1987). Position paper on definition and identification of students with behavioral disorders. *Behavioral Disorders, 13*(1), 9–18.

Fagen, S. (1986). Conducting an LSI: A process model. *Perceptions, 4–5.*

Fagen, S. A., & Hill, J. M. (1987). Teaching acceptance of frustration. *Teaching Exceptional Children, 19*(4), 49–51.

Fagen, S. A., & Long, N. J. (1975). Teaching children self-control: A new responsibility for teachers. *Focus on Exceptional Children, 7*(8), 1–10.

Fagen, S. A., Long, N. J., & Stevens, D. J. (1975). *Teaching children self-control: Preventing emotional and learning problems in the elementary school.* Columbus, OH: Merrill Publishing.

Fancher, R. E. (1985). *The intelligence men: Makers of the IQ controversy.* New York: W. W. Norton.

Fager, P., Andrews, T., Shepherd, M.J., & Quinn, E. (1993). Teamed to teach: Integrating teacher training through cooperative teaching experiences at an urban professional development school. *Teacher Education and Special Education, 16* (1), 51–59.

Farber, B. (1960). Family organization and crisis: Maintenance of integration in families with a severely mentally retarded child. *Monographs of the Society for Research in Child Development, 25* (Serial No. 75).

Farber, B. (1963). Interaction with retarded siblings and life goals of children. *Marriage and Family Living, 25,* 96–98.

Farber, B. (1972). Effects of a severely retarded child on the family. In E. P. Trapp & B. P. Himelstein (Eds.), *Readings on the exceptional child.* New York: Appleton–Century–Crofts. 225–245.

Farley, J. W. (1986). An analysis of written dialogue of educable mentally retarded writers. *Education and Training of the Mentally Retarded, 21*(3), 181–191.

Farnham-Diggory, S. (1978). *Learning disabilities: A psychological perspective.* Cambridge: Harvard University Press.

Farrell, E. E. (1909). Special classes in the New York city schools. *Journal of Psycho-Asthenics, 13*(1–4), 91–96.

Featherstone, H. (1980). *A difference in the family.* New York: Basic Books.

Federal Domestic Assistance Catalog. (1997). www.gsa.gov/fdac/query fdac.htm.

Fein, E. B. (1995). An educational oasis on Rikers Island. *New York Times,* B 1, January 6, 1995.

Feingold, B. (1975). *Why your child is hyperactive.* New York: Random House.

Feiter, F., & Tokar, E. (1982). Getting a handle on teacher stress. *Educational Leadership, 39*(6), 456–457.

Ferguson, P. M., & Ferguson, D. L. (1987). Parents and professionals. In P. Knoblock (Ed.), *Understanding exceptional children and youth* (pp. 346–388). Boston: Little, Brown.

Fine, E. (1987). Are we preparing adolescents with learning disabilities to cope with social issues? *Journal of Learning Disabilities, 20*(10), 633–635.

Fishbaugh, M.S.E. (1997). *Models of collaboration.* Boston: Allyn and Bacon.

Fisher, C. W., Filby, N. N., Marliave, R. S., Cahen, L. S., Dishaw, M. M., Moore, J. E., & Berliner, D. C. (1978). *Teaching behaviors, academic learning time and student achievement.* Final Report of Phase III–B, Beginning Teacher Evaluation Study. (Technical Report V–1). San Francisco, CA: Far West Laboratory for Educational Research and Development.

Fiske, E. B. (1988, February 12). Standardized test scores: Voodoo statistics? *New York Times.*

Flatley, J. K. (198__). *Homework—and Why.* Bloomington, IN: Phi Delta Kappa Educational Foundation. (Phi Delta Kappa Fastback Series #218).

Floord, C., & Floord, R. (1989). Living with David: Excerpts from the parents dairy. *Perceptions, 24*(4), 18–21.

Ford, B. A. (1992). *Multicultural education training for special educators working with African-American youth. Exceptional Children, 59*(2), 107–114.

Forness, S. R. (1985). Effects of public policy at the state level: California's impact on MR, LD and ED categories. *Remedial and Special Education, 6,* 36–43.

Forness, S. R., & Kavale, K. A. (1984). A Meta-analysis of the validity of Wechsler scale profiles and recategorizations: Patterns or parodies? *Learning Disability Quarterly, 7,* 136–156.

Forness, S., & Polloway E. (1987). Physical and psychiatric diagnoses of pupils with mild mental retardation currently being referred for related services. *Education and Training in Mental Retardation, 22*(4), 221–228.

Fowle, C. (1968). The effect of the severely mentally retarded child on his family. *American Journal of Mental Deficiency, 73,* 468–473.

Frankenberger, W. (1984). A survey of state guidelines for identification of mental retardation. *Mental Retardation, 22,* 17–20.

Friedrich, W. N. (1979). Predictors of the coping behavior of the mothers of handicapped children. *Journal of Consulting and Clinical Psychology, 47,* 1140–1141.

Frymier, J., & Gansneder, B. (1989). The Phi Delta Kappa study of students at risk. *Phi Delta Kappan, 71*(21), 142–146.

Fuchs, D., & Fuchs, L. S. (1988a). Evaluation of the adaptive learning environments model. *Exceptional Children, 55*(2), 115–127.

Fuchs, D., & Fuchs, L. S. (1988b). Response to Wang and Walberg. *Exceptional Children, 55*(2), 138–146.

Fuchs, D., & Fuchs, L. S. (1989). Effects of examiner familiarity on Black, Caucasian and Hispanic children: A Meta-analysis. *Exceptional Children, 55,* 303–308.

Fuchs, L. S., & Deno, S. L. (1992). Effects of curriculum within curriculum-based measurement. *Exceptional Children, 58*(3), 232–242.

Fuchs, L., & Fuchs, D. (1986). Effects of systematic formative evaluation: A Meta-analysis. *Exceptional Children, 53*(3), 199–208.

Fuchs, L. S., & Shinn, M. R. (1989). Writing CBM IEP objectives. In M. R. Shinn, *Curriculum-based measurement: Assessing special students*. New York: Guilford Press.

Gage, N. L. (1990). Dealing with the dropout problem? *Phi Delta Kappan, 72*(4), 280–285.

Gallagher, J. J. (1972). The special education contract for mildly handicapped children, *Exceptional Children,28*(7), 527–535.

Gallagher, J. J., Beckman, P., & Cross, A. H. (1983). Families of handicapped children: Sources of stresses and its amelioration. *Exceptional Children,50*(1), 10–19.

Gallagher, J. J., Cross, A., & Schartman, W. (1981). Parental adaptation to a young handicapped child: The father's role. *Journal to the Division for Early Childhood, 3*, 3–14.

Gallagher, P. A. (1988). *Teaching students with behavior disorders: Technique and activities for classroom instruction* (2nd ed.). Denver, CO: Love Publishing.

Garmen, N. B., & Hazi, H. M. (1988). Teachers ask: Is there life after Madeline H____? *Phi Delta Kappan, 69*(9), 669–672.

Garrett, J. E., & Brazil, N. M. (1989). *Categories of exceptionality: A ten-year follow up*. Manuscript submitted for publication.

Gartner, A., & Lipsky, D. K. (1987). Beyond special education: Toward a quality system for all students. *Harvard Educational Review, 57*(4), 367–395.

Gazaway, R. (1969). *The longest mile*. Garden City, NY: Doubleday.

Gelzheiser, L., & Meyers, J. (1990). Special and remedial education in the classroom: Theme and variations. *Journal of Reading, Writing, and Learning Disabilities, 6*, 419–436.

Gearheart, B.R. (1974). *Organization and administration of educational programs for exceptional children*. Springfield, IL: Charles C. Thomas, Publisher.

Georgia Department of Education, Program for Exceptional Children. (1986). *Mild mentally handicapped* (Vol. I), Atlanta, GA: Office of Instructional Services, Division of Special Programs, Program for Exceptional Children. Resource manuals for Program for Exceptional Children.

Georgia Department of Education (1989). Revised flow chart. (Correspondence from Dr. Joan Jordan, State Director of Special Education.)

Gersten, R., Walker, H., & Darch, C. (1988). Relationship Between teachers' effectiveness and their tolerance for handicapped students. *Exceptional Children, 54*(5), 433–438.

Gickling, E., & Havertape, J. (1981). *Curriculum-based assessment (CBA)*. Minneapolis, MN: National School Psychology Inservice Training Network.

Gillet, P. K. (1988). Career development. In G. A. Robinson, J. R. Patton, E. A. Polloway, & L. R. Sargent (Eds.), *Best practices in mild mental disabilities*. Reston, VA: The Division on Mental Retardation of the Council for Exceptional Children.

Gillie, O. (1980). Burt: The scandal and the coverup. *Supplement to the Bulletin of the British Psychological Society, 33*, 9–16.

Ginott, H. (1971). *Teacher and child*. New York: Macmillan.

Ginott, H. (1973). Driving children sane. *Today's Education, 62*, 20–25.

Ginsburg, H. (1972). *The myth of the deprived child: Poor children's intellect and education*. Englewood Cliffs, NJ: Prentice Hall.

Glasser, W. (1985). *Control theory in the classroom*. New York: Perennial Library.

Glavin, J., Quay, H., Annesley, F., & Werry, J. (1971). An experimental resource room for behavior problem children. *Exceptional Children, 38*, 131–138.

Glick, D., & Norton, F. (1973). Perspectives on the recent upturn in divorce and remarriage. *Demography, 10*, 301–304.

Glickman, C. D. (1987). good and/or effective schools: What do we want? *Phi Delta Kappan, 68*(8), 622–624.

Glidewell, J., & Swallow, C. (1968). *The Prevalence of maladjustment in elementary schools.* Chicago, IL: University of Chicago Press.

Gloeckler, T., & Simpson, C. (1988). *Exceptional students in regular classrooms: Challenges, services, and methods.* Mountain View, CA: Mayfield Publishing.

Goddard, H. H. (1912). How shall we educate mental defectives? *Training School Bulletin, 9,* 43.

Goldberg, D.C. (1997, October). *Early Intervention.* Presentation to Georgia Southwestern State Univesity Special Education Tests and Measurement Class, Americus, Georgia.

Goldberg, M. F. (1990). Portrait of Madeline Hunter. *Educational Leadership, 47*(5), 41–43.

Goldstein, H. (1974). *Social learning curriculum.* Columbus, OH: Charles E. Merrill.

Goldstein, H., Mischio, G. S., & Minskoff, E. (1969). A demonstration-research project in curriculum and methods of instruction for elementary level mentally retarded children. *Final Report.* ERIC Document: ED058–696.

Goldstein, K. (1942). *After effects of brain injuries in war.* New York: Grune & Stratton.

Good, R. H., & Salvia, J. (1987). Curriculum bias in published, norm-referenced reading tests: Demonstrable effects. *School Psychology Review, 17,* 51–60.

Good, T. L., & Brophy, J. E. (1986). School effects. In M. C. Wittrock (Ed.), *Handbook of research on teaching* (3rd ed.). New York: Macmillan.

Goodlad, J. I. (1984). *A place called school.* New York: McGraw-Hill.

Gorham, K. A. (1975). A lost generation of parents. *Exceptional Children, 41,* 521–525.

Gorham, K. A., Des Jardins, C., Page, R., Pettis, E., & Scherber, B. (1976). Effect on parents. In N. Hobbs (Ed.), *Issues in the classification of children* (Vol. 2). San Francisco: Jossey-Bass.

Gough, P. B. (1987). The key to improving schools: An interview with William Glasser. *Phi Delta Kappan, 68*(9), 656–662.

Gould, S. J. (1981). *The mismeasure of man.* New York, NY: W. W. Norton.

Grady, M. P., & Luecke, E. A. (1978). Education and the brain. (Phi Delta Kappan Series #108). Bloomington: Phi Delta Kappa.

Gresham, F. M. (1983). Social validity in the assessment of children's social skills: Establishing standards for social competency. *Journal of Psychoeducational Assessment,* 297–307.

Gresham, F. M. (1989). Utility of cognitive-behavioral procedures for social skills training with children: A critical review. *Journal of Abnormal Child Psychology, 13,* 411–423.

Gresham, F. M., & Reschly, D. J. (1986). Social skill deficits and low peer acceptance of mainstreamed learning disabled children. *Learning Disability Quarterly,* (9), 23–32.

Grosenick, J. K., & Huntze, S. L. (1979). *National needs analysis in behavior disorders.* Columbia, MO: University of Missouri, Department of Special Education.

Grossman, F. K. (1972). *Brothers and sisters of retarded children: An exploratory study.* Syracuse, NY: Syracuse University Press.

Grossman, H. J. (1973). *Manual on terminology and classification in mental retardation.* Baltimore: Garamond/Pridemark Press.

Grossman, H. J. (1983). *Classification in mental retardation.* Washington, DC: American Association on Mental Deficiency.

Grunwald, P. (1990). The new generation of information systems. *Phi Delta Kappan, 72*(2), 113–114.

Guetzloe, E. (1988, Summer). Suicide and depression: special education's responsibility. *Teaching Exceptional Children, 20*(4), 25–28.

Guralnick, M. J., & Groom, J. M. (1988). Peer interactions in mainstreamed and specialized classrooms: A comparative analysis, *Exceptional Children, 54*(5), 415–425.

Guskey, T. R. (1990). Integrating innovations. *Educational Leadership, 47*(5), 11–15.

Guttman, B., & Henderson, A. (1987). *A summary of state Chapter 1 participation and achievement information for 1984–85.* Washington, DC: Decision Resources Corporation.

Hagerty, C. J., Abramson, M. (1987). Impediments to implementing a national policy change for mildly handicapped students. *Exceptional Children, 53,* 315–323.

Hahn, A. (1987). Reaching out to America's dropouts: What to do? *Phi Delta Kappan, 69*(4), 256–263.

Hallahan, D., & Cruickshank, W. (1973). *Psychoeducational foundations of learning disabilities.* Englewood Cliffs, NJ: Prentice Hall.

Hallahan, D. P., & Kauffman, J. M. (1977). Categories, labels, behavioral characteristics: ED, LD, and ENR reconsidered. *Journal of Special Education, 11,* 139–149.

Hallahan, D. P., & Kauffman, J. M. (1978). Categories, labels, behavioral characteristics: ED, LD, and ENR reconsidered. *Journal of Special Education, 11,* 139–147.

Hallahan, D. P., & Kauffman, J. M. (1982). *Exceptional children: Introduction to special education* (3rd ed.). Englewood Cliffs, NJ: Prentice Hall.

Hallahan, D. P., & Kauffman, J. (1986). *Exceptional children.* Englewood Cliffs, NJ: Prentice Hall.

Hallahan, D. P., & Kauffman, J.M. (1994). *Exceptional children: Introduction to special education* (6th ed.). Boston: Allyn and Bacon.

Hallenbeck, M., & Beernink, M. (1989). A support program for parents of students with mild handicaps. *Teaching Exceptional Children, 21*(4), 44–47.

Hammill, D. D., & Bartel, N. R. (1986). *Teaching students with learning and behavior problems* (4th ed.). Boston: Allyn and Bacon.

Hammill, D. D., Brown, L., & Bryant, B. (1989). *A Consumer's guide to tests in print.* Austin, TX: Pro-Ed.

Hammill, D. D., Leigh, E., McNutt, G., & Larsen, S. E. (1981). A new definition of learning disabilities. *Learning Disability Quarterly, 4*(Fall).

Hardman, M. L., Drew, C. J., & Egan, M. W., & Wolf B. (1993). *Human exceptionality: Society, school and family.* Boston: Allyn and Bacon.

Hargrove, L. J., & Poteet, J. A. (1984). *Assessment in special education.* Englewood Cliffs, NJ: Prentice Hall.

Haring, N. G., & Phillips, E. L. (1962). *Educating emotionally disturbed children.* New York: McGraw-Hill.

Harris, K. R., & Pressley, M. (1991). The nature of cognitive strategy instruction: Interactive strategy instruction. *Exceptional Children, 57,* 392–401.

Hawking, S. W. (1988). *A brief history of time.* New York: Bantam Books.

Hearne, J. D., Cowles, R. V., DeKeyzer, J. O. (1987). Spelling: A brief study of three instructional approaches with learning disabled students. *Reading Improvement, 24*(3), 198–201.

Hebb, D. O. (1966). *A textbook on psychology* (2nd ed.). Philadelphia, PA: W. B. Saunders.

Heller, K., Holtman, N., & Messick, S. (Eds.) (1982). *Placing children in special education: A strategy for equity?* Washington, DC: National Academy Press.

Heller, K., & Monahan, J. (1977). *Psychology and community change.* Homewood, IL: Dorsey Press.

Heller, T. (1930). About dementia infantalis. Reprinted in J. G. Howells (Ed.) (1969), *Modern perspectives in international child psychiatry.* New York: Bruner/Mazel.

Henderson, A. (1987). *The evidence continues to grow: Parent involvement improves student achievement.* Columbia, MD: National Committee for Citizens in Education.

Hendrick, I. G., & MacMillan, D. L. (1987). Coping with diversity in city school systems: The role of mental testing in shaping special classes for MR children in Los Angeles, 1900–1930. *Education and Training in Mental Retardation, 22,* 10–17.

Henley, J. (1987). Discipline, process or product? *The Pointer, 3*(4), 36–39.

Henley, M. (1985). *Teaching mildly retarded children in the regular classroom.* (Phi Delta Kappa Fastback series #220). Bloomington, IN: *Phi Delta Kappan.*

Henley, M. (1986–1990). Unpublished interviews with parents, Westfield, MA.

Henley, M. (1986). Training teachers to manage the feelings and behavior of emotionally disturbed students. Paper presented at the National Adolescent Conference, Minneapolis, MN.

Henley, M. (1987). Ego function and dysfunction: A guide to understanding discipline problems. *The Pointer, 31*(4), 24–30.

Henley, M. (1991, January). Unpublished interview with special education teacher, Westfield, Massachusetts.

Henley, M. (1994). A self-control curriculum for troubled youngsters. *The Journal of Emotional and Behavioral Problems, 3*(1), 40–46.

Henley, M. (1997). *Teaching self-control: A curriculum for responsible behavior.* National Educational Service: Bloomington, IN.

Hersh, A. (1970). Changes in family functioning following placement of a retarded child. *Social Work, 15,* 93–102.

Hewett, F. M., & Taylor, F. D. (1980). *The emotionally disturbed child in the classroom: The orchestration of success.* Boston: Allyn and Bacon.

Hobbs, N. (1966). Helping disturbed children: Ecological psychological strategies. *American Psychologist, 21,* 1105–1115.

Hobbs, N. (Ed.) (1975). *Issues in the classification of children* (Vol. II). San Francisco: Jossey-Bass.

Hobbs, N. (1978). Perspectives on re-education. *Behavioral Disorders, 2,* 65–66.

Hobbs, N. (1982). Help's on the way for the learning disabled. *Salt Lake Tribune,* 102.

Holland, B. V. (1987). Fundamental motor skill performance of non-handicapped and educable mentally impaired students. *Education and Training in Mental Retardation, 22*(3), 197–203.

Holroyd, J. (1974). The questionnaire on resources and stress: An instrument to measure family responses to a handicapped family member. *Journal of Community Psychology, 2,* 92–94.

Holt, J. (1977). *How children fail.* New York: Dell.

Holt, J. (1989, November). Learning all of the time. *Parents,* pp. 231–233.

Hops, H. (1983). Children's social competence and skill: Research practices and future direction. *Behavior Therapy, 14,* 3–18.

Horn, J. L. (1924). *The education of exceptional children: A consideration of public school problems and policies in the field of differentiated education.* New York: Century.

Horn, J. L., O'Donnell, J. P., & Leicht, D. J. (1988). Phonetically inaccurate spelling among learning-disabled, head-injured, and nondisabled young adults. *Brain and Language, 33*(1), 55–64.

Houts, P. L. (1977). *The myth of measurability.* New York: Hart Publishing.

Howell, K. W., & Lorson-Howell, K. A. (1990). Fluency in the classroom. *Teaching Exceptional Children, 22*(3), 20–23.

Hresko, W. P., & Reid, D. K. (1980). Five faces of cognition: Theoretical influences on approaches to learning disabilities. *The Forum,* Summer, 14–23.

Hu-DeHart, E. (1993). The history, development, and future of ethnic studies. *Phi Delta Kappan, 75*(1), 50–54.

Hyman, I., & D'Alessandro, J. (1984). Good old fashioned discipline: The politics of punitiveness. *Phi Delta Kappan, 66*(1), 39–45.

Hynd, G. W., & Hynd, C. R. (1984). Dyslexia: Neuroanatomical/neurolinguistic perspectives. *Reading Research Quarterly, 19*(4), 482–498.

Idol, L., Paolucci-Whitcomb, P., & Nevin, A. (1981). *Collaborative Consultation*, Aspen Publishers.

Inhelder, B. (1968). *The diagnosis of reasoning in the mentally retarded.* New York: John Day.

An interview with B. F. Skinner. (1987, August 25). *New York Times*, p. A1.

Jackson, P. W. (1968). *Life in the classrooms.* New York: Holt, Rinehart, & Winston.

Jacobs, L. (1984). Cognition and learning disabilities. *Teaching Exceptional Children, 16*(3), 213–216.

Jenkins, J. R. & Heinen, A. (1989). Students' preferences for service delivery: Pullout, in class or integrated model. *Exceptional Children, 55*(6), 516–523.

Jenkins, J. R., & Jenkins, L. M. (1981). *Cross age and peer tutoring: Help for children with learning problems.* Reston, VA: The Council for Exceptional Children.

Jenkins, J. R., & Pany, D. (1978). Standardized achievement tests: How useful for special education. *Exceptional Children, 44,* 448–453.

Jenkins, J. R., Pious, C. G., & Peterson, D. L. (1988). Categorical programs for remedial and handicapped students: Issues of validity. *Exceptional Children, 55*(2), 147–158.

Jensen, A. R. (1969). How much can we boost IQ and scholastic achievement? Environment, heredity, and intelligence. *Harvard Medical Review, 39,* 1–123.

Johnson, D. W. (1972). *Reaching out: interpersonal effectiveness and self-actualization.* Englewood Cliffs, NJ: Prentice Hall.

Johnson, D. W., & Johnson, R. T. (1986). Mainstreaming and cooperative learning strategies. *Exceptional Children, 52*(6), 553–561.

Johnson, D. W., & Johnson, R. T. (1990). Social skills for successful group work. *Educational Leadership, 47*(4), 29–33.

Johnson, D. W., & Johnson, R.T. (1991). *Learning together and alone: Copperative, compeitive, and individualistic learning* (3rd ed.). Boston: Allyn and Bacon.

Johnstone, E. R. (1908). The functions of the special class. National Education Association Journal of Proceedings and Address of the 46th Annual Meeting, 114–118.

Jones, F. (1987). *Positive classroom discipline.* New York: McGraw-Hill.

Jones, F. (199). Positive classroom discipline. *Teaching Kids Responsibility, 1*(1), 2.

Jones, V. F., & Jones, L. S. (1981). *Responsible classroom discipline: Creating positive learning environments and solving problems.* Boston: Allyn and Bacon.

Jones, V. F., & Jones, L. S. (1986). *Comprehensive classroom management: Creating positive learning environments* (2nd ed.). Boston: Allyn and Bacon.

Jordan, J. B. (1989). *1988 Special Education Yearbook.* Reston, VA: Council for Exceptional Children. *Journal of Special Education* (1989).

Kamin, L. J. (1977). The polities of IQ. In P. L. Houts (Ed.), *The myth of measurability.* New York: Hart Publishing.

Kanner, L. (1943). Autistic disturbances of affective contact. *Nervous Child, 2,* 217–250.

Kauffman, J. M. (1985). *Characteristics of children's behavior disorders* (3rd ed.). Columbus, OH: Charles E. Merrill.

Kauffman, J. M., Gerber, M. M., & Semmel, M. I. (1988). Arguable assumptions underlying the regular education initiative. *Journal of Learning Disabilities, 21*(1), 6–11.

Kelly, T., Bullock, L., and Dykes, M. K. (1974). *Teacher perceptions of behavioral disorders in children.* Gainesville, FL: Florida Educational Research and Development Council.

Keogh, B. K. (1977). Working together: A new direction. *Journal of Learning Disabilities, 10,* 478–482.

Kephart, N. C. (1971). Foreword. In T. S. Ball (Ed.), *Itard, Sequin, and Kephart: Sensory education, a learning interpretation.* Columbus, OH: Charles E. Merrill.

Kerr, M., & Nelson, M. (1983). *Strategies for managing behavior problems in the classroom.* Columbus, OH: Charles E. Merrill.

Kinsbourne, M., & Caplan, P. J. (1979). *Children's learning and attentional problems.* Boston, MA: Little, Brown.

Kirk, S. A. (1962). *Educating exceptional children.* Boston, MA: Houghton Mifflin.

Kirk, S. A. (1976). In J. K. Kauffman & D. P. Hallahan, *Teaching children with learning disabilities: Personal perspectives.* Columbus, OH: Charles E. Merrill.

Kirk, S. A., & Kirk, W. D. (1983). On defining learning disabilities. *Journal of Learning Disabilities, 16*(1), 20–21.

Knapp, M. S., Turnbull, B. J., & Shields, P. M. (1990). New directions for educating the children of poverty. *Educational Leadership, 48*(1), 4–8.

Knoblock, P. (1983). Teaching emotionally disturbed children. Dallas, TX: Houghton Mifflin.

Knoblock, P. (1987). *Understanding exceptional children and youth.* Boston: Little, Brown.

Knopf, I. J. (1979). *Childhood Psychopathology.* Englewood Cliffs, NJ: Prentice Hall.

Kohl, H. (1967). *36 children.* New York: New American Express.

Kohlberg, L. (1973). The claim to moral adequacy of a highest stage of moral judgement. *Journal of Philosophy, 70,* 630–636.

Kohn, A. (1988, November). Suffer the restless children. *The Atlantic Monthly,* pp. 90–100.

Kohn, A. (1991). Caring kids: The role of schools. *Phi Delta Kappan, 72*(7), 496–506.

Kokaska, C. J., & Brolin, D. E. (1985). *Career education for handicapped individuals* (2nd ed.). Columbus, OH: Charles E. Merrill Publishing Company.

Koppitz, E. M. (1972–1973). Special class pupils with learning disabilities: A five year follow-up study. *Academic Therapy, 8,* 133–138.

Kounin, J. (1977). *Discipline and group management in classrooms.* New York: Holt, Rinehart and Winston.

Kozol, J. (1991). *Savage inequalities: Children in America's schools.* Crown Publishers: New York.

Kraeplin, E. (1923). *Textbook of Psychiatry* (8th ed.). New York: Macmillan.

Kronick, D. (1988). *New approaches to learning disabilities: Cognitive, metacognitive, and holistic.* Philadelphia, PA: Grune & Stratton.

Kuveke, S. (1983). School behaviors of educable mentally retarded children. *Education and Training of the Mentally Retarded, 14*(2), 134–137.

Lambert, N. M. (1988). Perspective on eligibility for and placement in special education programs. *Exceptional Children, 54*(4), 287–304.

Langdon, H. (1983). Assessment and intervention strategies for the bilingual language-disordered student. *Exceptional Children, 50*(1), 37–46.

Lapointe, A. (1986). The state of instruction in reading and writing in U.S. elementary schools. *Phi Delta Kappan, 68*(2), 135–138.

Larivee, B. (1988). Effective strategies for academically handicapped students in the regular classroom. In R. E. Slavin, N. L. Karweit, & N. E. Madden (Eds.), *Effective programs for students at risk.* Boston: Allyn and Bacon.

Larsen, S. C., & Poplin, M. S. (1980). *Methods for educating the handicapped: An individualized education program approach.* Boston: Allyn and Bacon.

Larson, K. A., Gerber, M. M. (1987). Effects of social metacognitive training for enhancing overt behavior in learning disabled and low achieving delinquents. *Exceptional Children, 54*(3), 201–211.

Lasley, T. J. (1989). A teacher development model for classroom management. *Phi Delta Kappan, 7*(1), 36–38.

Lazr, I., & Darlington, R. (1982). Lasting effects of early education: A report from the consortium for Longitudinal Studies. *Monograph of the Society for Research in Child Development, 47,* (Serial No. 175).

Leitch, L. M., & Tangri, S. S. (1988). Barriers to home-school collaboration. *Educational Horizons,* Winter, 70–74.

Lemeshow, S. (1982). *Handbook of clinical types in mental retardation.* Boston: Allyn and Bacon.

Lerner, J. (1985). *Learning disabilities: Theories, diagnosis, and teaching strategies* (4th ed.). Boston: Houghton Mifflin.

Lerner, J. (1997). *Learning disabilities.* Boston, MA: Houghton Mifflin.

Lerner, J. (1988). *Learning disabled: Theories, diagnosis, and teaching strategies* (5th ed.). Boston: Houghton Mifflin.

LeTendre, M. J. (1991). Improving Chapter 1 programs: We can do better. *Phi Delta Kappan, 72*(8), 577–585.

Leverault, A. H. (1990). Preventive discipline in the secondary school. Unpublished research paper.

Levinson, E. (1990). Will technology transform education or will school co-opt technology? *Phi Delta Kappan, 72*(2), 121–126.

Lewis, A. C. (1990). Tracking the national goals. *Phi Delta Kappan, 72*(7), 496–506.

Lewis, R. B., & Doorlag, D. H. (1987). *Teaching special students in the mainstream* (2nd ed.). Columbus, OH: Merrill Publishing.

Lickona, T. (1988). Four strategies for fostering character development in children. *Phi Delta Kappan, 69*(6), 419–423.

Lilly, M. S. (Ed.) (1979). *Children with exceptional needs: A survey of special education.* New York: Holt.

Lindsley, O. R. (1964). Direct measurement and prothesis of retarded behavior. *Journal of Education, 147,* 62–81.

Lindsley, O. R. (1990). Precision teaching: By teachers for children. *Teaching Exceptional Children, 22*(3), 10–15.

Lipsky, D., & Gartner, A. (1989). *Beyond separate education: Quality education for all.* Baltimore, MD: Brookes.

Lloyd, J. (1980). Academic instruction and cognitive behavior modification: The need for attack strategy training. *Exceptional Education Quarterly, 1*(1), 53–63.

Lobav, W., Cohen, C., & Lewis, J. (1968). *A study of the non-standard English of Negro and Puerto Rican speakers in New York City.* New York: Columbia University (Research Project No. 3288).

London, P. (1987). Character education and clinical intervention: A paradigm shift for U.S. schools. *Phi Delta Kappan, 68*(9), 667–673.

Long, N. L. (1986). The nine psychoeducational stages of helping emotionally disturbed students through the reeducation process. *The Pointer, 30*(3), 5–20.

Long, N. (1990). Life space interviewing. *Beyond 2*(1), 10–15.

Long, N. J., & Newman, R. G. (1965). Managing surface behavior of children in school. In N. J. Long, W. Morse, & R. G. Newman (Eds.), *Conflict in the classroom.* Belmont, CA: Wadsworth Publishing.

Love, H. (1973). *The mentally retarded child and his family.* Springfield, IL: Charles C. Thomas.

Lovitt, T. C. (1989). *Introduction to learning disabilities.* Boston: Allyn and Bacon.

Lovitt, T. C., Fister, S., Freston, J. L., Kemp, K., Moore, R. C., Schroeder, B., and Bauernschmidt, M. (1980). Using precision teaching techniques: Translating research. *Teaching Exceptional Children, 22*(3), 16–18.

Lund, N. J., & Duchan, J. F. (1988). *Assessing children's language in naturalistic contexts.* Englewood Cliffs, NJ: Prentice Hall.

Lynch, E. W., & Stein, R. C. (1987). Parent participation by ethnicity: A comparison of hispanic, black, and anglo families. *Exceptional Children, 54*(2), 105–111.

Mack, J. H. (1980). An analysis of state definitions of severely emotionally disturbed. Reston, VA: Council for Exceptional Children. (ERIC Document Reproduction Service No. ED 201 135).

MacKeith, R. (1973). Parental reactions and responses to a handicapped child. In F. Richardson (Ed.), *Brain and intelligence* (pp. 131–141). Hyattsville, MD: National Educational Consultants.

MacMillan, D. L. (1989). Incorporating adaptive behavior deficits into instructional programs. In G. A. Robinson, J. R. Patton, E. A. Polloway, & L. R. Sargent (Eds), *Best Practices in mild mental retardation.* Reston, VA: The Division of Mental Retardation Council for Exceptional Children.

MacMillan, D. L., & Bothwick, S. (1990). The new educable mentally retarded population: Can they be mainstreamed? *Mental Retardation, 18,* 155–158.

Maeroff, G. I. (1988). Withered hopes, stillborn dreams: The dismal panorama or urban schools. *Phi Delta Kappan, 69*(9), 632–638.

Mager, R. F. (1962). *Preparing educational objectives.* Palo Alto, CA: Fearon.

Maheady, L., Sacca, K. M., & Harper, G. F. (1988). Classwide peer tutoring with mildly handicapped high school students. *Exceptional Children, 55*(1), 52–59.

Mallery, D. (1971). High school students speak—An excerpt. In M. L. Silberman (Ed.), *The experience of schooling.* New York: Holt, Rinehart, and Winston.

Mandelbaum, L. H. (1989). Reading. In G. A. Robinson, J. R. Patton, E. A. Polloway, & L. R. Sargent (Eds), *Best practices in mild mental retardation.* Reston, VA: The Division of Mental Retardation Council for Exceptional Children.

Mandell, L., & Gold, M. (1984). *Teaching handicapped students.* St. Paul, MI: West Publishing.

Mangrum, C.T., & Strichart, S.S. (1984). *College and the learning disabled student.* London: Grune & Stratton.

Mann, L., & Sabatino, D. (1985). *Foundations of cognitive process in remedial and special education.* Rockville, MD: Aspen Systems.

Mannix, J. B. (1960). The number concepts of a group of ESN children. *British Journal of Educational Psychology, 30,* 180–181.

Marchi, J. U. (1971). Comparison of selected Piagetian tasks with the Weschler Intelligence Scale for children as measure of mental retardation. *Dissertation Abstracts International, 31,* 6442A.

Margalit, M., & Shulman, S. S. (1986). Autonomy perceptions and anxiety expressions of learning disabled adolescents. *Journal of Learning Disabilities,19* (5), 291–293.

Margolis, R. J. (1988). *Out of harm's way: The emancipation of juvenile justice.* New York: Edna McConnel Clark Foundation.

Markowitz, J. (1983). *Participation of fathers in early childhood special education programs: An exploratory study of factors and issues.* Washington, DC: George Washington University.

Marshall et al. v. *Georgia U.S. District Court for the Southern District of Georgia.* C.V. 482–233. June 28, 1984.

Marston, D. (1987). Does categorical teacher certification benefit the mildly handicapped child? *Exceptional Children, 53*(5), 423–431.

Marston, D. (1988). The effectiveness of special education: A time series analysis of reading performance in regular and special education settings. *Journal of Education, 21,* 13–26.

Marston, D. B. (1989). A curriculum-based measurement approach to assessing academic performance: What it is and why do it. In M. Shinn (Ed.), *Curriculum-based measurement: Assessing special children.* New York: Guilford Press.

Marston, D., & Magnusson, D. (1985). Implementing curriculum-based assessment in special and regular education settings. *Exceptional Children, 52*(3), 266—277.

Maslow, A. (1966). *The psychology of science.* New York: Harper & Row.

Massachusetts Department of Education (1991). Tracking: It's bad practice to identify ability groups, educators told. *Massachusetts Education Today, 6*(5), 1, 7.

Mayron (1979). *Correlates of success in transition of mentally retarded to regular class* (Vols. I and II). Final Report, Pomona, California. Los Angeles, CA: New Psychiatric Institute, Pacific State Hospital. (ERIC Document Nos. EC 081–038 and EC 081–039).

Mazin, L. (1994). Stress-free discipline. *Teaching Kids Responsibility, 1*(1), 2.

McConaughy, S. H. (1986). Social competence and behavioral problems of learning disabled adolescents. *Journal of Learning Disabilities, 19*(2), 101–106.

McConaughy, S. H., & Ritter, D.R. (1985). Social competence of learning disabled boys aged 6-11. *Journal of Learning Disabilities, 118* (9), 547–552.

McCoy, K. (1987). *Solo Parenting: Your essential guide.* New York: Signet.

McCoy, K. M. & Prehm, H. J. (1887). *Teaching mainstreamed students: Methods and techniques.* Denver, CO: Love Publishing.

McDaniel, E. A., & Dibella-McCarthy (1989). Enhancing teacher efficacy in special education. *Teaching Exceptional Children, 21*(4), 34–38.

McDaniel, T. R. (1986). A primer on classroom discipline: Principles old and new. *Phi Delta Kappan, 68*(1), 63–67.

McFall, R. M. (1982). A review and reformulation of the concept of social skills. *Behavioral Assessment, 4,* 1–33.

McGinnis, E., & Goldstein, P. (1984). *Skillstreaming the elementary school child: A guide for teaching pro-social skills.* Champaign, IL: Research Press.

McGinnis, E., Goldstein, A. P. (1990). *Skillstreaming in early childhood. Teaching prosocial skills to the preschool and kindergarten child.* Champaign, IL: Research Press.

McGuffey's Fourth Eclectic Reader (1920). New York: H. H. Vail, 38–39.

McKey, R., Condelli, L., Ganson, H., Barret, B., McConkey, C., and Plantz, M. (1985). *The impact of Head Start on children, families, and communities.* Washington, DC: DHHHS. Publication #85–31193 (OHDS).

McKinney, J. D., McClure, S., & Feagans, L. (1982). Classroom behavior of learning disabled children. *Learning Quarterly, 5*(1), 45–52.

McLanahan, S. (1983). Family structure and stress: A longitudinal comparison of two-patient and female-headed families. *Journal of Marriage and the Family, 45,* 347–357.

McLoughlin, J. A., & Lewis, R. B. (1986). *Assessing special students* (3rd ed.). Columbus, OH: Charles E. Merrill.

McLoughlin, J. A., & Lewis, R. B. (1990). *Assessing special students* (4th ed.). Columbus, OH: Charles E. Merrill.

McManis, D. (1970). Seriation and transitivity performance by retarded and average individuals. *American Journal of Mental Deficiency, 74*(6), 384–392.

McWhirter, J. J., McWhirter, R. J., & McWhirter, M. C. (1985). The learning disabled child: A retrospective review. *Journal of Learning Disabilities, 18*(6), 315–318.

Meese, R. L. (1994). *Teaching learners with mild disabilities.* Pacific Grove, CA: Wadsworth.

Meichenbaum, D. (1977). *Cognitive behavior modification: An integrative approach.* New York: Plenum.

Meichenbaum, D. (1985). Teaching thinking: A cognitive-behavioral perspective. In S. F. Chipman & J. W. Segal (Eds.), *Thinking and learning skills: Research and open questions* (Vol. 2). Hillsdale, NJ: Erlbaum Associates.

Meichenbaum, D., & Goodman, J. (1971). Training impulsive children to talk to themselves: A means of developing self-control. *Journal of Abnormal Psychology, 77,* 115–126.

Menacker, J., Weldon, W., & Hurwitz, E. (1889). School order and safety as community issues. *Phi Delta Kappan, 71*(1), 39–40, 55–56.

Mendler, A., & Curwin, R. (1994). Discipline with dignity. *Teaching Kids Responsibility, 1*(1), 1.

Mercer, C. D., & Mercer, A. R. (1985). *Teaching children with learning problems* (2nd ed.). Columbus, OH: Charles E. Merrill.

Mercer, C. D., & Mercer, A. R. (1998). *Teaching students with learning problems* (5th ed.). Upper Saddle River, N.J.: Merrill.

Mercer, J. (1973). The pluralistic assessment project. *School Psychology Digest, 2,* 10–18.

Meyen, E. L., Vergason, G. A., & Whelan, R. J. (Eds.) (1988). *Effective instructional strategies for exceptional children.* Denver, CO: Love Publishing.

Meyer, D. J. (1986). Fathers of handicapped children. In R. Fewell & P. Vadasy (Eds.), *Families of handicapped children: Needs and supports across the life span* (pp. 121–148). Austin, TX: Pro-Ed.

Meyers, C. E., MacMillan, D. L., & Yoshida, R. K. (1975). *Correlates of success in transition of mentally retarded to regular class. Volume 1 and II: Final report.* Los Angeles, CA: New Psychiatric Institute Pacific State Hospital (ERIC documents EC 081–038 & EC 081–039).

Miller, L. G. (1968). Toward a greater understanding of the parents of the mentally retarded. *Journal of Pediatrics, 73,* 699–705.

Miller, T. L., & Davis, E. E. (1982). The mildly handicapped: A rationale. In T. L. Miller & E. E. Davis (Eds.), *The mildly handicapped student.* New York: Grune and Stratton.

Mills v. the Board of Education of the District of Columbia, 348F. Supp. 866 (D.C. 1972).

Mitchell, P. B. (1988). Tower of Babel or shared vision. *Teaching Exceptional Children, 21*(1), 49–50.

Moore, B. C., & Moore, S. M. (1977). *Mental retardation: Causes and prevention.* Columbus, OH: Charles E. Merrill Publishing.

Moores, D. F. (1982). *Educating the deaf: Psychology, principles, and practices* (2nd ed.). Boston: Houghton Mifflin.

Morgan, C., & Demchak, M. (1996). *Addressing administrative needs for successful inclusion of students with disabilities.* (ERIC document, ED 394 767).

Morse, W. C. (1985). *Pursuit of excellence for educating the behavior disordered.* Paper presented at the Midwest Symposium for Leadership in Behavioral Disorders. Kansas City, MO.

Morse, W. (1987). Introduction. *Teaching Exceptional Children, 19*(4), 4–6.

Morsink, C. V. (1984). *Teaching special needs students in regular classrooms.* Boston: Little, Brown.

Morsink, C. V., Thomas, C. C., & Correa, V. I. (1991). *Interactive teaming, consultation and collaboration in special programs.* New York: MacMillan Publishing.

Moskowitz, F. C. (1988, July/August). Success strategies: Help for struggling students. *Learning,* 46–47.

Myers, P. I., & Hammill, D. D. (1982). *Learning disabilities: Basic concepts, assessment practices, and instructional strategies.* Austin, TX: Pro-Ed.

Myklebust, H. R. (1964). Learning disorders: Psychoneurological disturbances in childhood. *Rehabilitation Literature, 25,* 354–359.

National Assessment of Reading Progress (1985). *The reading report card: Progress towards excellence in our schools: trends in reading over four national assessments.* 1971–1984. Princeton, NJ: NAEP.

National Committee on Excellence in Education. (1983). *A nation at risk: The imperative for educational reform.* Washington, DC: U.S. Government Printing Office.

Neill, M. D., & Medina, N. J. (1989). Standardized testing: Harmful to educational health. *Phi Delta Kappan, 70*(9), 668–697.

Neisworth, J. T., & Greer, J. G. (1975). Functional similarities of learning disability and mild retardation. *Exceptional Children, 42,* 17–21.

Nelson, C. M. (1988). Social skills training for handicapped students. *Teaching Exceptional Children, 20*(4), 19–22.

Nelson, M. C., Rutherford, R. B., Jr., & Wolford, B. I. (Eds.) (1987). Special education in the criminal justice system. Columbus, OH: Charles E. Merrill.

Norwacek, J. E., McKinney, J. D., & Hallahan, D. P. (1990). Instructional behaviors of more and less effective beginning regular and special educators. *Exceptional Children, 57*(2), 140–149.

Noyes, K. G., & McAndrew, G. L. (1971). Is this what schools are for? In M. L. Silberman (Ed.), *The experience of schooling.* New York: Holt, Rinehart, & Winston.

Oakes, J. (1990). *Multiplying inequalities: The effects of race, social class, and tracking on opportunities to learn math and science.* Santa Monica, CA: RAND.

Office of Special Services, Division for Exceptional Students (1994). Resource manual: Specific Learning Disabilities. Atlanta, GA: Office of Special Services, Division for Exceptional Students.

Ohanian, S. (1991). P.L. 94–142: Mainstream or quicksand? *Phi Delta Kappan, 72*(3), 217–222.

Orlich, D. C. (1984). Education reforms: Mistakes, misconceptions, miscues. *Phi Delta Kappan, 70*(7), 512–517.

Ornstein, R. (1978, May). The split and the whole brain. *Human Nature,* 76–83.

Osman, B. B. (1979). *Learning disabilities: A family affair.* New York: Warner.

Palinesar, A. S. (1982). *Improving the reading comprehension of junior high students through reciprocal teaching of comprehension-monitoring strategies.* Unpublished doctoral dissertation, University of Illinois, Urbana-Champaign.

Pallas, A. M., Natriello, G., & McDill, E. L. (1989, June/July). The changing nature of disadvantaged population: Current dimensions and future trends. *Educational Leadership,* 16–22.

Pasamanick, B., & Knoblock, H. (1973). The epidemiology of reproductive casualty. In S. Sapir & A. Nitzburg (Eds.), *Children with learning problems.* New York: Brunner/Mazel.

Pate, J. (1963). Emotionally disturbed and socially maladjusted children. In L. Dunn (Ed.). *Exceptional children in the schools.* New York: Holt, Rinehart, & Winston.

Patton, J. R., Cronin, M. E., Polloway, E. A., Hutchison, D., & Robinson, G. A. (1989). Curricular considerations: A life skills orientation. In G. A. Robinson, J. R. Patton, E. A. Polloway, & L. R. Sargent (Eds.), *Best practices in mental disabilities.* Des Moines: Iowa Department of Education, Bureau of Special Education.

Patton, J. R., Kauffman, J. M., Blackbourn, J. M., & Brown, B. G. (1991). *Exceptional children in focus* (5th ed.). New York: Macmillan.

Paul, J. L., & Epanchin, B. C. (1991). *Educating emotionally disturbed children and youth: Theories and practices for teachers* (2nd ed.). New York: Merrill Publishing.

Peck, J. R., & Stephens, W. B. (1960). A study of the relationship between behavior of parents and that of their mentally defective child. *American Journal of Mental Deficiency, 64*, 839–844.

Pennsylvania Association for Retarded Children (PARC) v. Commonwealth of Pennsylvania, 334 F. Supp. 1257 (E.D. Pa., 1971), 343 F. Supp. 279 (L. D. Pa., 1972).

Perry, J. (1984, August 17). Migrant children may miss special education services. *San Antonio Light.*

Peterson, N. L. (1987). *Early intervention for handicapped and at-risk children.* Denver, CO: Love Publishing.

Phi Delta Kappa Commission on Discipline. (1982). *Handbook for developing schools with good discipline.* Bloomington, IN: Phi Delta Kappa.

Phillips, V., & McCullough, L. (1990). Consultation based programming: Instituting the collaborative work ethic. *Exceptional Children, 56*(4), 291–304.

Phillips, L., Sapona, R., & Lubic, B. (1995). Developing partnerships in inclusive education. One school's approach. *Intervention in School and Clinic* 30 (5), 262-272.

Piaget, J. (1950). *The psychology of intelligence.* New York: International Universities Press.

Piaget, J. (1977). *The development of thought: Equilibration of cognitive structures.* New York: Viking Press.

Plessy v. *Ferguson* (1894). La, 16 SCt. 1138, 163 US 537, 41, LEd 256—Const Law 83(2); RR 226; Slaves 24.

Polloway, E. A., & Epstein, M. H. (1985). Current issues in mild mental retardation: A survey of the field. *Education and Training of the Mentally Retarded, 20,* 171–174.

Polloway, E. A., & Patton, J. R. (1993). *Strategies for teaching learners with special needs* (5th ed.). New York: Merrill.

Polloway, E. A., Patton, J. R., Epstein, M. H., Cullinan, D., & Luebke, J. (1986). Demographic, social, and behavioral characteristics of students with educable mental retardation. *Education and Training of the Mentally Retarded, 21*(1), 27–34.

Polloway, E. A., Patton, J. R., Payne, J. S., and Payne, R. A. (1989). *Strategies for teaching learners with special needs* (4th ed.). Columbus, OH: Charles E. Merrill.

Polloway, E. A., & Smith, J. D. (1983). Changes in mild mental retardation: Population, Programs, and Perspectives. *Exceptional Children, 50*(2), 149–159.

Poplin, M. S. (1989). The reductionistic fallacy in learning disabilities: Replicating the past by reducing the present. *Journal of Learning Disabilities, 21*(7), 389–400.

Prasse, D. P., & Reschly, D. J. (1986). Larry P. A case of segregation, testing, or program efficacy? *Exceptional Children, 52,* 333–346.

Pressley, M., & Harris, K. R. (1990). What we really know about strategy instruction. *Educational Leadership, 48*(1), 31–33.

Price-Bonham, S., & Addison, S. (1978). Families and mentally retarded children: Emphasis on the father. *The Family Coordinator, 3,* 221–230.

Przychodin, J. (1981). Improving classroom discipline. *Clearing House, 55*(1), 16.

Public Law 94-142 (1975). Part B of the Education for All Handicapped Children Act.

Public Law 101-476 (1990). Individuals with Disabilities Education Act.

Pugach, M. C., & Johnson, L. J. (1989a). The challenge of implementing collaboration between general and special education. *Exceptional Children, 56*(3), 232–235.

Pugach, M. C., & Johnson, L. J. (1989b). Prereferral interventions: Progress, problems, and challenges. *Exceptional Children, 56*(3), 217–226.

Putnam, J. W., Rynders, J. E., Johnson, R. T., & Johnson, D. W. (1989). Collaborative skill instruction for promoting positive interactions between mentally handicapped and non-handicapped children. *Exceptional Children, 55*(6), 550–558.

Quay, H. C., & Peterson, D. R. (1967). *Manual for the Behavior Problem Checklist.* Unpublished.

Quay, H., & Peterson, D. (1977). *Manual for Quay-Peterson-Revised.* Unpublished manuscript.

Ralph, J. (1989). Improving education for the disadvantaged: Do we know whom to help? *Phi Delta Kappan, 70,* 395–401.

Ramirez, B. A. (1988). Culturally and linguistically diverse children. *Teaching Exceptional Children, 29*(4), 45–46.

Ramsey, R. S. (1981). *Perceptions of disturbed and disturbing behavioral characteristics by school personnel.* Unpublished doctoral dissertation, University of Florida, Gainesville.

Ramsey, R. S. (1988). *Preparatory guide for special education teacher competency tests.* Boston: Allyn and Bacon.

Ramsey, R. S. Dixon, M. J., & Smith, G. G. B. (1986). *Eyes on the special education: Professional knowledge teacher competency test.* Albany, GA: Southwest Georgia Learning Resources System Center.

Ramsey, R. S. (1995a). Preparatory guide for special education teacher competency tests—revised. (formerly published by Allyn and Bacon, Inc.)

Ramsey, R. S. (1995b). Students with Learning Disabilities in College. Presentation to Andrew College Faculty, Cuthbert, Georgia, April 12 and September 6, 1995.

Ramsey, R. S. (1995c). Learning styles. Consultant to Faculty, Crisp County High School, Cordele, Georgia, July 20 and 21, October 2, 1995.

Ramsey, R. S. (1996). Working with college students with learning disabilities. Session Presenter at the Georgia Council for Exceptional Children State Conference, Columbus, Georgia, November 8, 1996.

Ramsey, R. S. (1997). *Learning Disabilities and Young Adults in College.* Unpublished manuscript.

Ratekin, N. (1979, March). Reading achievement of disabled learners. *Exceptional Children, 45*(16), 454–458.

Reavis, G. H. (1953). "The Animal School." *Educational Forum, 17* (2), 141.

Redl, F. (1971). The concept of the life space interview. In N. Long, W. Morse, & R. Newman (Eds.), *Conflict in the classroom.* Belmont, CA: Wadsworth Publishing.

Redl, F., & Wineman, D. (1951). *Children who hate.* Glencoe, IL: The Free Press.

Redl, F., & Wineman, D. (1957). *The aggressive child.* Glencoe, IL: The Free Press.

Reed, E. W., & Reed, S. C. (1965). *Mental retardation: A family study.* Philadelphia: Saunders.

Reed, S., & Sauter, C. R. (1990). Children of poverty, the status of 12 million young children. *Phi Delta Kappan,* K1–K12.

Reid, D. (1978). *Toward the application of development epistemology to the education of exceptional children.* Proceedings of The Eighth Annual Conference on Piagetian Theory and the Helping Professions (8th). Los Angeles, California.

Reid, D. K., & Hresko, W. P. (1981a). Thinking about it in that way: Test data and instruction. *Exceptional Education Quarterly, 1*(3), 47–57.

Reid, D. K., & Hresko, W. P. (1981b). *A cognitive approach to learning disabilities.* New York: McGraw-Hill.

Reinert, H. (1976). *Children in conflict.* St. Louis, MO: C. V. Mosby.

Renzulli, J. S., Reis, S. M., & Smith, L. H. (1981). *The revolving door identification model.* Mamsfield Center, CN: Creative Learning.

Research Brief for Teachers (1988). *Curriculum based assessment.* (ERIC/OSEP Special Project). Reston, VA: The Council for Exceptional Children.

Reschly, D. J. (1988). Minority overrepresentation and special education reform. *Exceptional Children, 54*(4), 316–323.

Reschly, D. J. (1989). Incorporating adaptive behavior deficits into instructional programs. In G. A. Robinson, J. R. Patton, E. A. Polloway, & L. R. Sargent (Eds.), *Best practices in mild mental retardation.* Reston, VA: The Division of Mental Retardation Council for Exceptional Children.

Restak, R. M. (1984). *The brain.* New York: Bantam Books.

Reynolds, M. C., & Balow, B. (1971). Categories and variables in special education. *Exceptional Children, 38*(4), 357–366.

Reynolds, W. M., & Miller, K. L. (1985). Depression and learned helplessness in mentally retarded and non-mentally retarded adolescents: An initial investigation. *Applied Research in Mental Retardation, 6*(3), 295–306.

Rezmierski, V. E. (1987). Discipline: Neither the steel nor the velvet, but the maturity inside the glove, that makes the difference. *The Pointer, 31*(4), 5–13.

Rhodes, W. C. (1967). The disturbing child: A problem of ecological management. *Exceptional Children, 33,* 449–455.

Rhodes, W. C. (1970). A community participation analysis of emotional disturbance. *Exceptional Children, 37,* 309–314.

Rhodes, W. C., & Tracy, M.L. (1966). *A study of child variance: Conceptual models.* (Vols. 1 & 2). Ann Arbor, MI: University of Michigan.

Rhodes, W. C., & Tracy, M. L. (1972a). *A study of child variance: Conceptual models* (Vol. 1). Ann Arbor, MI: University of Michigan.

Rhodes, W. C., & Tracy, M. L. (1972b). *A study of child variance: Interventions* (Vol. 2). Ann Arbor, MI: University of Michigan.

Rich, H. L., & Ross, S. M. (1989). Students' time on learning tasks in special education. *Exceptional Children, 55*(6), 508–515.

Ritschl, C., Mongrella, A. J., & Presbie, R. L. (1972). Group time out from rock and roll music and out of seat behavior of handicapped children while riding a school bus. *Psychological Reports, 31,* 967–873.

Ritter, D. (1989). Teachers perceptions of problem behavior in general and special education. *Exceptional Children, 58*(6), 558–564.

Rivers, W. L. (1977). *The disruptive student and the teacher.* Washington, DC: National Education Association.

Roberts, M. (1986). Three mothers: Life span experiences. In R. Fewell & P. Vadasy (Eds.), *Families of handicapped children: Needs and supports across the life span* (pp. 193–218). Texas: Pro-Ed.

Roberts, S. (1983). A focus on learning disabilities at the college level. *Times-Argus, 89,* 90.

Robinson, G. A., Patton, J. R., Polloway, E. A., & Sargent, L. R. (Eds.) (1989). *Best practices in mild mental retardation.* Reston, VA: The Division of Mental Retardation Council for Exceptional Children.

Robinson, N., & Robinson, H. (1976). *The mentally retarded child.* New York: McGraw-Hill.

Robinson, N., & Robinson, H. (1982). *The mentally retarded child* (2nd ed.). New York: McGraw-Hill.

Robinson, S. M. (1989). Oral language: Developing pragmatic skills and communicational competence. In G. A. Robinson, J. R. Patton, E. A. Polloway, & L. R. Sargent (Eds.), *Best practices in mild mental retardation*. Reston, VA: The Division of Mental Retardation Council for Exceptional Children.

Robinson, W. A. (1965). The elaborated code in working class language. *Language and Speech, 8,* 243–252.

Roit, M. L., & Pfohl, W. (1984). The readability of P.L. 94–142. Parent materials: Are parents truly informed? *Exceptional Children, 50*(6), 496–504.

Rosenshine, B. V. (1979). Content, time, and direct instruction. In P. L. Peterson & H. L. Walberg (Eds.), *Research on teaching: Concepts, findings, and implications*. Berkeley, CA: McCutchan Publishing.

Rosenshine, B., & Stevens, R. (1984). *Classroom instruction in a reading research*. New York: Longman.

Rothstein, L. F. (1995). *Special education law* (2nd ed.). New York: Longman Publishers.

Rourke, B. P. (1989). Cole's learning mystique: The good, the bad, and the irrelevant. *Journal of Learning Disabilities, 22*(5), 274–277.

Rubin, R., & Balow, B. (1971). Learning and behavior disorders: A longitudinal study. *Exceptional Children, 38,* 293–299.

Ryan, E. B., Short, E. J., & Weed, K. A. (1986). The role of cognitive strategy training in improving the academic performance of learning disabled children. *Journal of Learning possibilities, 18,* 521–529.

Salend, S. J. (1987). Contingency management systems. *Academic Therapy, 22*(3), 245–253.

Salend, S. J., & Lutz, J. G. (1984). Mainstreaming or mainlining: A competency based approach to mainstreaming. *Journal of Learning Disabilities, 17,* 27–29.

Salvia, J., & Ysseldyke, J. E. (1998). *Assessment in special and remedial education* (7th ed.). Boston: Houghton Mifflin.

Samuels, S. J., & Miller, N. L. (1985). Failure to find attention differences between learning disabled and normal children on classroom and laboratory tasks. *Exceptional Children, 51,* pp. 358–375. Boston: Houghton Mifflin.

Sandford, J. A. (1987). Putting parents in their place in public schools. NASSP *Bulletin, 47.* 99–103.

Sarason, S. B., & Doris, J. (1979). *Educational handicap, public policy, and social history*. New York: Free Press.

Sattler, J. M. (1982). *Assessment of children's intelligence and special abilities* (2nd ed.). Boston: Allyn and Bacon.

Schloss, P. J., & Sedlak, R. A. (1986). *Instructional methods for students with learning and behavior problems*. Boston, MA: Allyn and Bacon.

Schroeder, C. S., & Riddle D. B. (1991). Behavior theory and practice. In J. L. Paul & B. C. Epanchin (Eds.), *Educating emotionally disturbed children and youth: Theories and practices for teachers* (2nd ed.). New York: Merrill Publishing.

Schulte, A. C., Osborne, S. S., & McKinney, I. D. (1990). Academic outcomes for students with learning disabilities in consulting and resource programs. *Exceptional Children, 57*(2), 162–172.

Schultz, E. W., & Heuchen, C. M. (1983). *Child stress and the school experience*. New York: Human Sciences Press.

Schulz, J. B., Carpenter, C. D., & Turnbull, A. P. (1991). *Mainstreaming exceptional students: A guide for classroom teachers*. Boston, MA: Allyn and Bacon.

Schumaker, J. B., & Hazel, J. S. (1984). Social skills assessment and training for the learning disabled: What's on second? Part I. *Journal of Learning Disabilities, 17*(7), 422–431.

Schumaker, J. B., Pederson, C. J., Hazel, J. S., & Meyen, E. L. (1983). Social skills curricula for mildly handicapped adolescents: A review. *Focus on Exceptional Children, 16*(4), 1–16.

Schwartz, L. W. (1979). *Psychopathology of Childhood.* New York, NY:Holt, Rinehart & Winston.

Scott, J., Wolking, B., Stoutimore, J., & Harris, C. (1990). Challenging reading for students with mild handicaps. *Teaching Exceptional Children, 22*(3), 32–35.

Scott, M. E. (1988). Learning strategies can help. *Teaching Exceptional Children, 20*(3), 30–34.

Scruggs, T. E., & Laufenberg, R. (1986). Transformational mnemonic strategies for retarded learners. *Education and Training of the Mentally Retarded, 21*(3), 165–173.

Scruggs, T. E., & Mastropieri, M. A. (1986). Improving the test-taking skills of behaviorally disordered and learning disabled children. *Exceptional Children, 53*(1), 63–68.

Seldes, C. (1985). *The great thoughts.* New York: Ballantine.

Selman, R. L. (1980). *The growth of interpersonal understanding: Developmental and clinical analysis.* New York: Academic Press.

Semmel, M. I., Abernathy, T. V., Butera, G., & Lesar, S. (1991). Teacher perception of the regular education initiative. *Exceptional Children, 58*(1), 3–23.

Senf, G. M. (1978). Implications of the final procedures for evaluating learning disabilities. *Journal of Learning Disabilities, 11,* 124–126.

Servakis, P., & Harris G. (1992), Co-teaching: Using the expertise of regular and special education for language arts instruction and remediation. *Reading and Writing Quarterly: Overcoming Learning Difficulties, 8,* 57–70.

Seyle, H. (1975). *Stress without distress.* New York: Signet.

Shanker, A. (1988). Joe Clark's school days: Teaching to the tune of a bullhorn. *The New York Times.*

Sheinker, A., Sheinker, J. M., & Stevens, L. J. (1988). Cognitive strategies for teaching the mildly handicapped. In E. L. Meyen, G. A. Vergason, & R. J. Whelan (Eds.), *Effective instructional strategies for exceptional children.* Denver, CO: Love Publishing.

Sherry, L. (1982). Non-task oriented behaviors of educable mentally retarded, emotionally handicapped, and learning disabled students. *Educational Research Quarterly, 4,* 19–29.

Shinn, M. R. (1986). Does anyone care what happens after the refer-test-place sequence: The systematic evaluation of special program effectiveness. *School Psychology Review, 15,* 49–58.

Shinn, M. (1989a). *Curriculum-based measurement.* New York: Guilford Press.

Shinn, M. R. (1989b). Identifying and defining academic problems: CBM screening and eligibility procedures. In M. Shinn (Ed.), *Curriculum-based measurement: Assessing special children.* New York: Guilford Press.

Shinn, M. R., Ysseldyke, J. E., Deno, S., & Tindal, G. (1986). A comparison of differences between students labeled learning disabled and low-achieving on measures of classroom behavior. *Journal of Learning Disabilities, 19,* 545–552.

Shumaker, J. B., & Deschler, D. D. (1988). Implementing the regular education initiative in secondary schools: A different ball game. *Journal of Learning Disabilities, 21*(1), 36–42.

Sigmon, S. B. (1989). Reaction to excerpts from *The Learning Mystique:* A rational appeal for change. *Journal of Learning Disabilities, 22*(5), 298–300, 327.

Silver, L. B. (1975). Acceptable and controversial approaches to treating the child with learning disabilities. *Pediatrics, 55*(3), 406–415.

Silver, L. B. (1989). Frequency of adoption of children and adolescents with learning disabilities. *Journal of Learning Disabilities, 22*(5), 325–327.

Silverman, R., Zigmond, N., & Sansome, J. (1981). Teaching coping skills to adolescents with learning problems. *Focus on Exceptional Children, 13*(6), 1–20.

Siperstein, G. N., & Goding, M. J. (1985). Teachers' behavior toward LD and non-LD children: A strategy for change. *Journal of Learning Disabilities, 18*(3), 139–144.

Slate, N. M. (1983). Nonbiased assessment of adaptive behavior; Comparison of three instruments. *Exceptional Children, 50,* 67–70.

Slavin, R. E. (1987). Ability grouping and student achievement in elementary schools. A best-evidence synthesis. *Review of Educational Research, 57* (3), 293–336.

Slavin, R. E. (1989a). PET and the pendulum: Faddism in education and how to stop it. *Phi Delta Kappan, 70*(10), 752–758.

Slavin, R. E. (1989b). Students at risk of school failure: The problem and its dimensions. In Slavin, R. E., Karweit, N. L., & Madden, N. A. (Eds.), *Effective programs for students at risk* P. 319. Boston: Allyn and Bacon.

Slavin, R. E., Karweit, N. C., & Madden, N. A. (1989). *Effective programs for students at risk.* Needham Heights, MA: Allyn and Bacon.

Slavin, R. E., Madden, N. A., & Leavey, M. (1984). Effects of cooperative learning and individualized instruction on mainstreamed students. *Exceptional Children, 50*(5), 434–443.

Smith, C. R. (1983). *Learning disabilities: The interaction of learner, task, and setting.* Boston, MA: Little, Brown.

Smith, C. R. (1991). *Learning disabilities: The interaction of learner, task. and setting.* Boston: Allyn and Bacon.

Smith C. R. (1994). *Learning disabilities: The interaction of learner, task, and setting.* Boston: Allyn and Bacon.

Smith, G. R. (1984). Desegregation and assignment of children to classes for the mildly retarded and learning disabled. *Integrated Education, 28,* 208–211.

Smith, J. E., & Patton, J. M. (1989). *A resource module on adverse causes of mild mental retardation.* (Prepared for the President's Committee on Mental Retardation).

Smith, R. A. (1987). A teacher's views on cooperative learning. *Phi Delta Kappan, 68*(9), 663–666.

Smith, S. (1980). *No easy answers: The learning disabled child at school and home.* New York: Bantam Books.

Smith, S.L. (1979) *No easy answers.* Cambridge: Winthrop.

Smith, T. E. C., Finn, D. M., & Dowdy, C. A. (1993). *Teaching students with mild disabilities.* Fort Worth: TX: Harcourt Brace Jovanovich.

Smith, T. E. C., Price, B. J., & Marsh, G. E., II. (1986). *Mildly handicapped children and adults.* St. Paul, MN, West Publishing.

Smith-Davis, J. (1989a, April). *A national perspective on special education.* Keynote presentation at the GLRS/College/University Forum, Macon, Georgia.

Smith-Davis, J. (1989b). Exceptional children in tomorrow's schools. In E. L. Meyen (Ed.), *Exceptional children in today's schools.* Denver, CO: Love Publishing.

Smothers, R. (1987, November 13). Jailed for paddling the paddler. *The New York Times,* A1.

Solnit, A. J., & Stark, M. H. (1961). Mourning and the birth of a defective child. *Psychoanalytic study of the child, 16,* 523–537.

Speece, S. L., McKinney, J. D., & Appelbaum, M. I. (1986). Longitudinal development of conservation skills in learning disabled children. *Journal of Learning Disabilities, 19*(5), 302–307.

Sperry, R. W. (1968). Hemisphere deconnection and unity in conscious awareness. *American Psychologist, 23,* 723–733.

Stafford, P., & Klein, N. (1977). Application of Piaget's theory to the study of thinking of the mentally retarded: A review of the research. *The Journal of Special Education, 11*(2).

Stagg, V., & Catron, T. (1986). Networks of social supports for parents of handicapped children. In R. R. Fewell, P. F. Vadsay (Eds.), *Families of handicapped children: Needs and supports across the life span.* Austin, TX: Pro-Ed.

Stainback, D., Stainback, W., & Forest, M. (1989). *Educating all students in the mainstream of regular education.* Baltimore, MD: Brookes.

Stainback, W., & Stainback, S. (1984). A rationale for the merger of special and regular education. *Exceptional Children, 51*(2), 102–111.

Stein, K. S., Leinhardt, B., & Bickel, W. (1989). Instructional issues for teaching students at risk. In R. E. Slavin, N. L. Karweit, & N. A. Madden (Eds.), *Effective programs for students at risk.* Boston: Allyn and Bacon.

Stephens, R. J., & Slavin, R. E. (1991). When cooperative learning improves the achievement of students with mild disabilities: A response to Tateyama-Sniezek. *Exceptional Children, 57*(1), 9–23.

Stephens, T. (1977). *Teaching skills to children with learning and behavior disorders.* Columbus, OH: Charles E. Merrill.

Stephens, T. M., Blackhurst, A. E., & Magliocca, L. A. (1988). *Teaching mainstreamed students* (2nd ed.). New York, NY: Pergamon Press.

Sternberg, R. J. (1990). Thinking styles: Key to understanding performance. *Phi Delta Kappan, 71*(5), 366–371.

Stevens, G. D., & Birch, J. W. (1957). A proposal for clarification of the terminology used to describe brain-injured children. *Exceptional Children, 23,* 346–349.

Stevens, R. J., & Slavin, R. E. (1991). When cooperative learning improves the achievement of students with mild disabilities: A response to Tateyama-Sniezek. *Exceptional Children, 57*(3), 276–280.

Strauss, A., & Lehtinen, L. S. (1947). Psychopathology and education of the brain injured child. New York: Grune & Stratton.

Strawser, S., & Weller, C. (1985). Use of adaptive behavior and discrepancy criteria to determine learning disabilities severity subtypes. *Journal of Learning Disabilities, 18*(4), 205–211.

Strong, R. W., Silver, H. F., Hanson, J. R., Marzano, R. J., Wolfe, P., Dewing, T., & Brock, W. (1990). Thoughtful education: Staff development for the 1990s. *Educational Leadership, 47*(5), 25–29.

Strother, D. B. (1985). Practical applications of research: Classroom management. *Phi Delta Kappan, 66*(10), 725–728.

Supplement to *Teaching Exceptional Children, 26*(3) (1994, January).

Swanson, H. L. (1988). Toward a metatheory of learning disabilities. *Journal of Learning Disabilities, 21*(4), 196–209.

Swanson, J. M., McBurnett, K., Wigal, T., Pfiffner, L. J., Lerner, M. A., Williams, L., Christian, D. L., Tamm, L., Wilcutt, E., Crowley, K., Clevenger, W., Khouzam, N., Woo, C., Crinella, F. M., & Fisher, T. D. (1993). Effects of stimulant medication on children with attention deficit disorder: A "Review of the reviews." *Exceptional Children, 60*(2), 154–162.

Tallamn, I. (1965). Spousal role differentiation and the socialization of severely retarded children. *Journal of Marriage, and the Family, 27,* 37–42.

Talley, R. C. (1979). Evaluating the effects of implementing the system of multicultural pluralistic assessment: A qualitative approach. *School Psychology Digest, 8,* 71–78.

Tarver, S. G. (1986). Cognitive behavior modification, direct instruction and holistic approaches to the education of students with learning disabilities. *Journal of Learning Disabilities, 19*(6), 368–375.

Tateyama-Sniezek, K. M. (1990). Cooperative learning: Does it improve the academic achievement of students with handicaps? *Exceptional Children, 57*(2), 426–427.

Taylor, R. L. (1993). *Assessment of exceptional students.* Boston: Allyn and Bacon.

Taylor, S. J., & Searle, S. J. (1987). The disabled in America: History, policy and trends. In P. Knoblock (Ed.), *Understanding Exceptional Children and Youth.* Boston: Little, Brown.

Telander, R. (1990). Senseless. *Sports Illustrated, 72*(2), pp. 36–49.

Tew, B. J., Lawrence, K. M., Payne, H., & Rawnsley, K. (1977). Marital stability following the birth of a child with spinal bifida. *British Journal of Psychiatry, 131,* 79–82.

Thomas, A., & Chess, S. (1977). Temperament and development. New York: Bruner/Mazel.

Thomas, A. M. (1960). Strategies for problem solving: A conversation with Herbert Goldstein about mildly retarded learners. *Education & Training of the Mentally Retarded, 15*(3), 216–223.

Tindal, G. (1985). Investigating the effectiveness of special education: An analysis of methodology. *Journal of Learning Disabilities, 18,* 101–112.

Torgesen, J. K. (1977). Memorization processes in reading disabled children. *Journal of Educational Psychology, 69,* 571–578.

Treible, C. (1996, February). Unpublished interview with Director of Learning Disability Support Services, Andrew College, Cuthbert, Georgia.

Tucker, J. (1985). Curriculum-based assessment: An introduction. *Exceptional Children, 52,* 199–204.

Turnbull, A. P., & Turnbull, R. H. (1982). Parent involvement in the education of handicapped children: A critique. *Mental Retardation, 20*(3), 115–122.

Udvari-Solner A. (cited). (September 1997). Effective accomodations for students with exceptionalities. *CEC today, 4* (3), 1, 9, 15.

Umbreit, J., & Ostrow, L. S. (1980). The fetal alcohol syndrome. *Mental Retardation, 18*(3), 109–111.

U.S. Bureau of the Census. (1995). Health insurance coverage: 1994. *Current Population Reports, Series* P60-P190, November, U.S. Government Printing Office: Washington, D.C.

U.S. Department of Education. (1985). *Tenth Annual Report to Congress on the Implementation of the Education of the Handicapped Act.* Washington, DC: Author.

U.S. Department of Education. (1990). *To assure the free appropriate public education of all handicapped children: Twelfth annual report to Congress on the implementation of The Education of the Handicapped Act.* Washington, DC: Office of Special Education Programs.

U.S. Department of Education. (1992). *Fourteenth annual report to Congress on the implementation of the Individuals with Disabilities Education Act.* Washington, DC: Author.

U.S. Department of Education. (1993). *Fifteenth annual report to Congress on the implementation of the Individuals with Disabilities Education Act.* Washington, DC: Author.

U.S. Department of Education. (1995). *Seventeenth Annual Report to Congress on the Implementation of The Individuals with Disabilities Education Act.* Washington, DC: Author.

U.S. Department of Education (1996). *Eighteenth annual report on the implementation of the individuals with disabilities education act.* Washington., D.C: Author.

Utley, C. A., Lowitzer, A. C., & Baumeister, A. A. (1987). A comparison for the AAMD's definition eligibility criteria an declassification schemes with state departments of education. *Education and Training in Mental Retardation, 22*(1), 35–43.

Uzgiris, I. C., & Hunt, J. M. (1966). *Assessment in infancy: Ordinal scales of psychologies development.* Urbana, IL: University of Illinois Press.

Vadasy, P. F. (1986). Single mothers: A social phenomenon and population in need. In R. Fewell & P. Vadasy (Eds.), *Families of handicapped children: Needs and Supports across the life span* (pp. 221–249). Austin, TX: Pro-Ed.

Vadasy, P. F., Fewell, R., Meyer, D. J., & Greenberg, M. T. (1985). Supporting the future of handicapped children: Preliminary findings of program young effect. *Analysis and Intervention in Development Disabilities, 5,* 125–137.

Van Sickle, J. H. (1908–1909). Provision for exceptional children in the public schools. *Psychological Clinic, 2,* 102–111.

Vaughn, S., Bos, C. S., & Schumm, J.S. (1997). *Teaching mainstreamed, diverse, and at-risk students in the general education classroom.* Boston: Allyn and Bacon.

Vaughn, S., Bos, C. S., & Lund, K. A. (1986). But they can do it in my room: Strategies for promoting generalization. *Teaching Exceptional Children, 18*(3), 176–180.

Venn, J. (1994). *Assessment of students with special needs.* New York: Merrill.

Vergason, G. A., & Anderegg, M. L. (1989). Save the baby! A response to 'Integrating the children of the second system.' *Phi Delta Kappan, 71*(1), 61–63.

Villa, R. A., & Thousand, J. S. (1988). Enhancing success in heterogeneous classrooms and schools: The powers of partnerships. *Teacher Education and Special Education, 11*(4), 144–154.

Wagschal, P. H. (1984). A last chance for computers in the school. *Phi Delta Kappan, 66*(4), 251–254.

Walker, D. K., Singer, J. D., Palfrey, J. S., Prza, M., Wenger, M., & Butler, J. A. (1988). Who leaves and who stays in special education? *Exceptional Children, 54*(5), 393–402.

Walker, H., & Rankin, R. (1983). Assessing the behavior expectations and demands of less restrictive settings. *School Psychology Review, 12,* 274–284.

Walker, J. E., & Shea, T. M. (1991). *Behavior management: A practical approach for educators.* New York: MacMillan.

Wallace, G., & Kauffman, J. M. (1986). *Teaching students with learning and behavior problems* (3rd ed.). Columbus, OH: Charles E. Merrill.

Wallace, H. (1972, October). The epidemiology of development disabilities. Paper delivered to the Annual Meeting of United Cerebral Palsy, Kentucky.

Walls, R. T., Wener, T. J., Bacon, F., & Zane, T. (1977). Behavior checklists. In J. D. Cone & R. P. Hawkins (Eds.), *Behavioral Assessment: New directions in clinical psychology.* New York: Brunner/Mazel.

Wang, M. C., & Baker, E. T. (1986). Mainstreaming programs: Design features and effects. *The Journal of Special Education, 19*(4), 503–520.

Wang, M. C., Reynolds, M. C., & Walberg, H. J. (1986). Rethinking special education. *Educational Leadership, 44*(1), 26–31.

Wang, M. C., & Walberg, H. J. (1988). Four fallacies of segregationism. *Exceptional Children, 55*(2), 128–137.

Wang, M. R., & Birch, J. W. (1984a). Effective special education in regular classes. *Exceptional Children, 50*(5), 391–398.

Wang, M. R., & Birch, J. W. (1984b). Comparison of a full time mainstreaming program and a resource room approach. *Exceptional Children, 51*(1), 33–40.

Warner, I. (1991). Parents in touch—District leadership for parent involvement. *Phi Delta Kappan, 72*(5), 372–375.

Weikert, D. P. (1984). *Changed lives: The effect of the Perry preschool project on youths through age 19.* Ypsilanti, MI: High/Scope Educational Research Foundation.

Weinstein, S., & Roschwalb, S. A. (1990). Is there a role for educators in telecommunications policy? *Phi Delta Kappan, 72*(2), 115–117.

Weintraub, M., & Wolf, B. M. (1983). Effects of stress and social supports on mother child interactions in single and two parent families. *Child Development, 54,* 1297–1311.

Weller, C., Strawser, S., & Buchanan, M. (1985). Adaptive behavior: Designator of a continuum of severity of learning disabled individuals. *Journal of Learning Disabilities, 18*(4), 200–203.

Werner, H. (1944). Development of visuo-motor performance on the marble board test in mentally retarded children. *Journal of Genetic Psychology, 64,* 269–279.

Werry, J. S., & Quay, H. C. (1971). The prevalence of behavior symptoms in younger elementary school children. *American Journal of Orthopsychiatry, 41,* 136–143.

Wesson, C. L. (1991). Curriculum-based measurement and two models of follow-up consultation. *Exceptional Children, 57*(3), 246–256.

West, R. P., Young, K. R., & Spooner, F. (1990). Precision teaching: An introduction. *Teaching Exceptional Children, 22*(3), 4–9.

Whelan, R. J., de Saman, L. M., & Fortmeyer, D. J. (1988). The relationship between pupil affect and achievement. In E. L. Meyen, G. A. Vergason, & R. J. Whelan (Eds.), *Effective instructional strategies for exceptional children.* Denver, CO: Love Publishing.

White, M. A. (1971). The view from the pupil's desk. In M. L. Silberman (Ed.), *The experience of schooling.* New York: Holt, Rinehart, and Winston.

White, O. R. (1986). Precision teaching—precision learning. *Exceptional Children, 52*, 522–534.

White, R. (1997). Unified discipline. In B. Algozzine (Ed.), *Problem behavior management: Educator's resource service* (pp. 11:28-11:36). Gaithersburg, MD: Aspen, Publishers.

Whiting, J., & Aultman, L. (1990). *Workshop for parents* (Workshop materials). Albany, GA: Southwest Georgia Learning Resources System Center.

Wickman, E. K. (1929). *Children's behavior and teachers' attitudes.* New York: The Commonwealth Fund.

Wiederholt, J. (1974). Historical perspectives in the education of the learning disabled. In L. Mann & D. Sabatino (Eds.), *The second view of special education.* Philadelphia: Journal of Special Education Press.

Wiederholt, J. L., Hammill, D. D., & Brown, V. L. (1983). *The resource room teacher: A guide to effective practices* (2nd ed.). Boston: Allyn and Bacon.

Wiggins, G. (1989). A true test: Toward more authentic and equitable assessment. *Phi Delta Kappan, 70*(9), 7.

Wikler, L. (1979). *Single parents of mentally retarded children: A neglected population.* Paper presented at the American Association of Mental Deficiency, Miami, Florida.

Will, M. (1986). *Educating students with learning problems: A shared responsibility.* Washington, DC: U.S. Department of Education.

William T. Grant Foundation Commission on Work, Family, and Citizenship (1988). The forgotten half: Non-college bound youth in America. *Phi Delta Kappan, 69*(6), 409–414.

Williams, L. D. (1988). A parent's opinion: Exceptional teachers. *Teaching K–8, 9–10,* 88.

Wilson, C. R. (1983). Teaching reading comprehension by connecting the known to the new. *The Reading Teacher, 36,* 382–390.

Winick, M. (1976). *Malnutrition and brain development.* New York: Exford Press.

Winton, P. J., & Turnbull, A. P. (1981). Parent involvement as viewed by parents of preschool handicapped children. *Topics in Early Childhood Special Education, 1,* 11–19.

Witcher, D. (1988, November). Perspective. *CCBD Newsletter,* 1.

Witt, J. C., Elliott, S. N. Kramer, J. J., & Greshan, F. M. (1994). *Assessment of children: Fundamental methods and practices.* Madison, WS: Wm. C. Brown Communications, Inc.

Wojnilower, D. A., & Gross, A. M. (1988). Knowledge, perception, and performance of assertive behavior in children with learning disabilities. *Journal of Learning Disabilities, 21*(2), 109–117.

Wolford, J. N. (1991, August 11). Discovering Columbus. *The New York Times Magazine,* pp. 25–29; 45–46; 48–49; 55.

Wolking, B. (1991). Personal correspondence.

Wolking, B. (1992). Precision Teaching Graph.

Wong, B. Y. L. (1979). Increasing retention of main ideas through questioning strategies. *Learning Disability Quarterly, 2,* 42–47.

Wong, B. Y. L. (1985). Potential means of enhancing content skills acquisition in learning disabled adolescents. *Focus on Exceptional Children, 17*(5), 1–8.

Wood, M. (1986). *Developmental therapy* (2nd ed.). Austin, TX: Pro-Ed.

Wood, M. M., & Long, N. J. (1991). *Life Space Intervention: Talking with Children and Youth in Crisis.* Austin, TX: Pro-Ed.

Woods, R. (1998). *An investigation of regular elementary teacher's knowledge about co-teaching methods as they could be implemented in an inclusive classroom.* Unpublished manuscript.

Woodward, M. (1959). The behavior of idiots interpreted by Piaget's theory of sensorimotor development. *British Journal of Educational Psychology, 29,* 60–71.

Wyne, M. D., & O'Connor, P. D. (1979). *Exceptional children: A developmental view.* Lexington, MA: D. C. Heath.

Yell, M.L., & Shriner, J. G. (1997). The IDEA Amendments of 1997: Implications for special and general education teachers, administrators, and teacher trainers. *Focus on Exceptional Children, 30* (1), 1-19.

Ysseldyke, J. E., & Algozzine, B. (1982). *Critical issues in special and remedial education.* Boston: Houghton Mifflin.

Ysseldyke, J. E., & Algozzine, B. (1984). *Introduction to special education.* Boston: Houghton Mifflin.

Ysseldyke, J. E., & Algozzine, B. (1990). *Introduction to special education* (2nd ed.). Boston, MA: Houghton Mifflin.

Ysseldyke, J. E., & Algozzine, B. (1995). *Special education: A practical approach for teachers.* Boston, MA: Houghton Mifflin.

Ysseldyke, J. E., Algozzine, B., & Epps, S. (1983). A logical and empirical analysis of current practice in classifying students as handicapped. *Exceptional Children, 50,* 160–166.

Ysseldyke, J. E., Algozzine, B., Shinn, M. R., & McGue, M. (1982). Similarities and differences between low achievers and students classified learning disabled. *The Journal of Special Education, 16*(1), 73–85.

Ysseldyke, J., Algozzine, B., & Thurlow, M. (1983). On interpreting institute research: A response to McKinney. *Exceptional Education Quarterly, 4*(1), 145–147.

Ysseldyke, J. E., Thurlow, M. L., Wotruba, J. W., and Nania, P. A. (1990). Instructional arrangements: Perceptions from general education. *Teaching Exceptional Children, 22*(4), 4–8.

Zargona, N., Vaughn, S., & McIntosh, R. (1991). Social skills interventions and children with behavior problems: A review. *Behavior Disorders, 16*(4), 260–275.

Zigler, E. (1978). National crises in mental retardation research. *American Journal of Mental Deficiency, 83,* 1–8.

Zigmond, N., & Baker, J. (1990). Mainstream experiences for learning disabled students (Project Meld): Preliminary report. *Exceptional Children, 57*(2), 176–185.

Zigmond, N., Levin, E., & Laurie, T. (1985). Managing the mainstream: An analysis of teacher attitudes and student performance in mainstream high school programs. *Journal of Learning Disabilities, 18,* 505–568.

Zigmond, N., & Miller, S. E. (1986). Assessment for instructional planning. *Exceptional Children, 52*(3), 501–509.

Zinmeister, K. (1990). Growing up scared. *The Atlantic, 265*(6), 49–66.

Zucker, S. H., & Polloway, E. A. (1987). Issues in identification and assessment in mental retardation. *Education and Training in Mental Retardation, 22*(2), 69–76.

INDEX